FOR REFERENCE

Do Not Take From This Room

AMERICAN JUSTICE

Ready Reference

AMERICAN JUSTICE

Volume I
Abington School District v. Schempp – Felony

A Magill Book
from the Editors of Salem Press

Consulting Editor

Joseph M. Bessette
Claremont McKenna College

Salem Press, Inc.

Pasadena, California   Englewood Cliffs, New Jersey

Editor in Chief: Dawn P. Dawson

Consulting Editor: Joseph M. Bessette   *Project Editors:* McCrea Adams and R. Kent Rasmussen
Research Supervisor: Jeff Jensen   *Photograph Editor:* Valerie Krein
Proofreading Supervisor: Yasmine A. Cordoba   *Production Editor:* Janet Long
Layout: James Hutson   *Maps:* Moritz Design

Library of Congress Cataloging-in-Publication Data
American Justice / from the editors of Salem Press, consulting editor, Joseph M. Bessette
   p. cm. — (Ready reference)
"A Magill Book"
Includes bibliographical references and index.
   ISBN 0-89356-761-2 (set : alk. paper). — ISBN 0-89356-762-0 (vol. 1 : alk. paper).
   1. Law—United States—Encyclopedias. 2. Justice, Administration of—United States—Encyclopedias.
I. Bessette, Joseph M.   II. Series.
KF154.A44 1996
349.73—dc20
[347.3]

95-51529
CIP

First Printing

PRINTED IN THE UNITED STATES OF AMERICA

Publisher's Note

Providing justice for its citizens is generally considered the most fundamental purpose of government. Justice in modern societies encompasses criminal law and the criminal justice system, civil law and civil courts, and social justice. In the United States, concepts of justice and law are based most directly on the U.S. Constitution and its Bill of Rights, but behind them is the extensive English common-law tradition brought to North American shores by the first English colonists. Discussions of justice in the United States may therefore touch on subjects ranging from the right of *habeas corpus* to the rules concerning the introduction of evidence at a trial to controversies over abortion, affirmative action, and the "right to die."

In *Ready Reference: American Justice*, it was the goal of the editors of Salem Press to assemble articles on a wide variety of American justice topics—including Supreme Court cases, federal legislation, civil justice, the criminal justice system, types of crime, legal terms, personages, organizations, historical events, and contemporary justice issues—and to present them in an alphabetical format for ease of access. This three-volume set, the third installment in the Ready Reference series, contains 843 articles ranging in length from 200 to 3,000 words. The encyclopedic format of the series enables readers to find information easily about subjects large and small. For example, readers seeking information about crime may begin with the overview articles "Crime" and "Criminal justice system" and then turn to articles on specific crimes, from "Arson" to "Vandalism." They will also find essays on law enforcement agencies (for example, "Federal Bureau of Investigation"), legislation ("Violent Crime Control and Law Enforcement Act of 1994"), and the gathering of crime statistics ("Uniform Crime Reports"). Similarly, the search for information on constitutional law could begin with "Constitution, U.S." or "Supreme Court of the United States" and lead to articles on concepts such as "Due process of law" and "Speech and press, freedom of," to individual biographies of chief justices, and to any of the 190 articles clearly explaining the significance of crucial Supreme Court decisions—from the pivotal 1803 case *Marbury v. Madison* to the 1995 *Adarand Constructors v. Peña* decision regarding affirmative action. In addition, numerous articles define legal concepts and terms such as "bench warrant," "litigation," "*mens rea*," and "*voir dire*." Also covered are historical events important to the development of justice in the United States, from the American Revolution to the Sacco and Vanzetti trial to the beating of Rodney King by Los Angeles police officers. Finally, social justice concepts are included—among them capitalism, the Civil Rights movement, natural rights, the welfare state, and discrimination based on age, race, and sex.

Each article begins with easily accessible ready-reference information. Articles on legal concepts, for example, define the concept, then encapsulate its importance; articles on historical events provide the date, location, and significance of the event. Articles on court cases list the court handing down the decision, the date of the decision, and the significance of the case. Where appropriate, articles are illustrated with photographs, maps, charts, and tables; the set contains more than 270 historical and contemporary photographs. Each article concludes with cross-references to other relevant articles in the set. Finally, articles of 1,000 words or more conclude with an annotated paragraph-style bibliography.

Each volume includes, in the front, an alphabetical list of all entries in the set and, in the back, a list of articles by category. Volume 3 contains a series of seven appendices. Two present the texts of the Declaration of Independence and the U.S. Constitution, and five provide information on criminal arrests, criminal victimization, famous American trials, Supreme Court cases, and Supreme Court justices. Following these are a time line, glossary, and bibliography. Finally, there are two indexes: a case index and a comprehensive index with numerous cross-references.

Many authors generously contributed their time and talents in order to make this set possible, and we thank them all for their contributions. A complete list of writers appears in the front of volume 1. We particularly wish to thank Consulting Editor Joseph M. Bessette of Claremont McKenna College for his invaluable expertise and advice.

List of Contributors

McCrea Adams
Independent Scholar

Richard Adler
University of Michigan, Dearborn

Roger W. Andersen
University of Toledo College of Law

William M. Apple
Independent Scholar

Kamala Arogyaswamy
University of South Dakota

H. C. Aubrey
Independent Scholar

James A. Baer
Northern Virginia Community College

Charles Bahmueller
Center for Civic Education

Barbara Bair
Independent Scholar

Douglas E. Baker
Welch, Wulff & Childers

Robert Baker
Union College

Thomas E. Baker
Texas Tech University School of Law

Timothy Bakken
Trenton State College

Richard Barrett
University of Alberta

Charles A. Bartocci
Independent Scholar

Paul Albert Bateman
Southwestern University School of Law

Jonathan J. Bean
Independent Scholar

Patricia A. Behlar
Pittsburg State University

Alberto Bernabe-Riefkohl
John Marshall Law School

Joseph M. Bessette
Claremont McKenna College

Denis Binder
Western New England College

Steve D. Boilard
Western Kentucky University

Alan E. Brownstein
*University of California, Davis
    School of Law*

Faith Hickman Brynie
Independent Scholar

William H. Burnside
John Brown University

Johnny C. Burris
*Nova Southeastern University Shepard
    Broad Law Center*

Malcolm B. Campbell
Bowling Green State University

Edmund J. Campion
University of Tennessee

David Carleton
Middle Tennessee State University

Brian J. Carroll
California Baptist College

Frederick B. Chary
Indiana University Northwest

Maxwell O. Chibundu
University of Maryland School of Law

James B. Christoph
Indiana University, Bloomington

Lawrence Clark III
Independent Scholar

Scot Clifford
Jett & Laquer

Robert G. Clouse
Indiana State University

William H. Coogan
University of Southern Maine

Randall Coyne
University of Oklahoma Law School

David A. Crain
South Dakota State University

Jennifer Davis
University of Dayton

Robert C. Davis
Pikeville College

Davison M. Douglas
William and Mary Law School

Jennifer Eastman
Clark University

Craig M. Eckert
Eastern Illinois University

Loring D. Emery
Independent Scholar

Daniel C. Falkowski
Canisius College

Sonia M. Lopez Falkowski
Independent Scholar

John L. Farbo
University of Idaho

Thomas G. Field, Jr.
Franklin Pierce Law Center

John W. Fiero
University of Southwestern Louisiana

Dale L. Flesher
University of Mississippi

Tonya K. Flesher
University of Mississippi

Carol Franks
Portland State University

Karen Garner
University of Texas at Austin

K. Fred Gillum
Colby College

Bradley R. Gitz
Lyon College

Robert F. Gorman
Southwest Texas State University

J. Kirkland Grant
Touro Law School

Gwendolyn Griffith
Willamette University College of Law

Richard S. Gruner
Whittier Law School

Michael Haas
University of Hawaii at Manoa

Cathy Moran Hajo
New York University

Sam Ramsey Hakim
University of Nebraska at Omaha

Timothy L. Hall
University of Mississippi Law School

Louise A. Halper
Washington & Lee University School of Law

Roger D. Haney
Murray State University

Robert M. Hardaway
University of Denver College of Law

Keith Harper
Mississippi College

Gregory Harris
Independent Scholar

Fred R. van Hartesveldt
Fort Valley State College

Sterling Harwood
San Jose State University

Megali S. D. B. Havens
*University of the Pacific, McGeorge School
    of Law*

Margaret Hawthorne
South Hadley High School

J. Denny Haythorn
Whittier Law School

Sarah E. Heath
University of Cincinnati

Peter B. Heller
Manhattan College

Mary A. Hendrickson
Independent Scholar

Murray Henner
Hofstra University

Stuart Henry
Eastern Michigan University

Maria A. Hernandez
Northern Arizona University

David G. Hicks
Independent Scholar

Marsha M. Huber
Otterbein College

Charles C. Jackson
Northern Kentucky University

Robert Jacobs
Central Washington University

Charles L. Kammer
The College of Wooster

Mara Kelly-Zukowski
Felician College

Theodore P. Kovaleff
Independent Scholar

Melvin Kulbicki
York College of Pennsylvania

Lisa Langenbach
Middle Tennessee State University

Ralph L. Langenheim, Jr.
University of Illinois at Urbana-Champaign

Karyn E. Langhorne
District of Columbia School of Law

Eugene Larson
Los Angeles Pierce College

Thomas T. Lewis
Mount Senario College

Harry van der Linden
Butler University

Ronald W. Long
West Virginia Institute of Technology

R. M. Longyear
University of Kentucky

William C. Lowe
Mount St. Clare College

David C. Lukowitz
Independent Scholar

Wei Luo
Southern Illinois University School of Law

Donna Echols Mabus
PLATO Associates

Robert McClenaghan
Independent Scholar

Arthur F. McClure
Central Missouri State University

Jean Sinclair McKnight
Southern Illinois University School of Law

Paul D. Mageli
Independent Scholar

Bill Manikas
Gaston College

Richard W. Mansbach
Iowa State University

S. A. Marino
*State University of New York
Westchester Community College*

Thomas D. Matijasic
Prestonburg Community College

Patricia C. Matthews
Mount Union College

Bruce E. May
University of South Dakota

Diane Kroeger May
Independent Scholar

Steve J. Mazurana
University of Northern Colorado

Dyan E. Mazurana
Clark University

Linda Mealey
College of St. Benedict

Joseph A. Melusky
Saint Francis College

William V. Moore
College of Charleston

Mario F. Morelli
Western Illinois University

Brian K. Morley
Master's College

Thomas J. Mortillaro
Nicholls State University

Jerry A. Murtagh
Fort Valley State College

Dale K. Nesbary
Oakland University

Cathal J. Nolan
*Institute of International Relations,
University of British Columbia*

Kathleen O'Brien
Independent Scholar

Victor Ortloff
Troy State University

David E. Paas
Hillsdale College

Lisa Paddock
Independent Scholar

W. David Patton
Boise State University

Darryl Paulson
University of South Florida

William E. Pemberton
University of Wisconsin, La Crosse

Steven L. Piott
Clarion University

C. Michelle Piskulich
Oakland University

Oliver B. Pollak
University of Nebraska at Omaha

Christina Polsenberg
Michigan State University

Srinivasan Ragothaman
University of South Dakota

Samory Rashid
Indiana State University

Betty Richardson
Southern Illinois University, Edwardsville

Michelle R. Royle
Northern Arizona University

Nadia M Rubaii-Barrett
New Mexico State University

Joseph R. Rudolph, Jr.
Towson State University

Sunil K. Sahu
Depauw University

Jerry Purvis Sanson
Louisiana State University at Alexandria

John E. Santosuosso
Florida Southern College

Daniel C. Scavone
University of Southern Indiana

Larry Schweikart
University of Dayton

Elizabeth Algren Shaw
Kitchen, Deery & Barnhouse

R. Baird Shuman
University of Illinois at Urbana-Champaign

Donald C. Simmons, Jr.
Troy State University

Donna Addkison Simmons
Troy State University

Kevin F. Sims
Cedarville College

Sanford S. Singer
University of Dayton

Andrew C. Skinner
Brigham Young University

Christopher E. Smith
Michigan State University

Ira Smolensky
Monmouth College, Illinois

David R. Sobel
Provosty, Sadler & deLaunay

Robert Sobel
Hofstra University

List of Contributors

John A. Sondey
South Dakota State University

Alene Staley
Saint Joseph's College

Ruffin G. Stirling
Independent Scholar

Leslie Stricker
Independent Scholar

Glenn L. Swygart
Tennessee Temple University

William Taggart
New Mexico State University

Robert D. Talbott
University of Northern Iowa

Harold D. Tallant
Georgetown College

Susan M. Taylor
Indiana University at South Bend

Leslie V. Tischauser
Prairie State College

Paul B. Trescott
Southern Illinois University

Mfanya D. Tryman
Mississippi State University

Diane C. Van Noord
Independent Scholar

Mary E. Virginia
Independent Scholar

William C. Ward III
Kent State University

Robert P. Watson
Northern Arizona University

Samuel E. Watson III
Midwestern State University

William L. Waugh, Jr.
Georgia State University

Donald V. Weatherman
Lyon College

Marcia J. Weiss
Point Park College

Ashton Wesley Welch
Creighton University

Scott A. White
University of Wisconsin, Platteville

Richard Whitworth
Ball State University

Robert R. Wiggins
Cedarville College

Richard L. Wilson
University of Tennessee at Chattanooga

Thomas Winter
University of Cincinnati

Clifton K. Yearley
State University of New York at Buffalo

Noah Zerbe
Northern Arizona University

CONTENTS

Contents

ALPHABETICAL LIST OF ENTRIES

Volume I

Volume II

Volume III

AMERICAN JUSTICE

Abington School District v. Schempp

COURT: U.S. Supreme Court

DATE: Decided June 17, 1963

SIGNIFICANCE: In this case the Supreme Court ruled that a state or school board violated the establishment clause (the clause in the First Amendment stating that Congress shall "make no law respecting an establishment of religion") by requiring Bible readings or the recitation of the Lord's Prayer at the beginning of the school day

The Supreme Court in *Abington School District v. Schempp* actually decided two cases that had been consolidated before the Court. The first involved a challenge to a Pennsylvania law that required ten verses of the Bible to be read at the beginning of each school day and allowed children to be excused from participation or attendance at the Bible readings if their parents or guardians so requested. The second case (*Murray v. Curlett*), brought by Madalyn Murray (O'Hair) and her son, William J. Murray III, challenged a rule adopted by a Maryland school board providing for the holding of opening exercises in public schools at which either a chapter from the Bible was to be read or the Lord's Prayer recited. This rule also permitted parents to have their children exempted from the exercises.

Justice Tom C. Clark wrote the opinion for the majority, significant less for its result than for its articulation of a formal test for determining establishment clause violations. "[T]o withstand the strictures of the Establishment Clause," the Court declared, "there must be a secular legislative purpose and a primary effect that neither advances nor inhibits religion." This test, supplemented in *Lemon v. Kurtzman* (1971) with a prohibition against excessive entanglements between government and religion, guided the law of the establishment clause for nearly thirty years. In an 8-1 decision, the Court held that both the Pennsylvania law and the Maryland school board's rule violated the establishment clause of the First Amendment. It had held the year before in *Engel v. Vitale* (1962) that recitation of a brief nondenominational prayer in public schools violated the establishment clause. The holding in *Abington* was therefore an expected application of *Engel* to roughly comparable facts.

Although the majority in *Abington* found that the required Bible readings and prayers at issue in the cases violated the establishment clause, it nevertheless cautioned that its holding was not intended to set in motion a general purging of religious references from the public schools. Justice Clark's majority opinion emphasized that the Bible was "worthy of study for its literary and historic qualities" and that studies of the Bible or of religion in general, "when presented objectively as part of a secular program of education," were not inconsistent with the establishment clause.

The decision in *Abington* elicited several concurrences, including a mammoth seventy-four-page concurring opinion by Justice William Brennan surveying the history of religious freedom and disestablishment in the United States, but only a single dissent. Justice Potter Stewart, who had dissented the year previously in *Engel*, continued to assert that the majority's reading of the establishment clause actually threatened the free exercise rights of parents who desired their children to receive some religious influence during the school day.

See also *Engel v. Vitale*; Establishment of religion; *Lemon v. Kurtzman*; School prayer.

Abolitionist movement

DEFINITION: The abolitionist movement called for the elimination of slavery in the United States

SIGNIFICANCE: Abolitionists helped set the United States on the course to the Civil War; they were also instrumental in making African American liberation a primary Civil War aim, and their efforts culminated in the Thirteenth Amendment to the Constitution

The earliest American antislavery sentiment came from Quakers, who believed that human bondage was immoral. A mass movement to abolish slavery developed slowly. Despite the fact that many slaveholders were ambivalent about the institution, the closest thing to large-scale antislavery legislation prior to the nineteenth century was the Ordinance of 1787, which forbade slavery in what was then called the Northwest Territory. The word "slavery" is not even mentioned in the Constitution until the Thirteenth Amendment, which outlawed human bondage in 1865.

Pressure to address the issue of slavery mounted throughout the early nineteenth century. In 1817 the American Colonization Society was formed with the hope of settling freed blacks in Africa. In 1821 this group acquired land which eventually became Liberia; its first colonists arrived in 1822. This venture was not very successful. Few slave owners would free their slaves without compensation. Moreover, freed blacks born in the United States were reluctant to leave their homes. In 1827 there were 130 abolitionist societies in the United States, 106 of which were in the South.

White Southerners had long feared the possibility of a massive slave uprising, and Nat Turner confirmed their worst nightmares in 1831. Turner, a Baptist minister and slave in Virginia, led a violent revolt that resulted in more than sixty white fatalities. In that same year, William Lloyd Garrison began publishing his abolitionist newspaper, *The Liberator*. Unlike earlier abolitionists, who advocated gradual emancipation, Garrison called for immediate black liberation with no compensation to slave owners. He also called for full civil, political, and social equality for freed slaves.

Senator Charles Sumner, a leading abolitionist, denounced the Kansas-Nebraska Act, calling it a "swindle." (Library of Congress)

In 1832 Garrison founded the New England Anti-Slavery Society. Inspired by his example, Arthur and Lewis Tappan founded a similar organization in New York. With Garrison's aid they established the American Anti-Slavery Society in 1833. This spirit of unity was short-lived. Garrison championed a variety of reforms ranging from abolitionism to women's rights, and critics saw him as a fanatic. In 1840 the abolitionist movement split into rival camps, essentially along pro- and anti-Garrisonian lines.

Garrison's bombastic rhetoric led to a shift in slavery apologetics. Whereas slavery had been traditionally defended as a necessary evil, proponents began defending it as a positive good. They argued that slavery maintained social order and exposed bondsmen to Christianity. Freed slaves, however, particularly Frederick Douglass, saw nothing positive in slavery and dismissed this argument as ridiculous.

Abolitionist dreams were realized in 1865 with the ratification of the Thirteenth Amendment to the Constitution. The Civil War, the bloodiest war in America's history, had finally gained freedom for all African Americans.

See also Civil War; Civil War Amendments; Douglass, Frederick; Fugitive Slave Laws; Lincoln-Douglas debates; Missouri Compromise of 1820; Republican Party; Slavery.

Abortion

DEFINITION: The intentional termination of a pregnancy by using a surgical or chemical technique for expelling the fetus from the uterus of the mother

SIGNIFICANCE: A fundamental source of political and social conflict in the contemporary United States, the abortion debate is centered on the right of a fetus to life as it conflicts with a woman's right to make decisions about pregnancy and motherhood

In the early nineteenth century there were no significant laws in the United States pertaining to abortion. Reflecting the country's Christian heritage, abortion was generally viewed as sinful but not serious until "ensoulment," at which it was believed the soul entered the body. This distinction was recognized in English common law and in American social practice, according to which abortion before "quickening," the mother's sensation of fetal movement, was accepted. Until the mid-nineteenth century, pregnancy and birth were handled privately by women and midwives. Recipes for abortifacients (drugs to induce abortion) were available, and abortion was quietly practiced. In the mid-nineteenth century, newspapers even carried advertisements for abortionists and abortifacients. Estimates have placed the abortion rate at 20 to 25 percent of pregnancies in the period from 1840 to 1870.

By the mid-nineteenth century, however, medicine had made advances in understanding fertilization and fetal development as well as in safer methods of delivery and abortion. The 1850's marked the first abortion debate, led primarily by physicians and the newly formed American Medical Association (AMA). Concerned about mothers' health (many folk procedures were useless or even dangerous) and interested in

wresting control of pregnancy and delivery from midwives, the American Medical Association adopted, in 1871, a statement declaring all abortions murder, but some medically necessary. Only physicians were deemed qualified to determine medical necessity. A public campaign to change state laws was so successful that, by 1910, all but one state had adopted laws making abortion illegal except when medically necessary. The religious leadership of the time remained neutral in the debate, leading to criticism from medical professionals.

These new statutes reduced the number of abortions but did not eliminate them. With no uniform standards for determining medical necessity, some doctors remained quite liberal in practice. After World War II, however, when the practice of abortion was shifted from doctors' offices to hospitals, increased public scrutiny caused the legal practice of abortion to become extremely restricted; it was limited to situations in which the mother's life or health was threatened. In response, the illegal practice of abortion increased dramatically, to perhaps 650,000 per year in the years preceding legalization.

In the 1960's, the issue again entered the arena of public debate. Social agreement on the immorality of abortion had eroded, and concerns over population growth and women's rights generated organizations working to legalize abortion. In 1967, the AMA adopted a statement supporting legalization. By the late 1960's, about one-third of the states had adopted laws permitting abortion under some circumstances, and by 1970 four states had totally decriminalized abortion during the first three months (first trimester) of pregnancy. In 1973, two Supreme Court cases, *Roe v. Wade* and *Doe v. Bolton*, established a woman's right to abortion, changing public policy and the abortion debate dramatically.

Legal Status Since *Roe v. Wade*. Until 1973, laws pertaining to abortion were at the discretion of individual states. In the Supreme Court rulings of 1973, the Court, drawing on the Fourteenth Amendment to the Constitution, ruled that a woman's right to abortion is protected under the "right to privacy." Since pregnancy is a private matter, the state impinges on a woman's freedom when it makes abortion illegal. The right to an abortion, however, was not ruled to be absolute. States were prohibited from regulating abortion during the first trimester, but they could regulate to assure the safety of abortion during the second trimester. During the third trimester, however, the state's interest in the developing fetus could override the woman's right. Abortion could then be prohibited except where the life or health of the mother was threatened. These decisions, based on 7-2 majority votes, surprised both proponents and opponents of abortion.

Challenged by opponents of abortion, the legal status of abortion has remained in a state of flux. While a woman's right to abortion has been consistently upheld by the Supreme Court, most notably in *Planned Parenthood v. Casey* (1992), the right to abortion has been restricted in a number of ways. The Court has struck down provisions requiring consent by the father and other restrictions which impose an "undue burden." Yet it has affirmed the right of states to impose a twenty-four-

A candlelight rally in 1990 protesting a Michigan law requiring parental consent for abortions for women under eighteen. (Jim West)

hour waiting period and to require parental consent for a minor providing there is the alternative of court approval in lieu of such consent. Additionally, the Hyde Amendment, upheld in *Harris v. McRae* (1980), prohibited the use of federal funds for abortions except to save the life of the mother. The Supreme Court has also ruled that states are not responsible for providing funding for nontherapeutic abortions (*Maher v. Roe*, 1977). In *Webster v. Reproductive Health Services* (1989) and *Rust v. Sullivan* (1991), it ruled that states and the federal government may restrict staff and physicians in government-funded facilities from offering abortion services, counseling, and referral.

Social and Political Conflicts. The debate in the 1960's was led by groups attempting to have abortion legalized. A significant countermovement did not appear until after the 1973 Supreme Court decisions. Initially led by the Catholic church, but including many non-Catholics, it focused on the passage of a Right to Life Amendment which, if adopted, would have constitutionally defined a fetus as a person from the moment of conception. By the late 1970's, organized conservative Protestant groups had become leading spokespersons in the self-described "pro-life movement." These groups increasingly focused on state legislatures and were quite effective in obtaining passage of very restrictive abortion laws, most of which were successfully challenged in the United States Supreme Court by "pro-choice" groups, often under the leadership of Planned Parenthood.

By the early 1980's, it was clear that the Supreme Court would continue to uphold a woman's right to abortion. Pro-life groups concentrated more on national politics, hoping to elect conservative presidents who could eventually alter the makeup of the Supreme Court itself. Also significant was the emergence of groups such as Operation Rescue that adopted methods of nonviolent resistance. They protested at abortion clinics, verbally challenged staff and clients, and physically blocked the entrances to clinics. The pro-choice movement in *NOW (National Organization for Women) v. Scheidler* (1992) unsuccessfully attempted to use antitrust and racketeering laws (the RICO statutes) to prevent such blockades. The U.S. court of appeals ruled against them, a ruling upheld by the U.S. Supreme Court. By the late 1980's, more radical members of the antiabortion movement began to utilize acts of violence, including the bombing of abortion clinics. In 1993, Michael Griffin shot and killed a physician, David Gunn, outside an abortion clinic in Pensacola, Florida, initiating a new phase in which such killings were justified by some on the grounds of defending the unborn.

The Moral Arguments. The most important moral argument centers on which value should take precedence, a woman's right to make decisions about pregnancy and parenting or the fetus' right to life. Related is the debate on when the fetus achieves human status. If personhood is present from the moment of conception, all abortion is wrong except, perhaps, to save the life of the mother. If birth is the defining moment, abortion is always permissible. One view sees personhood as

PUBLIC OPINION, 1993: SHOULD ABORTION BE LEGAL?

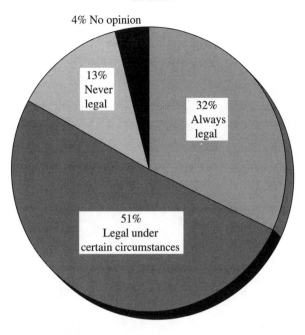

4% No opinion

13% Never legal

32% Always legal

51% Legal under certain circumstances

Source: U.S. Department of Justice, Bureau of Justice Statistics, *Sourcebook of Criminal Justice Statistics—1993*. Washington, D.C.: U.S. Government Printing Office, 1994. Primary source, *The Gallup Poll Monthly*, April, 1993.

Note: The question asked was, "Do you think abortions should be legal under any circumstances, legal only under certain circumstances, or illegal in all circumstances?"

emerging during the process of fetal development. Hence abortion before certain stages may be permissible, but after certain stages must be seriously limited. Such a view is reflected in the Supreme Court's position, which as of 1994 supported unrestricted abortion during the first trimester and highly restricted access during the last trimester as the fetus approaches viability (the ability to live independent of the mother).

Other arguments relate to empirical factors or assumptions concerning social realities. Opponents argue that widespread use of abortion undermines respect for life, culminating in a society in which the powerless and socially useless will routinely be killed. They also argue that legalized abortion encourages sexual promiscuity, increasing the incidence of sexually transmitted diseases and births to unwed teenage mothers. Others focus on the long-term mental health of the mother and possible feelings of guilt and depression. In response, supporters of legalization note that women are disproportionately left alone to bear the results of unwanted pregnancies, as fathers often desert. Additionally, they say, social stigmas against unwed mothers, the lack of job guarantees related to preg-

Operation Rescue antiabortion activists blocking the entrance to a clinic in Livonia, Michigan. (Jim West)

nancy leaves, and the financial effects of additional children on low-income families make abortion a responsible act. Further, proponents argue, social conditions make unwanted pregnancies so traumatic that women will resort to dangerous illegal abortions. Finally, they argue that population increases are stretching the world's resources beyond their limits to support human life, causing widespread poverty and ecological deterioration. Even in the United States, one-fourth of all children live in poverty, lacking adequate food, housing, and medical care.

A final argument centers not on the morality of abortion per se but on the appropriateness of having laws prohibiting abortion. Central to the argument is the debate over church-state separation. The Constitution of the United States affirms that government should not act to favor the religious views of one group or to prevent the free exercise of religion. The antiabortion movement is predominantly a religious movement, reflecting the beliefs of the hierarchy of the Roman Catholic church and some of its laity, various fundamentalist and conservative Protestant groups, and Orthodox Jews. The prochoice opposition includes a large number of Catholics, many liberal Protestants, and many Conservative and Reformed Jews, but also the vast majority of persons who consider themselves to be nonreligious or humanist. According to this argument, a person's view of abortion reflects their religious beliefs. To prohibit abortion is to favor a particular set of religious beliefs and to limit others' freedom of religious expression. Some argue that, because public opinion is so sharply divided, prohibiting abortion will lead to open defiance of the law, thus undermining the authority of law itself.

The abortion debate is far from resolved, and legal, political, and social conflict will continue. While the Supreme Court has continued (at least through 1995) to uphold a woman's right to an abortion, this right has also been somewhat restricted since *Roe v. Wade*. The Court's majority in affirming such a right declined to a 5-4 majority in the 1992 *Planned Parenthood v. Casey* decision, indicating that at some future date *Roe v. Wade* might be overturned. Medical advances may also impinge on the future of the debate. The ability to sustain prematurely born infants at earlier dates (now as early as twenty weeks) may lead to reconsideration of the issue of fetal viability. Additionally, the invention by a French company of a pill, RU-486, which is a safe and effective (up to 95 percent) abortifacient when used in the first eight weeks, would make abortion a private, relatively simple procedure that would be hard to monitor. Consequently, antiabortion activists have worked to restrict the drug's availability in the United States.

—Charles L. Kammer

See also *Akron v. Akron Center for Reproductive Health*; Birth control, right to; *Doe v. Bolton*; Feminism; *Harris v. McRae*; *Maher v. Roe*; National Organization for Women (NOW); *Planned Parenthood of Central Missouri v. Danforth*; *Planned Parenthood v. Casey*; Religion, free exercise of; *Roe v. Wade*; *Rust v. Sullivan*; *Thornburgh v. American College of Obstetricians and Gynecologists*; *Webster v. Reproductive Health Services*.

BIBLIOGRAPHY

The Guide to American Law: Everyone's Legal Encyclopedia (12 vols. St. Paul, Minn.: West, 1983-1985), along with its annual supplements, is an excellent source for pertinent court cases. Barbara Hinkson Craig and David M. O'Brien, *Abortion and American Politics* (Chatham, N.J.: Chatham House, 1993), is a comprehensive discussion of the political battle since the *Roe v. Wade* decision. James C. Mohr, *Abortion in America: The Origins and Evolution of National Policy, 1800-1900* (New York: Oxford University Press, 1978), provides a history of the practice and policy concerning abortion in the nineteenth century. J. Douglas Butler and David F. Walbert, eds., *Abortion, Medicine, and the Law* (4th ed. New York: Facts on File, 1992), is an extensive anthology presenting a variety of perspectives on the abortion debate in the areas of law, medicine, ethics, and religion. Beverly Wildung Harrison, *Our Right to Choose: Toward a New Ethic of Abortion* (Boston: Beacon Press, 1983), while written from a feminist perspective, provides a thorough, balanced history of the Christian, Western debate over abortion.

Abrams v. United States

COURT: U.S. Supreme Court

DATE: Ruling issued November 10, 1919

SIGNIFICANCE: The Abrams case involved questions of the meaning of free speech and the definition of the clear and present danger test, as defined by Judge Oliver Wendell Holmes, Jr.

In August of 1918, Jacob Abrams, Mollie Steimer, Hyman Lachowsky, Samuel Lipman, and Jacob Schwartz were arrested by New York police authorities for distributing leaflets opposing American intervention in Soviet Russia. They were charged with violating the 1918 Sedition Act, which made it a crime willfully to "utter, print, write, or publish any disloyal, profane, scurrilous, or abusive language" about the United States, its government and its officials.

The defendants were indicted on charges of conspiracy before the Southern District Court of New York by U.S. Attorney Francis Gordon Caffey. Harry Weinberger took on the defense of Abrams and the others. Throughout the trial, judge Henry DeLamar Clayton, Jr., actively aided the prosecution's case. The defendants were convicted on October 21, 1918, and the sentence was issued on October 25. Abrams, Lipman, and Lachowsky received twenty years each and fines of up to $1,000. Mollie Steimer was sentenced to fifteen years in the Missouri penitentiary and was fined $500. Jacob Schwartz died of pneumonia, possibly exacerbated by the effects of police torturing, while awaiting his trial.

Weinberger appealed the ruling before the Supreme Court, which gave the case a first hearing on October 21, 1919. The Court upheld the sentence with a vote of 7 to 2 on November 10, 1919, with Oliver Wendell Holmes, Jr., and Louis D. Brandeis dissenting. Free on $10,000 bail each, Abrams, Steimer, and Lipman tried to escape but were captured. Weinberger negotiated with American and Russian authorities for their deportation, which was granted at the defendants' own expense in 1921.

The significance of the Abrams case lies in its importance for the meaning of free speech and its limitations under the clear and present danger test. In the *Schenck v. United States* (1919), *Frohwerk v. United States* (1919), and *Debs v. United States* (1919) rulings, Holmes had imposed limitations to the right to free speech by introducing the clear and present danger test: "The question in every case is whether the words used are used in such circumstances and are of such a nature as to create a clear and present danger that they will bring about the substantive evils that Congress has a right to prevent" (*Schenck*). In his dissenting opinion in the Abrams case, Holmes modified the test significantly. He argued "that the best test of truth is the power of the thought to get itself accepted in the competition of the market." Only in extreme cases, Holmes said, should the law check the expression of opinions. Holmes's permissive redefinition of the clear and present danger test in his dissent in the Abrams case was invoked by justices into the 1960's to protect the right to freedom of expression.

See also Brandeis, Louis D.; *Brandenburg v. Ohio*; Civil liberties; Clear and present danger test; Holmes, Oliver Wendell, Jr.; *Schenck v. United States*; Speech and press, freedom of; Supreme Court of the United States.

Accessory, accomplice, and aiding and abetting

DEFINITION: Closely related concepts that apply to individuals accused of helping another in the commission of a crime

SIGNIFICANCE: The liability of an accomplice is an important concept in American criminal law

The terms "accessory" and "accomplice" are often used interchangeably and are roughly similar, but they have different derivations and slightly differing meanings today. "Accessory" comes from English common law, which divides participants in a crime into principals and accessories. In this classification, there are two types of accessories. Accessories before the fact aid, command, or encourage another person to commit a felony but are not present at the crime scene. Accessories after the fact knowingly give aid to a felon after the crime has been committed to help the felon evade apprehension or conviction. (By contrast, a "principal," in either the first or second degree, must have been present at the scene of the crime.)

Most criminal statutes in the United States no longer maintain this distinction. Rather, they emphasize the legal accountability of the "accomplice." An accomplice may be defined as anyone who contributes to the commission of a crime or encourages another party, in certain specified ways, to commit a crime. The criminal liability of an accomplice is an important concept in criminal law. In some jurisdictions it is governed by statute, in others by common-law concepts; either way, an accomplice is subject to the same criminal punishments as the perpetrator, although frequently an accomplice receives a lesser sentence. On the other hand, there are cases—as when a powerful crime boss orders or pressures another to commit a crime—in which the accomplice can receive a harsher sentence than the actual perpetrator.

Under common law, "aiding and abetting" may refer either to the actions of an accessory before the fact or to the actions of a principal in the second degree in helping the perpetrator (the principal in the first degree). The term has been incorporated into modern law and is generally held to mean either physical aid or activity that instigates, commands, procures, incites, or counsels another in ways that lead the other party to commit a crime. It is stipulated that the one aiding and abetting must be doing so with the intent of causing a crime to be committed—ambiguous or accidental connections between activities or exhortations and crimes are not prosecutable. Although there are broad areas of agreement among jurisdictions regarding accomplice law, there are also differences as to who should be considered an accomplice and how severe the punishment should be.

See also Attempt to commit a crime; Common law; Conspiracy; Criminal; Discretion.

Acquired immune deficiency syndrome (AIDS)

DEFINITION: AIDS is a fatal viral disease that destroys the human immune system

SIGNIFICANCE: AIDS has generated more litigation than any other disease in U.S. history

In 1982, the Centers for Disease Control (CDC, later renamed the Centers for Disease Control and Prevention) adopted the term acquired immune deficiency syndrome (AIDS) to describe a disease that attacks the immune system, producing susceptibility to rare and lethal forms of pneumonia, carcinoma, and opportunistic infections. The previous year, the CDC had noted a statistical relationship between AIDS and homosexuality.

In 1983, scientists in Paris isolated the human immunodeficiency virus (HIV), which causes AIDS. Sexual contact, intravenous drug abuse involving unsterilized needles, and contaminated blood were soon identified as the major modes of transmission. The disease may also pass from mother to child *in utero*. Asymptomatic persons who carry HIV antibodies in their blood are said to be HIV-positive.

In 1987, Ronald Reagan created a presidential commission to recommend federal policy on AIDS. In 1988, the National Institutes of Health (NIH) established the Office of AIDS Research. Congress' first major legislative response to AIDS came that same year with support for education, prevention, and home health care. By 1990, the federal budget for AIDS research topped the $1 billion mark.

In 1994, the World Health Organization estimated that seventeen million people worldwide were infected with AIDS.

The U.S. Agency of Health Care Policy and Research predicted that the care of one million HIV-positive Americans in 1995 would cost $15 billion. The CDC ranked AIDS as the number one killer of men and the number four killer of women ages twenty-five to forty-four. A 1993 report in *The New York Times* showed that AIDS cases had increased 3.5 percent in 1992. The number of known heterosexually transmitted cases doubled in 1993.

Curbing the Spread. Testing for HIV antibodies has been used in an attempt to slow the spread of AIDS. State laws and practices concerning consent, reporting, and confidentiality vary widely. In several states, minors can consent to HIV testing without parental approval. In 1988, the Illinois legislature amended the state's marriage laws to require an HIV test, then quickly repealed the law in 1989. Confidentiality is usually protected, but some states have adopted exceptions—for example, health care workers who risk transmitting the virus to their patients.

By 1995, more than half the states had passed laws concerning AIDS testing for sex offenders, some emphasizing the rights of the victim, some the rights of the accused. Some states permit compulsory testing of rape suspects. The Supreme Court of Illinois has upheld a statute requiring convicted prostitutes to submit to testing.

The transmission of AIDS has raised questions of criminal culpability. By 1992, twenty-four states had passed laws against knowingly exposing another person to HIV, and in 1993 the Supreme Court of Illinois held constitutional a state law making it a felony for one who knows he or she has HIV to engage in "intimate contact" with another. Some jurists assert a common-law duty to inform a sexual partner of HIV status or previous high-risk sexual activity or drug use.

Research and Treatment. In March, 1987, the Food and Drug Administration (FDA) approved the use of azidothymidine (AZT) as a drug treatment for AIDS. Other promising drugs and possible vaccines followed. In response to pressure from AIDS advocates, the FDA relaxed its approval process, allowing new AIDS drugs onto the market faster. Within months, the agency was criticized for rushing AIDS drugs into circulation without adequate testing.

AIDS advocates have consistently denounced the federal government for paying little attention to the disease, despite growing support for AIDS treatment and research programs in Congress and the White House. In 1993, President Bill Clinton announced a 20 percent increase in funding in AIDS research and a 66 percent increase in care through the Ryan White Comprehensive AIDS Resources Emergency Act of 1990. Also in 1993, the National Institutes of Health Revitalization Act centralized the federal government's AIDS-research program.

Provision of Health Care. The denial of health care to HIV-positive individuals has received much attention in the media and the courts. For example, in 1993, the Department of Justice used the Americans with Disabilities Act (ADA) to sue two dental offices for allegedly withholding care. The high

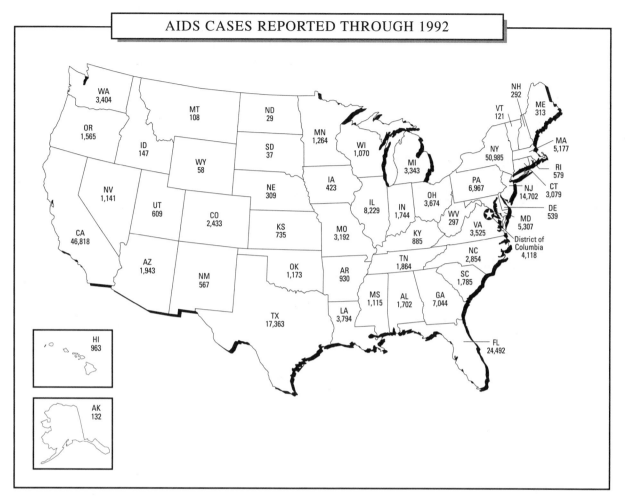

AIDS CASES REPORTED THROUGH 1992

WA 3,404
OR 1,565
MT 108
ND 29
MN 1,264
ID 147
SD 37
WI 1,070
NV 1,141
WY 58
NE 309
IA 423
MI 3,343
UT 609
CO 2,433
KS 735
IL 8,229
IN 1,744
OH 3,674
CA 46,818
AZ 1,943
NM 567
OK 1,173
MO 3,192
AR 930
KY 885
WV 297
VA 3,525
TN 1,864
NC 2,854
SC 1,785
MS 1,115
AL 1,702
GA 7,044
TX 17,363
LA 3,794
FL 24,492
NH 292
VT 121
ME 313
MA 5,177
NY 50,985
RI 579
PA 6,967
NJ 14,702
CT 3,079
DE 539
MD 5,307
District of Columbia 4,118
HI 963
AK 132

Source: Data are from U.S. Department of Health and Human Services, Public Health Service, *Health, United States, 1992* (DHHS publication PHS 93-1232). Washington, D.C.: U.S. Government Printing Office, 1993.

Note: The five states with the highest AIDS rates for 1993, according to the National Center for Health Statistics, were New York, Florida, New Jersey, California, and Delaware.

cost of treatment is an actuarial problem for insurers, who routinely reject HIV-positive individuals seeking life or medical coverage. Many refuse payment for experimental treatments, including AZT. In 1992, the U.S. Supreme Court refused to overturn a lower court ruling which allowed self-insured employers to cap health coverage for employees with AIDS.

The transmission of AIDS through blood transfusions and blood products (such as Factor VIII for hemophiliacs) has instigated a number of product liability cases. Manufacturers of blood products can be held liable for negligence if they fail to screen blood donors adequately. AIDS has also challenged both the legality and the morality of euthanasia. Laws against assisted suicide have been struck down in Michigan and Washington.

Employment. Most courts have sided with employees in AIDS-related cases. The California Court of Appeals has de-

fined AIDS as a physical handicap subject to the California Fair Employment and Housing Act. In 1992, the Westchester County (New York) Medical Center was found to have violated the federal Rehabilitation Act of 1973 by refusing to hire an HIV-positive applicant as a pharmacist. In 1994, a federal judge cited the ADA in permitting an antidiscrimination suit against a Philadelphia law firm that fired an AIDS-infected associate.

The 1990 ADA and the 1991 Civil Rights Act are generally agreed to prohibit employers from dismissing an HIV-positive employee. Nevertheless, the Equal Employment Opportunity Commission has affirmed employers' rights to limit or exclude coverage for AIDS under the ADA.

Discrimination. More than forty states have antidiscrimination laws to protect people with disabilities in matters of employment, housing, education, and civil rights. In 1992, the Minnesota Court of Appeals ruled that people with AIDS are

The AIDS epidemic has created the need for national and local organizations to provide support and services. (James L. Shaffer)

protected under the state's Human Rights Act. The U.S. Supreme Court has ruled that persons with a contagious disease are protected by the Rehabilitation Act of 1973. Nevertheless, immigration policies have banned HIV-positive persons from entering the United States, and schools in some states have had to be forced by the courts to accept HIV-positive children.

—Faith Hickman Brynie

See also Americans with Disabilities Act (ADA); Gay rights; Medical and health law.

BIBLIOGRAPHY

Legal issues involving AIDS have been the subject of many books and articles; among the best overviews are Allan H. Terl, *AIDS and the Law: A Basic Guide for the Nonlawyer* (Washington, D.C.: Taylor & Francis, 1992); Mona Rowe and Caitlin Ryan, *A Governor's Policy Guide on AIDS* (Washington, D.C.: National Governors' Association, 1989); American Bar Association, AIDS Coordinating Committee, *AIDS: The Legal Issues* (Chicago: American Bar Association, 1988); Wiley Law editorial staff, *AIDS and the Law* (2d ed. New York: Wiley, 1992); Scott Burris and Yale AIDS Law Project, eds., *AIDS Law Today: A New Guide for the Public* (New Haven, Conn.: Yale University Press, 1993); Padraig O'Malley, ed., *The AIDS Epidemic: Private Rights and the Public Interest* (Boston: Beacon Press, 1989).

Adamson v. California

COURT: U.S. Supreme Court
DATE: Decided June 23, 1947
SIGNIFICANCE: This case reaffirmed the "fundamental rights" interpretation of the due process clause of the Fourteenth Amendment; Justice Hugo Black wrote a widely noted dissent in which he argued that the clause should be read to incorporate all Bill of Rights guarantees against encroachment by state governments

Admiral Dewey Adamson was convicted of murder in the first degree in California in 1946 and condemned to death. California's criminal procedure at that time authorized the judge and prosecutor to comment on the defendant's refusal to testify. Adamson had committed earlier offenses which would have been revealed to the jury on cross-examination had he testified in his own defense. The prosecutor pointed out to the jury Adamson's refusal to take the stand. After his conviction, Adamson appealed on the ground that the due process clause of the Fourteenth Amendment protects his privilege against self-incrimination. Justice Stanley F. Reed, writing for a Supreme Court majority of five, held that the privilege against self-incrimination is not part of the right to a fair trial protected by the due process clause of the Fourteenth Amendment. Reed argued that "the purpose of due process is not to protect a defendant against a proper conviction but against an unfair conviction. When evidence is before a jury that threatens conviction, it does not seem unfair to require him to choose between leaving the adverse evidence unexplained and subjecting himself to impeachment through disclosure of former crimes." In short, California's procedure was not "fundamentally unfair."

Justice Felix Frankfurter concurred, arguing that the due process clause of the Fourteenth Amendment was not meant by its framers to include the whole Bill of Rights: "It would be extraordinarily strange for a Constitution to convey such specific commands in such a roundabout and inexplicit way" as the due process clause.

Justice Hugo Black's dissenting opinion argued that inclusion of the entire Bill of Rights in the Fourteenth Amendment had been the intention of its framers. He attached to his opinion a long historical appendix citing many of the speeches of Congressman Jonathan Bingham and other influential members of Congress who had participated in the drafting and ratification of the Fourteenth Amendment. Black argued further that the "fundamental fairness" rule was too open-ended; it gives too much power to judges to include and exclude rights according to their personal wishes rather than on the basis of principled constitutional analysis.

Frankfurter's position prevailed in theory and Black's in practice. By 1970 nearly the entire Bill of Rights had been incorporated into the Fourteenth Amendment. The major exceptions are the Second Amendment's right to keep and bear arms and the Fifth Amendment's command that criminal defendants are entitled to indictment by grand jury. The Court's specific decision in *Adamson* was overruled in 1964 in *Malloy v. Hogan*.

The open-ended character of the due process clause of the Fourteenth Amendment permitted later courts to expand personal liberty and privacy rights. *Griswold v. Connecticut* (1965) and *Eisenstadt v. Baird* (1972) established constitutional rights to receive and use birth control devices and information; *Roe v. Wade* (1973) established a constitutional right to an abortion in the first trimester of pregnancy. Had the Supreme Court accepted Justice Black's interpretation of the Fourteenth Amendment, these expansions of individual autonomy would have been much more difficult to achieve.

See also Black, Hugo L.; Due process of law; *Griswold v. Connecticut*; Incorporation doctrine; *Malloy v. Hogan*; *Roe v. Wade*.

Adarand Constructors v. Peña

COURT: U.S. Supreme Court
DATE: Decided June 12, 1995
SIGNIFICANCE: In this case the Supreme Court held that broad affirmative action programs involving employment and contracts were unconstitutional but preserved the applicability of affirmative action to specific and limited circumstances of discrimination

Randy Pech, a white contractor in Colorado Springs, Colorado, submitted the lowest bid for a federal road-repair project.

The contract, however, was awarded to a company owned by a Latino man because of a 1987 law requiring that the Department of Transportation award at least 10 percent of its funds to companies owned by minorities or women. Pech took his complaint to the courts. The case was decided by the Supreme Court at a time when criticism of affirmative action had become widespread both among the public and in Congress. In addition, the makeup of the Court itself had changed since the last federal affirmative action case in 1990; notably, Thurgood Marshall, a staunch liberal, had retired and been replaced by another African American jurist, Clarence Thomas, a conservative.

Overturning previous decisions offering support of federal affirmative action, the Court voted 5 to 4 that the type of affirmative action program involved in the case was unconstitutional. In an opinion written by Justice Sandra Day O'Connor, the Supreme Court stated that the Constitution protects individuals but was not intended to offer special protections to groups. Treating "any person unequally because of his or her race" causes the person to suffer an injury that is not acceptable under the Constitution's guarantee of equal protection under the law. The law can treat people differently because of race "only for the most compelling reasons," and racial classifications by government agencies are "inherently suspect and presumptively invalid." The Court did say, however, that affirmative action programs could be acceptable to remedy specific, provable cases of discrimination.

The decision severely undercut all federal affirmative action programs, most notably those involving jobs or contracts required to go to minorities ("minority set-asides"). In addition, federal law at the time of *Adarand* required firms that did more than $50,000 of business a year with the federal government and had more than fifty employees to have a written affirmative action policy, a fact which meant that the *Adarand* decision could affect the policies of nearly all major employers in the United States. Reaction to the decision was strong and immediate. A leader of the Anti-Defamation League called it a "sea change" in the law. Many civil rights leaders protested the decision and urged the government not to abolish all affirmative action efforts. Conservative Republican leaders in Congress, in contrast, vowed to pass legislation to eliminate all "racial preferences" in federal hiring and contracting.

See also Affirmative action; Equal protection of the law; *Fullilove v. Klutznick*; *Griggs v. Duke Power Co.*; *Regents of the University of California v. Bakke*; *Richmond v. J. A. Croson Co.*; *United Steelworkers of America v. Weber*.

Addams, Jane (Sept. 6, 1860, Cedarville, Ill.—May 21, 1935, Chicago, Ill.)

IDENTIFICATION: Social reformer
SIGNIFICANCE: Jane Addams' Hull House, founded in 1889, became the best-known American settlement house and the center of agitation to improve conditions in slums, sweatshops, and factories, protect child laborers, secure a juvenile court system, and obtain women's suffrage

Daughter of an abolitionist, Addams, after being graduated from Rockford (Illinois) Female Seminary in 1882, toured England and was impressed by Toynbee Hall, a London settlement house. In 1889, she established Hull House on that model in Chicago's Nineteenth Ward, the center of immigrants who then made up three-quarters of Chicago's million inhabitants. Increasingly aware that no settlement house could cure urban problems, Addams soon sought social legislation; she inspired and coordinated the efforts of a committed group of women who included Grace Abbott, Alice Hamilton, Julia Lathrop, and Florence Kelley. Their work, described in *Hull-House Maps and Papers* (1895), *Twenty Years at Hull-House* (1910), and *The Second Twenty Years at Hull-House* (1930), resulted in juvenile legislation, the first Illinois factory inspection act (1893), the first Chicago juvenile court (1899), and, through involvement with the National Consumers' League, legislation to secure fire safety and protection against occupational diseases. Addams, in 1912, was a delegate to the first national convention of the Progressive Party. She received the Nobel Prize in 1931.

See also Dix, Dorothea Lynde; Progressivism.

Administrative law

DEFINITION: The body of law that deals with the powers and procedures of administrative agencies; it includes judicial review of agency actions

SIGNIFICANCE: Administrative law is designed to prevent abuses of authority, and it stresses agency procedure, fairness, due process, accountability, and responsibility; administrative law provides a mechanism for aggrieved parties to seek redress

Administrative agencies implement and interpret government policies at the federal and state levels. Agencies are granted these responsibilities by the legislative branch of government. These agencies have the power of discretionary authority when implementing laws made by the legislature. The executive branch of government also maintains control over administrative agencies by its authority to set budget priorities for programs and through executive appointment of agency directors.

In order for administrative agencies to implement policy successfully, they must have discretion and enforcement authority. Without the power of enforcement, an agency cannot perform its mission. Administrative agencies fulfill their policy implementation obligations by adjudication, rule making, and other similar functions. The concept of administrative law developed from several sources, including both constitutional law and common law (law that is accepted although generally unwritten). Agencies promulgate policy through policy initiatives which they develop themselves. The rules and regulations enforced by agencies are created to control the functions and activities of private citizens and companies that operate within the jurisdiction assigned to each agency.

Enforcement of these rules and regulations is also carried out by the agencies. Violations of administrative law, either by individuals or by companies, are dealt with by the agency responsible for the law. Agencies can impose fines and sanctions, deny benefits, and perform inspections or audits to ensure compliance. The aggrieved party can seek redress for agency actions through an agency hearing or through the judicial process with the courts. During an agency hearing, an aggrieved party can retain legal counsel and is entitled to fair and impartial due process throughout the proceedings. These hearings are similar to regular court hearings in that careful documentation, pleading, rulings, objections, evidence, and the verdict are all recorded in the event the case is appealed to the judicial system.

Administrative law is intended to guard against abuses of agency power and thereby to provide justice for society at large as well as for individual participants in the case at issue. The three major areas of administrative law are rule making, adjudication, and judicial review. Each of these areas continues to define the direction and authority of administrative law. The ability to combine management, legal, and political considerations is critical in resolving problem areas in administrative law.

See also Civil service system; Due process of law; Judicial review.

Admiralty law

DEFINITION: The body of law controlling legal issues which arise on public navigable water involving maritime activity or transactions

SIGNIFICANCE: Federal district courts exercise jurisdiction over torts involving traditional maritime activity occurring on public navigable water and over contracts whose nature and subject matter involve maritime service or transactions

The United States Constitution, Article III, section 2, and the United States Code at Title 28, section 1333 establish exclusive admiralty jurisdiction in the federal district courts. This jurisdiction extends to public navigable waters that include (in addition to the ocean and tidal reaches) rivers, lakes, and other waterways, natural or otherwise, on which a vessel may travel among the states or to foreign countries. Jurisdiction will not include questions arising on a body of water lying entirely within an individual state. For tort questions, jurisdiction includes incidents involving a vessel on public navigable water regardless of whether the activity is commercial in nature. Courts also broadly define what may be considered a "vessel," though floating structures that are permanently chained to the bank are not vessels. Jurisdiction over contract questions depends upon whether the nature and subject matter of the transaction relate to maritime activity. While the Constitution and the United States Code do allow exceptions, it is seldom possible for state courts to exercise jurisdiction, and virtually all maritime cases are heard in federal district court.

Procedure. The Federal Rules of Civil Procedure include specific admiralty exceptions to the typical procedural rules. For example, admiralty courts allow a jury only when specifically provided for in a statute. There are also Supplemental Rules for Certain Admiralty and Maritime Claims Rules of Practice located in the Federal Code of Civil Procedure.

Among these rules is one of the more unusual aspects of admiralty practice, the arrest of a ship. The theory is that the vessel itself is responsible for some act, and the action is therefore brought directly against the ship. Arrest of the vessel by a U.S. marshal begins this *in rem* proceeding. Unless the owner appears in court, the district court may sell the vessel to satisfy the plaintiff's claim. In this proceeding, the notice requirements afforded to debtors on land do not apply. Actions against publicly owned vessels are brought under the Public Vessels Act or Suits in Admiralty and not under the Federal Tort Claims Act.

The basis of the *in rem* action is a maritime lien. These common-law liens were developed by English and American courts. Maritime liens include claims against the vessel for crew wages, salvage, collision and tort, repairs, and for providing necessaries, such as fuel, to the vessel. Preferred ship mortgages and "later repair and necessaries" liens are the only statutory maritime liens. The priority of ranks of liens is subject to interpretation by the court in the *in rem* proceeding. Within a priority rank, more recent liens often have a right superior to earlier liens. There may be further refinement to this order such that these proceedings become extremely complex. Generally, all maritime liens take priority over all land-based liens, even those which would otherwise have a high priority such as those with preferences in a bankruptcy proceeding.

Shipment of Goods. Material is transported by sea through contracts to lease a vessel, referred to as charters, or under bills of lading. Charters may be "demise," in which situation the charterer has control of the vessel as if the charterer were the owner, "time," in which the charterer controls the vessel's destinations and cargos for a calendar period, or "voyage," in which the charterer merely directs a vessel to a specific port. Depending on the type of charter, control and liability may shift to the charterer, though the vessel may still be liable. Transportation of goods under a bill of lading is controlled by two statutes: The Harter Act and the Carriage of Goods by Sea Act. A difficulty with the interpretation of these statutes is that there are few U.S. Supreme Court cargo cases, and some rulings of federal circuit courts of appeal are in conflict.

Remedies for Workers. Maritime shipboard workers are afforded common-law and statutory remedies for injury and death. A seaman permanently attached to a vessel may recover damages for the common-law remedies of maintenance, cure, and wages. These include wages to the end of the voyage, costs of return to the port where the seaman joined the voyage, medical expenses until the individual has recovered to the greatest extent possible, and board during the period of recovery. A second remedy is for unseaworthiness. The ship owner has an obligation to provide a vessel and crew which are fit for the venture. If they are not, even temporarily, the owner is liable to a seaman injured as a result of the unseaworthy condition. Unseaworthiness also affects defenses to damage claims regarding the cargo. The Jones Act provides a statutory remedy to seamen for injury and death and allows a jury.

These three remedies are generally tried together, and a Jones Act jury may also rule on the common-law remedies.

Recovery for death in maritime settings is governed by statute, as there was no remedy at common law. Actions for wrongful death are allowed under the Jones Act and the Death on the High Seas Act. The Death on the High Seas Act applies only to deaths which occur more than three miles from the United States. Federal courts have held that dependents of individuals who die within the three-mile limit and are not covered under the Jones Act may bring an action under the local state's wrongful death statute, adopted by the federal district court as federal common law.

Other subjects with unique admiralty rules include collision, salvage, finds, limitations on owner liability, passenger claims, crimes on the high seas, and marine insurance. Admiralty law applies to certain airline accidents as well. Questions regarding pollution, natural resources in the ocean, rights-of-way, and boundary issues are also addressed under admiralty law.   —*J. Denny Haythorn*

See also Coast Guard, U.S.; Environmental law; International law.

BIBLIOGRAPHY

Texts for further reading include Frank L. Maraist, *Admiralty in a Nutshell* (2d ed. St. Paul, Minn.: West, 1988); Thomas J. Schoenbaum, *Admiralty and Maritime Law* (2d ed. St. Paul, Minn.: West, 1994); and the looseleaf treatise by Erastus C. Benedict and Steven F. Friedell, *Benedict on Admiralty* (7th ed. New York: Matthew Bender, 1989).

Adultery

DEFINITION: The violation of the marriage vows through voluntary and consensual sexual intercourse with a third party

SIGNIFICANCE: Adultery is widely considered one of several offenses against morality; society and public policy have interests in moral issues, marital infidelity, and the preservation of the sanctity of family relationships

The biblical Ten Commandments considered adultery a violation of the moral code and thus sinful. Christian canon law continued this view. At first, adultery was dealt with by ecclesiastical courts. In turn, English common law prohibited such behavior, not only in its effort to embody community values but also because of the possible threat to the integrity of the family and the danger of illegitimate offspring. Later, British statutes made adultery a crime.

Most American states have followed suit, not so much to criminalize consensual relations between adults as to obviate harmful public results. Beyond its moral considerations, adultery is viewed as a possible source of disorder—for example, when a cuckolded spouse seeks revenge—or as prejudicial to the couple's children in case of public scandal or as an affront to community standards.

Laws vary regarding whether adultery or adulterous cohabitation is a felony or merely a misdemeanor, whether the unmarried person in the case of single adultery (where only one of the parties is married to someone else) is as guilty as the married partner, whether coitus needs to have occurred only once or more often to rate as a criminal act, and whether the illicit relationship must necessarily have been open and notorious. Adultery is sometimes considered to be "normal" sexual intercourse, so that "deviate" relations such as oral or anal sex between two consenting adults (of the same or opposite gender) may not be considered adulterous by the law regardless of marital status. Such activity may be considered illegal for other reasons. When legal action on charges of adultery is brought, a number of defenses—for example, ignorance of a partner's marital status—may obviate conviction.

Opposition to these laws has grown on the grounds of evolving mores and the widespread violation of traditional moral codes. Infrequent and inconsistent enforcement of laws prohibiting adultery has led to charges of discrimination and arbitrariness and thus contempt for the law. Regardless of whether there is criminal prosecution, proven adultery is legal grounds for divorce or separation in civil courts. State laws against adultery have survived the constitutional challenge that they infringe on the right of privacy.

See also Common law; Criminal law; Family law; Mitigating circumstances; Ninth Amendment; Privacy, right of; Rape and sex offenses; Victimless crimes.

Advisory opinion

DEFINITION: A judicial decision or opinion that is rendered on an issue when there is not a particular case or controversy before the court

SIGNIFICANCE: The fact that advisory opinions are not given by U.S. federal courts helps maintain the separation between the branches of the federal government; some state governments allow their courts to offer advisory opinions

An advisory opinion is a judicial decision rendered when there is not a case or controversy before the court. Such decisions are prohibited by Article III, section 2 of the United States Constitution, which limits the jurisdiction of federal courts to "Cases" and "Controversies." This restriction on the power of federal courts ensures that they will not decide important constitutional issues prematurely or invade the functions of the executive or legislative branches of the government. The practice of not offering advisory opinions has been consistently adhered to by the Supreme Court. As Justice Robert H. Jackson noted in *Chicago and Southern Air Lines v. Waterman Steamship Corporation* (1948), "It has . . . been the firm and unvarying practice of Constitutional Courts to render no judgments not binding and conclusive on the parties and none that are subject to later review or alteration by administrative action." To do otherwise would put the Court in the potential position of offering advice to another branch of the government when it has not asked for it but a private litigant has demanded it. Such a result would be an intolerable invasion of the other branch's authority by the Court.

The prohibition on offering advisory opinions was adopted even though at the time of the American Revolution it was accepted practice for English courts to do so. The earliest example of the use of advisory opinion doctrine occurred in 1793, when Secretary of State Thomas Jefferson sought the Supreme Court's advice on the legality of positions that President George Washington wanted to take in the wars which arose between European powers after the French Revolution. The Supreme Court refused to offer any advice, because to do so would require it to act outside its constitutionally assigned judicial role. In *Muskrat v. United States* (1911), the Supreme Court emphasized that federal courts could not hear lawsuits when there was no real controversy between the parties, because any decision rendered would be advisory in nature. In 1937, however, in *Aetna Life Insurance Co. v. Haworth*, the Court held that the advisory opinion doctrine did not prohibit federal courts from hearing declaratory judgment action. According to *Ex parte Bakelite Corp.* (1929), Congress may authorize Article I courts to render advisory opinions, because such courts are not subject to the "Cases" and "Controversies" requirement found in Article III.

See also Retroactivity of Supreme Court decisions; Supreme Court of the United States.

Affirmative action

DEFINITION: Policies or programs specifically designed to increase the numbers of minorities and women in employment and education where their representation has been sparse or nonexistent

SIGNIFICANCE: Since the 1960's, affirmative action has been considered a major strategy in the attempt to eliminate institutional discrimination in the areas of employment and education by providing minorities and women with greater access to opportunity; it has also been controversial and widely debated

Affirmative action policies and programs have created tremendous controversy since their introduction in the 1960's under the John F. Kennedy and Lyndon B. Johnson administrations. Affirmative action programs involve strategies designed to increase the participation of women and minorities, particularly in the areas of employment and education. Typically, affirmative action programs are gender-conscious and/or race-conscious measures designed to assist minorities in overcoming past and present discrimination.

Purpose of Affirmative Action. Affirmative action policies have been applied to a host of situations involving discrimination in employment and education. The underlying purpose is to increase the prospect for equality of opportunity while eliminating systemic discrimination against specific populations. Equality of opportunity has historically been the social agenda pushed by civil rights organizations. They believe that affirmative action is an important strategy in the struggle for equal opportunity.

The enforcement of affirmative action is predicated almost exclusively on Title VII of the 1964 Civil Rights Act (and to a lesser degree on Executive Order 11246, a 1965 order requiring equal employment opportunity clauses in all federal contracts). The U.S. Department of Justice, the Equal Employment Opportunity Commission, the Office of Federal Contract Compliance Programs (of the Department of Labor), and the federal courts have used Title VII to dismantle long-standing patterns of discrimination in employment and education. Affirmative action programs are actually considered remedial strategies.

Ideally, affirmative action is a twofold approach. First, it is an analysis of the existing workforce to determine if the percentages of "protected groups" in a given job classification are similar to the percentage of those groups in the surrounding community. Second, if it can be substantiated that certain practices have an exclusionary effect in the selection process, affirmative (race- and gender-conscious) measures may be required to remedy the situation. A number of steps may be taken to alter the existing selection process, including the establishment of goals and timetables for hiring, the development of recruitment programs, a redesigning of jobs and job descriptions, substantiation of the use of testing as a selection instrument, and attempting to improve the opportunity for advancement training for those in positions with limited career paths.

An affirmative action program may involve some or all of these steps. Additionally, affirmative action may be either voluntary or mandated by the courts. A court order or consent decree may force an offending enterprise to make restitution and to submit a detailed plan specifying its intentions to provide back pay and strategies for equitable promotion opportunities to those it has victimized. It may also include a provision on how it proposes to restructure its recruitment and hiring practices to come into compliance with federal guidelines. A primary concern of affirmative action is to encourage that additional measures be taken that go beyond the mere cessation of discriminatory practices.

Without the invoking of goals and timetables, the responsibility for providing equal opportunity would rest solely with the employer. Goals and timetables provide a type of indicator for employers; they are different from quotas, which are rigid and inflexible. Quotas do not allow for flexibility above or below the stated numbers.

Distributive Justice and Compensatory Justice. Since the Supreme Court's decision in the "reverse discrimination" case of *Regents of the University of California v. Bakke* in 1978, the debate on affirmative action has been framed within interpretations of Title VII of the 1964 Civil Rights Act, the 1965 Executive Order 11246, and subsequent decisions by the Supreme Court. The Court's decisions have appeared to oscillate between limiting and expanding affirmative action. Two major questions are considered in such decisions: whether affirmative action is permissible and appropriate under the law, and whether it should be limited to victims of discrimination or should include distributive remedies.

According to Kathanne W. Greene, in *Affirmative Action and Principles of Justice* (1989), affirmative action rests on two basic principles: distributive justice and compensatory justice. Distributive justice is concerned with the distribution of the benefits, rights, and burdens shared by members of society. These benefits and rights can be distributed in several ways; they may be based on equality of opportunity, for example, or based on need, effort, and utility. Therefore, there is no one best way to effectuate distributive justice.

Compensatory justice is essentially concerned with compensation (or reparation) for past injustices against individuals or groups by the government: a victim is entitled to fair compensation or entitled to be returned to a situation comparable to that which existed prior to the injustice. There is little debate that the U.S. government was a participant in the injustices perpetuated against certain groups (see *Plessy v. Ferguson*, 1896).

Levels of Preferential Consideration. There are arguably three levels at which preferential considerations or affirmative measures may be accorded women and minorities in employment and education under affirmative action. First, an affirmative measure can be accorded minorities or women who are less qualified than their white male counterparts. Second, an affirmative measure can be granted to minorities and women when they and their white male counterparts are equally qualified. Third, minorities and women can be accorded an affirmative measure when they are more qualified than their white male counterparts.

The Affirmative Action Controversy. Critics of affirmative action argue that it accords special privilege to entire categories of people whose individual members may or may not have experienced discrimination. Moreover, they maintain that affirmative action policies establish rigid quotas and may therefore extend opportunities to individuals that are otherwise unqualified. The resulting argument is that affirmative action programs create "reverse discrimination" against white males. Proponents, on the other hand, argue that race-conscious and gender-conscious measures are needed because race and gender have long been bases for discrimination. Race and gender, they say, still limit opportunities for minorities and women in certain areas of society. Consequently, minorities and women will only be able to achieve equal opportunity through the use of race- and gender-conscious strategies.

Affirmative action and equality of opportunity have been inextricably linked in the minds of some Americans. Yet over the years affirmative action has become associated with concepts that have served to bias many others against it. For example, terms such as "preferential treatment," "minority set-asides," "quotas," "managing diversity," and "reverse discrimination" have caused many whites to become hostile to the concept of affirmative action. Few Americans would dispute the fact that minority populations and women have experienced widespread discrimination in the past. Many, however, disagree that they continue to experience discrimination. One reason has to do with the perception that there is already widespread application of affirmative action programs in both the public and private sectors.

"Reverse Discrimination." Some opponents of affirmative action insist that such policies and programs amount to social engineering and violate the Constitution: They virtually sanction discrimination against white males, thereby simply reversing the object of discrimination. The reverse discrimination argument maintains that women and members of minority groups receive preferential treatment in employment (for example, in obtaining promotions) and in admission to institutions of higher education, particularly where a past history of discrimination can be documented. In such situations white males who may demonstrate greater academic skill, may have accrued more seniority on the job, or may have scored higher on an entrance examination may be passed over so that the institution can increase the numbers of an underrepresented population. Consequently, and controversially, such decisions are not based on merit. It might be noted that very little objection has been heard concerning episodes of nepotism and widespread preferential treatment offered to veterans (which are clearly not based on merit).

In the well-known 1978 *Regents of the University of California v. Bakke* litigation, a white applicant with a higher score on a medical school entrance examination than some minority applicants was rejected because of the practice of reserving fifteen spaces for minority applicants. Tremendous controversy ensued. (Little was said about the sons and daughters of upper-level university officials who also happened to receive special consideration over more qualified applicants.) Al-

though affirmative action policies are attempts to rectify past and present discriminatory practices, they do undeniably have a negative impact on the opportunities of some white males (as argued in *Weber v. Kaiser Aluminum & Chemical Corp.*, 1976). Opponents of affirmative action argue that all that can be hoped to be achieved legally is the eradication of discrimination. Nothing else, constitutionally, can be done. Any attempt to compensate victims of discrimination—especially if they are given preferential consideration in hiring, promotion, or admission to an institution of higher education—simply results in another form of discrimination. Compensation, if it were to be considered, should be offered only to the actual victims of discrimination, not to individuals simply because they belong to a particular group. Departing from its previous rulings on affirmative action, the Supreme Court gave support to this view in 1995 in its decision in *Adarand Constructors v. Peña*.

Limited Success of Affirmative Action. It has been argued that affirmative action programs have experienced only limited success, despite the fact that they have been an accepted strategy for many years. Augustus J. Jones, Jr., in *Affirmative Talk, Affirmative Action: A Comparative Study of the Politics of Affirmative Action*, suggests a number of reasons for this. First is poor communication between policy makers and those

Alan Bakke, central figure in the landmark 1978 Supreme Court case Regents of the University of California v. Bakke, *graduating from medical school in 1982.* (AP/Wide World Photos)

responsible for implementing the policies. If policies are not clearly delineated they cannot be effectively administered. Second, a lack of adequate resources may prohibit successful implementation. Money, information, authority, and the necessary staff must all be in place. Third, those responsible for implementation may be antagonistic to affirmative action and may operate opposite to their directives. Fourth, dysfunctional organization structure may preclude the effective implementation of policies. Fifth, political leadership (especially at the national level) may sour the social climate for the acceptance of affirmative action. In particular, inflammatory rhetoric using such terms as "preferential treatment," "racial quotas," and "reverse discrimination" has helped to create reservation and even anger among some whites regarding the legitimacy of affirmative action. Presidents Ronald Reagan and George Bush, for example, consistently referred to affirmative action policies as reverse discrimination and quota legislation.

Ronald Reagan, in particular, was an outspoken critic of affirmative action policies and programs. He believed that they were unfair and that they led to rigid quotas, and he appointed men and women during his administration that shared his views. It has been noted that Reagan put together a conservative team of legal experts in the Department of Justice that shared his opposition to affirmative action. His administration also challenged the use of statistical data as a means of substantiating discriminatory patterns by employers.

Both Reagan and Bush appointed to posts in their administrations and in federal agencies minority individuals who opposed affirmative action. Reagan completely restructured the U. S. Commission on Civil Rights and selected Clarence Pendleton, an African American, to be chairman of the commission. Pendleton proved to be so extreme in his opposition to affirmative action that he was rejected by much of the African American community and rebuffed by black Republicans. Linda Chávez, a Hispanic, was selected staff director of the U.S. Civil Rights Commission. Criticizing affirmative action programs in a number of speeches, she argued that affirmative action actually endangered the progress made by African Americans since *Brown v. Board of Education* (1954) and that it was a new type of paternalism.

Clarence Thomas, as chairman of the Equal Employment Opportunity Commission (EEOC), applied a more restrictive interpretation of Title VII than his predecessors had. He decided that the EEOC would pursue only individual claims of discrimination that could be explicitly proved. Therefore, neither statistical data nor the underrepresentation of certain populations in the workforce would be sufficient to demonstrate systemic discrimination. The individual complainant had to provide undeniable proof of discrimination. This policy virtually eliminated the conception of "pattern and practice" discrimination for filing suit.

Congress and the federal courts also manifested some degree of retrenchment regarding affirmative action during the 1980's. Amendments were introduced in Congress to eliminate affirmative action, while the federal courts, in particular

the Supreme Court, vacillated on the applicability of affirmative action policies. A number of decisions by the Court in the 1980's and 1990's, particularly *Adarand Constructors v. Peña*, called into question the use of broad affirmative action programs.   *—Charles C. Jackson*

See also *Adarand Constructors v. Peña*; Equal protection of the law; *Griggs v. Duke Power Co.*; *Regents of the University of California v. Bakke*; *Richmond v. J. A. Croson Co.*; *United Steelworkers of America v. Weber*.

BIBLIOGRAPHY

An excellent explanation of affirmative action goals and discussion of timetables versus quotas can be found in Robert K. Fullinwider's *The Reverse Discrimination Controversy: A Moral and Legal Analysis* (Totowa, N.J.: Rowman & Littlefield, 1980). A discussion of the justification for reverse discrimination can be found in chapter 3 of Tom Regan and Donald VanDeVeer's *And Justice for All: New Introductory Essays in Ethics and Public Policy* (Totowa, N.J.: Rowman & Allanheld, 1982). An analysis of the effort to dismantle affirmative action is provided by Charles C. Jackson in "Affirmative Action: Controversy and Retrenchment," *The Western Journal of Black Studies* 16 (no. 4, Winter, 1992). Other discussions of affirmative action include Kathanne W. Greene, *Affirmative Action and Principles of Justice* (New York: Greenwood Press, 1989); Marshal Cohen, Thomas Nagel, and Thomas Scanlon, eds., *Equality and Preferential Treatment* (Princeton, N.J.: Princeton University Press, 1977); Mary G. Miner and John B. Miner, *Employee Selection Within the Law* (Washington D.C.: Bureau of National Affairs, 1979); Daniel C. Maguire, *A New American Justice* (Garden City, N.Y.: Doubleday, 1980). A good look at the application of affirmative action programs at the local level can be found in Augustus J. Jones, *Affirmative Talk, Affirmative Action: A Comparative Study of the Politics of Affirmative Action* (New York: Praeger, 1991).

Age discrimination

DEFINITION: The denial of access, benefits, or services solely on grounds of age

SIGNIFICANCE: The concept of age discrimination extends the concept of civil rights to age by presuming that justice requires nondiscriminatory treatment of all persons, irrespective of chronological age

The term "ageism" was coined by Robert N. Butler in his 1975 book *Why Survive? Being Old in America*. He defined it as the "process of systematic stereotyping of and discrimination against people because they are old." Arthur S. Flemming, while serving both as commissioner on aging for the Department of Health, Education, and Welfare (HEW) and as chairman of the United States Commission on Civil Rights, introduced this terminology into political rhetoric that same year. Ageism, he told the House Education and Labor Committee, was equivalent to racism and sexism, and he "hope[d] that the day will come when the Civil Rights Act will be amended to include age . . . as one of the factors that must be taken into consideration under the Civil Rights Act." The expression "ageism" later became integral to the rhetoric of protest groups such as the Gray Panthers, while advocacy groups such as the American Association of Retired Persons (AARP) lobbied against age discrimination.

The Age Discrimination Act of 1975. Most civil rights legislation is modeled on the Civil Rights Act of 1964, which categorically prohibits any discrimination on the basis of race, color, or national origin. The first law protecting older people, however, the Age Discrimination in Employment Act of 1967, banned only workplace discrimination against people between the ages of forty and sixty-five. The narrow scope of the 1967 law was one reason Flemming hoped that Congress would incorporate age discrimination into a broad civil rights law. By the end of 1975, Congress had granted his wish and passed the Age Discrimination Act of 1975. The act categorically prohibited discrimination on the basis of age: "[N]o person in the United States shall, on the basis of age, be excluded from participation in, be denied the benefits of, or be subjected to discrimination under, any program receiving Federal financial assistance." In 1978 Congress amended the Age Discrimination in Employment Act to extend protection to all workers up to age seventy and to prohibit mandatory retirement prior to age seventy.

Although the 1964 Civil Rights Act and all subsequent civil rights laws seek to remedy discrimination against certain specific groups (African Americans, female Americans) they are written to protect every American (white or black, male or female). Consequently, although the Age Discrimination Act was motivated by a desire to protect the elderly, the civil rights paradigm required that it protect Americans of all ages—the young as well as the old. Despite this affirmation of universal rights, however, the Age Discrimination Act willingly suspends its egalitarian strictures for programs—such as Medicare—that assist members of the discriminated-against group.

The Case for Prohibiting Age Discrimination. Martin Luther King, Jr., dreamed of an America in which all people would be judged by the content of their character, not the color of their skin. The Age Discrimination Act seeks to create an America in which people are judged by their ability, not the wrinkles on their face or the date on their birth certificate. Civil rights laws impose a moral vision upon a recalcitrant reality: To envision all persons as equal is, in a sense, to blind oneself to a world in which everyone is different—differently colored, differently gendered, differently abled, and differently aged. To argue for a civil right to equal treatment is thus to argue that there is a compelling moral reason for ignoring these differences. The reason most commonly cited is a history of denying people opportunities to realize their potential as persons—denials of access, participation, or benefit—because of some unrelated biological or physiological fact (such as skin color, gender, or disability).

Age, like skin color, gender, and disability, is a biophysiological fact. As testimony before the House Education and Labor Committee quickly established, this biological fact was used by businesses, private organizations, and governmental agencies to deny the elderly access to credit, education, employment, housing, mortgage financing, and scarce medical resources, irrespective of their abilities or physical condition. Thus the biophysiological fact of old age per se, like the biophysiological facts of skin color and sex, had become associated with negative stereotypes that effectively denied individuals the opportunity to function fully as persons.

Moreover, the primary source of legal redress, the courts, had long refused to recognize, much less to remedy, discrimination against the elderly. Article III of the U.S. Constitution implicitly rejects the idea of mandatory retirement by guaranteeing life tenure to federal judges. Yet in a 1976 case, *Massachusetts Board of Retirement v. Murgia*, the U.S. Supreme Court upheld the right of the states to retire all police officers over age fifty, irrespective of their physical condition or their ability to perform their jobs. The Court also rejected the claim that age, like race, should be constitutionally protected under the equal protection and due process doctrines:

> While the treatment of the aged in this Nation has not been wholly free of discrimination, such persons, unlike, say, those who have been discriminated against on the basis of race or national origin, have not experienced a "history of purposeful unequal treatment" or been subjected to unique disabilities on the basis of stereotyped characteristics not truly indicative of their abilities. . . . [O]ld age does not define a discrete and insular group . . . in need of "extraordinary protection from the majoritarian political process." Instead, it marks a stage that each of us will reach if we live out our normal span.

Only one justice, Thurgood Marshall, dissented from the decision—and he was the only justice who could compare age and race discrimination on the basis of personal experience.

A number of other Supreme Court cases have addressed age discrimination, with a variety of results. In *Vance v. Bradley* (1979), the Court held that it was constitutional for the government to require Foreign Service employees to retire at age sixty, emphasizing the special needs of the Foreign Service. In *Johnson v. Mayor and City Council of Baltimore* (1985), on the other hand, the Court held that Baltimore's requirement that firefighters be under the age of fifty-five was not a bona fide occupational qualification.

Children's Rights. The Age Discrimination Act protects the young as well as the elderly, but no evidence of discrimination against the young was presented to Congress. The Age Discrimination Act was drafted to protect all age groups against discrimination simply because it was modeled on earlier civil rights legislation that protected against all forms of racial and gender bias. Nevertheless, a compelling case has since been made for the protection of children's rights.

It is probably not coincidental that the civil rights legislation of the 1960's and 1970's was enacted by the generation that fought both World War II and the Cold War (which flared into "hot" wars in Korea and Vietnam). To justify fighting these wars abroad, American administrations continually evoked the democratic and egalitarian ideals of the United States' foundational charters, the Declaration of Independence and the Constitution. The stage was thus set for civil rights reformers to appeal to these same foundational ideals to remedy undemocratic and inegalitarian social conditions at home.

The Declaration of Independence and the Constitution say little about the rights of children and youths. The Declaration declares that all "men" are created equal but says nothing specifically about children. The Constitution expressly denies children and youths the right to hold the office of president or vice president (minimum age thirty-five), senator (thirty), or representative (twenty-five). The Twenty-sixth Amendment bars federal and state governments from setting the minimum voting age higher than eighteen (thus implicitly empowering them to deny anyone younger than eighteen the right to vote). Children's rights advocates, therefore, sought inspiration not in the United States' foundational documents but in the works of John Locke, the seventeenth century philosopher whose ideas inspired the founders to write these documents. Chapter six of Locke's *Second Treatise of Government* (1690) is an eloquent yet searing critique of "paternal power," the presumed right of parents, particularly fathers, to control the lives of their offspring:

> Though I have said that *All Men by Nature are equal* . . . *Children*, I confess are not born in this full state of *Equality*, though they are born to it. Their Parents have a sort of Rule and Jurisdiction over them when they come into the World, and for some time after, but 'tis but a temporary one. The Bonds of this Subjection are like the Swaddling Cloths they are wrapt up in . . . in the weakness of their Infancy. Age and Reason as they grow up, loosen them till at length they drop quite off, and leave a Man at his own free disposal.

Locke does not specify a chronological age when children attain the age of reason. He offers instead a criterion for emancipation: Parents have a right "To inform the Mind and govern the Actions of their yet ignorant Nonage [children], till Reason shall take its place, and ease them of that Trouble." Thus, for Locke, children come of age when they can reason well enough to understand the consequences of their actions and to take responsibility for them.

Until the end of World War II, American courts eschewed Locke's rationality criterion, preferring to mark maturity chronologically. In a 1944 case, *Prince v. Massachusetts*, the U.S. Supreme Court upheld a state statute prohibiting "boys under twelve and girls under eighteen" from selling newspapers and magazines, thereby denying a nine-year-old girl the right to sell Jehovah's Witnesses literature despite her guardian's consent. In language that is grandiloquent (but overblown, given the facts of the case), the Court declared that parents cannot "make martyrs of their children before they have reached the age of full and legal discretion." Thus the Court not only denied a guardian the right to raise her child as she believed best, but also, by insisting that chronological age

defined maturity, denied the child herself the possibility of deciding whether to "martyr" herself by selling magazines.

In the postwar era, most state and federal courts have used the "mature minor rule" to empower young people to make decisions for themselves, especially about health care. Angela Holder, in an essay in *Children and Health Care: Moral and Social Issues* (1989), has characterized this rule as "the legal principle . . . that if a young person . . . understands the nature of the proposed [medical] treatment and its risks and can give the same degree of informed consent as an adult patient, and the treatment does not involve very serious risks, the young person may validly consent to receiving it." Thus the courts have been moving toward Locke's view that that decision-making capacity, rather than chronology, defines maturity—in other words, they are implementing the underlying age-blind conception of the 1975 Age Discrimination Act.

Arguments Against the Age Discrimination and Age Discrimination in Employment Acts. Criticisms of age discrimination legislation generally fall into two major categories: arguments that the elderly do not truly constitute a separate and distinct group and arguments that societal resources, if they must be unevenly distributed, should go to younger people first. Law professor Peter Schuck has noted that the Age Discrimination Act could not live up to its age-blind ideals, and he argues that other civil rights legislation has the justification of protecting a separate disadvantaged group, whereas the elderly do not constitute such a group. As the Supreme Court pointed out in the *Murgia* case, the elderly are ourselves at a different stage in the normal life cycle. Therefore, to some, the analogy of comparing age to gender and race is false. According to Schuck, in "The Graying of Civil Rights Law" (*The Yale Law Journal*, 1979), the Age Discrimination Act "leaves a conceptual void concerning the nature of the age discrimination problem."

Others, including Daniel Callahan and Norman Daniels, argue that intergenerational justice requires society to prioritize access to scarce resources in favor of young people. This argument is based on the idea that it is unfair to deny resources to those who have not reached their full natural life span in order to extend the lives of those who have already lived beyond their full natural life span. Both Callahan and Daniels maintain that this life span is seventy-five years.

Ideals and Reality. Egalitarian ideals always conflict with inegalitarian reality. In reality, the young and the elderly are treated differently because they are more vulnerable. In reality, the elderly were all once young, so in that sense there is no separate class of elderly persons. Yet American justice was founded on John Locke's seemingly unrealistic ideal of an egalitarian society in which all rational persons have equal opportunities to realize themselves as persons. Locke believed that education was crucial to realizing this ideal and that parents (and, by extension, all middle-aged people) are obligated to support and to educate each new generation of youth. Justice, however, requires reciprocity; it requires that the younger generation, when grown, then honor and support the elderly generation that educated them. Locke never discussed age discrimination, but one suspects that he would have argued that respecting someone equally, as a person, is a minimal requisite of honoring them.   —*Robert Baker*

See also Affirmative action; Age Discrimination in Employment Act; Aid to Families with Dependent Children (AFDC); Americans with Disabilities Act (ADA); Civil rights; Civil Rights Act of 1964; Civil Rights Act of 1968; Commission on Civil Rights; *Illinois v. Krull*; *Massachusetts Board of Retirement v. Murgia*.

BIBLIOGRAPHY

John Locke's *Two Treatises of Government*, edited by Peter Laslett (Cambridge, England: Cambridge University Press, 1960) is the classic edition of a classic work. Robert N. Butler's *Why Survive? Being Old in America* (New York: Harper & Row, 1975) introduced the concept of ageism. Two good introductions to the children's rights movement are William Aiken and Hugh La Follette, *Whose Child? Children's Rights, Parental Authority, and State Power* (Totowa, N.J.: Littlefield Adams, 1980), and Jeffrey Blustein, *Parents and Children: The Ethics of the Family*, (Oxford University Press, N.Y. 1982); Loretta Kopelman and John Moskop's *Children and Health Care: Moral and Social Issues* (Boston: Kluwer Academic Publishers, 1989) presents the debate over "mature minors." Two important challenges to the ideal of an age-blind society are Daniel Callahan, *Setting Limits: Medical Goals in an Aging Society* (New York: Simon & Schuster, 1987), and Norman Daniels, *Am I My Parents' Keeper?: An Essay on Justice Between the Young and the Old* (New York: Oxford University Press, 1988). Peter Schuck's critique of the Age Discrimination Act of 1975, "The Graying of Civil Rights Law," is in *The Yale Law Journal* 89 (November, 1979).

Age Discrimination in Employment Act

DATE: Enacted 1967

DEFINITION: Legislation that protects workers age forty and older from discrimination in employment

SIGNIFICANCE: Age discrimination, not addressed in the Civil Rights Act of 1964, was prohibited by this act except in rare cases involving "bona fide occupational qualifications"

The Age Discrimination in Employment Act (ADEA) is designed to "promote the employment of older persons based on their ability rather than their age" and to prevent age discrimination in employment. The ADEA applies to all private employers with twenty or more employees, state and local governments, employment agencies serving covered employers, and labor unions with twenty-five or more members. High-level managers in bona fide executive or policy-making positions and public safety personnel such as police and firefighters are partially exempt from the provisions of the act.

Under the ADEA (as amended in 1987), employers are prohibited from discriminating against any person who is forty years of age or older on the basis of age. Under the act, however, an employer may use age as a basis for employment decisions when there is a bona fide occupational qualification (BFOQ). An employer asserting a BFOQ must prove three things: that the age limit is "reasonably necessary to the normal operation of the particular business," that all or substantially all individuals excluded from the job are in fact not qualified, and that age is the only means to identify which individuals are not qualified. The decision on whether there is a valid BFOQ is based on the facts of each situation. The courts have narrowly construed BFOQ claims.

Although Congress debated issues of age discrimination in the 1950's, age was not included as a protected class under Title VII of the Civil Rights Act of 1964. The reasons for its exclusion include Congress' perception at the time that age discrimination is not intentional but based on false stereotypes. Further, Congress wanted time to identify the extent of age discrimination on older workers and the economy. The secretary of labor was asked to study and report on the matter, and the findings of that study formed the basis of the ADEA. The provisions of the statute also include features from Title VII and the Fair Labor Standards Act. Since enactment of the ADEA in 1967, there have been numerous amendments. In 1974 the law was extended to state, local, and federal entities. The ADEA initially extended protection only between the ages of forty and sixty-five. In 1978 the upper age limit was increased from sixty-five to seventy, and in 1987, the upper limit was eliminated entirely. In 1984, coverage was extended to U.S. citizens employed by U.S. corporations even when they are employed outside the United States.

Related legislation and executive orders include the Age Discrimination Act of 1975, which extends coverage to recipients of federal assistance; Executive Order 11141, which prohibits federal contractors and subcontractors from age discrimination; and the Older Worker Benefit Protection Act, which prohibits age discrimination in benefits and establishes minimum standards for determining waivers and claims under the ADEA. Until July 1, 1979, the Department of Labor administered the ADEA, but after that date the Equal Employment Opportunity Commission (EEOC) became responsible for its enforcement. The EEOC has since issued its own interpretation of the act.

See also Age discrimination; Equal Employment Opportunity Commission (EEOC); *Massachusetts Board of Retirement v. Murgia*.

Aid to Families with Dependent Children (AFDC)

DEFINITION: The joint federal-state program designed to provide relief to disadvantaged families with children

SIGNIFICANCE: Aid to Families with Dependent Children (AFDC) seeks to guarantee a minimum economic standard for the millions of poor children in the United States

The idea of government payments to families started at the state level; it originated with the mothers' aid movements of the early twentieth century. Originally intended to provide relief to mothers who would otherwise have left children alone while they went to work, these programs proved ineffective in

A 1995 rally in support of programs such as AFDC and against congressional Republicans' plans to cut social spending. (Jim West)

serving or protecting the increasing number of children in poverty. The Social Security Act of 1935 established the first federally mandated program directed at providing relief for children. Title IV of the act, "Grants to States for the Aid to Dependent Children [ADC]," established a dual-level program: The federal level provided funding through grants-in-aid to the states and set national guidelines, while the state level actually administered the program.

Initially, the program concentrated on families wherein the father, for whatever reason, was absent. Seeing a need to provide some level of economic security for these families, the system offered monthly payments to those who qualified based on family income and other criteria. Subsequent amendments to the Social Security Act extended the qualifications to cover families with a disabled or unemployed parent.

Several socioeconomic factors led to a dramatic increase in program recipients during the 1950's and 1960's. This increase, coupled with a systemwide reform of Social Security in the early 1960's, resulted in a name change from Aid to Dependent Children (ADC) to Aid to Families with Dependent Children (AFDC) in 1962. Along with the name change came a new direction for the program as it sought to add new services in addition to monthly payments, including medical coverage, day care programs, and job training. AFDC and the Child Welfare Services programs were formally combined in 1967.

Although AFDC has been instrumental in helping families across the country, the program has fallen under harsh criticism. Charges against the system have ranged from invasions of privacy to excessive bureaucracy. In addition to these administrative criticisms, the program has often faced social condemnation. Some studies, for example, have concluded that AFDC guidelines punished fathers and even promoted illegitimacy.

Despite criticism, challenges to funding, and changes in its program goals, AFDC has continued to move forward. Since the early 1960's, when the federal government began reworking social service programs, changes in federal budgetary demands have threatened to decrease the number of families AFDC could service, while economic realities increased the number of families in need. That factor, coupled with ever-changing directions in child welfare philosophies, has brought increased national attention to the program. AFDC must attempt to remain effective in providing services to needy children while adapting to societal and economic changes.

See also *Dandridge v. Williams*; Family law; Social Security system; Welfare state.

Aiding and abetting. *See* **Accessory, accomplice, and aiding and abetting**

Akron v. Akron Center for Reproductive Health
COURT: U.S. Supreme Court
DATE: Decided June 15, 1983
SIGNIFICANCE: In the face of challenges to the *Roe v. Wade* trimester framework, the Court struck down a range of abortion regulations and reaffirmed *Roe*'s principle that the right of privacy encompasses a qualified right to obtain an abortion

An Akron, Ohio, city ordinance required that (1) all abortions after the first trimester of pregnancy would be performed in hospitals; (2) parents of unmarried minors would be notified, and their consent would be obtained before such minors could have abortions; (3) physicians would advise their patients that "the unborn child is a human life from the moment of conception"; (4) except in an emergency, there would be a twenty-four-hour waiting period between the signing of a consent form and the abortion; and (5) fetal remains would be disposed of in a humane and sanitary fashion. The United States District Court for the Northern District of Ohio invalidated some of the provisions and upheld others. The U.S. Court of Appeals for the Sixth Circuit affirmed in part and reversed in part. On appeal, the U.S. Supreme Court found these provisions unconstitutional.

Justice Lewis Powell, joined by Chief Justice Warren Burger and Justices William Brennan, Thurgood Marshall, Harry Blackmun, and John Paul Stevens, wrote the majority opinion. Recalling *Roe v. Wade* (1973), Powell noted that the right of privacy encompasses the right to an abortion but that this right must be considered against important state interests. A state can regulate to further its "legitimate interest in protecting the potentiality of human life." This interest, however, becomes compelling only at the point of fetal viability. Further, a state has an important interest in safeguarding the health of women who undergo abortions, but this health interest does not become compelling until "approximately the end of the first trimester" of pregnancy. The majority was unconvinced that the challenged regulations furthered legitimate state interests and, citing the importance of the doctrine of *stare decisis*, reaffirmed *Roe*.

In a dissent joined by Justices Byron White and William Rehnquist, Justice Sandra Day O'Connor stopped short of advocating that *Roe* be overruled, but she did argue that "the trimester approach is a completely unworkable method." Improvements in medical technology will make later abortions safer, thus postponing the point at which the state's maternal health interests become compelling. Conversely, technological developments will enable fetuses to reach viability earlier, thus advancing the point at which this state interest becomes compelling. Therefore, O'Connor wrote, "The *Roe* framework is clearly on a collision course with itself." Instead, O'Connor would hold that an abortion regulation "is not unconstitutional unless it unduly burdens the right to seek an abortion." The minority concluded that the Akron regulations were not un-

duly burdensome. This case is important because, although the *Roe v. Wade* decision survived, its analytical framework was severely challenged.

See also Abortion; *Griswold v. Connecticut*; *Harris v. McRae*; Privacy, right of; *Roe v. Wade*; *Thornburgh v. American College of Obstetricians and Gynecologists*; *Webster v. Reproductive Health Services*.

Alcohol, Tobacco, and Firearms (ATF), Bureau of

DATE: Given bureau status in 1972

SIGNIFICANCE: The Bureau of Alcohol, Tobacco, and Firearms was historically important for its role in the prosecution of Prohibition-era gangsters; today it oversees the regulation and taxation of three multibillion-dollar industries

The Bureau of Alcohol, Tobacco, and Firearms (ATF) is a division of the United States Department of the Treasury. It has responsibilities for regulating the alcohol, tobacco, and firearms industries and for ensuring the collection of the federal taxes imposed on alcohol and tobacco products. The bureau has the authority to prosecute the illegal sale and distribution of firearms and to assist federal, state, and local enforcement agencies in reducing crime and violence. Other responsibilities of the ATF include investigating violations of

ATF agents at the airport in Waco, Texas, on April 19, 1993, the day the Branch Davidian compound burned. (AP/Wide World Photos)

federal explosives laws, regulating the alcohol, tobacco, and firearms industries by issuing licenses and permits, collecting taxes on these items, and investigating charges of bribery and consumer fraud within the alcohol industry.

In 1791, a U.S. Congress facing debts incurred during the American Revolution imposed the first federal tax on distilled spirits. Years later, to help finance the Civil War, Congress passed legislation that created the Internal Revenue Service and allowed the hiring of three detectives to help collect and enforce the collection of taxes on alcohol.

The Prohibition era began in 1919 with the ratification of the Eighteenth Amendment to the U.S. Constitution; the sale of alcoholic beverages became illegal. A new division of the Internal Revenue Service, known as the Prohibition unit, was created to enforce Prohibition. This unit had jurisdiction over the manufacture, sale, and transportation of alcohol. The enforcement of firearm laws, enacted largely because of crime associated with the illegal trafficking of alcohol, became another duty of the agents responsible for controlling alcohol.

The increasing responsibilities of the Alcohol, Tobacco, and Firearms Division of the Internal Revenue Service, particularly after passage of the Gun Control Act of 1968, prompted the separation of the two agencies. The ATF was given bureau status within the U.S. Department of the Treasury in 1972. The ATF investigates and prosecutes many violent crimes and gang-related activities. This bureau collects more than $14 billion annually in taxes associated with the industries it regulates. The ATF promotes and advocates strong antiviolence and antigang legislation. The bureau was partly responsible for new firearm restrictions and regulations that were created under the Gun Control Act of 1986, which established mandatory sentences for armed drug traffickers and violent criminals.

The ATF has drawn considerable criticism since the 1970's, and the agency has had problems with both outside complaints and internal dissent. The bureau received intense scrutiny for its disastrously mishandled 1993 raid on the compound of the Branch Davidian sect in Waco, Texas, in which six Branch Davidians and four agents were killed. After a nearly two-month stand-off, eighty-one more people died in a conflagration at the compound. A Treasury Department investigation found numerous examples of ineptness in the raid and the ATF intelligence gathering that preceded it. The National Rifle Association has been the agency's most vocal critic through the years, going so far in 1995 as to circulate a fund-raising letter referring to ATF agents as "jack-booted thugs." A new ATF director, John Magaw, was appointed in 1993 after the Waco raid, and he began efforts to reform the agency.

See also Branch Davidians, federal raid on; Internal Revenue Service (IRS); National Firearms Act and Federal Firearms Act; Organized Crime Control Act; Treasury, U.S. Department of the.

Alexander v. Holmes County Board of Education

COURT: U.S. Supreme Court
DATE: Decided October 29, 1969

SIGNIFICANCE: In this case, the U.S. Supreme Court ruled that southern school boards must desegregate their schools immediately and refused to grant several school districts a one-semester delay in proceeding with school desegregation

In the late 1960's, many southern school districts still operated segregated schools, notwithstanding pressure from both the U.S. Office of Education and the federal courts to integrate. In the late 1960's, African American parents throughout Mississippi, with the assistance of the National Association for the Advancement of Colored People (NAACP) Legal Defense and Educational Fund, filed lawsuits challenging segregation in thirty Mississippi school districts. In 1969, the U.S. Court of Appeals for the Fifth Circuit ordered the districts to file desegregation plans by August 11, 1969, to take effect by the beginning of the 1969-1970 school year. With the support of President Richard M. Nixon's Department of Justice, however, the school districts requested the court to allow them to postpone the submission of school desegregation plans until December 1, 1969. The proceedings, which marked the first time that the Department of Justice had asked for a delay in a school desegregation case, reflected the Nixon Administration's lukewarm support for school desegregation. The Fifth Circuit granted the request, and the parents who had filed the original suits appealed to the U.S. Supreme Court.

The Supreme Court considered the case in an expedited fashion. On October 29, 1969—only twenty days after deciding to hear the case, and only six days after oral argument—the Court held that the court of appeals had erred in permitting the delay; the Court's decision stated that "the obligation of every school district is to terminate dual school systems at once." The Court ordered every affected school district to "begin immediately to operate as unitary school systems."

The *Alexander* decision signaled an unprecedented sense of urgency in school desegregation cases. After allowing local school boards to desegregate at a slow pace for much of the prior fifteen years, the Court had now indicated that further delays would not be tolerated—even delays until the end of a school semester or school year. In a sense, the *Alexander* decision constituted the Court's atonement for the "all deliberate speed" language of its 1954 decision in *Brown v. Board of Education*; although the *Brown* decision had been a landmark in the battle against segregation, the muted language of the Court's opinion had allowed another generation of African American children to remain in segregated schools. Beginning with its *Green v. County School Board of New Kent County* decision (1968), the Court had finally begun to insist upon meaningful desegregation. Faced for the first time with Justice Department recalcitrance in a desegregation case and a presidential administration with a questionable commitment to school integration, the Court acted in dramatic fashion to signal that the time for delay and "deliberate speed" had come to an end.

In the wake of the *Alexander* decision, courts throughout the South began to insist on immediate desegregation, in some instances in the middle of the school year. The *Alexander* decision dramatically altered the time frame within which school boards were required to meet their desegregation obligations.

See also *Brown v. Board of Education*; *Green v. County School Board of New Kent County*; Segregation, *de facto* and *de jure*.

Alien and Sedition Acts

DATE: Became law June-July, 1798

DEFINITION: The four laws collectively known as the Alien and Sedition Acts ostensibly were passed to aid in avoiding war with France

SIGNIFICANCE: The Alien and Sedition laws led to further debate regarding the function of the Bill of Rights during wartime, the role of the federal government in legislating for the states, and the process of judicial review

Under the threat of imminent war with France, the Federalist-controlled Congress, tacitly supported by Federalist president John Adams, passed several acts designed to lessen seditious activity and to limit immigration and naturalization. The Alien Act and the Alien Enemy Act empowered the president to deport dangerous aliens in peacetime and, in wartime, to imprison aliens who were citizens of an enemy country. Residency requirements for the naturalization of immigrants were extended from five to fourteen years in the Naturalization Act. While all of the acts were condemned by Republican Party leaders, the Sedition Act was considered most odious.

The Sedition Act, unconstitutional by modern standards for its limitations on freedom of speech, sought to punish any person who publicly opposed or conspired to interfere with any United States law. It further censured public expressions of political dissent in the form of criticism of individual government officials. While President Adams refrained from implementing the Alien Acts, he invoked the Sedition Act to indict fifteen men and to sentence ten men, all of whom were rival Republicans. The act was construed by Republicans, therefore, as an attempt to silence their criticism of the Federalist administration.

Organized Republican opposition to the Alien and Sedition Acts was immediate and hostile. At the forefront were Thomas Jefferson and Virginia political theorist James Madison, who authored what became known as the Virginia and Kentucky Resolutions. As expressed in the resolutions, the Constitution was a compact between the states, with sovereignty arising from the states, not from the federal government. The Alien and Sedition Acts, therefore, were denounced as flagrant violations not only of individual constitutional rights but also of states' rights.

The Virginia and Kentucky resolves were further expounded upon by John C. Calhoun in the 1830's. In formulating his theory of nullification, Calhoun argued that since the federal government is granted power by the states, the states therefore reserve the right to nullify any federal law.

The Alien Acts, although angering Republicans, were nevertheless constitutional by modern standards. Indeed, while the Naturalization Act was repealed in 1802 and the Alien Act expired in 1880, the Enemy Alien Act is still in effect and was upheld in the U.S. Supreme Court decision *Ludecke v. Watkins* (1940). The Sedition Act, however, was deemed a violation of an individual's right to freedom of speech. The debate over military necessity and the Bill of Rights was partially clarified by *Ex parte Milligan* (1866) and in the clear and present danger doctrine expressed during passage of the 1917 Espionage Act.

See also Censorship; Clear and present danger test; Espionage Act; Federalist Party; *Milligan, Ex parte*; Smith Act; Treason.

Alternative dispute resolution. *See* Arbitration and mediation

Alvarez-Machain, United States v.

COURT: U.S. Supreme Court

DATE: Decided June 15, 1992

SIGNIFICANCE: The Supreme Court held that nothing in the extradition treaty between the United States and Mexico and nothing in general international law prohibited the trial of a defendant whose arrest was the result of a forcible abduction from Mexico

Humberto Alvarez-Machain, a physician and a citizen of Mexico, was believed by the Drug Enforcement Administration (DEA) to have been partly responsible for the torture and murder of a DEA agent. Alvarez-Machain was indicted by a federal court for kidnapping and murder. After U.S. negotiations with Mexico for his extradition failed, he was forcibly abducted from his office in Guadalajara, flown to the United States, and arrested on arrival. His abductors, though not employees of the federal government, had been solicited by the DEA and promised a reward. When Alvarez-Machain was brought to trial, he moved to dismiss the indictment because his arrest had been illegal. The district court judge found that although the Drug Enforcement Administration did not directly participate in the kidnapping, it was responsible for it. The indictment was dismissed on the ground that the extradition treaty between the United States and Mexico had been violated by the illegal arrest. The court of appeals upheld the district court, arguing that the abduction violated the purpose of the extradition treaty. The government appealed to the Supreme Court.

Justice William Rehnquist wrote the opinion for a 6-3 majority. He held that the complicity of the United States government in Alvarez-Machain's abduction did not nullify the indictment. The case turned on a narrow question: Does the extradition treaty between the United States and Mexico provide the only means by which a defendant can legally be brought from one of the two countries to the other? As the majority saw the case, the extradition treaty does not establish an exclusive means of bringing potential defendants from Mexico to the United States. It does not specifically exclude kidnapping or unlawful arrest. Therefore the illegality of U.S. actions in Mexico did not affect the validity of the indictment. The case was remanded to the lower courts so that Alvarez-Machain's trial could go forward.

Justice John Paul Stevens wrote a strong dissenting opinion in which he argued that the extradition processes set out in the treaty are designed to provide an orderly means of dealing with cross-border crimes. The dissent argued that by substituting kidnapping for extradition, the United States had violated the treaty. Stevens also argued that the decision would encourage the government to engage in additional acts of international lawlessness.

Although the decision cleared the way for Alvarez-Machain to be put on trial in the United States, Mexican protests about U.S. violation of Mexican sovereignty resulted in an executive decision to return Alvarez-Machain to Mexico. He was repatriated within a few months of the Court's decision.

See also Arrest; Drug Enforcement Administration (DEA); Extradition; Rehnquist, William.

American Bar Association (ABA)

DATE: Established 1878

SIGNIFICANCE: The American Bar Association (ABA) has sought to maintain high educational and ethical standards in the legal profession and has contributed significantly to shaping the American sense of justice; it also speaks out on matters of public policy and advises elected federal officials on appointments to the judiciary

The development of the legal profession and the laws on which it is based occurred almost contemporaneously. Prior to the American Revolution, disputes were generally heard by laymen. "Attorneys" were often laymen who were tradespeople. Throughout most of the seventeenth century, lawyers were widely deemed to be individuals of poor reputation and moral character. They were viewed with suspicion by those in the more powerful strata of society. The law and lawyers were of little consequence to the majority of citizens, having little if any impact on their everyday existence.

With the dawn of the eighteenth century, the social milieu of the colonies began undergoing subtle change. Concepts of education as well as the founding of various educational institutions such as Yale, Columbia, and Princeton began changing the appearance of various professions. Newspaper publication was initiated in the colonies. Communication both within and among the colonies was vastly improved with the implementation of a government position, deputy postmaster general for the colonies, which significantly improved the exchange of information. Commerce flourished and property rights became central to the implementation of a merchant class and upper-class values. There was then a need for seasoned attorneys and judges. The reputation of those practicing law improved, as there were more disciplined, educated professionals expounding the rule of law.

Establishment and History of the ABA. Against this background, the first bar association of any kind was established in the colonies in New York in 1745. Others soon followed. Ironically, as the stature of the bar improved, the justice system itself came under increasing attack. Simeon E. Baldwin, a member of the Connecticut Bar Association, proposed that the Connecticut Bar Association form a committee under its auspices to investigate the formation of a national bar. This committee of senior lawyers concluded that such an association was desirable and circulated a letter which included a proposal that a body of delegates, representing the profession in all parts of the country, should meet annually for a comparison of views and friendly intercourse.

The first meeting was attended by one hundred lawyers from twenty-one states on August 21, 1878, in Saratoga Springs, New York. They determined to coordinate themselves as the American Bar Association and appointed committees to draft a constitution and by-laws. The constitution, which was adopted, states the primary objectives of the association in Article I. Its object was to "advance the science of jurisprudence, promote the administration of justice and uniformity of legislation throughout the union, uphold the honor of the profession of the law and encourage cordial intercourse among the members of the American Bar."

The organization's first president was James O. Broadhead of Missouri. The American Bar Association began with 289 members representing twenty-nine states. The association established a number of standing committees: on jurisprudence and law reform, judicial administration and remedial procedure, legal education and admission to the bar, international law, publications, and grievances. In early years, the association focused more on technical aspects of legal administration than on controversial social and economic public policy issues. Improvement of the law was a goal; revolutionary reformation and political polarization were not.

The early years of the American Bar Association found an organization struggling to establish itself among individual attorneys and local and regional bar associations as the representative of the profession. Focus was on organizing, building personnel, and determining policies. One of the major accomplishments in these early years was the establishment of the Association of American Law Schools for the sole purpose of improving legal education. Eventually the connection between the ABA and the AALS was broken, with the AALS maintaining an independent existence, overseeing the quality of legal education.

The Twentieth Century. In 1936, the ABA was completely reorganized. Focus shifted from an autonomous association of individuals to an association of limited autonomy operating within the framework of a house of delegates, representation of state and local bar associations, and respected juridical groups which maintained all powers relating to the administration and organization of the ABA.

The ABA comprises more than 370,000 members representing all fifty states and the District of Columbia. It is said to be the largest voluntary organization in the United States. The association is far more complex than at its initiation, yet it still maintains many of the same goals. The goals continue to be met through an interplay of standing committees and special committees with operating units and sections. The mission of the ABA is to be the national representative of the legal profession, serving the public and the profession by promoting justice, professional excellence, and respect for the law. These goals are reflective of a more activist ABA, which plays a significant and vocal role in public and political discussions.

—*Murray Henner*

See also Attorney; Bar, the; Bar examinations and licensing of lawyers; Law schools; Legal ethics.

BIBLIOGRAPHY

Overviews of various bar organizations include Glenn R. Winters, *Bar Association Organization and Activities: A Handbook for Bar Association Officers* (Ann Arbor, Mich.: American Judicature Society, 1954). For a history of the American Bar Association, see Charles Warren, *A History of the American Bar* (Buffalo, N.Y.: W. S. Hein, 1990), and Edson R. Sunderland, *History of the American Bar Association and Its Work* (1953). For an in-depth discussion on the role of the ABA in formulating policy and law, see *The ABA in Law and Policy: What Role?* (Washington, D.C.: Federalist Society for Law and Public Policy Studies, 1994).

American Civil Liberties Union (ACLU)

DATE: Founded January 19, 1920

SIGNIFICANCE: This group, the most important civil liberties organization in the United States, uses the courts to protect the rights of controversial and ordinary individuals

The American Civil Liberties Union (ACLU) has its origins in the movement to protect the right of pacifists to protest American entrance into World War I. The basic objective of the organization is to monitor and protect the constitutional rights of all American citizens and groups. Although the ACLU has earned notoriety by defending unpopular organizations and being involved in controversial court cases, it has over the decades taken thousands of routine cases as well, from the firing of a public librarian for refusing to remove a book from her shelves to the right of employees to join a labor union.

Methods. The ACLU uses the courts to achieve its objectives. Although it often petitions state courts, its main course of action takes place in the federal courts. Almost all its cases bear on constitutional issues, and some have led to landmark decisions by the U.S. Supreme Court.

Its critics accuse the ACLU of having a specific political agenda, but the organization claims to be neutral in politics and, in fact, has championed individuals and organizations from both extremes of the political spectrum. It has worked to overturn laws banning the Communist Party and defended the right of Nazis to march in Jewish neighborhoods. It has forced local communities to dismantle religious displays and defended the right of police officers to join the Ku Klux Klan and the John Birch Society. The organization has thus been strongly chastised by both the Left and Right. In general, however, the organization clearly has been part of left-of-center politics in the United States.

The ACLU's single purpose is an uncompromisingly rigid protection of civil liberties for all, no matter how unpopular, outrageous, or despicable the cause or individual. Its most controversial cases are the standard by which it measures its success. For the ACLU, opposition to all censorship means defending the rights of pornographers. Opposition to illegal searches means opposition to unannounced police sweeps of public housing to root out drug traffickers. Strict separation of church and state means absolute opposition to the most bland prayers in public schools and to the display of any religious symbol on public grounds or documents.

Structure. The ACLU is a private organization of volunteers whose membership in the mid-1990's numbered about 300,000. The organization relies on more than four thousand volunteer lawyers for its litigation; they are the heart of the organization. Its paid staff is fewer than a hundred people, but it has eleven paid lobbyists. Besides its two national offices in New York and Washington, it has affiliates in forty-six states and has eleven special project offices.

History. The positions of the ACLU have evolved over the decades of its existence. It has not always opposed censorship or the separation of church and state so rigidly. Some of its issues, such as the right of women to have abortions, have reflected changes in society rather than initiated them.

The ACLU was born out of the United States' entry into World War I. Wartime hysteria and widespread popular support for American participation led to the censorship of opposition to the war and harassment or imprisonment for individuals opposing American entry. To protect the right of free speech, members of the pacifist American Union Against Militarism (AUAM) formed the Civil Liberties Board (CLB). Because the AUAM and its branch CLB publicly embraced the radical left, a number of members resigned and formed the nonpartisan National Civil Liberties Board (NCLB).

The NCLB was unable to fight successfully the curtailment of civil liberties during the war or during the postwar "red scare" when the government harassed and prosecuted thousands of citizens suspected of harboring Marxist and other left-wing ideas. In 1920 its members created the restructured ACLU under the leadership of Roger Baldwin, a Boston attorney, who had been the guiding spirit of the NCLB. The broad base of the organization and its commitment to consider all violations of civil liberties distinguished it from other existing civil rights groups such as the National Association for the Advancement of Colored People (NAACP) and the Anti-Defamation League, founded by B'nai B'rith.

Over the next seven decades the ACLU was involved in some of the most renowned cases in American jurisprudence and issues in American society—the Scopes "monkey" trial, the internment of Japanese Americans during World War II, the rights of conscientious objectors, the Smith and McCarran anti-Communist Acts, the Scottsboro case, abortion rights, antiwar protests, and many others.

The Skokie March Case. The organization's most unpopular cause among its membership was the defense of the 1976 proposed march by the American Nazi Party in Skokie, Illinois, a largely Jewish suburb of Chicago. The party planned the march after the city of Chicago refused them a permit for a rally there. Skokie also denied a parade permit on the grounds that it would cause a public nuisance. The ACLU took up the Nazis' petition, and although the controversy was resolved without a march through the suburb, the championing of the Nazis' cause split the organization almost to the point of extinction. This was not the first time the organization took on a case on behalf of the Nazis, but the reaction of its membership, the overwhelming majority of whom are leftists and many of whom are Jews, was unprecedented. The union suffered a 15 percent drop in membership renewal and found itself with a half-million-dollar deficit. The ACLU reorganized and cut its staff, and new leadership moved into position. In the years following Skokie, a new conservative era in the United States, the organization faced the issues of the day: abortion rights, gay rights, the rights of sufferers of acquired immune deficiency syndrome (AIDS), and the war on drugs. It became a favorite whipping boy of the Republican Party, but its function as the protector of the individual against the conforming impulse of society revitalized it as the country's leading civil rights organization.   —*Frederick B. Chary*

See also *Amicus curiae* brief; Civil liberties; Civil rights; *Miranda v. Arizona*; *Palko v. Connecticut*; Palmer raids and the "red scare"; *Reed v. Reed*; *Tinker v. Des Moines Independent Community School District*; *Village of Skokie v. National Socialist Party of America*; *West Virginia State Board of Education v. Barnette*.

BIBLIOGRAPHY

The standard work on the ACLU is Samuel Walker, *In Defense of American Liberties: A History of the ACLU* (New York: Oxford University Press, 1990). Other good sources include Alan Reitman, ed., *The Pulse of Freedom: American Liberties, 1920-1970's* (New York: W. W. Norton, 1975); Paul L. Murphy, *World War I and the Origin of Civil Liberties in the United States* (New York: W. W. Norton, 1979); and Peter Irons, *The Courage of Their Convictions* (New York: Free Press, 1988). William Donohue, *The Politics of the American Civil Liberties Union* (New Brunswick, N.J.: Transaction Books, 1985) is a polemical attack on the ACLU. On Skokie, see Aryeh Neier, *Defending My Enemy* (New York: Dutton, 1979); David Hamlin, *The Nazi/Skokie Conflict* (Boston: Beacon Press, 1980); and James L. Gibson and Richard D. Bingham, *Civil Liberties and Nazis: The Skokie Free-Speech Controversy* (New York: Praeger, 1985).

American Federation of Labor-Congress of Industrial Organizations (AFL-CIO)

DATE: Established December 5, 1955

SIGNIFICANCE: The AFL-CIO, a vast confederation of American labor unions, exerts a strong influence on business and American politics

The American Federation of Labor-Congress of Industrial Organizations (AFL-CIO) was formed in 1955 by the merger of

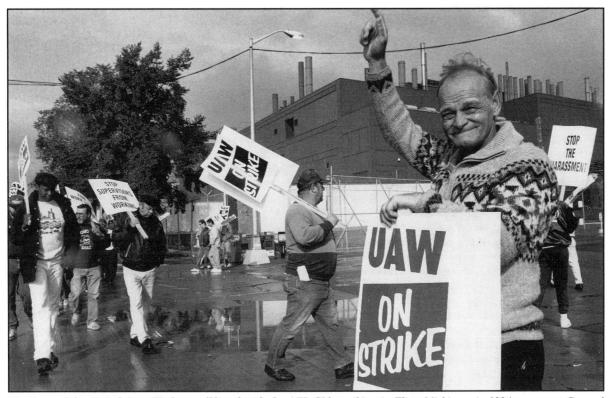

Members of the United Auto Workers, affiliated with the AFL-CIO, striking in Flint, Michigan, in 1994 to protest General Motors speed-up and overtime policies. (Jim West)

the two largest labor organizations in the United States. Each organization was composed of a large number of individual labor unions. Many of the oldest unions were organized on the basis of a particular craft or skill; for example, there were unions of bricklayers, carpenters, plumbers, and electricians. Craft unions predominated in the original AFL, which was formed in 1886. The AFL's longtime president, Samuel Gompers, stressed "business unionism," aimed at achieving better wages and working conditions through collective bargaining rather than radical political activism. Craft unions were sometimes elitist, enrolling better-paid workers and neglecting unskilled workers in mass-production industries. Many excluded women and racial minorities and erected barriers against newcomers to the craft.

As the United States economy sank into serious depression after 1929, the federal government adopted measures to promote the formation of unions. John L. Lewis, head of the United Mine Workers, saw a great opportunity to unionize mass-production industries. When the conservative leaders of the AFL dragged their feet, Lewis led his union (and others like it) out of the AFL to form the CIO, officially separate in 1938. Taking advantage of the National Labor Relations Act of 1935, Lewis promoted the formation of unions in key industries such as automobiles and steel. Employer resistance was strong, and industrial violence was common in the late 1930's. Favorable court decisions and the coming of World War II helped to spread union membership.

CIO "industrial" unions were organized by the employer's industrial classification rather than the worker's occupation. They enrolled far more women and racial minorities and supported government measures to relieve discrimination against them. CIO unions tended to support the Democratic Party and were active proponents of such governmental action as increases in the statutory minimum wage, transfer payments for low-income families, and government-supported medical benefits.

In the decades following the formation of the AFL-CIO in 1955, union membership declined slightly in numbers and substantially in proportion to nonfarm employment. By 1993 about one-sixth of employed wage and salary workers were union members. Four-fifths of these (13 million members) were in unions affiliated with the AFL-CIO.

Unions have sought "due process" on the job, seeking rules for decisions affecting worker welfare and grievance procedures for complaints about their application. Ideally, collective bargaining can be a form of workplace democracy, giving workers' representatives some influence in decision making. When union efforts are directed toward higher wages, however, the social justice aspects of union efforts become complex and difficult to assess. Wage increases improve the lives of union members, but critics argue that union gains tend to raise product prices and possibly to reduce wage levels for nonunion workers, who are even more likely to be in low-income conditions.

See also Gompers, Samuel; Labor unions; Landrum-Griffin Act; Lewis, John L.; National Labor Relations Act (NLRA); United Farm Workers (UFW).

American Indian Movement (AIM)

DATE: Founded July 28, 1968, Minneapolis, Minnesota
SIGNIFICANCE: This militant Native American organization, seeking to revitalize Indian peoples on the basis of traditional spirituality and practices and struggling for native rights, has produced some dramatic confrontations

The American Indian Movement (AIM) has its origins in the summer of 1968 as a reaction to police brutality and harassment of native peoples in the Minneapolis-St. Paul metropolitan area. Initially, efforts were made to unite the approximately twenty local Indian organizations for the purpose of providing victims with assistance in the form of foot and car patrols and witness reports. Although the names of some founders are now unknown, several urban Indians coming from Minnesota Ojibwa reservations—among them Dennis Banks, Clyde Bellecourt, and George Mitchell—were prominent cofounders. By 1969, AIM was an organization in its own right with an agenda addressing the needs of American Indian peoples. In the mid-1970's, AIM maintained about eighty chapters, including eight in Canada and several overseas. Membership totaled five thousand in the early 1990's.

AIM's philosophy and goals identify the organization as a spiritual movement seeking to reawaken the traditional values by which Indian people have lived since time immemorial. AIM members become bona fide after participation in the Sun Dance ceremony on the Pine Ridge reservation in South Dakota. AIM's short-range goals for urban and reservation people included improving housing, working with youth, creating jobs and raising living standards, encouraging active involvement in community affairs, educating the dominant society about Native American culture, keeping Indian people informed about developments affecting them, and rendering active assistance where appropriate. To realize its goals, AIM established training sessions called "survival schools" in Minneapolis and other places to promote school curriculum development and to instill pride as an alternative to loss of identity.

In the early 1970's, AIM launched a series of actions which made it the best known and most controversial American Indian group. Confrontational measures intended to highlight Indian grievances, such as the seizure of Alcatraz Island in 1969, the brief takeover of the Bureau of Indian Affairs' Washington headquarters in 1972, and the dramatic and sometimes violent 1973 standoff with federal authorities during a ten-week occupation of Wounded Knee on the Pine Ridge reservation, focused considerable national attention on AIM and leaders such as Dennis Banks and Russell Means.

AIM's militant confrontational tactics have been condemned by some Indian leaders. These critics cite increased racial tensions, brutal crackdowns by federal authorities involving systematic violations of the civil rights of non-AIM members, and a retardation of potential economic investment on reservations as negative results of AIM's actions. On the other hand, AIM and its supporters argue that the organization's efforts have served to awaken the dominant culture to legitimate Indian demands and civil liberties issues and to the consequences of not honoring them. Moreover, AIM can point to lobbying successes such as its sponsorship of international treaty conferences on various Lakota Sioux reservations, which led to the 1977 International Treaty Conference of the United Nations in Geneva, Switzerland, and to the adoption of several major points from AIM's national program by the Minnesota Democratic Party in 1974.

See also American Indians; Civil Rights movement.

American Indians

DEFINITION: Descendants of the original inhabitants of the American continent who are affiliated with officially recognized tribes within the United States

SIGNIFICANCE: As members of distinct political communities with limited sovereignty, American Indian tribal people share a legal status unique among American citizens

When Europeans first reached the Americas, they encountered native peoples whose ancestors had occupied the entire landmass for more than twenty thousand years. The numerous North American tribes utilized many different legal systems which functioned successfully under natural law without police, formal courts, or prisons. Decisions affecting individual rights were resolved in a manner that gave considerable weight to the best interests of the group and sought restoration of community harmony and balance. Around the fifteenth century, the indigenous peoples encountered Europeans holding different views of legal rights and posing a serious threat to native sovereignty and rights.

The Old Colonialism. English colonizers in North America generally pursued the treaty-making process as the chief means for acquiring land. Their diplomacy recognized Indian tribes as sovereign foreign nations. When the American Revolution ended British rule in the thirteen seaboard colonies, the new American republic displaced England and continued the old colonialism in its diplomatic relationships with the tribes. The United States initially viewed American Indians as members of small nations who would remain permanently outside American political institutions.

Tribal Sovereignty and Indian Rights, 1781-1840. Early American statesmen, including Thomas Jefferson, formulated ideal rules for the peaceful and voluntary extinction of Indian title through legal land purchases. Government policy encouraged Native Americans to enter the mainstream of the dominant culture and live alongside white settlers.

The United States abandoned this policy when it concluded that the tribal lands were too valuable to recognize Indian rights within them. Presidential administrations responded to pressure from anti-Indian frontiersmen and the desire of new southern states to appropriate Indian lands and dismantle tribal governments. Between 1815 and 1840, most eastern and southern tribes were removed—with great hardship and loss—west of the Mississippi, to the southern plains region designated Indian Territory.

As removal proceeded, a defining moment in the legal relationship between tribes and the United States came with the Cherokee court cases of the 1830's. The Cherokees, a highly advanced and acculturated southeastern tribe that was implementing Jefferson's advice, sought justice through the U.S. legal system, resisting impending removal from Georgia and the state's effort to dissolve their government and subject them to its laws. In *Cherokee Nation v. Georgia* (1831), Chief Justice John Marshall ruled that the case was not eligible to be heard by the Supreme Court because Indian tribes did not qualify as independent foreign nations. This decision characterized Indian tribes as "domestic dependent nations" whose relationship with the U.S. government was that of a ward to its guardian.

In a second case, *Worcester v. Georgia* (1832), Marshall reached different conclusions using the same legal background. He cited earlier treaties with the Cherokees recognizing their national character and right to self-government as distinct, independent political communities retaining natural rights as the original possessors of the soil. Georgia's actions interfered with the federal government's exclusive authority to make treaties with Indian tribes and were therefore invalid. The Cherokee legal victory was short-lived, as President Andrew Jackson refused to enforce the ruling, and the tribe was removed forcibly to Indian Territory within a few years. Yet on this important decision, cited frequently in later cases, hinged issues such as Indian title to lands, tribal independence, and the validity of treaty rights.

Dispossession and Warfare, 1840-1870's. Unexpectedly rapid American expansion westward beginning in the 1840's jeopardized the political autonomy and security of person and possessions that had been promised to removed tribes in their new lands. A final round of violent confrontation played out after 1860, as American movement into tribal lands of the West and Great Plains forced further cessions and destroyed the tribes' traditional economic base. Tribal sovereignty received a new setback in 1871, when the United States ceased negotiating treaties with tribal nations. Although previous treaties were to remain valid, from this point onward the federal government would unilaterally subject the tribes to congressional legislation and presidential orders.

The New Colonialism, 1870's-1920's. Under this new colonialism, the situation of American Indians reached its lowest point. Tribal peoples were confined to reservations under authoritarian paternalistic control; there the government ruthlessly pursued assimilation goals through forced acculturation, while corrupt U.S. Indian agents plundered tribal resources. Furthermore, the General Allotment Act of 1887 forced tribal members to break up communal holdings by accepting 160-acre tracts and opened unallotted reservation land to sale. The eventual result was loss of both "surplus" land and many private allotments to whites.

By 1934, this process had reduced the tribal estate from 138 million to 48 million acres, half of which was desert. The Native American population, once numbering over ten million, fell to 250,000 toward the end of the nineteenth century. By the 1920's, tribal peoples suffered from impoverishment, poor health conditions, and lack of education—a situation from which they have not fully recovered.

After 1870, court rulings and congressional legislation upheld Marshall's legal precedents but further refined and narrowed the scope of tribal sovereignty. Moreover, the Bill of Rights did not protect tribal peoples' rights. In legal disputes with the government, Indians were denied freedom of choice of counsel (Sixth Amendment). The First Amendment right to assemble was violated through forced confinement on reservations, which Indians were unable to leave without permission. Cultural genocide and loss of property contradicted the Fifth Amendment.

The late 1870's and early 1880's witnessed the creation of tribal police forces and courts as instruments to enforce the government's determined assault on traditional Indian culture. The tribal courts' authority soon became controversial because of the Supreme Court ruling *Ex parte Crow Dog* (1883). Tribal magistrates on the Rosebud Reservation in South Dakota allowed a murder case to be handled in the traditional manner of restitution to the victim's family. Federal officials then arrested the assailant, Crow Dog, and convicted him of murder in the territorial district court. On appeal, the Supreme Court ordered him released on grounds that a federal court had no jurisdiction over crimes committed by Indians against other Indians on reservation land. In response, Congress passed the 1885 Major Crimes Act, which placed seven serious crimes under federal jurisdiction even when they were committed on reservation land. This list of crimes was further expanded in the twentieth century, leaving tribal courts with jurisdiction only over minor offenses.

A devastating blow to sovereignty came in the court case *Lone Wolf v. Hitchcock* (1903). This litigation involved the Kiowa tribe's attempt to halt the sale of "surplus" reservation lands based on a former treaty guarantee requiring the signed consent of at least three-fourths of male occupants. Ignoring the Constitution's Fifth Amendment protection of life, liberty, and property, the Supreme Court upheld lower court opinions that Congress had full authority over tribal land which superseded treaty guarantees.

In 1924, the government bestowed U.S. citizenship on American Indians. This gesture did not halt the loss of lands to whites or the campaign to suppress Indian culture. Moreover, some states successfully prevented these new citizens from voting.

The Indian New Deal, 1934-1946. A major policy shift followed the election of President Franklin Delano Roosevelt in 1932. The Indian Reorganization Act (IRA), or "Indian New Deal," the inspiration of Roosevelt's Bureau of Indian Affairs chief, John Collier, ended allotment, helped tribes purchase some lost land, encouraged the recovery of traditional native culture, and attempted to revitalize the tribal system of self-government. The IRA improved conditions for Native Americans and gave them new hope; it is still considered the most important piece of Indian legislation in U.S. history. About half of the tribes refused participation, however, resisting Collier's paternalistic attempt to impose guidelines for U.S.-style constitutions. They preferred traditional forms of self-rule.

Termination, 1946-1960. After World War II, a conservative Congress mounted the most serious threat to date against tribal sovereignty under the label "termination." This policy's most ominous components were congressional bills authorizing termination of various designated tribes, thereby liquidating federal treaty obligations and payments, and Public Law 280, which authorized states to assume jurisdiction over criminal and civil cases involving Indians.

Termination failed badly. States faced escalating welfare costs and were often reluctant to assume the added expense of policing or taking control of judicial matters in Indian country. As the injustice and impracticality of this policy became clear, it was put on hold after 1960. Congress eventually restored the status of most terminated tribes, and Public Law 280 was amended to the point where it ceased to be a threat to tribal sovereignty.

Indian Civil Rights Act, 1968. Earlier rulings recognizing tribes as distinct political entities exempted their courts from external regulation. Concern that basic rights guaranteed to other Americans were sometimes violated in tribal judicial proceedings prompted passage of the Indian Civil Rights Act. The legislation extended many (though not all) constitutional protections to tribal members. Some Indians welcomed this measure, and most tribal courts already adhered to its provisions. Traditionalists, however, saw it as another attempt to force the dominant white culture on tribal peoples with distinct sociocultural traditions. The legislation did give rise to some situations in which procedures consistent with Native American culture were challenged in court by both Indian and non-Indian litigants.

Post-1970 Developments and Issues. The period since the late 1960's has been marked by mixed success for Indian rights and tribal sovereignty. The late 1960's gave rise to political militancy among urban Indians who reacted against racism and sought to reconnect with their roots. Pride in being Indian and efforts to seek renewal through the recovery of language, religion, and other traditions, nearly eradicated by past U.S. policy, have contributed to a Native American cultural rebirth.

President Richard M. Nixon denounced termination and handed the Taos Pueblo tribe a major victory with the return of its sacred Blue Lake area. Renewed tribalism and self-determination empowered tribes by allowing them to contract with the government to assume management of numerous government programs and services on the reservation. Although contested at every step, tribes have also had some success in asserting control over natural resources.

During the Reagan presidency, Indian rights suffered a setback in Supreme Court rulings that restricted First Amendment religious freedoms. In *Lyng v. Northwest Indian Cemetery Protective Association* (1988), the new conservative Court majority ruled against Native American efforts to protect sacred sites from development. A 1990 decision threatened the

The occupation of Wounded Knee, South Dakota, in 1973 was representative of Indian activism in the late 1960's and early 1970's. (AP/Wide World Photos)

traditional use of the sacramental plant and drug peyote in religious ceremonies of the Native American Church, likened to the use of wine in the Christian Communion rite.

Since 1990, progress has occurred on the sensitive issue of repatriating the remains of tribal people from museums and private and government collections. Nevertheless, the exercise of tribal sovereignty and treaty rights continues to bring tribes into conflict with state and local interests. Also uncertain is the future of tribally owned gambling casinos on reservation land, a financially successful business venture for many tribes which is regulated under the Indian Gaming Act of 1989. The long struggle of Native Americans to defend and preserve their rights in American society continues.   —*David A. Crain*

See also American Indian Movement (AIM); Bill of Rights, U.S.; *Cherokee Nation v. Georgia*; Constitution, U.S.; Due process of law; *Employment Division, Department of Human Resources of Oregon v. Smith*; New Deal; Racial and ethnic discrimination; Religion, free exercise of.

BIBLIOGRAPHY

A very useful source on the legal status and rights of tribal peoples and a historical account of Indian nations' struggle to maintain sovereignty is John R. Wunder, *Retained by the People: A History of American Indians and the Bill of Rights* (New York: Oxford University Press, 1994). Other good overviews are Vine Deloria, Jr., and Clifford M. Lytle, *American Indians, American Justice* (Austin: University of Texas Press, 1983); Wilcomb Washburn, *Red Man's Land, White Man's Law: A Study of the Past and Present Status of the American Indian* (New York: Charles Scribner's Sons, 1971); Charles F. Wilkinson, *American Indians, Time, and the Law: Native Societies in a Modern Constitutional Democracy* (New Haven, Conn.: Yale University Press, 1987). A relevant documentary collection of court cases, treaties, congressional legislation, government studies, and reports is Francis Paul Prucha, ed., *Documents of United States Indian Policy* (2d ed. Lincoln: University of Nebraska Press, 1990).

American Revolution

DATE: 1763-1783

PLACE: Eastern seaboard of North America

SIGNIFICANCE: Separation from Great Britain led to the creation of the United States as an independent state with its own system of justice

The American Revolution was the culmination of a number of trends that finally resulted in open conflict in 1775 at the battle of Lexington and Concord. Those trends were a mixture of economic, social, and constitutional matters that stretched back to the settlement of the colonies and that became seriously divisive in 1763 with the conclusion of the French and Indian War (in Europe, the Seven Years' War).

The British War Debt. The Peace of Paris of 1763 left Britain with an enormous empire and with what for the day seemed an enormous debt. The government determined to both economize and increase revenues to deal with its problems. To reduce the cost of defense against Indians in North

America (Pontiac's Rebellion in 1763-1764 proved the need for such defense), London issued the Proclamation of 1763, which forbade westward expansion. This was intended to buy time for resolving the question of Indian resistance. The colonists, who generally regarded Indians with disdain, saw expansion as their right and were outraged.

Raising revenue provoked more questions about the rights of the colonists. The mercantilist economic philosophy of the day required governmental involvement in commerce, and there was no question that taxes could be used to regulate trade. The colonists, however, argued that they had the right to consent to any taxation for revenue. Although many Whig Party political leaders, including William Pitt, agreed, the chief ministers of the 1760's (Pitt was too ill when he returned to power in 1766 to be effective) did not. A series of revenue measures provoked increasing colonial defiance and assertion of rights.

The Sugar and Stamp Acts. The first effort to tax for revenue came with the Sugar Act (1764), which revised (downward, to increase activity) duties on sugar and molasses. The problem was that this act contained a provision for enforcement. Earlier duties, whatever the rate, had been largely dead letters, and the colonists had come to regard smuggling as virtually a right. The next year the Stamp Act required tax stamps on a variety of luxury items, publications, and legal documents. The latter two hit journalists and lawyers, groups particularly well situated to protest. Groups called the Sons of Liberty formed, a Stamp Act Congress drew delegates from most of the colonies, and an effective boycott of British goods was established.

The loss of trade quickly led to the repeal of the Stamp Act, but Parliament passed a Declaratory Act (1766) asserting the British right to tax colonies. Since the British constitution is the acts of Parliament and customs of the realm, this act technically made such taxation constitutional. The colonists, accustomed to not being taxed and used to a large degree of autonomy—a trip across the Atlantic typically took six weeks, making close control from London impossible—ignored the technicality. When a new set of duties was imposed in 1767, another boycott was established. Once again the duties were repealed, except the one on tea; it was retained to establish the principle. This was the worst possible move the English government could have made. The colonists were not fools, and although they could smuggle tea to avoid paying the duty, they did not miss the implication of the remaining toll. All the British had hoped to gain from taxing the colonists was future defense costs in North America, but the revenue from the one duty on tea would have come nowhere near paying it. The government had, in other words, ensured continuing animosity without achieving even the possibility of meaningful revenue collection.

The Road to Confrontation. In 1770, the year that the second duties were repealed, a tragic incident further marred British-American relations. Modern police forces had not yet been developed, so soldiers were commonly used to maintain

The Boston Tea Party of 1773 was one of the actions preceding widespread rebellion in the colonies. (Library of Congress)

order. To the outrage of the citizens, a garrison had been established in Boston. In March, a mob led by, among others, Crispus Attucks was harassing some of the Redcoats, who fired on them, killing several, including Attucks. The violence gave both sides pause, but in a failure of leadership, no compromise was advanced. In the next several years Committees of Correspondence appeared in colony after colony with the goal of maintaining communications in case of renewed disputes.

A final incident precipitated the actual military confrontation. The East India Company, holder of the British monopoly of trade in and around India, was exempted from the navigation laws and allowed to ship tea directly to North America. This tea, even with the duty paid, would undercut both legal and smuggled supplies already in the colonies. In December, 1773, colonists seized several ships in Boston harbor and threw the tea overboard. London insisted that the colony pay for the lost cargo and passed a series of acts—called "intolerable" by the colonists—closing the port, revoking the colonial charter, and quartering troops in Boston. The colonists responded with the first Continental Congress in 1774. When, the next year, colonial irregulars fired on British troops sent to confiscate munitions at Lexington and Concord, the chance of compromise was gone. The British were not willing to negotiate with rebels in arms. In 1776 the Americans declared their independence, asserting "inalienable" rights based on the philosophy of natural rights expressed in the writings of John Locke.

The revolutionary war would continue until 1783, but the issue of colonial rights was resolved. The Americans had declared George III a tyrant and separated themselves from his domain. They embarked on a struggle to determine what rights citizens of their new state would have, drawing much from the English experience but making innovations as well.

—*Fred R. van Hartesveldt*

See also Bill of Rights, U.S.; Declaration of Independence; Federalism; Federalist Party; Natural law and natural rights; Rush, Benjamin.

BIBLIOGRAPHY

The classic study of the British background which should underlie any study of the American Revolution is Lewis Namier, *The Structure of Politics at the Accession of George III* (2d ed. London: Macmillan, 1968). An excellent study of the whole period is Robert Middlekauff, *The Glorious Cause: The American Revolution, 1763-1789* (New York: Oxford University Press, 1982). More narrowly American concentrations can be found in John R. Alden, *The American Revolution* (New York: Harper, 1954), and James Kirby Martin and Mark Edward Lender, *A Respectable Army: The Military Origins of the Republic, 1763-1789* (Arlington Heights, Ill.: Davidson, 1982). The question of colonial and American rights can be pursued in Carl L. Becker, *The Declaration of Independence: A Study in the History of Political Ideas* (New York: Vintage Books, 1942).

Americans with Disabilities Act (ADA)

DATE: Enacted 1990; different sections of the law became effective at different times

DEFINITION: Legislation mandating that access be provided to people with disabilities and prohibiting employment discrimination against them

SIGNIFICANCE: The ultimate purpose of the Americans with Disabilities Act is to bring those who have disabilities into the mainstream of American life by enabling them to obtain and hold jobs and providing access to all public facilities

The Americans with Disabilities Act (ADA) was the culmination of seventy-two years of legislation, beginning with the Sears-Smith Act of 1918. The Sears-Smith Act provided training for disabled World War I veterans. Following this act, various other laws were enacted, including the immediate precursor to the ADA—the Rehabilitation Act of 1973. The Rehabilitation Act covered federal executive agencies. The ADA was intended to extend the rights that existed under the Rehabilitation Act. The measure enjoyed bipartisan support in Congress, passing 91 to 6 in the Senate and 377 to 27 in the House. The ADA was also supported by presidents Ronald Reagan and George Bush. The ADA may be viewed as adding a new "protected" category to the Civil Rights Act of 1964. In addition to existing categories such as race, color, sex, and national origin, the ADA protects persons with disabilities from being discriminated against. Through its various provisions, it makes it easier for a person with a disability to participate in mainstream American life. Under the ADA, a person is considered to have a disability when a physical or mental impairment substantially limits one or more of the person's life activities (such as speaking, seeing, or caring for oneself), when the person has a record of such impairment (such as cancer that is in remission), or when a person is regarded as being so impaired.

There are five titles to the ADA: Title I covers employment, Title II covers transportation and state and local services, Title III covers public accommodations, Title IV covers telecommunications, and Title V covers miscellaneous provisions. Under Title I, employers with fifteen or more employees may not discriminate against an individual with a disability in any employment decision, such as hiring or promoting, if the person is otherwise qualified. Further, as long as it does not create "undue hardship," employers are expected to make "reasonable accommodation" to individuals with disabilities. The act does not require an employer to favor a disabled person in any employment decision, nor does it require an employer to hire a person who will be a hazard to the health of coworkers or the public.

Under Title II, federal, state, and some private transportation companies must make their facilities, services, and communications "accessible" to people with disabilities. Under Title III, businesses that provide goods or services to the public should also make their facilities accessible if reasonably possible. Further, any renovations or construction undertaken after January, 1992, must include provisions for making the end result accessible. Under Title IV, telecommunications companies providing voice services to the general public should provide telecommunications relay services (TRS) for people with hearing or speech disabilities. Title V covers miscellaneous provisions. Although the act does not include a list of disabilities, in Title V it provides a list of things that are not covered as disabilities. For example, current drug users are not protected, although those who have used drugs in the past and are in a rehabilitation program are covered.

See also Bush, George; Civil rights; Civil Rights Act of 1991.

Title III of the Americans with Disabilities Act requires that businesses providing services to the public make their facilities accessible to people with disabilities. (James L. Shaffer)

Amicus curiae brief

DEFINITION: A written brief by a person or organization that is not a party to the litigation in question

SIGNIFICANCE: An *amicus curiae* ("friend of the court") brief gives an opportunity to people who may be affected by the decision of a particular case, but are not a party to the case, to influence the reasoning process that will lead judges to a decision

An *amicus curiae* brief explains rational arguments as to how and why a case should be decided a certain way. The judges or justices are not under any obligation to follow the line of reasoning set forth in the *amicus curiae* brief. *Amicus curiae* briefs are often filed in appeals that may affect a large category of people in the United States, such as cases dealing with broad public policy matters. These briefs may be filed only with the written consent of all parties or by permission of the recipient court.

See also Appellate process; *Certiorari*, writ of; Class action; Dictum; Supreme Court of the United States.

Animal rights movement

DEFINITION: A loosely organized effort to extend certain rights to nonhumans, including pets and laboratory animals

SIGNIFICANCE: The ascription of rights to animals gives rise to legal protections, but it extends beyond that to a possible reconceptualization of the meaning of human rights. Americans have long maintained an interest in the ethical and humane treatment of animals in work and in medical experiments. The boundaries of that interest have varied over time, as prevailing moral standards are weighed against changing technological and medical capabilities. Over the years laws and policies have been established to ensure minimum humane standards in such areas as trapping, farming, hunting, and sport.

In the 1970's and 1980's the focus of these efforts expanded beyond merely preventing cruelty to animals as undesirable, and it began to frame animal cruelty as a violation of animals' rights. The term "animal rights" is intended to carry the same resonance as "civil rights" and "human rights," and some in the animal rights movement refer to the concept that human rights outweigh animal rights as "speciesism," analogous to "racism." The animal rights movement opposes as patent rights violations such practices as fur trapping and vivisection (the dissection of live laboratory animals). Organizations such as the Animal Liberation Front have gone so far as to use deadly force against persons involved in animal research, implying that to them some human rights are subordinate to the protection of animal rights. The issue of exactly what "rights" animals should have is hotly contested, and the implications are broad. Medical researchers argue, for example, that if animal rights include the right not to be used in laboratory experimentation, medical research will be severely limited in ways that could have an impact on human lives; animal rights activists have attempted to dispute this claim. People for the Ethical Treatment of Animals (PETA) is probably the most widely known animal rights group.

See also Food and Drug Administration (FDA); Medical and health law; Nuclear radiation testing with human subjects.

Anthony, Susan B. (Feb. 15, 1820, Adams, Mass.—Mar. 13, 1906, Rochester, N.Y.)

IDENTIFICATION: American social reformer and organizer for women's rights

SIGNIFICANCE: Anthony's efforts paved the way for the Nineteenth Amendment to the Constitution (1920), granting women the right to vote

The daughter of a cotton manufacturer, Susan B. Anthony attended Quaker schools and became a teacher at a female academy near Rochester, N.Y. In 1849, she made her first public speech, decrying intemperance and urging women to assume moral leadership in society. Three weeks later she left teaching, and her career as a political reformer began. Frustrated by the restricted role of women in the temperance movement, she helped establish the Women's State Temperance Society of New York.

She was a vigorous opponent of slavery, active in the abolitionist movement. She traveled extensively and organized meetings under the motto No Compromise with Slaveholders. Immediate and Unconditional Emancipation. She was an agent for the American Anti-Slavery Society until 1861.

Her campaigns for women's rights, begun in 1852, expanded after the end of the Civil War. From 1868 to 1870, she worked with friend Elizabeth Cady Stanton to publish the New York liberal weekly *The Revolution*. Espousing the concept of equal pay for equal work, she helped found the New York Working Women's Association. Her public speeches enjoined lawmakers to accord women the same rights granted black males under the Fourteenth and Fifteenth Amendments to the U.S. Constitution.

In 1872, on behalf of her National Woman Suffrage Association, she visited President Ulysses S. Grant at the White House. She asked him to make votes for women a plank in the Republican platform. Grant made no promises, but Anthony believed that he represented women's best hope for effecting her organization's goal: "Men—their rights and nothing more. Women—their rights and nothing less." On November 5, 1872, she and fifteen other women went to the polls and cast ballots. Three weeks later, she was arrested for voting illegally.

At her trial, Judge Ward Hunt directed the jury to deliver a guilty verdict. Anthony refused to pay her fine, and Hunt refused to jail her until her fine was paid, thus effectively blocking appeal. Never pardoned because she was never jailed, she kept her promise to "rebel against . . . unjust, unconstitutional forms of law that tax, fine, imprison and hang women while denying them the right of representation in the government."

From 1890 until her death, she lectured widely on behalf of the National American Woman Suffrage Association. With Stanton and Matilda Joslyn Gage, she wrote and published *The History of Woman Suffrage* in four volumes (1881-1902). Her efforts were not confined to the United States. In 1888 she organized the International Council of Women and in 1904 the International Woman Suffrage Alliance. Susan B. Anthony envisioned a future in which "the true woman . . . will be her own individual self,—do her own individual work,—stand or fall by her own individual wisdom and strength." In campaigning for her vision, she pointed the way not only to suffrage for women but also to equality with men in all aspects of economic, social, and political life.

See also Seneca Falls Convention; Stanton, Elizabeth Cady; Woman suffrage.

Anti-Defamation League (ADL)

DATE: Established 1913

SIGNIFICANCE: The Anti-Defamation League was founded in 1913 by the Jewish fraternal organization B'nai B'rith to fight anti-Semitism and bigotry

B'nai B'rith was founded in New York in 1843 as a counterpart to the fraternal orders thriving in the United States in the nineteenth century. Its objective was to fulfill the traditional functions of Jewish societies in Europe that cared for the sick, elderly, and orphaned. In 1913, Leo Frank, a Jewish factory owner in Atlanta, was arrested and charged with the murder of a female employee. After his trial and conviction, he was kidnapped from prison and lynched. Shortly thereafter, Frank was fully exonerated. The incident led B'nai B'rith to form the Anti-Defamation League (ADL) to counter defamatory statements about Jewish people and to secure fair treatment for all people.

With a staff of more than four hundred and a $35 million budget, the ADL puts out a number of regular publications and supports studies involving anti-Semitism, racism, and other forms of bigotry. The group also maintains a speakers' bureau and gives annual awards that include a human rights prize and a First Amendment freedoms prize. Through its extensive publications, political lobbying activities, media campaigns, and education programs, the ADL wields considerable influence. Because the ADL also monitors the activities of hate groups and militias, the organization is often consulted by those seeking information and statistics on neo-Nazi groups and other hate groups in the United States. The ADL also collects and provides information on a broad range of first amendment concerns.

The ADL is led by a National Commission, which consists of 151 members and meets once a year. In the interval between the commission's annual meetings, the National Executive Committee runs the organization. Membership in the ADL is by nomination or invitation. The organization has twenty-eight regional offices in major metropolitan areas, and each office has its own board of local Jewish leaders and prominent citizens.

See also Hate crimes; Mack, Julian William; Racial and ethnic discrimination.

Anti-Racketeering Act

DATE: Became law May 18, 1934
DEFINITION: Legislation enacted to protect trade and commerce from interference by criminal threats of violence or coercion
SIGNIFICANCE: The Anti-Racketeering Act of 1934 was the first federal law enacted to fight the control that organized crime was suspected of holding over local communities

During the 1920's and 1930's, there was a significant increase in gangster activity and organized crime in the United States. Groups of criminals used bribery, extortion, threats, and violence to manipulate and control political officials, judges, and policemen and to harass local businesses. These groups were suspected of controlling gambling, prostitution, and the sale of illegal alcohol. Local authorities felt helpless in their fight to end criminally controlled rackets.

The 1934 Anti-Racketeering Act was proposed by Assistant Attorney General Joseph B. Keenan. Keenan, who testified before the Senate Judiciary Subcommittee on March 2, 1934, asserted that federal authorities needed an antiracketeering law to help fight organized crime. Racketeers were debilitating legitimate businesses and communities. To fight back, local authorities needed assistance from the federal government. The Anti-Racketeering Act was one of six changes in the criminal justice code recommended by Keenan to aid the Department of Justice in its goal to put every gangster, racketeer, and kidnapper out of business and into jail.

The Anti-Racketeering Act was one of several crime-fighting bills submitted to Congress by Senator Hy Ashurst of Arizona and Senator Royal Copeland of New York. Reflecting the recommendations made by Keenan, these bills aimed to reduce crime in the United States by increasing the powers of the federal government to assist local communities. The crime bills were vigorously supported by President Franklin D. Roosevelt. The House of Representatives quickly approved all six bills on May 5, 1934, and the Senate passed them on May 15. Numerous criminals were subsequently arrested and convicted under the Anti-Racketeering Act.

Under the Anti-Racketeering Act, racketeering was defined as any act or threat of violence committed to divert or interfere with interstate commerce and any actual or intended attempts at extortion in connection with interstate commerce transactions. Racketeering included any acts or coercions used to force an individual or business to join or not to join any organization or to buy or not to buy goods. It included any acts of violence to individuals in connection with such activities. Those convicted of racketeering would receive a maximum of ninety-nine years in prison and a fine commensurate with the profits derived from racketeering transactions.

The Anti-Racketeering Act remained unchanged until 1946, when Congress passed the Hobbs Act. The Hobbs Act placed previously exempted illegal labor-union activity within the reach of federal prosecutors. In 1970, Congress passed the Racketeer Influenced and Corrupt Organizations Act (RICO), which increased penalties for those convicted of racketeering and permitted the seizure of assets acquired or used at the time of the criminal activity.

See also Blackmail and extortion; Bribery; Hobbs Act; Organized crime; Police corruption and misconduct; Political corruption; Racketeer Influenced and Corrupt Organizations Act (RICO).

Antitrust law

DEFINITION: A series of laws and court decisions that regulate and limit business mergers, practices, and behavior
SIGNIFICANCE: No other capitalist nation has attempted to legislate marketplace competition on such a large scale as the United States has, making U.S. antitrust laws unique in the world

There are three major antitrust legislative acts: the Sherman Antitrust Act of 1890, the Clayton Antitrust Act of 1914, and the Federal Trade Commission Act of 1914. There were also three major amendments: the Robinson-Patman Act of 1936, the Miller-Tydings Act of 1937, and the Celler-Kefauver Act of 1950.

Sherman Antitrust Act of 1890. In the period after the Civil War, the United States enjoyed rapid economic growth that transformed the nation from an agrarian society with high transportation costs and a limited internal market into a nation with a national railroad system, an emerging modern capital market, and national markets for many industrial goods. Many small regional manufacturers found themselves facing large national competitors that enjoyed a lower cost of production because of economies of scale. The small regional producers could either fold and leave the business or merge with other firms.

A popular way to join forces was to form a "trust." The stock certificates of a number of corporations would be turned over to a trust in exchange for shares in the trust. The trust would then operate the various firms as though they were a single company. John D. Rockefeller's Standard Oil Company, which was organized as a trust, was extremely aggressive and notorious; Standard Oil did much to make "trust" a pejorative term. Many areas of commerce came to be dominated by trusts and other business monopolies. Trusts developed in a number of areas, including the tobacco, oil, and sugar industries. Some of these trusts were more predatory than others, but they all acted in restraint of trade to stifle competition.

The Sherman Antitrust Act of 1890 contains two main sections. First, it stipulated that "[e]very contract, combination in the form of a trust or otherwise . . . in restraint of trade or commerce among the several states or with foreign nations, is declared to be illegal." Second, it said, "Every person who shall monopolize, or attempt to monopolize, or combine or conspire . . . to monopolize any part of the trade or commerce among the several states or with foreign nations, shall be deemed guilty of a felony." Both sections provided for criminal penalties of fines of up to one million dollars for corporations and one hundred thousand dollars for individuals and/or up to three years of imprisonment.

Clayton Antitrust and Federal Trade Commission Acts of 1914. These two legislative acts should be viewed as complementary. The Clayton Antitrust Act outlaws certain specific practices, and it exempts labor and the legitimate activities of labor unions from all federal antitrust laws. The Federal Trade Commission (FTC) was to take action against unfair and deceptive practices, which were deemed to be anticompetitive, and to enforce the antitrust laws. Creating the FTC put U.S. antitrust policy under the continuous supervision of an independent, quasi-judicial commission.

Enforcement of the Sherman Act was never very vigorous until the "trust-busting" era of President Theodore Roosevelt (president from 1901 to 1909). The act was used with more consistent success against labor unions than against trusts and other business monopolies. There was widespread dissatisfaction with the Sherman Act as well as political agitation against trusts and other business monopolies in the first decade of the

It was during "trust-busting" Theodore Roosevelt's administration that antitrust legislation was first taken seriously. (Library of Congress)

twentieth century. The Sherman Act was too brief, and its language too general to be effective. In addition, the courts had considerable latitude in interpreting and applying the law. The legislative history of the act did not seem to indicate that Congress had intended to apply it to labor unions; nevertheless, several federal district courts used it to limit union activities.

The Clayton Antitrust Act, in section 6, declared that "the labor of a human being is not a commodity or article of commerce. Nothing in the antitrust laws shall . . . restrain individual members . . . [or labor unions] . . . from carrying out . . . [their legitimate goals]." Other sections of the act outlawed price discrimination, kickbacks or bribes in the forms of unearned commissions, interlocking directorates, and tying agreements whereby the purchase or lease of one item was tied to the purchase of another (such as a requirement that, if one wants to buy or lease a particular machine, one must agree to purchase supplies from the same source).

The Sherman and Clayton Antitrust acts can be enforced by either the United States Department of Justice or the Federal Trade Commission. Both criminal and civil actions can be brought under these statutes. The court may award triple damages plus attorneys' fees in civil cases. The Federal Trade Commission was given the power to enforce the Sherman and

MAJOR ANTITRUST CASES AND LEGISLATION

Date	Action	Significance
1890	Sherman Antitrust Act	Banned every "contract, combination . . . or conspiracy" in restraint of trade or commerce.
1898	*United States v. Addyston Pipe and Steel Co.*	Ruled that an agreement to set prices was illegal because it gave the parties power to set unreasonable prices.
1904	*Northern Securities v. United States*	Supreme Court ruled against holding companies that control the stock of competing companies.
1911	*Standard Oil Co. v. United States*	Supreme Court ordered the breakup of Standard Oil.
1911	*United States v. American Tobacco Co.*	Supreme Court ordered the breakup of American Tobacco Company. Along with the Standard Oil case, established the "rule of reason" approach to antitrust prosecution.
1914	Clayton Antitrust Act	Specified actions that are subject to antitrust prosecution.
1914	Federal Trade Commission Act	Established the Federal Trade Commission as an administrative agency to police "unfair methods of competition."
1920	*United States v. U.S. Steel Corp.*	Supreme Court ruled that size alone, in the absence of abuse of power, did not make a monopoly illegal.
1921	*American Column and Lumber Co. v. United States*	Ruled that competitors could be convicted if they had discussed prices and later set identical prices, even if no agreement to do so had been reached.
1936	Robinson-Patman Act	Specified the types of price discrimination that are illegal.
1936	*International Business Machines Corp. v. United States*	Established conditions under which it is illegal to tie the sale of one product to the sale of another.
1937	Miller-Tydings Act	Exempted manufacturers and retailers from prosecution for agreeing to set minimum prices if the states in which they operate allow such agreements.
1938	Wheeler-Lea Act	Strengthened enforcement powers of the Federal Trade Commission.
1945	*United States v. Aluminum Co. of America* (Alcoa)	Supreme Court ordered breakup of Alcoa, ruling that a monopoly is illegal even if not accompanied by abuse of power.
1948	*Federal Trade Commission v. Cement Institute*	Supreme Court ruled illegal agreements by producers to base prices on manufacturing costs plus transportation from a given location (base-point pricing).
1950	Celler-Kefauver Act	Clarified the Clayton Antitrust Act, making it enforceable against mergers accomplished by sale of assets in addition to those accomplished by sale of stock.
1967	*Federal Trade Commission v. Procter & Gamble Co.*	Supreme Court forced Procter & Gamble to divest itself of Clorox because P&G's market power could have allowed Clorox to dominate the bleach market.
1976	Antitrust Improvements Act	Allows state attorneys general to sue on behalf of residents.
1976	*United States v. American Telephone and Telegraph Co.*	Ruled that even though the company was subject to regulation it still was subject to antitrust prosecution. The decision led to the breakup of AT&T.

Clayton acts because the Department of Justice is a highly politicized agency. With the attorney general, the head of the department, being a member of the president's cabinet, the department follows the political philosophy of the administration. The Federal Trade Commission, by contrast, is an independent, quasi-judicial agency. The commission consists of five commissioners appointed by the president for staggered seven-year terms, with the advice and consent of the U.S. Senate. No more than three members of the commission may be of the same political party. The only way the president can remove a member of the commission is for "inefficiency, neglect of duty, or malfeasance in office."

The Robinson-Patman Act of 1936. During the 1920's, chain stores and other mass distributors grew in importance. The Great Depression of the 1930's and the aggressive tactics used by these mass merchandisers put independent retailers and wholesalers under pressure. A politically well-organized group of these independents was able to force the passage of this act, sometimes referred to as the "anti-chain store act." The Robinson-Patman Act amended section 2 of the Clayton Act. It was aimed at limiting price discrimination among buyers in cases where price differences give an unfair competitive advantage that hurts competition. The law prohibited the quantity discounts manufacturers gave to chain stores unless they could be justified on the basis of lower cost or they were intended to match the price of a competitor.

Miller-Tydings Act of 1937. The twentieth century saw the development of advertising and brand-name loyalty, and many consumers, for one reason or another, associated quality with price. The aggressive price competition of the mass merchandisers of the 1930's led independent retailers to press for the passage of "fair trade" or retail price maintenance laws. Most states passed such legislation during the 1930's. The manufacturers of the day went along with independent retailers for their own reasons. The Miller-Tydings Act exempted retail price maintenance laws, which prohibited retailers from discounting brand name products, from all federal antitrust laws.

Celler-Kefauver Act of 1950. Corporations were prohibited from merging, in cases where the effect of the merger "was to substantially reduce competition or tend to create a monopoly," by section 7 of the Clayton Antitrust Act. A loophole in the law existed, in that a corporation could buy the physical assets and equipment of a competitor with impunity.

The Celler-Kefauver Act amended the Clayton Act to prohibit "directly or indirectly [the purchase of] . . . the whole or any part of the stock or . . . any part of the assets of another corporation . . . where . . . the effect of such acquisition may be to substantially lessen competition or tend to create a monopoly."

American Telephone and Telegraph Cases. On November 20, 1974, the U.S. Justice Department brought an antitrust action against American Telephone and Telegraph (AT&T). The lengthy antitrust case against AT&T illustrates the complexity of the issues involved and the difficulty of attempting to resolve industrial concentration through antitrust court actions. The government accused AT&T of monopolizing the telecommunications business. The Justice Department wanted AT&T to divest itself of Western Electric, its manufacturing subsidiary, and either to divest itself of some or all of the regional Bell Telephone companies or to leave the long distance telephone business.

Almost a decade later, in 1983, an out-of-court settlement was reached. AT&T was split into eight separate companies. A new AT&T, freed from Federal Communications Commission (FCC) regulations, would handle long distance telecommunications and be able to enter areas of business that had previously been closed to the company. AT&T would compete with other companies offering long distance telephone service. The seven separate regional operating companies, largely remaining regulated monopolies, would handle the local telephone business. This was the largest antitrust divestiture in history, dwarfing the Standard Oil and American Tobacco cases of 1911.

The breakup of the AT&T monopoly was made possible by technological developments and made inevitable as the government allowed bits of competition to be inserted into a monopoly structure. AT&T had long been a "natural monopoly" in that the cost of wiring the nation for several competing telephone companies with copper cable would have been ex-

tremely expensive and a waste of scarce resources. The development of microwave transmission and communication satellites, however, made a competitive market structure possible. The government allowed some competitors into the market for long distance service using this technology, thus setting the stage for the breakup of AT&T.

Many years after the 1983 settlement, the AT&T divestitures still generated controversy. Some observers questioned whether the breakup was necessary. In the words of Charles Wholstetter (chairman of the board of Continental Telecom), AT&T was supplying "telephone service which was the envy of the world in quality and reliability and placed all the financial strains on those who could best afford to pay."

Changing Government Attitude Toward Enforcement. The 1980's were a somnolent period for antitrust enforcement. Few cases were initiated during the decade. In 1989, however, James F. Rill was appointed to head the Justice Department's Antitrust Division, and antitrust enforcement came back with a vengeance. Ivy League universities, airlines, the Salomon Brothers, and Arizona dentists were investigated by the Justice Department. In 1990, the Justice Department brought actions against eleven proposed mergers, the greatest number of cases filed in any year since 1973. Congress substantially increased the budget for antitrust activities and stiffened the penalties for violations.
                                                —*Daniel C. Falkowski*

See also Capitalism; Clayton Antitrust Act; Federal Trade Commission (FTC); Price fixing; Sherman Antitrust Act.

ANTITRUST CONVICTIONS IN U.S. DISTRICT COURTS

Source: U.S. Department of Justice, Bureau of Justice Statistics, *Sourcebook of Criminal Justice Statistics—1993*. Washington, D.C.: U.S. Government Printing Office, 1994.

BIBLIOGRAPHY

For the historical development of antitrust policy, see Donald Stevenson Watson, *Economic Policy: Business and Government* (Cambridge, Mass.: Riverside Press, 1960). For economic analysis and economic models of antitrust cases, see Eugene M. Singer, *Antitrust Economics: Selected Legal Cases and Economic Models* (Englewood Cliffs, N.J.: Prentice-Hall, 1968), and Eugene M. Singer, *Antitrust Economics and Legal Analysis* (Columbus, Ohio: Grid, 1981). For cases, see Irwin M. Stelzer and Howard P. Kitt, *Selected Antitrust Cases: Landmark Decisions* (Homewood, Ill.: Richard D. Irwin, 1976), and William Breit and Kenneth G. Elzinga, *The Antitrust Casebook: Milestones in Economic Regulation* (Chicago: Dryden Press, 1982). For a good critical analysis of the basic philosophy behind antitrust laws and policy, see Robert H. Bork, *The Antitrust Paradox: A Policy at War with Itself* (New York: Basic Books, 1978).

Appellate process

DEFINITION: The judicial mechanism by which decisions of lower courts are reviewed by higher courts

SIGNIFICANCE: The appellate process allows a higher court to correct errors committed by a lower court or administrative agency

Although the possibility of an appeal has not typically been viewed as a fundamental right or as essential to due process, Anglo-American legal systems have traditionally provided mechanisms for the review of decisions rendered by lower courts. All states and the federal judicial system provide for one or more levels of appellate review. In the federal system, for example, appeals may be taken from the decision of a trial court to the court of appeals and from there to the U.S. Supreme Court. Appeals to some appellate courts may be a matter of right. Appeals to others, as to the Supreme Court of the United States, are discretionary. A party aggrieved with the decision of a lower court is allowed to request review of the lower court's proceeding, but the decision of whether to grant the review lies within the discretion of the higher court.

See also *Certiorari*, writ of; Civil procedure; Criminal procedure; Due process of law; Judicial system, U.S.; Miscarriage of justice; Pardoning power; Scottsboro cases; Supreme Court of the United States.

Arbitration and mediation

DEFINITION: Arbitration and mediation are processes in which neutral private citizens called arbitrators and mediators help parties resolve disputes without litigation going to court

SIGNIFICANCE: In the United States, arbitration and mediation are increasingly being used in place of or before litigation, sometimes because courts require it

Arbitration and mediation are collectively known as "alternative dispute resolution," or ADR. In mediation, or "conciliation," neutrals help the parties themselves resolve disputes. Mediators do not decide the parties' rights. Following informal trials, however, arbitrators do, in a decision called an award.

In the most general sense, alternative dispute resolution has been used for thousands of years; disputes were resolved informally long before courts were invented. Among friends and relatives, it is almost always used to resolve disputes. The world is full of experienced, if not formally trained, mediators and arbitrators. For example, a large (and difficult) job of parents is to resolve sibling disputes. In China and Japan, ADR is the standard approach for resolving disputes between strangers; people who sue are seen as unreasonable. In the United States, people are more likely to sue—sometimes even members of their own families. This situation is changing, however: A mid-1990's survey of attorneys showed significant increases in the use of ADR, particularly mediation, since 1980.

An example of the use of ADR would be a situation in which newly installed plumbing begins to leak. The homeowner might refuse to pay the plumber and might seek money for water damage. If so, either the homeowner or the plumber could sue—or both could ask any neutral person to help resolve their disagreement.

A neutral party's role must be clearly defined. People often tell mediators things they would not tell an arbitrator or judge. Also, it is good to know the rules in advance. Thus, people generally call on experienced organizations. Better Business Bureaus often provide ADR services for customer complaints. The American Arbitration Association (AAA) has sets of rules and panels of neutrals for many kinds of controversies. Although its main office is in New York, the AAA has offices throughout the United States. Often, the easiest way to find a suitable ADR organization is to call a local court.

General Advantages of ADR. ADR is increasingly popular for a number of reasons. First, it is often quicker and cheaper than litigation. People who do not want their differences aired in public courtrooms also prefer ADR because it is private. Additionally, litigation is generally more likely than ADR to spoil long-term relationships, which is probably the reason people do not ordinarily sue their friends or family. This fact is also reflected by the fact that arbitration and mediation have long been part of labor-management contracts. Finally, because people using ADR have more control over how their disputes will be resolved, it is regarded as being at least as fair as litigation.

Mediation. Mediators help parties resolve disputes, but they cannot decide what must be done—that is up to the parties themselves. Any dispute can be mediated. The agreement to mediate, and any resulting settlement, are governed by contract law. Courts have the power to reject agreements, such as those involving child custody disputes, regardless of how they are reached. Courts rarely disapprove, however, because settlement is encouraged.

Mediation often begins with all parties gathered together so the mediator can understand the dispute and spot major problems quickly. Eventually, mediators discuss disputes with the parties separately and convey offers and counter-offers back and forth. The main job of a mediator is to nudge parties toward settling their differences. A simple dispute might be resolved in an hour or two, but, as with any negotiations, agreement can take much longer. Mediation concludes when the parties agree or when it becomes clear that the parties are too far apart to settle the dispute.

Arbitration. When disputing parties cannot agree, with or without mediation, they can use an arbitrator rather than a judge or jury. To do so, they must agree to arbitrate and to be bound by the arbitrator's award. After arbitrators are chosen, parties tell their stories in a trial-like hearing. They can call witnesses and introduce documents as evidence. If necessary, an arbitrator can go see evidence that cannot be effectively presented in a hearing room. Arbitrators must not have discussions with one party without the other party present.

When disputes are simple, arbitration can be very informal. In simple cases, the AAA, for example, uses expedited procedures. If the amount in controversy is large, the procedure can be more complex; for example, three arbitrators, instead of one, might be used. Yet even complex arbitration is simpler than litigation, at least partly because arbitrators are chosen for their expertise in the subject matter at the heart of a dispute.

Title 9 of the U.S. Code makes agreements to arbitrate and arbitration awards enforceable when federal courts have jurisdiction. That statute also allows judges to set aside arbitration awards in a few situations—as when one party did not get an opportunity to participate or when arbitrators failed to report prior party relationships. State statutes also govern such matters, but with a few important differences. Alabama courts, for example, will not enforce agreements to arbitrate future disputes, but they will enforce contracts to arbitrate existing disputes.

Nonbinding Arbitration. Judges used to seem hostile to arbitration, but, faced with crowded dockets, they may now require pretrial arbitration. Under the Seventh Amendment, many parties are entitled to a jury trial. Yet few parties disappointed with pretrial arbitration pursue that right. For one thing, a better result may seem unlikely; for another, there will be additional expenses. Even in the rare instances when arbitrations have been procedurally flawed, arbitrations may still encourage settlement. —*Thomas G. Field, Jr.*

See also Civil procedure; Contract, freedom of; Contract law; *Elrod v. Burns*; Judicial review; Judicial system, U.S.; Jury system; Justice; Reversible error; Small-claims court.

BIBLIOGRAPHY

Good sources include the American Arbitration Association's *A Guide to Mediation for Business People*, *Resolving Your Disputes*, and *A Guide to Arbitration for Business People* (New York: American Arbitration Association, 1992, 1993, and 1993, respectively). One may also contact the AAA at any regional office or at its New York headquarters. Court clerks can help identify local ADR organizations. See also John W. Keltner, *The Management of Struggle: Elements of Dispute Resolution Through Negotiation, Mediation, and Arbitration* (Cresskill, N.J.: Hampton Press, 1994), and Abraham P. Ordover, *Alternatives to Litigation: Mediation, Arbitration, and the Art of Dispute Resolution* (Notre Dame, Ind.: National Institute for Trial Advocacy, 1993).

Argersinger v. Hamlin

COURT: U.S. Supreme Court

DATE: Decided June 12, 1972

SIGNIFICANCE: Defendants have the right to counsel at criminal trials whenever they may be imprisoned for any offense, whether it be classified as a felony or misdemeanor

The police arrested Jon Richard Argersinger for carrying a concealed weapon. The potential punishment was up to six months in jail and/or a fine of one thousand dollars. Being indigent, Argersinger was unable to afford counsel. He was convicted and sentenced to serve ninety days in jail. At that time the Florida courts did not provide counsel, except for nonpetty offenses punishable by more than six months in jail. In a *habeas corpus* petition to the Florida Supreme Court, Argersinger argued that because he was poor and had not been provided with counsel, the charge against him could not effectively be defended. The Florida appellate court rejected the claim, and the U.S. Supreme Court agreed to hear the case.

In a unanimous decision, the Court ruled that the right to counsel not only applied to state defendants charged with felonies but also applied in all trials of persons for offenses serious enough to warrant a jail sentence. Prior to *Argersinger*, some doubt had existed as to whether the constitutional right to appointed counsel applied to any misdemeanor prosecutions. In *Gideon v. Wainwright* (1963), the Court had established a right to counsel only in felony prosecutions.

The Court in *Argersinger* held *Gideon* to be applicable to all misdemeanor defendants who could be sentenced to a jail term. The Court rejected the state's contention that the Sixth Amendment's right to counsel should not apply to petty offenses even when a jail sentence might be imposed. Nothing in the history of the right to counsel, the Court said, suggested a retraction of that right in petty offenses; conversely, the common law previously did require that counsel be provided.

The problems associated with petty offenses often require the expertise of counsel. The legal questions involved in a misdemeanor trial, or in a guilty plea, are not necessarily less complex simply because the jail sentence would not exceed six months. Indeed, petty misdemeanors may create a special need for counsel because the great volume of such cases may provide a tendency for speedy dispositions regardless of the fairness of the results.

Since the defendant had been sentenced to jail, the Court found it unnecessary to rule on the defendant's right to appointed counsel where "a loss of liberty was not involved." The opinion laid the foundation for distinguishing between cases involving sentences of imprisonment and those in which only fines are imposed. The Court noted the special qualities of imprisonment, "for however short a time," including its possible serious repercussions affecting the defendant's career and reputation.

Argersinger v. Hamlin established that, under the Sixth and Fourteenth Amendments to the U.S. Constitution, without a knowing and intelligent waiver, no person may be imprisoned for any offense, whether classified as petty, misdemeanor, or felony, unless represented by counsel at trial.

See also Counsel, right to; Criminal procedure; *Gideon v. Wainwright*; Public defender.

Arizona v. Fulminante

COURT: U.S. Supreme Court

DATE: Decided March 26, 1991

SIGNIFICANCE: The Supreme Court ruled that a coerced confession wrongly admitted as evidence could be subjected to "harmless error" analysis and might not be grounds for automatic invalidation of a criminal conviction

In 1983, Oreste C. Fulminante, incarcerated in a federal prison for an unrelated crime, confessed to another inmate, a paid informant for the Federal Bureau of Investigation, that he had raped and murdered his eleven-year-old stepdaughter. He also confessed to a woman who later married the informant. The next year, when tried for first-degree murder in the Superior Court, Maricopa County, Arizona, Fulminante sought to have his confessions suppressed on grounds that they violated his due process rights guaranteed by the Fifth and Fourteenth Amendments. The motion was denied, and Fulminante was convicted of first-degree murder and sentenced to death. On appeal, Fulminante's conviction was first upheld by the Arizona Supreme Court; later, however, under reconsideration, that same court ordered a retrial on the grounds that the "harmless error" basis of admitting Fulminante's confession was inapplicable because the first confession was coerced.

On *certiorari*, the U.S. Supreme Court upheld the ruling of the Arizona Supreme Court. It confirmed that Fulminante's first confession had been coerced and that admission of his confession was not harmless under the specific circumstances. Yet part of the majority opinion, argued by Chief Justice William H. Rehnquist, advanced the 5-4 majority's conclusion that in a state criminal trial an involuntary confession admitted in violation of the Fourteenth Amendment's due process clause is, in fact, subject to harmless-error analysis. This opinion was rooted in a distinction made between due process violations and "trial error," holding that the admission of an involuntary confession does not transcend the criminal trial process and that it is similar in kind and degree to other evidence admitted in court. It noted, too, that confessions secured in violation of *Massiah v. United States* (1964) and *Miranda v. Arizona* (1966) had already been subject to harmless-error analysis.

Justice Byron R. White, vigorously dissenting, argued that the admission of a coerced confession in a criminal trial violated the defendant's constitutional rights and should not be subject to harmless-error analysis, and, further, that no sufficient reason had been presented for departing from the Supreme Court's time-honored "rule of automatic reversal" in coerced-confession cases. According to that rule, if a coerced, involuntary confession was erroneously admitted in criminal proceedings, any conviction had to be overturned regardless of how much other evidence of guilt supported it.

In effect, the Supreme Court's *Fulminante* decision overturned earlier decisions such as that rendered in *Chapman v. California* (1967), one of the last cases prior to *Fulminante* upholding the rule of automatic reversal. This departure from that rule raised questions whether admission of a coerced confession as evidence must always be interpreted as a violation of a defendant's constitutional rights or of those protected by the rulings in the *Massiah* and *Miranda* decisions. The finding has been criticized for eroding those rights.

See also *Brown v. Mississippi*; Due process of law; *Escobedo v. Illinois*; Harmless error; *Malloy v. Hogan*; *Miranda v. Arizona*.

Arms, right to keep and bear

DEFINITION: A right guaranteed to the American people by the Second Amendment because a "well regulated militia" is crucial to the security of a free state

SIGNIFICANCE: The constitutional right to "keep and bear arms" has not been interpreted by the Supreme Court as absolute or as prohibiting gun control legislation

Quoted in its entirety, the Second Amendment to the U.S. Constitution states, "A well regulated militia, being necessary to the security of a free state, the right of the people to keep and bear arms, shall not be infringed." These twenty-seven words have generated tremendous debate and controversy since the 1960's. Opposing sides in arguments over gun control—that is, arguments over whether the government should be allowed to regulate firearms and, if so, to what extent—disagree heatedly about the meaning of this sentence. On the one hand, it clearly proclaims the right to keep and bear firearms; on the other, it also clearly links that right to a "well regulated militia" and to the issue of state security.

The debate over gun control, although it must by nature center on constitutional issues, also by nature involves people's emotional reactions to the national prevalence of violent crime. Do citizens need to have sophisticated firearms to protect themselves against criminals? Will banning the sale of assault weapons lessen incidents of senseless mass murder? Can imposing a waiting period on the purchase of handguns lessen the number of people killed in crimes of passion? Statistics that support any of these positions reliably are hard to obtain and always arguable.

The Origin of the Second Amendment. The Second Amendment was passed because of the colonial American experience under the British. Both the king and the British Parliament had sought to increase their control of the colonies and had partially succeeded in their attempt to seize many citizens' privately held firearms in Boston. Based on that experience, the framers of the Bill of Rights included the amendment out of a fear that the national U.S. government might someday similarly attempt to disarm the state militias. The use of state militias was actually declining at the end of the eighteenth century. They essentially became a dead issue during the nineteenth century and were replaced by the National Guard system in the twentieth century. This historical perspec-

Teenagers target shooting in rural Iowa; the right to such activities is protected by the Second Amendment. (James L. Shaffer)

tive is of considerable importance for understanding the Supreme Court's rulings on the Second Amendment. While the amendment seems to have been intended to prevent the (now obsolete) fear of national disarmament of state militias, some organizations, such as the National Rifle Association (NRA), maintain that the amendment prohibits even modest gun control legislation by federal, state, or local authorities. This view has never received any significant support from even a minority of members of the Supreme Court.

"The People." The NRA and other opponents of gun control tend to quote only the last fragment of the Second Amendment, which seems to assert flatly that "the people" have an absolute "right to keep and bear arms." While this position is problematic in that it ignores the other half of the clause, it does provide a particular avenue for arguing against restrictions on gun ownership. If the framers had intended only states (rather than individuals) to have the right to keep and bear arms to protect them against the federal government, it seems likely that they would have used the word "states" instead of "people" in the amendment. This is precisely what they did in other amendments, particularly the Tenth Amendment, in which the Constitution is said to protect both the "people" and the "states respectively"—clearly drawing a distinction between the two.

This argument is even stronger if one recognizes that the original militias were collections of individuals who owned their own firearms and kept them in their homes. (The practice of today's National Guard, on the other hand, is to maintain publicly owned weapons in centralized locations.) Supporters of gun control attempt to counter this line of reasoning by maintaining that the colonial militias were not actually vague entities consisting of all the colony's men; they were organized, and membership involved a number of legal requirements.

Application to the Federal Government. The Supreme Court has held consistently that the Second Amendment does not prohibit the federal government from passing gun control legislation. Nevertheless, in spite of the protestations of the NRA and other groups, one could argue that federal restrictions on firearms have been few. Until the violence and unrest of the late 1960's and a growth in the national crime rate, there was little demand for regulation. The first federal firearms law

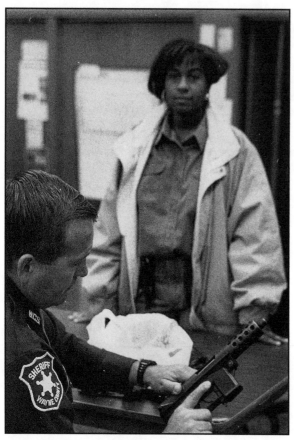

Many advocates of gun control would argue that the Second Amendment should not be interpreted to allow unregulated possession of weapons such as this semi-automatic pistol, here turned in by a high school girl in a "guns for cash" exchange program. (Jim West)

was the War Revenue Act of 1919, a tax measure; the second was the 1927 Firearms in the U.S. Mails Act, forbidding the interstate mailing of most guns to private individuals. The National Firearms Act of 1934 made it a crime to carry certain types of weapons, notably short-barreled or "sawed-off" shotguns, across state lines and imposed a tax on sales of automatic weapons. The 1938 Federal Firearms Act required gun dealers to obtain federal licenses and to keep records of interstate gun sales; it also prohibited sales to people convicted of violent crimes. The Gun Control Act of 1968, which increased the licensing requirements of gun dealers, was passed largely in response to the assassinations of John and Robert Kennedy and Martin Luther King, Jr.

The 1980's and 1990's saw further legislation. Laws in 1984 and 1986 limited sales of "armor-piercing" bullets; the 1986 law also limited the manufacture, sale, and possession of fully automatic weapons. In 1993 Congress enacted a five-day waiting period for handgun purchases (the "Brady bill"), and in 1994 it banned nineteen types of "assault weapons" and other semiautomatic firearms. No challenges to these laws had

been heard by the Supreme Court as of the mid-1990's. As of 1995, in fact, the most recent Supreme Court case on which lower court decisions could be based was the 1939 case *United States v. Miller*.

Application to State Governments. Whether the individual states can regulate (or even confiscate) individually owned firearms is another question. According to the Supreme Court, as long as there is no stipulation to the contrary in the respective state's constitution, the states are free to regulate firearms as they see fit. In the first Supreme Court case to deal with the matter, *United States v. Cruikshank* (1876), the Court determined that the Second Amendment was "one of those amendments that has no other effect than to restrict the powers of the National Government." Ten years later, the Court quoted and reaffirmed *Cruikshank* in *Presser v. Illinois* (1886). Even more directly on point, the Court unanimously upheld a state law "prohibiting the carrying of dangerous weapons" in *Miller v. Texas* (1894) and reaffirmed that position in *Robertson v. Baldwin* (1897).

Selective Incorporation. All these cases predated the current Supreme Court procedure of "selectively incorporating" sections of the Bill of Rights into the due process clause of the Fourteenth Amendment—and thus applying them to the states as well as to the federal government. One might therefore wonder whether these rulings are still valid; this question has been answered in the affirmative by the cases decided in the federal courts since the 1930's. In *United States v. Miller* (1939), the Supreme Court held that the registration of sawed-off shotguns did not violate the Second Amendment, since these guns would not be used by a militia. The Court's decision in *Miller* did not go beyond this particular question to address any larger issues, however, a fact which has encouraged continuing debate over the constitutionality of gun control.

In more than a dozen cases since *Miller*, the federal courts of appeals have held that the Second Amendment protects state militias rather than individual ownership. Of the six cases appealed upward to the Supreme Court, all have been denied a hearing, thus allowing the appeals court rulings to stand. The Court has never attempted to apply the Second Amendment to the states although it has had more than a dozen opportunities to do so. —*Richard L. Wilson*

See also Bill of Rights, U.S.; National Firearms Act and Federal Firearms Act; National Guard; National Rifle Association (NRA).

BIBLIOGRAPHY

The best single policy analysis of gun control, with an excellent chapter on the mainstream "states' rights minimalist" theory of what the Second Amendment means, is Robert J. Spitzer's *The Politics of Gun Control* (Chatham, N.J.: Chatham House, 1995). For a sharply contrasting view, consider Stephen P. Halbrook's "The Original Understanding of the Second Amendment" and Don B. Kates, Jr., "Minimalist Interpretation of the Second Amendment," both in Eugene W. Hickok, Jr., ed., *The Bill of Rights: Original Meaning and Current Understanding* (Charlottesville: University of Virginia Press, 1991). Wallace Mendelson's *The American Constitution and Civil Liberties* (Homewood, Ill.: Dorsey Press, 1981) contains useful excerpts from the most important Supreme Court cases on civil liberties. Another comprehensive symposium on the entire Bill of Rights is Geoffrey R. Stone, Richard A. Epstein, and Cass R. Sunstein, eds., *The Bill of Rights in the Modern State* (Chicago: University of Chicago Press, 1992).

Arraignment

DEFINITION: A hearing at which the accused is informed of charges being brought and is given the opportunity to plead

SIGNIFICANCE: An accused person cannot be held without being charged

The Seventh Amendment to the U.S. Constitution provides that an accused person must be informed of the nature of the accusation being brought. The arraignment fulfills that right. At the arraignment, the accused is called by name, informed of the charges, and given the opportunity to enter a plea of guilty, not guilty, or *nolo contendere* (no contest).

If the charge is serious, an attorney may be present with the accused or may be appointed by the court if the accused requests. The defense may use the arraignment to determine the merits of the case and, if appropriate, attempt a plea bar-

gain, pleading guilty to a lesser offense in return for a reduced sentence.

A plea of guilty or *nolo contendere* leads to immediate sentencing without trial. A plea of not guilty leads to a trial. *Nolo contendere*, which the court considers an implied confession of guilt, does not lessen liability in criminal matters. Such a plea may reduce liability in civil matters, however, because there is no confession of guilt.

See also Arrest; Assigned counsel system; Competency to stand trial; Criminal procedure; Grand jury; Indictment; Information; Plea bargaining; Sentencing.

Arrest

DEFINITION: The process by which suspected offenders are formally taken into custody and transferred for processing into the criminal justice system

SIGNIFICANCE: Arrest is the point of entry into the criminal justice system and one of the main functions of police officers

An arrest takes place when a police officer has probable cause to believe that an individual has committed a crime. An essential part of the arrest procedure involves taking the suspect into secure custody. That is, persons suspected of committing crimes are taken to police stations against their will. When

Colin Ferguson on his way to arraignment on six counts of murder; he was convicted of the crimes in 1995. (AP/Wide World Photos)

arrests take place, the suspected offenders are taken, often in handcuffs, to booking facilities at police stations, where their identities, fingerprints, and details of the crime are recorded.

Arrest is the point of entry into the criminal justice system for people who are caught violating the law. For some offenders, their journey through the criminal justice system continues to trial and sentencing. For others, whose cases are dismissed, the events following arrest are inconsequential. Regardless, every suspected offender apprehended by the police experiences the arrest procedure. The bulk of police officers' work involves arresting suspects.

Arrest Warrants. Police officers may arrest suspects only if they believe that there is probable cause to do so. Probable cause exists when a reasonable person would believe (given the evidence) that there is sufficient cause to bring a suspect into custody. The facts must reasonably point to the individual to be arrested. Probable cause is necessary whether an officer is arresting an individual with a warrant or without one.

Arrest warrants are given to police officers by judges, who must find probable cause before issuing them. An arrest warrant is a paper that authorizes an officer to arrest a suspect without actually seeing the suspect committing a crime. This paper must contain specific details about the nature of the offense committed, where the individual will be apprehended, and why a warrant is desired. An officer may arrest a suspect without an arrest warrant if he or she has seen the suspect violate the law. The majority of arrests are made without warrants.

Police officers make arrest decisions based on the information available about the offense and their past experience. Because of the large number of differences in arrestees and arrest situations, there is no way to anticipate all the situations police officers will encounter. Police officers are said to have "discretion" in the arrest decision, which means that they must use their own judgment in deciding whether to arrest a suspect. While they must always abide by the doctrine of probable cause, they must still rely on their own judgment. Some critics of police procedure have argued that the police have too much discretion in the arrest decision and that racism or sexism may play a part in some officers' decisions to arrest.

Arrest Procedures. Arrest involves taking a suspect into secure custody. A police officer making an arrest must have intent to arrest. Simply stopping a motorist to write a ticket or ask a question does not constitute intent to arrest. In some cases, an arrestee will voluntarily submit to the arrest procedure. When this occurs, there is no need for the officer to take the suspect into custody forcibly. In most cases, however, it is more difficult to take a suspect into custody, and some amount of force is required. Officers also must have authority to arrest a suspect. "Authority" refers to the power that police have to deprive a citizen of liberty through arrest. While ordinary citizens have limited powers to arrest someone suspected of committing a felony (in some states), they do not have the legal authority to take an offender into custody.

Finally, suspects must be informed that they are being arrested. That is, they are told that they are not merely being stopped for

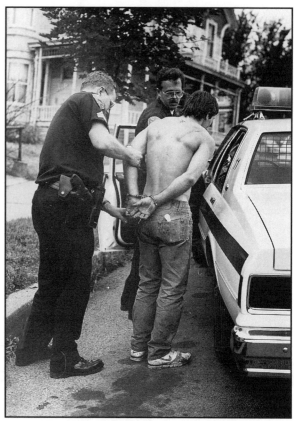

Police have the authority to arrest an individual when there is "probable cause" to do so; most arrests do not involve arrest warrants. (James L. Shaffer)

questioning but have been taken into custody because there is probable cause to believe that they committed a crime.

Rights of Arrestees. Special constitutional rights apply to people arrested by the police. They include the right to counsel and the right against self-incrimination. In other words, arrestees are entitled to attorney representation, and they are accorded the right not to incriminate themselves in a crime. This latter right was written into the Constitution of the United States to keep officers from coercing arrestees into confessing to a crime. Specifically, the Fifth Amendment to the Constitution states (in part) that an arrestee shall not "be compelled in any criminal case to be a witness against himself." Historically, arrestees were often physically assaulted or tortured in order to obtain confessions.

The U.S. Supreme Court case *Miranda v. Arizona* (1966) established that arrestees must be notified of their rights under the Constitution. They must be aware that they are entitled to an attorney and that if they cannot afford an attorney, one will be provided for them by the court. They are also notified that they have the right to remain silent, but if they choose to speak it can be used against them at their trial. This notification is called a Miranda warning, and it must be given to all arrestees immediately following their arrest.   —*Christina Polsenberg*

See also Citizen's arrest; Counsel, right to; Criminal justice system; Criminal procedure; Discretion; Felony; *Miranda v. Arizona*; Police; Probable cause; Self-incrimination, privilege against; Sex discrimination.

BIBLIOGRAPHY

Police discretion is discussed extensively in Michael K. Brown, *Working the Street: Police Discretion and the Dilemmas of Reform* (New York: Russell Sage Foundation, 1988), and Jerome H. Skolnick, *Justice Without Trial: Law Enforcement in Democratic Society* (2d ed. New York: John Wiley & Sons, 1975). A detailed discussion of police arrest procedure and relevant Supreme Court cases can be found in Rolando V. Del Carmen, *Criminal Procedure for Law Enforcement Personnel* (Monterey, Calif.: Brooks/Cole, 1987).

Arson

DEFINITION: Crime involving the deliberate and wanton destruction of property by fire or explosion, either for private revenge, material gain, destruction of evidence, or fulfillment of an irrational urge

SIGNIFICANCE: Arson is a major crime, first designated "index crime" in the Federal Bureau of Investigation's *Uniform Crime Reports* in 1979; arson is considered a serious problem because detection is difficult, evidence hard to obtain, and conviction rates low

Arson has a long legal history. In English common law, the basis of most arson statutes in the United States, the term originally referred to the burning of a house, but in contemporary law the term has a much more inclusive definition, referring to the burning of property of any kind.

Degrees of Arson. Most current statutes now recognize degrees of arson. Many state laws distinguish three degrees:

Arson investigator examines a burned building, seeking evidence of the cause of the fire. (James L. Shaffer)

ARSON BY TYPE OF PROPERTY, 1993		
Property Classification	Number of Offenses	Percent Distribution
Total	**82,348**	**100.0**
Total structure	42,867	52.1
Single occupancy residential	17,795	21.6
Other residential	7,516	9.1
Storage	3,753	4.6
Industrial/manufacturing	681	.8
Other commercial	4,968	6.0
Community/public	5,049	6.1
Other structure	3,105	3.8
Total mobile	21,617	26.3
Motor vehicles	20,094	24.4
Other mobile	1,523	1.8
Other	17,864	21.7

Source: U.S. Department of Justice, Federal Bureau of Investigation, *Crime in the United States* (Uniform Crime Reports). Washington, D.C.: U.S. Government Printing Office, 1994.

Note: Because of rounding, percentages may not add to totals.

the first, or aggravated degree, which involves the destruction of an inhabited domicile; the second, which involves the destruction of an uninhabited building; and the third, which involves the destruction of personal or real property for some illegal purpose. A factor in some jurisdictions is the time of the occurrence, whether the crime is committed in the nighttime or daytime hours.

Arson's Alarming Growth. Arson has always been a particularly pernicious crime. It may reap material benefits for the arsonist with few risks; on the other hand, in the case of pyromaniacs, it can be motivated by totally irrational urges. Fueled in part by mob violence and urban blight, and in part by economic incentives, arson has reached new and alarming epidemic proportions. In 1970, it was called the fastest-growing crime in the United States, and statistics confirmed that assessment. From 1970 to 1977, the number of fires begun by arsonists in any single year doubled. By 1980, arson annually accounted for more than a thousand deaths and was costing insurance companies more than $1.6 billion. In 1990, the direct cost of arson exceeded $2 billion, with an indirect cost estimated at four times that amount. It is now believed that at least one in four fires in the United States is deliberately set.

Types of Arsonists. Arsonists generally fall into one of several, somewhat overlapping categories. A common type is the arsonist who seeks to gain revenge by setting fire to property, most often inhabited. The victim is known to the arsonist, and often the two are related; this type of arsonist is therefore identified and convicted relatively often. Statistically, revenge is the motive for arson in about 23 percent of the cases.

A second type is the vandal arsonist, the most common, who accounts for 42 percent of cases. Typically, offenders are juveniles who destroy property for sport, although they may be motivated to act against what appear to be repressive symbols in their lives. Usually they act with accomplices, often in a climate of group or mob violence.

Next there is the arsonist who uses fire to conceal another crime, such as burglary or murder. This arsonist acts to destroy evidence. Typically, the property destroyed is an uninhabited dwelling or business establishment.

There is also the thrill arsonist, one who derives pleasure from the spectacle of the fire and the efforts of firefighters to put it out. This arsonist works alone and is not out to make the crime a defiant gesture against authority. Abandoned buildings are likely nighttime targets for this breed of arsonist. Thrill and concealment arsonists, linked with other miscellaneous types, account for less than 7 percent of all occurrences.

Far more troublesome is the fire-for-profit arsonist. Often this type is an insurance fraud arsonist, one who resorts to the destruction of property to escape financial difficulty. The aim of this arsonist is to collect the insurance on what the arsonist destroys. Closely related is the professional arsonist or torch, who sets fires for hire, allowing a conspirator, usually an insurance fraud arsonist, to cover his or her complicity with an alibi. This individual is a professional, a repeat offender, a student of the art, and one who is careful to conceal the crime. Arson for profit accounts for about 14 percent of all deliberate fires.

Finally, there is the pyromaniac, whose motives arise from a pathological need not clearly understood. These arsonists may set fires in a serial pattern or on a rampage. Although they may also reveal resentment for authority, pyromaniacs are driven by an inexplicable need, possibly related to a low level of intelligence or a sense of sexual inadequacy. They also account for about 14 percent of all deliberate fires.

Losses and Punishment. Despite constantly improving arson prevention and detection techniques, there had been no significant reduction in the rate of the crime in the United States as of the mid-1990's. In fact, if statistics compiled between 1989 and 1992 reflect an ongoing trend, the situation continues to worsen. In 1989, fire accounted for $7.2 billion in property loss or damage, with incendiary or suspicious fires accounting for $1.56 billion of that total. While the total loss or damage amounted to less in 1992 ($6.96 billion), the amount accounted for by incendiary or suspicious fires rose to $2 billion.

While in some countries arson carries the death penalty, in the United States sentencing tends to be lenient. For example, between 1986 and 1993, federal arson prisoners were serving sentences averaging less than three years. That does not seem like much of a risk to professional arsonists, convinced, as some are, that they can set a hundred fires with little fear of detection. —*John W. Fiero*

See also Common law; Crime Index; Criminology; Felony; Fraud; Insurance law.

BIBLIOGRAPHY

Overviews of arson and the criminal investigation thereof include John M. McDonald, Robert B. Shaughnessy, and James A. V. Galvin, *Bombers and Firesetters* (Springfield, Ill.: Charles C Thomas, 1977); Wayne S. Wooden and Martha Lou Berkey, *Children and Arson: America's Middle Class Nightmare* (New York: Plenum Press, 1984); Wayne W. Bennett and Karen Matison Hess, *Investigating Arson* (Springfield, Ill.: Charles C Thomas, 1977); and Brendan P. Battle and Paul B. Weston, *Arson: Detection and Investigation* (New York: Arco, 1978). Statistics on arson are printed annually in the FBI's *Crime in the United States*, also called *Universal Crime Reports for the United States* (Washington, D.C.: U.S. Government Printing Office) and the U.S. Department of Justice's *Sourcebook of Criminal Justice Statistics* (Washington, D.C.: U.S. Government Printing Office).

Assault

DEFINITION: Crime involving either an attempt at inflicting bodily harm or the threat of doing so

SIGNIFICANCE: Both a common crime and a tort, assault often goes unreported, especially when it occurs in domestic or private quarrels

Assault is usually linked to battery, a more serious offense involving physical contact, and is sometimes defined as an attempt at battery. In some jurisdictions it is not otherwise defined. Although the expression "assault and battery" is common, persons tried for battery are not normally charged with assault because the lesser charge is contained in the more serious offense.

Conditional, Simple, and Aggravated Assault. In addition to attempted battery, in most jurisdictions assault can include threats used to frighten victims. Here the assault may also take a conditional form, whereby the victim is threatened with physical harm if he or she fails to comply with the perpetrator's demands. In any case, assault must be overt. A threat in words alone is insufficient; it must be accompanied by a gesture, such as a raised arm and fist, indicating that physical harm is both intended and imminent.

Assault may also be simple or aggravated. Simple assault, normally a misdemeanor, involves no clear threat of permanent bodily harm. Aggravated assault, a felony, is one of the "index crimes" tracked by the Federal Bureau of Investigation. It occurs when there is a clear intent to kill, torture, maim, or sexually abuse the victim. An offender's actions may make intent irrelevant; this is the case, for example, if he or she threatens the victim with a handgun, even if the gun is unloaded. Assault with a deadly weapon, such as a knife or firearm, is usually classified as aggravated assault. There are, however, jurisdictional differences as to what constitutes a lethal weapon.

Assault can also involve civil suits. Victims must prove that they were in imminent danger of harm or at least had good reason to think they were. The threat must be physical. Normally, abusive language without threatening gestures, as in criminal cases, does not constitute assault in civil codes.

Proof and Defense. Complex considerations may make assault, without actual battery, difficult to prove, especially when the assault involves only an attempt to frighten the victim. It

WEAPONS USED IN AGGRAVATED ASSAULT, 1993

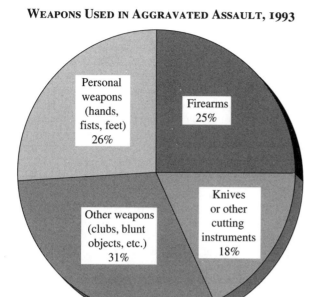

Personal weapons (hands, fists, feet) 26%

Firearms 25%

Knives or other cutting instruments 18%

Other weapons (clubs, blunt objects, etc.) 31%

Source: U.S. Department of Justice, Federal Bureau of Investigation, *Crime in the United States* (Uniform Crime Reports). Washington, D.C.: U.S. Government Printing Office, 1994.

must be established that the defendant had a serious intent and that his or her behavior might induce fear in the average person.

Two principal legal defenses against the charge of assault are self-defense and consent. In the former, defendants argue that their behavior was prompted by a need to protect either themselves, their property, or others from physical harm threatened by their victims. In the latter, defendants claim that their victims, by word or gesture, consented to their actions. This last is a common defense in cases of sexual assault, as in threatened conjugal or date rape. It may also be used as a defense when both parties have agreed to their violent encounter, as in many private fights. Most state courts, however, disallow consent as a defense in personal fights if they exceed a level of violence tolerated by public policy.

Special Problems: Sports and Domestic Violence. Assessing what constitutes either assault or consent can be made difficult by special circumstances. For example, in some sports, such as football, where potentially harmful physical contact is required, consent is usually construed as a contractual obligation of the athletes engaging in the sport. Excessively violent behavior in the field, however, especially when play is not in progress, may be construed as assault or battery and the consent defense invalidated. A player's violent behavior toward a field judge or referee would be a clear example. Less clear might be one player's assault on another after play has ended or when, as possible battery, a player commits a deliberate and flagrant personal foul.

In recent years, assault cases relating to spouse and child abuse have begun to crowd court agendas. Domestic violence may or may not be more prevalent than it was before, but it is certainly more widely exposed to public purview and censure. Encouraged by women's rights organizations and frank media treatment, criminal justice agencies have been much less reluctant to prosecute domestic crimes than in former years. Both witnesses and victims, notably battered wives, are now more willing to report the crime and testify in court, particularly since domestic abuse no longer bears the stigma of shame and the threat of familial or social ostracism. Nevertheless, conviction in assault cases is still comparatively difficult to obtain. In 1992, in U.S. district courts, the conviction rate for assault was 68 percent—but 84 percent of the convictions resulted from a plea of guilty. Twenty-six percent of assault cases were simply dismissed.

Slowing Crime Rate. Statistics indicate that reported instances of aggravated assault in the United States have grown at a dangerous rate, outstripping all other crimes on the FBI's Crime Index. In a nineteen-year period, from 1974 to 1993, the rate of recorded aggravated assaults rose from 218 to 440 per 100,000 inhabitants. The total number of aggravated assaults annually reported in that same period more than doubled, from about 456,000 to 1,135,000. Between 1984 and 1993, the rate increased by an alarming 65 percent. There was, however, one somewhat hopeful sign: in the last four years of that period, the rate increased by only 19 percent. Clearly, the rate of increase was slowing. Still, by 1993, it was estimated that an aggravated assault in the United States was occurring every twenty-eight seconds. —*John W. Fiero*

See also Battered child and battered wife syndromes; Battery; Crime Index; Domestic violence; Felony; Misdemeanor; Self-defense; Tort.

BIBLIOGRAPHY

Overviews of assault within the context of crimes of violence include James A. Inciardi and Anne E. Pottieger, eds., *Violent Crime: Historical and Contemporary Issues* (Beverly Hills, Calif.: Sage Publications, 1978); Jeffrey H. Goldstein, *Aggression and Crimes of Violence* (New York: Oxford University Press, 1975); and Keith D. Harries, *Serious Violence: Patterns of Homicide and Assault in America* (Springfield, Ill.: Charles C Thomas, 1990). Statistics on aggravated assault are printed annually in the FBI's *Crime in the United States*, also called the Uniform Crime Reports (Washington, D.C.: U.S. Government Printing Office), and on assault in the U.S. Department of Justice's *Sourcebook of Criminal Justice Statistics* (Washington, D.C.: U.S. Government Printing Office).

Assembly and association, freedom of

DEFINITION: The First Amendment guarantee that Americans are free to assemble and associate peaceably

SIGNIFICANCE: Along with other guarantees of free expression, the ability to meet with others for that purpose is protected by the Bill of Rights

"Peaceably" is the key word in the First Amendment's statement that "Congress shall make no law . . . abridging . . . the right of the people peaceably to assemble." Assembly means more than a group of people gathered in one place; it also applies to an organization whose members may rarely, if ever, meet in one spot. The right of association is thus derivative of the right of assembly.

The First Amendment divides the free expression of ideas into two major categories: speech/press and "peaceable" assembly. Congress (and, since the 1930's, state legislatures and local governing bodies) may not exercise prior restraint (or censorship) over either speech or press. The presence of the word "peaceably" in connection with assembly means that assemblies can be, and routinely are, subject to prior restraint. Speech and press are assumed to have a more passive character, enabling the government to grant them greater protection. While it is possible to imagine someone making a speech that incites its hearers to riot, it is very difficult to imagine a crowd silently reading a magazine or newspaper, reaching the punch line at the same time, and then rioting.

John Stuart Mill takes the same position in *On Liberty* (1859), one of the most famous defenses of free expression. While arguing that society has no right to silence a dissenting view even if it is held by only one individual, Mill maintains that no one would ever suggest that actions could be as unrestrained as speech, which loses its immunity if used to incite a riot. Many Supreme Court opinions on free speech, press, and assembly maintain this distinction between the expression of ideas and actions, although an absolutely clear line between the two may not be drawn in all cases.

The Fourteenth Amendment and Incorporation. Originally, none of the First Amendment rights—nor indeed any part of the Bill of Rights—applied to the states. Section 1 of the Fourteenth Amendment, however, required that no state deny any person the "right to life, liberty, or property without due process of law." This language has been held to incorporate most of the important rights in the Bill of Rights and apply them to the states. Application has been on a case-by-case basis. The right of assembly was incorporated and applied to the states at least partially in the case of *DeJonge v. Oregon* (1937), although it was more clearly stated in *Hague v. Congress of Industrial Organizations* (1939).

Conflict with Riotous Assemblies Laws. The Constitution's framers never intended to prohibit prior restraints on assembly. There are many federal, state, and local laws that forbid or limit the size of assemblies—for example, limiting the numbers permitted to ride a bus or occupy an auditorium or an elevator. One cannot allow seventeen people in a sixteen-person elevator even if the seventeenth person wants to praise the current U.S. president to all of those who are the captive audience. In a similar vein, regulations may require advance permission for parades or may prohibit parades during "rush hour" to allow the free movement of traffic for people going to and from work. Neither kind of regulation has anything to do with the content of the ideas expressed in an assembly. Naturally, if the police knew that a speaker intended to incite a crowd to riot, such an assembly could also be restrained in advance.

Difficulties arise when speakers address a peaceful assembly with no intention of starting a riot, but express ideas so offensive to the audience that some people seek to silence the speakers with violence. When the Supreme Court first considered such a case in *Feiner v. New York* (1951), they decided that the police could arrest speakers even if the speakers had no intention of starting a riot; this apparently put the blame on the peaceable speaker but not the violent audience. Eighteen years later, in *Brandenburg v. Ohio* (1969), the Court reversed itself, holding that the police should protect those who assemble peaceably, even if they express unpopular ideas, from members of the audience who might threaten them.

How far the Court has gone to protect those who express unpopular ideas is evident in the famous case of the American Nazi Party members who announced that they would parade in Skokie, Illinois. Although they had no direct ties to the German Nazi Party, the American Nazis used the swastika, flags, and paraphernalia of the German Nazi Party and espoused similar vicious views that Jews should be isolated, shipped off, or killed. Skokie residents reacted with horror to the prospect of the Nazis marching, and Jewish groups threatened violence if the march was allowed. Skokie responded by passing three separate ordinances aimed at preventing the march, on grounds that the audience would not be peaceable, even if the Nazis were.

The American Civil Liberties Union (ACLU) joined in a suit on behalf of the Nazi Party, despite the ACLU's opposition to all the Nazis' ideas. The ACLU thought it vital to protect free assembly. The federal district court struck down the Skokie ordinances, and the U.S. Supreme Court upheld the lower courts' rulings in *Smith v. Collin* (1978) and *Village of Skokie v. National Socialist Party of America* (1978). Despite the lack of a Supreme Court opinion in the case, the Court's decision strengthened freedom of assembly. Ironically, after the case was over, the Nazis did not actually march: They had achieved their real goal of nationwide publicity.

Freedom of Association. Freedom of association is derived from the freedom of peaceable assembly. Normally, the members of a single organization would not be violent with one another. The question is: Do individuals have the right to join associations that advocate violent overthrow of the government, even if they make no concrete plans to be violent? In the U.S. legal tradition, "conspiracy to commit a crime" is a crime itself, and some say the advocacy of violent overthrow is a conspiracy. Unlike physical commission of a crime, however, conspiracy is hard to define, and statutes against it are often unconstitutionally vague.

The government can act only if there is clear evidence of direct violent action. Yet the "clear and present danger" test used by the Supreme Court in the past has often been twisted into a "bad tendency" test that is so vague as to pose a threat to almost any group. At the height of U.S. animosity toward the Soviet Union, the Supreme Court in *Dennis v. United States* (1950) upheld the jailing of Communist Party members simply for attending a meeting in which they discussed publishing a newsletter. Associate Justices Hugo L. Black and William O. Douglas vigorously dissented from this decision.

Black and Douglas both lived long enough to see the Supreme Court move steadily away from the position taken in the *Dennis* case. By the time of *Yates v. United States* (1957), the Court seemed to be changing its mind, although technically it did not overturn *Dennis* until later. In *Noto v. United States* (1961), the Supreme Court held that membership in the Communist Party was not in itself evidence of conspiracy to overthrow the government; this made it even more difficult to gain any convictions for membership or registration in a so-called subversive organization.

After 1982, the Supreme Court actually protected the Communist Party from some government threats by ruling that campaign finance laws did not require that the names of party members and contributors be published. Since the Communist Party was an unpopular minority party and a published list might have a chilling effect on its contributors, it was exempted from such laws. The Communist Party has been allowed to run candidates for president of the United States or any other office as long as it can gather enough signatures to get names on the ballot. In some states, the laws for petition signatures to place names on the ballot are very lenient, so that a mere handful of signatures (as few as twenty-five in Tennessee) are sufficient to get a party's candidates on the ballot.

Importance in the Civil Rights Movement. The Court did not develop this enlightened attitude toward subversive organizations solely through disinterested thought. By the 1950's, the Supreme Court faced a problem in defending its own position that segregation and discrimination against blacks were unconstitutional, and it needed political support from black organizations. The Court then discovered that its decisions against the Communist Party were being used against civil rights organizations in the South. Many southern officials were claiming that the National Association for the Advancement of Colored People (NAACP) was a subversive organization and were harassing its members. Thus, in the case of *National Association for the Advancement of Colored People v. Alabama ex rel. Patterson* (1958), the Supreme Court ruled unconstitutional an Alabama law requiring the NAACP to disclose its membership list. A similar local ordinance in Little Rock, Arkansas, was ruled unconstitutional in *Bates v. Little Rock* (1960). These civil rights cases provided a strong impetus for the Court to revise its position on the Communist Party and other unpopular organizations. Ironically, the 1969 *Brandenburg v. Ohio* case extended this protection to the Ku Klux Klan, at the other extreme of the political spectrum.

—*Richard L. Wilson*

See also Bill of Rights, U.S.; Breach of the peace; Censorship; Civil liberties; Civil rights; Disorderly conduct; Speech and press, freedom of.

BIBLIOGRAPHY

Two fine books that discuss these First Amendment freedoms are M. Glenn Abernathy, *The Right of Assembly and Association* (2d rev. ed. Columbia: University of South Carolina Press, 1981), and David Fellman, *The Constitutional Right of Association* (Chicago: University of Chicago Press, 1963). Robert A. Horn, *Groups and the Constitution* (Stanford, Calif.: Stanford University Press, 1956), although dated, is also useful. Good general discussion may be found in Henry J. Abraham and Barbara A. Perry, *Freedom and the Court* (6th ed. New York: Oxford University Press, 1994); Walter Berns, *Taking the Constitution Seriously* (New York: Simon & Schuster, 1987); and Eugene W. Hickok, Jr., ed., *The Bill of Rights: Original Meaning and Current Understanding* (Charlottesville: University of Virginia Press, 1991). Wallace Mendelson's *The American Constitution and Civil Liberties* (Homewood, Ill.: Dorsey Press, 1981) contains useful excerpts from important Supreme Court cases on censorship and other free expression issues.

Assigned counsel system

DEFINITION: A system of assigning attorneys to represent indigent defendants in criminal cases

SIGNIFICANCE: The assigned counsel system improves the fairness of the criminal justice system for defendants who cannot afford to hire counsel

The Sixth Amendment of the U.S. Constitution guarantees criminal defendants the right to counsel, even if they cannot afford one. In *Gideon v. Wainwright* (1963), the U.S. Supreme Court held that the Sixth Amendment extended to state courts by virtue of the due process clause of the Fourteenth Amendment. According to the Court, the right of an indigent defendant in a criminal trial to have the assistance of counsel was a fundamental right essential to a fair trial.

The state determines whether defendants are "indigent" by interviewing them after arrest. Defendants who prove indigent are entitled to an attorney assigned to them and paid by the state. That attorney owes the same duties to indigent defendants as to any other clients, even though the attorney is paid by the state. The duty of representation usually ends at the entering of a final judgment, although many appointed attorneys will also participate in the notice of appeal. A different attorney usually represents the defendant on appeal.

See also Arraignment; Counsel, right to; *Gideon v. Wainwright*; Public defender.

Attempt to commit a crime

DEFINITION: An act that includes three elements: the intent or purpose to commit a crime, overt act(s) in pursuit of the intention, and a failure to complete the crime

SIGNIFICANCE: Statutes banning attempted crimes help control dangerous behavior and dangerous persons, but criminal law consistently imposes lesser penalties on attempted crimes than on completed crimes

Attempted crime has a history dating back to the ancient Greeks, approximately two thousand years ago. The philosopher Plato wrote, "One who has a purpose and intention to slay another and . . . wounds him should be regarded as a murderer" (*Laws*). He argued, however, that punishment for attempted murders should be less harsh than for murderers. English common law defined attempted crime more clearly. English jurists found that the elements of intent and act must both be present prior to a finding of guilt in a case involving an attempted crime. By the sixteenth century, acts considered to be crimes in English common law included threats, challenges, "fighting words," and lying in wait. An important legal distinction is between preparation and attempt. Criminal law requires action (the *actus reus*) beyond mere thought or preparation (the *mens rea*).

See also Conspiracy; Crime; Criminal intent; *Mens rea*; Solicitation to commit a crime.

Attica prison riot

DATE: September 9-13, 1971

PLACE: Attica Correctional Facility, Attica, New York

SIGNIFICANCE: More than a thousand inmates in this maximum security prison, angry over prison conditions, took control of four of the five prison blocks and held forty hostages

The unrest that became the Attica prison riot had been building for months prior to the outbreak of hostilities. A report of the New York Committee on Crime and Correction in January of 1971 warned of possible prison violence at Attica. In June, a number of prisoners drafted a petition asking for better food and medicine and for better training for the guards, among other demands. The new correctional commissioner, Russell Oswald, began to move forward on the demands, and in early Septem-

ber he outlined a series of reforms intended to address the problems identified by the prisoners. He asked that the prison population give him more time to put these changes into effect.

On Wednesday, September 8, however, two inmates were placed in solitary confinement for fighting. The next morning just before 9 A.M., twelve hundred prisoners rioted, overpowering the unarmed guards. During this initial breakout, twenty-eight guards were seized, along with eleven civilian employees. Quickly the hostages were herded to cell block D, which would become the prisoner stronghold for the next four days. Throughout the confrontation, Oswald played an active part, but the prisoners demanded and received a group of fifteen observers/negotiators consisting of people who were sympathetic to their cause. Since the committee had no real power to change any of the conditions, the demands had to be taken to Oswald and Prison Superintendent Vincent Mancusi.

Amnesty for all misdeeds was in every list of demands that was made. By Saturday, September 11, the inmates had a list of twenty-eight demands, including things such as wages, health care, education, food, and recreation. Commissioner Oswald agreed to support all the reforms he had the power to implement, except for two: amnesty and the ouster of Mancusi. Saturday evening things worsened when prison guard William Quinn died of injuries sustained during the initial uprising. There was now no chance of amnesty.

At 9:46 A.M. Sunday, under the cover of tear gas, rifle, and shotgun fire, two hundred state policemen quickly subdued the prisoners. In what was the bloodiest confrontation in United States prison history, thirty inmates were killed outright, with another two hundred injured. Nine of the thirty-nine hostages were also killed by state police gunfire. A total of forty-two people died. Many of the reforms that the prisoners wanted were reasonable, and except for positions taken by some of the more extreme members of the convict leadership, the bloodbath might have been avoided. There was also some evidence that prison authorities had invented stories about harsh treatment of hostages in order to gain support for the Sunday police attack.

The battle lasted only four minutes, but the impact was felt through the entire correctional system. The public attention generated by the riot and deaths focused on the inhumane conditions that had existed at the prison. Food, hygiene, and medical care in prisons have generally been improved since 1971, and recreational and educational opportunities have been provided to many inmates. In 1974, a civil suit claiming civil rights violations and "cruel and unusual punishment" at the time the authorities retook the prison was filed by 1,281 Attica

On September 11, 1971, attorney William Kunstler tells Attica inmates he will represent them in negotiations (in foreground are state senator Robert Garcia and U.S. congressman Herman Badillo). (AP/Wide World Photos)

inmates. They sought $2.8 billion in damages. It took eighteen years for the case to come to trial. In 1992, a jury ruled that the constitutional rights of the inmates had been violated but exonerated three of the four former prison officials named in the suit, holding liable only Karl Pfeil, a deputy warden.

See also Cruel and unusual punishment; New Mexico State Penitentiary riot; Prison and jail systems; Punishment.

Attorney

DEFINITION: A person trained in the law and admitted by a state's highest court to practice law in that state

SIGNIFICANCE: An attorney provides the knowledge that laypeople may lack in matters of law

An attorney is a person learned in the law who gives legal advice and is licensed to represent a person, or client, who hires the attorney. Originally, attorneys were minor court officials, tutored by judges or others with legal knowledge, who represented a client. The modern attorney is a graduate of an accredited four-year college and spends three years at an accredited law school to receive the degree of Juris Doctor. The graduate must pass an examination given under the auspices of a state's bar association. An attorney may perform legal duties related to both criminal and civil matters. In both venues, an attorney offers counsel concerning the law, drafts documents, and represents the client in court.

Much of the communication between attorney and client is subject to privilege (confidential) and may not be divulged to a third party unless the client agrees to it. For the attorney to do otherwise would be a serious breach of professional conduct. Attorney-client privilege is so important that an attorney must receive permission from the court to withdraw from representation of a client once proceedings are begun.

The professional conduct of attorneys is governed by the *Model Rules of Professional Conduct* (first published in 1984), established by the American Bar Association and accepted by individual state bar associations. A serious breach of professional conduct or ethics may subject an attorney to censure or suspension from practice and, in extreme cases, to disbarment.

An attorney may be in private practice, work for a private corporation, or work for the government. An attorney engaged in private practice, whether a sole practitioner, a member of a partnership, or a member of a large law firm, may handle diverse duties such as estate planning, business law, and civil or criminal litigation. Many law firms specialize in an area of law, so that the attorney becomes a specialist. An attorney may also have expertise that is unrelated to the firm's general practice but enhances the services offered to a client. The private-practice attorney is hired by, and works directly for, a client. The majority of lawyers are engaged in private practice.

Attorneys working for private corporations may represent the corporation in labor or contract negotiations and may handle routine litigation filed against the corporation. Major litigation, or any lawsuit that may take a long time to resolve, is often turned over to a private law firm hired for the purpose.

Attorneys meeting with a judge (right) in the judge's chamber. (James L. Shaffer)

Corporate attorneys may also provide low-cost or no-cost legal advice to employees of the corporation.

Attorneys engaged in government service may work directly for the U.S. Department of Justice or in any of the government's numerous agencies. The ultimate in government service may be election to the legislative or executive branch in either state or federal government. Because the business of government is law, attorneys are often considered particularly qualified to serve in elective offices.

See also American Bar Association (ABA); Bar, the; Bar examinations and licensing of lawyers; Defense attorney; Law; Law schools; Legal ethics; Privileged communications; Prosecutor, public; Public defender.

Attorney, United States

DEFINITION: Chief legal representative of the United States Department of Justice in its regional offices

SIGNIFICANCE: Each United States attorney supervises the operation of one of the department's ninety-four offices spread throughout the country and its possessions

The ninety-four United States attorneys stationed in the United States, Guam, Puerto Rico, and the Virgin Islands are appointed by the Department of Justice and report to the director of the Executive Office for United States Attorneys, who in turn reports to the deputy attorney general of the United States. United States attorneys work cooperatively with the United States marshals assigned to their offices and supervise the work of assistant United States attorneys and special assistant United States attorneys in their jurisdictions.

United States attorneys coordinate the work of their offices, which deal with legal situations that include such responsibilities as doing regional investigations of matters about which other branches of the Department of Justice need information. Their offices, for example, might be asked to gather data about federal prisoners being considered for pardons and transmit such information to the Office of the Pardon Attorney.

See also Attorney general, state; Attorney general of the United States; Judicial system, U.S.; Justice, U.S. Department of.

Attorney general, state

DEFINITION: As the chief legal officer of the state, the attorney general serves as counselor for state government agencies, the legislature, and the citizenry

SIGNIFICANCE: The attorney general provides legal advice and legal representation for state agencies and the public on diverse matters such as drug abuse, the environment, business regulation, and criminal appeals

The development of state attorneys general in the United States can be traced to England. The king of England had specially designated lawyers to represent his legal interests. The attorney general of England served as legal adviser to the king and all government departments and was responsible for all litigation. During the American colonial era, the attorney general provided legal advice to the king and governance over the colonies. After the revolution, American officials adapted

the English version of the office of attorney general to govern their own legal interests. Constitutional provisions were enacted to create the office of the attorney general to have jurisdiction of legal affairs of the federal government. As the new nation grew, the states also adopted the office of attorney general, and many had constitutional provisions for the office.

Attorneys general are popularly elected in forty-three states, appointed by the governors in five states and six jurisdictions, appointed by the state supreme court in Tennessee, and selected by the state legislature in Maine. New legislation and conceptions of the office have significantly expanded the powers and duties of the state attorneys general. There is much diversity in the role of the attorney general from state to state.

In response to needs identified by governors and legislatures, attorneys general have become active in areas of consumer protection, antitrust law, toxic waste, child-support enforcement, organized crime, and many other areas. The most common duties of the attorney general involve controlling litigation concerning the state, serving as chief legal officer, writing opinions which clarify law, acting as public advocate, enforcing criminal law, and investigating issues of public interest.

Public advocacy is a growing field for attorneys general in nearly all states. In addition to providing legal service in such areas as consumer protection and child-support enforcement, relatively new areas of concern for states' chief legal officers include utility regulation and advocacy regarding the provision of services to crime victims. These new areas of interest put attorneys general in the position of being the initiator of legal action, or plaintiff, which is a role reversal that provides a new opportunity to implement and interpret public policy. One of the most important functions of the state attorney general is writing opinions. Opinions clarify law for the executive and legislative branches. Attorneys general use their opinions to identify legislative oversight that is in need of correction and to resolve issues that are not likely to be solved through litigation.

See also Attorney, United States; Attorney general of the United States; District attorney; Prosecutor, public.

Attorney general of the United States

DEFINITION: The attorney general of the United States is the cabinet-level officer who heads the Department of Justice

SIGNIFICANCE: Attorneys general, although responsible for the impartial enforcement of federal law, are politically appointed and are involved in the partisan political process

The office of attorney general of the United States has existed since the administration of George Washington, the nation's first president. The office has, however, evolved into something quite different from what it was at the time of its creation.

Evolution of the Office. A major enactment of the first Congress under the U.S. Constitution was the Judiciary Act of 1789. It set forth the structure of the federal court system and created the office of attorney general. The law set forth no qualifications for the position other than that the person appointed be learned in the law. The president was to appoint the attorney general, subject to the consent of the Senate.

Washington wanted to appoint Edmund Randolph of Virginia to be the first attorney general. The Virginian was not eager to have the position, however, because Congress had appropriated funds for only a low salary without any allowance for expenses. Moreover, Congress had created no department for the attorney general to head, which meant that if Randolph were to need help with the work, or if he needed supplies, all such expenses would have to come out of his pocket. Congress apparently interpreted the position as that of legal adviser to the president and the heads of the executive departments and did not foresee the attorney general incurring expenses or being sufficiently busy to warrant a larger salary (even though the attorney general was to represent the United States before the Supreme Court). Edmund Randolph, who was Washington's personal attorney, accepted appointment as the nation's first attorney general because Washington was able to convince him that his private law practice would benefit from the prestige of the office.

Since the attorney general was not the head of an executive department, that official was not initially a member of the president's cabinet. During cabinet meetings, however, discussions often revolved around legal issues; therefore, Washington brought Randolph into his cabinet. This set the precedent for future attorneys general being considered regular members of the cabinet.

The office of attorney general underwent its greatest change when the Department of Justice was created. The bill creating it was signed into law by President Ulysses S. Grant on June 22, 1870. One of the things it did was create the position of solicitor general of the United States. The solicitor general became the official who represented the United States before the Supreme Court, with strong ties to the Court as well as to the Department of Justice. Attorneys general ceased to represent the United States regularly before the Court, which they had done in the early years, and became primarily administrators and presidential advisers. By the late twentieth century, the attorney general headed a large and complex organization. Among the major units of the Justice Department in the 1990's were the Criminal Division, Civil Division, Civil Rights Division, Antitrust Division, Tax Division, Immigration and Naturalization Service, Federal Bureau of Investigation, and Drug Enforcement Agency.

Politics and the Attorney General. Many twentieth century attorneys general were politically active persons who played major roles in the campaigns of the presidents who appointed them. Such was Attorney General Robert F. Kennedy. Although he did not have legal experience, his brother, President John F. Kennedy, appointed him attorney general because he relied on his advice and could be confident of his loyalty. President Richard M. Nixon appointed John Mitchell, his former law partner, who had managed his campaign.

Mitchell ultimately was discredited because he had been a major participant in the Watergate scandal. Presidents Gerald Ford and Jimmy Carter therefore sought attorneys general who would be less involved in the partisan politics of their administrations. Ford appointed Edward Levi, a law professor who was not even a registered member of a political party. Carter appointed Griffin Bell, who had been a federal appeals court judge of impeccable reputation. Carter and Bell had known one another since they were boys, but they had not maintained a close relationship over the years.

President Bill Clinton appointed Janet Reno, the first woman to hold the office of attorney general. Reno took an interest in children's issues and in supporting the Immigration and Naturalization Service's efforts to prevent illegal immigrants from entering the United States. She sometimes displayed a degree of independence from the president who appointed her.

Judicial Selection. Attorneys general have played important roles in the process of selecting federal judges, who are appointed by the president with the consent of the Senate. President Dwight D. Eisenhower's attorney general, Herbert Brownell, worked hard at maintaining good relations with state and local Republicans as well as with the Senate Judiciary Committee. Attorney General Griffin Bell urged President Carter to create merit selection commissions to identify prospective nominees, including more minorities and women, which he did. The commissions were abandoned by succeeding presidents.
                                        —Patricia A. Behlar

See also Attorney general, state; Daugherty, Harry M.; Justice, U.S. Department of; Kennedy, Robert F.; Organized crime; Palmer raids and the "red scare"; Solicitor general of the United States; Watergate scandal.

BIBLIOGRAPHY

Overviews of the office of attorney general include Nancy V. Baker, *Conflicting Loyalties: Law and Politics in the Attorney General's Office, 1789-1990* (Lawrence: University Press of Kansas, 1992); Cornell W. Clayton, *The Politics of Justice: The Attorney General and the Making of Legal Policy* (Armonk, N.Y.: M. E. Sharpe, 1992); U.S. Department of Justice, *200th Anniversary of the Office of the Attorney General, 1789-1989* (Washington, D.C.: U.S. Department of Justice, 1990). Works on or by specific attorneys general include Herbert Brownell, with John P. Burke, *Advising Ike: The Memoirs of Attorney General Herbert Brownell* (Lawrence: University Press of Kansas, 1993), and Victor Navasky, *Kennedy Justice* (New York: Atheneum, 1971).

Auburn system

DEFINITION: A type of prison in which prisoners work together during the day and remain in individual cells at night

SIGNIFICANCE: The Auburn penitentiary system represented an early reformist effort to create a physical and moral environment in which imprisoned criminals could be rehabilitated

Prison reform swept the United States in the postrevolutionary war generation, facilitated by the pioneering efforts of the

Philadelphia Society for Alleviating the Miseries of Public Prisons. In this context, New York State constructed its first new penitentiary at Auburn, New York, in 1816. It was designed to house prisoners together (the congregate system), but reformers soon introduced small individual cells, roof-ventilated and windowless. Such confinement produced illness and even insanity, and in 1823 prison policy makers led by Elam Lynds confined prisoners to their cells only at night and forced them to labor together during the day. Although the purpose was the reformation of prisoners, discipline was draconian. Prisoners went to work in lockstep, were forbidden to speak, and were flogged even for minor infractions. The Auburn system, however, required relatively few guards and proved economical. The chairman of the state commission on prison reforms, Thomas Mott Osborne, who served a voluntary term in Auburn, fought for changes in the system during the early twentieth century.

See also Prison and jail systems; Walnut Street Jail.

Autopsy

DEFINITION: A postmortem examination revealing the physical abnormalities and chemical makeup of a person's body at the time of death

SIGNIFICANCE: The performance of an autopsy is the only way to be certain of what caused a person's death

There are three levels of examination that are performed on the body, tissue, and fluids to help the medical examiner determine what caused death. At the primary level is a visual examination of the exterior of the body for any abnormalities, recent wounds, and punctures. The body is opened to allow inspection of the organs, including the brain, to see to what extent any trauma has led to the death, including whether exterior and interior damage is related. Part of this process involves the removal of the organs in related groups to see more closely any abnormal relationships between the affected organs. An example of this approach would be removing the liver, pancreas, bile duct, and gall bladder together and studying their relationship to one another.

At the secondary level is the examination of sections of each organ under a microscope. A thin slice of each organ is embedded in wax, and very thin slices are prepared. After the sample is stained to enhance the fine structure of the tissue, it is examined under a microscope. This procedure can reveal a degenerative problem that could have been aggravated by injuries. At the ultimate level, organs and body fluids are analyzed to detect traces of drugs, toxins, and any other chemical imbalances. Deoxyribonucleic acid (DNA) testing may also be a part of this procedure. The time spent on the first stage will range from two hours for a limited autopsy to four or more hours for a total autopsy. The second step is more time consuming, and the final stage is the most lengthy of all.

In the United States about 75 percent of all autopsies are total, with homicide being the main reason that an autopsy is performed. An autopsy is done in more than 90 percent of all homicide cases. There is also much knowledge to be gained in the performance of autopsies after normal deaths. Toxic-shock syndrome and Legionnaires' disease, for example, were both discovered through autopsies. In spite of the possible benefits derived from this procedure, the practice has been declining in most areas. This decline may be attributable to a fear of malpractice lawsuits (an autopsy examination can conceivably reveal that medical diagnosis or treatment was incorrect). It also may partly be because there is little emphasis placed on the study of autopsy procedure in medical schools. At one time it was required, but by the early 1990's it was not even an option for many medical students.

See also Coroner; DNA testing; Forensic science and medicine; Medical examiner.

Bail system

DEFINITION: The bail system allows an individual accused of a criminal offense to be released prior to court appearance by securing funds to assure his or her appearance in court

SIGNIFICANCE: This highly debated practice has been criticized for discriminating against poor and minority arrestees; it has also been criticized for the practice of preventive detention, which uses exorbitant bail to keep accused offenders from committing crimes while awaiting trial

The United States bail system operates on the premise that some individuals can be released prior to their appointed court date by leaving an amount of money with the court. Individuals are expected to return for their subsequent court appearance to have the amount of bail returned to them. Many argue that this practice discriminates against poor arrestees who cannot afford a monetary bail and thus must remain incarcerated while awaiting trial.

Tradition in English Law. The bail system in the United States is rooted in the traditional court systems of England. In feudal England (prior to the Battle of Hastings in 1066), law was dispensed by judges who would travel from county to county. Sheriffs would typically keep accused offenders in local jails with the promise to turn the offender in when the judge returned. As the number of offenders increased and jail space became limited, offenders were occasionally entrusted to the custody of a friend or relative who would ensure their appearance. In some cases, these individuals were required to sign a bond promising a specific sum of money to the king if the accused failed to appear when the judge next visited the area.

Over time (and eventually in the American colonies), the practice of having an individual step forward for an accused was replaced by the use of financial security, or monetary bail. In exchange for freedom prior to trial, the accused would deposit a certain amount of money with the court, which would be returned following appearance. Even before the colonization of America it was recognized that the practice discriminates against individuals who cannot afford to leave a monetary bail. Arrestees who could not afford to leave bail were frequently incarcerated until their appearance at trial, a time period which could encompass years. Thus, the first formal regulations governing the use of bail were written in England in the year 1275. These statutes set forth specific conditions under which bail could be imposed, defining which crimes were "bailable" and which were not. That is, they specified for which crimes bail must be denied and the accused must be incarcerated prior to trial. Laws forbidding excessive bail eventually appeared in England, but not until they were included in the English Bill of Rights in 1688.

History of the American Bail System. Like the English system, early Americans also protected against excessive bail. The Eighth Amendment to the U.S. Constitution begins with the phrase, "Excessive bail shall not be required." The meaning of this phrase, however, has not been successfully decided by the U.S. Supreme Court. For example, does excessive bail refer to the defendant's ability to pay, or does it relate to the seriousness of the crime committed? In addition, is there a constitutional right to bail?

The Judiciary Act of 1789 gave offenders a right to bail unless arrested for a capital offense. For a capital offense, maximum penalties can consist of life imprisonment or death. Assuming that these offenders may be likely to flee, considering the severity of punishment, bail is typically denied. Thus, every defendant in a noncapital case was guaranteed to receive bail. The appropriate amount of bail was not discussed in the Judiciary Act of 1789.

A recommended or appropriate amount of bail was not dealt with in the United States until 1951, when the Supreme Court, in *Stack v. Boyle*, decided that bail must be of sufficient amount to ensure the defendant's appearance at trial. In other words, the amount of bail must be enough to assure the defendant's appearance, but it cannot be more than that amount, or else it would be considered excessive. The vagueness of this decision has left many experts speculating about the appropriate amount of bail.

Bail Reform. During the 1960's, it became apparent that the United States bail system was not operating as it was designed. Judges were accused of having an excessive amount of discretion in setting amounts for bail. In addition, judges were responsible for setting bail based on which defendants were at high risk for flight and which were not. These decisions were supposed to be based on criminal characteristics, such as the seriousness of the crime committed and prior appearance history. It became clear, however, that among the factors taken into account in the assessment of flight risk were race and sex. Thus, judges' decisions were discriminatory against certain racial groups and against male offenders.

Another form of discrimination emerged in the practice of pretrial detention. Although the primary purpose of bail is to assure a defendant's appearance at trial, there is another purpose. Preventive detention is the practice of holding an arrestee prior to trial so that he or she does not commit any crimes during the time between arrest and court appearance. If a defendant is deemed to be a danger to the community during the pretrial period, a high amount of bail might be set in order to keep the arrestee locked up. Judges are responsible for making the determination regarding the "dangerousness" of an offender. Again, it was found that these decisions were influ-

BAIL SET FOR FELONY DEFENDANTS, 1990

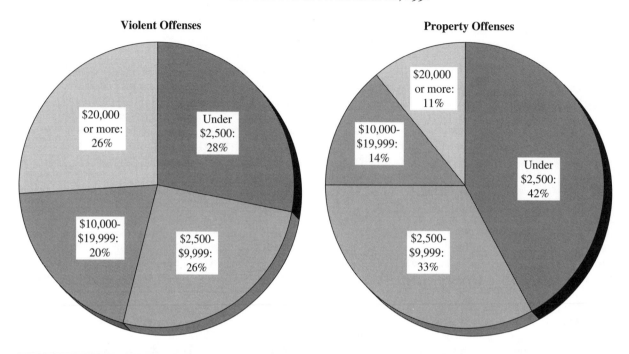

Violent Offenses

$20,000 or more: 26%

Under $2,500: 28%

$10,000-$19,999: 20%

$2,500-$9,999: 26%

Property Offenses

$20,000 or more: 11%

$10,000-$19,999: 14%

Under $2,500: 42%

$2,500-$9,999: 33%

Source: U.S. Department of Justice, Bureau of Justice Statistics, *Sourcebook of Criminal Justice Statistics—1993.* Washington, D.C.: U.S. Government Printing Office, 1994.

Note: Data are based on a sample of 39 of the 75 most populous U.S. counties.

enced by noncriminal characteristics such as sex and race. Thus, the type of discrimination that appeared when assessing risk of flight also occurred when judges attempted to assess how likely an offender was to commit a crime while awaiting trial.

In the face of these problems, the first bail reform movement developed. Beginning in the early 1960's, bail came to the forefront as a serious problem within the criminal justice system. The Bail Reform Act of 1966 was an attempt to limit judicial discretion and remove discrimination from the bail process. There were two important developments that came from the Bail Reform Act of 1966. First, judges were expected to release all defendants on their own recognizance unless the judge had some good reason to set bail. In other words, the judge had to have solid grounds for setting bail. Second, "pretrial service agencies" were created to collect information about defendants, thus allowing the judge to have more—and more correct—information about each defendant.

Although preventive detention was a reality in the bail system, there were no laws in the United States stating that it was legal. The second bail reform movement occurred in the early 1970's, and it focused on the issue of legalizing preventive detention. In 1970, the District of Columbia enacted a law which authorized the detention of arrestees without bail if they were deemed a danger to the community. This was the first

statute to set standards for the detention of arrestees for preventive reasons.

The issue of preventive detention was not a legal one until the year 1984. In this year, the United States bail system was a central focus of the Comprehensive Crime Control Act of 1984. The Bail Reform Act of 1984 legitimated two federal judicial practices that were informally used before 1984. First, this act gave judges the power to assess defendants on their level of "dangerousness" to the community if released. It gave federal judges the legal right to use preventive detention. While the District of Columbia had its own provisions for preventive detention in 1970, it was not until 1984 that federal judges were given that right. Second, judges were given the right to deny bail in certain circumstances. Traditionally, bail was denied to offenders arrested for capital crimes; the Bail Reform Act of 1984 permitted judges to deny bail to those offenders who were judged to be at extremely high risk for nonappearance. Most notable in this group of offenders were drug traffickers, who were usually able to make extremely high bail and then flee the country.

The Bail Reform Act of 1984 was challenged in 1987, when *United States v. Salerno* was heard before the Supreme Court. This case challenged the idea of preventive detention, arguing that incarcerating alleged offenders violates their right to due process of law. Opponents of preventive detention argue that incarcerating offenders because of *potential* threat violates the presumption of innocence to which every arrestee is entitled. The Supreme Court did not agree with Salerno and upheld the judicial right to preventive detention. As long as judges have convincing evidence that the offender is likely to commit a crime while awaiting trial, they may set bail at a level higher than the typical amount.

Types of Bail. Judges must make a decision for every offender regarding the likelihood that the offender will appear for trial. They take several factors into account in making this decision, usually including prior arrest record, whether the defendant has appeared at previous hearings, stable family ties, and steady employment. After judges weigh these factors, they make a determination about how likely the defendant is to appear at trial. If offenders are classified as good risks—that is, if they are likely to appear for trial—they are typically released on their own recognizance. Release on recognizance (ROR) allows offenders to remain free before trial with the expectation that they will appear at the appropriate time.

Not all offenders are judged as good risks for appearance. For those expected to be bad risks, or those who are unlikely to appear at trial, some type of bail is usually required. While bail itself involves leaving some type of financial security with the court, the type of security can vary. The most obvious type of bail is typically called a cash bond, and this occurs when the defendant turns over money in the exact amount of bail to the court. Money is not the only type of bail that a defendant can leave with the court. In some cases, a defendant can post a property bond instead, which entails leaving property (per-

sonal possessions) with the court to ensure appearance. If the defendant does not appear for the next court appearance, all money and property is forfeited to the court.

Courts are aware that not everyone has the financial ability to post the exact amount of bail or to put up a substantial amount of property. For these individuals, a deposit bond is available. In a deposit bond, the accused offender deposits only a portion of the full bail amount to the court. If the defendant fails to appear, the deposit is kept by the court. If the defendant appears for trial, the majority of the bond is returned, with a small percentage kept by the court to cover court costs.

Finally, the most common type of bail is a surety bond. In this arrangement, a third party (not the court nor defendant) promises the court that if the defendant does not appear, they will turn over the amount of bail to the court. In exchange for this service, the defendant pays a fee to the third party. Usually, this third party is a bailbondsman.

Bailbondsmen. When defendants are required to pay bail prior to release, they may enlist the aid of a bailbondsman in securing funds. Bondsmen are independent businessmen who loan bail money to defendants with only a small amount of cash used as a fee. Bondsmen typically require 10 percent of the amount of bail for the fee. They use part of this fee to purchase a surety bond from an insurance company, which actually pays the bail if the defendant does not appear. In addition, bondsmen usually require some collateral as assurance that the defendant will not default on the loan. Many bond businesses also serve as pawn shops in their spare time,

RELEASED FELONY DEFENDANTS WHO FAILED TO MAKE A SCHEDULED COURT APPEARANCE IN THE 75 LARGEST U.S. COUNTIES, 1990					
			Percent Failing to Appear in Court		
Defendant Characteristics	*Number of Defendants*	*Percent Making All Scheduled Court Appearances*	*Total*	*Returned to Court*	*Remained a Fugitive*
All released defendants	34,831	76%	24%	16%	8%
Most Serious Arrest Charge					
Violent offenses	8,606	81	19	12	6
Property offenses	11,990	72	28	19	9
Drug offenses	11,466	74	26	17	8
Public-order offenses	2,769	87	13	9	4
Type of Release					
Recognizance	13,543	71	29	18	11
Surety bond	7,841	86	14	11	3
Conditional	4,297	86	14	10	4
Full cash bond	3,520	76	24	15	9
Unsecured bond	2,738	64	36	26	10
Deposit bond	1,451	81	19	10	8
Emergency	520	51	49	44	5

Source: U.S. Department of Justice, Bureau of Justice Statistics, *Sourcebook of Criminal Justice Statistics—1993*. Washington, D.C.: U.S. Government Printing Office, 1994.

Note: Data are from a sample of 39 of the 75 most populous U.S. counties. "Failure to appear" occurs when the court issues a bench warrant for a defendant's arrest. A "fugitive" is a defendant who failed to appear and was not returned to court within a one-year study period. Percentages may not add to 100 because of rounding.

Bailbondsmen typically require that defendants pay them 10 percent of their bail amounts. (James L. Shaffer)

selling the collateral left by those who jump bail. Not all defendants will qualify for a bondsman's services. If defendants have a prior history of jumping bail, they will most likely be denied the bondsman's service.

Even those defendants judged as good risks for the bondsman's service sometimes jump bail. When a defendant fails to appear for trial after securing a bondsman, the bailbondsman has legal authority to retrieve the defendant. The bondsman hires individuals referred to as "bounty hunters" or "skip tracers," people who search for those who jump bail. These skip tracers have virtually unlimited discretion in apprehending the defendant. Unlike state and local police officers, skip tracers are allowed to cross state lines to retrieve individuals who jump bail and are allowed to enter a residence without an arrest warrant.

A major criticism of the bailbondsman trade is the ease with which corruption can flourish. Officers of the court, for example, are sometimes paid by bondsmen to refer defendants to their offices. These officers are typically given kickbacks for each defendant referred to the bondsmen. Judges are not immune from inappropriate behavior—some judges may set unreasonably high bail so that defendants are forced to utilize the bondsman's services. In return for these "referrals," judges are

paid by the bondsman. Finally, the bondsman trade also discriminates against indigent offenders, as most poor people cannot afford the fees.

Trends and Statistics. Approximately half of all defendants are held prior to trial, according to 1991 statistics. This figure includes individuals who do not make bail (44 percent of all defendants) and those who are held without bail (9 percent of all defendants). Only about 18 percent are released on their own recognizance. The amount of bail also varies across individuals and is usually dependent on the seriousness of the crime committed and prior criminal record. Property offenders are likely to receive lower bail (under $2,500), while violent offenders are more likely to receive high bail (sometimes over $20,000).

Of those who are released prior to trial, about one-fourth fail to appear for trial. Drug offenders are most likely to jump bail, and public order offenders are most likely to appear for trial. There also appears to be a relationship between the type of bond and rates of appearance. For example, offenders who are released on their own recognizance and offenders who leave a deposit bond have the highest rates of failure to appear. Offenders who use a bondsman are most likely to appear at their appointed court date. —*Christina Polsenberg*

See also Arraignment; Bill of Rights, U.S.; Comprehensive Crime Control Act of 1984; Criminal justice system; Discretion; Due process of law; Preventive detention.

BIBLIOGRAPHY

A general review and history of the American and English bail systems can be found in Ronald Goldfarb, *Ransom: A Critique of the American Bail System* (New York: Harper & Row, 1965). The felony bail process is summarized in Roy B. Flemming, *Punishment Before Trial: An Organizational Perspective of Felony Bail Processes* (New York: Longman, 1982), and an overview of bail reform in the United States can be found in Wayne H. Thomas, Jr., *Bail Reform in America* (Berkeley: University of California Press, 1976). Bail reform is also discussed in Samuel Walker, *Taming the System: The Control of Discretion in Criminal Justice, 1950-1990* (New York: Oxford University Press, 1993). Information on released and detained defendants is contained in the Bureau of Justice Statistics' annual *Sourcebook of Criminal Justice Statistics* (Washington, D.C.: U.S. Government Printing Office).

Bailiff

DEFINITION: An official charged with the care of others

SIGNIFICANCE: A court bailiff is responsible for maintaining order in the courtroom

In the judicial sense, a bailiff is an officer of the court who is specifically charged with the duty of preserving and protecting order in a courtroom, thereby allowing proceedings to continue unimpeded. During trial, the bailiff serves as the liaison between judge and jury. The bailiff ensures that the jury is present in the courtroom when required and is responsible for maintaining the integrity of the jury. Bailiffs are generally appointed to their positions by the judge in whose courtroom the bailiff serves. A bailiff may be a private individual or a sheriff's deputy.

Bailiffs also serve in other capacities. A bailiff may be appointed by the court to act as guardian of a mental incompetent, in which case the bailiff must report regularly to the court. A bailiff may also stand in the place of an owner of lands or goods, as a manager, and owes an accounting of that management to the owner.

See also Judicial system, U.S.; Jury system; Sheriff.

Baker v. Carr

COURT: U.S. Supreme Court

DATE: Decided March 26, 1962

SIGNIFICANCE: In this case, the Supreme Court held that federal courts can decide cases involving state voting rights when the case is brought on equal protection grounds, thereby opening the door for future decisions requiring state legislatures to redesign legislative districts

Prior to 1962, federal courts routinely refused to hear cases dealing with the rights of voters in state elections, holding that under the "political question doctrine" such issues are reserved for resolution by Congress or the president.

The scope of that doctrine was narrowed considerably in

Baker v. Carr, a federal lawsuit brought by several Tennessee voters. Those plaintiffs claimed that their voting rights had been diminished because Tennessee had not redrawn its legislative districts since 1901, even though the population of most districts had changed dramatically. The plaintiffs said that the result was discrimination against voters who lived in the more populated districts. The plaintiffs argued that this discrimination was a denial of their equal protection rights guaranteed by the Fourteenth Amendment to the United States Constitution.

The federal district court dismissed the case as involving a political question, relying on the case of *Colegrove v. Green* (1946), in which the United States Supreme Court had called reapportionment cases "political thicket[s]" to be avoided by the courts.

In *Baker v. Carr*, however, the Supreme Court, by a vote of 6 to 2 (one justice abstained) held that the district court should hear the case. The Supreme Court explained, in the majority opinion by Justice William Brennan, that not every voting rights lawsuit is necessarily a political question case. The determining factor is the underlying cause of action. If resolving the case would require a court to make decisions that are constitutionally or practically reserved to the executive and legislative branches of the federal government, then a nonjudicial political question is involved. Otherwise, the federal courts may hear it.

The Supreme Court said that the doctrine should be reserved for cases involving issues which the courts lacked the experience, expertise, or authority to resolve. The Supreme Court said that *Colegrove* had been such a case, pointing out that the issue there had involved application of the so-called guaranty clause, Article IV, section 4 of the United States Constitution. That clause provides that the United States "shall guarantee to every state . . . a Republican Form of Government." According to the Supreme Court, the question of whether a state government meets that standard, and the question of how to make sure it does, are clearly questions better resolved by Congress. By contrast, the Supreme Court said that *Baker* involved the equal rights provision of the Fourteenth Amendment to the United States Constitution, an issue with which courts are familiar and are best capable of resolving, as they had been doing since the amendment had been adopted.

Although in *Baker v. Carr* the Supreme Court did not address the underlying question of reapportionment, the decision opened the judicial doors for such lawsuits. The *Baker* plaintiffs ultimately succeeded in the Tennessee federal district court, and in 1964 the Supreme Court held, in *Reynolds v. Sims*, that legislative districts must be apportioned so that every vote is roughly equal.

See also Civil War Amendments; *Colegrove v. Green*; Equal protection of the law; Representation: gerrymandering, malapportionment, and reapportionment.

Bakke case. *See* **Regents of the University of California v. Bakke**

Bank robbery

DEFINITION: The unlawful taking of money or other assets from a bank through the use of force or the threat of force, typically involving firearms or explosives

SIGNIFICANCE: Bank robbery historically has been one of the most visible and publicized crimes, and it affects larger numbers of citizens than do many other types of crimes, but in total numbers it remains relatively minor among robbery crimes

Only a small percentage of all reported robberies in the United States are bank robberies. In 1981, for example, fewer than 2 percent of all robberies involved banks. Convenience stores represent the most frequent robbery targets; banks are one of the least-robbed businesses. Typically, bank robberies involving member banks of the Federal Deposit Insurance Corporation (FDIC) fall under the purview of the Federal Bureau of Investigation (FBI) rather than local police.

In 1993, according to FBI statistics, there were 8,578 bank robberies, 310 bank burglaries, and 78 bank larcenies, for a total of 8,966 bank crimes. In addition, armored carriers suffered 90 robberies. California was the leading state for bank robberies during 1993, and the western region led the nation in bank robberies largely because of California. Money was not

taken in 675 of the robberies during calendar year 1993. Total robbery losses were $89 million. More important, acts of violence accompanied 470 of the 8,966 robberies, with eighteen deaths occurring. The majority of those injured in bank crimes were employees, although some guards and perpetrators also were injured.

Those numbers represent sharp increases from 1989, when 6,691 commercial banks, savings banks, credit unions, and armored cars were robbed. During that year, 273 burglaries and 142 larcenies were directed at banks. Losses in 1989 came to just over half the 1993 total ($50 million). Increasingly, white collar crime, such as embezzlement, which was not classified as bank robbery, and other types of insider lending, grew much more significant than traditional "holdups."

Historical Background. Prior to the Civil War, bank robbery was virtually nonexistent. It did not become a crime of serious proportions until the 1920's. Contrary to popular images, few bank robberies occurred in the Old West: Excluding Texas, the West witnessed a scant handful of robberies prior to 1900. Bank protection and location accounted for the security of banks. Bank buildings were established in the centers of towns, usually protected on each side by another building. A vault was constructed against an interior wall, with a safe placed inside the vault. The vaults were all but impregnable, and even if robbers got inside they still had to make their escape through a town full of armed men. Consequently, most robberies took place in transit, perpetrated against trains or stagecoaches.

In the 1920's, however, advances in transportation allowed robbers to strike quickly and escape via back roads before law enforcement officials could react. Many of those robberies occurred in the Midwest, with its extensive network of dirt roads, and where state boundaries provided effective barriers to pursuit. As a result, insurance for banks against robberies soared, contributing to the instability of many Midwest banks. Ultimately, improvements in law enforcement and rewards posted by bankers' associations succeeded in reducing the number of bank robberies, but criminals such as Bonnie Parker and Clyde Barrow gained notoriety for their bank robberies.

Bank Robbery Since the 1960's. Until the 1960's, bank robberies remained under control, but a new outburst of bank robberies occurred between 1960 and 1970, during which time FBI statistics showed bank robberies rising at a rate of 409 percent. The new wave of robbery was characterized by increasing violence and led to new preventative measures. Banks installed bulletproof glass for tellers, alarm systems, and dye markers for money. Identifying robbers still proved difficult until the introduction of security cameras that allowed law enforcement officials to match bank photographs with "mug shots." Perpetrators found a new target, however, with the advent of automated teller machines (ATMs), which could be attacked through forged cards or through code-cracking. More typically, thieves could simply wait until patrons withdrew their money and then hold up the customer.

Bonnie and Clyde, infamous midwestern bank robbers of the 1930's (AP/Wide World Photos)

Increasingly, noncash transactions and the withdrawal of large-denomination bills from circulation have contributed to a steady decline of bank robberies. Credit card fraud has taken over much of the crime that used to be directed at banks themselves. Other types of bank-related crimes continue, however, including robberies of armored vehicles carrying cash to and from banks.

Bank robbery statistics are extremely spotty: Bank robbery against a state institution was a state crime until the creation of the Federal Reserve System in 1913, and even then a state bank had to be a member bank before it came under any federal protection. Usually a U.S. marshal handled federal issues related to state banks. Meanwhile, state authorities dealt with crimes against state banks. At present, the FBI compiles bank robbery statistics.

Bank security systems include "bait money," tear gas and/or dye packs, guards, alarm systems, surveillance cameras, or bullet-resistant enclosures (or combinations of those systems). In the 1920's, some Arizona banks experimented with teller-operated tear gas guns mounted in the bank, but those guns malfunctioned and were removed after releasing gas inside the banks. Alarms and surveillance cameras were maintained at most of the banks that were robbed in 1992, but very few robberies (seven) occurred where guards were employed, and only three robberies occurred where guards were on duty. Most bank robberies occurred in metropolitan or suburban areas; only seven robberies out of seventy-five occurred in small towns or rural areas.

The war against drugs in the 1970's and 1980's had a side effect on bank and other robberies. Large-denomination bills disappeared from use, and although banks received $500 and $100 bills in transactions, the Federal Reserve began to collect all bills larger than $100 from every bank on a weekly basis. Thus, banks increasingly carried less physical cash—and more of it in smaller bills—and more "electronic cash."

In 1934 the New Deal government of Franklin Roosevelt instituted federal deposit insurance. Even though the banks themselves had previously carried insurance, the federal backing of the money in the banks made deposits seem safer. Runs or "white-collar" crimes within the banks suddenly represented a much greater threat to the public than did bank robbers. Indeed, during interviews with bankers in twelve western states in the late 1980's conducted by two authorities on banking, none of the bank owners, presidents, or officers even mentioned bank robberies as a concern. Likewise, in commercial banks, safeguards against embezzlement have reduced embezzlement crimes to a negligible level.

By the 1990's, banks were much more susceptible to the problems of mismanagement of investments or sudden shifts in interest rates than robbery or embezzlement. While a single well-placed official could invest millions of dollars into risky ventures, and profit by participating with his own funds in those investments, the ability of employees to siphon large amounts of money from banks has decreased significantly since the early part of this century.

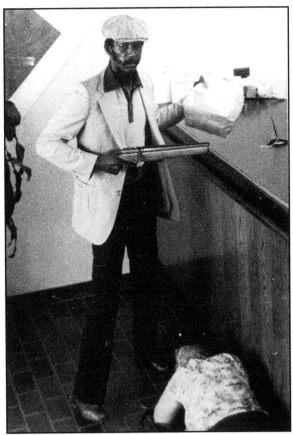

Bank robbery in Garland, Texas, 1978, photographed by bank's security camera. (AP/Wide World Photos)

A growing but little-measured type of crime involves the use of computers to gain access to bank accounts. Specialists known as "hackers" use computers to obtain other people's account numbers, identification numbers, and credit card information. In early 1993, one such hacker was apprehended when he electronically broke into the credit card processing center for a number of banks in the eastern United States. Banks responded by modifying their telephone transaction policies. It is now difficult or impossible to transfer money by telephone at many banks; others have special code words or identification symbols they use to authorize transactions. In a related vein, credit card fraud had reached high levels in the United States by the early 1990's.

The Criminals. More than eleven thousand people participated in the 8,966 bank crimes reported in 1993. The overwhelming majority of bank robbery felons were male, but the racial breakdown was almost evenly divided between white and black. Hispanics made up almost 10 percent of the criminals. In most cases, criminals used a demand note or a telephone call. Surprisingly, more banks were threatened with explosive devices than with handguns or other firearms. When violence actually occurred, it was unprovoked in more than a third of the occasions. More than 130 hostages were taken in the course of forty-six of the robberies. No information was reported on incarceration rates for bank robbers in particular, nor did the FBI keep specific statistics on age or education of the perpetrators. Information is available regarding the times banks are robbed. In 1992, for example, the day and time that a robbery was most likely to occur was Friday between 3 and 6 P.M., with the second most likely time being Tuesday between 9 and 11 A.M. Yet at neither of those times would a bank have its largest holdings of cash. Instead, on Monday mornings after 10 A.M., banks are bulging with weekend deposits, but prior to the bank's opening a robber could gain access only by securing a hostage. On Friday afternoons—the most popular time for a robber to strike—banks are very low on cash because they are cashing checks for customers. —*Larry Schweikart*

See also Banking law; Computer crime; Crime; Embezzlement; Pinkerton, Allan; Robbery.

BIBLIOGRAPHY

Useful information can be found in *Report to the Nation on Crime and Justice: The Data* (Washington, D.C.: U.S. Department of Justice, Bureau of Justice Statistics, 1983); Kristen M. Williams and Judith Lucianovic, *Robbery and Burglary: A Study of the Characteristics of the Persons Arrested and the Handling of Their Cases in Court* (Washington, D.C.: Institute for Law and Social Research, 1979); and U.S. Department of Justice, Federal Bureau of Investigation, *Bank Crime Statistics (BCS), Federally Insured Financial Institutions*, various years, 1989-1993. Lynne Pierson Doti and Larry Schweikart, *Banking in the American West: From the Gold Rush to Deregulation* (Norman: University of Oklahoma Press, 1991), includes brief discussions of bank robbery in the West.

Banking law

DEFINITION: The collection of laws, both civil and criminal, that apply to those who operate, manage, are employed by, or deal with financial institutions, the largest of which are commercial banks

SIGNIFICANCE: The financial services industry, including the commercial banking industry, is involved with every type of business, commerce, government agency and individual; the fact that money is the product they have to sell requires them to be a highly regulated industry

James Conboy, in *Law and Banking* (1982), describes the legal environment of banking by noting that "while certain laws and regulations apply only to banks, banks must also transact business within a legal environment common to all individuals and entities within the United States. . . . Nearly every relationship a bank has is a contract, whether it is labeled as such or not." In the area of civil law, banks fall under many different regulations. They are bound by the basic principles spelled out in contract law. They also must conform to the laws outlined in the Uniform Commercial Code. In the area of criminal law, banks again are subject to compliance with many different laws. Bank robbery, burglary, fraud, embezzlement, money laundering, forgery, blackmail, and extortion all are crimes perpetrated against financial institutions and banks.

In the area relating strictly to banking regulation, banks have many regulators who oversee their operation. The comptroller of the currency is the primary regulator for national banks, while the Federal Reserve Bank is the primary regulator of state chartered banks. Other regulators include the Federal Deposit Insurance Corporation and the state in which the bank operates. There are many areas covered within the scope of bank regulation. Consumers are protected by regulations such as the Equal Credit Opportunity Act, truth in lending legislation, the Fair Debt Collections Practices Act, and the Fair Credit Reporting Act. The Community Reinvestment Act requires banks to give something back to the communities that they operate within. Most banks have a major portion of their assets in real estate, a situation that opens up an additional area of rules and regulations with which an institution must comply.

See also Bank robbery; Bankruptcy; Commercial law; Contract law; Counterfeiting and forgery; Embezzlement; Fraud; Money laundering; Truth in Lending Act; White-collar crime.

Bankruptcy

DEFINITION: Bankruptcy is the legal process by which debts that cannot be paid in full are discharged through a federal court; the inability to pay debts as they become due is also called insolvency

SIGNIFICANCE: As the major forum in which financially stressed individuals and businesses sort out their legal obligations, bankruptcy court provides for the orderly disposition of debtor assets and resolution of creditor claims

The concept of bankruptcy, or debt cutting, goes back at least as far as the Old Testament. Both Deuteronomy (15:1-6) and Leviticus (25:1-55) set forth rules for the legal cancellation of debts. The ancient Greek statesman Solon canceled debts in Athens in 594 B.C.E. These independent responses to debt indicate the complex natures of economies ranging from agricultural to capitalist.

Article I, section 8 of the U.S. Constitution provides that Congress shall have the power "to establish . . . uniform Laws on the subject of Bankruptcies throughout the United States." The intent was to give creditors long-arm jurisdiction to reach debtors fleeing from one state in the republic to another. Debtors' prisons existed in America until the early nineteenth century.

The longest continuous legislation was the Bankruptcy Act of 1898, which prevailed until the passage of the Bankruptcy Reform Act in 1978, effective October 1, 1979, which has been variously amended in 1980, 1984, 1986, 1990, and 1994. These amendments have generally limited and narrowed the access of debtors to broad bankruptcy relief. The goal of bankruptcy is to provide a fresh start for the honest debtor. The cause of bankruptcy may be poor business decisions, loss of employment or reduced income, divorce, substance or gambling abuse, illness and lack of health insurance, improvidence, and the uncertain shifts in a capitalist economy.

Current statute provides for types of bankruptcies known as Chapters 7, 9, 11, 12, and 13. Chapter 7 is a general liquidation, sometimes called straight bankruptcy; Chapter 9 is for municipalities (such as California's Orange County in 1994); Chapter 11 generally is for businesses that may liquidate or reorganize; Chapter 12 is for family farmers (introduced in 1986); and Chapter 13 is commonly called the wage earner's plan. Chapters 7 and 13, the most frequently used by individual or married debtors, are usually referred to as consumer bankruptcies. Bankruptcies may range from a few thousand dollars in a consumer Chapter 7 to several billion dollars in a Chapter 11.

Exemptions. In bankruptcy certain of the debtor's property is protected from creditors. In the nineteenth century, state statutes specifically exempted items such as cattle, sheep, a horse and wagon, bedding, and a family Bible from execution. Today's list includes household goods, tools of the trade, and automobiles. States may adopt the generous federal exemptions or use state exemptions. About thirty-three states chose not to use the federal exemptions, thus creating wide diversity in exemptions. The federal homestead exemption is $15,000 per individual debtor and $30,000 for a married couple. In Florida, Iowa, Kansas, Minnesota, Texas, and Washington, 100 percent of the debtor's homestead is exempt from creditor claims. In seventeen other states the homestead exemption is $7,500 or less. Workers' compensation and employment benefits are also generally exempt. There is some concern about the good-faith motives of debtors planning bankruptcy who move from stingy to generous jurisdictions.

The U.S. Bankruptcy Court is part of the Department of Justice. There is a United States Trustee network at the national, regional, and state levels. At the local level, a Chapter 7, 12, or 13 trustee manages the disposition of the case. Before 1978 a referee served the function of the trustee. From filing to discharging Chapter 7 takes three to five months. Most Chapter 7

Billionaire Donald Trump in 1990 announcing a plan to put his Atlantic City casino under bankruptcy-court protection and give investors a 50 percent stake in it. (AP/Wide World Photos)

	BANKRUPTCY PETITIONS FILED AND PENDING, 1981 TO 1991								
Item	*1981*	*1984*	*1985*	*1986*	*1987*	*1988*	*1989*	*1990*	*1991*
Total filed	**360,329**	**344,275**	**364,536**	**477,856**	**561,278**	**594,567**	**642,993**	**725,484**	**880,399**
Business	47,415	62,170	66,651	76,281	88,278	68,501	62,534	64,688	69,193
Nonbusiness	312,914	282,105	297,885	401,575	473,000	526,066	580,459	660,796	811,206
Voluntary	358,997	342,828	362,939	476,214	559,658	593,158	641,528	723,886	878,626
Involuntary	1,332	1,447	1,597	1,642	1,620	1,409	1,465	1,598	1,773
Chapter 7	265,721	232,994	244,650	332,679	397,551	423,796	457,240	505,337	612,330
Chapter 9	1	4	3	7	10	3	7	7	20
Chapter 11	7,828	19,913	21,425	24,443	22,566	18,891	17,465	19,591	22,495
Chapter 12	(X)	(X)	(X)	(X)	4,824	3,099	1,717	1,351	1,358
Chapter 13	86,778	91,358	98,452	120,726	136,300	148,771	166,539	199,186	244,192
Section 304	1	6	6	1	27	7	25	12	4
Total pending	**361,664**	**577,567**	**608,945**	**728,577**	**808,504**	**814,195**	**869,340**	**961,919**	**1,123,433**

Source: U.S. Department of Commerce, Bureau of the Census, *Statistical Abstract of the United States, 1992.* Washington, D.C.: U.S. Government Printing Office, 1992.

Note: Covers only bankruptcies filed under the Bankruptcy Reform Act of 1978. "Filed" means proceedings have been commenced; "pending" means the administration of a proceeding has not been completed. (X) means "not applicable."

cases do not contain assets for the trustee to distribute to creditors. A Chapter 13 bankruptcy runs from three to five years. Chapter 13 has a superdischarge, because it discharges problems such as fraud that cannot be discharged in a Chapter 7.

Litigation in bankruptcy court is heard by a bankruptcy judge who is appointed by the president of the United States for a renewable fourteen-year term. There are two types of proceedings: motions and adversary proceedings.

Types of Debts and Dischargeability. There are three types of debt: Secured (lien on collateral); priority (taxes, wages, and certain other specified claims); and unsecured (everything else, including medical bills, credit cards, and back rent). In addition, there are administrative claims and executory contracts (leases and the like). Congress has determined that some debts cannot be discharged. These include child support, alimony, personal injury claims based on automobile accidents involving alcohol, willful and malicious action, student loans under certain circumstances, criminal restitution, and some taxes.

Section 362 of the bankruptcy code, which is called the automatic stay, provides injunctive relief against creditors. It stops creditor harassment, lawsuits, foreclosure, eviction, and garnishment. There are exceptions to the automatic stay, however. For example, it does not stop the prosecution of a criminal charge or the collection of child support. Bankruptcy is only a civil court matter. Filing fees are $160 for debtors, $200 for Chapter 12, and $800 for Chapter 11, making bankruptcy court one of the most expensive court costs within the American judicial system. Preferences involve the improper payment of selected debts on the eve of filing bankruptcy. After they receive a discharge, the code provides that certain lenders and employers are proscribed from discriminating against the discharged debtor "solely" on the basis of filing bankruptcy.

The number of bankruptcies filed increased considerably after the passage of the 1978 code. There is some correlation between bankruptcy and the state of the economy. In 1980, 331,098 cases were filed. Filings peaked in 1991 at 943,987. In 1993, 875,202 cases were filed, of which 92 percent were consumer cases and 70 percent were Chapter 7. In 1994, 832,829 cases were filed.

The 1994 Bankruptcy Reform Act created a National Bankruptcy Review Commission to report to Congress on the effectiveness of the 1978 code and subsequent amendments in the late twentieth century American economy. —*Oliver B. Pollak*

See also Banking law; Commercial law; Contract law; *Ogden v. Saunders*; *Sturges v. Crowninshield*.

BIBLIOGRAPHY

A humane overview is provided in Teresa A. Sullivan, Elizabeth Warren, and Jay Lawrence Westbrook, *As We Forgive Our Debtors: Bankruptcy and Consumer Credit in America* (New York: Oxford University Press, 1989). *Collier on Bankruptcy* (15th ed. New York: Matthew Bender, updated regularly) is a technical treatise. Douglas G. Baird, *The Elements of Bankruptcy* (Westbury, N.Y.: Foundation Press, 1992), is also helpful.

Bar, the

DEFINITION: The full court, or a particular place in a courtroom, or attorneys in the aggregate, or an association of lawyers, or an examination taken by aspiring lawyers

SIGNIFICANCE: Originally a rail that set the judge off from the rest of the courtroom, "the bar" now designates a variety of law-related entities and procedures

The name for a rail that enclosed the judge in early courts has become a synecdoche. Closest to its original meaning is use of the expression to designate a full court, as opposed to a single judge. In this sense, matters under consideration by such a court are said to be "cases at bar." A prisoner, too, can be said to be "at the bar"—that is, standing in a particular spot in the courtroom. The bar can also designate all lawyers or an association of lawyers grouped by where they have been admitted to practice (for example, the Supreme Court bar or the Arizona bar) or by specialty (such as the plaintiff's bar, attorneys who customarily represent parties instituting suits). Such use of "the bar" distinguishes lawyers from judges, collectively referred to as "the bench." Lawyers are admitted to practice after having passed a qualifying examination, also called "the bar."

See also American Bar Association (ABA); Attorney; Bar examinations and licensing of lawyers; Law schools; Legal ethics.

Bar examinations and licensing of lawyers

DEFINITION: Examinations administered by the National Conference of Bar Examiners and many state boards of law examiners to graduates of accredited law schools (or, in rare cases, to individuals who may qualify to take the examination based on study and internship under the direction of a licensed attorney) in order to certify their qualifications for admission to the practicing bar of the state

SIGNIFICANCE: The bar examination serves the purposes of the legal profession in maintaining standards for admission to the legal profession; the screening for legal knowledge provides the public with evidence of the competency of the candidate to practice law in each respective state

A primary objective of the American Bar Association (ABA) at its inception, as written in its constitution, was "to advance the administration of justice and uniformity of legislation throughout the union, uphold the honor of the profession of the law, [and] encourage cordial intercourse among the members of the American Bar." To this end, one of the original standing committees established was that on legal education and admission to the bar. At that time, each of the states had its own standards for admission to the state bar. The ABA's section on legal education was the first organizational section created in 1893 to supplement the standing committee on legal education. In 1898, this section invited members of state boards of law examiners to meet in conjunction with the annual meeting of the American Bar Association. The purpose was to discuss the similarities and discrepancies in how the state boards administered their responsibilities.

Discussion topics included the organization of examining boards, the nature and scope of the exams, grading, eligibility requirements, ratio of failing grades, fees, exams for moral character, and retesting. A committee was appointed to study the feasibility of forming a National Association of Bar Examiners. In 1900, this committee suggested that representatives of the state boards meet contemporaneously with the annual ABA meeting to discuss the various aspects of legal education.

At the 1904 annual meeting of the ABA it was resolved "that it is desirable that the members of the Boards of Law Examiners in the different states form an association for the purpose of adopting uniform methods in their work establishing and maintaining standards of excellence." No significant changes occurred until the standing committee's presentation of nine recommendations in 1918. These included the recommendation that state bar membership be contingent on more than successful completion of a course of legal study at an accredited law school. Further requirements should take the form of passing a state examination under the direction of the highest appellate court of that state. In 1921, the ABA adopted the resolution that "graduation from a law school should not confer the right of admission to the Bar, and . . . every candidate should be subjected to an examination by public authority to determine his fitness."

Today, the National Conference of Bar Examiners is a permanent agency that assists the state boards in carrying out their mandates. Every state administers its own examination for licensure in that state, commonly known as the bar exam. Generally, these exams may be separated into three parts: an exam testing one's knowledge of the canon of ethics of the profession; an objective, or multiple-choice exam covering generalities of law in all respective disciplines (focusing on aspects of constitutional law, criminal law, contracts, evidence, torts, and real property, known as "multi-state" subjects); and an essay portion focusing on aspects of state law.

The bar exam is considered a comprehensive testing of an applicant's knowledge of the law. Each state weighs the various aspects of the examination differently. Some states do not administer a "multi-state" examination at all. The bar examination's overt purpose is to indicate to the public, as well as to the legal profession itself, that a candidate for licensing is well equipped to assist in the general appreciation of justice.

See also American Bar Association (ABA); Attorney; Bar, the; Law schools; Legal ethics.

BIBLIOGRAPHY

An overview of the organization of various bar organizations and examinations administered is Glenn Winters, *Bar Association Organization and Activities: A Handbook for Bar Association Officers* (Ann Arbor, Mich.: American Judicature Society, 1954). For a discussion of the role of the bar association in licensing, see *The ABA in Law and Policy: What Role?* (Washington, D.C.: Federalist Society for Law and Public Policy Studies, 1994).

Barenblatt v. United States

COURT: U.S. Supreme Court

DATE: Decided June 8, 1959

SIGNIFICANCE: Previously, the Court had recognized the Fifth Amendment's privilege against compulsory self-incrimination as a legal limit upon the authority of congressional investigating committees; here the Court held that the First Amendment provides less protection against congressional interrogations

Congress has long conducted legislative investigations and provided criminal penalties for uncooperative witnesses. In *Kilbourn v. Thompson* (1881), the Court ruled that Congress can investigate only where it has the power and intent to legislate. During the Cold War era, congressional committees had roving commissions to investigate subversive activities. Some congressmen noted that public exposure of persons of questionable loyalty—rather than crafting new legislation—was a primary function of such investigations. In *Watkins v. United States* (1957), the Court ruled, on Fifth Amendment due process grounds, that congressional investigations must clearly relate to legislating.

Lloyd Barenblatt, a former psychology instructor at Vassar College, was called to testify before a subcommittee of the House Committee on Un-American Activities (HUAC) investigating communist infiltration into the field of education. He invoked the First Amendment rather than the Fifth Amendment in refusing to answer questions about his affiliation with the Communist Party and was convicted for contempt of Congress in the United States District Court for the District of Columbia. The Court of Appeals for the District of Columbia Circuit affirmed—and subsequently reaffirmed—his conviction. In light of *Watkins'* ban on exposure "for the sake of exposure," some observers expected the Supreme Court to shut down HUAC. Instead, on *certiorari*, the U.S. Supreme Court upheld Barenblatt's conviction.

Justice John M. Harlan wrote the majority opinion in this 5-4 decision. Harlan found that the subcommittee was authorized to conduct this investigation and that Barenblatt could ascertain the pertinency of the subcommittee's questions to the subject of the inquiry. First Amendment protections against government interrogations involve "a balancing by the courts of . . . competing private and public interests." Harlan balanced the public's interest in preventing government overthrow against an individual's right to refrain from revealing Communist Party affiliations, and he found the former to be weightier.

Justice Hugo L. Black, joined by Chief Justice Earl Warren and Justice William O. Douglas, dissented on grounds that the committee's mandate to investigate "un-American" activities was vague and that First Amendment freedoms should not be evaluated through a balancing test. Further, Black argued that the majority overstated the government's self-preservation interests and understated the interest of the people as a whole to be able to join organizations, advocate causes, and make political mistakes without being penalized. Black found these societal interests to be weightier. In a separate dissent, Justice William Brennan agreed with Black that the only purpose for the investigation was "exposure purely for the sake of exposure."

This case is important because the Court refused to provide legislative witnesses with a "right to silence" based on the First Amendment. In the 1960's, however, the Court did recognize the related claim of "associational privacy."

See also Bill of Rights, U.S.; Civil liberties; Communist Party, American; House Committee on Un-American Activities (HUAC); McCarthyism; Self-incrimination, privilege against.

Barker v. Wingo

Court: U.S. Supreme Court
Date: Decided June 22, 1972
Significance: The Supreme Court, for the first time, gave substantive content to the Constitution's guarantee of a speedy trial

In 1958 Silas Manning and Willie Barker were arrested for the murder of an elderly Kentucky couple. Kentucky had a stronger case against Manning, and the state decided to try him first. If Manning were convicted, then he could be required to testify against Barker. Kentucky sought and obtained the first of what would be sixteen continuances of Barker's trial. Meanwhile, the prosecution had great difficulty in getting a conviction against Manning. The first trial ended in a hung jury, and a second trial, at which Manning was convicted, was annulled because of the admission of illegally seized evidence. Barker finally objected to additional delay when the state requested a twelfth continuance. Even after Manning's conviction—after a third trial—became final, the Kentucky court granted a further continuance because of the illness of the former sheriff who had been the investigating officer in the case. Barker finally came to trial in 1963, more than five years after his arrest. During ten months of that period he had been held in jail. He moved to dismiss the charge on the ground that his right to a speedy trial had been violated. After several unsuccessful appeals, Barker asked the U.S. Supreme Court to review his claim.

In an opinion for a unanimous Supreme Court, Justice Lewis F. Powell, Jr., held that Barker's right to a speedy trial had indeed been violated. Justice Powell pointed out that the notion of a "speedy" trial is slippery because there is no clearly definable standard. The circumstances of each case are likely to determine whether any postponements are reasonable. Powell saw two possible alternatives. The first would be to set a rigid time period and to apply it to every case. This the Court rejected because it would amount to law making, a function reserved to the legislature. The second alternative would be to restrict the speedy trial right to defendants who demand it. Justice Powell rejected that solution because it would amount to waiving constitutional rights except for those who ask for them. That would be inconsistent with the Court's general approach to constitutional liberties.

The Court adopted a "balancing test" in which the conduct of both the prosecution and the defendant is considered. This approach requires courts to approach speedy trial issues on an *ad hoc* basis, but once the defendant has asserted the right to a speedy trial, the state must move forward expeditiously. Among the factors which courts must consider are the reasons for any delays, the strength and frequency of the defendant's objections, if any, and the length of any pretrial incarceration defendants have suffered.

The *Barker v. Wingo* balancing test did not prove satisfactory in practice, and the federal government and many states passed statutes to establish rigid time limits for trial. Typically, if no continuances are at the defendant's request, trial must proceed within ninety to one hundred days or the charges against the defendant must be dismissed with prejudice.

See also Bill of Rights, U.S.; Criminal procedure; Speedy trial, right to.

Barnes v. Glen Theatre, Inc.

Court: U.S. Supreme Court
Date: Decided June 21, 1991
Significance: In this case the Supreme Court recognized that nude dancing was a form of expression but held that a public indecency statute which prohibited nude dancing did not violate the First Amendment's free speech clause

An Indiana statute prohibited individuals from appearing in a public place nude. Dancers in adult establishments were effectively required by the statute to wear "pasties" and "G-strings." Two establishments and the dancers employed by them wished to offer totally nude dancing for their customers and brought suit seeking to enjoin enforcement of the statute. They claimed that it violated the First Amendment's freedom of speech guarantee since the dancing they wished to provide was a form of communication. In a narrowly divided decision, five members of the Court concluded that the Indiana public indecency statute was constitutional, although the justices disagreed on the reasons for this holding. Chief Justice William Rehnquist, joined by Justices Sandra Day O'Connor and Anthony Kennedy, argued that the statute was constitutional because it only incidentally limited expressive activity and was not expressly intended to suppress speech, because it furthered the state's substantial interests in protecting morals and public order, and because its requirement that dancers wear "pasties" and "G-strings" was narrowly tailored to achieve these interests. Justice David Souter also believed that the statute was constitutional, but he differed from the chief justice in concluding that the interest served by the statute was not in protecting morals but in preventing certain secondary effects of nude dancing, such as prostitution. Justice Antonin Scalia found the statute constitutional as well but believed that it did not even raise a First Amendment issue since the state of Indiana had not specifically targeted expressive conduct for restraint.

Four dissenters who joined in an opinion by Justice Byron White argued that the very purpose of the statute as applied to dancing was to prevent the communication of the message conveyed by nude dancing: thoughts of eroticism and sensuality. This kind of censorship was, the dissenters contended, the very kind prohibited by the First Amendment.

Barnes v. Glen Theatre, Inc. revisited a constitutional issue most famously addressed in the 1960's when opponents of the Vietnam War burned their draft cards in symbolic protest of the war. Congress responded to these protests by making it a criminal offense to burn a draft card. In *United States v. O'Brien* (1968), the Supreme Court held that protesters of the Vietnam War could be punished for destroying their draft cards, even though the destruction was a kind of speech. Ever since, speakers who wished to express their ideas through nonverbal conduct have not fared well against general laws prohibiting the conduct they wished to use expressively. *Barnes* is one example. So long as government does not appear to target only the individuals who wish to convey a message through particular conduct, its ability to proscribe such conduct is broad.

See also Bill of Rights, U.S.; Commercialized vice; *O'Brien, United States v.*; Speech and press, freedom of.

Barron v. Baltimore

COURT: U.S. Supreme Court
DATE: Decided February 16, 1833
SIGNIFICANCE: The Bill of Rights, restricting governmental power on behalf of individual liberty, was added to the U.S. Constitution shortly after its ratification; in this case, the Supreme Court held that these restrictions applied only against the national government

While paving its streets, the city of Baltimore diverted certain streams from their natural courses. As a result, deposits of sand and gravel built up near Barron's wharf, making the water shallow and rendering the wharf useless. Barron claimed that the city's action had deprived him of his private property for public use. The Fifth Amendment provides that individuals so injured are entitled to just compensation. The amendment makes no mention of state or local action. Nevertheless, since the amendment is a guarantee of individual liberty, Barron maintained that it should be interpreted as restraining states (and cities) as well as the national government.

In this, his last constitutional decision, Chief Justice John Marshall observed that the question was "of great importance, but not of much difficulty." He agreed that Barron had been denied effective use of his property without just compensation, but he held that the Fifth Amendment affords protection against the national government alone. Had the framers of the Bill of Rights intended them to limit the powers of state governments, Marshall reasoned, "they would have . . . expressed that intention . . . in plain and intelligible language." Since the amendments "contain no expression indicating an intention to apply them to the State government," Marshall concluded that the Fifth Amendment did not protect Barron against the city.

Prior to the Civil War, the Constitution provided individuals with little protection against state actions. This situation changed with the postwar ratification of the Thirteenth, Fourteenth, and Fifteenth Amendments. The Fourteenth Amendment provides that no state shall "deprive any person of life, liberty, or property, without due process of law." Over the years, many rights and liberties deemed essential to due process have been "incorporated" or "absorbed" into the Fourteenth Amendment, providing protection against state encroachment. While *Barron v. Baltimore* has not been overruled, its practical effect has been limited. Today a case such as Barron's could be brought under the Fourteenth Amendment's due process clause, according to which individual rights are now afforded greater national protection against state infringements.

See also Bill of Rights, U.S.; *Gideon v. Wainwright*; *Gitlow v. New York*; Incorporation doctrine; Marshall, John; *Near v. Minnesota*; *Palko v. Connecticut*; *Powell v. Alabama*; *Wolf v. Colorado*.

Batson v. Kentucky

COURT: U.S. Supreme Court
DATE: Decided April 3, 1986
SIGNIFICANCE: The decision altered the peremptory system, which had remained essentially unaltered since medieval times

On the surface, *Batson v. Kentucky* was one of a long string of efforts to eliminate discrimination from the judicial system. It departed from the Supreme Court's 1965 holding in *Swain v. Alabama*, in which case the Court first considered the use of the peremptory challenge for discriminatory purposes.

In *Swain*, asked whether the equal protection clause of the Fourteenth Amendment prevented the total exclusion of blacks from a jury, the Supreme Court declared that the "presumption in any particular case must be that the prosecutor is using the State's challenges to obtain a fair and impartial jury. . . . [even if] all Negroes were removed because they were Negroes." To overcome the presumption, the Court ruled, a defendant would have to demonstrate that the state followed a consistent pattern of discrimination in "case after case."

Swain prevailed until 1986. Challengers were unable to meet the standards of systematic exclusion established in the decision. State and federal courts alike refused to countenance presentation of evidence from only cases which involved black defendants. Over the repeated objections of Justice Thurgood Marshall, the Supreme Court waited to allow "states to serve as laboratories in which the issue receives further study before it is addressed by this Court" again. Marshall called the experimentation cruel, noting that "there is no point in taking elaborate steps to ensure Negroes are included in venires [pools of prospective jurors] simply so they can be struck because of their race by a prosecutor's use of peremptory challenges."

The reconsideration came in *Batson v. Kentucky*. Batson's counsel asked the Court:

In a criminal case, does a state trial court err when, over the objection of a black defendant, it swears an all-white jury constituted only after the prosecutor had exercised four of his six peremptory challenges to strike all of the black veniremen from the panel in violation of constitutional provisions guaranteeing the defendant an impartial jury and a jury composed of persons representing a fair cross section of the community?

James Kirkland Batson had been charged with burglary and the receipt of stolen goods. The prosecutor used four of his six peremptory challenges to create, in his words, an "all-white jury." The defense counsel's motion to discharge the panel before it was sworn in on grounds that the panel did not represent a cross-section of the community and that to use it would be a denial of equal protection was denied by the trial judge. Tried and convicted, Batson appealed to the Kentucky Supreme Court, which upheld the conviction in 1984, based on the *Swain* doctrine. The U.S. Supreme Court disagreed. Reversing the conviction, it held that the impaneling of the jury resulted in a denial of equal protection. It ruled that when objection is lodged against an alleged racially discriminatory use of the peremptory challenge, the trial court must examine the validity of the claim.

Thus, for the first time, a federal court agreed that an attorney can be forced to explain his or her reason for invoking a peremptory challenge. In the process, the Court created a second category of peremptory challenges, ones to be explained.

See also *Duncan v. Louisiana*; Equal protection of the law; Jury system; Marshall, Thurgood.

Battered child and battered wife syndromes

Definition: Reactions to violence perpetrated by a parent, guardian, or spouse that lead victims to adopt coping mechanisms that may lock them into a cycle of violence; they have been likened to post-traumatic stress disorders

Significance: The development of the battering syndrome concept changed police and court procedures by sensitizing the criminal justice system to the behavioral and psychological characteristics of domestic abuse victims

Under English common law, battering that was not considered excessive was commonly accepted as a part of familial relationships. As a result, the criminal justice system was long unwilling to intervene in cases involving domestic violence, arguing that such conflicts are private matters. Sensitizing the criminal justice system to the power differential between men and women and women and their children led the way to more active interventions.

Awareness of the particular problems faced by women and children when someone is abusing them began to surface in the 1960's. C. Henry Kempe's "The Battered Child Syndrome" (1962) and Lenore Walker's *The Battered Woman Syndrome* (1984) raised the consciousness of the public to the problems of child and wife abuse in the United States. Recognition of battered child syndrome involves evidence that the child is failing to thrive, radiological evidence of breaks in

bones, and psychological coping strategies that may include a close identification with the abusing parent. Battered woman syndrome, as described by Walker, includes various coping mechanisms related to survival, including manipulation, minimization of the violence directed at them, and alcohol and drug abuse.

The problems of women and children are intertwined, given their subordinate status in society. Estimates suggest that in 70 percent of homes in which the wife is battered and children are present, child abuse will also occur. Women and children in battering relationships often have an acute perception of what constitutes "normal" violence and behavior for their batterers and what is abnormal and life-threatening. In the latter situation, battered children or spouses may be so focused on survival that they see homicide as their only alternative. The identification of these syndromes has stretched the ability of the criminal justice system to protect victims of abuse and to provide a fair trial for victims who kill their batterers.

Criminal Justice. The coping mechanisms and "cycles of violence" common to victims of abuse present challenges to those charged with prosecuting perpetrators and protecting the abused. The children and wives of batterers are locked into a violent cycle in which tension builds, a battering incident occurs, and then kindness follows. Children and women will sometimes go so far as to provoke the violence in attempts to control the conditions under which it occurs. Evidence suggests that victims of domestic violence are hypervigilant in their observations of the batterer's behavior and can predict an impending violent episode. This pattern, while helpful to the victims, creates difficulty for law enforcement officials when they must determine who is at fault in a violent incident. Compounding the problem is the victims' frequent reticence to implicate the batterer either because they fear that they will be in more danger once the perpetrator is released, because they rely on the individual for support, or because they believe the violence will end if they can control the batterer.

Procedures for handling domestic violence began changing in the 1980's with better understanding of the victim's response to violence. Laws vary by state, but major changes have included not requiring an officer to witness the violence to make an arrest, allowing an arrest without a warrant, requiring officers to respond to domestic violence calls, informing victims of their legal rights, and providing transportation to hospitals and shelters when needed. Court procedures changed to increase protection by enforcing restraining orders, not requiring visitation, and requiring counseling. Again, however, these changes are not universal, but vary by state. Under such changes, battered women and children can receive greater protection from the criminal justice system regardless of whether they are able to realize their need for this protection, thereby reducing the likelihood that a homicide will result.

Battering Syndrome as a Defense for Homicide. The battered child and wife syndromes have been used as a defense tactic in homicide cases to establish that the murder was in self-defense. The traditional view of self-defense holds that a

Programs to aid battered women now exist throughout the United States. (James L. Shaffer)

person must reasonably believe that he or she is in imminent danger of extreme bodily harm or death in order for a homicide to be ruled self-defense. The battered woman and child syndromes are used to show that a child or woman's actions were reasonable when they killed their batterer. Defense attorneys use the cycle of violence and learned helplessness theories to explain why the homicides occur in calm periods and why other alternatives to the killing were not pursued. In one case, for example, a jury was given information about the history of the violence, the woman's broken leg, and the woman's size relative to her husband's to help establish that her act was reasonable.

The battering syndromes have been used to bolster self-defense arguments in a variety of cases; they began gaining support in the 1980's. This defense was controversial at first because the syndrome was not generally accepted as a scientific reality and because judges disagreed about whether experts were necessary to explain the woman's or child's state of mind to the jury. The courts have upheld the introduction of evidence on the syndromes in a number of cases. The cases of

Madelyn Diaz and Diana Goodykoontz are instructive. Diaz shot her husband, a police officer, while he slept, after he had threatened to kill the children and kill her if she did not behave as he expected. She was acquitted by the jury after a trial in which a self-defense case was based on the battered wife syndrome. Goodykoontz shot her father after fleeing to the bedroom and deciding that escape was not possible. A victim of sexual abuse and battering, she was found not guilty after evidence was introduced that she was a victim of battered child syndrome. The case, argued in 1989, was the first in which the battered child syndrome was used successfully in a nonjury trial.   —*C. Michelle Piskulich*

See also Child abuse; Domestic violence; Family law; Murder and homicide; National Organization for Victim Assistance (NOVA); Self-defense.

BIBLIOGRAPHY

Among the best sources for further information on these syndromes are Kathleen M. Heide, *Why Kids Kill Parents: Child Abuse and Adolescent Homicide* (Columbus: Ohio State University Press, 1992); Sara Lee Johann and Frank Osanka, eds., *Representing . . . Battered Women Who Kill* (Springfield, Ill.: Charles C Thomas, 1989); and two books by Lenore Walker, *Terrifying Love: Why Battered Women Kill and How Society Responds* (New York: Harper & Row, 1989) and *The Battered Woman Syndrome* (New York: Springer, 1984).

Battery

DEFINITION: Striking (or touching) a person with criminal intent

SIGNIFICANCE: Battery is one of the most frequently committed personal crimes, although it is usually not recorded by police agencies as a battery; battery often occurs with another crime such as aggravated assault, simple assault, rape, or robbery

There is much confusion regarding what constitutes a battery. As a result, battery and assault are often considered a single offense but are actually distinct. Threatening to or attempting to strike a person is an assault, while actually striking a person is a battery. Assault may be considered an incomplete battery, while battery may be considered a completed assault. Most criminal codes define battery as purposefully, recklessly, or negligently causing bodily injury with a weapon. Actual body contact must take place for battery to occur. Assaults are categorized in two ways. Simple assaults include verbal and physical threats. Aggravated assaults usually include an assault combined with a battery.

There are many kinds of battery. One's fist, a gun, or an object may be used to attack a person, and all of these are forms of battery, although most criminal codes include distinct crime categories for these offenses. Sexual contact with the intent of transmitting disease, such as acquired immune deficiency syndrome (AIDS), is a more recent example of battery. Criminal sexual contact, such as molestation or rape, is a battery, although this offense has its own distinct crime category.

See also Assault; Domestic violence; Rape and sex offenses; Robbery.

Bench warrant

DEFINITION: An order issued by the court in session for a person's immediate arrest

SIGNIFICANCE: The bench warrant permits the matter at bar to continue without lengthy delay in obtaining a warrant

A bench warrant, issued by the court, is an order that follows the failure of earlier attempts to resolve a problem. It permits police to seize a person, but not usually property, immediately. The bench warrant may be issued in a case of contempt, a refusal to abide by an order of the court. The court may have issued a written order requiring the performance of certain duties, such as payment of support, or during a trial the court may have issued an order that is not obeyed, such as an order to a witness to disclose certain information. A bench warrant also follows if the court issues a subpoena or another order commanding a witness to appear and testify at trial, but the witness ignores the order. The bench warrant differs from a warrant issued by the court which permits search and seizure of persons and property for evidence.

See also Arrest; Contempt of court; Subpoena power.

Bentham, Jeremy (Feb. 15, 1748, London, England— June 6, 1832, London, England)

IDENTIFICATION: English philosopher

SIGNIFICANCE: Bentham's ideas on the reform of law, and on constitutional thought, were read with interest in America and provided a challenge to the influential intuitionist position on the foundations of law

After his legal training, Jeremy Bentham wrote on jurisprudence and attempted to codify and simplify both civil and penal law. The main works published during his lifetime were *A Fragment on Government* (1776) and *An Introduction to the Principles of Morals and Legislation* (1789). He was at the forefront of utilitarian moral philosophy and founded a radical journal called *Westminster Review*. His many followers included James Mill, John Stuart Mill, and John Austin. Bentham thought that much of what occurred in the courts was chaotic, and he blamed this on intuitionist theories which held some acts to be inherently wrong irrespective of whether they caused any harm. He took issue with the notions of natural law and social contract and proposed that laws should prohibit acts only on grounds of their consequences for human welfare, in terms of the balance of pain and pleasure. This led to "the greatest happiness principle," which is at the heart of utilitarianism and which has been a force in moral and legal thinking in the United States and elsewhere ever since.

See also Blackstone, William; Jurisprudence; Model Penal Code; Natural law and natural rights.

Bill of attainder

DEFINITION: A legislative act that punishes specific individuals or groups without a trial in a court of law

SIGNIFICANCE: In order to protect individuals from arbitrary punishment, the U.S. Constitution (Article I, sections 9 and 10) specifically forbids both the Congress and the states from enacting bills of attainder

In English common law, bills of attainder were legislative pronouncements of death sentences. Lesser punishments such as forfeiture of property or loss of a job were known as bills of pains and penalties. Under U.S. law, all legislative punishments are known as bills of attainder and are forbidden. For legislation to be a bill of attainder it must contain three elements: a clear and definite punishment, the absence of a judicial trial, and a clear specification of individuals or groups to which it applies. The legal standard for each of these elements is high, or else the ban on bills of attainder would seem to apply to almost any legislation that burdens some groups or individuals but not all. Many bills of attainder have been *ex post facto* laws (laws applied retroactively "after the fact"), but they need not necessarily be so.

See also Common law; Constitution, U.S.; Due process of law; *Ex post facto* law; Treason.

Bill of particulars

DEFINITION: A defendant's request of the detailed information supporting the charges presented in the prosecutor's indictment

SIGNIFICANCE: A bill of particulars allows the defendant the opportunity to better prepare a defense and receive a fair trial

In the past, prosecutors deliberately drafted loose indictments and gave defendants only the information that the prosecutors thought they should have. Under these conditions the defense counsel had to rummage through hundreds and perhaps thousands of the prosecutor's documents to find the specific information supporting the prosecutor's charge. In addition, the prosecutor could spring a surprise against the defense at the trial.

In *United States v. Davidoff* (1988), however, the court of appeals ruled that a bill of particulars cannot be ignored by the prosecutor, and in *United States v. Bortnovsky* (1987), the court required that prosecutors advise the defendant which specific documents the government intends to use in the trial. In these two cases the U.S. Court of Appeals for the Second Circuit recognized that the defendant must have optimum opportunity to understand the charges and prepare an adequate defense. A bill of particulars is designed to define and limit the government's case. There can be no variance between the bill of particulars and the evidence presented at the trial.

See also Evidence, rules of; Indictment; Information.

Bill of Rights, U.S.

DEFINITION: The first ten amendments to the U.S. Constitution, proposed in 1789 and ratified in 1791

SIGNIFICANCE: The Bill of Rights is the Constitution's most concentrated statement of civil liberties

The Bill of Rights consists of the first ten amendments to the U.S. Constitution, although some scholars believe that the differences between the first eight and the final two mean that only the first eight should really be counted. The first eight provide specific prohibitions against government action, while the last two appear to be more explanatory. British common law had evolved many rights that British citizens had in relation to their government, but these rights were not necessarily granted to American colonists; this was one of the grievances that led to the American Revolution. There was a direct relationship, in fact, between certain British actions and certain amendments in the Bill of Rights.

Not only grievances against the British but also fear of the potential power of the national government under the newly proposed Constitution led to the Bill of Rights. Some opponents of the proposed document seized on the lack of a list of citizens' rights as an argument against adopting the Constitution. The inclusion of a Bill of Rights was accepted by the Constitution's proponents as a means to sway undecided voters to vote for ratification. Still, not all proponents liked the idea. In one of the Federalist Papers, Alexander Hamilton argued that the entire Constitution was so limited as to be itself a "Bill of Rights," that no further list was needed, and that there might even be the danger that a narrow list of rights would be regarded as the only rights people had. To meet Hamilton's objection, the Ninth Amendment stated explicitly that the mere enumeration of these rights was not meant to preclude other rights belonging to Americans. The Ninth Amendment and the Tenth Amendment (which reserves power to the states and people, respectively) therefore are explanatory and do not have the same character as the first eight. The decision to promise inclusion of a Bill of Rights was a great strategic success for the Constitution's proponents and was a key feature in several wavering states' support for the new union.

Early in the First Congress under the new Constitution, James Madison led in suggesting the amendments that, after committee deliberation, became the text of the Bill of Rights. There were twelve amendments, but only ten were ratified initially. For all of the twentieth century celebration of the Bill of Rights, at their centennial in 1891 there was almost no mention of them. At that time they were understood to apply only to the federal government, which was not significantly involved in regulating individual behavior. Even after the passage of the Fourteenth Amendment, which the Supreme Court later used to extend the Bill of Rights to the states, the actual incorporation of these rights for use of citizens against either level of government did not come until much later. In the twentieth century, the "selective incorporation" process has applied most essential provisions to the states under the "due process" clause of the Fourteenth Amendment.

The First Four Amendments and Their Current Significance. The First Amendment's promise that "Congress shall pass no law" establishing religion or blocking the free exercise of religious belief, speech, press, peaceful assembly, or petition is of core importance to the whole realm of free expression. Of all the sections of the Bill of Rights, the provisions of the First Amendment were the first to be incorporated under the due process clause of the Fourteenth Amendment and applied to the states. All of its sections have been the subject of considerable litigation.

Most scholars believe that the Second Amendment's language—"a well regulated militia, being necessary to the security of a free state, the right of the people to keep and bear arms, shall not be infringed"—is misunderstood by those who attempt to find in it a broad individual right to own unregulated firearms. Adopted because of the British attempt to disarm the colonial militias before the Revolution and the fear that the new U.S. national government might do the same, this amendment has never been interpreted by the Supreme Court to establish an absolute individual right to own guns or to bar regulation of them. It has not been applied to state regulation of firearms. The amendment was intended to prevent national disarmament of state militias, which is no longer a substantial concern. Clearly, Congress cannot regulate guns in such a way as to disarm state militias, but not much more is banned by this amendment. For example, *United States v. Miller* (1939) held

THE BILL OF RIGHTS

Amendment I
Congress shall make no law respecting an establishment of religion, or prohibiting the free exercise thereof; or abridging the freedom of speech, or of the press; or the right of the people peaceably to assemble, and to petition the Government for a redress of grievances.

Amendment II
A well regulated Militia, being necessary to the security of a free State, the right of the people to keep and bear Arms, shall not be infringed.

Amendment III
No Soldier shall, in time of peace be quartered in any house, without the consent of the Owner, nor in time of war, but in a manner to be prescribed by law.

Amendment IV
The right of the people to be secure in their persons, houses, papers, and effects, against unreasonable searches and seizures, shall not be violated, and no Warrants shall issue, but upon probable cause, supported by Oath or affirmation, and particularly describing the place to be searched, and the persons or things to be seized.

Amendment V
No person shall be held to answer for a capital, or otherwise infamous crime, unless on a presentment or indictment of a Grand Jury, except in cases arising in the land or naval forces, or in the Militia, when in actual service in time of War or public danger; nor shall any person be subject for the same offence to be twice put in jeopardy of life or limb; nor shall be compelled in any criminal case to be a witness against himself, nor be deprived of life, liberty, or property, without due process of law; nor shall private property be taken for public use without just compensation.

Amendment VI
In all criminal prosecutions, the accused shall enjoy the right to a speedy and public trial, by an impartial jury of the State and district wherein the crime shall have been committed, which district shall have been previously ascertained by law, and to be informed of the nature and cause of the accusation; to be confronted with the witnesses against him; to have compulsory process for obtaining Witnesses in his favor, and to have the assistance of counsel for his defence.

Amendment VII
In Suits at common law, where the value in controversy shall exceed twenty dollars, the right of trial by jury shall be preserved, and no fact tried by a jury, shall be otherwise reexamined in any Court of the United States, than according to the rules of the common law.

Amendment VIII
Excessive bail shall not be required, nor excessive fines imposed, nor cruel and unusual punishments inflicted.

Amendment IX
The enumeration in the Constitution, of certain rights, shall not be construed to deny or disparage others retained by the people.

Amendment X
The powers not delegated to the United States by the Constitution, nor prohibited by it to the States, are reserved to the States respectively, or to the people.

that a ban on sales of sawed-off shotguns did not violate the amendment, since these guns would not be used by a militia.

The Third Amendment was written in response to British stationing of troops in the homes of civilian colonists without compensation for the service—purportedly to cut the cost of the army needed to defend against American Indians, but probably also as a device for controlling rebellious colonists. The Third Amendment bans such a practice: "No soldier shall, in time of peace, be quartered in any house, without the consent of the owner, nor in time of war, but in a manner to be described by law." The Supreme Court has not heard any cases contesting the Third Amendment because the language is so clear, the quartering of soldiers in civilian houses is impractical in modern times, and the amendment has not been applied to the states under the incorporation theory.

The Fourth Amendment's promise—"the right of the people to be secure in their persons, houses, papers, and effects, against unreasonable searches and seizures, shall not be violated, and no warrant shall be issued but upon probable cause, supported by oath or affirmation, and particularly in describing the place to be searched, and the persons or things to be seized"—arose out of British colonial practices. Although British citizens had gained some protection against unreasonable searches and seizures in England itself, the British government did not extend this protection to the colonists. To protect citizens from such abuses by the new national government, the requirement for a search warrant provided an important judicial control on search and seizure actions by the police. Although the police may both search and seize, they must obtain court approval, which is to be granted only with probable cause. Any material seized through an unreasonable search and seizure may be found inadmissible as evidence in federal courts, under a legal doctrine known as the "exclusionary rule," which was applied to the states as a result of incorporation in *Mapp v. Ohio* (1961). In the early history of the United States, searches and seizures were largely physical acts, but later, as of *Katz v. United States* (1967), the Court held that electronic eavesdropping and wiretapping also require a warrant from a judge based on probable cause.

The Fifth Amendment. The Fifth Amendment is so comprehensive that each section must be examined separately. The first section provides that "no person shall be held to answer for a capital, or otherwise infamous crime, unless on a presentment or indictment by a grand jury, except in cases arising out of the land and naval forces or in the militia, when in actual service when in time of war or public danger." While the grand jury (not the petit jury which sits at a trial) is one of the oldest institutions in Anglo-American law, its use has declined, and this right has not been incorporated and applied to the states. Many states do not use a grand jury and proceed to a trial with an indictment or presentment by the prosecutor.

The second section prohibits "double jeopardy": "Nor shall any person be subject for the same offense to twice be put in jeopardy of life or limb." The double jeopardy provision covers only criminal cases and was not applied to the states until the case *Benton v. Maryland* (1969). The double jeopardy provision is important as a safeguard against a government that seeks to try to retry a person until it finally gains a conviction, as the British did in colonial times. It is an important individual protection against the government, but the provision does not always prohibit a retrial if a mistrial has occurred or if the defendant appeals a conviction.

The third widely known provision of the Fifth Amendment protects against self-incrimination "Nor shall [any person] be compelled in any criminal case to be a witness against himself." Churches' and monarchs' ancient practice of torturing people to force them to confess to crimes was gradually overcome in England in the sixteenth and seventeenth centuries, and it was natural for Americans to include protection against it. The Supreme Court did not consider this right so fundamental that it needed to be applied to the states until the case of *Malloy v. Hogan* (1964). Those who testify before some congressional committees are not protected by this section, although most congressional committees now voluntarily allow witnesses "to take the Fifth." With this exception, the U.S. legal system does provide a broad, significant protection against self-incrimination.

The fourth section states, "Nor [shall any person] be deprived of life, liberty, or property without due process of law." Identical words are used in the Fourteenth Amendment, and subsequent judicial interpretation has applied the due process clause of the Fourteenth Amendment to all the other protections included in the Fifth Amendment and many other protections as well. For most of U.S. history, the Supreme Court has treated the due process clause of the Fifth Amendment as if it were redundant (merely reincorporating the procedural due process guarantees listed elsewhere). On some occasions, the due process clause has been interpreted as meaning that substantive due process issues (such as reasonableness or fairness) can also be examined under the Fifth Amendment. The Fifth Amendment was used in this way to strike down national economic legislation under a substantive due process concept early in the twentieth century, but more recently the Court has departed from this practice without completely abandoning the substantive due process notion. Specifically, the Supreme Court has allowed this section of the Fifth Amendment to be used to resolve substantive due process questions in the civil rights area. This represents a substantial shift in the meaning of substantive due process. In *Bolling v. Sharpe* (1954), the Court

included the legal equal protection concept of the Fourteenth Amendment under the due process portion of the Fifth Amendment. In this way, the notion of equal protection of the law was applied on the federal level, whereas previously it had applied only on the state level through the Fourteenth Amendment.

The last provision, "nor shall private property be taken for public use without just compensation," represented an attempt by the framers to limit the power of eminent domain, or the government's power to reclaim private land for society's benefit. Clearly, in war property owners might need to yield their property for the good of all, or lose it to the enemy. Such situations make any limit on government difficult, so the U.S. drafters should be credited for trying. This restraint has been seriously weakened in the twentieth century. As the courts have stopped second-guessing legislatures on what constitutes a "public purpose," the phrase has become vague and meaningless. The Supreme Court has even allowed the government to take land from one private party and sell it to another for a commercial use, so that all any owner can do is haggle over the sales price. Even this is difficult, because "just compensation" should match the "fair market value," which implies a willing seller. This was the first portion of the Bill of Rights to be incorporated under the due process clause of the Fourteenth Amendment—in *Chicago, Milwaukee and St. Paul Railway Co. v. Minnesota* (1890), and even more clearly so in a second case, *Chicago, Burlington and Quincy Railroad Co. v. Chicago* (1897).

The Sixth Amendment. The Sixth Amendment enumerates basic rights for those accused of committing crimes. First, "in all criminal prosecutions, the accused shall have the right to a speedy and public trial, by an impartial jury of the state and district wherein the crime shall have been committed, which district shall have previously been ascertained by law." These are virtually the same words used in Article III of the Constitution; clearly, the framers were convinced that these rights were absolutely vital. These rights, which had evolved over time in Anglo-Saxon law, had not been extended to the American colonists by the British, and the framers wanted to avoid the possibility of similar difficulties recurring. These provisions did not apply to the states until *Duncan v. Louisiana* (1968).

A second speedy, public trial section was applied to the states in *Klopfer v. North Carolina* (1967). Klopfer had been indicted by North Carolina for criminal trespass for taking part in a sit-in demonstration in a restaurant. At the trial, the jury failed to reach an agreement; the resulting mistrial allowed the state to retry Klopfer. The state elected to delay the trial indefinitely, but the U.S. Supreme Court ruled unanimously against North Carolina, stating that the resulting uncertainty and delay deprived Klopfer of his liberty without due process of law. "Public" trials have turned out to be an even more difficult issue for the courts because they readily bring the rights of the accused into conflict with the rights of the press under the First Amendment.

The Sixth Amendment's requirement of an impartial jury has been used on occasion to prevent racial discrimination in the selection of local juries as well as discrimination based on sex, nationality, and religion. Prior to the American Revolution, the British had hauled American colonists across the Atlantic to stand trial in England. Not only was the expense prohibitive for the accused colonist, but also the chances of bringing witnesses in the accused's defense or of a fair trial were nonexistent. Thus the right to a "local" jury was included to prevent the federal government from doing the same to residents of various states. Other rights basic to the common-law tradition of the Anglo-Saxon judicial tradition, including the right to be informed of the nature and cause of an indictment, to be confronted by witnesses, to have compulsory process (subpoenas) for obtaining reluctant witnesses in one's behalf, and to have the assistance of counsel for defense, are also in the Sixth Amendment.

Notable among the Sixth Amendment guarantees applied to the states is the right to the assistance of counsel in the defense of criminal cases, as established in the case *Gideon v. Wainwright* (1963). Prior to this time, the right to counsel in capital cases had been granted to criminal defendants, but until 1963 it was not clear that all defendants in criminal proceedings should have counsel provided. Later, the more controversial *Escobedo v. Illinois* (1964) and *Miranda v. Arizona* (1966) cases provided for the assistance of counsel not only at the trial but also at the time an accused is arrested by the police.

Provisions of the Seventh and Eighth Amendments. The Seventh Amendment states, "In suits at common law, where the value in controversy shall exceed twenty dollars, the right of trial by jury shall be preserved, and no fact tried by a jury, shall be otherwise reexamined in any court of the United States according to the rules of common law," providing guarantees in federal civil cases. Because civil cases are held to be less directly related to an individual's basic rights and civil liberties, and because the original limit of twenty dollars is unrealistically low, the Supreme Court has not applied the Seventh Amendment to the states.

The Eighth Amendment provides that "excessive bail shall not be required, nor excessive fines imposed, nor cruel or unusual punishment inflicted." The ban on excessive bail (not yet applied to states) means that bail should not be set higher than would be reasonable to ensure the presence of the defendant at the trial. It also allows the denial of bail when no bail could guarantee the presence of the accused at trial, as in capital cases or those where the accused might commit other crimes pending trial. The prohibition of excessive fines has been extended to states; it means that an indigent person does not have to pay a fine, since failure to pay a fine cannot result in imprisonment unless imprisonment is otherwise a penalty for the same crime.

Controversy has emerged over the Eighth Amendment's prohibition of cruel and unusual punishment, since opponents of capital punishment argue that it is "cruel and unusual." Throughout U.S. history, however, capital punishment has existed in most states, and the prevailing view is that capital punishment is not cruel and unusual. Former U.S. Supreme Court Justices Harry A. Blackmun, William J. Brennan, and William O. Douglas have maintained that public sensibilities have gradually changed and that capital punishment is now, by nature, "cruel and unusual." These justices did not persuade a court majority to this view, but in *Furman v. Georgia* (1972) a majority did rule that capital punishment as administered in the various states was cruel, unusual, and discriminatory in its impact because vastly more blacks were executed than whites. Subsequently, many states revised their capital punishment laws, and the revisions were upheld.

The Ninth and Tenth Amendments. The Ninth Amendment was added to try to overcome the objections of those who opposed adding a Bill of Rights for fear that such a list would lead people to conclude that only those rights would be protected. The Ninth Amendment states, "The enumeration in the Constitution, of certain rights, shall not be construed to deny or disparage others retained by the people." The Ninth Amendment has been used principally to include a broad range of rights under the general notion of privacy, which can be found in the Fourth, Fifth, and Sixth Amendments.

Technically, the Tenth Amendment adds nothing to the Constitution, because it simply makes explicit what everyone regarded as understood: that the power of the federal government consisted in certain delegated or enumerated powers which could not expand. The framers considered it important, however, to make clear that certain rights were retained by the states or the people, so they added the words "The powers not delegated to the United States by the Constitution, nor prohibited to the states, are reserved to the states respectively, or to the people."

—Richard L. Wilson

See also Arms, right to keep and bear; Assembly and association, freedom of; Civil liberties; Civil rights; Constitution, U.S.; Constitutional law; Due process of law; Equal protection of the law; Establishment of religion; Incorporation doctrine; Religion, free exercise of; Speech and press, freedom of; Speedy trial, right to.

BIBLIOGRAPHY

The best way to approach this complex subject is to turn to a helpful book of general scholarship, such as Henry J. Abraham and Barbara A. Perry, *Freedom and the Court* (6th ed. New York: Oxford University Press, 1994). For a contrary view on incorporation, see Raoul Berger, *The Fourteenth Amendment and the Bill of Rights* (Oklahoma City: University of Oklahoma Press, 1989). A comprehensive examination of each element of the entire Bill of Rights can be found in Eugene W. Hickok, Jr., ed., *The Bill of Rights: Original Meaning and Current Understanding* (Charlottesville: University of Virginia Press, 1991). A comprehensive symposium on the entire Bill of Rights can be found in Geoffrey R. Stone, Richard A. Epstein, and Cass R. Sunstein, eds., *The Bill of Rights in the Modern State* (Chicago: University of Chicago Press, 1992).

Birth control, right to

DEFINITION: The right to use a method or object that aids in regulating or preventing the birth of children

SIGNIFICANCE: Based on definitions of individual liberties and the right to privacy, the American justice system has been involved in changing notions of the permissibility of individual citizens' use of birth control

Throughout American history, midwives and health professionals have always recorded ways in which couples could restrict or prevent pregnancies. In the nineteenth century, however, increasingly stringent moral standards and emphasis on women's domesticity led reformers to identify the prevention of pregnancy as a moral evil. Such moral views were made a legal formality in 1873, when Anthony Comstock pressed for legislation that made illegal the possession, sale, or gift of any obscene materials or articles for the prevention of conception (the Comstock Law). Comstock was made an assistant postal inspector, which gave him expanded power to investigate and prosecute the dissemination of literature dealing with planned parenthood through the mail. In the 1870's and 1880's, several states passed similar laws, making the use of contraceptives and the spread of information about pregnancy prevention punishable under obscenity statutes.

The Birth Control Movement. Some reformers, however, viewed this legislation as damaging to the development of American families. Pointing to large immigrant families and to mothers who were always in ill health, they suggested that the spread of information about contraception would help to prevent unchecked growth of American cities. One reformer in particular, Margaret Sanger, was joined by Protestants, social reformers, Malthusian scholars, and others who believed that American cities suffered from unchecked population growth. Sanger chose to confront the viability of the Comstock Law. She founded planned parenthood clinics, and she reproduced contraception information to send to women by mail.

Although doctors could prescribe contraceptives for health reasons (to prevent the spread of disease, broadly defined), Sanger and several other reformers, including her sister, were arrested and jailed under the terms of the Comstock Law. In spite of numerous penalties and court appearances, Sanger continually agitated for changes in the laws to permit the use of contraception by married couples. Eventually, activists in the state of Connecticut made a direct challenge to the legal validity of such statutes.

In 1935, the Birth Control League of Connecticut began to operate clinics for married women who could not afford doctors. Because this action violated Connecticut's obscenity statutes, the directors of the clinic were arrested and found guilty, and the clinics were closed. In the 1960's, however, Estelle

Planned Parenthood, founded by Margaret Sanger in 1916, has been in the forefront of offering birth-control information and services. (James L. Shaffer)

Griswold, executive director of the Planned Parenthood League of Connecticut, opened another Planned Parenthood center for married women in the state. In *Griswold v. Connecticut* (1965), what was at issue were fundamental principles of individual freedoms and rights to privacy within the home. Griswold and her coworker both maintained that they had the right to practice their occupations and that the state's effort to limit their right to property was arbitrary. Even more important, attorneys maintained that obscenity statutes such as those in Connecticut were a violation of due process, since they unfairly invaded the privacy of the home and the private decisions of couples regarding their sexual practices and family planning. The Supreme Court, in a 7-2 ruling, agreed that laws passed under the terms of the Comstock Law were unfair invasions of privacy.

Privacy and Birth Control Since *Griswold*. *Griswold v. Connecticut* was one of several decisions that have dealt with the question of rights to privacy. In *Mapp v. Ohio* (1961; right to privacy within one's home), *Bowers v. Hardwick* (1986; permissibility of consensual sodomy), and *Roe v. Wade* (1973; the right of a woman to obtain an abortion), courts have had to address the extent to which the American judicial system protects individual liberties and citizens' rights to privacy.

Since the *Griswold* case, contraception has become widely available to individuals, through both private purchases and public programs. More recently, the spread of venereal diseases and acquired immune deficiency syndrome (AIDS) has added to public acceptance of the use of contraceptives. Nevertheless, public funding for the dissemination of information about contraception and of condoms and other preventive devices has come under increasing criticism. Some groups have organized protests against the use of public monies for private relations. In particular, Catholics and religious fundamentalists protest the spread of information and contraceptives for moral and religious reasons. Some cities have engaged in debates regarding whether the desire to protect public health outweighs the need to respect the religious and moral convictions of those opposed to the use of condoms and of family planning in general. —*Sarah E. Heath*

See also Abortion; Comstock Law; *Doe v. Bolton*; Feminism; *Griswold v. Connecticut*; Privacy, right of; *Roe v. Wade*; Sanger, Margaret; Sterilization and American law.

BIBLIOGRAPHY

A good survey of the birth control movement which places birth control activism in historical perspective is Linda Gordon's *Woman's Body, Woman's Right: A Social History of Birth Control in America* (New York: Penguin Books, 1977). On Margaret Sanger, see Margaret Sanger, *My Fight for Birth Control* (New York: Maxwell Reprint, 1969); Vivian L. Werner, *Margaret Sanger: Woman Rebel* (New York: Hawthorn Books, 1970); Gloria Moore and Ronald Moore, *Margaret Sanger and the Birth Control Movement: A Bibliography, 1911-1984* (Metuchen, N.J.: Scarecrow Press, 1986); and David M. Kennedy, *Birth Control in America: The Career of Margaret Sanger* (New Haven, Conn.: Yale University Press, 1970).

Bivens v. Six Unknown Named Agents

Court: U.S. Supreme Court

Date: Decided June 21, 1971

Significance: This case established that, under certain conditions, plaintiffs have the right to claim civil damages when federal officials violate the Fourth Amendment guarantee against unreasonable search and seizure

The plaintiff in this case filed a civil action against federal employees of the Federal Bureau of Narcotics who had entered his house, searched it, and arrested him for possession of narcotics. He alleged that the entry and search had been without probable cause and was therefore in violation of the Fourth Amendment of the U.S. Constitution. He sought $15,000 in damages from each federal official.

The lower courts denied him relief on the ground that in the absence of a federal statute giving him the right to sue federal officials for violation of his constitutional rights, he could not sue the federal officials in a federal court for monetary relief. The Supreme Court disagreed. In his opinion for the Court, Justice William J. Brennan held that federal law permitted the plaintiff to bring the action. He reserved the question of whether the action might nevertheless be defeated by a claim of immunity by the officials.

Justice Brennan reasoned that the Fourth Amendment "guarantees to citizens of the United States the absolute right to be free from unreasonable searches and seizures carried out by virtue of federal authority" and that, "where federally protected rights have been invaded, it has been the rule from the beginning that courts will be alert to adjust their remedies so as to grant the necessary relief." He saw no reason to depart from this rule simply because there was no specific congressional authorization of the suit or because the plaintiff might have been able to bring an action under state law for the invasion of his privacy.

Dissenting opinions argued against the decision on the grounds that it invaded Congress' prerogative to define the rights of persons to sue in federal courts, that it would result in an avalanche of unmeritorious claims against federal officials, and that, like the exclusionary rule in criminal prosecutions, it would hamper the capacity of law enforcement officers to carry out their duties because they would be fearful of direct personal liability for violation of the Fourth Amendment.

Bivens established that federal courts may, at least in some circumstances, hear and adjudicate civil actions for monetary damages against federal officials predicated on violation of constitutional rights even though Congress has not explicitly created the right to sue. It therefore raises questions regarding the distribution of lawmaking (or "right-creating") power between the judicial and the legislative branches of the federal government. The issue, generally referred to as the "implication of a private right of action," continues to be a difficult and challenging one for the courts: When should the courts find that the existence of a federal law (a statute, a constitutional provision, a treaty, or even a prior decision) gives a plaintiff a right to seek damages for violation of the law? Despite *Bivens* and numerous other cases since, the Supreme Court has failed to give a clear and concise answer to the question and has proceeded on a case-by-case basis.

See also Evidence, rules of; Immunity of public officials; Privacy, right of; Probable cause; Search and seizure.

Black, Hugo L. (Feb. 27, 1886, Harlan, Ala.—Sept. 25, 1971, Bethesda, Md.)

IDENTIFICATION: U.S. Supreme Court justice, 1937-1971

SIGNIFICANCE: From 1937 until 1971, Black served on the U.S. Supreme Court and contributed significantly to the protection of constitutional rights, especially in the areas of free speech and civil rights

Hugo L. Black was born in the small Alabama town of Harlan on February 27, 1886. His father was a storekeeper, and his family was rather poor. He received his law degree in 1906 from the University of Alabama and began practicing law in Birmingham the following year. He became active in the Alabama Democratic Party and was elected twice to the U.S. Senate, first in 1926 and then in 1932. After Franklin D. Roosevelt became president in March, 1933, Senator Black became one of the most outspoken defenders of the New Deal, and he criticized several U.S. Supreme Court decisions which had invalidated certain New Deal legislation approved during Roosevelt's first term. In August, 1937, when President Roosevelt had the opportunity to make his first appointment to the U.S. Supreme Court, he nominated Senator Hugo Black. His colleagues in the Senate confirmed Hugo Black by a vote of 63 to 16. He served on the U.S. Supreme Court from October, 1937, until September, 1971, when very poor health forced him to resign. He died only eight days later.

During his thirty-four years of service as an associate justice of the Supreme Court, Black played a very influential role in protecting individual rights. He believed firmly that the protections of the U.S. Constitution needed to be interpreted literally, and he always kept in his jacket a paperback copy of the Constitution so that he could make sure that lawyers appearing before the Supreme Court had quoted it correctly. He firmly believed the Fourteenth Amendment's guarantee that all citizens receive equal treatment required the U.S. Supreme Court to declare unconstitutional all discriminatory laws and practices. He joined all other members of the Supreme Court in *Brown v. Board of Education* (1954) in deciding that it was incompatible with the Fourteenth Amendment to prevent black pupils from attending school with whites. Justice Black also believed that constitutional rights applied equally to both federal and state cases. For this reason, he voted in several cases in the 1950's and 1960's to annul state laws which placed onerous burdens on blacks who tried to register to vote as well as "Jim Crow" laws which prevented whites and blacks from eating together in restaurants.

He also believed that the First Amendment guarantee of the right to free speech was absolute. He voted to overrule many state laws which placed undue burdens on citizens who wished to protest against laws they considered to be unjust. He also played a major role in establishing the rights of prisoners. In *Gideon v. Wainwright* (1963), he wrote the majority decision that affirmed the right to representation by court-appointed lawyers of paupers who had been accused of felonies.

See also *Brown v. Board of Education*; Civil rights; Constitutional interpretation; Constitutional law; Douglas, William O.; Frankfurter, Felix; *Gideon v. Wainwright*; Roosevelt, Franklin D.; Speech and press, freedom of; Supreme Court of the United States.

Black codes

DEFINITION: Black codes were repressive legal measures that were designed to control African Americans by restricting their social, political, and economic freedom in the nineteenth century

SIGNIFICANCE: The black codes led to constitutional guarantees of civil liberties for black Americans, most notably in the Fourteenth Amendment

In their broadest sense, black codes were laws aimed at controlling African American life in the nineteenth century. Some of these laws, the slave codes, applied only to slaves. As America's indigenous black population grew, free blacks became increasingly subject to discriminatory laws designed to ensure their acquiescence to white rule. For example, some states refused to allow black people to carry canes, a widely recognized symbol of authority, and free blacks in nearly all states could be sold into slavery for failure to pay their taxes. Moreover, fearing that free blacks might incite or assist slave insurrections, especially in the wake of Nat Turner's revolt, antebellum black codes became increasingly severe. In most Southern states, free black status was barely distinguishable from slave status on the eve of the Civil War.

The term "black codes" most commonly refers to laws passed by former Confederate state legislatures in response to the Thirteenth Amendment to the Constitution (1865). These laws bestowed certain civil liberties on the newly freed black population. While these codes varied from state to state, all black codes legitimized African American marriages, recognized the right to own property, and permitted blacks to sue and be sued, enter into contracts, and testify in court cases involving other blacks. On the other hand, most black codes forbade interracial marriage, denied blacks the right to bear arms, and prohibited blacks from testifying against whites in courts of law. On an even more negative note, the black codes merely granted African Americans an apprentice-like status that in no way conferred genuine freedom. They also attempted to tie black employment to a socioeconomic system that closely resembled slavery. Most states required newly freed blacks to secure employment with a local landowner or face involuntary service in plantation labor. Free blacks were also subject to involuntary service for civil offenses ranging from vagrancy and derogatory gestures to "mischief" and preaching the Gospel without a license. Moreover, in some states white landowners were subject to a fine or imprisonment for attempting to hire black laborers who were already under contract to someone else.

Appalled by southern actions, northern congressmen began calling for legislation that would ensure civil rights for all African Americans. The result was the Fourteenth Amendment to the Constitution, which forbade denial of "life, liberty, and property without due process of law" and guaranteed citizenship to all persons born or naturalized in the United States. This amendment, ratified on July 28, 1868, constitutionally guaranteed civil liberties that had been stipulated earlier in the Civil Rights Act of 1866.

See also Civil rights; Civil Rights Acts of 1866-1875; *Civil Rights Cases*; Civil War Amendments; Enforcement Acts; Jim Crow laws; Reconstruction; Segregation, *de facto* and *de jure*; *Slaughterhouse Cases*; Slavery.

Black Panther Party

DATE: Established 1966
SIGNIFICANCE: The Black Panther Party was one of the most militant of the urban civil rights organizations promoting black power

By the mid-1960's, many black civil rights advocates were unhappy with the slow pace of change and with the prevailing movement tactic of passive nonviolence. Increasingly, African Americans in inner cities viewed the police as an army of occupation, willing and able to engage in police brutality to

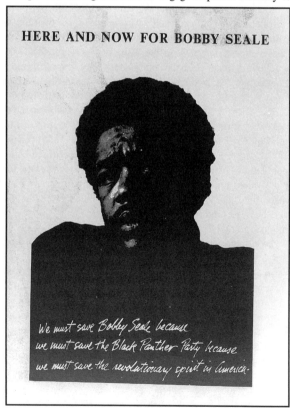

HERE AND NOW FOR BOBBY SEALE

We must save Bobby Seale because we must save the Black Panther Party because we must save the revolutionary spirit in America.

A 1968 poster to gain support for Bobby Seale, cofounder of the Black Panther Party, on trial for conspiring to riot. Seale was acquitted. (Library of Congress)

enforce white rule. In response, the Black Panther Party, begun in Oakland, California, by leaders including Huey P. Newton and Bobby Seale, advocated "picking up the gun"—in effect, fighting violence with violence.

Though primarily known for their philosophy of violent retribution, the Panthers also organized community action programs such as health clinics, breakfast programs, food pantries, and alternative schools. Their avowed militancy made the Panthers the focus of intense and lethal repression by law enforcement agencies; Panther leader Fred Hampton's shooting death at the hands of Chicago police is the best-known example.

Ideological splits and effective government repression led to the demise of the Black Panthers by the mid-1970's. Nevertheless, at least partly as a result of the party's campaign, virtually all urban police departments significantly increased the percentage of minorities on the force, many going so far as to institute residency requirements. In addition, self-help programs remain an important part of inner-city life.

See also Black Power movement; Chicago seven trial; Civil Rights movement; COINTELPRO; Police brutality; Race riots, twentieth century.

Black Power movement

DEFINITION: A movement, influential during the late 1960's, that espoused black pride and demanded equal justice
SIGNIFICANCE: The Black Power movement, initiated by young blacks who rejected black assimilation, signified a growing impatience with American racial injustice

In 1967 Stokely Carmichael and Charles V. Hamilton argued that "black power" as a concept rests on the premise that before a group can enter the open society it must first close ranks. Carmichael, head of the Student Nonviolent Coordinating Committee (SNCC), and Charles Hamilton, a professor at Columbia University, captured the mood of many young blacks in 1966 who rejected the nonviolent, assimilationist, Civil Rights movement led by Martin Luther King, Jr. Carmichael, who had marched with King in the South, split with King to adopt a more militant approach to combating American racism. By the summer of 1966, black power became the rallying cry for angry young blacks. As a movement it demanded an end to social injustice and a redefinition of the black liberation struggle that would be shaped by blacks themselves.

Although the movement was first associated with Stokely Carmichael (now Kwame Toure), other prominent leaders of the movement included H. Rap Brown (now Jamil al-Amin), who led a protest delegation to the U.N., Huey P. Newton and Eldridge Cleaver, major figures in the Black Panther Party in Oakland, California, Bobby Seale of the Black Panthers, author-poet Amiri Baraka, author-professor Angela Davis, and Ron (Maulana) Karenga, founder of the black cultural holiday known as Kwanza.

Although united by their militant opposition to what they saw as injustice toward blacks, black power groups differed in

U.S. Olympic athletes Tommie Smith and John Carlos raising their fists in the Black Power salute at the 1968 Olympics in Mexico City. (Library of Congress)

their vision of the future and in the political strategies they embraced. For example, groups associated with Karenga redefined black culture in terms of Kwanza, while Baraka and Jamil al-Amin redefined black culture in terms of Islam. Cleaver and Newton's Black Panthers gained notoriety for violent encounters, including shoot-outs with police. Regardless of their ideological differences, black power groups frightened many whites. Another aspect of the Black Power movement was the joining of some black militants with white radicals to forge a potent antiwar movement (members of the Black Panther Party, for example, worked with white radical groups such as Students for a Democratic Society).

Like many white radicals, Black Power leaders modified their political views over time, creating a decline in the movement. For example, Carmichael became a pan-Africanist and emigrated to the West Africa state of Guinea. Newton earned a Ph.D. degree but died violently in 1989 at the hands of drug lords in California. Karenga and Davis are college professors in California, while Cleaver is a born-again Christian and a Republican. Jamil el-Amin leads a large Islamic community in Atlanta, Baraka is a Marxist college professor in New York, and Bobby Seale wrote a cookbook in the early 1990's. The presence of blacks in various fields today can be seen as a reminder of the legacy of both the Civil Rights and Black Power movements and their impact on social justice in the United States.

See also Black Panther Party; Civil Rights movement; COINTELPRO; Congress of Racial Equality (CORE); Race riots, twentieth century; Racial and ethnic discrimination; Student Nonviolent Coordinating Committee (SNCC).

Blackmail and extortion

DEFINITION: Criminal conduct involving demand for payment by threats of future exposure or harm

SIGNIFICANCE: Extortion is generally considered a crime by public officials against the government; blackmail is a crime against an individual or group

At common law, extortion was a misdemeanor that resulted when public officials, under color of their office, obtained payments to which they were not entitled or payments in excess of payments due. These payments were collected in exchange for official duties or governmental acts. Although extortion is now defined by statute rather than the courts in most states, in some jurisdictions, extortion remains a crime against the administration of justice or against the government. In these states, extortion is a crime committed exclusively by public officers and involves collecting money or other advantages in exchange for governmental duties or favors, like the common-law crime.

Distinctions and Variations. The relationship between blackmail and extortion is evident in the definition of blackmail. Blackmail has been traditionally defined as extortion by threat of exposure or criminal prosecution, thus incorporating the concepts of threat and future damage to reputation or business with the notion of payments to which one is not entitled. Blackmail, then, is a kind of extortion but with a broader legal application. Blackmail, unlike extortion, can be applied not only against government officials but also against anyone who solicits payments. Blackmail includes a wider range of acts than extortion does. Extortion targets money accepted by public officials in exchange for performing their official duties. Blackmail focuses on any money obtained through threats or intimidation. While extortion is considered a crime against the government, blackmail is a crime against an individual or group of individuals.

Although common law distinguishes between the two, some modern criminal codes have merged the terms extortion and blackmail into a single crime. In some states, extortion has been expanded to include any person who obtains money or property by threatening to expose another's failings or inflict future injury on the person or the person's family or property. Other jurisdictions use the term blackmail to refer to both public and private theft by threat, reasoning that public officials who accept money do so under the threat that if they are not paid, they will not complete the duties of their office. Still other jurisdictions use blackmail to refer to persons not acting in the capacity of a public official and extortion to refer to the conduct of public officials who accept payments in exchange for the performance of their official duties. Like those states which have merged blackmail and extortion into one crime, the Model Penal Code considers blackmail and extortion not as separate crimes but as members of the family of offenses which are called generally "theft."

Statutory Language. The language of blackmail and extortion statutes varies greatly from state to state, and consequently, the allegations necessary to prove a charge of blackmail or extortion also vary from jurisdiction to jurisdiction. In most states, threats which encompass future bodily harm, destruction of property, and damage to one's business or reputation form grounds for a charge of blackmail or extortion. Threats may be oral or written in most states, but a few recognize only a written threat. Most jurisdictions recognize a claim for blackmail or extortion based on any threats accompanied by a demand for money, property, or pecuniary advantage. Broader statutes allow recovery for threats accompanied by a demand for "anything of value" or even "any act against one's will." Sometimes the blackmailer or extortionist must actually obtain the money, property, or other item or act demanded in order to be prosecuted for blackmail. If the demand is not successful, a charge of "attempted blackmail" or "attempted extortion" might be brought. Still other states do not distinguish between the presence or absence of a successful demand for money; these jurisdictions focus on the fact that a demand was made rather than whether money was obtained as a result of it.

Blackmail and extortion are closely related to the crimes of robbery and false pretenses. Robbery, which has been traditionally defined as taking the property of another against his or her will, is distinguished from blackmail in that the person being blackmailed consents to turn over property to the blackmailer. False pretenses, a crime that deals with obtaining property as a result of lies or deception, resembles blackmail in the use of threats (which may or may not be true) to obtain property. Despite their differences, robbery, false pretenses, blackmail, and extortion share the same result: A person relinquishes property that he or she would not have otherwise surrendered.

Several federal statutes prohibit extortion and blackmail. Government employees, members of Congress, and the executive branch are all governed by statutes that prohibit accepting payments in exchange for public duties. The Hobbs Act specifically focuses on extortion that affects, obstructs, or delays interstate commerce. Other statutes deal with blackmail or extortion aimed at jurors or foreign officials or with demands made through the mails. Any person who receives the proceeds of extortion, regardless of whether the person was involved in the demand for payment, can be sentenced to up to three years in prison. —*Karyn E. Langhorne*

See also Hobbs Act; Model Penal Code; Organized crime; Political corruption; Robbery; Theft; White-collar crime.

BIBLIOGRAPHY

See Richard L. Clutterbuck, *Kidnap, Hijack, and Extortion: The Response* (New York: St. Martin's Press, 1987); R. H. Coase, *Blackmail* (Chicago: University of Chicago Law School, 1988); and Steven Shavell, *An Economic Analysis of Threats and Their Illegality: Blackmail, Extortion, and Robbery* (Cambridge, Mass.: 1992).

Blackstone, William (July 10, 1723, London, England— Feb. 14, 1780, London, England)

IDENTIFICATION: English jurist

SIGNIFICANCE: Blackstone's *Commentaries on the Laws of England* were widely read in the early American republic and greatly influenced the practice of American law and the understanding that law rests on general principles of justice

A British lawyer, William Blackstone was professor of law at Oxford University, a member of Parliament, and a judge. In 1753 he was the first person to lecture on English law at a university. His lectures grew into the four-volume *Commentaries on the Laws of England* (1765-1769), which became immensely popular within the legal profession in both England and the American colonies. More than a mere codification of English law, the *Commentaries* were an effort to ground statutory rules of human conduct, or positive law, on "the natural foundations of justice." Blackstone's connection of positive law to nature and justice accounts for the warm reception that his *Commentaries* received in America. Even as the American colonists were throwing off the authority of the British king and Parliament, they were founding their new political order on the "laws of nature and of nature's God" (in the words of the Declaration of Independence), laws that, in Blackstone's view, provided the deepest justification of civil rights and duties under English law.

See also Common law; Deadly force, police use of; Jurisprudence; Positive law.

Blue laws

DEFINITION: State or local regulations banning certain activities on Sunday; one type of blue law is the "Sunday closing law"

SIGNIFICANCE: Although Sunday closing laws originated for religious reasons, the Supreme Court has held them constitutional; nevertheless, in most areas blue laws have little significance today

The origin of the term "blue laws" is uncertain; it may refer to the color of the paper on which colonial New Haven, Connecticut, printed its laws. During the early colonial period the Puritans established their civil government as an outgrowth of their religious convictions. Many of their laws had the purpose of enforcing moral behavior; it was for moral and religious reasons that they restricted or required certain activities, especially on Sunday. As the Christian Sabbath, Sunday was to be a day of rest in compliance with the Fourth Commandment: "Remember the Sabbath day and keep it holy . . . you shall not do any work." In addition to regulations against work, there were prohibitions against selling liquor and against such activities as dancing, card playing, cooking, traveling, public sports, and smoking. In the early 1600's, Virginia (not a Puritan colony) passed a law requiring church attendance on Sunday.

Blue laws restricting activities ranging from general labor to retail sales to clam digging have remained on the books in many states and localities, although in most areas they gradually fell into disuse in the twentieth century. Blue laws have been challenged in the courts, and in two cases in 1961 (the first was *McGowan v. Maryland*) the Supreme Court upheld the constitutionality of blue laws. The Court held that a blue law requiring businesses to close on Sunday did not violate the freedom of religion clause of the First Amendment, saying that the state has a legitimate interest in designating a day of rest for its citizens. Nevertheless, since the 1960's blue laws have been a relatively minor issue. In some areas they have been repealed; in others they are still on the books but are ignored.

See also Establishment of religion; Prohibition; Religion, free exercise of; *Sherbert v. Verner*; Temperance movement; Vagrancy laws.

Bolling v. Sharpe

COURT: U.S. Supreme Court

DATE: Decided May 17, 1954

SIGNIFICANCE: In ruling that racially segregated schools in the District of Columbia were a violation of the Fifth Amendment, the Supreme Court interpreted the due process clause to prohibit invidious racial discrimination

In this companion case to *Brown v. Board of Education*, the issue of segregated public schools in the nation's capital, a matter of congressional jurisdiction, was treated in an opinion separate from *Brown* because the Fourteenth Amendment did not apply to the federal government and because the applicable Fifth Amendment did not include an equal protection clause. From the perspective of practical politics, it would have been highly embarrassing for the Court to allow segregated schools in Washington, D.C., while ruling them unconstitutional in the rest of the country.

Speaking for a unanimous Supreme Court, Chief Justice Earl Warren first noted that the petitioners were African American minors who had been refused admission to a public school "solely because of their race." He then declared that the Court had long recognized that certain forms of governmental discrimination violated the constitutional mandate for due process of law. For precedents, he looked to an 1896 *dictum* by Joseph M. Harlan and to *Buchanan v. Warley*, a 1917 decision that had defended the equal right of citizens to own property based on a substantive due process reading of the Fourteenth Amendment. Also, Warren referred to *obiter dicta* in the Japanese American cases which acknowledged that racial classifications were inherently suspect, requiring that they be "scrutinized with particular care."

Warren gave an expansive interpretation of the "liberty" protected by the Fifth Amendment, explaining that it extended to the "full range of conduct which the individual is free to pursue." The government could restrict liberty only when justified by a "proper governmental objective," and racial segregation in education was not related to such an objective. Thus, the Washington schools were imposing an "arbitrary deprivation" on the liberty of black children. In addition, Warren noted that it was "unthinkable" that the federal government might practice the kind of discrimination prohibited in the states.

Bolling v. Sharpe had major theoretical implications, for the case indicated that the Supreme Court continued to interpret the due process clauses as protecting substantive rights as well as procedures, although the substantive focus had shifted from property interests to liberty interests. Also, the decision affirmed that the ideas of liberty and equality are often overlapping and that constitutional due process of law prohibits government from practicing invidious discrimination.

See also *Brown v. Board of Education*; Civil liberties; Civil rights; Due process of law; *Hirabayashi v. United States*; Segregation, *de facto* and *de jure*.

Boot camps

DEFINITION: Facilities that emulate Marine boot camps and provide "shock incarceration" for first-time offenders

SIGNIFICANCE: Boot camps are intended both to relieve prison overcrowding and to offer first-time offenders an alternative to traditional incarceration that will instill self-reliance and discipline

The United States prison population increases annually, severely straining prison resources and state budgets. Nationally the prison population doubled between 1970 and 1980 and grew from more than 200,000 in 1980 to 1.1 million in 1995.

After Georgia established the first boot camp in 1983, twenty-nine other states created similar facilities aimed at reforming nonviolent first offenders. Such prisoners are given their choice of prison sentences or confinement, usually for ninety days, in a facility practicing "shock incarceration." Fifty-seven such camps serve more than seven thousand inmates in the United States. Additional facilities accommodating sixty-six thousand inmates and costing roughly a billion dollars are planned.

Prison boot camps, imitating United States Marine boot camps, aim to instill self-reliance and discipline in their subjects during a brief training period. Each inmate follows an undeviating routine that emphasizes stringent discipline, unquestioning obedience to authority, respect for superiors, hard work, and, frequently, humiliation. Shock incarceration seeks to brainwash young offenders so that they will strive to become productive citizens.

See also Diversion; Juvenile justice system; Prison and jail systems; Punishment; Rehabilitation.

SHOCK INCARCERATION/BOOT CAMP PROGRAMS		
Jurisdiction	Length of Program	Maximum Capacity
Alabama	3 to 6 months	180
Arizona	120 days	150
Arkansas	105 days	150
California	(a)	176
Colorado	3 months	100
Florida	3 months	100
Georgia	(b)	1,265
Illinois	120 days	430
Kansas	180 days	104
Kentucky	(c)	50
Louisiana	90 to 180 days	148
Massachusetts	4 months	256
Michigan	3 months	360
Minnesota	6 months	72
Mississippi	4 months	287
Nevada	150 days	96
New Hampshire	4 months	75
New York	6 months	1,850
North Carolina	3 months	90
Oklahoma	45 days to 5 months	430
Pennsylvania	6 months	197
Tennessee	3 months	150
Texas	3 months	400
Virginia	3 months	96
Wisconsin	6 months	40
Federal Bureau of Prisons	6 months	299

Source: U.S. Department of Justice, Bureau of Justice Statistics, *Sourcebook of Criminal Justice Statistics—1993*. Washington, D.C.: U.S. Government Printing Office, 1994. Primary source: *Corrections Compendium* (Lincoln, Nebraska, Contact Publications, 1993).

Note: Data are based on a survey; Hawaii, Idaho, Maryland, Ohio, South Carolina, and Wyoming did not respond.

(a) 3 months while in prison, 2 months of work training, 4 months on parole.

(b) 3 months for probation facilities, 4 months for incarceration facilities.

(c) 120 days plus another 6-day week.

Booth v. Maryland

COURT: U.S. Supreme Court

DATE: Decided June 15, 1987

SIGNIFICANCE: In this case, a sharply divided Supreme Court ruled that victim impact evidence was not admissible in capital sentencing proceedings

John Booth and an accomplice robbed and murdered an elderly couple in West Baltimore, Maryland, to obtain money to buy heroin. A jury sentenced Booth to die after considering information contained in a victim impact statement (VIS). The VIS emphasized the victims' outstanding personal characteristics and stressed how deeply the murdered couple would be missed. The VIS also reported the emotional and personal problems suffered by family members as a result of the murders. Finally, the VIS set forth the family members' opinions and characterizations of the crime and of Booth.

In death penalty cases, the Supreme Court requires the jury to make an individualized determination about whether the defendant should be executed, based on the character of the defendant and the circumstances of the crime. Booth argued that the victim impact evidence presented in his case was irrelevant to the question of his character and/or the circumstances of his crime. Worse, because of its inflammatory nature, the VIS had unduly influenced the jury to return a death sentence.

By a 5-4 vote, the Supreme Court agreed. Writing for the majority, Justice Lewis F. Powell, Jr., said that permitting the jury to consider the VIS in Booth's case had violated the Eighth Amendment by increasing the risk that Booth's death sentence was arbitrary and capricious. Justice Powell said that victim impact evidence diverts the jury's attention from the defendant's background and record and focuses it on the victim and surviving family members. Consequently, whether a defendant is sentenced to death might turn on such irrelevant factors as the degree to which surviving family members are willing and able to articulate their grief, or the relative worth of the victim's character. Thus, defendants whose victims were assets to the community would be punished more harshly than those whose victims were considered less worthy. This in turn would run contrary to the promise, engraved on the Supreme Court building itself, of "Equal Justice Under Law."

Four justices dissented. Justice Byron White argued that because victim impact evidence was admissible in noncapital cases it should also be permitted in death penalty cases. In Justice Antonin Scalia's view, a criminal's personal responsibility is very much a function of how much harm he or she causes. Victim impact evidence provides a more complete picture of the defendant's personal responsibility. Justice Scalia also wrote that admitting victim impact evidence in death penalty cases would accomplish an additional benefit: It would help offset the evidence the defendant offered to mitigate his moral guilt.

In 1989, only two years after *Booth*, the Court reaffirmed its principles in *South Carolina v. Gathers*, again by a 5-4 margin. In *Gathers*, a bare majority extended the rule in *Booth* to prohibit prosecutors from commenting on the personal characteristics of the victim during closing arguments to the jury. Nevertheless, the *Booth* decision proved to be impermanent. After two members of the *Booth* majority retired and were replaced by more conservative justices, the Court decided to revisit the victim impact evidence issue. In a dramatic reversal in 1991, only four years after *Booth* and two years after *Gathers*, the Court overruled both decisions in *Payne v. Tennessee*.

See also *Payne v. Tennessee*; Sentencing; Victim assistance programs; Victims of Crime Act.

Boston police strike

DATE: September 9-September 22, 1919

SIGNIFICANCE: This strike raised the question of how to balance public safety and the right of police officers to unionize, bargain collectively, and strike for economic justice

The Boston police strike lasted from September 9 to September 22, 1919. Of the city's 1,544 policemen, 1,117 went on strike. Immediately after the policemen walked out, acts of violence broke out in the South End area of Boston. On September 11, Governor Calvin Coolidge brought in the state guard, which quickly established control over the city. On September 22, the police gave in, ending the strike, and the recruiting of new policemen began. None of the striking policemen was allowed back to duty.

The Boston police strike was only one of many labor disturbances in 1919. During World War I, inflation had driven prices up, while unions had gained government backing for the right to organize and bargain collectively in exchange for wage concessions. In 1919, 4 million workers, or 22 percent of the work force, engaged in strikes. In Boston, telephone operators and transit workers had gone on strike and succeeded before the policemen walked out.

Work conditions for policemen in Boston had deteriorated significantly over the decades. Their pay scale dated back to 1898, while prices had gone up 79 percent, city government had increased their obligations, promotion regulations were arbitrary, and the quality of police facilities was generally poor. When Mayor Andrew J. Peters and Police Commissioner Edwin Upton Curtis responded hesitatingly to the policemen's demands, offering only a two-hundred-dollar annual increase, they decided to organize and affiliate themselves with the American Federation of Labor (AFL). The Boston Police Union was part of a larger movement: By August of 1919, the police forces of thirty-seven large cities had unionized and affiliated themselves with the AFL. Commissioner Curtis suspended the nineteen policemen who had been elected officers of the new union, among them union president John F. McInnes. The bad pay and work conditions, along with the city officials' hostile response to their demands, convinced the policemen to strike: They voted 1,134 to 2 for the walkout.

From the perspective of the city officials, the policemen, by joining the AFL, had entered a conflict of interest. City government argued that policemen were officers of the state, bound to the impartial enforcement of the law. Any affiliation, then, with an outside group that represents only a part of the population would compromise police officers in the exercise of their duty. The policemen, on the other hand, could point to pay and work conditions that undermined their ability to carry out their mission effectively.

For police unions, the Boston strike had important consequences. Most police unions remained and remain independent. Those that are affiliated with the AFL-CIO carry a no-strike rule in their charters. The Boston policemen eventually reorganized as the Boston Police Patrolmen's Association in 1965. In 1968, the police officers arbitrated a labor contract with the city of Boston.

See also American Federation of Labor-Congress of Industrial Organizations (AFL-CIO); Labor law; Labor unions; Police.

Bowers v. Hardwick

COURT: U.S. Supreme Court

DATE: Decided June 30, 1986

SIGNIFICANCE: In this case the Supreme Court held that the fundamental right to privacy protected by the due process clause of the Fourteenth Amendment did not extend to create a right for homosexuals to engage in consensual acts of sodomy

Bowers v. Hardwick involved a Georgia statute making it a criminal offense to commit sodomy. Hardwick was charged with violating the statute by committing sodomy with another male in Hardwick's bedroom, but the district attorney in charge of the prosecution ultimately decided not to pursue a conviction. Hardwick then brought suit, seeking a declaration that the Georgia statute was unconstitutional. In a 5-4 decision, the Supreme Court held that the statute did not violate the due process clause of the Fourteenth Amendment.

Prior to the decision in *Bowers*, the Supreme Court had held that the Constitution protected a right to privacy in matters such as abortion and the use of contraceptives. In *Bowers*, Hardwick argued that consensual sexual acts, including sodomy, should also fall within this right to privacy and should therefore be free from government regulation. In an opinion by Justice Byron R. White, a narrowly divided Court emphasized that previous privacy cases had involved family, marriage, and procreation. White insisted that homosexual conduct fell into a different category. Normally, he wrote, the Court determined whether a particular interest was a fundamental right by considering whether the interest was "implicit in the concept of ordered liberty" such that "neither liberty nor justice would exist if [it] were sacrificed," or whether the interest was "deeply rooted in this Nation's history and tradition." Sodomy, Justice White suggested, clearly failed to satisfy either of these definitions of a fundamental right. Nor was it fatal to the statute that it used the criminal sanction to enforce morality. The law, Justice White declared, "is constantly based on notions of morality, and if all laws representing essentially moral choices are to be invalidated under the Due Process Clause; the courts will be very busy indeed."

Justice Harry Blackmun, joined by Justices William Brennan, Thurgood Marshall, and John Paul Stevens, vigorously dissented from the majority's holding, arguing that the right to engage in intimate sexual relationships should be considered a fundamental right. For the dissenters, at issue in *Bowers* was the right that Justice Louis Brandeis had once described as "the most comprehensive of rights and the right most valued by civilized men": "the right to be let alone."

Bowers is significant because it signified a reluctance by the Court to recognize fundamental rights not explicitly guaranteed by the Constitution. Prior to the decision in *Bowers* it had seemed that the Court might soon recognize a fundamental right to sexual privacy between consenting adults protected by the due process clauses of the Fifth and Fourteenth Amendments. *Bowers* disappointed these expectations. It also suggested that the era in which the Court had looked to the doctrine of "substantive due process" to declare certain rights "fundamental" might be nearing a close.

See also Civil liberties; Due process of law; Gay rights; Privacy, right of.

Brady v. United States

COURT: U.S. Supreme Court

DATE: Decided May 4, 1970

SIGNIFICANCE: In this decision the Supreme Court first acknowledged the validity of plea bargaining, asserting that it offered a "mutuality of advantage" for both the defendant and the state

In 1959, Robert M. Brady, in a kidnapping case that involved the death of the victim, changed a plea of innocent to guilty when a codefendant in the case pled guilty and became available as a witness against him. Before admitting the new plea, the judge twice asked Brady if his plea was voluntary. Brady was convicted, but in 1967 he sought a reversal of his conviction in the U.S. District Court for the District of New Mexico, arguing that his guilty plea had not been voluntary. The petitioner argued that the death-penalty provisions of the Federal Kidnapping Act had coerced his plea. The district court denied Brady relief, upholding the constitutionality of the federal statute and arguing that Brady changed his plea because of his codefendant's confession. The Court of Appeals for the Tenth Circuit affirmed the lower court's finding.

On *certiorari*, the U.S. Supreme Court concurred. In the various opinions issued by the Court, it was argued that an earlier case, *United States v. Jackson* (1968), which struck down the section of the Federal Kidnapping Act under which Brady had originally been tried, did not mandate that every guilty plea previously entered under the statute be deemed invalid, even when the threat of death was a consideration. It was further argued that a guilty plea was not a violation of the Fifth Amendment protection against self-incrimination when it was entered to ensure a lesser penalty than the maximum provided for by a criminal statute. It was also noted that the Fifth Amendment did not bar prosecutors or judges from accepting pleas of guilty to lesser, reduced, or selected charges in order to secure milder penalties. Brady's guilty plea was held to have been made voluntarily, despite the fact that it was influenced by the death-penalty provision of the statute that *United States v. Jackson* later declared unconstitutional.

The formal recognition of plea bargaining as a valid procedure for obtaining criminal convictions was very important because plea bargaining has been widely used in the United States, despite the fact that there is no statutory or constitutional basis for it. In fact, almost four-fifths of all convictions in serious state and federal criminal cases are obtained through guilty pleas made to secure either reduced charges or milder punishments. Although the procedure has its critics, it is a practical way of speeding up justice and clearing court dockets. It also mitigates against long pretrial imprisonment and anxiety and protects the public from the criminal activities of habitual offenders who would be free on bail for indefinite periods.

See also Kidnapping; Plea bargaining; Retroactivity of Supreme Court decisions; *Rummel v. Estelle*; *Santobello v. New York*; Self-incrimination, privilege against.

Branch Davidians, federal raid on

DATE: February 28, 1993-April 19, 1993
PLACE: Waco, Texas
SIGNIFICANCE: The federal government's attack on an armed cult's compound resulted in scores of deaths, galvanizing an extremist antigovernment movement in the United States

A religious cult led by messianic leader David Koresh had established a compound about twelve miles from Waco, Texas. The Branch Davidians, as they were known, practiced a religion very loosely based on the Old and New Testaments, although Koresh's word bore the ultimate authority within the group. Federal and state authorities were monitoring the cult. Besides violating a variety of state and federal laws concerning such issues as polygamy and child abuse, the Branch Davidians had amassed a large cache of weapons and ammunition.

This situation was gaining increased media attention, and the federal government decided to act. On February 28, 1993, agents of the Bureau of Alcohol, Tobacco, and Firearms (ATF) launched a raid against the Branch Davidians' compound with the goal of seizing the illegal weapons. Four ATF agents and six Davidians were killed in the ensuing gun battle before the ATF called a halt to the raid. The ATF agents were replaced by the Federal Bureau of Investigation's (FBI's) Hostage Rescue Team, which surrounded the compound. For the next fifty-one days, federal negotiators worked for the release of persons from the compound. Several persons were freed during this period.

On April 19, the Hostage Rescue Team used tanks and tear gas to storm the Branch Davidians' stronghold. During the operation a massive fire, perhaps fueled by the stored munitions, broke out in the compound. Eighty-one Branch Davidians, including twenty-five children and David Koresh himself, died. Only nine of those in the compound at the time survived.

The Branch Davidians' compound in flames on April 19, 1993; David Koresh and eighty others died in the fire. (AP/Wide World Photos)

The federal government tried eleven surviving Branch Davidians for conspiring to murder federal agents. Although the jury found them guilty only of lesser charges, the judge sentenced five of the defendants to prison terms of up to forty years. At the same time, numerous charges of governmental mishandling of the standoff and raid were circulating. Survivors and families of the dead cultists filed lawsuits seeking damages of more than $1.5 billion. Some claimed that the FBI's firing of tear gas had caused the fatal fire. The government responded that the Davidians themselves had set the fire. Attorney General Janet Reno ordered a review of the FBI's actions. The resulting report cleared the FBI and placed the blame for the deaths upon David Koresh and some of his followers.

The raid on the Branch Davidians served as a rallying point for extremists believing that the federal government is systematically working to deprive Americans of their weapons and their freedom of religion. Exactly two years after the FBI raid, on April 19, 1995, a federal building in Oklahoma City was bombed, allegedly by a man who was aggrieved about the Waco raid. In the wake of the Oklahoma City bombing, the U.S. Senate held hearings in the summer of 1995 to examine the federal government's actions with regard to the Branch Davidians.

See also Alcohol, Tobacco, and Firearms (ATF), Bureau of; Arms, right to keep and bear; Conspiracy; Deadly force, police use of; Federal Bureau of Investigation (FBI); MOVE, Philadelphia police bombing of; Religion, free exercise of; Religious sects and cults.

Brandeis, Louis D. (Nov. 13, 1856, Louisville, Ky.—Oct. 5, 1941, Washington, D.C.)

IDENTIFICATION: American jurist, reformer, and U.S. Supreme Court justice, 1916-1939

SIGNIFICANCE: Brandeis' use of sociological jurisprudence as an acceptable method of legal argumentation and his belief that the meaning given to the law should evolve in relation to social need have become important elements in the judicial process

As a student at Harvard Law School and as a successful Boston attorney, Louis Brandeis established a reputation as an exceptional legal scholar. In a landmark article, "Right of Privacy" (*Harvard Law Review*, December 15, 1890), Brandeis showed that he could expand the boundaries of legal reasoning in presenting an original argument for the right to be left alone. During the 1890's he became increasingly interested in questions of social justice and in matters of civic and economic reform, and he constantly looked for ways to protect the interests of consumers, taxpayers, and workers. In this regard he helped reform Boston's municipal gas rate structure and devised a savings-bank insurance plan for workers. His concern about the growth of trusts and monopolies and about the inequities involved in modern business methods and interlocking financial interests led him to publish an important document for the Progressive movement entitled *Other People's Money and How the Bankers Use It* (1914).

As an advocate of trade unionism and with a growing reputation as a champion of the rights of the working class, Brandeis was retained by the state of Oregon in 1907 to defend a statute limiting the employment of women in industrial establishments to not more than ten hours a day. In his famous brief, in which only two pages dealt with legal principles, Brandeis presented more than one hundred pages of scientific information, expert opinion, and examples from other states and countries to argue that the right to sell one's labor was a liberty protected by the Constitution but subject to reasonable restraint to protect the health, safety, morals, or general welfare. Overriding the contention of opposing counsel that the freedom of women workers to bargain with their employers was impaired by the statute, the U.S. Supreme Court sustained the Oregon law in *Muller v. Oregon* (1908).

The capstone of Brandeis' legal career came with his appointment to the Supreme Court in 1916. During his twenty-three years on the Court Brandeis consistently argued in support of his belief that the law should accommodate changing social and economic need, and he stood as a constant defender of freedom of speech, press, assembly, and religion, and the protection of civil liberties. His dissenting opinions have become classic defenses in the struggle to liberalize judicial interpretation of the Constitution. In one especially eloquent dissent, in *Olmstead v. United States* (1928), Brandeis condemned the use of wiretapping by federal authorities in violation of state law and admonished the federal government for assuming that in the administration of the criminal law the ends justified the means. During the 1930's Brandeis saw his long-standing belief in judicial self-restraint in the review of legislative acts realized with the enactment of New Deal programs that included collective bargaining, minimum wages, unemployment insurance, regulation of securities and stocks, and restraints on holding companies.

See also *Abrams v. United States*; Clear and present danger test; Electronic surveillance; *Muller v. Oregon*; *Olmstead v. United States*; Progressivism; Supreme Court of the United States.

Brandenburg v. Ohio

COURT: U.S. Supreme Court

DATE: Decided June 9, 1969

SIGNIFICANCE: Climaxing a long line of cases about the limits of free expression, the Court ruled that government may not punish the advocacy of illegal actions except when the advocacy is aimed at imminent action and is likely to have such a result

Charles Brandenburg, a Ku Klux Klan leader, had addressed a rally of twelve hooded men on a farm near Cincinnati and declared that if the government continued "to suppress the white, Caucasian race, it's possible that there might have to be revengeance taken." Based on films of the rally, Brandenburg was convicted under the Ohio Criminal Syndicalism statute of 1919 for advocating unlawful or violent means in pursuit of political reform, and he was fined $1,000 and sentenced to imprisonment from one to ten years. Although the Court had protected the advocacy of abstract beliefs in *Yates v. United States* (1957), the precedent of *Whitney v. California* (1927) still allowed government to prosecute the advocacy of illegal acts when such advocacy tended to cause such acts.

At conference, the judges voted unanimously to reverse *Whitney*, to overturn Brandenburg's conviction, and to rule the Ohio law a violation of the First and Fourteenth Amendments. Chief Justice Earl Warren assigned Justice Abe Fortas to write the opinion for the Court, but after Fortas resigned from the Court in May, the Court issued its ruling as an unsigned, *per curiam* opinion. The Court declared that the constitutional guarantees of free speech and free press meant that government might not "forbid or proscribe advocacy of the use of force or of law violation except where such advocacy is directed to inciting or producing imminent lawless action and is likely to incite or produce such action."

Brandenburg v. Ohio did not make use of the exact words of the controversial "clear and present danger" test, but in referring to imminence and likelihood, the opinion seemed to accept Judge Learned Hand's modification of the basic idea. Justices Hugo Black and William Douglas wrote concurring opinions to explain that while they agreed with the outcome of the case, they took an absolutist view on freedom of expression and believed that the clear and present danger test had no place in the interpretation of the First Amendment.

Since 1969, the Court has pointed to *Brandenburg* as controlling precedent in regard to First Amendment protection for advocating those very evils against which the state may act. While it is impossible to know how the courts might interpret the *Brandenburg* standard in an emergency or wartime situation, the standard presents the state with a hurdle that makes it very difficult to prosecute most forms of advocating illegal actions.

See also *Abrams v. United States*; Clear and present danger test; *Dennis v. United States*; *Gitlow v. New York*; Hand, Learned; *Herndon v. Lowry*; Ku Klux Klan (KKK); *R.A.V. v. City of St. Paul*; Smith Act; Speech and press, freedom of; *Yates v. United States*.

Breach of the peace

DEFINITION: Behavior that might cause someone to respond in a violent manner even if the guilty party acted peacefully

SIGNIFICANCE: Breach of the peace laws have been used by police to deal with persons who have committed no crime but are still considered undesirable, such as vagrants

Breach of the peace laws are closely related to disorderly conduct and vagrancy statutes. They date to the 1300's in English common law and resulted from the social chaos of the times. Thousands of unemployed peasants roamed the countryside looking for work. To stabilize conditions, the king issued a law requiring every able-bodied citizen to work. Those who did not could be arrested and imprisoned. "Disorderly people" were declared vagrants and could be charged with "breach of peace" if they created a hazardous or physically offensive condition in the community.

In recent years the U.S. Supreme Court has challenged the very basis of these types of laws. In *Terminiello v. Chicago* (1949) the Court ruled that a speaker could not be prevented from making a controversial speech on grounds that the audience might become disruptive. In *Papachristou v. City of Jacksonville* (1972) the Supreme Court threw out Florida's vagrancy and breach of peace law because it was so loosely drawn that it failed to give a person of ordinary intelligence a fair definition of what conduct constituted these crimes.

See also Assembly and association, freedom of; Disorderly conduct; Homelessness; Public order offenses; Vagrancy laws; Victimless crimes.

Bribery

DEFINITION: The illegal act of offering money or favors to a public official (or the acceptance of such an offer by an official) in order to influence the official's actions

SIGNIFICANCE: Bribery has existed since the origins of civilization; it is generally discovered only by accident, and only the most flagrant cases are prosecuted

The crime of bribery usually goes unreported, because both parties—the person paying the bribe and the person accepting the payment—stand to benefit from keeping it secret. Therefore, there are no reliable statistics regarding the number of bribes offered each year or for the amount of money involved. Since neither the number of attempted bribes offered nor the number of successful bribes accepted can be counted, the success of antibribery laws can never be measured.

Bribes involving police, judges, and government officials are considered the worst offenses. For example, a judge could take money in return for finding a criminal not guilty, a citizen could offer a police officer money to forget about a speeding ticket, a multinational corporation could pay money to an official of a foreign government to get a contract, or a gambler could "fix" a sporting event by offering money to a participant to lose the game on purpose.

Bribery is condemned in the Bible, in ancient law codes, in Roman law, and in English law. Judges and public officials who accept bribes receive the most severe condemnation. The Constitution of the United States lists only two specific crimes terrible enough to lead to impeachment of a public official: treason and bribery. Since 1787, only two federal judges have been impeached for taking bribes, though sixteen others have resigned rather than face an impeachment trial.

Eighteenth and Nineteenth Centuries. Controlling bribery among elected officials has proven far more troublesome. Bribery scandals have afflicted every period of American history, beginning with the Yazoo Land Fraud of 1795. Land companies bought off the entire Georgia legislature to receive a favorable land grant. Other notorious scandals include the Crédit Mobilier affair exposed by the *New York Sun* in 1872. In this case lobbyists bribed more than a hundred U.S. congressmen to vote for railroad land grants. Only two representatives were censured for this incident, and both kept their seats, though the House mandated expulsion of any member convicted of taking bribes. The period after the Civil War, especially during the presidency of Ulysses S. Grant (1869-1877), is known as one of the most corrupt in American history. The Grant era included a scandal involving payments to one of the president's closest advisers by whiskey distillers evading taxes. It was also during this time that the Tweed ring was broken in New York City, again by a crusading newspaper, and William "Boss" Tweed was sent to prison for receiving millions of dollars in bribes through his Tammany Hall political organization.

Twentieth Century. The aftermath of World War I witnessed a period of major corruption in Washington, D.C. The Teapot Dome scandal was the worst incident, involving a cabinet secretary and several congressmen and senators in bribery and payoffs from the oil industry. Because of this and other scandals during his presidency, the brief tenure of Warren G. Harding (1921-1923) is regarded as one of the most corrupt in American history. During the administration of Richard M. Nixon (1969-1974), the public again became aware of the crime of bribery when the president was found to have authorized illegal payments to the Watergate burglars during the election of 1972. When the House of Representatives voted two years later to impeach the president, authorizing bribes was one of the key charges against him.

Concern about bribery increased in the aftermath of the Watergate affair, and the Federal Bureau of Investigation (FBI) investigated corruption in Congress. The investigation culminated in the Abscam indictments in 1979 as a dozen House members and one U.S. senator were accused of taking bribes offered by an undercover FBI agent. Congress expelled one member for his conduct, and all the others were defeated in subsequent elections.

There have been few attempts by state officials to uncover all bribe takers; in general, only outrageous cases have been prosecuted. After passage of the Racketeer Influenced and Corrupt Organizations Act (RICO) of 1970, the federal government increased its prosecution of state and local government officials found taking bribes. The law declared any "pattern" of bribery, meaning two or more acts, a federal offense. It covered sheriffs, police officers, traffic court employees, and higher-level government workers. Hundreds of local officials were prosecuted, and many were convicted, but bribery continued. Some public employees defended the custom as a method of supplementing their relatively low salaries.

Difficulties in Enforcement. The difficulty of enforcing anticorruption laws is illustrated by the Foreign Corrupt Practices Act of 1977. It forbids offering any money to a foreign official for the purpose of influencing a decision on contracts, a practice admitted to by hundreds of American corporations. It excludes, however, "grease payments," such as money to speed up shipments or obtain special permits to build new factories. These payments are considered necessary requirements for doing business and therefore legitimate. In practice, the loophole for "grease" is so large that only a few persons have been convicted of illegal behavior under the law.

All members of society are victimized by bribery since it increases citizen suspicion of government and makes people less trusting of the fairness of the system. Punishment offers little deterrence to the crime, since bribery so often evades detection. Shame appears to have worked best in the past to reduce bribery. Only when it is considered an act unworthy for humans to engage in has it been reduced.

—*Leslie V. Tischauser*

See also Anti-Racketeering Act; Blackmail and extortion; Malfeasance, misfeasance, and nonfeasance; Organized crime; Police corruption and misconduct; Political corruption; Watergate scandal; White-collar crime.

BIBLIOGRAPHY

Interesting works on bribery include W. Michael Reisman, *Folded Lies: Bribery, Crusades, and Reforms* (New York: Free Press, 1979); Joseph Borkin, *The Corrupt Judge* (New York: C. N. Potter, 1962); John J. McCloy, *The Great Oil Spill* (New York: Chelsea House, 1976); and Stanley I. Kutler, *The Wars of Watergate* (New York: Alfred A. Knopf, 1990).

Brown, John (May 9, 1800, Torrington, Conn.—Dec. 2, 1859, Charlestown, Va.)

IDENTIFICATION: Abolitionist

SIGNIFICANCE: Brown's efforts to incite a slave rebellion encouraged the South to withdraw from the Union prior to the Civil War and encouraged Northerners to emancipate slaves during the war

BRIBERY CONVICTIONS IN U.S. DISTRICT COURTS

Bar graph showing Convictions by year: 1986: 200; 1987: 182; 1988: 184; 1989: 238; 1990: 220; 1991: 242; 1992: 302.

Source: U.S. Department of Justice, Bureau of Justice Statistics, *Sourcebook of Criminal Justice Statistics—1993*. Washington, D.C.: U.S. Government Printing Office, 1994.

John Brown spent the first fifty-five years of his life in obscurity and near-poverty. He experienced numerous business failures and lived a nomadic life while providing for his family of twenty children. Since early childhood, Brown had an unusually strong concern for the slaves. This concern, along with Brown's violent personality, ultimately transformed him into one of the most important figures of his era.

In 1854, Congress passed the Kansas-Nebraska Act, which allowed the settlers of Kansas themselves to decide whether slavery should enter the territory. Subsequently, thousands of settlers rushed to Kansas to gain political control of the territory. Among these settlers were John Brown and his family. Fighting soon erupted among the free-state and slave-state settlers. Brown and his sons killed five proslavery settlers who lived along the banks of Pottawatomie Creek.

Brown's actions made him a hero to some abolitionists. Though most abolitionists favored a peaceful means of emancipation, some were increasingly frustrated with their failure to free the slaves through nonviolent means. Brown found a ready audience among these people. He toured the North in 1857-1858, raising money for an ill-defined effort to destroy slavery.

Brown received significant financial assistance from a group of abolitionists known as the Secret Six: Samuel Gridley Howe, Thomas Wentworth Higginson, Franklin B. Sanborn, Theodore Parker, Gerrit Smith, and George Luther Stearns. To the Secret Six, Brown revealed his ultimate purpose: to end slavery by inciting a massive slave rebellion in the South. Brown planned to train a small band of men to attack the federal arsenal at Harpers Ferry, Virginia (now West Virginia). Seizing weapons stored there, Brown's men would march south, arming slaves and stirring rebellion.

Brown launched his raid on October 16, 1859. He and his twenty-one followers captured and held the Harpers Ferry arsenal for thirty-six hours before federal troops regained control and arrested Brown and six of his followers. Seventeen people were killed in the raid, including ten of Brown's men.

Brown's raid provoked intense sectional animosities. Most white Southerners strongly condemned the raid. They had long maintained that the ultimate goal of the abolitionists was to stir up a slave rebellion. Brown's raid strengthened this belief and prompted Southerners to see all opponents of slavery as potential John Browns. When a moderate opponent of slavery, Abraham Lincoln, was elected president one year after Brown's raid, there was sufficient alarm in the South that seven states withdrew from the Union.

The overwhelming majority of Northerners initially condemned Brown's violent actions. Yet as Virginia officials rushed Brown to his execution with undue haste and as Brown faced his impending martyrdom with courage, many Northerners came to admire him. While continuing to criticize his methods, they praised Brown's moral outrage concerning slavery. Thus, shortly before the start of the Civil War, Northerners embraced as a hero someone who proposed using violence to end slavery.

See also Abolitionist movement; Civil War; Douglass, Frederick; Free Soil Party; Fugitive Slave Laws; Garrison, William Lloyd; Kansas-Nebraska Act.

Brown v. Board of Education

COURT: U.S. Supreme Court

DATE: Decided May 17, 1954

SIGNIFICANCE: This landmark case struck down the "separate but equal" doctrine upheld by the U.S. Supreme Court in *Plessy v. Ferguson* (1896) and subsequent court decisions, ending legal racial segregation in public schools

Brown et al. v. Board of Education of Topeka et al., usually referred to as *Brown v. Board of Education*, was but one case dealing with segregation in public schools that came before the Supreme Court in 1954. Similar suits were filed in South Carolina (*Briggs v. Eliot*), Virginia (*Davis v. County School Board*), and Delaware (*Gebbart v. Belton*). The cases all addressed the same basic problem: the exclusion of black children from all-white schools by state laws maintaining racial segregation.

Litigants and the District Court Ruling. The plaintiffs in the Kansas case were elementary schoolchildren in Topeka. The case was initiated in 1951, after the daughter of a black clergyman was denied admission to an all-white public school. As a class action suit, it went before the U.S. District Court for the District of Kansas. Although the three-judge court found that public school segregation had a "detrimental effect upon the colored children," contributing to "a sense of inferiority," it denied them relief, upholding the separate but equal doctrine. The case then went to the U.S. Supreme Court, which reversed the lower court's decision unanimously.

The Supreme Court's Argument. In writing the Court's decision, Chief Justice Earl Warren stated that "in the field of public education the doctrine of 'separate but equal' has no place" because segregated schools are "inherently unequal." The decision held that the plaintiffs were in fact "deprived of the equal protection of the laws guaranteed by the Fourteenth Amendment."

A second *Brown* opinion, generally known as *Brown II*, was issued a year later, on May 31, 1955. It remanded impending desegregation cases to lower federal courts, ordering them to issue equitable decrees in accordance with "varied local school problems." Although this decision directed the district courts and school boards to desegregate public schools "with all deliberate speed," it opened the door to judicial and political evasion at the local level. Thus, despite the fact that in *Cooper v. Aaron* (1958) the Court unequivocally reaffirmed the 1954 decision, strong resistance to both *de jure* and *de facto* desegregation delayed the implementation of the Supreme Court's ruling for many years.

***Brown* and the Civil Rights Movement**. While the *Brown* decision theoretically ended *de jure* (by law) segregation in public education, it did not bring an immediate end to the segregation of schools or any other public facilities. More than a decade of turmoil followed. Integration was strategically

NAACP lawyers George E. C. Hayes, Thurgood Marshall, and James M. Nabrit after their victory in Brown v. Board of Education. (AP/Wide World Photos)

delayed or phased in, notably in big urban centers with large black populations.

In the South, change was particularly painful and slow, in both urban and rural areas. According to the U.S. Commission on Civil Rights, in 1963, nine years after the *Brown* ruling, less than half of 1 percent of southern black students were attending integrated schools. It would take marches, boycotts, sit-ins, and more aggressive racial agitation by blacks and sympathetic whites, plus growing media coverage and strong public pressure, to force change.

The Civil Rights movement took a dramatic turn in 1956, in Montgomery, Alabama, when Rosa Parks, a black woman, refused to surrender her bus seat and move to a section reserved for blacks. Her action began a boycott that led to other demonstrations throughout the South under the leadership of Martin Luther King, Jr. The movement culminated in the Civil Rights Act of 1964, the Voting Rights Act of 1965, and the Fair Housing Act of 1968, which, together, and in conjunction with antisegregation suits initiated by the Justice Department, rang the death knell of *de facto* segregation (segregation "in fact" rather than by law).

The fact remains, however, that the *Brown* decision was the most important legal precedent in the Civil Rights movement. It was also inevitable. In earlier cases, the Supreme Court, even while upholding the "separate but equal" doctrine, had begun to undermine it. As early as 1938, in *Missouri ex rel. Gaines v. Canada*, the Court rejected the practice of funding law schooling for blacks outside a state in lieu of providing equal facilities within the state. In 1950, in *Sweatt v. Painter*, the Court further determined that a separate public law school for blacks (in Texas) violated the equal protection clause of the Fourteenth Amendment because the school was not equal to the state's white law school in prestige or quality of faculty and facilities. Thereafter, by 1952, the Court had begun to review cases dealing with public schools, not only the professional schools.

Brown's **Legal Legacy**. *Brown v. Board of Education* set a legal precedent that would be used to overturn laws upholding segregation, not only in public schools but also in other public facilities. The argument that separate facilities are "inherently unequal" is the cornerstone of much civil rights legislation that has effectively ended apartheid in the United States. New ground would be broken two decades later, in 1976, when the Supreme Court, in *Runyon v. McCrary*, ruled that even private, nonsectarian schools violated federal civil rights laws if they denied admission to students because they were black. Although some problems implementing these important rulings remain, the landmark decision in *Brown* made it clear that segregation would no longer be tolerated in a democratic society.

—*John W. Fiero*

See also *Bolling v. Sharpe*; Busing; Civil rights; Civil Rights movement; *Cooper v. Aaron*; Equal protection of the law; Equality of opportunity; Little Rock school integration crisis; National Association for the Advancement of Colored People Legal Defense and Educational Fund; *Plessy v. Fer-*

guson; Racial and ethnic discrimination; *Runyon v. McCrary*; Segregation, *de facto* and *de jure*; *Sweatt v. Painter*; Warren, Earl.

BIBLIOGRAPHY

The role of the U.S. Supreme Court in school desegregation and the general impact of school integration are extensively covered in several studies, including Leon Jones, *From Brown to Boston: Desegregation in Education, 1954-1974* (Metuchen, N.J.: Scarecrow Press, 1979); Christine H. Rossell and Willis D. Hawley, eds., *The Consequences of School Desegregation* (Philadelphia: Temple University Press, 1983); Derrick Bell, ed., *Shades of Brown: New Perspectives on School Desegregation* (New York: Teachers College Press, 1980); Larry W. Hughes, William M. Gordon, and Larry W. Hillman, *Desegregating American Schools* (New York: Longman, 1980); and Jennifer L. Hochschild, *The New American Dilemma: Liberal Democracy and School Desegregation* (New Haven, Conn.: Yale University Press, 1984).

Brown v. Mississippi

COURT: U.S. Supreme Court

DATE: Decided February 17, 1936

SIGNIFICANCE: This was one of the first cases in which the U.S. Supreme Court held that a state's criminal process had deprived the defendant of due process of law under the Fourteenth Amendment; it paved the way for later cases requiring states to exclude coerced confessions and to provide humane and fair procedures for defendants

Brown and his two codefendants were tried and convicted of murder in Mississippi in 1934. Confessions had been obtained from them by deputy sheriffs and jailers by means of torture. They were repeatedly hanged until nearly dead and then flogged unmercifully with a leather strap with buckles on it. After initially denying their guilt they confessed, adjusting or changing their statements until these had been provided in the exact form demanded by the deputies. After being allowed to recuperate for a day, they were put through the farce of repeating these confessions to witnesses. On the basis of the confessions alone, the defendants were convicted of murder and condemned to death. Although the deputies and others who had participated in the whippings freely admitted to the fact on the witness stand, the trial judge and later the Mississippi Supreme Court refused to reverse the convictions. The defendants appealed to the U.S. Supreme Court.

Under the Fourteenth Amendment, states are forbidden to "deprive any person of life, liberty, or property without due process of law." At that time this clause had been interpreted to mean that states had to provide a fundamentally fair procedure in criminal cases. Although they could establish their own court policies, the policies could not "offend some principle of liberty and justice so rooted in the traditions of conscience of our people as to be ranked as fundamental." Under this rule the Supreme Court reversed Brown's conviction. Chief Justice Charles Evans Hughes, writing for a unanimous Court, held that Mississippi could not substitute the rack and torture chamber for the witness stand. The defendants had been deprived of a fundamental aspect of due process of law. Hughes gave short shrift to Mississippi's argument that Brown's counsel had made a technical procedural error in not asking more clearly to have the confessions suppressed: "The duty of maintaining constitutional rights of a person on trial for his life rises above mere rules of procedure."

Brown v. Mississippi was the first case in which the Supreme Court held that a coerced confession was inadmissible in a state criminal trial. It mirrored *Weeks v. United States* (1914), in which the same rule had been applied to federal trials. In the three decades that followed *Brown*, the rule was broadened to include more and more forms of coercion. This line of cases culminated in 1966 when, in *Miranda v. Arizona*, the Court decided that no confession obtained once a defendant is in custody is admissible unless the defendant has been fully informed of his constitutional rights.

See also *Argersinger v. Hamlin*; Criminal procedure; Due process of law; Hughes, Charles Evans; *Malloy v. Hogan*; *Miranda v. Arizona*; *Weeks v. United States*.

Bryan, William Jennings (Mar. 19, 1860, Salem, Ill.— July 26, 1925, Dayton, Tenn.)

IDENTIFICATION: Social justice advocate and political figure

SIGNIFICANCE: Bryan was an editor, politician, and populist leader who ran for president three times and was secretary of state, 1913-1915

Reared in Illinois, William Jennings Bryan attended Illinois College and received a law degree from Union College of Law in Chicago (1883). He moved to Nebraska, where he was elected to Congress. At the Chicago Democratic Convention of 1896, he ensured his nomination for president with his famous "cross of gold" speech. A popular spokesman for the free silver movement, which was fighting for a monetary policy that would use both silver and gold instead of gold alone as its standard, Bryan declared, "You shall not crucify mankind upon a cross of gold." Losing the election, he became the spokesman for western and southern interests who wanted the addition of cheap money (silver) to the currency. After losing the presidential elections of 1900 and 1908, he nominated Woodrow Wilson in 1912 and as a result was appointed secretary of state. During his term of office he expanded U.S. control in the Caribbean and negotiated the Bryan-Chamorro Treaty (1914). As a peace advocate he obtained the agreement of thirty nations to arbitrate international disputes. Fearing that Wilson's pro-English policies would lead to war, he resigned in 1915.

The end of his political career opened the way for his religious activities. These included a significant role in the passage of the Eighteenth Amendment outlawing alcoholic beverages after June, 1920, and serving with the prosecution in the famous Scopes trial. Bryan, called the Great Commoner, expressed the feelings of many rural people of his time as he advocated tariff reform, control of trusts, direct elections, free silver, anti-imperialism, prohibition, and fundamentalism.

See also Populism; Scopes "monkey" trial.

Buck v. Bell

COURT: U.S. Supreme Court

DATE: Decided May 2, 1927

SIGNIFICANCE: This case established the right of a state to perform sexual sterilization on any person deemed to be mentally defective

On June 17, 1924, the General Assembly of Virginia passed into law a sterilization bill which authorized state governments to impose "eugenical sterilization" on mental defectives. At the time, the terms "mental defective" and "feebleminded" were broad designations which incorporated any person judged to be "so weak mentally that he or she is unable to maintain himself or herself in the ordinary community at large." Many people, especially women, were incarcerated for being "morally deficient."

The driving force behind this law was the superintendent of the Virginia State Colony for Epileptics and Feebleminded, Albert S. Priddy. Soon after the bill was signed into law, the colony's board voted that Carrie Buck undergo sexual sterilization for the promotion of her own welfare and that of society. It also instructed Aubrey Strode, the attorney for the colony, to take to court a test case to ensure the constitutionality of this action. Carrie Buck's case was selected.

Carrie Buck, the daughter of Emma and Frank Buck, had been taken as a ward by the Dobbs family at an early age because of her mother's alleged loose ways. Carrie attended school in Charlottesville for five years, until the Dobbses withdrew her to help with housework, maintaining good academic progress. In 1923, the Dobbs family petitioned the court to commit Carrie to the colony. They cited symptoms of feeblemindedness and epilepsy that made controlling her impossible. They did not mention the fact that Carrie had accused their nephew of raping her and that she was now pregnant. The court acquiesced, and on June 4, 1924, Carrie entered the colony. The Dobbses kept her baby.

Carrie was considered an ideal test case, since her mother and daughter were both alleged to be feebleminded, supporting statements of genetically based mental deficiency. The case went to the Circuit Court of Amherst County on November 18, 1924, as *Buck v. Priddy*. That the Virginia State Colony paid the fees for Carrie's defense as well as her prosecution was not called into question. The court decided in favor of the state in February, 1925. In June, 1925, the case, now *Buck v. Bell* (Priddy had died and the case was renamed for his successor) was taken to the Virginia Court of Appeals, which affirmed the decision and so enabled it to proceed to the U.S. Supreme Court in September, 1926. Justice Oliver Wendell Holmes delivered the opinion of the Court on May 2, 1927, upholding the lower court decisions and concluding that "three generations of imbeciles are enough." The only dissenting judge was Justice Pierce Butler.

On October 19, 1927, Carrie Buck was sterilized by Bell in the colony's infirmary. The legal precedent set the stage for more than four thousand sterilizations at the colony alone, until the practice was discontinued in 1972. More than fifty thousand people were sterilized nationwide under *Buck v. Bell*, and the law stands today.

In 1980, the American Civil Liberties Union brought a lawsuit on behalf of 8,300 people sterilized in institutions in the state of Virginia. In 1985, a settlement was approved which provided for psychological counseling for the individuals.

See also Sterilization and American law.

Buckley v. Valeo

COURT: U.S. Supreme Court
DATE: Decided January 30, 1976
SIGNIFICANCE: This decision upheld the constitutionality of publicly financed presidential election campaigns while striking down limitations on the amount of money that candidates may spend in their own behalf

Growing concern over the political influence wielded by large contributors and the potential for corruption that such activities represented led Congress to pass the Federal Election Campaign Act (FECA) in 1971 and to strengthen its provisions substantially in the wake of the Watergate scandal in 1974. The major provisions of the act as amended included the establishment of the Federal Elections Commission (FEC), whose members would be appointed by Congress; restrictions on the amount that individuals or political action committees might contribute to campaigns; restrictions on the amount that candidates or their organizations might spend on campaigns; and provision of public financing of presidential campaigns.

FECA sought to bring about significant changes in the ways political campaigns were financed, and many opposed the act. A challenge to the act was mounted by New York's Republican senator James Buckley. The U.S. Supreme Court took the case as an opportunity to review FECA's constitutionality.

The Court's decision in the case was given in a long and complicated *per curiam* opinion (one not signed by individual justices). Different majorities of justices decided different points of controversy that the law had raised. Ultimately, the decision upheld some parts of the act while invalidating others. The decision had four major points. First, the appointment of the members of the FEC by Congress was held to be an unconstitutional violation of the appointments clause. (This part of the act was subsequently rewritten to provide for appointment by the president.) Second, restrictions on campaign contributions were upheld as a valid exercise of Congress' responsibility to provide for the general welfare. Third, restrictions on expenditures by candidates themselves were struck down as violating their right of free expression. In addition, it was noted that candidates spending their own money were less susceptible to corruption than those dependent on contributions from others. Finally, the decision upheld the provision of public financing of presidential campaigns.

The decision in the *Buckley* case left standing some of the most significant campaign-reform legislation in American history. Nevertheless, the scope of FECA was restricted in important ways. The invalidating of limits on campaign expenditures allowed an advantage to wealthy candidates. The court also found that indirect expenditures in behalf of candidates were not limited by the act. This left an important loophole through which increasing numbers of political action committees could operate.

See also Political campaign law; Political corruption; Speech and press, freedom of; Spoils system and patronage; Watergate scandal.

Burden of proof

DEFINITION: The duty or responsibility of proving a disputed charge or allegation in a court of law
SIGNIFICANCE: The prosecution's burden of proving guilt "beyond a reasonable doubt" in criminal cases is considered a crucial part of the constitutional right to due process of law

Few ideas are more central to litigation—and therefore more disputed—than that of the "burden of proof." Stated in simple terms, the issue concerns who (the plaintiff or the defendant) must bring forward evidence on a particular issue at a trial, as well as the quantity or quality of the evidence that must be brought forward. The answers to these questions are affected by whether the trial is a civil or a criminal one and by the definition of the "elements" of the claim or case.

The general rule is that in a criminal case, the government (the prosecution) must prove all elements of the offense "beyond a reasonable doubt." This rule has been upheld by the Supreme Court, most notably in *In re Winship* (1970). The rule in civil cases is less straightforward. The plaintiff has the burden of proving all material elements of his or her claim. In the majority of cases the required standard of proof is that of "preponderance of the evidence"—in other words, that it is "more likely than not" that the truth of the matter is as told by the plaintiff. In some cases, however, a higher burden is imposed on the plaintiff, usually phrased in some combination of the words "clear," "convincing," and "unequivocal," as in "clear and convincing evidence."

Even if the plaintiff satisfies the burden of proof, a defendant may, in a civil case, avoid liability by satisfying what is called an "affirmative defense." For example, the law may say that a person who goes onto another person's land without invitation is a trespasser who may be liable in damages to the owner of the land, but it may add that if the trespasser openly occupies the land for twenty-one years, then ownership of the land shall pass to the trespasser. In this situation, even though a plaintiff successfully shows ownership of land and its uninvited occupation by the defendant, the defendant may still win if he or she can prove under one of the standards above that he or she has openly occupied the land for the prescribed period of time. One of the most difficult questions in law is determining what constitutes an "affirmative defense" (in which the burden of proof is on the defendant), and what is simply a regular defense (under which the burden remains with the plaintiff).

Whether the standard for the burden of proof is expressed in terms of the "preponderance of the evidence" or a higher burden, and whether a given element of a case must be proved by the plaintiff or the defendant, is related to society's conception of fairness—its interest in distributing the rights at issue. One question, for example, would be which party society believes to have the easier access to the necessary information or evidence with which to meet the burden.

See also Civil procedure; Criminal procedure; Presumption of innocence; Reasonable doubt; Standards of proof.

Bureaus, U.S. *See name of bureau*

Burger, Warren (Sept. 17, 1907, St. Paul, Minn.—June 25, 1995, Washington, D.C.)

IDENTIFICATION: Chief justice of the United States

SIGNIFICANCE: Chief justice from 1969 to 1986, Burger was only partially successful in his efforts to move the Court in a more conservative direction

From a family of modest means, Warren Earl Burger sold insurance while attending evening classes at the St. Paul College of Law. He taught and practiced law in Minnesota from 1931 until 1953 and then served for three years as attorney general in charge of the U.S. Justice Department's Civil Division. In 1956 he was appointed to the U.S. Court of Appeals for the District of Columbia; on the bench he developed a reputation as a judge with conservative views, especially in matters of criminal justice. President Richard Nixon was impressed with his defense of a "strict constructionist" approach to the Constitution, and in 1969 Burger was appointed and easily confirmed as the fifteenth chief justice. Under his leadership, the Supreme Court's decisions were somewhat more conservative than under his predecessor Earl Warren, but the Burger Court also established liberal precedents in several controversial areas, including abortion, affirmative action, and busing as a means of desegregation. For this reason, some observers have described those years as "the revolution that wasn't." Burger was outspoken in advocating administrative reform of the judicial system.

See also *Lemon v. Kurtzman*; *Miller v. California*; Nixon, Richard M.; *Reed v. Reed*; *Roe v. Wade*; *Swann v. Charlotte-Mecklenburg Board of Education*; Watergate scandal.

Warren Burger, chief justice from 1969 to 1986. (Supreme Court Historical Society)

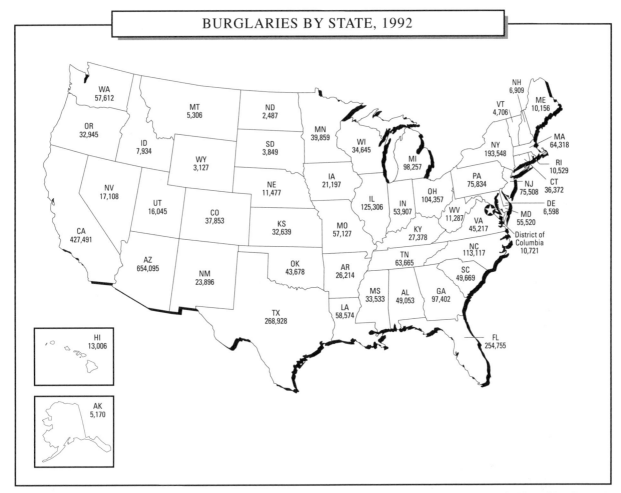

BURGLARIES BY STATE, 1992

WA 57,612
OR 32,945
MT 5,306
ND 2,487
MN 39,859
ID 7,934
SD 3,849
WI 34,645
WY 3,127
NE 11,477
IA 21,197
MI 98,257
NV 17,108
UT 16,045
CO 37,853
KS 32,639
MO 57,127
IL 125,306
IN 53,907
OH 104,357
CA 427,491
AZ 654,095
NM 23,896
OK 43,678
AR 26,214
KY 27,378
WV 11,287
VA 45,217
TN 63,665
NC 113,117
TX 268,928
LA 58,574
MS 33,533
AL 49,053
GA 97,402
SC 49,669
FL 254,755
NH 6,909
VT 4,706
ME 10,156
NY 193,548
MA 64,318
RI 10,529
PA 75,834
NJ 75,508
CT 36,372
DE 6,598
MD 55,520
District of Columbia 10,721
HI 13,006
AK 5,170

Source: Data are from U.S. Department of Justice, Federal Bureau of Investigation, *Crime in the United States, 1992* (Uniform Crime Reports). Washington, D.C.: U.S. Government Printing Office, 1993.

Note: The five states with the highest burglary rates, as opposed to total numbers of burglaries, were, in descending order, Florida, North Carolina, Texas, New Mexico, and Georgia.

Burglary

DEFINITION: Crime involving unlawful entry of a building for the purpose of committing a felony or theft

SIGNIFICANCE: Listed among the eight index crimes tabulated in the federal government's Uniform Crime Reports, burglary is considered one of the most serious nonviolent crimes, especially when it takes the form of residential burglary

Burglary is one of the most common property offenses in the United States. In 1992, for example, law enforcement authorities received 2,979,884 reports of burglaries, which are included in the Uniform Crime Reports (UCR). For that same year, the National Crime Victimization Survey (NCVS), which measures crimes based on a survey of more than 100,000 residents of the United States, estimated that the actual number of burglaries was 5.8 million. The NCVS figure is nearly double that of the UCR because its survey measures criminal

victimizations, regardless of whether they are reported to the police. Over a two-decade period, the NCVS found that about half of all burglaries are never reported to police. According to Federal Bureau of Investigation (FBI) figures for 1992, burglary victims suffered losses of nearly $4 billion—at an average of $1,215 in residential burglaries and $1,400 in nonresidential burglaries.

The essence of burglary is unlawful entry into a structure. It may be by force—such as by breaking a window—or it may be unforced—such as by climbing through an open window. Nearly half of all burglaries do not involve forcible entry. In general, residential burglaries are more likely to occur during the day, while most nonresidential burglaries occur at night. According to the UCR, about two-thirds of all burglaries are of residences and the rest are of nonresidential structures, such as stores, offices, and warehouses. Although residential burglary is not in itself a violent crime, its victims often suffer substantial psychological trauma and a distinct loss of their sense of personal security—particularly when their homes are violated in this way.

The Criminals. Of all burglaries reported to the police, only 13 percent—fewer than one in seven—result in arrests. In court, burglaries are usually filed as felonies (crimes that can result in prison sentences of at least a year). About two-fifths of all burglary arrests lead to felony convictions. Just over half of convicted burglars are sentenced to state prisons; the rest are about evenly divided among those sentenced to local jails (for an average of nine months) and those placed on probation (a period of supervision in the community). Convicted burglars placed in state prisons serve an average of twenty-two months behind bars, with a median term of about fifteen months.

Burglars, like robbers, tend to have exceptionally high recidivism rates. Extensive national studies show that 70 percent of burglars released from prison are rearrested for felonies or serious misdemeanors within three years and that half are reincarcerated. Many burglars tend to specialize in this crime, with some perpetrating hundreds of burglaries each year. Others commit an assortment of crimes including drug offenses, robberies, and assaults. For example, one-fifth of burglars released from state prisons are rearrested for violent crimes within three years.

The Victims. Burglary victimization follows the patterns that characterize many other crimes. Blacks are about 50 percent more likely than whites to be burglarized; Hispanics are somewhat more likely to be victimized than non-Hispanics; lower-income families are more likely to be burglarized than upper-income families; and central city residents are more likely than suburbanites and rural residents to be burglarized. These differences among communities, however, are not as great as those associated with many violent crimes. For exam-

Although a variety of tools such as this lock-picking "gun" are available, most burglars simply break a window or force open a door. (McCrea Adams)

ple, although central city residents are four times more likely than rural residents to be robbed, they are only about half as likely to be burglarized.

One of the most controversial issues surrounding the crime of burglary is what steps homeowners may take to protect their property from burglars. Although only a small number of states permit the use of deadly force to protect personal property generally, most states authorize the use of deadly force against burglars in at least some circumstances—particularly in cases of forcible entry. It is significant, however, that in more than four-fifths of residential burglaries, the residents are not home when the crimes occur so that contact between burglars and their victims is infrequent.

Declining Burglary Rates. Like some other property offenses, the rate of burglaries dropped considerably after the 1970's. During the two decades after the National Crime Victimization Survey began in 1973, burglary rates decreased to nearly half the 1973 rate throughout the United States. Most of this drop occurred after 1980, with a 42 percent drop between 1980 and 1992. The Uniform Crime Reports of crimes reported to the police indicate a somewhat smaller drop, of 31 percent, during this same period.   —*Joseph M. Bessette*

See also Crime; Crime Index; Criminal justice system; Criminal law; Felony; National Crime Victimization Survey; Neighborhood watch programs; Robbery; Self-defense; Theft; Uniform Crime Reports (UCR).

BIBLIOGRAPHY

Overviews of burglary include John M. MacDonald, C. Donald Brannan, and Robert E. Nicoletti, *Burglary and Theft* (Springfield, Ill.: Charles C Thomas, 1980); Kristen M. Williams and Judith Lucianovic, *Robbery and Burglary: A Study of the Characteristics of the Persons Arrested and the Handling of Their Cases in Court* (Washington, D.C.: Institute for Law and Social Research, 1979); and Paul F. Cromwell, *Breaking and Entering: An Ethnographic Analysis of Burglary* (Newbury Park, Calif.: Sage Publications, 1991). Burglary statistics are summarized in the FBI's annual *Crime in the United States* (Washington, D.C.: U.S. Government Printing Office) and the Bureau of Justice Statistics' *Report to the Nation on Crime and Justice* (2d ed. Washington, D.C.: U.S. Government Printing Office, 1988). Other relevant bureau publications include Jacob Perez, *Patterns of Robbery and Burglary in Nine States, 1984-88* (Washington, D.C.: U.S. Department of Justice, 1992).

Bush, George (b. June 12, 1924, Milton, Mass.)

IDENTIFICATION: President of the United States, 1989-1993

SIGNIFICANCE: As president, Bush guided the Persian Gulf War and oversaw the end of the Cold War

As forty-first president of the United States, George Bush signed into law the Americans with Disabilities Act of 1990, the Clean Air Act of 1990, and the Civil Rights Act of 1991. Bush's popularity soared during the 1991 Persian Gulf War, but an economic recession led to his defeat by Bill Clinton in the 1992 election. In legal matters, Bush nominated David H.

President George Bush signed into law the Americans with Disabilities Act as well as a number of antidrug bills. (Library of Congress)

Souter and Clarence Thomas to the U.S. Supreme Court, and both were confirmed. In 1989, Bush banned the importation of semiautomatic assault rifles and signed into law a bill that provided drug-fighting assistance to several Latin American countries (the International Narcotics Control Act, or the Andean initiative) and a bill that required schools to implement drug abuse prevention programs (the Drug-Free Schools and Communities Act). The Crime Control Act of 1990 included increased funding for local law enforcement, and it strengthened federal law enforcement agencies. In 1992, Congress passed a limited Weed and Seed program to "weed" drug dealers and other criminals out of inner cities and to "seed" the areas with social programs.

See also Americans with Disabilities Act (ADA); Civil Rights Act of 1991; Drug use and sale, illegal; Iran-Contra scandal; Reagan, Ronald; *Webster v. Reproductive Health Services*.

Busing

DEFINITION: The transportation of elementary and secondary students to educational facilities

SIGNIFICANCE: Busing as a tool for desegregating public schools has been controversial, and both Congress and the Supreme Court have dealt with the issue

School desegregation has been the most controversial American educational issue of the twentieth century. Busing, one of the more feasible strategies for achieving school desegregation, generated tremendous controversy as desegregation plans were implemented during the late 1960's, 1970's, and 1980's. Consequently, school desegregation and busing have become inextricably linked in the minds of many people. Busing actually predates school desegregation by many decades, and it was originally simply a means of transporting students in rural areas to schools that were better-equipped and staffed than traditional one-room country schools. In rural areas of the South, however, busing simultaneously served as a means of facilitating school segregation.

Busing to Facilitate Segregation. Many school districts in the South encompass entire rural counties, so transportation to school must be provided to students. Busing proved to be the most feasible means to transport large numbers of students. Until the Supreme Court's *Brown v. Board of Education* decision in 1954, segregated schools were legal in the South. Typically, segregation meant busing black and white children to different schools regardless of what school was closest to a child's house. Black children could be bused many miles even if a white school was right next door. Similar circumstances would apply for the white child if the nearest school was a black one.

The 1954 *Brown* decision was supposed to bring an end to *de jure* ("by law") segregation, the practice of state-imposed segregation. A subsequent decision (*Brown II*) in 1955 addressed the issue of remediation and ordered that the elimination of segregated dual school systems proceed "with all deliberate speed." Yet thirteen years passed before the Supreme Court became disillusioned with the delay tactics and obstructions employed by many southern school districts and began enforcement of its desegregation decree. During that time, an entire generation of schoolchildren, both black and white, was subjected to the continuation of busing that facilitated segregation.

Busing to Facilitate Integration. Busing became an effective strategy for transporting students reassigned under desegregation plans. In *Swann v. Charlotte-Mecklenburg Board of Education* (1971), the Supreme Court established that busing was an acceptable strategy for desegregating school systems. In upholding the use of busing, the Supreme Court was aware that it might prove to be administratively awkward for school districts, burdensome, bizarre and that it might impose a degree of hardship on some districts. While busing was sanctioned in the *Swann* decision, it was done so only in regard to *de jure* segregation (segregation enacted by law). In *Keyes v. Denver School District No. 1* (1973), busing was ordered for the first time outside the South. Also in this case, the Supreme Court ruled on the issue of *de facto* segregation (segregation "in fact," generally resulting from discriminatory residential patterns) for the first time. In evaluating the Denver school system, the Court concluded that when segregative intent exists in a substantial portion of the school system, then a systemwide remedy to assure nondiscrimination is acceptable. A

Busing was so controversial when it began in Boston in 1974 that buses were stoned by angry whites and massive police escorts were required. (AP/Wide World Photos)

systemwide remedy necessitates the reassignment of significant numbers of students, which typically requires some degree of busing. In a number of desegregation cases, the federal courts used busing when forced to develop their own desegregation plans, especially when recalcitrant school districts refused to restructure long-standing dual systems of education.

A number of school districts in the South developed desegregation plans that were premised on voluntary integration strategies, such as freedom-of-choice plans, voluntary transfer plans, and magnet schools. The Fifth Circuit Court, in *United States v. Jefferson County Board of Education* (1966), argued that the only desegregation plans that would be acceptable to the federal courts would be those that work—those that are practical and that actually accomplish the goal of desegregation.

In *Green v. County School Board of New Kent County* (1968), the Supreme Court rejected the freedom-of-choice plan implemented by the New Kent County school board. The Court concluded that freedom-of-choice plans did not demonstrate significant levels of desegregation and did not remove the racial identification attached to specific schools. While freedom of choice was rejected as the primary strategy in a desegregation plan, however, it was not precluded from being used as a supplemental component in a more comprehensive desegregation plan.

The federal courts came to a similar conclusion regarding voluntary transfer plans. White parents saw no benefit in having their children attend a segregated black school that was perceived to be educationally inferior. On the other hand, many African American parents did not see the value in having their children attend segregated white schools where they were unwelcome. They were hesitant to expose their children to the physical threat posed by some segregated white schools.

Magnet schools have unquestionably been the most successful of the voluntary desegregation plans. Magnet schools have grown tremendously since their inception in 1972. Generally, these are racially integrated public schools that have innovative programs and activities that attract students from throughout a school district.

Freedom-of-choice, voluntary transfer, and magnet programs all required some degree of busing if they were to be properly executed. In some instances voluntary desegregation plans involved a greater degree of busing than did the mandatory pupil reassignment plans initiated by the federal courts. Yet parents had little difficulty in accepting the notion of a voluntary desegregation plan. Voluntary plans permit parents and children who do not wish to participate in the desegregation effort to remain outside the process while remaining within the public schools. Many of the voluntary desegregation plans, however, proved to be unacceptable to the courts.

Resistance to Busing. Busing to achieve integration met with considerable opposition at the local, state, and federal levels. Although busing was merely a strategy to facilitate meaningful integration, it eventually became symbolic of all that some people found distasteful about the desegregation process. Opponents of desegregation characterized it as "forced busing." The issue of forced busing, for many, was associated with the reluctance of white parents to send their children to what had previously been inferior all-black schools. Actually, considerably more minority students (African American and Hispanic) than white students were bused for desegregation purposes. Over the decades of the 1960's, 1970's, and early 1980's, white parents took to the streets in their opposition to forced busing. The problem was exacerbated when some political leaders—instead of seeking to mollify and encourage the desegregation process—took advantage of the controversy for political gain.

During the time of the *Keyes* decision, when the use of busing was being established as a remedy in *de facto* segregation cases, there was substantial political force growing in opposition to busing. According to Derrick A. Bell, Jr., in *Race, Racism, and American Law* (1980), Richard M. Nixon used an antidesegregation plank in his presidential campaign in 1968 to help defeat the Democratic presidential candidate, Hubert H. Humphrey. His opposition to forced busing assumed an even greater role in his reelection campaign for 1972.

Although the legitimacy of busing was upheld in the *Keyes* decision, the parameters for its use were questioned the following year in *Milliken v. Bradley* (1974). The Supreme Court failed to support metropolitan busing in Michigan that would have involved the city of Detroit and fifty-three surrounding suburban school districts. Detroit, at the time, was more than 63 percent African American, while the neighboring suburban districts were almost exclusively white. The Supreme Court reasoned that the plaintiffs did not demonstrate constitutional violations on the part of the suburban communities. The plaintiffs' request to include the suburban school districts in the desegregation effort was denied.

During this same period, Congress was reevaluating busing and its proper place in school desegregation. Congress attempted to pass legislation that would have either eliminated or limited the use of busing. It failed to pass antibusing legislation designed to reduce federal jurisdiction. It succeeded, however, in passing legislation that placed restrictions on the use of busing for desegregation beyond the next-nearest school. This permitted many students to remain at their neighborhood school, and since many neighborhoods were racially segregated, the legislation actually contributed to school segregation. Congress also passed legislation that prioritized remedies in school desegregation cases and prohibited the issuance of administrative or judicial orders requiring student reassignment at any time other than the beginning of an academic year.

Despite the guidelines established in the *Milliken* decision regarding metropolitan busing, the restrictive busing legislation passed by Congress, and other precedent-setting decisions in the federal courts, school desegregation continued to move forward. The responsibility of proof had changed, however—from demonstrating the mere existence of segregation in a school system to the more difficult to prove standard of segregative intent on the part of school officials.

Much concern surfaced in Congress and in the federal courts about "white flight," the movement of white families to areas outside racially mixed school districts as well as the increasing tendency of white parents to place their children in private schools. While part of the decline in the number of white students can be attributed to desegregation and busing, white enrollment had actually begun to decline almost a decade before integration began. This decrease was a function of the declining white birthrate, departures to private schools, and departures to the suburbs. It should be noted that some suburban school districts not subject to desegregation actually lost more students proportionally than did city districts undergoing desegregation.

Although the phenomenon of white flight is generally associated with the desire to avoid school desegregation, technically the term is a misnomer. It would be more accurately characterized as middle class flight. The African American middle class, along with other minority middle class populations, has continually sought to remove itself from the inner cities when presented with the opportunity.

Diminished Opposition to Busing. Opposition to busing appeared to diminish in the 1980's. The Reagan Administration tended to focus on other domestic and foreign issues (especially the economy and the Cold War). Nevertheless, the Reagan Administration was firmly opposed to busing. It even threatened to reopen desegregation cases already settled through extensive busing if it believed that the remedy was too drastic. The Reagan Administration argued that desegregation should occur on a voluntary basis. Consequently, it supported voluntary desegregation plans such as magnet schools, tuition tax credits, and school "choice" programs. Busing became a side issue as debates focused on the impact that tuition tax credits and choice programs would have on public schools.

—*Charles C. Jackson*

See also *Brown v. Board of Education*; Civil rights; Civil Rights movement; *Green v. County School Board of New Kent County*; *Keyes v. Denver School District No. 1*; *Milliken v. Bradley*; School law; *Swann v. Charlotte-Mecklenburg Board of Education*.

BIBLIOGRAPHY

A thorough examination of busing can be found in *School Desegregation: Hearings Before the Subcommittee On Civil and Constitutional Rights of the Committee on the Judiciary, House of Representatives, Ninety-seventh Congress* (Washington, D.C.: U.S. Government Printing Office, 1982). Other excellent discussions are the Citizens Commission on Civil Rights, *"There Is No Liberty . . . "* (Washington, D.C.: Citizens Commission on Civil Rights, 1982); Derrick A. Bell, Jr., *Race, Racism, and American Law* (2d ed. Boston: Little, Brown, 1980); Harvard Sitkoff, *The Struggle for Black Equality: 1954-1992* (New York: Hill and Wang, 1993); and S. Alexander Rippa, *Education in a Free Society: An American History* (7th ed. New York: Longman, 1992).

Calhoun, John C. (Mar. 18, 1782, Abbeville District, S.C.—Mar. 31, 1850, Washington, D.C.)

IDENTIFICATION: United States senator

SIGNIFICANCE: Calhoun achieved renown as a defender of states' rights

John C. Calhoun, admitted to the bar in 1807, was a South Carolina legislator from 1808 to 1810. Elected to Congress in 1811, he agitated for the War of 1812 and avoided sectionalism. In 1817, James Madison appointed him secretary of war.

In 1824, Calhoun was elected vice president under John Quincy Adams and was reelected with Andrew Jackson in 1828. After the protective tariff of 1828 passed, Calhoun wrote the "South Carolina Exposition," asserting that states could refuse enforcement of unconstitutional acts, such as the protective tariff. Compromise failing, he published his doctrines of nullification, secession, and concurrent majorities in mid-1831. A South Carolina convention then adopted ordinances nullifying the 1818 and 1832 tariff acts. Jackson asked Congress to impose the tariff by force. Calhoun opposed the Force Bill, but, with Henry Clay, advanced a compromise gradually reducing duties to a revenue basis by 1840. The South Carolina convention then repealed tariff nullification.

By 1836 Calhoun was publicly opposing abolition, and in 1837 he asserted that slavery was a positive good. As secretary of state he supported annexing Texas as a slave state. He opposed the Wilmot proposal, 1846, barring slavery from annexed Mexican lands. He argued that territories were the states' common property, that citizens could bring property, including slaves, into any territory, and that citizens were entitled to federal protection of their property until a territory achieved statehood. Calhoun also opposed the Compromise of 1850. Calhoun's *Disquisition on Government* and *Discourse on the Constitution of the United States* (both 1851) outline his governmental philosophy.

See also Clay, Henry; Constitution, U.S.; Slavery; States' rights; Tariff; Whig Party.

Campus Unrest, President's Commission on

DATE: Established May, 1970

SIGNIFICANCE: Formed in response to the killing of students by National Guard troops, the commission released a report that raised serious concerns about the excessive use of state power against protesters

On May 4, 1970, Ohio National Guard troops fired on students at Kent State University who were protesting American military involvement in Cambodia. Four of those students died. Ten days later, two students were killed at Jackson State College in Mississippi under similar circumstances. In response, President Richard M. Nixon convened the President's Commission on Campus Unrest to investigate the shootings and campus unrest in general. The commission was headed by William Scranton, a former governor of Pennsylvania.

The commission held three days of hearings at KSU. In October, the commission released a report describing the political tensions at KSU as part of a national problem that required addressing. The report found that the Kent State shooting "was unnecessary, unwarranted and inexcusable." It further found the Jackson State shooting to be "an unreasonable over-reaction." In subsequent months and even years, a variety of grand jury inquiries, investigative newspaper reports, governmental investigations, and other analyses debated the commission's findings.

See also Chicago seven trial; Civil disobedience; Conscription; Kent State student killings; Nixon, Richard M.; Students for a Democratic Society (SDS); Vietnam War; Weather Underground.

Capital punishment

DEFINITION: Punishment by death for serious crimes such as murder or treason

SIGNIFICANCE: The United States is one of the few democracies in the world that maintains the death penalty for particularly serious crimes; whether it should maintain it has been a matter of practical, moral, and constitutional debate

During the 1600's, the colonials in British America maintained many English legal practices, including capital punishment. Murder, rape, and religious blasphemy were considered the most serious of crimes. Because no central authority existed, executions were carried out under local control. Most executions were held in public to serve as a warning to the populace and to celebrate the fact that justice was being done.

Executions in America during the 1600's totaled 162; in the 1700's executions increased to nearly 1,400. Between 1800 and 1865, more than 2,400 persons fell victim to capital punishment; from 1866 to 1899, more than 2,900 persons did. As the number of executions increased, so did interest in reforming the capital punishment laws. Reformers of the 1800's succeeded in reducing dramatically the number of capital crimes (from some two hundred acts to about three), in establishing capital punishment under centralized state rather than local control, and in making executions private rather than public. They also aided in the abolishment of capital punishment in such states as Michigan (except for treason, 1846), Rhode Island (1852), and Wisconsin (1853).

Between 1900 and 1929, more than 3,600 individuals suffered the death penalty. From 1930 to 1967, there were 3,859 executions in the United States, with 1935 as the peak year (199 executions). Most executions were for murder, but a

METHODS OF EXECUTION IN STATES AUTHORIZING THE DEATH PENALTY, 1992

Lethal Injection	Electrocution	Lethal Gas	Hanging	Firing Squad
Arkansas	Alabama	Arizona	Montana	Idaho
Colorado	Arkansas	California	New Hampshire	Utah
Delaware	Connecticut	Colorado	Washington	
Idaho	Florida	Maryland		
Illinois	Georgia	Mississippi		
Louisiana	Indiana	Missouri		
Mississippi	Kentucky	North Carolina		
Missouri	Louisiana			
Montana	Nebraska			
Nevada	Ohio			
New Hampshire	South Carolina			
New Jersey	Tennessee			
New Mexico	Virginia			
North Carolina				
Oklahoma				
Oregon				
Pennsylvania				
South Dakota				
Texas				
Utah				
Washington				
Wyoming				

Source: U.S. Department of Justice, Bureau of Justice Statistics, *Sourcebook of Criminal Justice Statistics—1993.* Washington, D.C.: U.S. Government Printing Office, 1994.

Note: Some states appear more than once because they authorize two methods of execution.

good number were for rape. The South had the highest number of executions, with a disproportionate number of African Americans executed. After 1967, executions dropped dramatically because of the power of two strong national movements: organized opposition to the death penalty and the Civil Rights movement.

Banning and Reinstatement. In 1972, a liberal-oriented U.S. Supreme Court declared existing death penalty laws unconstitutional as part of its deliberations in the case *Furman v. Georgia.* The Court believed that death sentences were inconsistent and unfairly applied, especially against the poor and minorities. These sentences, according to the Court, violated both the Eighth Amendment's section on "cruel and unusual punishment" and the Fourteenth Amendment, which guarantees "equal protection of the law." The Court's decision in *Furman* resulted in the overturning of more than six hundred other death sentences and, in effect, banned executions from 1972 to 1976.

Because the Court did not ban capital punishment outright, various state legislatures enacted death penalty statutes in attempts to satisfy the Court's ruling. Some legislatures attempted to develop "mandatory death sentences," whereby the death penalty was imposed on all persons guilty of a particular crime. The Court rejected this approach, however, saying that all aggravated murders are not alike. The Court reasoned that juries and judges need to consider "mitigating circumstances" surrounding each crime along with the character and record of each defendant to render fair justice.

With the mandatory death penalty ruled out, some states, including Georgia, proposed using "guided discretion" statutes. One of the first cases to follow guided discretion was that of *Gregg v. Georgia* (1976). The jury first determined the defendant's guilt for armed robbery and murder. Then the jury was given a checklist of ten "aggravating circumstances." They had to agree on at least one circumstance before recommending capital punishment (for example, "Was the murder committed for money?"). Finally, the jury had to consider whether there were mitigating circumstances (for example, the defendant's youth or a clean prior record).

The Supreme Court in 1976—its membership now more conservative—found guided discretion statutes acceptable because the juries and judges had guidelines on how to make their decisions on life-and-death matters. A number of states, among them Florida, Texas, and Ohio, soon had similar models. The innovation of guided discretion, although not exempt from problems of implementation, transformed the capital punishment process, making it more fair by narrowing the class of people subject to the death penalty.

Once capital punishment was reinstated in 1976, the sentencing of people to "death row" increased rapidly. As of 1993, the number of inmates housed on death row had reached 2,716. Yet executions were infrequent, primarily because of the lengthy appeals process; for example, in 1993, thirty-eight executions (or 1.39 percent of death row inmates) took place. Critics of the system began to argue that the ratio of inmates

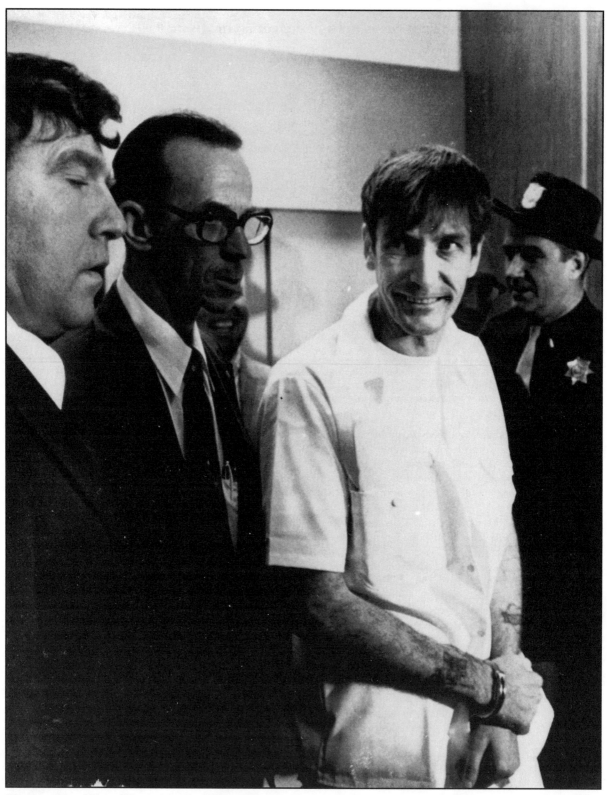

The execution of Gary Gilmore in early 1977 was the first in the United States since the 1972 Furman v. Georgia *decision; Gilmore himself wished to be executed.* (AP/Wide World Photos)

awaiting execution to those actually executed was grotesque and inhumane. Public concern about violent crime during the 1990's led politicians to demand an increase in the number of capital crimes, thereby worsening the situation.

The 1990's also saw the Supreme Court tighten the appeals process for the condemned. For example, in 1991 the Court ruled that "attorney error" could not be the basis of an appeal. In 1992, the Court struck down the "probable innocence" standard for exemption from the death penalty. In 1993, the Court decreed that unless so-called new evidence in a case was incontrovertible, an execution was to proceed. Critics worried that in the Court's zeal to reduce lengthy appeals it might be violating the basic tenet of "due process," a situation which could result in the execution of the innocent.

Usefulness of Capital Punishment. The capital punishment issue may be debated from three perspectives: on utilitarian or practical grounds, on ethical or moral grounds, and from the perspective of political ramifications.

Advocates of capital punishment believe that executions protect the public by removing any chance that the criminal will obtain a parole or commutation of sentence. They cite examples of murder-for-hire criminals and serial killers as types of criminals who should be destroyed for the public good. Opponents counter that the bulk of condemned prisoners are of a different sort—people who were caught up in the passion of their crimes or people never intending to kill who became entangled in situations leading unexpectedly to lethal violence. A study in the 1980's concluded that criminals indicted for murder were unlikely to repeat violent crimes.

Capital Punishment as a Deterrent. Supporters avow that capital punishment strikes fear in the hearts of potential killers—for example, a husband thinking about killing his mate for insurance money. Logically, harsh punishment should be a strong deterrent in keeping people from carrying out heinous schemes. Supporters of capital punishment often cite the "econometric" studies of Isaac Ehrlick. After statistically controlling his data for demographic characteristics, Ehrlick concluded that each execution deters some seven or eight potential murders. Challengers of capital punishment argue that Ehrlick's methodology and data were flawed and cite a number of studies which tried to determine the deterrent effects of the death penalty when executions were abolished within a state (states were also compared with neighboring states which still had the death penalty). The murder rates did not change significantly.

Some on both sides of the argument about capital punishment favor a return to public executions, via television. Supporters argue that looking at executions directly on television would deter potential criminals. Opponents believe that such a public spectacle would arouse revulsion against capital punishment.

Retribution. When outrageous criminals—such as mass poisoners or political assassins—are found guilty, the cry for justice and vengeance is almost instinctual in humans. The public looks to government to punish criminals appropriately. This process, one argument goes, acts as a safety valve for discharging instinctual vengeance. If the government fails in its responsibilities, then people may take justice into their own hands, forming lynch mobs and sowing the seeds of anarchy. It has happened at various times in the history of the United States. For example, Colorado briefly abolished capital punishment in 1897; however, the death penalty was quickly reinstituted when mobs began to lynch accused suspects, believing that they were murderers who would otherwise not be adequately punished.

Financial Costs of Capital Punishment. It is commonly believed that it is more expensive to maintain life-sentenced prisoners than it is to execute them. "Lifers," after all, must be housed and fed, given medical attention, and provided with vocational and recreational activities.

Surprisingly, however, studies have demonstrated that executions are significantly more costly than life sentences. To begin with, court trials in capital cases are more expensive than those for noncapital cases. Trial costs involve both the prosecution and defense teams preparing for two separate trials: to determine whether the defendant is guilty and, if the defendant is found guilty, to determine whether capital punishment is warranted. The trial phase also involves selecting a "death qualified" jury (one whose members are not opposed to capital punishment). The most expensive aspect is the extensive appeals process, which takes an average of eight years. During the 1980's, when the average execution cost about $1.8 million per case, Florida estimated that it spent six times more per person to execute a person than to maintain that individual in prison for life without parole.

Ethical and Constitutional Implications. Beyond the practical considerations, capital punishment raises moral questions about the sacredness of human life. Advocates believe that capital punishment actually affirms human life because it exalts the value of innocent victims. Some also argue that it is ethical to execute someone who has committed a particularly heinous crime. Opponents counter that capital punishment cheapens human life and puts government on the same low moral level as criminals who have taken life.

Opponents of capital punishment object on moral grounds to mentally impaired individuals receiving the death penalty because these people often do not understand their crimes. The courts have upheld the constitutionality of executing mentally retarded persons but have suggested that in jury deliberation "diminished mental capacity" be considered as a mitigating factor. Those challenging the death penalty on moral grounds also object to the execution of juvenile murderers. Although relatively few offenders under the age of eighteen are executed, it does occur. The courts have upheld the constitutionality of capital punishment for youthful offenders, leaving the minimum age requirement for execution to the discretion of state legislatures. They caution that juveniles should rarely receive capital punishment.

Some of the controversy over capital punishment stems from the interpretation of the U.S. Constitution and its first ten amendments, the Bill of Rights. The Fifth Amendment explic-

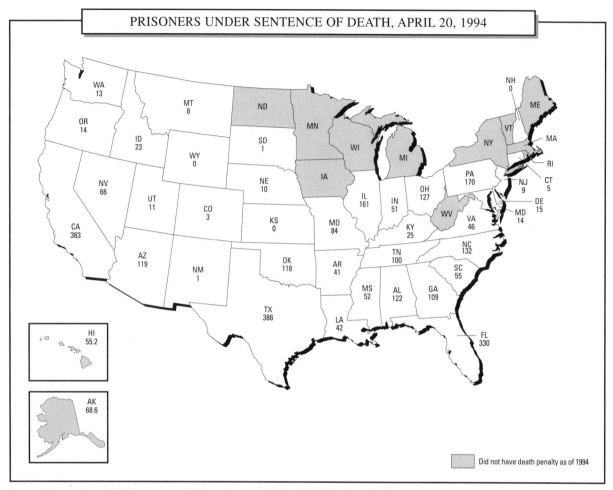

PRISONERS UNDER SENTENCE OF DEATH, APRIL 20, 1994

WA 13
MT 8
ND
MN
NH 0
ME
OR 14
ID 23
SD 1
WI
MI
VT
NY
MA
RI
NV 66
WY 0
NE 10
IA
PA 170
NJ 9
CT 5
DE 15
UT 11
CO 3
IL 161
IN 51
OH 127
WV
MD 14
CA 383
KS 0
MO 84
VA 46
AZ 119
NM 1
OK 118
AR 41
KY 25
NC 132
TN 100
SC 55
MS 52
AL 122
GA 109
TX 386
LA 42
FL 330

HI 55.2

AK 68.6

Did not have death penalty as of 1994

Source: Data are from U.S. Department of Justice, Bureau of Justice Statistics, *Sourcebook of Criminal Justice Statistics—1993.* Washington, D.C.: U.S. Government Printing Office, 1994. Primary source, NAACP Legal Defense and Educational Fund.

Note: Thirty-seven states had the death penalty in 1994; 13, and the District of Columbia, did not. In addition to those individuals under state death sentences, 5 people were under federal death sentences and 8 were under U.S. military death sentences. U.S. total was 2,848.

itly refers to capital crimes twice, thereby rendering capital punishment constitutional. The Eighth Amendment, however, can be argued to restrict capital punishment by authorizing the courts to decide whether punishments rendered are "cruel and unusual." During the early 1970's, the U.S. Supreme Court interpreted this to mean that the Court could determine "evolving standards of decency," implying that punishments tolerated in 1800 might not be acceptable in contemporary society.

Opponents of capital punishment have seized the phrase "cruel and unusual" as a rallying cry to protest the lack of uniform standards of courts in handing down death sentences. They have also used the phrase to question the treatment of inmates on death row, who lead a miserable existence and alternate between fear and hope during the lengthy appeals process. Moreover, opponents of capital punishment have used the phrase "cruel and unusual punishment" to challenge the methods of execution (most commonly electrocution or

lethal injection) as inhumane. Nevertheless, since 1976, when executions resumed, the Supreme Court has usually rejected the moral grounds of "cruel and unusual punishment" as espoused by opponents of capital punishment.

Fairness in the System. It has been argued that capital punishment is most often applied to indigents, minorities, the mentally retarded, and violent youths. Defenders of capital punishment contend that the death penalty itself is not biased against these groups; the fact that disproportionate numbers of them have been sentenced to death, they say, has to do with the aberrant behaviors exhibited by these groups. Opponents, however, offer statistical data demonstrating that death row inmates most often come from the lower economic strata. The disadvantaged cannot afford top-level lawyers to defend them. A 1987 study found that court-appointed lawyers in Texas were more than twice as likely to have clients receive the death penalty than were those able to hire their own lawyers.

The Civil Rights movement of the 1950's and 1960's was instrumental in the U.S. Supreme Court's decision in 1972 to impose a moratorium on death sentences until fair and equitable procedures were established for all races. The Court was influenced by studies showing that from 1930 to 1967 African American males suffered an excessive number of executions (50 percent of the executions for murder; 89 percent for rape) when they made up less than 20 percent of the entire population. Once the Court revamped sentencing procedures and allowed for the resumption of executions, the proportion of African American executions dropped. In 1991, for example, 1,464 whites (58.98 percent) and 982 blacks (39.56 percent) were on death row; seven whites and seven blacks were executed that year.

Some critics complain that racial bias still exists in the sentencing of black criminals to death. A 1990 study by David Baldus, for example, showed that African Americans who killed whites were more likely to receive the death penalty than those who killed African Americans. Moreover, since the enactment of the federal "drug kingpin law" (the 1988 law that allows the death penalty for drug-related killings), federal prosecutors sought, from 1988 to 1993, the death penalty against thirty-seven individuals. Twenty-nine of them were black (78.4 percent). Of the six defendants sentenced to death, only two were white.

Political Ramifications. In 1966, public support for capital punishment reached a low point of 42 percent. Public approval rose steadily thereafter; by 1993, the public approval of capital punishment reached 72 percent, with those opposed at only 21 percent. Much of the shift can be attributed to frightening crime statistics, such as those provided for the year 1993 by the U.S. Department of Justice: "one violent crime every sixteen seconds; one murder every twenty-one minutes; one forcible rape every five minutes; one robbery every forty-eight seconds; one aggravated assault every twenty-eight seconds."

Political leaders often take their cues from public opinion polls and media representations of public opinion, ranging from talk shows to editorials. During the 1990's, successful politicians supported crime bills, tougher sentencing practices, a reduced number of appeals, and capital punishment. Even governors seldom granted executive clemency for fear of appearing "soft on crime."

In spite of the significant amounts of money, time, and effort expended in the United States on capital punishment, it represents a minor aspect of the criminal justice system. Only a small percentage of murderers receive the death penalty, and an even smaller percentage are actually executed. Nevertheless, because of the finality of execution and the difficult moral issues presented by capital punishment, it has received much attention and will continue to engender considerable controversy.   —*Richard Whitworth*

See also *Coker v. Georgia*; Criminal justice system; Criminal law; Cruel and unusual punishment; Deterrence; *Ford v. Wainwright*; *Furman v. Georgia*; *Gregg v. Georgia*; Murder

and homicide; Murders, mass and serial; Prison and jail systems; Punishment.

BIBLIOGRAPHY

Constitutional issues, court proceedings, and the roles of juries in capital punishment cases are fully discussed in Mark Tushnet, *The Death Penalty* (New York: Facts on File, 1994), and in Lee Epstein and Joseph Kobylka, *The Supreme Court and Legal Change: Abortion and the Death Penalty* (Chapel Hill: University of North Carolina Press, 1992). For the origins, history, and changing nature of capital punishment, see Michael Kronenwetter, *Capital Punishment: A Reference Handbook* (Santa Barbara, Calif.: ABC-Clio, 1993), and Raymond Paternoster, *Capital Punishment in America* (New York: Lexington Books, 1991). Crime statistics may be found in the Department of Justice's annual *Sourcebook of Criminal Justice Statistics* (Washington, D.C.: U.S. Government Printing Office) and in *Crime State Rankings 1994: Crime in the Fifty United States* (Lawrence, Kans.: Morgan Quitno, 1994). On the mental capacities of condemned killers, see Kent Miller and Michael Radelet, *Executing the Mentally Ill* (Newbury Park, Calif.: Sage Publications, 1993), and Emily Reed, *The Penry Penalty: Capital Punishment and Offenders with Mental Retardation* (Lanham, Md.: University Press of America, 1993). Eyewitness accounts of executions and the effects of capital punishment on the families of the condemned and their victims are detailed in Helen Prejean, *Dead Man Walking* (New York: Random House, 1993), and in Michael Radelet et al., *In Spite of Innocence: Erroneous Convictions in Capital Cases* (Boston: Northeastern University Press, 1992).

Capitalism

DEFINITION: An economic system based on a free market and on private ownership of property and industry, with the goal of making profits

SIGNIFICANCE: The U.S. economic system depends on the safeguarding of private property and on the use of the marketplace to promote economic efficiency

American justice has a reciprocal relationship with capitalism, with the character of capitalism influencing the legal system, and the legal system influencing capitalism. Capitalism rests on private ownership of property and promotes economic efficiency through the market. The market is any location in which an exchange takes place between a willing buyer and willing seller of land, commodities, or labor. Capitalists believe that a "fair market price" is possible for everything that is traded and that optimum prices and allocation of resources will take place with everyone seeking to buy low and sell high.

The pursuit of individual gain or profit is said to be the motivating force of the system, and the most successful operation of the entire system is said to result if the market is allowed to function without undue government interference. Capitalists tend to lament excessive government interference in business, but not even the staunchest capitalists believe that private property or the market can exist without government or a framework of laws. While they like to say, "That government

Early twentieth century cartoon of capitalists earning dividends on the backs of the poor. (Library of Congress)

governs best which governs least," they do not say, "That government governs best which governs not at all." Government may be a necessary evil, but it is necessary. If government is necessary, what are the particular laws that capitalism needs? Capitalism certainly appears to require order and stability in which agriculture, industry, and commerce can take place, but it requires more than that.

Laws Protecting Private Property. Beyond the universal requirement of protecting human life, capitalism needs laws protecting private property, such as laws against theft, robbery, burglary, and so forth, so that the fruits of agricultural, industrial, and commercial activity can be protected from those who would steal it. Such prohibitions also rest on the notion that anyone able to steal money would also probably be able to kill or otherwise assault or harm their victims.

Laws Protecting the Market. Capitalism also requires laws that protect the market, starting with the protection of contracts or agreements between willing buyers and sellers detailing what exchanges will take place and for what amounts of money. The influence of capitalism on the American judicial system is demonstrated in Article I, section 10 of the U.S.

Constitution, which forbids state governments from passing laws "impairing the obligation of contracts." In some of the thirteen original states, groups had forced the legislatures to pass laws rendering contracts meaningless or had blocked the courts from enforcing existing contracts. The framers inserted this language not only to protect commerce but also to stop violence that was arising as a result of interference with interstate commerce.

Capitalism also requires laws against fraud. The most basic fraud laws are those specifying and insisting on accurate weights and measures, widely recognized as a governmental duty. From this necessity it is comparatively easy to find reasons for laws against fraud, forgery, and embezzlement, which also impair contracts. By the late twentieth century, capitalism was reliant on an enormous array of electronic and computerized capabilities that clearly required additional regulatory measures. In addition, modern technology has created new foods and drugs, the quality and safety of which consumers have difficulty evaluating. These also require regulation. Arguably, all of these regulations and laws flow from capitalism and its need to protect the market.

Laws Creating Specific Market Conditions. Capitalism, operating without regulation, tends to produce very wealthy holders of private property who may be able to purchase market positions in which they—solely or in the company of a few others—control certain property so that monopolies and oligopolies are created. While economists disagree over the extent to which monopolies and oligopolies evolve naturally, they have developed enough times that most business and government leaders believe the government should prevent monopolies and other restraints to trade. The U.S. government uses various antitrust, antimonopoly, and antirestraint of trade laws to preserve the competitive system. Such laws are also connected with fraud statutes in the area of securities. There is considerable disagreement about how many and what kinds of laws are necessary in this regard.

Currency. One key relationship between capitalism and the legal system is the regulation of the amount and kind of legal tender or currency the government permits. In ancient times, legal tender was nearly always a durable good, such as a precious metal. The government's job was basically to set accurate standards of weight and quality for such metals. Some capitalists, such as the "Austrian school economists," argue that governments should avoid regulating currency altogether by returning to the gold standard as a measure of all currencies, since that would avoid the dangers of inflation that can result from substituting paper currency for gold. Austrian school economists argue that the inflationary tendency of governments to print excessive amounts of paper money aggravates the "boom and bust" characteristics of the business cycle. Other economists, probably a majority, believe that governments can take prudent actions to regulate currency through systems such as the U.S. Federal Reserve banking system. The Austrian school doubts this, citing what they believe is an ever-present temptation for democratic governments to print inflationary money. From either perspective, the government is responsible for establishing the rules for the legal tender, currency, or money supply.

Taxation. Every government needs revenue, derived from taxes, to pay for even minimal police, firefighting, and military services. This fact leads to the question of how taxes should be raised. Capitalists, who wish for the maximum amount of private ownership, usually argue for minimal taxation. Arguments abound in economics over what types of taxes are most intrusive on the marketplace. Most capitalists favor taxes on consumption rather than on wealth (for example, property taxes) or income. If more than one kind of taxation is deemed necessary, capitalist economists favor consumption taxes first, income taxes second, and property taxes third. Almost without exception, capitalist economists oppose so-called business or privilege taxes. They also typically note that business taxes usually generate the least amount of revenue. Capitalists do not object to user taxes, which shift the burden of taxation on those persons who can be clearly identified as the beneficiaries of governmental services.

Additional Regulation of the Economy. Capitalist economists have a strong tendency to oppose regulatory agencies, which have become increasingly common in the twentieth century in the United States. One key problem with regulatory agencies is that they are often established by vague legislation that creates the agency and then directs it to write such additional rules and regulations as it deems necessary. Decisions by regulatory agencies represent a delegation of power in which the arena of legislation shifts from the legislative branch (Congress) to the executive branch (regulatory agencies).

—*Richard L. Wilson*

See also Antitrust law; Banking law; Clayton Antitrust Act; Commercial law; Communist Party, American; Contract law; Copyrights, patents, and trademarks; Labor unions; Marxism; Property rights; Socialism.

BIBLIOGRAPHY

A classic statement of neoclassical thought and its relationship to government is Milton Friedman, *Capitalism and Freedom* (Chicago: University of Chicago Press, 1965). An instructive comparison between capitalist and Marxist legal systems is available in Mary Ann Glendon, Michael W. Gordon, and Christopher Osakwe, *Comparative Legal Traditions* (St. Paul, Minn.: West, 1985). An excellent critique of the central planning necessary for all socialist and communist regimes that, by comparison, underscores the logic of the free market system may be found in Friedrich A. Hayek, *The Road to Serfdom* (Chicago: University of Chicago Press, 1944). See also Herbert Hovenkamp, *Enterprise and American Law, 1836-1937* (Cambridge, Mass.: Harvard University Press, 1991), and Arthur Selwyn Miller, *The Supreme Court and American Capitalism* (New York: Free Press, 1968).

Capone, Alphonse (Al) (Jan. 17, 1899, Brooklyn, N.Y.— Jan. 25, 1947, Palm Island, Fla.)

IDENTIFICATION: Notorious criminal

SIGNIFICANCE: The most publicized gangster of the early twentieth century, Al Capone ruled Chicago in the 1920's through violence, public popularity, and political corruption

Born in Brooklyn, New York, to Italian immigrant parents, Al Capone became a criminal as a child. In 1919, he was sent to Chicago by Johnny Torrio, who ran First Ward vice for his uncle, Jim Colosimo. With passage of the Volstead Act legislating Prohibition in 1919, Capone foresaw American demand for alcohol. Colosimo was killed, Torrio retired, and Capone became master of Chicago vice, rejecting involvement only with narcotics. Capone's reign coincided with the thirteen years of Prohibition. Of the many killings in which he was implicated, the most famous was the Saint Valentine's Day massacre of 1929, which left seven dead. Yet Capone remained popular with much of Chicago, paying immigrant Italians to manufacture alcohol in their homes, opening a private soup kitchen during the Depression, and forcing through a fresh milk law.

Apparently invulnerable to conventional prosecution because of political corruption, he and other gang members were eventually sentenced for income tax evasion, the first use of tax laws against organized crime. Brought to trial on Octo-

Al Capone, Kingpin of Chicago crime in the 1920's. (AP/ Wide World Photos)

ber 6, 1931, Capone received an eleven-year sentence. He was released, his health ruined, in 1939. Glamorized by the media, Capone was featured in at least seven films between 1932 and 1976; his legendary corruption and homicides have strongly influenced portrayals of organized crime in the mass media.

See also Blackmail and extortion; Commercialized vice; Internal Revenue Service (IRS); Organized crime; Prohibition; Saint Valentine's Day massacre; Tax evasion.

Cardozo, Benjamin Nathan (May 24, 1870, New York, N.Y.—July 9, 1938, Port Chester, N.Y.)

IDENTIFICATION: American judge and jurist; U.S. Supreme Court justice, 1932-1938

SIGNIFICANCE: The internationally renowned Cardozo devoted his life to the principle of applying traditionally worded rules of law to changing conditions of life by insisting that the meaning of any rule of law lies in its purpose or spirit, not in its words or letter

Benjamin Cardozo was of Portuguese Jewish ancestry. His boyhood tutor was writer Horatio Alger, who helped mold Benjamin's character and fostered the boy's enduring love for English and classical literature. At age nineteen, Cardozo was the youngest graduate of Columbia University in 1889, graduating with highest honors. In 1890 he obtained an M.A. while still attending Columbia's law school. He passed the New York bar in 1891 and, after twenty-four years in private practice,

gained a seat on New York State's court of appeals in 1914. During Cardozo's eighteen years in that post, from 1927 to 1932 as chief judge, the decisions of the New York Court of Appeals exerted a great influence on American law. Cardozo himself gained a reputation among lawyers as a legal consultant. On February 15, 1932, upon the retirement of Oliver Wendell Holmes, and on the recommendation of virtually the entire legal profession, President Herbert Hoover appointed Cardozo the seventy-fifth justice of the U.S. Supreme Court. He served with distinction until his death six years later.

Those years were among the most controversial in Supreme Court history. Against the opinion of the majority of justices, Cardozo voted in favor of the constitutionality of New Deal legislation. The majority joined Cardozo in upholding federal Social Security legislation. Cardozo's views—he wrote some 150 opinions—generally prevailed. His Supreme Court opinions often were cited in cases before the British House of Lords. His lasting contribution was to make the law of the land more responsive to modern social needs and forces.

Cardozo wrote a number of books. In 1904 he published his authoritative *The Jurisdiction of the Court of Appeals of the State of New York. The Nature of the Judicial Process* (1921) analyzed the material and psychological circumstances that can influence a judge's decisions. It showed that the common law is a living and ongoing process capable of growth consonant with changing social values. This was also the theme of *The Growth of the Law* (1924). In *The Paradoxes of Legal Science* (1928), he considers the relationship between justice and law. His last books were *What Medicine Can Do for the Law* (1930) and *Law and Literature and Other Essays* (1931), a collection of his essays and addresses.

Cardozo's ability to adapt traditional wisdom to changing social requirements and the highly literary style in which he articulated his legal pronouncements made him one of the few American judges famous throughout the English-speaking world. In his own time he was unanimously acclaimed by his peers as one of the great jurists in American legal history.

See also Constitutional interpretation; Court-packing plan of Franklin D. Roosevelt; Jurisprudence; Motor Vehicle Theft Law Enforcement Act; New Deal; *Palko v. Connecticut*; Supreme Court of the United States.

Carjacking

DEFINITION: The illegal receiving of any motor vehicle while the vehicle is occupied

SIGNIFICANCE: Unlike many other property crimes, motor vehicle theft has risen in frequency since the mid-1980's, and carjacking is the most violent kind of vehicle theft

Carjacking is a form of motor vehicle theft and may be associated with other offenses, including assault, battery, or kidnapping. While carjackings make up less than 1 percent of all motor vehicle thefts nationwide, it is arguably the most violent form of property crime. In carjacking, the perpetrator usually takes the motor vehicle by force and may use a weapon. The victim is threatened verbally or physically and removed from the vehicle, and the perpetrator drives the vehicle to a remote location, where it is sold or "chopped" so that its parts may be distributed to buyers. Because victims are often threatened or assaulted, carjacking is a hybrid crime, part violent crime and part property crime. It is estimated that carjacking grew from fewer than one thousand known offenses in 1987 to approximately twenty-eight thousand offenses in 1992.

In the 1990's, carjacking and auto theft became the initiation rite of choice of many urban gangs. Because cars could be disposed of quickly and police agencies had limited resources for follow-up, gangs found it relatively risk free to promote carjacking. For example, a gang in Pontiac, Michigan, required its members to steal or carjack a motor vehicle from an open parking lot. This practice showed their belief that there was little or no risk in carjacking. Unfortunately, it takes little time to steal a car. Law-enforcement agencies estimate that the average motor vehicle theft takes just under five minutes and the average carjacking takes approximately thirty seconds.

While carjacking is not new, its growth has been significant since 1990. The Federal Bureau of Investigation estimated that approximately seventy cars were carjacked each day in 1994. This growth has prompted a number of responses. Insurance companies have alerted policyholders to the dangers of carjacking and have developed guidelines for maximizing the safety of drivers and passengers who are threatened. In 1993, President Bill Clinton signed a law designating carjacking as a federal crime.

See also Assault; Battery; Motor vehicle theft; Motor Vehicle Theft Act; Motor Vehicle Theft Law Enforcement Act.

Carter, Jimmy (b. Oct. 1, 1924, Plains, Ga.)

IDENTIFICATION: Thirty-ninth president of the United States
SIGNIFICANCE: Carter's four-year presidency in the late 1970's represented the only Democratic control of the White House between 1969 and 1993

Jimmy Carter was elected president in 1976 on a wave of anti-Republican and anti-Washington sentiment spawned by the Watergate scandal a few years earlier. Carter's presidency was known for its commitment to American civil rights (notably affirmative action) and to a foreign policy emphasizing human rights abroad. Among Carter's contributions were the appointment of many women and minorities to policy positions and federal judgeships and the passage of the Civil Service Reform Act of 1978. No Supreme Court justices retired during his presidency, so Carter was not able to nominate anyone to the Court.

Carter was hard working, and he obviously had strong moral principles, but he faced many frustrations as president, including the fact that his status as a self-proclaimed Washington outsider made it difficult for him to work with Congress once he became president. Critics labeled Carter's efforts to reform the cynicism and conservative drift of American politics as misguided and naïve. A perception that indecisiveness and managerial ineptness, combined with the relatively liberal domestic policies of the Carter Administration, were causing a

Jimmy Carter appointed more women and minorities to government posts than had any previous president. (Library of Congress)

"malaise" in the United States set the stage for Republican Ronald Reagan's presidency in the 1980's, which put a decidedly conservative stamp on the U.S. Supreme Court, American foreign policy, and civil rights legislation. In the 1980's and 1990's, Carter continued to crusade for human rights both in the United States and elsewhere in the world.

See also Democratic Party; Ford, Gerald R.; Liberalism, modern American; Morality and foreign policy; President of the United States; Reagan, Ronald.

Carter v. Carter Coal Co.

COURT: U.S. Supreme Court
DATE: Ruling issued May 18, 1936
SIGNIFICANCE: The decision declared unconstitutional the chief provisions of the Bituminous Coal Conservation Act of 1935 and helped provoke the "Court-packing" controversy

When the National Industrial Recovery Act of 1935, a New Deal program, was held unconstitutional in 1935, Congress attempted to reenact parts of the program for individual industries to relieve the impact of the economic depression. The [Guffey] Bituminous Coal Act of August, 1935, created the Bituminous Coal Commission to help formulate and administer a Bituminous Coal Code. The country was divided into twenty-three districts, each with a board, including representatives of management and labor. These organizations were empowered to fix minimum prices for coal and to negotiate labor provisions limiting hours of work and setting minimum wages. Coal producers were subjected to a 15 percent sales tax, 90 percent of which would be refunded to producers who accepted the code. The goal was to raise the market price of coal and thereby to enable coal producers to pay higher wages.

A number of lawsuits were initiated to block payment of the tax and adherence to the codes. These were consolidated on *certiorari* from federal district and appellate courts. The Supreme Court decision thus involved several cases, though it is best known for the first, namely *Carter*.

The Court's decision closely resembled that in *Schechter Poultry Corp. v. United States* (1935). Delegation of code-drafting authority to representatives of industry and labor was held to be improper. Neither the production and sale of coal nor the employment of labor in the mines constituted interstate commerce: "Production is a purely local activity." Granting the hardships faced by coal miners, "the evils are all local evils over which the federal government has no legislative control."

The *Carter* case, with the better-known *Schechter* case and *United States v. Butler* (1936), placed the Supreme Court squarely in opposition to measures which President Franklin D. Roosevelt considered central to his program for economic recovery. The Court came under heavy criticism. After President Roosevelt's landslide reelection in 1936, he proposed a number of "reforms" which would have enabled him to appoint new Supreme Court justices. The proposal aroused a storm of protests and was withdrawn, but the Court gave way to the political pressures of the times. The decision in *National Labor Relations Board v. Jones & Laughlin Steel Corp.* (1937) essentially reversed the *Carter* position regarding labor relations. The restrictive view of the commerce clause with regard to commodities was removed in *United States v. Darby Lumber Co.* (1941) and *Wickard v. Filburn* (1942).

Congress passed a second Bituminous Coal Act in 1937 with provisions very similar to those of 1935. The detailed labor provisions of the 1935 law were omitted, and the authority of the commission was clarified. It remained in effect until August, 1943.

See also Commerce clause; Court-packing plan of Franklin D. Roosevelt; Labor law; Labor-Management Relations Act; Lewis, John L.; New Deal; *Wickard v. Filburn*.

Case law

DEFINITION: The entire body of reported cases forming all or part of the law in a particular jurisdiction

SIGNIFICANCE: Case law is a defining characteristic of common law legal systems, which use cases to declare rules and principles of law

The common law, as developed in England and transplanted to colonial America, was unwritten and based on custom. It had no authoritative statement in a code or statute such as may be found in civil law systems. Legal rules and principles were "found" or "declared" by judges as they decided cases. A judicial decision can be viewed in two parts: first, the decision on who won and the relief granted, and second, the reasoned explanation of the judge in reaching the decision. It is the reasoned explanation which gives rise to a case law system, even if the reasons must be skillfully extracted or inferred from the written decision.

Cases, including their explanations, are used to decide future cases. If the facts of a future case are similar to the facts of an old case, the rule or principle of the old case will be used to decide the new case. The old case is called a precedent, and the general procedure whereby courts use old cases to decide new ones is called *stare decisis*. Over time *stare decisis* causes a refinement of old rules and principles, adapting them to changes in law and society. In addition, judges will change an old rule or principle if they believe it is wrong, outdated, or otherwise unacceptable. For example, the law of products liability changed in the early twentieth century as judges rejected established legal rules which did not allow consumers to recover damages when injured by defective products except under the most extreme circumstances. Today, the common-law rules allow recovery in most circumstances.

Case law is also used to interpret positive law, such as constitutions, statutes, and administrative regulations. This is particularly true if the language of the positive law is open-ended, vague, ambiguous, susceptible to different interpretations, or simply ill-defined. A court which applies the positive law in a particular case will announce a decision accompanied by a reasoned explanation. This explanation will be read by lawyers to discover a legal rule or principle, which will then be applied to future cases arising under the same or a similar positive law. For example, cases arising under the free speech clause of the First Amendment to the United States Constitution have created a rich case law defining the boundaries of protected speech. The Constitution does not define what is meant by freedom of speech, so it is up to the courts to give meaning to this concept as they decide individual cases.

See also Civil law; Common law; Fiduciary trust; Judicial system, U.S.; Law; *Milligan, Ex parte*; *Stare decisis*.

Cease and desist order

DEFINITION: An order requiring that a citizen cease illegal behavior or face arrest or punishment

SIGNIFICANCE: Cease and desist orders are warnings given before a formal arrest takes place

When the police become aware of illegal behavior, they do not always opt for formal arrest procedure. In some cases, they can use a cease and desist order to request that the illegal behavior stop. The wording of the order will specify that if the illegal behavior does not stop, an arrest will follow. Occasionally, a judge may also issue a cease and desist order to stop illegal behavior, and an arrest may not be the end result. For example, a judge may issue a cease and desist order to a company that is engaging in illegal hiring practices or discriminates against job candidates. While a company would not be arrested if it does not cease illegal behavior, the order may specify that certain fines may be levied against the company unless the behavior ceases.

See also Arrest; Discretion; Police.

Censorship

DEFINITION: The examination of any material in advance of publication, performance, or broadcast with the aim of preventing "objectionable" materials from being distributed

SIGNIFICANCE: Censorship is commonly used by dictators to prevent the spread of ideas hostile to their rule, but modern democracies abhor censorship of nearly all expression except obscenity, where prior restraints are sometimes allowed

Repressive governments such as dictatorships have given censorship, or "prior restraint" (the suppression of materials before publication, performance, or broadcast), a very bad name. It is easy to understand why prior restraint is so important in a dictatorship. If a dictator waits until after publication, the dangerous ideas are already widespread, and extreme penalties may not deter some critics from voicing their opposition to a regime. In modern democracies, on the other hand, censorship is generally shunned. In the United States, censorship is allowed by the federal or state governments (or their agents) only if such prior restraint can be made compatible with the free expression portions of the First Amendment to the U.S. Constitution, which read: "Congress shall make no law . . . abridging the freedom of speech, or of the press; or the right of the people peaceably to assemble."

The First Amendment divides the free expression of ideas into two major categories: freedom of speech and the press, and freedom of peaceable assembly. Neither speech nor press is to be restrained, but the presence of the word "peaceably" in connection with assemblies indicates that assemblies can be, and routinely are, subject to prior restraint or censorship. Yet even in the case of assembly, prior restraints are allowed only for a reason such as allowing the "free movement of traffic in public areas." They must not be used to block the presentation of ideas simply because they are objectionable to the authorities.

Freedom of speech and the press is different from freedom of assembly because of its more passive character, although the U.S. Supreme Court has not always consistently and officially said so. The press, in particular, is regarded as a less dangerous medium for the expression of ideas, since reading is a far more passive activity than speaking to an audience. While it is possible to imagine someone making a speech that would incite a riot, it is very difficult to imagine a crowd reading a newspaper and then rioting. Because speech is frequently given before an assembly, speech falls partially under the First Amendment's requirement that assembly must be peaceable to avoid being restrained. This requirement rests on a distinction between ideas and actions. Pure ideas, as expressed in the press or in speeches to peaceable assemblies, are fully protected, but the requirement that an assembly must be peaceable

may lead to some restraints on speech, even if there are no prior restraints on the press.

The essence of freedom of speech and the press is that there shall be no prior restraint—no censorship of any material in advance of its distribution. This requirement clearly implies that there may be punishments or restraints applied afterward, a view that is part of a long Anglo-Saxon legal tradition. In an age when censorship laws were focused against "blasphemy," John Milton argued in his *Areopagitica* (1644) against such laws: "Let [Truth] and falshood grapple; who ever knew truth put to the worse in free and open encounter?" By the eighteenth century, the battle against censorship had been sufficiently successful that the great jurist William Blackstone could write in book four of his *Commentaries on the Laws of England*: "The liberty of the press is indeed essential to the nature of a free state; but this consists of laying no *previous* restraints upon publications."

This tradition carried over into the colonies and led to the adoption of the First Amendment in 1791. Freedom of the press became an issue only a few years after the passage of the Bill of Rights when the Federalists passed the Alien and Sedition Acts in 1798 to punish their political opponents. Despite considerable controversy, the Federalists justified the acts by saying they did not impose a prior restraint. The political outcry was so great that Federalist John Adams lost the 1800 election to Thomas Jefferson, who pardoned all who had been convicted under the acts. Shortly thereafter the Federalists ceased to be a cohesive political party, and the Alien and Sedition Acts were considered such a black mark that no attempt was made to pass anything like them for more than a hundred years.

Throughout the 1800's, the common understanding of the First Amendment was that the federal government could not pass a law that restricted freedom of the press. Since the Bill of Rights was interpreted as applying only to the national government, however, sedition laws existed in various states. After the Fourteenth Amendment was passed following the Civil War, a basis for applying the principles of the Bill of Rights to the states was established, although the U.S. Supreme Court did not immediately accept this interpretation. During World War I, Congress passed two acts, the Sedition Act and the Espionage Act, which produced the first "free speech" cases, but no restraints on the press in advance of publication were enacted.

Prior Restraint Cases. The first U.S. Supreme Court decision on prior restraint was *Near v. Minnesota* (1931). Near published an anti-Semitic newsletter in Minneapolis, Minnesota, which charged that local government officials were Jewish-influenced and corrupt. Authorities sought to use a state statute to prevent Near from publishing, but the U.S. Supreme Court held that this was an impermissible prior restraint. Also, for the first time, it applied the free press portion of the First Amendment to state governments, utilizing the due process clause of the Fourteenth Amendment "selectively incorporating" part of the Bill of Rights.

Daniel Ellsberg (at microphone), who leaked the top-secret "Pentagon papers" to The New York Times *in 1971.* (AP/Wide World Photos)

The second Supreme Court prior restraint case, *New York Times Co. v. United States* (1971, the "Pentagon papers" case), involved hundreds of top-secret government documents that were photocopied by Daniel Ellsberg, knowing he was in violation of the security clearance laws. The documents were printed by *The New York Times* and other newspapers. The documents disclosed U.S. violations of international law and other matters damaging to the government. The Pentagon papers were clearly stolen government property, but the legal question was whether the newspapers could be restrained in advance from publishing them. The Supreme Court ruled against the government by a 6-3 vote. All nine justices upheld the "no prior restraint" concept, but they disagreed whether the restraint was justified by the extraordinary issues in this case. While each judge wrote a separate opinion, three major groups can be distinguished. The first group (justices Hugo Black, William O. Douglas, William Brennan, and Thurgood Marshall) maintained that no circumstances justified any prior restraint. Justices Warren Burger, Harry Blackmun, and John Harlan upheld prior restraint but requested more time to exam-ine the documents before deciding whether a permanent re-straining order should be issued.

Justices Potter Stewart and Byron White, the swing votes who voted with the first four justices to allow publication of the Pentagon papers, believed that the "no prior restraint" presumption was too strong to overrule in this case but held open the idea mentioned in *Near* that there might be extreme circumstances in which prior restraint would be justified—such as a newspaper's attempt in wartime to publish the secret route of naval convoy through submarine-infested waters. Given the Court's disregard of the U.S. government's anger and embarrassment at publication of the Pentagon papers, it is hard to imagine circumstances which would justify prior re-straint. In two hundred years, the Supreme Court has never found a case that justified prior restraint and, since 1931, has never allowed any state or local government to exercise prior restraint, even when the expression of ideas is embarrassing to the government.

Obscenity. Not all ideas are political ideas, and the question of whether censorship can be justified also includes the artistic and scientific arenas. In particular, the Supreme Court has found it necessary to confront obscenity and pornography, particularly when applying the First Amendment to the states, many of which long had restrictive statutes on such subjects.

Despite the clear language of the First Amendment that "Congress shall make no law" abridging freedom of the press or speech, there have long been other rights which the Court has counterbalanced against the right of free expression. For example, there is a right of the adult population to avoid being assaulted in public by widespread display of materials that they might regard as offensive. There is an even more important need to protect children from pornographic materials which might damage their growth and development as human beings. Prior restraint is allowable for any pornography involving sexual acts by children, as the Court made clear in *New York v. Ferber* (1982). Sex acts involving children are against the law in every jurisdiction within the United States.

Regarding the publication of pornographic materials depicting adults for the use of other adults in the privacy of their own homes, the Supreme Court has found grounds to provide prior restraint of some materials. It has had great difficulty in doing so in practice, however, principally because of the strong constitutional opposition to prior restraint. Also, although the Supreme Court has consistently held that obscene materials are not protected under the First Amendment, it has had serious problems defining obscenity.

Roth v. United States. In *Roth v. United States* (1957), the Supreme Court attempted to define obscenity for the first time in the modern era. The first premise of the Court's *Roth* decision was that "all ideas having even the slightest redeeming social importance—unorthodox ideas, controversial ideas, even ideas hateful to the prevailing climate of opinion—have the full protection of the [First Amendment] guarantees." Because the First Amendment has been interpreted to protect virtually all ideas against prior restraint except obscene ones, the definition of obscenity was crucial, but it proved very difficult. Earl Warren, U.S. Chief Justice from 1953 to 1969, once said that defining obscenity presented the Court with its "most difficult" area of adjudication. In *Roth*, the Court said that to be obscene, expression had to be "utterly without redeeming social importance." Obscenity was fully defined by the following phrase: "Whether to the average person applying contemporary community standards, the dominant theme of the material taken as a whole appeals to prurient interests."

"Prurient" was defined as "material having a tendency to excite lustful thoughts." The Court asserted that "sex and obscenity are not synonymous," however, because the Court could not equate sex and obscenity without legitimizing the

The Supreme Court has found it tremendously difficult to define obscenity and thus to decide what sexually oriented materials may legally be censored. (McCrea Adams)

banning of a wide range of artistic, medical, and scientific materials. While there is a certain logic to the Supreme Court's decision in the *Roth* case, the decision itself involves a number of words which are not easy to define. Obscenity is difficult to define, but so are the words "lustful" and "prurient." A number of questions quickly became apparent. How can one decide that something is "utterly without redeeming social importance"? What "community standards" should be followed? Is the community a particular town, a particular state, or the nation as a whole? Moreover, exactly who is an "average person"? Lower courts quickly found that reaching judicial determinations on whether particular works fit within a definition that includes so many vague words was extremely daunting.

Ideally, the Supreme Court should provide clear definitions that can serve as workable guidelines for legislators, courts, and attorneys all across the nation. When the Court does not do so, it invites a flood of litigation, because only the Court can determine what its own vague guidelines mean. Since it did not do so in *Roth*, it found a huge number of obscenity cases being presented to it. Furthermore, the Court's own agreement on the *Roth* definition was short-lived.

Per Curiam Rulings. By 1967, several distinct positions were evident. Justices Black and Douglas maintained that the principle of "no prior restraint" is so strong that neither federal, state, nor local governments have any power to regulate any sexually oriented matter on the ground of obscenity. Justice Harlan took the opposing view that the federal government could control the distribution of "hard-core" pornography by using its enumerated powers and that states were entitled to even greater freedom to ban any materials which state courts had reasonably found to treat sex in a fundamentally offensive manner. A variety of other views were held by the other justices.

From 1967 until 1973, the Court followed the practice, established in *Redrup v. New York* (1967), of issuing *per curiam* reversals of convictions for the dissemination of obscene materials if at least five members of the Court, applying their separate tests, deemed them not to be obscene. *Per curiam* decisions are generally unsatisfactory in that they do not include any accompanying opinions as guidance for lower courts. As with vague guidelines, they invite endless litigation. At one point in the struggle to define hard-core pornography, Justice Stewart, with evident frustration, said of obscenity, "I can't define it, but I know it when I see it." While this statement became the butt of many jokes, it was essentially an accurate description of the Court's approach from 1967 to 1973. The Court was deciding obscenity cases on an individual and retroactive basis, which was unsatisfactory for lower courts, prosecuting attorneys, police officers, defense attorneys, the producers of the materials, and the public.

Miller v. California. Sixteen years after *Roth* a new definition of obscenity was offered in the case *Miller v. California* (1973) and the companion case *Paris Adult Theatre v. Slaton*. Since five justices voted for the definition, it became the new definitive holding (or leading case) on the subject, but it proved little better than its predecessor.

The new definition made two major changes. First, it specifically rejected the standard "utterly without redeeming social value," which had been established in *Memoirs v. Massachusetts* (1966), in favor of a broader standard. The obscenity label can be applied only to a work which, "taken as a whole, appeals to the prurient interest," which depicts or describes sexual conduct in a "patently offensive way," and which, "taken as a whole, lacks serious literary, artistic, political, or scientific value." Second, the Court rejected the notion of national community standards in favor of local community standards. The Court explained that the United States "is simply too big and too diverse for this Court to reasonably expect that such standards could be articulated for all 50 States in a single formulation, even assuming the prerequisite consensus exists."

Promptly some communities began defining obscenity very restrictively. A Georgia community banned the 1971 film *Carnal Knowledge*. The case reached the Supreme Court, and once again, in *Jenkins v. Georgia* (1974), it was faced with making a decision on a case-by-case basis. The Court held that the film could not be found to appeal to the prurient interest or be found patently offensive under Georgia community standards, thus setting a guideline for the limits of allowable differences in local community standards.

Censorship and prior restraint are so alien to the American system that the Supreme Court has found it virtually impossible to apply censorship in any area. On the one hand, the Court acknowledges that adults have a right to be protected from unwanted public obscenity and that children must be protected. On the other, the Court is uncomfortable with any form of prior restraint. It may be that there is no way to write a clear obscenity law, but the Court's failure to provide clear standards has led to considerable litigation: There have been only two Supreme Court cases concerning prior restraint of political ideas, but there have been hundreds of obscenity cases.

The Broadcast Media. The issue of obscenity becomes still more complicated when one addresses the issue of electronic broadcasting. While the freedom to express political ideas is well protected, this protection is not as great for the broadcast media as it is for print media. The reason is that radio and television must use broadcast or microwave frequencies which are considered public property. Therefore the owners of radio and television stations must receive a license from the Federal Communications Commission (FCC). The licensing requirement can be viewed as a form of prior restraint. The government does not seek to control news broadcasts, however, generally granting them the same freedom as the print media; similarly, there is no government control of individual broadcasts of artistic, scientific, or medical materials.

Yet broadcasters, knowing that their licenses (which may be extremely lucrative) can be revoked or denied renewal, engage in considerable self-censorship, which also occurs in the film industry. Generally, self-censorship has been sufficiently effective that only a few cases of license nonrenewal exist. Some conservative commentators and politicians have argued that this self-censorship does not go far enough. In fact, a fairly sizeable minority of citizens are concerned by what they describe as a climate of permissiveness with regard to sex and violence, particularly on television. In mid-1995, for example, Congress heatedly debated whether to require manufacturers of television sets to include a "V-chip" that would allow parents to block their children's viewing of programs with violent or sexual content.

Public Live Presentations. Public live presentations fall into the category of assemblies and are therefore subject to the restriction that they must be "peaceable." Since the question of riots or violent behavior is not often at stake, an issue more often debated is the extent to which governments (primarily local but occasionally state) can restrain public live presentations of a sexual nature. Public displays in areas of public traffic, where such presentations might assault the sensibilities of some adults or be viewed by children, are widely prohibited by indecent exposure laws.

The problem is more complex for public live presentations in private businesses or in publicly or privately owned and operated theaters. Those who favor censorship of sexually explicit materials have been most successful in restricting sexually explicit presentations in establishments that sell alcoholic beverages or those in which activities that come close to prostitution can be documented. For other privately owned establishments open exclusively to adults, local governments have generally found it difficult to write statutes or ordinances which are specific enough to avoid being declared unconstitutionally vague without at the same time being declared unconstitutional for restraining freedom of expression. Even publicly owned and operated theaters have been forced to permit their use by productions that include nudity. Officials in Chattanooga, Tennessee, discovered this in the 1970's when they attempted to bar the presentation of the musical *Hair* from being performed in a publicly owned and operated theater (*Southeastern Promotions, Ltd. v. Conrad*, 1975). —*Richard L. Wilson*

See also Alien and Sedition Acts; Assembly and association, freedom of; *City of Renton v. Playtime Theaters*; Civil liberties; Clear and present danger test; Comstock Law; *Miller v. California*; *Near v. Minnesota*; *New York Times Co. v. United States*; *New York v. Ferber*; *Roth v. United States*; Speech and press, freedom of; *Village of Skokie v. National Socialist Party of America*; Zoning.

BIBLIOGRAPHY

The best book of general scholarship on the subject is Henry J. Abraham and Barbara A. Perry, *Freedom and the Court* (6th ed. New York: Oxford University Press, 1994). For a concise, thoughtful summary of the reasons it is so difficult to fashion a rule or definition of pornography, see Kent Greenwalt, "Pornography," in his *Speech, Crime, and the Uses of Language* (New York: Oxford University Press, 1989). Wallace Mendelson's *The American Constitution and Civil Liberties* (Homewood, Ill.: Dorsey Press, 1981) contains useful excerpts from important Supreme Court cases on censorship. For a detailed history of the free speech clause, see Stephen A. Smith, "The Origins of the Free Speech Clause," in Raymond S. Rodgers, *Free Speech Yearbook: The Meaning of the First Amendment 1791-1991* (Carbondale, Ill.: Southern Illinois University Press, 1991).

Certiorari, writ of

DEFINITION: An order from an appellate court issued in cases in which the court has discretion over whether to hear an appeal from the decision of a lower court and determines to exercise its discretion to hear the case

SIGNIFICANCE: The writ of *certiorari* is the legal mechanism by which the United States Supreme Court accepts almost all cases it decides, giving the Court almost complete discretion in the choice of which cases to hear

At common law the writ of *certiorari* was a writ issued by a superior court to a lower tribunal directing the tribunal to deliver a certified record of its proceedings in a particular case to the superior court. The record thus certified was the basis for the superior court's review of the lower tribunal's proceeding. The most familiar use of the writ of *certiorari* in the American system is by the U.S. Supreme Court. In most cases, the Court has almost complete discretion in the choice of cases to hear, and it exercises this discretion by either granting—and thus choosing to hear—or denying the writ of *certiorari* or "cert."

See also *Amicus curiae* brief; Appellate process; Supreme Court of the United States.

PETITIONS FOR REVIEW ON WRIT OF CERTIORARI TO THE U.S. SUPREME COURT, FISCAL YEAR 1992

Nature of Proceeding	Pending October 1, 1991	Filed	Terminated			Pending September 30, 1992
			Granted	Denied	Dismissed	
Total	**1,645**	**4,635**	**127**	**4,104**	**12**	**2,037**
Criminal	729	1,849	17	1,717	1	843
U.S. civil	170	526	24	464	0	208
Private civil	674	2,128	80	1,799	11	912
Administrative appeals	72	132	6	124	0	74

Source: U.S. Department of Justice, Bureau of Justice Statistics, *Sourcebook of Criminal Justice Statistics—1993*. Washington, D.C.: U.S. Government Printing Office, 1994. Data are from Administrative Office of U.S. Courts.

Note: U.S. civil filings involve suits against the federal government in U.S. district courts. Private civil filings involve suits in which litigation is between states and/or private citizens. Administrative appeals include applications for enforcement or petitions for review of orders of an administrative agency.

Chambers v. Florida

Court: U.S. Supreme Court

Date: Decided February 12, 1940

Significance: This case established that confessions elicited by compulsion short of actual physical duress cannot be used in state criminal proceedings

In May, 1933, an elderly white man was murdered in Pompano, Florida. Within the next twenty-four hours, twenty-five to forty black men were arrested. Isaiah Chambers and three others were questioned by relays of law enforcement officers and deputies continuously for the next five days. There were two all-night sessions. During this period they were not permitted to consult counsel or to see family or friends. On the fifth day they confessed. Although Florida admitted that they had been held incommunicado, there was considerable dispute whether physical force had been used against the four defendants. The Florida state courts found that all allegations of physical coercion were false and that the confessions were therefore admissible. On the basis of the confessions, Chambers and his co-defendants were convicted and sentenced to death.

The Supreme Court unanimously reversed the convictions. At that time the only relevant precedent was *Brown v. Mississippi* (1936). In that case the Court reversed a conviction based on a confession which had been obtained by torture. Forced by jurisdictional rules to accept the Florida state court findings that Chambers and the others had not been tortured, the Court nevertheless held the convictions invalid. Justice Hugo L. Black wrote the Court's opinion. He stated that the circumstances by which the confessions had been obtained rendered them involuntary even though physical coercion may not have been applied. Justice Black focused on incommunicado interrogation. The defendants had been questioned for five days; they were held at the will of their jailers without formal charges having been brought against them. They were terrified: "[T]he haunting fear of mob violence was around them in an atmosphere charged with excitement and public indignation." They had no opportunity to consult friends or family. Once they did confess, the interrogators insisted that they redo the confessions so as to conform their words to the physical facts of the crime. Black insisted that the confessions were compelled, not voluntary, and consequently they were inadmissible.

In the immediate sense, *Chambers v. Florida* establishes that compulsion that stops short of physical coercion can still render a confession invalid. It prevents incommunicado and protracted interrogation of criminal suspects. In the broader development of American criminal procedure, this case is an important precursor of *Miranda v. Arizona* (1966), which requires law enforcement officers to obtain a knowing waiver of a potential defendant's right to remain silent in situations of custodial interrogation.

See also Black, Hugo L.; *Brown v. Mississippi*; Evidence, rules of; *Miranda v. Arizona*.

Change of venue

Definition: The removal of a suit from the locality in which it was filed to another locality

Significance: Change of venue rules allow for suits to be transferred to new locations where the interests of convenience or of justice will be better served

"Venue" concerns the place at which a case is to be tried. The appropriate venue for civil cases is typically the county in which the defendant resides, events underlying a controversy occurred, or where subject matter such as land is located. For criminal actions, Article III, section 2 of the Constitution specifies that a trial shall occur in the state where the underlying offense was committed. The Sixth Amendment provides for a jury from the state and district where the crime was committed.

A case filed originally in one location may be moved to another place under certain circumstances. A criminal defendant, for example, may seek a change of venue on the grounds that a fair trial cannot be obtained in the original venue. In civil cases, a case may be transferred from one venue to another for the convenience of the parties or witnesses or in the interests of justice generally.

See also Bill of Rights, U.S.; Civil procedure; Constitution, U.S.; Criminal procedure; King, Rodney, case and aftermath.

Charles River Bridge v. Warren Bridge Co.

Court: U.S. Supreme Court

Date: Decided February 12, 1837

Significance: This decision overturned monopoly rights of the holder of a charter but upheld the sanctity of contract law as long as contracts are well designed

This 1837 case involving the sanctity of contracts and monopoly rights came before the Supreme Court on a writ of error from the Massachusetts Supreme Court. Acting under a 1785 charter from the state of Massachusetts, the Charles River Bridge Company erected a toll bridge across the Charles River, assuming that such a charter (as had been prior practice) included a monopoly over bridges built in that region. The company had compensated Harvard College for impairing an exclusive franchise, previously granted to Harvard in 1650 to operate a ferry across the Charles River. In 1828, however, the state of Massachusetts authorized a second bridge company, the Warren Bridge Company, to erect a second toll bridge near the Charles River Bridge. The Charles River Bridge Company filed a suit maintaining that the legislature had set aside its constitutional rights, and the case reached the Massachusetts Supreme Court.

In colonial days, charters, such as those given to the London Company in the early 1600's that led to the Jamestown settlement in 1607, had contained an implied grant from the crown of monopoly power in the charter area. No other joint-stock trading companies could settle in the Jamestown area, for example, without violating the London Company's charter. For two hundred years, American business had operated under the impression that charters authorized by state legislatures also contained such monopoly powers. Typically, organizations receiving such charters—banks, hospitals, schools—faced little competition because of the regional nature of the charters, which tended to spread chartered companies throughout a state. The proximity of the Warren Bridge, however, threatened the business of the Charles River Bridge directly.

Chief Justice Roger B. Taney of Maryland wrote the U.S. Supreme Court's opinion. He cited a case (*Proprietors of the Stourbridge Canal v. Wheeley and others*) which stated that any ambiguity in contract terms should operate against "adventurers" and in favor of the public and that the plaintiffs could only claim what the act promised them. As for the Charles River Bridge Company, all the "franchises and rights of property enumerated in the charter . . . remain unimpaired." Did the construction of the Warren Bridge, however, destroy the income of the Charles River Bridge? In other words, did it impair the "enumerated" rights in the charter, as the counsel for the company, Daniel Webster, argued? Taney ruled that "in charters of this description, no rights are taken from the public, or given to the corporation, beyond those which the words of the charter, by their natural and proper construction, purport to convey." Since no such words existed, none could be implied.

The Court thus took a narrow definition of contract law, namely that conditions had to be stipulated explicitly, but did not undermine the sanctity of contracts well designed; the Court did not undermine *Dartmouth College v. Woodward* (1819). Monopoly powers, once assumed to accompany all charters, could no longer be implied in contracts. At the same time, the Court reflected the support in the American economic system for competition, with competition as seen in the public interest. Consequently, the justice system increasingly supported economic opportunity and open trade and ruled against arrangements by business or labor that resulted in "restraint of trade," a concept that became a key feature of American antitrust law.

See also Antitrust law; Contract, freedom of; Contract law; *Dartmouth College v. Woodward*; Taney, Roger Brooke.

Chase, Samuel (Apr. 17, 1741, Somerset County, Md.—June 19, 1811, Baltimore, Md.)

IDENTIFICATION: U.S. Supreme Court justice, 1796-1811
SIGNIFICANCE: Perhaps the most partisan Federalist to sit on the Court, Chase was the only Supreme Court justice ever to have been impeached

Samuel Chase's entire career was fraught with controversy. In the early 1780's, he was dropped from the Maryland delegation to the Continental Congress, accused of war profiteering. One of the signers of the Declaration of Independence, he publicly opposed adoption of the Constitution in 1787. In 1790, while he held two Maryland judgeships simultaneously, the state assembly tried to remove him from both, but the vote went in his favor by the narrowest of margins. After he was appointed to the high bench, he became the intellectual leader of the Court headed by Oliver Ellsworth, but he also developed a reputation as a "hanging judge" for his harsh enforcement of the controversial Alien and Sedition Acts of 1798. His 1803 tirade before a grand jury—delivered in the wake of the election of the Republican Thomas Jefferson as president—in

which he denounced democracy as "mobocracy" led to his impeachment in the House of Representatives the next year. When he was tried before the Senate in 1805, however, there were not enough votes to convict him. He served on the Court for six more years, a considerably subdued presence.

See also Alien and Sedition Acts; Ellsworth, Oliver; Federalist Party; Impeachment; Supreme Court of the United States.

Chávez, César (Mar. 31, 1927, near Yuma, Ariz.—Apr. 23, 1993, San Luis, Ariz.)

IDENTIFICATION: Labor leader
SIGNIFICANCE: Chávez organized farmworkers in California into the United Farm Workers Union, an affiliate of the AFL-CIO, and initiated nationwide boycotts of farm produce to gain recognition from growers

Chávez grew up the son of farmworkers in migrant labor camps. In 1952 he joined the Community Service Organization (CSO). He became general director in 1958 but resigned when the CSO resisted efforts to create a farmworkers' union. He thus began his commitment in 1962 to establish the first important farmworkers' union by organizing the National Farm Workers Association. By 1965, seventeen hundred families were organized when he supported migrant Filipino grape pickers in a strike against growers that lasted for years and brought national attention to Chávez's cause. From 1966 until 1978 Chávez organized nationwide boycotts of farm produce such as grapes, lettuce, and citrus fruits. His efforts met with success when California growers signed contracts with the United Farm Workers union (UFW) improving work conditions and wages and providing health care and retirement programs. Although the UFW lost some membership when the

César Chávez in 1971 announcing a contract agreement between the UFW and Coca-Cola's foods division. (AP/Wide World Photos)

Teamsters organized farmworkers, the two groups came together in 1977, agreeing to UFW representation of field workers and Teamster jurisdiction over cannery employees and truck drivers.

Chávez continued his work in the late 1980's, protesting the use of pesticides that contributed to high cancer rates among migrant workers and birth defects among their children. Although his nonviolent boycotts, marches, and fasts often resulted in physical violence toward workers and the jailing of Chávez himself, his protests earned him a nation's respect and the Medal of Freedom from President Bill Clinton.

See also Labor unions; United Farm Workers (UFW).

Cherokee Nation v. Georgia

Court: U.S. Supreme Court

Date: Ruling issued March 18, 1831

Significance: In this case, the Cherokee nation, claiming sovereign immunity from the Georgia state government's legal jurisdiction, sought a Supreme Court injunction which failed but was the prelude to a later short-lived legal victory

In 1830, Congress, urged on by President Andrew Jackson, passed the national Indian Removal Act. It was aimed especially at several southern tribes whose ancestral lands were coveted by white southerners. The Cherokee nation, of northern Georgia, had experienced a high degree of acculturation, adopting American political, legal, and social norms through the work of Protestant missionary societies and close contacts with Anglo-American merchants. Under the leadership of Principal Chief John Ross, the tribe took legal action against the threat of removal and the increasing depredations on the part of Georgia citizens and state officials.

After Georgia adopted laws which disbanded the Cherokees' U.S.-style government and court system and passed laws that organized Cherokee lands into counties under Georgia law, the Cherokees hired prominent Washington attorney William Wirt to represent them.

Wirt appeared before the Court on March 5, 1831, seeking an injunction to restrain the state from enforcing its laws on the Cherokee nation, arguing that Georgia had violated Cherokee sovereignty. While Chief Justice John Marshall and his fellow justices were sympathetic to the Cherokees' cause, Marshall refused to hear the case on the grounds that the Cherokees did not constitute a "foreign state." Rather, Marshall classified Indian tribes as "domestic dependent nations" who were wards of their guardian, the United States government.

In spite of this setback, there were hopeful signs. The possibility of a future legal challenge was suggested on the issue of property rights. Marshall was troubled by the results of the case and apparently moved by the strong dissenting opinion of Justice Smith Thompson. Thompson concluded that the Cherokees did (barely) meet criteria for sovereignty. He also observed that Georgia's attack on a people's attempt to model their own government after that of the United States struck at the heart of American political ideals—the Constitution and Bill of Rights.

Shortly thereafter, the Supreme Court under Marshall adopted the dissenting views of Thompson in *Worcester v. Georgia* (1832). This case involved the arrest of white missionaries for residing on Cherokee land in violation of Georgia law. This time the court upheld Wirt's arguments that Georgia laws were void because they violated and interfered with the government's constitutional treaty-making powers with Indian nations. Marshall now characterized Indian tribes as "distinct, independent political communities retaining their original natural rights" and essentially like "other nations of the earth."

Regardless of the ruling, justice did not prevail at the time. Jackson refused to enforce the decision, and the Cherokees were compelled by military force to set out on the long, arduous trek to Indian Territory (Oklahoma). One-fourth of the tribe perished on this genocidal "Trail of Tears." Later nineteenth century court cases tended to interpret "domestic" and "dependent" in ways that legitimized the ongoing grab for Indian lands. Since 1945, however, the courts have broadened their definition of "nation" in a manner more favorable to tribal peoples.

See also American Indians; Marshall, John.

Chicago seven trial

Date: August, 1968, to November, 1972

Place: Chicago, Illinois

Significance: The "Chicago seven" trial was the federal government's first attempt to prosecute under the antiriot provisions of the 1968 Civil Rights Act

During August, 1968, the city of Chicago hosted the Democratic National Convention. During convention week protesters held numerous antigovernment demonstrations, several of which led to confrontations between protesters and police. Wednesday, nomination day, saw continuous demonstrations with as many as ten thousand protesters involved. In the early evening hours, police and demonstrators clashed violently for twenty minutes before the national press and network news cameras. Violent attacks ensued, and police, demonstrators, reporters, and passersby became victims.

On March 20, 1969, a federal grand jury indicted eight civilians and eight police officers in connection with the incidents that had occurred during the convention. The eight civilians were Abbie Hoffman and Jerry C. Rubin, leaders of the Youth International Party (Yippies); David T. Dellinger, chairman of the National Mobilization Committee to End the War in Vietnam; Rennard C. Davis, leader of Students for a Democratic Society (SDS); Thomas C. Hayden, SDS founder and member; Lee Weiner, research assistant of sociology at Northwestern University; John R. Froines, assistant chemistry professor at the University of Oregon; and Bobby G. Seale, the founder of the Black Panthers. Seale was later tried separately because of the illness of his attorney. The other seven defendants were charged with conspiracy to cross state lines to incite a riot and teach the use of riot weapons, in this case Molotov cocktails.

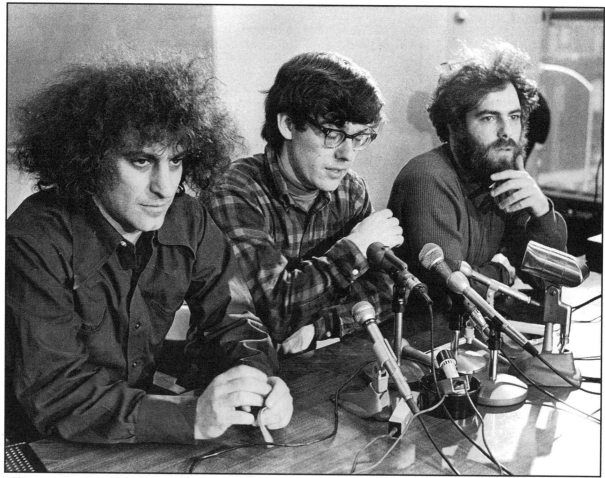

Chicago seven defendants Abbie Hoffman, Rennie Davis, and Jerry Rubin at a press conference. (AP/Wide World Photos)

The trial began on September 24, 1969, with Judge Julius J. Hoffman presiding. During twenty weeks of testimony from almost two hundred witnesses, U.S. prosecuting attorney Thomas Foran accused the defendants of luring potential demonstrators to Chicago in order to further their own revolutionary agenda. Defense attorneys Leonard I. Weinglass and William M. Kunstler compared their clients to Jesus Christ, Susan B. Anthony, and Mohandas K. (Mahatma) Gandhi. The defense contended that the federal government was using the defendants as scapegoats to justify the police violence that had occurred during convention week.

After deliberating for forty hours, the jury acquitted all seven defendants of charges that they had conspired to incite a riot. Dellinger, Davis, Hayden, Hoffman, and Rubin were found guilty, however, of crossing state lines to prompt a riot. Froines and Weiner were cleared of all charges. Judge Hoffman sentenced the convicted defendants to five years in prison and fined them five thousand dollars each, plus court costs. All seven defendants and defense attorneys Kunstler and Weinglass were charged with numerous counts of contempt of court for repeated outbursts, name-calling, and disruption of court

proceedings. Of the eight police officers charged in the matter, seven were acquitted; charges against the eighth were dropped after a mistrial. Demonstrations were held across the country to protest the verdicts and sentences. The Chicago seven immediately appealed their convictions.

On November 21, 1972, the U.S. Court of Appeals for the Seventh Circuit overturned the convictions of the five defendants, citing improper rulings and conduct on the part of Judge Hoffman during the trial and his deprecatory and antagonistic attitude toward the defendants.

See also Black Panther Party; Civil disobedience; Contempt of court; Police brutality; Speech and press, freedom of; Students for a Democratic Society (SDS); Vietnam War.

Chief of police

DEFINITION: Generally considered to be the senior uniformed police officer in a community

SIGNIFICANCE: Chiefs of police exert a powerful influence in police departments and in their communities because of their leadership of the departments and their interaction with community officials and the public

The chief of police is the administrative head of a unique public service entity, the police department. The services that the police perform are well known by most Americans and include protecting life and property, preserving law and order, and providing a wide range of emergency services. From a management point of view, police forces are unique in that they are considered paramilitary organizations adhering to policies developed to implement laws created by legislative bodies. In the process of carrying out their duties, chiefs of police are subject to a variety of organizational and external political pressures. These pressures come not only from union leadership internal to the department but also from political leadership in the municipality, politically active citizens' groups, and the general public. Their training is increasingly dependent upon years of hands-on experience coupled with a variety of advanced degree programs.

See also Civilian review boards; International Association of Chiefs of Police; Police; Sheriff; State police.

Child abuse

DEFINITION: Physical, sexual, or emotional mistreatment or neglect of a child, typically by the person responsible for the child's care

SIGNIFICANCE: Child abuse is both a crime and a basis for civil proceedings through which the state supervises a child's family or places a child in the care of others to protect the child from harm

Child abuse comprises every type of harm inflicted upon children. Physical abuse may range from excessive discipline to murder. As society's attitude toward children has changed, so have beliefs about appropriate discipline. Although serious efforts to protect children from physical mistreatment began in the nineteenth century, the evolution of legal and social protection for children was slow. Today, in most jurisdictions, spanking with any object that leaves marks on the child may result in intervention in the family by welfare agencies, police, or the court. Physical abuse may result in grievous injuries: massive welts and bruises, severe burns, or multiple fractures. Parental ignorance, frustration, or inability to control impulses is often the cause.

Sexual abuse is often more difficult to identify because of the absence of physical evidence. The victim is usually female, the perpetrator a stepfather or boyfriend of the child's mother; however, incest is not uncommon. Such abuse may begin with inappropriate touching when the child is young and lead to intercourse as the child matures. Attempts at sexual intercourse with very young children results in obvious physical trauma. Sexual abuse causes severe and prolonged emotional damage, but it may go unreported and undetected for years. An older victim may not complain about sexual misconduct until it appears that a younger sibling will be threatened with a similar assault.

Child neglect may have consequences as life threatening as physical abuse. Neglect is often the consequence of poor judgment or a lack of parenting skills, as when a parent leaves a young child unattended. The age of the child and the length of the parent's absence are factors that courts consider in determining whether the neglect constitutes a crime or warrants judicial intervention in the family. Some circumstances pose obvious and grave risks to the welfare of the child, such as abandonment of a newborn. Infants and young children need not only constant supervision but also food, water, and clothing. Failure to provide these necessities can lead to malnutrition, dehydration, and death. Neglecting to provide a clean, safe home may also be grounds for authorities to file a criminal complaint and remove children from an unsafe environment.

Physical abuse, sexual abuse, and neglect can each cause disastrous emotional consequences for the child victim. Some caretakers inflict severe emotional trauma, however, without ever touching the victim. Emotional abuse is not commonly prosecuted because of the difficulty in detection and proof. Misuse of alcohol or other drugs is sometimes an underlying cause of abuse or neglect. Babies born to mothers who are addicted to dangerous drugs suffer direct physical harm because the drugs pass through the mother's placenta to the child before birth, sometimes causing physical abnormalities or mental impairment. Exposure to certain drugs can produce painful withdrawal symptoms for newborns.

The Victims. The nature of the victims is a significant obstacle to prosecuting abusive adults and protecting abused children. Infants and very young children are unable to seek help; older children are often too intimidated to complain. In many societies throughout history, children have been treated cruelly, often with the sanction of religious or secular authority. The first organized effort in the United States to protect children began in 1875 with the founding of the New York County Society for the Prevention of Cruelty to Children in response to a notorious case involving a child, Mary Ellen, who had been beaten and neglected. Concerned citizens found that no remedy was available to aid abused children. They sought assistance from the Society for the Prevention of Cruelty to Animals, which successfully petitioned the court on Mary Ellen's behalf. The favorable outcome inspired the founding of organizations throughout the United States to prevent cruelty to children.

In the twentieth century, the development of the X ray enabled pediatricians to diagnose and study injured infants and children more accurately. Radiological studies showed a common association of injuries to the brain and abnormal findings in the long bones that appeared to be willfully inflicted. In 1961, Doctor C. Henry Kempe identified and described the "battered child syndrome" to focus attention on the many children who appeared to be suffering from nonaccidental injury.

The increased awareness of child abuse that was inspired by attention from the medical community and advances in diagnostic techniques fundamentally altered the response of the legal system not only in the prosecution of child abuse but also in civil proceedings to protect dependent children. Medical

NUMBER OF ABUSED CHILDREN REPORTED TO STATE AGENCIES

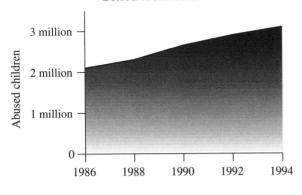

Source: Data are from the National Committee to Prevent Child Abuse.

evidence was available to the courts in many instances when the victim could not testify. Such evidence could show that injuries or symptoms of neglect were not medically consistent with the explanations provided by the child's guardians. The consequences of child abuse are significant to society for a number of reasons. Studies show that abused children, when they become parents, tend to abuse their own children. Moreover, many juvenile delinquents and adult criminals were mistreated or neglected children. Having an effective legal system to prevent abuse and ameliorate its consequences is therefore of paramount importance.

The Abusers. Abusive behavior is not confined to any particular race or class, but families from lower socioeconomic groups tend to be overrepresented in judicial child abuse proceedings. This tendency may be attributable to the greater contact such families have with police and social service agencies or to the fact that, with fewer resources, they tend to suffer greater stress and frustration, leading to physically aggressive treatment of children. Cases of sexual abuse are divided more evenly among the various races and socioeconomic groups. Many authorities believe that pedophiles cannot be cured. Counseling and education can be effective remedies, however, for other types of abuse and neglect and have been utilized successfully by courts and social service agencies to assist in keeping families together. State laws typically provide that willfully causing or permitting a child to suffer is a crime punishable either as a misdemeanor or as a felony, depending upon the severity of the harm. Adults who abuse children may also be guilty of violating general criminal statutes such as those proscribing battery, mayhem, rape, or murder.

Legal Intervention. Two distinct and separate judicial proceedings exist to cope with suspected child abuse. The state may file criminal charges against one accused of mistreating a child to ascertain guilt or innocence of the accused and to impose punishment mandated by statute on those convicted.

Broadly worded child endangerment statutes in the various states supplement other laws that apply to adult victims as well. The public prosecutor has considerable discretion in determining whether to file criminal charges. The severity of the crime and the availability of resources to prosecute are considerations in each case.

Successfully prosecuting child abuse is often difficult. Guilt must be established beyond a reasonable doubt to convict, and the victim may be unable or unwilling to testify against the accused. A criminal defendant has a right to confront and cross-examine witnesses for the prosecution. Children are understandably reluctant to testify against a parent or other adult authority figure. If the defendant is convicted and incarcerated, the child may benefit temporarily by the abuser's absence while in prison, but the solution is temporary because most defendants are released after, at the most, several years in prison.

In all states, an additional legal proceeding, civil in nature, permits the court to intervene in troubled families and provide protection for abused and neglected children. The juvenile court hears cases involving juvenile crime; it also may assert its jurisdiction over mistreated children. State law gives police, probation officers, and social workers the authority to take abused or neglected children into temporary custody to ensure their safety. Parents are given notice of a hearing to determine whether continued protective detention is required. The initial hearing is like a criminal arraignment; the parent or guardian is apprised of the allegations, and the judge determines where the child will live until the trial to adjudicate the child's need for protection. The trial is a civil, not criminal, proceeding, in which the justification for court supervision is typically proved by a preponderance of the evidence rather than the more difficult evidentiary burden ("beyond a reasonable doubt") of criminal prosecutions. Once the court has determined that the child will benefit by court supervision, a second hearing determines whether the child should remain in the custody of parents or guardians or be placed with relatives or in a foster home, group home, or shelter. A social worker is assigned to supervise the family, and the matter is reviewed periodically in court.

The juvenile court must balance the need to protect the child with respect for the right of parents to have custody. The majority of cases do not require removal of the child from home. Only when serious or life-threatening harm or injuries have been sustained or threatened are children placed with surrogate parents. The modern approach is either to reunite families quickly or to move the child into a permanent, stable family in which adoption is possible. Separate legal proceedings may be employed to terminate parental rights permanently.

Family courts which hear divorce cases may receive evidence regarding child abuse or neglect when resolving child custody and visitation issues between divorcing parents. Such courts, however, usually refer serious matters of abuse to social service agencies or to the juvenile court and defer to the juvenile court's jurisdiction when the state seeks to protect an abused child.

A successful government effort to protect children depends on early detection, but friends and neighbors are often reluctant to notify authorities that a child is being harmed. In the past, doctors were also slow to report suspected child abuse, fearing that it would damage the relationship with the patient, reveal a privileged communication, or expose the reporting party to civil liability for slander, libel, or invasion of privacy. All states now have child abuse reporting laws, and a few impose the duty on all persons. Most, however, require specific classes of professionals, health care workers, school personnel, and social workers to report abuse. These laws also shield those having a mandatory duty to report from civil or criminal liability. Other laws extend a limited immunity to those who report child abuse, without being compelled to do so by statute, in all cases in which the reporter had a good-faith belief that abuse was occurring. Considering the serious consequences of a criminal prosecution for child abuse and the removal of a child from home, legislatures must balance the need to encourage reporting to protect abused children with the goal of protecting innocent parents and healthy families from government intrusion based on false accusations.

Criminal prosecutions for child abuse can be hampered by the inability or unwillingness of the victim, who may be the only witness, to testify. To qualify as a witness, a child must understand the obligation to testify truthfully and must comprehend the difference between telling the truth and telling a lie. Rarely can young children articulate this knowledge. Furthermore, criminal defendants have a constitutional right to confront and cross-examine witnesses against them. An abused child who can qualify as a witness must take the stand in a courtroom filled with strangers, face an abusive authority figure, and submit to cross-examination. Understandably, many victims refuse to testify. Often successful prosecutions rely on expert medical evidence to win convictions.

In contrast, proceedings in juvenile court are not constrained by the same procedural protections afforded criminal defendants. Some juvenile courts permit children to testify in the judge's chambers without the presence of other family members. The rules of evidence may be relaxed to allow findings of abuse based on a probation officer's or social worker's report. Such reports contain hearsay evidence which would not be admissible in more formal proceedings. An accused criminal defendant has a right to a jury trial; child protective proceedings in juvenile court are tried before a judge. The trend throughout the United States has been to facilitate and encourage the reporting of child abuse and to structure a juvenile court process which ensures the safety, comfort, and welfare of minor children and which augments the parallel criminal proceedings to punish more serious offenses against children.   —*Scot Clifford*

See also Battered child and battered wife syndromes; Child molestation; Domestic violence; Family law; Incest; Juvenile justice system; Kidnapping; Statutory rape.

BIBLIOGRAPHY

Ray E. Helfer, *The Battered Child* (Chicago: University of Chicago Press, 1968), presents an informative overview of child abuse and contains a comprehensive summary of child abuse legislation in each state. For a readable analysis of the causes and prevention of abuse and neglect of children, see Blair Justice, *The Abusing Family* (New York: Human Sciences Press, 1976). Also see James Garbarino, *Protecting Children from Abuse and Neglect* (San Francisco: Jossey-Bass, 1980), and Alfred Kadushin, *Child Abuse: An Interactional Event* (New York: Columbia University Press, 1981), which contains a careful historical account of the development of governmental interest and intervention in child protection in the United States. A volume with no author listed, *Psychological Approaches to Child Abuse* (Totowa, N.J.: Roman and Littlefield, 1981), sets forth an extensive bibliography of useful and informative works on the subject.

Child molestation

DEFINITION: The sexual exploitation of a child who is not developmentally capable of understanding or resisting the contact or who may be psychologically and socially dependent upon the abuser

SIGNIFICANCE: Child molestation includes a wide variety of acts; for a number of reasons child molestation cases are difficult to bring to trial and are very difficult to prove

Child molestation is governed by both criminal and civil statutes. The incidence of child molestation is unknown because it is almost certainly underreported, often going unidentified. It has been estimated that one in five female children and one in eleven male children in the United States will be sexually molested by the age of eighteen. It is also estimated that half of all child molestation is incestuous. Child molestation has been found to occur in families of every racial and ethnic background and at every income and educational level.

Sexual activities involved in child molestation vary in intensity. They can include stroking a child's hair, holding a child close, fondling a child, and having sexual intercourse with a child. Any act that is designed to stimulate the child or to use the child for another's stimulation is child molestation.

Myths. There are a number of myths associated with child molestation. One is the idea that homosexual men are the only ones who molest children. Another is that children enjoy, provoke, or are partially responsible for the sexual act. Yet another myth is that child molestation is committed mainly by strangers. In reality, twice as many abusers are oriented toward opposite-sexed children. Males are predominantly the abusers, but females may also be abusers. Also contrary to common belief, studies have shown that in about 85 percent of the reported cases of child molestation, the abuser is someone known to the child. Molesters range in age from adolescence through the late seventies, but a significant percentage are in their middle to late thirties. The least understood aspect of molestation is the trauma to the child, whether it be physical trauma from violent molestation or the emotional trauma that accompanies any type of child molestation.

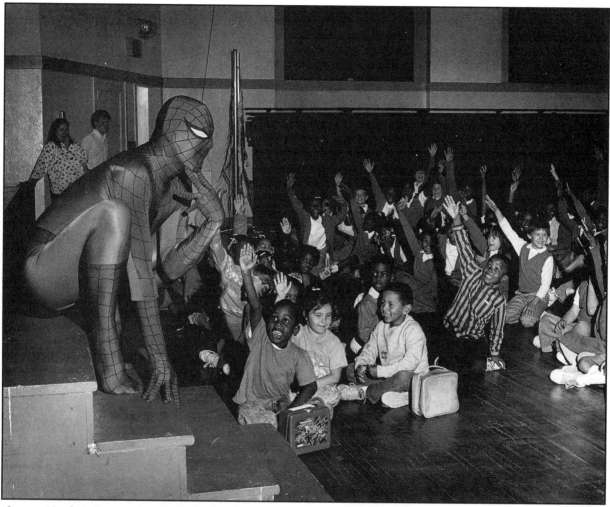

In an antimolestation program in the St. Paul schools, "Spiderman" teaches young children the difference between "good touching" and "bad touching." (James L. Shaffer)

Dynamics of Abuse. Factors that motivate child molesters vary according to the age of the perpetrator. Some teen abusers are sexually inexperienced with persons of their own age, and they prefer younger children because the child is less psychologically threatening. These abusers are typically callous and exploitative in their behavior. They normally seek vulnerable children. Adult abusers manifest other maladjustments, such as alcoholism, which are frequently associated with the aberrant sexual act. Older abusers may suffer from feelings of loneliness and isolation, and they may reach out to children for intimate human contact. Adult abusers may have difficulties relating to people their own age. These difficulties, and therefore the appeal of children to them, may increase when they are experiencing a stressful situation. Some have antisocial personalities which predispose them to prey on children in quest of new sexual thrills.

Child molesters tend to seek passive, quiet, trusting, and unhappy children. They especially gravitate toward children from divorced homes who have low self-esteem. Once the abuser identifies such a child, the abuser desensitizes the child to sexual activity by gradually grooming the child. Grooming may include material enticements (such as gifts), misrepresentation of standards and values (such as telling the child that sexual activity is normal), verbal threats, and overt aggression, such as overpowering the child.

Secrecy is an essential element of child molestation. Several factors contribute to secrecy. The child victim may fear repercussions, such as the breakup of the family. The abuser often offers positive inducements to the child, such as gifts of candy and toys. There may be an emotional bond between the abuser and the child, especially in cases of incest, so that the child feels the need to remain quiet in order to protect his or her mother, father, or other loved one. Developmental variables may contribute to delayed disclosure as well. Naïveté is one such variable. The young child may not understand that the sexual act is wrong or may not be able to verbalize it. Younger children are more likely to accommodate the adult, whereas older children are likely to feel embarrassed or guilty.

Effects of Abuse. Effects on the victims of molestation vary according to such factors as the frequency of the molestation. Among the effects, both short-term and long-term, are affective disturbances, such as anxiety and depression; physical problems, such as genital injury; psychosomatic problems, such as enuresis (bed-wetting); cognitive disturbances, such as poor school achievement; and sociobehavioral disturbances, such as aggressive behavior. The symptoms most commonly identified with victims of child molestation are oversexualized behavior, which includes sexual "acting out" toward adults or children, sexual promiscuity, and a high level of sexual curiosity. Emotional consequences include depression, distrust in interpersonal relations, phobias, cognitive reactions such as flashbacks, and behavioral problems such as eating disorders.

A percentage of cases exists in which allegations of child molestation are unfounded (the size of this percentage is a matter of considerable debate). Accused abusers who are innocent represent a separate class of victims. When an allegation becomes public knowledge, the accused person suffers immediate and serious consequences and will never be viewed in the same way by neighbors, friends, or family. The person begins to carry a stigma which is likely to last a lifetime. The best outcome that he or she can hope for is a finding of "not guilty," which merely signifies that there was not enough evidence for a conviction—it does not prove that the person is innocent.

Legal Issues. Child molestation is governed by both criminal and civil statutes. The act of molesting a child is a crime, punishable by a term of imprisonment and/or a fine. Decisions to prosecute offenders are made on a very subjective basis. Child molestation cases are very difficult to prove. Part of that difficulty is a statutory provision that very young children must be judged competent before they can testify. Another problem is that young children often do not have the vocabulary to describe a sexual assault accurately. The younger the child, the more acute this problem is. Because it can be very difficult for a child to remember and pinpoint exact instances when molestation occurred, the law usually does not require noting specific dates and times when an offense took place. This situation has been cited as a serious problem in child molestation cases.

Yet another problem lies in the sentencing. Most convicted offenders do not receive lengthy prison terms. They normally are out of prison within two years. The victim usually does not feel that justice has been done.

Child molestation is also governed by civil statutes. An abuser can be personally sued by the victim in civil proceedings. If the abuser is found liable, monetary damages are awarded to the victim in civil proceedings. The victim may be seeking compensation for the "pain and suffering" and the emotional trauma that he or she has experienced because of the abuse. In most cases, the victim is primarily seeking validation. He or she wants to heal and move beyond the abuse.

The statute of limitations is different in civil and criminal cases. In civil cases, the period of time during which a victim can bring a lawsuit is based on when the victim remembers the act, rather than on when the act was committed (as in criminal cases). Thus, a victim who has repressed the abuse until he or she is an adult may still bring a civil suit even though it is too late for the prosecutor to file criminal charges.

Accusations of child molestation based on "recovered memories"—most typically these memories are recalled when a person is undergoing counseling or psychotherapy in adulthood—became a heatedly debated issue in the mid-1990's. There was considerable polarization among both psychologists and legal experts as to the reliability of newly recalled memories concerning traumatic events long past. Some experts argued that people's overwhelming emotional reactions to newly recovered memories attest their reliability, while others argued that the reconstructive process of memory (particularly if influenced by a therapist's guidance) essentially may result in false memories. Legal cases in which people accused of molestation sued their accusers' therapists began to appear, with results of the trials being widely varied.

Survivors of child molestation have shown an impressive capacity to handle testifying during a trial. Whether it be a criminal or civil trial, the experience of testifying can serve as a catharsis, a way for the victim to put the sexual abuse behind him or her and to heal.

—*Susan M. Taylor*

See also Child abuse; Domestic violence; Incest; Rape and sex offenses; Statutory rape.

BIBLIOGRAPHY

Among the good sources for further information on child molestation and its legal ramifications are Joseph E. Crnich, *Shifting the Burden of Truth: Suing Child Sexual Abusers, a Legal Guide for Survivors and Their Supporters* (Lake Oswego, Oreg.: Recollex, 1992); Eleanor C. Goldstein, *Confabulations: Creating False Memories, Destroying Families* (Boca Raton, Fla.: Social Issues Resources Series, 1992); Becca Cowan Johnson, *For Their Sake: Recognizing, Responding to, and Reporting Child Abuse* (Martinsville, Ind.: American Camping Association, 1992); Rosamund L. Murdock, *Suffer the Children: A Pediatrician's Reflections on Abuse* (Santa Fe, N.Mex.: Health Press, 1992).

Chimel v. California

COURT: U.S. Supreme Court

DATE: Decided June 23, 1969

SIGNIFICANCE: *Chimel v. California* was the Supreme Court's most significant pronouncement concerning the permissible extent of a warrantless search of a criminal suspect conducted pursuant to making a lawful arrest

Chimel, who was suspected of having committed a burglary at a coin shop a month earlier, was arrested at his home, where the police—who had a warrant for his arrest but not one authorizing a search—at the same time conducted a search. Over Chimel's objections, police searched his entire three-bedroom house, seizing some coins found there that were later entered into evidence at Chimel's trial. Chimel was convicted, and his conviction was twice upheld by California state courts before he petitioned the Supreme Court for review, claiming that the warrantless search of his house had been unreasonable and violated the Fourth Amendment.

In overturning Chimel's conviction, the Supreme Court held that police may search only the person of the arrested criminal suspect and the area "within his immediate control" in order to uncover a concealed weapon and prevent the destruction of evidence. In so deciding, the Court overruled two earlier precedents, *Harris v. United States* (1947) and *United States v. Rabinowitz* (1950), in which a warrantless search was limited only by the nature of what was sought.

As Justice John M. Harlan had stated in *Katz v. United States*, which the Court decided the year before *Chimel* was handed down, "searches conducted outside the judicial process [that is, without a warrant] are per se unreasonable under the Fourth Amendment—subject only to a few specifically established and well-delineated exceptions." One long-standing exception is that permitting a warrantless search that is made incident to a lawful arrest. The justification for this exception is often that the police have not had time to obtain a search warrant, but the open-ended interpretation given the exception by the Harris-Rabinowitz rule gave police tremendous latitude for abuse. In *Chimel*, the offense precipitating the search and the arrest was committed a month before police arrested Chimel, and in the interim Chimel clearly had neither fled nor destroyed all the evidence against him. After obtaining the arrest warrant, police delayed several days before serving it, and they provided no explanation of why there was no time to obtain a search warrant from the court.

In *Weeks v. United States* (1914), the Court made the exclusionary rule, banning introduction at trial of evidence obtained in any unconstitutional fashion, binding on federal courts. Because most crimes are tried at the state level, however, reaction against the exclusionary rule became pronounced only when the Court, led by Chief Justice Earl Warren, extended it to state court proceedings in *Mapp v. Ohio* (1961). The Warren Court was accused of coddling criminals, and when Earl Warren retired in 1969, President Richard Nixon, who had made the Warren Court a campaign issue in 1968, replaced him with an outspoken critic of the exclusionary rule, Warren Burger.

See also Evidence, rules of; *Illinois v. Krull*; *Katz v. United States*; *Leon, United States v.*; *Mapp v. Ohio*; Search and seizure.

Chinese Exclusion Act

DATE: Became law May 6, 1882

DEFINITION: Legislation designed to limit the number of Chinese immigrants to the United States

SIGNIFICANCE: This act represents the first time the United States sought to exclude immigrants by race and nationality; it marked a turning point in what had been, until then, an open door to immigrants from around the world

The Chinese Exclusion Act of 1882 suspended immigration by Chinese laborers to the United States for a period of ten years

and prohibited Chinese residents in the United States from becoming naturalized citizens. Merchants, students, and tourists, however, were still permitted to enter the United States for visits. Although the Chinese Exclusion Act of 1882 was established as a temporary suspension of immigration by Chinese laborers, it was only the first of many laws designed to exclude Asians from entry into the United States.

This law was both a political and social reaction to increasing non-European immigration in the second half of the nineteenth century. As the country became more industrialized and its frontier began to disappear, there was increased apprehension about employment and the role of immigrants in the United States. American labor organizations objected to what they perceived as unfair competition by Chinese laborers.

Background. Chinese immigration to the mainland United States began in earnest after the Taiping Rebellion in 1848. Most Chinese immigrants headed for California, where the Gold Rush of 1849 led to an increased need for labor. In 1854 there were 13,100 Chinese immigrants to the United States. This immigration, regulated by the Burlingame Treaty in 1868, was unrestricted; by 1880, the number of immigrants had risen to 105,465. The majority remained in California, where they were hired as laborers by the railroads, worked as domestics, and opened small businesses. San Francisco was the port of entry for many Chinese; the population of its Chinatown grew from two thousand to twelve thousand between 1860 and 1870.

The size and nature of this early Chinese immigration brought a long-lasting prejudice. Californians thought of Chinese laborers as "coolies"—that is, as cheap labor brought to the United States to undercut wages for American workers. Chinese workers were also accused of being dirty. Authorities in San Francisco suspected that crowded areas of Chinatown were the focus for disease and passed the Cubic Air Ordinance, prohibiting rental of a room with fewer than five hundred cubic feet of space per person. This municipal ordinance was later declared unconstitutional.

Discrimination and violence increased during the 1870's. In 1871 a mob attacked and killed nineteen Chinese people in Los Angeles. Dennis Kearney, a naturalized citizen from Ireland, organized the Workingmen's Party in 1877 to oppose Chinese immigrants. Shouting, "The Chinese must go!" Kearney threatened violence to all Chinese immigrants. In July, 1877, men from an "anti-coolie club" led workers into San Francisco's Chinatown on a rampage that lasted several days.

Since most local ordinances against the Chinese were declared unconstitutional, people who opposed Chinese immigration turned to Congress for new legislation. Congress responded in 1879 with a bill to limit Chinese immigration by prohibiting ships from bringing more than fifteen Chinese immigrants at a time. The bill was vetoed by President Rutherford B. Hayes on the grounds that it violated the Burlingame Treaty. With popular sentiment against continuing Chinese immigration, however, the treaty was amended in 1880, allowing the United States to limit the number of Chinese immigrants.

Exclusionary Legislation. The Chinese Exclusion Act of 1882 was a response to the intensity of anti-Chinese feelings in the West and to close political elections which made western electoral votes critical. As signed into law by President Chester A. Arthur, the act suspended immigration by Chinese laborers for ten years. The vote in the House of Representatives reflected the popularity of the measure. There were 201 votes in favor, 37 against, and 51 absent. Representatives from every section of the country supported the bill, with southern and western House members voting unanimously for the legislation.

Later laws were even more draconian. An amendment in 1884 excluded all Chinese and Chinese residents living in other countries from entering the United States except as students, merchants, or tourists. The Scott Act of 1888 prohibited outright the entry of Chinese laborers and denied reentry to those who traveled abroad, even if they held reentry visas. The law also placed additional restrictions on those who were still permitted to come to the United States. In 1892 the Geary Act extended for an additional ten years the exclusion of Chinese immigrants, prohibited the use of *habeas corpus* by Chinese residents in the United States if arrested, and required all Chinese people to register and provide proof of their eligibility to remain in the United States. The act was renewed in 1902, and Congress made permanent the exclusion of Chinese immigrant laborers in 1904.

These exclusionary laws reflected a significant bias in American attitudes toward immigration by non-Europeans and increasing racial discrimination. Restrictions on intermarriage and land ownership by Chinese in many western states in the early 1900's led to a reduction in the number of Chinese residing in the United States from more than 100,000 in 1890 to 61,639 by 1920.

On December 17, 1943, the Chinese Exclusion Act was repealed. By then the threat of competition by Chinese labor was no longer an issue, and China was an ally of the United States in the war with Japan. —*James A. Baer*

See also Immigration, legal and illegal; Immigration laws; Racial and ethnic discrimination.

BIBLIOGRAPHY

Corinne K. Hoexter, *From Canton to California: The Epic of Chinese Immigration* (New York: Four Winds Press, 1976), looks at Chinese immigration specifically; Maldwyn Allen Jones, *American Immigration* (2d ed. Chicago: University of Chicago Press, 1992), takes a broader view of immigration issues and history. Other valuable works include Tricia Knoll, *Becoming Americans: Asian Sojourners, Immigrants, and Refugees in the Western United States* (Portland, Oreg.: Coast to Coast Books, 1982); Ronald Takaki, *Strangers from a Different Shore: A History of Asian Americans* (Boston: Little, Brown, 1989); United States Commission on Civil Rights, *The Tarnished Golden Door: Civil Rights Issues in Immigration* (Washington, D.C.: U.S. Government Printing Office, 1980).

Church of the Lukumi Babalu Aye v. Hialeah

Court: U.S. Supreme Court

Date: Decided June 11, 1993

Significance: Striking down a ban on animal sacrifices, the Court ruled that a law targeting religious conduct for special treatment must be justified by compelling state interests and must be narrowly tailored to advance those interests

Santeria, a religion combining East African traditions with elements of Roman Catholicism, teaches that rituals of animal sacrifice influence benevolent spirits, and believers perform sacrifices for the cure of the sick and at ceremonies such as marriages and funerals. After most sacrifices, the resulting meat is cooked and eaten by church members. In 1987 a Santeria church was announced for Hialeah, Florida, and the Hialeah city council responded to a public outcry by passing a series of ordinances which had the effect of outlawing the killing of animals in religious rituals while allowing such killing when exclusively done for food or other secular reasons.

Church attorneys attacked the ordinances as a violation of freedom of religion under the First and Fourteenth Amendments. After federal district and appellate courts upheld the ordinances, the church then appealed the case to the Supreme Court, where the justices voted 9 to 0 that the ordinances were unconstitutional.

Justice Anthony Kennedy's opinion for the Court explained that when a law, as in the Hialeah ordinances, is plainly directed at restricting a religious practice, the law must satisfy two tests: justification by a compelling state interest and use of the least restrictive means to promote that interest. Kennedy, however, displeased libertarians in reaffirming *Employment Division, Department of Human Resources of Oregon v. Smith* (1990), a rule that a neutral law of general applicability would not be required to pass the two tests when the law burdens religion incidentally. General and neutral laws might proscribe cruelty to animals or require the safe disposal of animal wastes; however, Hialeah could not place a direct burden on unpopular religious rituals without a secular justification.

Justices David Souter, Harry Blackmun, and Sandra Day O'Connor issued concurring opinions expressing agreement with the ruling while disagreeing with the *Smith* precedent. These three justices wished to return to *Sherbert v. Verner* (1963) and require a compelling state interest and narrowly tailored laws for both direct and indirect burdens on religious practice.

While *Lukumi Babalu* gave First Amendment protection against direct assaults on unpopular religions, many agreed with the concurring justices' opposition to the *Smith* rule. Congress in 1993 responded with the Restoration of Religious Freedom Act, which mandated the compelling state interest test when a federal or state restriction imposed a "cruel choice" by penalizing any significant practice based on sincere religious convictions.

See also *Employment Division, Department of Human Resources of Oregon v. Smith*; Religion, free exercise of; Religious sects and cults; *Reynolds v. United States*; *Sherbert v. Verner*; *Wisconsin v. Yoder*.

Citizen's arrest

DEFINITION: An arrest without a warrant made by a private citizen rather than by an officer of the law

SIGNIFICANCE: Citizen's arrest allows private citizens to detain criminals either for a felony or for a breach of the peace; it also allows law enforcement officials to call for the assistance of a citizen in making an arrest

Citizen's arrest has its roots in English common law, formalized in the Statutes of Winchester in 1285. During the first century of United States history, citizen's arrest was abused for individual self-interest, such as bounty hunting, causing most states to restrict citizen's arrest laws in the nineteenth century. Some of these restrictions limited citizen's arrests by making citizens responsible for wrongful arrests and by placing boundaries on ways of getting information that led to arrests. In *Aguilar v. Texas* (1964), for example, restrictions were placed on the use of citizen informers: The informant must be reliable and credible, and the informant's information has to be corroborated. In addition, the resulting arrest must comply with the standards of "probable cause" contained in the Fourth Amendment.

Although citizens in all states may make arrests for both felonies and misdemeanors, usually the arrests involve a breach of peace committed in the presence of the arresting citizen. Other crimes, especially in the case of felonies, need not be committed in the arrester's presence if the arrester has reasonable cause for believing that the person arrested has committed the crime. When a citizen makes an arrest without the assistance of a police officer, the arrester is responsible for turning the arrested person over to an officer of the law as soon as possible. In other instances, a police officer may request the help of a citizen in making an arrest. In these instances, because the private citizen is legally bound to assist the officer, the officer is responsible for the actions of the private citizen assisting in the arrest.

Most arrests made under citizen's arrest laws are not, however, made by private citizens. Most are made by other individuals or groups covered by these laws, including postal inspectors, private security personnel, bank guards, store employees detaining shoplifters, customs inspectors, private investigators, and state and federal agents. Because not all these groups are registered or licensed, accurate statistics regarding their numbers and their arrests are impossible to obtain.

The degree of physical force that can be used is a critical issue in making a citizen's arrest. State laws vary on the degree of physical force allowable. Deadly force in making a citizen's arrest is generally reserved for situations of protecting other people, and private citizens making such arrests act at their own legal peril in using deadly force. In contrast, when a citizen assists a police officer in making an arrest or in preventing an escape, deadly force may usually be used for self-defense, for the defense of a third party, or at the authorization of a police officer. Because the assisting citizen cannot take time to verify an officer's authority, good-faith assistance is justified, even if the officer misdirects the assisting citizen.

According to Les Johnson, in his book *The Rebirth of Private Policing* (1992), private policing by individual citizens and private groups was increasing in the early 1990's. Even though psychologists and sociologists contend that most citizens avoid intervening in situations of criminal activity, citizens are forming groups such as neighborhood watch groups to lower crimes of theft and personal injury. These groups are especially strong in neighborhoods with high rates of crime and understaffed police forces.

See also Criminal law; Criminal procedure; Deadly force, police use of; Neighborhood watch programs; Police and guards, private; Probable cause; Vigilantism.

Citizenship

DEFINITION: The status of being a citizen, or an inhabitant of a country (or other political entity) who enjoys its full privileges and rights; in the United States, these include the right to vote, to hold elective office, and to enjoy the protections of government

SIGNIFICANCE: Citizenship is a legal term recognizing certain rights and protections; it implies responsibilities as well as privileges

Residence in a particular place does not automatically give a person citizenship. Citizenship must be conferred by law or by constitution. The definition of a citizen was not spelled out in the United States Constitution until the Fourteenth Amendment was passed in 1868. That amendment states, "All persons born or naturalized in the United States, and subject to the jurisdiction thereof, are citizens of the United States and of the State wherein they reside."

Birthright Citizenship. Americans are accustomed to the concept of automatic citizenship granted to persons born in the United States, who are called "natural-born citizens." Historically, this was not a common concept. Most nations were more like ancient Rome, which had different degrees of citizenship while the majority of people in the Roman empire were merely "subjects" of Rome and did not have the rights of citizenship. Many were slaves of Rome. Rome had two classes of citizens: full citizens and those who could own property and engage in business but could not hold public office. The children of these "half citizens" received the same political status as their parents.

English Heritage. The concept of American citizenship grew from English roots. During the Middle Ages political loyalties and protections came from the feudal system that operated in Europe for a thousand years. A characteristic of modern times was the development of the idea of nation-states and with that the concept of nationality. Both obligations and rights were intrinsic to the status of having a nationality.

The English common law held that people born within the royal dominions were automatically the "king's subjects." If one's parents were "natural-born subjects," then one had an inherent claim to the "rights of Englishmen." As early as 1350 it was clear that in English law the place of birth was not so important as the citizenship of a child's parents. In legal terms,

In a swearing-in ceremony that connected inductees at Miami's Orange Bowl with Chief Justice Warren Burger via satellite, more than fourteen thousand people became citizens on July 4, 1986. (AP/Wide World Photos)

citizenship was affected by *jus soli* (birthplace) and *jus sanguinis* (descent).

Colonial Background. The American colonists were merely English people residing in America, and they claimed all their rights as Englishmen. The Virginia Charter of 1606 recognized that situation, and in it the king granted to all his subjects living in the "Colonies and Plantations," as well as to any children born there, "all Liberties, Franchises, and Immunities, within any of our other Dominions, to all intents and purposes, as if they had been abiding and born, within this our Realm of England."

In fact it was this very concept of equality of Englishmen, regardless of where in the realm they lived, that provided a philosophical basis for the American war for independence. The Americans demanded equal treatment and claimed that their own "American parliaments" (assemblies) should rule over them rather than the British Parliament in London. Not all American colonists were English, however, and that fact raised questions of citizenship. It was much easier to become naturalized citizens in America than in England. English Americans from the earliest days of settlement had accepted "foreigners" as equal subjects of the king.

Citizenship: Limited or Absolute? Are the obligations of citizenship and allegiance limited or absolute? This was a key question in the disputes between England and the American colonies before the American Revolution. In the Declaratory Act of 1766 the British Parliament claimed to have "full power and authority to make laws and statutes of sufficient force and validity to bind the colonies and people of America, subjects of the crown of Great Britain, in all cases whatsoever."

The Americans categorically rejected that idea of unlimited political authority over them. They claimed their rights as Englishmen to make their own laws within their colonial assemblies. They rejected the idea that the British Parliament could dictate to them and accepted the authority of the English king only in a limited constitutional sense. Citizenship required allegiance, but as freemen, not as slaves. Patrick Henry eloquently expressed the attitude of his countrymen: "Is life so sweet and peace so dear as to be purchased at the price of chains and slavery? Forbid it, Almighty God! I know not what course others may take, but, as for me, give me Liberty or give me Death!"

Contractual American Citizenship. The result was an independent United States and a constitution that spelled out the limits of governmental authority. The government was to be strong enough to provide for the common defense and a stable society, but it was to be limited in its interference in the lives of the free citizens of the United States. Citizens owed obedience to governments only in exchange for the protection of their fundamental rights. It was essentially a contract with mutual obligations on both sides.

The new state governments had the authority to grant citizenship within their borders. They did so and welcomed many new immigrants. Typically the states required a year or two of residence within the state and an oath of allegiance and good moral character for a person to become a citizen.

After the United States Constitution went into effect, the Naturalization Act of 1802 required five years of residence, a loyalty oath accepting the principles of the Constitution, and proof of good character and behavior for a person to become a United States citizen. The law also required all immigrants to register with the government.

Citizenship Denied. During the nineteenth century there were two classes of people born in the United States who were denied citizenship in that country: slaves and American Indians. Even the 250,000 free blacks in the United States did not have equal protection of the law and political opportunities associated with citizenship during the first half of the nineteenth century.

The conscience of many Americans was stirred, but it took a civil war and further political upheaval before these matters were addressed. Former slaves were—at least on paper—granted citizenship and guaranteed civil rights with the Thirteenth, Fourteenth, and Fifteenth Amendments to the Constitution (1865-1870). Some American Indians were granted citizenship with the Dawes Act of 1887; others had to wait until the Citizenship Act of 1924.

Foreign-Born Americans. "Natural-born citizens" are either born in the United States or born in a foreign country of one or two parents who are United States citizens. A "certificate of citizenship" is issued to confirm that fact, but normally a five-year period of continuous residency in the United States is required between the ages of fourteen and twenty-eight years.

Naturalization. A "naturalization paper" is issued for naturalized citizens when they acquire citizenship. They must have been lawful residents of the United States for five years and must demonstrate a knowledge of the fundamentals of American government and history, and they must be of good moral character. They must also promise to obey the laws of the United States and defend its Constitution and laws and agree to serve in the United States military if required to do so. The process includes a hearing before a United States district court or certain state courts of record. That hearing is followed, at least thirty days later, by the administering of the oath of allegiance.

Foreign Visitors. Aliens visiting the United States have certain rights and protections, but remaining in the United States is not one of them. Aliens are sometimes expelled from the United States for subversion, criminal or immoral behavior, violation of narcotic laws, or mental or physical defects. More often, however, expulsion is for failure to comply with conditions of nonimmigrant status or for entering the United States without legal documents or by false statements. Approximately ten thousand aliens a year are thus deported from the United States. Deportation of aliens is an administrative enforcement of the laws and not a judicial procedure, so court trials are not involved.

Expatriation. American citizens have the right, if they choose, to relinquish their citizenship. This process is called "expatriation." They cannot, however, lose their citizenship simply by fleeing the country to avoid serving in the military or by serving in a foreign military without United States consent. A request to renounce citizenship can be accomplished in the United States only in time of war. In a foreign country a person can make the renunciation before a diplomatic officer or can take an oath of allegiance to another government.

Expatriation is a very rare occurrence among American citizens because citizenship is so highly prized. There are many millions of people in other parts of the world who would quickly take American citizenship if they had the opportunity. Many do immigrate to the United States, but American immigration laws slow the flow of naturalization, and many people must wait many years before becoming American citizens.

—*William H. Burnside*

See also Alien and Sedition Acts; Civil Rights Acts of 1866-1875; Extradition; Illegal aliens; Immigration, legal and illegal; Immigration and Naturalization Service (INS); Immigration laws; Immigration Reform and Control Act; *Scott v. Sandford*.

BIBLIOGRAPHY

For a historical perspective on this subject, see James H. Kettner, *The Development of American Citizenship, 1608-1870* (Chapel Hill: University of North Carolina Press, 1978). Henry C. Black, *Black's Law Dictionary* (5th ed. St. Paul, Minn.: West, 1979), gives concise discussions of legal terms pertaining to immigration and citizenship; somewhat more detail is given in Bryan Garner, *A Dictionary of Modern Legal Usage* (New York: Oxford University Press, 1987). For comparative systems of citizenship see A. N. Sherwin-White, *Roman Society and Roman Law in the New Testament* (Oxford: Clarendon Press, 1965). Samuel MacClintock, *Aliens Under the Federal Laws of the United States* (Chicago: Illinois Law Review, 1909), and J. Mervyn Jones, *British Nationality Law and Practice* (Oxford: Clarendon Press, 1947), provide American and English background.

City of Renton v. Playtime Theaters

COURT: U.S. Supreme Court
DATE: Decided February 25, 1986
SIGNIFICANCE: In rejecting a First Amendment challenge to a dispersal zoning ordinance specifically directed at motion picture theaters that show sexually explicit films, the Supreme Court substantially expanded the authority available to local governments seeking to limit the sites at which adult film theaters might be located in a community

The city of Renton, Washington, adopted an ordinance prohibiting any adult film theater from locating within 1,000 feet of any residential area, school, church, or park. The new owners of two theaters who intended to show sexually explicit films to the public at their theaters brought suit in federal court to enjoin (negate) the ordinance on the grounds that it unconstitutionally regulated their expressive activities. The federal court of appeals held that the ordinance violated the First Amendment. The U.S. Supreme Court reversed the decision and ruled that the ordinance was constitutional.

Laws that regulate expressive activity based on the content of speech are presumed to violate the First Amendment. Such content-discriminatory laws receive strict scrutiny and are struck down in all but the most compelling of circumstances. Since the ordinance in question in *Renton* restricted the location of theaters showing sexually explicit films but did not regulate the location of other movie theaters, the ordinance appeared to be directed at the content of speech in violation of this basic rule of First Amendment jurisprudence.

By a 7-2 vote, however, the Supreme Court held that a different free speech principle applied to the Renton zoning law. While "the ordinance treats theaters that specialize in adult films differently from other kinds of theaters," Justice William Rehnquist, writing for the majority, explained, "the Renton ordinance is aimed not at the *content* of the films shown at 'adult motion picture theaters,' but rather at the *secondary effects* of such theaters on the surrounding community." The city's goal in adopting the ordinance was not to suppress the presentation of adult films, but rather to prevent the crime and neighborhood blight that adult movie theaters may cause. Since these objectives are unrelated to an attempt to silence the message being communicated by adult films, the Renton ordinance was more properly characterized as a content-neutral regulation. Accordingly, the ordinance could be upheld under a relatively lenient standard of review.

The importance of the *Renton* decision extends beyond its particular facts. The secondary-effects analysis utilized by the Court in *Renton* not only makes it easier for cities to regulate the location of adult theaters and bookstores but also arguably creates a new basis for justifying restrictions on other kinds of speech. In *Boos v. Barry* (1988), for example, the District of Columbia unsuccessfully attempted to justify a content-discriminatory ordinance prohibiting protests outside foreign embassies on the grounds that the challenged law was aimed at the secondary effects of speech. Although the Court did not accept the District's argument in *Boos*, the applicability of the secondary effects doctrine to speech that lies at the core of the First Amendment, such as political speech, remains unresolved.

See also Censorship; *O'Brien, United States v.*; Speech and press, freedom of; Zoning.

Civil disobedience

DEFINITION: A deliberate act of law breaking to protest a law or governmental policy that is regarded as immoral

SIGNIFICANCE: Civil disobedience is an important type of political dissent that goes beyond legal means of protest; it was widely employed by the Civil Rights and anti-Vietnam War movements

Notable discussions of the conflict between the individual and legal authority are found in Plato's *Apology* and *Crito* and Sophocles' *Antigone*. The classic discussion of civil disobedience, however, is in the essay "Civil Disobedience" by Henry David Thoreau, first presented in a public lecture at Concord, Massachusetts, in January of 1848 under the title, "On the Relation of the Individual to the State." Thoreau defended his refusal to pay the Massachusetts poll tax because of his opposition to government policies, specifically the Mexican War and governmental acceptance of slavery. He contended that the claims of individual conscience were superior to those of the state and should be followed, even if the individual must violate the law and be subject to arrest and imprisonment. Thoreau himself had been arrested for his refusal to pay taxes, and he spent one night in the Concord jail until an anonymous friend made the tax payment owed by Thoreau.

Early in the essay, Thoreau posed the question: "Must the citizen ever for a moment, or in the least degree, resign his conscience to the legislator?" His famous answer was: "I think that we should be men first, and subjects afterward. It is not desirable to cultivate a respect for the law, so much as for the right. The only obligation which I have a right to assume, is to do at any time what I think right." He added the observation that "Law never made men a whit more just; and by means of their respect for it, even the well-disposed are daily made the agents of injustice." For Thoreau, the emphasis is placed on the appeal to individual conscience to justify the breaking of law.

The best-known contemporary manifesto on civil disobedience is Martin Luther King, Jr.'s "Letter from a Birmingham Jail," written in April, 1963. King's letter was a response to a public appeal made by eight white Alabama clergymen who urged King and his associates not to engage in mass protests against segregation in Birmingham. Instead they recommended negotiation and dialogue. King in reply insisted that sit-ins, marches, and other forms of nonviolent direct action were a means of creating a crisis and thereby establishing "such creative tensions that a community that has constantly refused to negotiate is forced to confront the issue." King also addressed the white ministers' criticism of King's readiness to resort to breaking the law, especially when he had urged officials in the South to obey the 1954 Supreme Court decision outlawing racial segregation in public schools. King wrote: "One may well ask, 'How can you advocate breaking some laws and obeying others?' The answer is to be found in the fact that there are two types of laws. There are *just* laws and there are *unjust* laws. I would agree with St. Augustine that 'An unjust law is no law at all.' " According to King, an unjust law is one that is out of harmony with the moral law. He thus offers what is sometimes called a "higher law" defense of civil disobedience, which differs from the appeal to individual conscience made by Thoreau.

Definition. In the writings of both Thoreau and King, one characteristic feature of civil disobedience is the deliberate violation of some established law or legal requirement. Civil disobedience is, after all, disobedience, although, as King and

Fifteen antiwar protesters were arrested in this 1969 demonstration in which they blocked the entrance to an Army induction center. (AP/Wide World Photos)

others have noted, the law violated may be only a putatively valid law. Especially in American legal contexts, a law may sometimes be challenged in order to test its constitutionality in court. Some have questioned whether such law-testing should be counted as civil disobedience. Other definitional concerns have been to distinguish civil disobedience from other forms of law-breaking such as "ordinary" criminal activity and revolutionary action. One contrast is in the type of typical motivation; unlike the ordinary criminal, motivated by self-interest or malice, the civil disobedient is often moved by moral or conscientious motivation, in the sense that a moral belief prompts the illegal act. The revolutionary aims, at least ultimately, at overturning the existing political or legal order, whereas the civil disobedient seeks change within the established system. King captured these points when he affirmed that the civil disobedient must break the law "openly, lovingly . . . , and with a willingness to accept the penalty" and that one who does this "to arouse the conscience of his community over its injustice, is in reality expressing the very highest respect for law."

There is considerable controversy over how precisely to define civil disobedience. The philosopher John Rawls, in his book *A Theory of Justice* (1971), defined civil disobedience as a "public, nonviolent, conscientious yet political act contrary to law usually done with the aim of bringing about a change in the law or policies of government." Rawls regards civil disobedience as breaking the law from motives of conscience (that is, not from self-interest) and also requires that it be nonviolent. Some critics have questioned whether nonviolence should be a defining feature of civil disobedience, suggesting instead that it is a tactical feature of civilly disobedient protest or a factor to be considered in determining whether such a protest is morally justified. Other critics have objected to requiring as part of the definition that acts of civil disobedience be public, with the likelihood of detection and arrest.

Types. Definitions such as that offered by Rawls construe civil disobedience quite narrowly. Thoreau's refusal to pay the poll tax, a pacifist's refusal to submit to military service, and a Jehovah's Witness' refusal to salute the flag are not counted as acts of civil disobedience but instead are classified as cases of "conscientious refusal." Rawls recognizes that his definition is narrower than Thoreau's but favors it because it enables him to call attention to the public and political character of those protests he chooses to label as "civil disobedience," and to relate them to political activity within a constitutional democracy. Conscientious refusal is not primarily aimed at political change and is not made in terms of principles shared by the community. Rawls also excludes from the category of civil disobedience militant acts of resistance and disruption. An example might be animal rights activists breaking into laboratories in order to spare the animals. It is possible to use a more generic definition of civil disobedience, classifying under it such phenomena as conscientious refusal, militant action, and civil disobedience (in its narrow sense).

A commonly drawn distinction is between direct and indirect acts of civil disobedience. The former are acts in which the law objected to is the one violated. A clear example is the sit-ins at segregated lunch counters by civil rights protesters in the 1960's in order to protest segregation laws. They were violating the laws they were protesting. Such direct action is not always possible, since the law or policy regarded as immoral cannot be violated. Indirect acts of civil disobedience are ones in which a law violated is not the one protested. In the late 1950's, Bertrand Russell and the Committee of 100, involved in the Campaign for Nuclear Disarmament, engaged in mass demonstrations involving civil disobedience. They were arrested for violating (morally unobjectionable) trespass law during the demonstrations. In a statement on the subject, "Civil Disobedience and the Threat of Nuclear Warfare," Russell observed: "By means of civil disobedience, a certain kind of publicity becomes possible." The aim of the group was to draw attention to the dangers of nuclear weapons policy, not to protest trespass law.

Some forms of indirect civil disobedience are concerned less with publicity than with interfering with what the civil disobedients regard as immoral activity. This is sometimes referred to as "direct action," although that expression is used in other ways as well. Activities associated with "Operation Rescue," a campaign of abortion opponents to shut down abortion clinics in the hopes of sparing the lives of the unborn who would have been aborted, constitute an example of direct action.

Justification. One of the most vexing questions is whether and when civil disobedience is morally justified. Thoreau seemed to be of the opinion that he and, presumably, others ought to do what they think is right. Many have taken a polar opposite position to the effect that, in a constitutional democracy at least, deliberately breaking the law is never justified. Others have argued that indirect civil disobedience is never justified. Former Supreme Court justice Abe Fortas, in the widely cited 1968 essay entitled "Concerning Dissent and Civil Disobedience," specifically condemned indirect civil disobedience. Fortas, writing at a time of massive protests in connection with racial discrimination, the military draft, and the Vietnam War, concluded: "So long as our governments obey the mandate of the Constitution and issue facilities and protection for the powerful expression of individual and mass dissent, the disobedience of laws which are not themselves the target of the protest—the violation of law merely as a technique of demonstration—constitutes an act of rebellion and not merely dissent."

In the background of this issue are large questions about the nature of law, morality, and democratic government. A number of grounds have been offered for a general obligation to obey the law. In Plato's *Crito*, Socrates cites several reasons why he should not escape from jail but should instead submit to the laws of Athens. Among them are gratitude for the protection the law has afforded him as well as an implicit agreement with the state. Another common appeal has been to considerations of fairness—in a democracy, laws and policies are arrived at by procedures in which people can exert their influence. Finally, others have cited the general value of respect for law and

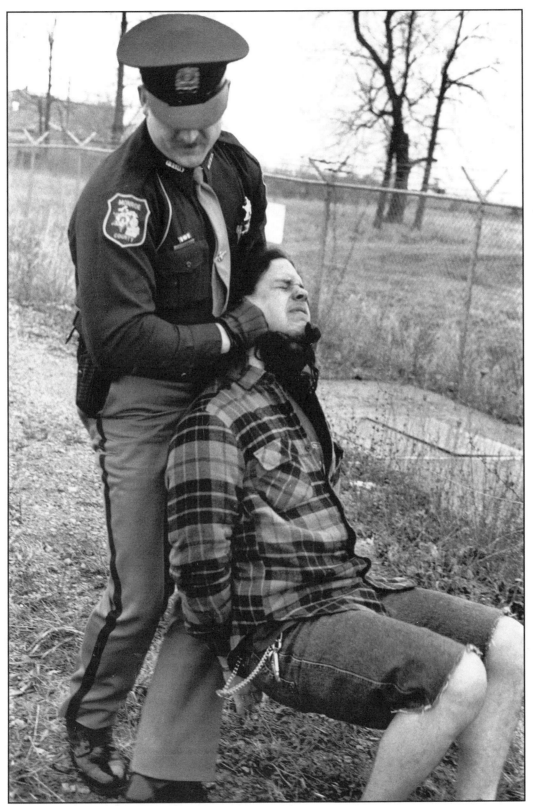

An antinuclear protester being arrested for blocking traffic in Monroe, Michigan, in 1994. (Jim West)

the threat to peaceful and orderly processes of collective decision posed by deliberate law breaking. If individuals are allowed to follow their diverse and sometimes erratic consciences, or if they are permitted to observe "higher laws," which are difficult to verify and to interpret, then the viability of the democratic process is seriously jeopardized. On the other hand, many defenders of civil disobedience have held that the obligation to obey the law is not absolute, because even in constitutional democracies the political process may yield morally unacceptable outcomes. Defenders of civil disobedience cite approvingly the nineteenth and twentieth century targets of protest and civil disobedience, including slavery and fugitive slave laws, the denial of suffrage to women, laws supporting segregation and discrimination, the war in Vietnam and the military draft, and nuclear weapons policies.

Few defenders of civil disobedience see its justification as an issue that lends itself to resolution by a simple and easy formula. Complex factors relating to the type of civil disobedience, the motives and aims of the practitioners, and the circumstances in which it must be carried out must be taken into account. Among the questions that must be answered are: How gravely wrong is the law or policy being protested; what are the motives of those engaging in civil disobedience (that is, whether they are predominantly moral or are heavily mixed with less admirable motives such as fame or greed); what is the likelihood of success; what are the dangers of violence, especially injury to persons; and what is the risk of encouraging or spreading lawlessness and disrespect for law? On this latter point, the distinction between direct and indirect civil disobedience comes into play. Furthermore, significance is also given to the character of civil disobedience—that it is nonviolent, that it is done openly and with an acceptance of the penalty, and that it is done as a last resort, after available political and legal resorts have been exhausted. These are perceived as important in demonstrating that civil disobedience can be, in Rawls's words, "a form of political action within the limits of fidelity to the rule of law."

While civil disobedience may be morally justified, courts and prosecutors have seldom shown any special leniency toward those who have broken the law for reasons of conscience. As noted earlier, in the context of American law, significant constitutional issues are implicated. In particular, there is the issue of whether an apparent illegal act is really that, since the law might subsequently be declared unconstitutional by judicial review. There are also First Amendment concerns, especially the extent to which protests are protected speech. For example, the U.S. Supreme Court has held that burning a draft card is not protected speech (*United States v. O'Brien*, 1968) but that burning an American flag as a political protest is protected speech (*Texas v. Johnson*, 1989).

—*Mario F. Morelli*

See also Civil Rights movement; Conscientious objection; Gandhi, Mahatma; King, Martin Luther, Jr.; Montgomery bus boycott; Nonviolent resistance; *O'Brien, United States v.*; *Texas v. Johnson.*

BIBLIOGRAPHY

Several excellent collections of essays that include Thoreau's famous essay are available, including Hugo Bedau, *Civil Disobedience: Theory and Practice* (New York: Pegasus, 1969), and Jeffrie Murphy, ed., *Civil Disobedience and Violence* (Belmont, Calif.: Wadsworth, 1971). Scholarly discussions include Peter Singer, *Democracy and Disobedience* (New York: Oxford University Press, 1974), and Kent Greenawalt, *Conflicts of Law and Morality* (New York: Oxford University Press, 1987).

Civil law

DEFINITION: That division of law, sometimes called "private law," which applies to the rights governing conduct between individuals who resort to the courts for redress

SIGNIFICANCE: The goals of civil law are compensation in the form of money damages or equitable relief (injunction, rescission, reformation, or specific performance) and the returning of the injured party to the status quo

Two major subdivisions of the law are criminal law and civil law. Because a crime is considered an offense against society, the government initiates criminal actions through the office of the public prosecutor or district attorney. Criminal law seeks to punish the wrongdoer for violating societal rules, generally through imposition of a penalty in the form of a fine payable to the state or imprisonment. Criminal law also aims to serve as a deterrent to other citizens in society. A basic premise of the criminal law concerns the presumption of innocence of the accused until proven guilty beyond a reasonable doubt. If that burden is not met, then the accused is released.

Civil cases, on the other hand, are primarily brought by private individuals or organizations against persons or entities who have allegedly injured or wronged them. Civil law seeks to compensate the plaintiff (the person initiating the lawsuit) for a wrong through an award of monetary damages or a remedy in equity. In most civil cases, the plaintiff must prove his or her case by the preponderance or weight of the evidence—which essentially means merely tipping the scales slightly in the plaintiff's direction. Other civil cases sometimes require proof by clear and convincing evidence, a standard more demanding than preponderance of the evidence but below the burden of proof required in criminal cases. Certain cases (such as battery) are actionable in independent criminal and civil proceedings.

Damages. The civil law awards money damages to right any wrong done to a plaintiff, assuming that the plaintiff has prevailed at trial. Damages awardable in a civil case are of four types: compensatory, punitive, nominal, and liquidated. Compensatory damages attempt to compensate the plaintiff for pecuniary (monetary) losses—past, present, and future—which resulted from the defendant's wrongful conduct. In awarding compensatory damages, the court attempts to put the plaintiff in the same financial position as existed before commission of the wrong or prior to the breach of contract. The law will not put the party in a better position. Recovery for future losses is not permitted for remote, speculative, or indirect consequences.

Punitive or exemplary damages punish the wrongdoer for unconscionable, willful, or wanton conduct. They also are awarded to deter others from similar conduct. Punitive damages are awarded to the plaintiff over and above the compensatory amount. They are additional damages for a civil wrong and are not a substitute for criminal punishment. In order to receive punitive damages, therefore, the plaintiff must prevail at trial.

Nominal damages, generally a token sum (such as one dollar), are awarded to vindicate a plaintiff's claim or establish a legal right in cases where no evidence of specific harm exists. Liquidated damages are stipulated in a contract by the parties as the amount to be paid as compensation for loss in the event of a breach.

Equity. Civil law may be subdivided into law and equity. Law, referring to the original common-law courts that developed in medieval England, granted money damages according to rigid and strict rules and procedures. Grievances where money was not the remedy sought were brought before a British religious and political leader called a chancellor, sometimes referred to as the "king's conscience." Attempting to mitigate the harshness of strict rules and statutes, equity courts applied flexible principles of fairness and discretion in individual cases. Instead of relying on rules of law to reach decisions, courts of equity use as guidelines in the decision-making process equitable maxims, or short statements containing the gist of equity law.

The dual system of law and equity became part of the American legal system. In fact, until the courts were merged and integrated in 1938, law and equity courts were completely divided, each having a separate administrative system. Distinctions between the two still exist in principle; the threshold requirement for entering equity is the existence of an incomplete or inadequate remedy at law. Because jury trials are unavailable in equity, the judge acting as chancellor has the discretion to fashion an appropriate remedy in the case. Among equitable remedies are injunctions, or judicial orders directing another to act or refrain from acting in a certain manner; reformation, used to rectify or reform an agreement to reflect the true intention of the parties; rescission, or cancellation of an agreement because of mistake, duress, fraud, or undue influence; and specific performance, requiring the defendant to fulfill contractual obligations. Hybrid actions seeking both common law and equitable remedies may be brought in one lawsuit, with the legal issues decided by a jury and the equitable issues by a judge/chancellor.

Certain landmark constitutional cases have been decided following equitable principles. Those include *Brown v. Board of Education* (school desegregation, 1954) and *Regents of the University of California v. Bakke* (racial quotas and preferential admissions programs, 1978). —*Marcia J. Weiss*

See also Burden of proof; Civil procedure; Civil remedies; Commerce clause; Compensatory damages; Contract law; Equitable remedies; Equity; Fiduciary trust; Punitive damages; Standards of proof; Tort.

BIBLIOGRAPHY

Civil law is covered in general introductory law texts such as Harold J. Grilliot and Frank A. Schubert, *Introduction to Law and the Legal System* (5th ed. Boston: Houghton Mifflin, 1992), and Beth Walston-Dunham, *Introduction to Law* (2d ed. St. Paul, Minn.: West, 1994). Books on equity include Peter Charles Hoffer, *The Law's Conscience: Equitable Constitutionalism in America* (Chapel Hill: University of North Carolina Press, 1990), and Gary L. McDowell, *Equity and the Constitution: The Supreme Court, Equitable Relief, and Public Policy* (Chicago: University of Chicago Press, 1982). A readable comparison of common law and civil law traditions, including historical development and the emergence of equity courts, is John Henry Merryman, *The Civil Law Tradition: An Introduction to the Legal Systems of Western Europe and Latin America* (2d ed. Stanford, Calif.: Stanford University Press, 1985).

Civil liberties

DEFINITION: Negative promises that a government will not do something contrary to the human or individual rights of a person in its jurisdiction

SIGNIFICANCE: Civil liberties represent one of the most basic of all conceptions of individual human rights

One of the most significant questions about any government has to do with how it handles its relations with individuals. Though individuals may form governments among themselves for their protection, the government they have created may become so powerful that it can crush any one of them. To paraphrase James Madison, one must first create a government to control the governed, and then require it to control itself. For a constitutional democracy, how well a regime protects its citizens individually is the acid test of its constitution.

There is a critical distinction between civil liberties and civil rights. Civil liberties are seen as negative promises by (or negative commands to) the government not to do certain things. The U.S. Constitution's Article I, sections 9 and 10 (the prohibitions against the federal and the state governments respectively) and the entire Bill of Rights (the first ten amendments) are clearly lists of negative commands. The First Amendment, "Congress shall make no law respecting an establishment of religion," is only one of a long list. Other negative commands in the Bill of Rights include "No soldier . . . shall be quartered in any house. . . . No person shall be held to answer for a capital . . . crime, unless on indictment. . . . Excessive bail shall not be required."

Still, negative commands would not help much if a government did not also act positively to protect its citizens from improper acts by others. Purely negative commands need to be balanced with certain affirmative obligations, and these are properly known as civil rights. These become particularly important to members of groups that suffered discrimination in the past, such as African Americans, Hispanic Americans, or females in the United States. Naturally, there is also an overlap between civil liberties and civil rights: A negative promise that the government will not interfere with free speech implies an affirmative promise that it will protect individuals who express their opinions, even in the face of majorities that wish to silence them. Still, distinguishing between the affirmative and the negative characteristics of two concepts is useful.

The Need for Negative Promises. The best way to understand the distinction between negative promises and affirmative guarantees is to compare the mainly negative wording of the U.S. Constitution with the constitution written by Joseph Stalin for the Soviet Union in 1936. The Soviet Constitution was revised a number of times before the collapse of the Communist regime in the early 1990's, but each version followed the general provisions of Stalin's 1936 draft. At the time of writing, Stalin had already defeated all rivals and stood at the height of his power. Apparently, he wanted a constitution for propaganda purposes. It would be easy to dismiss this

document by saying that Stalin never intended to live up to it, but it is still instructive to see how its provisions were worded.

Stalin's constitution contained a "Bill of Rights and Duties"—affirmative promises of numerous material benefits not provided by the U.S. Constitution. Among these were "the right to work," or guaranteed full adult employment (that is, no unemployment), and a "right to rest and leisure," including a maximum forty-hour workweek, lengthy paid vacations, and resorts for working people. Also guaranteed were rights to education, medical care, and maintenance in old age. Women were granted "equal rights"—a promise still not explicitly included in the U.S. Constitution.

Stalin's constitution also promised religious freedom and free expression, typically called "civil liberties." Unlike the U.S. Bill of Rights wording, "Congress shall make no law . . . ," Stalin's promise is affirmatively worded: "In conformity with the interests of the working people, and in order to strengthen the socialist system, the citizens of the Soviet Union are guar-

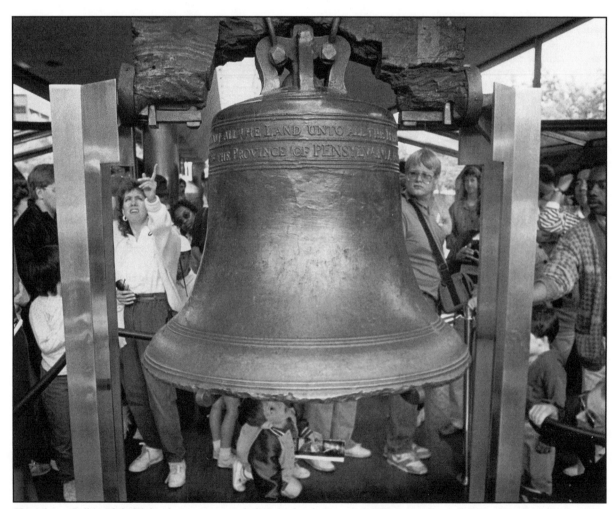

The Liberty Bell in Philadelphia has come to symbolize the freedoms and civil liberties guaranteed Americans by the "negative promises" of the Bill of Rights. (James L. Shaffer)

anteed by law: (a) freedom of speech; (b) freedom of the press; (c) freedom of assembly, including the holding of mass meetings; (d) freedom of street processions and demonstrations. These civil rights are ensured by placing at the disposal of the working people and their organizations printing presses, stocks of paper, public buildings, the streets, communications facilities, and other material requisites for the exercise of these rights."

Stalin's free-expression promise is remarkably generous, providing for an unrestrained right to "street processions and demonstrations," while the U.S. Constitution limits its protection only to those who "peaceably assemble." Still more generous is the promise to supply paper and printing presses. This is in stark contrast to the situation in the United States, where exercising "free" speech can cost considerable money for media advertising. Yet the extensive record of persecution of dissident Russian writers belies Stalin's promises. Why did Stalin's constitution not protect individuals? In fact, the innocent-sounding, presumably nonbinding introductory clause, "In conformity with the interests of the working people, and in order to strengthen the socialist system," acted as a limit on the promise of free expression that followed. Only press or speech that was in the "interests of the working people" or "strengthen[ed] the socialist system" was ever allowed in the Soviet Union.

Stalin's constitution promised a whole range of economic benefits, far beyond the financial ability of even the wealthiest government to provide for all citizens. How could any government fulfill a promise to give all citizens all the free paper, radio time, and printing presses they might want? What would prevent a citizen from collecting huge amounts of materials and using them for other purposes? Clearly, this document was a mere wish list for the future, not a constitution.

In a November, 1936, speech announcing the constitution, Stalin explained not only that free expression must be in the interests of the working class but also that the Communist Party, which "defends the interests of the workers and peasants to the very end," would decide how this would be accomplished. Citizens would have to work to produce economic resources to be given to the Communist Party, which would freely express its views on the "interests of the working people." The lack of any negative limits on government, then, clearly stands the whole notion of free speech on its head.

While the U.S. Bill of Rights contains only negative promises, those promises are far more effective, for it costs nothing for Congress *not* to pass a law. Under Stalin, speech was declared "free," but one could not even buy it. In the United States, speech may cost money, but it is freely available in the marketplace. Starting with a broad affirmative promise, the Soviet Union ended with no free speech at all. The United States began with a limited, negatively worded promise of free speech and has found itself with an overwhelming flood of information.

This is not to suggest that a constitution is satisfactory with only negative promises, for both civil liberties and rights are vital. One cannot have an effective government with only negative limits, but history's lessons clearly demonstrate that a constitution filled with affirmative promises does virtually no good at all.

Tradition in English Common Law. The U.S. Constitution's commands against government action are not the only examples of negative commands—nor were they the first. Actually, the Constitution evolved out of negative commands against the British monarchy that had evolved over roughly seven hundred years, since the Magna Carta in 1215. Some of these negative guarantees were contained in documents, such as the Magna Carta and the Petition of Right of 1628, but the British experience also includes successive judicial enactments known as the "common law." Originally, the common law was an idea developed by the British kings to ensure that their rule was uniform throughout the country—the "common" law of the land. The king's courts were supposed to compare their decisions on particular cases and render like decisions in like cases. Once cases were decided, they were to serve as precedents for all future cases.

The early kings saw the common law as a way to strengthen their control; as the courts came under the Parliament's control, however, they limited the monarch's power by creating precedents for the future. Both the documents and the common law limited the government's power negatively. Since the American colonists were reacting to what they perceived to be an overly powerful British government, they naturally bound up their new government—especially the national government—with negative bans.

Historical Trends in Court Cases. Originally, the most important purpose of the U.S. Bill of Rights was to protect the states from the danger of an overly powerful national government. The period from the adoption of the U.S. Constitution in 1789 to the Civil War was devoted to protecting the state governments (and only indirectly the citizens) from the federal government. During this period, perhaps the most important of the entire Bill of Rights was the Tenth Amendment's promise that "the powers not delegated to the [national government] by the constitution, nor prohibited by it to the states are reserved for the states respectively, or to the people." The First Amendment begins with the phrase "Congress shall make no law," clearly making the federal government its only target; none of the other nine original amendments, however, includes this language. One might assume that the intention was for the entire Bill of Rights to apply to only the federal government, but, given the doubt, it was natural for someone to test this assumption.

Perhaps the most important test case to determine to which level of government the Bill of Rights applied was the case of *Barron v. Baltimore* (1833). The city of Baltimore paved a number of streets and dumped leftover construction materials into the water near a wharf that Barron owned. The floor of the bay was raised so high that ships could no longer use Barron's Wharf; thus he was deprived of his property interest in his livelihood without due process or just compensation. Barron decided to sue the city of Baltimore to recover damages. Baltimore was a subunit, however, under the "sovereign" state of Maryland, which did not provide the same guarantee against eminent domain actions which the federal constitution included. Since Barron could not succeed in the Maryland courts, he turned to the federal courts, only to discover upon reaching the Supreme Court that it regarded the Fifth Amendment as applying only to the federal government. In effect, Barron was told that if the Maryland Constitution did not offer him protection, he could not receive it from the federal government. With this decision, the Supreme Court declared that the first ten amendments to the Constitution applied only to the federal government and not to the states. This reflected the reality of the situation before the Civil War, especially with regard to the slavery of African Americans in southern states. No slave could claim the right of free speech by citing the First Amendment.

After the Civil War, Congress sought to reverse the *Barron* decision with the Fourteenth Amendment, which begins: "All persons born or naturalized in the United States, and subject to the jurisdiction thereof, are citizens of the United States and of the State wherein they reside." The point was to undo the notion of citizenship established in *Barron*, which held persons to be primarily citizens of the state in which they resided and only secondarily, through that state, citizens of the United States. This constitutional language certainly appears to mean that all persons, black or white, were to be citizens of the United States and of the state in which they lived simultaneously and that citizenship could not be denied to African Americans as it had been in southern states. Thus the U.S. Constitution was to reach through the boundaries of each state, to each individual citizen.

Then the Fourteenth Amendment, in negative language, states, "No State shall make or enforce any law which shall abridge the privileges or immunities of citizens of the United States; nor shall any State deprive any person of life, liberty, or property, without due process of law." Arguably, this section of the Fourteenth Amendment applies the negative commands contained in the Bill of Rights and elsewhere in the Constitution to the citizens of each state. Once the Fourteenth Amendment was ratified, it would appear that *Barron* had been overturned by an act of the American people.

The Changing Composition of the Supreme Court. Though the Supreme Court did not initially interpret the Fourteenth Amendment in this way, it started to do so beginning in the 1920's. The Court has been guided by the so-called doctrine of selective incorporation, which holds that parts of the Bill of Rights are so basic to the notion of due process that the states cannot deny them to any persons residing within their borders. Thus, the words "Congress shall make no law" now mean that no government within the United States shall make any law that abridges the freedom of speech or of the press.

For most civil liberties, the process began in 1925 with the case of *Gitlow v. New York*, in which the Court applied the free-speech section of the First Amendment to the states. This act of selective incorporation set in motion a set of cases that applied most of the rest of the First Amendment to the states. In *Near v. Minnesota* (1931), the Court applied the free press section, and *Hague v. Congress of Industrial Organizations* (1939) applied the assembly section to the states. Free exercise of religion came partly in *Hamilton v. Regents of the University of California* (1934) and more completely in *Cantwell v. Connecticut* (1940). The nonestablishment of religion followed in *Everson v. Board of Education of Ewing Township* (1947). These cases maintained that the First Amendment (at least) had such a crucial relationship to due process that states could not deprive the citizens of its benefits without denying them due process.

The Court did not advance much toward incorporation until Earl Warren was named chief justice in 1953, for only portions of the First Amendment and a single clause of the Fifth Amendment had been applied to the states by then. Warren joined Associate Justices Hugo L. Black, William O. Douglas, and (partially) Tom C. Clark, who had long argued for a much fuller incorporation, in support of the application of more sections of the Bill of Rights. Later, the appointment of William J. Brennan (and others) made it possible for the Court to incorporate eventually nearly all of the Fourth, Fifth, Sixth, and Eighth Amendments—that is, nearly all the important sections of the Bill of Rights. Thus, the civil liberties familiar to U.S. citizens against the actions of both the federal and state governments are a rather recent addition to the understanding of civil liberties in the United States.   — *Richard L. Wilson*

See also American Civil Liberties Union (ACLU); Assembly and association, freedom of; *Barron v. Baltimore*; Bill of Rights, U.S.; Civil rights; Civil War Amendments; Constitution, U.S.; Gay rights; *Gitlow v. New York*; Incorporation doctrine; Religion, free exercise of; Speech and press, freedom of.

BIBLIOGRAPHY

A general study of the subject, such as Henry J. Abraham and Barbara A. Perry, *Freedom and the Court* (6th ed. New York: Oxford University Press, 1994), is a good place to begin. For one view of incorporation, see Raoul Berger, *The Fourteenth Amendment and the Bill of Rights* (Oklahoma City: University of Oklahoma Press, 1989). Eugene W. Hickok, Jr., ed., *The Bill of Rights: Original Meaning and Current Understanding* (Charlottesville: University of Virginia Press, 1991), examines each element of the Bill of Rights. The 1936 Soviet constitution and Stalin's defense of it are found in Thomas Riha, ed., *Readings in Russian Civilization* (Chicago: University of Chicago Press, 1964). A comprehensive symposium on the Bill of Rights can be found in Geoffrey R. Stone, Richard A. Epstein, and Cass R. Sunstein, eds., *The Bill of Rights in the Modern State* (Chicago: University of Chicago Press, 1992).

Civil procedure

DEFINITION: The rules and practices relating to the practice of civil, rather than criminal, law; included are pretrial, trial, and post-trial activities as well as certain alternative dispute resolution mechanisms

SIGNIFICANCE: Civil law and civil procedure are intended to ensure that litigants have opportunities to present their claims and defenses before an impartial judicial tribunal and to ensure that such claims and defenses receive evenhanded and fair treatment

The rules and practices that regulate the conduct of "civil" (that is, noncriminal) litigation before judicial tribunals form the basis of civil procedure. While many of these rules and practices are codified, some are temporary and informal understandings driven by immediate needs and circumstances. Whatever their nature, these rules and practices are the product of experience, and they embody contemporary societal values and aspirations.

The Structure of Civil Procedure. In the United States, although each state is, broadly speaking, free to adopt unique rules and practices regarding litigation within its courts, there is a high level of uniformity in the schemes that the states have adopted. These systems, at least in their broad outlines, generally parallel the federal scheme contained in the rules of civil procedure that prescribe the rules for the conduct of civil trials in the federal district courts of the United States. Therefore, discussion of federal procedure is generally descriptive of the states as well.

The predominant characteristic of civil litigation is the intervention of the state in resolving what are viewed essentially as private disputes. In Anglo-American practice (as distinguished from the Continental European approach), the mechanism for doing this is the "adversarial" method. Under the adversarial approach, the parties to litigation have primary responsibility for preparing and presenting their cases to more-or-less neutral representatives of the state: the judge and jury. Procedural rules are constructed to facilitate the active role of the parties and to maintain the neutrality of the state.

The central and organizing event in civil litigation is the trial. This is true even though fewer than 6 percent of all cases filed in courts in the United States ever reach the trial stage. The trial is central because it brings all the participants face to face with one another and with the issues at stake. It is convenient, therefore, to look at the structure of civil procedure in terms of pretrial, trial, and post-trial rules and practices.

Pretrial Procedure. Litigation typically begins when someone (the plaintiff) who believes that he or she has been injured by the unlawful act of another (the defendant) files a claim for relief from the injury (the complaint). The plaintiff invokes the power of the state to help obtain the relief by asking for and receiving a summons from the court. The summons orders the defendant to appear and respond to the complaint.

Defendants' responses to a complaint ordinarily fall into three classes; a defendant is entitled to take all three positions, even if they appear contradictory. First, the defendant may contest the accuracy of the plaintiff's story. Second, the defendant may concede the accuracy of the story but nevertheless assert that the plaintiff may not obtain relief. Third, the defendant may take no position on the correctness of the plaintiff's version of events, but rather may argue that the case may not go on because the court lacks the power to hear the case. The first position ordinarily is conveyed through an "answer," the second and third through written arguments to the court known as motions.

If the defendant files an answer, the parties immediately begin "discovery." Discovery is basically the gathering of facts using methods sanctioned by the court. It involves direct communication between the parties (usually through their lawyers) in which they seek documents and take written and oral answers to specific questions that they pose to each other. The court is generally not involved in this process; it remains in the background and steps in only when one of the parties, asserting that the other party is being uncooperative, directly invites the court to resolve a dispute.

Much of the high cost of litigation in the United States is associated with the discovery stage. That cost is primarily the result of the numerous hours spent by lawyers examining documents in minute detail for the proverbial "smoking gun" as well as in taking lengthy depositions of parties and witnesses to develop the evidence to use at trial. Moreover, discovery is a highly invasive process. In the United States, the boundaries of discovery are quite broad. Unless information is "privileged," either side is typically entitled to obtain the information if it has any relevance to the subject matter of the lawsuit, regardless of whether it will be used at trial. It is sufficient that the information may lead to other information that will be used at trial. Most defendants, therefore, would like to avoid discovery both to minimize cost and to limit the invasion of their privacy or disclosure of trade or business secrets. Thus, typically, rather than filing an answer, a defendant will respond to a complaint by a pre-answer motion.

A pre-answer motion may raise a variety of procedural defenses to the complaint. In essence, the defendant asserts that regardless of the facts, the plaintiff is not entitled to continue with the lawsuit. A defendant may argue that the plaintiff, although feeling injured, has no legally recognized right, that the claim has not been properly stated, that the court lacks power over the defendant or the subject matter of the lawsuit, or that the defendant has not been properly notified of the suit. These defenses may raise constitutional questions related to the due process clause of the Fourteenth Amendment of the United States Constitution or to the structure of the judicial power between the federal and state governments.

When a pre-answer motion is made, a judge is required to resolve the issues raised by the motion. The ruling is always on a matter of law and does not involve the truthfulness or untruthfulness of the plaintiff's factual assertions.

Trial Procedure. It is commonly suggested that in an adversarial system, a modern trial is—like its medieval predecessor—a form of ritualized combat. The underlying philosophy is that truth emerges from the direct confrontation of the parties (or, generally, the parties' lawyers) as they feint, thrust, and parry each other's blows. First, the plaintiff, through a highly partisan opening statement, the calling of favorable witnesses, and the introduction into evidence of documents and other records that support the plaintiff's story, seeks to convince the jury of the defendant's unlawful acts and of the injuries to the plaintiff. Second, the defendant, by cross-examining and impeaching the plaintiff's witnesses, and by introducing witnesses and records favorable to the defendant's side, seeks to undermine the plaintiff's case. Finally, both sides summarize the evidence from their respective vantage points and strenuously urge that the judge and/or jury decide the case in their favor. Each side prepares instructions for the jury which are reviewed and modified by the judge and then given to the jury. The jury then deliberates on these submissions and renders a verdict. The rendition of the verdict is often the climax of the litigation process.

In reaching its verdict, the jury weighs the evidence and applies the law (on which it has been instructed by the judge) to the facts. Where there is conflicting testimony, the jury must decide whom to believe. The jury's decision is based on "the preponderance of the evidence" (in certain exceptional cases, it must be based on "clear and convincing evidence"). In other words, unlike in criminal cases, in civil cases the jury is not required to find guilt beyond a "reasonable doubt" before it finds in favor of one or the other party. Rather, it decides whose case is more likely to be right.

A judge will then enter a "judgment on the verdict" unless there is a "mistake of law" but for which the outcome would have been different or unless the factual findings of the jury are so clearly erroneous that no reasonable jury could have reached the verdict given by the jury. If this happens, the judge determines whether to grant a new trial or, as may happen in exceptional cases, to enter a judgment for the other side as a matter of law. The decision taken by the judge very much depends on the motions made by the parties (or, more accurately, by their lawyers).

The role of the jury in the trial process has generated considerable discussion. The Seventh Amendment to the United States Constitution guarantees to parties in particular types of actions (those that would have been heard in a law court as opposed to an equity court in 1791) in the federal courts the right to present their case to a jury of their peers. Although this constitutional requirement does not apply to the states, all the states have similar provisions within their constitutions. It is therefore the case that in all civil cases involving a demand for the award of monetary compensation, the parties are entitled, if they so choose, to have a trial by a jury. Many people have argued that in today's complex and pluralistic society the institution of the jury has outlived its usefulness. It is inefficient because the outcome of a trial depends on persuading a supermajority of laypersons to reach a simple verdict on a set of highly complex and technical issues. Indeed, the United States is virtually alone in the use of juries in civil trials.

Post-Trial Procedure. Once a judgment has been entered, the losing party is entitled to an appeal. An appeal, however, can be taken only as to those matters that the losing party "preserved" for appeal. This means that the losing party must have objected to or "taken exceptions" to rulings and determinations made by the judge during, before, or after trial. If the issue was not preserved, it is, with one exception, deemed to have been waived and is therefore not subject to appellate review. The one exception is where the trial court did not have subject matter jurisdiction over the case. This exception is important because it goes to the very structure of the United States as a federal union of states in which the central government possesses only those powers that are delegated to it under the federal constitution.

Questions of law ordinarily are reviewed *de novo*—that is, on the assumption that the court of appeals is as competent to decide them as was the trial court. There are, however, instances where the applicable law grants the trial court discretion as to what choices it can make under specified situations. In such cases, the review is for "abuse of discretion," which means that the trial court's rulings are given deference and will be overruled only if they fall outside the zone of permissible choices available to the trial court. Finally, appellate courts are very reluctant to overrule factual findings of a jury or a trial court. Such findings are overruled only where they are "clearly erroneous."

Within the federal system, and in all but a handful of states, there is a second tier of appellate review, a "supreme court" (in New York and Maryland, this tier is called the "court of appeals"). No parties have an automatic right to have their civil cases reviewed at this second tier. Typically, the loser in the first tier of appellate review seeks *certiorari* (a request for discretionary review) from the court. The likelihood of obtaining a grant of *certiorari* is generally small. In the case of the Supreme Court of the United States, fewer than one in twenty such requests are granted. The Supreme Court will generally grant a petition only in cases of exceptional importance to society or if it wishes to provide a uniform guideline or statement of the law where there has been significant disagreement among the lower courts on the interpretation of the law. In other words, the argument that a trial court or court of appeals made a mistake of law or of fact is ordinarily not a sufficient reason for Supreme Court review.

Fairness, Justice, and Systemic Values. Although the main purpose of civil procedure is generally framed in terms of resolving private disputes and of doing justice among the parties, civil procedure also implicates significant societal interests. These interests range from substantive social norms and values regarding what constitutes justice and fairness to issues of administrative and economic efficiency. They also include the nature of the relationships between the various levels of governance in the federal union—local, state, and central governments—as well as the relationships between the legislative, executive, and judicial arms of those governments.

At a very basic level, there is some disagreement about the primary role of civil procedure in contemporary society. If the purpose is to assure fairness and justice, much debate centers on whether the adversarial system is the fairest means of reaching the result. Criticism is especially forceful among those who contend that the purpose of civil procedure is not and has never been to discover the truth of past events, but only to resolve disputes authoritatively and allow the disputants to get on with their lives and with each other. Many people who hold this view maintain that alternative dispute resolution (ADR) mechanisms such as professional counseling, formalized negotiation processes, and mediation and conciliation practices are superior to adversarial adjudication as fairer means of resolving disputes. In any event, they further argue, even if one assumes that justice lies in discovering the truth or falseness of a plaintiff's claim and in providing the appropriate relief, the contemporary adversarial system is an unfair method for doing so for a variety of reasons. Such persons generally concede that the current system is an improvement over previous ones in that there is less emphasis on the "sporting theory of law"—that is, today's system depends less on a lawyer's capacity to pull rabbits out of a hat and to win simply by overwhelming the other side with surprises. Nevertheless, they say, this "evening out" of the playing field has been bought at a very high price. Procedural rules continue to be complicated and well beyond the mastery of laypersons; they impose significant financial and psychological costs on participants, costs that in turn mean that more often than not, litigants are forced to settle for unsatisfactory results rather than proceeding to trial.

In response to these criticisms, there has been a movement toward the use of alternative dispute resolution approaches, including arbitration, mediation, and conciliation, as well as an encouragement of privately crafted rules and increased experimentation within the courts of simplified rules of procedure. Thus, concepts such as notice pleading, adequate investigation of the facts before the filing of a lawsuit, less-adversarial procedures in the use of discovery procedures, and easier dismissal of claims that are unmeritorious on their face are all being emphasized by the courts and by the legislatures that enact procedural rules for courts.

Administrative and Financial Costs. The extremely high economic cost to the private individual or corporate entity of litigating a case in the United States is a well-known criticism of the system. Of no less significance, however, are the administrative and economic costs imposed on the system by the desire to do not merely individual, but systemic justice. Some of the most profound changes in civil procedure in recent years have come from the use of the courts by disadvantaged members of society to protect their collective rights. Thus, victims of school segregation, asbestos pollution, securities fraud, and sexual harassment have all employed the "class action" device to obtain collective relief. Rules originally adopted to deal with individualized claims have had to be modified to take these types of claims into account.

The class action (and similar multiple-party devices) may promote administrative efficiency, but it also raises the issue of the "roughness" of the justice being done. Are the members of the class receiving fair and adequate representation? Are the individual defendant's procedural protections being eroded by the search for efficiency in the processing of grouped claims? Can and should a judge involved in a collectivized suit continue to remain passive, or must the judge become an active case manager? There are no simple answers to these questions, and the answers that have been proposed raise additional issues about the nature of the relationship of the state and the court system to individuals and to groups within society.

These issues are further complicated by the fact that much modern litigation is instituted by or against the government, throwing into doubt the capacity of the judicial system to act as an impartial arbiter between similarly placed litigants. In other words, there is a serious question as to whether the same rules can be meaningfully applied both to the private individual or corporation and to the government. The interests of the state may be such that the state as a litigant must be treated differently, with the ordinary rules of civil procedure being waived to accommodate or compensate for those interests.

Federalism. As already observed, civil procedure has direct implications for the structure and functioning of the federal union. Substantial concerns include such issues as when a state or federal court can assert "personal jurisdiction" over an out-of-state defendant; the distribution of cases between federal and state courts; whose law—federal or state (and if state, which state)—governs actions brought in federal and state courts; and what effect a state or federal court should give to the decisions of another state or federal court. Another issue is the question of when practices within a state court can be said to violate the United States Constitution. The answers to these questions under American civil procedure directly affect the structure, relationship, and character of the federal union, and they remain areas of inquiry, divergent views, and societal manipulation.   —*Maxwell O. Chibundu*

See also Appellate process; Arbitration and mediation; Civil law; Civil remedies; Class action; Criminal procedure; Jury system; Litigation; Suit; Tort; Tort reform.

BIBLIOGRAPHY

Excellent overviews of civil procedure may be found in the following one-volume works: Charles Alan Wright, *The Law of Federal Courts* (4th ed. St. Paul, Minn.: West, 1983); Fleming James, Jr., Geoffrey C. Hazard, Jr., and John Leubsdorf, *Civil Procedure* (4th ed. Boston: Little, Brown, 1992); Geoffrey C. Hazard and Michele Taruffo, *American Civil Procedure: An Introduction* (New Haven, Conn.: Yale University Press, 1993); and Jack H. Friedenthal, Mary K. Kane, and Arthur Miller, *Civil Procedure* (2d ed. St. Paul, Minn: West, 1993). The standard multivolume treatments of the subject are Charles Alan Wright, Arthur R. Miller, and Edward H. Cooper, *Federal Practice and Procedure* (2d ed. St. Paul, Minn.: West, 1982, updated periodically), and James William Moore et al., *Moore's Federal Practice* (New York: Mathew Bender, 1984, updated periodically). Robert M. Cover and Owen M. Fiss, *The Structure of Procedure* (Mineola, N.Y.: Foundation Press, 1979), is a useful compilation of edited versions of interesting academic articles written on the subject prior to 1980.

Civil remedies

DEFINITION: The resolution to a suit at law or in equity, including money damages, injunction, restitution, reformation, rescission, or specific performance

SIGNIFICANCE: Civil remedies are the means awarded by a court to redress a civil wrong

Remedies at law are generally limited to money damages—a sum awarded as compensation for an injury resulting from a wrongful act or breach of contract. The object is to return the plaintiff to the status quo, or the position that existed prior to the offensive conduct or the breach.

When something other than money damages is sought, or where the legal remedy is inadequate, the plaintiff may resort to a court of equity or chancery. An injunction is a judicial order directing a party to act or refrain from acting in a certain manner. Reformation is granted when a written agreement (contract) fails to express the intent of the parties because of fraud, mistake, or ambiguity of language. Its purpose is to reform the contract so that it accurately reflects the parties' intent.

Rescission is granted when one party's consent to a contract was obtained through duress, fraud, undue influence, or misrepresentation. Rescission cancels the agreement entirely and compels each party to return any property or money received in performance of the contract (restitution).

The remedy of specific performance requires defendants to fulfill their obligations under a contract and is generally applied to contracts for the sale of land or unique goods such as antiques, sculpture, or racehorses. A valid contract is required.

The Seventh Amendment to the Constitution and most state constitutions guarantee jury trials in cases at common law. Cases in equity, however, are not entitled to jury trials.

See also Civil law; Compensatory damages; Contempt of court; Contract law; Equitable remedies; Punitive damages; Restitution; Tort.

Civil rights

DEFINITION: Affirmative promises that a government will do something fairly specific to protect the human or individual rights of persons in its jurisdiction

SIGNIFICANCE: Civil rights are among the most basic of all conceptions of human individual rights, but must be paired with civil liberties to be effective

Civil rights are typically paired with civil liberties; together they constitute the realm of human individual rights. Civil liberties are negative limits on government's treatment of private citizens. In the United States, civil rights are affirmative obligations that various levels of government have to protect citizens from coercion (often called discrimination) by the government or by private citizens. In Canada, civil rights are exclusively defined as the government's obligation to protect one person from actions by another individual. Both are important parts of human rights, particularly for democratic governments, since how well a regime protects its citizens individually is of paramount concern.

Civil liberties have a longer, clearer relationship to American government than do civil rights, given that U.S. history began with the Constitution's negative commands. From the country's founding in 1787 to the Civil War, constitutional theory protected state governments (and only indirectly their citizens) from the federal government's power. During this period, the provision considered to be the most important of the Bill of Rights was the Tenth Amendment: "The powers not delegated to the United States by the constitution, nor prohibited by it to the states are reserved for the states respectively, or to the people."

The argument that the Bill of Rights restrained only the national government stemmed from the wording of the First Amendment, which begins: "Congress shall make no law." While this phrase was omitted from the other nine amendments, the unwritten assumption was that the word "Congress" should be applied to all ten. It was natural for this assumption to be tested, as it was in *Barron v. Baltimore* (1833). Barron's livelihood came from a wharf that was rendered useless when the city of Baltimore dumped paving debris in the water, raising the bottom of the bay too high near the wharf. Barron decided to sue for money to recompense himself for his loss of livelihood. Baltimore was a subunit under Maryland State, whose constitution did not provide for the guarantee against such losses which the federal constitution's Fifth Amendment did. Thus, aware that he could not succeed in the Maryland courts, Barron turned to the federal courts, only to discover upon reaching the Supreme Court that it regarded the Fifth Amendment as applying only to the federal government. In effect, Barron was told, if the Maryland constitution did not offer him protection, he could not receive it from the federal government. With this decision, the Supreme Court made clear that the first ten amendments to the U.S. Constitution applied only to the federal government and not to the states.

The pre-Civil War conception of civil rights showed clearly in the case of *Scott v. Sandford* (1857). Dred Scott was an African American slave sold to a new owner who took him into a free state, into a free territory, and then back into a slave state. Since the Constitution's language did not include the word "slavery," it was not clear whether Scott's time in free areas meant that he had become free. In the highly politically charged pre-Civil War atmosphere, the Supreme Court might well have found that Scott was still a slave on narrow technical issues, but it went far beyond that by declaring unconstitutional the 1820 Missouri Compromise. This was the first congressional enactment to be invalidated since *Marbury v. Madison* (1803). Since the 1820 compromise had prevented a clash between North and South over slavery, the decision had explosive consequences leading to the Civil War. Another critical effect of the *Scott* decision was to reinforce the notion that one had citizenship in one's home state as well as another set of rights acquired only through that state in the national government, and that the limits on the national government did not necessarily apply to the state government.

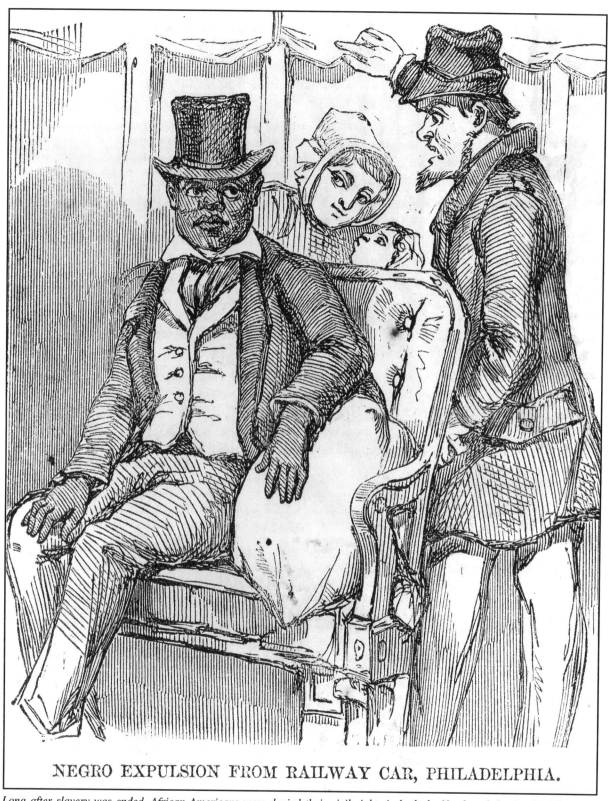

NEGRO EXPULSION FROM RAILWAY CAR, PHILADELPHIA.

Long after slavery was ended, African Americans were denied their civil rights in both the North and the South. (Library of Congress)

The Fourteenth Amendment. After the Civil War, Congress sought to insert language into the Constitution that would at least potentially reverse both *Barron* and *Scott*. The Fourteenth Amendment's first section has four parts, the first of which reads, "All persons born or naturalized in the United States, and subject to the jurisdiction thereof, are citizens of the United States and of the State wherein they reside." This first statement seeks to undo the notion of citizenship established in *Barron*, whereby persons are primarily considered citizens of the state in which they reside and only secondarily, through that state, citizens of the United States. The Fourteenth Amendment's constitutional language certainly appears to mean that all persons, black or white, were to be citizens both of the United States and of the state in which they lived simultaneously, and that African Americans could not be denied citizenship as they had in southern states. This allowed the U.S. Constitution to reach through the boundaries of the state to reach each individual citizen.

The Fourteenth Amendment then states, "No State shall make or enforce any law which shall abridge the privileges or immunities of citizens of the United States; nor shall any State deprive any person of life, liberty, or property, without due process of law, nor deny to any person within its jurisdiction the equal protection of the laws." From a reading of the "plain meaning of the text," these words would seem to reverse the Court's decision in *Barron* by insisting that in subsequent comparable cases, whose who found themselves in situations like Barron's could not be denied their property without "due process of law." Once the Fourteenth Amendment had been ratified, it would appear that *Barron* had been overturned by an act of the American people.

The Supreme Court's Response. The Supreme Court, however, did not initially respond as if such were the case; instead, it seemed to resurrect the pre-Fourteenth Amendment constitutional understanding. In one important case, hundreds of butchers in New Orleans, operating as small individual businesses typical of nineteenth century America, were thrown out of business after what is widely regarded as the corrupt passage of a law in the Louisiana legislature granting a state franchise (monopoly) to one company. The butchers sued, arguing that they had been deprived of their property (their livelihood) by the state "without due process of law." In what seems a very curious decision today, the Supreme Court ruled (in what are known as the *Slaughterhouse Cases*, 1873) that the Fourteenth Amendment sought only to make African American citizens equal with white citizens and did not affect the relationships between white persons (that is, butchers as butchers).

A few years later, in the *Civil Rights Cases* (1883), the Supreme Court invalidated the 1875 Civil Rights Act. This act had made it a federal crime for public conveyances, hotels, restaurants, or amusement halls to refuse admission to anyone because of race, color, or previous condition of servitude, but the Court found that the Fourteenth Amendment stopped only government discrimination, not that of individuals or businesses. The Court's outlook was even more damaging to civil rights when it confronted a case of governmental discrimination in *Plessy v. Ferguson* (1896). Homer Plessy, only one-eighth African American in descent, was classified as an African American and was denied the opportunity to ride in the segregated first-class sections of public transportation in Louisiana. He sued on grounds that segregation in public transportation denied him "equal protection of the laws" under the last clause in the first section of the Fourteenth Amendment. The Court ruled, however, that Plessy was provided "equal protection" as long as the state provided him with "equal" facilities, even if the facilities were separate. By this means, the doctrine of "separate but equal" came to be the binding interpretation of the equal protection clause. This seems even more curious (if not outrageous) in view of the Court's contention in the *Slaughterhouse Cases* that the Fourteenth Amendment solely protected the rights of blacks.

The end result of these cases was that the late nineteenth century Supreme Court treated the Fourteenth Amendment as if it did not exist for ordinary citizens. If one was a white butcher in New Orleans, one was not covered by the Fourteenth Amendment, because the Court said that the "original intent" of those who proposed the amendment was merely to bring blacks to the level of whites. If one were an African American citizen, one could claim no protection from the amendment if a state provided any kind of remotely comparable separated facilities, even if they were quite unequal in fact. From a current perspective, the Fourteenth Amendment seems not to have provided much protection for U.S. citizens.

Applying the Equal Protection Clause. For nearly sixty years, the Court did not go very far toward reversing itself on civil rights, but it did chip away at *Plessy* around the edges. It had still not gone very far when Earl Warren was named chief justice in 1953, but his leadership made it possible for the Court to move toward protecting civil rights by applying the equal protection clause. The first decision in this direction was the famous *Brown v. Board of Education* (1954), which overturned the *Plessy* case by deciding that "separate but equal" was an impossibility because segregated schools were inherently unequal.

By overturning *Plessy*, the Court was announcing a new jurisprudence with revolutionary implications. Perceiving this, some legal scholars wrote searching challenges to *Brown*, but the Court won, not simply because it was the highest court in the land but because its interpretation of the Fourteenth Amendment rang truer to the original language than did the earlier view. In fact, segregated schools had not been equal to integrated schools, and the "separate but equal" doctrine had been used fundamentally to discriminate against African Americans by maintaining grossly unequal facilities.

State action was the principal focus toward which *Brown* was directed. Southern states had been taxing all of their citizens, black and white, but had been using that tax money to benefit whites far more than blacks. Since African American citizens had no effective way to vote in most southern states, they had no political remedy against discrimination. The states' abusive use of coercive power gave the Supreme Court its greatest moral justification for ending segregation in schools and other facilities.

The Supreme Court, the least powerful of American national institutions, must lead largely by persuading citizens that its decisions are correct. American courts do have sufficient legitimate strength so that the national and state executive branches will respond to court orders, and individuals who defy the courts will find themselves in great difficulty. In *Brown*, however, the Court was seeking not to influence an individual but to persuade large masses of people who had the force of the state on which to counterpoise their power against the courts. Many southern states responded to *Brown* by erecting legal and constitutional barriers against the Supreme Court decision, continuing to use their coercive power to deny African Americans "equal protection." At the same time, they failed to protect African Americans from private racist groups such as the Ku Klux Klan.

Lacking support from the U.S. government's executive and legislative branches, the Court was unable on its own power to achieve the end of segregation. In the decade between the 1954 *Brown* decision and the passage of the 1964 Civil Rights Act, the courts decided case after case striking down discriminatory laws in southern states, a process that was so slow and tedious that only 1 percent of southern students were attending integrated schools by 1964. Only with the passage of the 1964 and 1965 Civil Rights Acts did all three branches of the national government begin to act in concert for equal protection. Only when these acts were enforced by a sympathetic administration in the 1960's did the country begin to make real progress toward eliminating the improper use of southern state governmental power.

The problem was enormous because it was a question of striking down not only a handful of specific laws giving preference to whites over African Americans but also a whole fabric of law that protected privileges acquired over years of discrimination. The U.S. Constitution is designed to protect minorities that already have legal protections. Within the nation as a whole, white southerners became a minority who used the legal system to maintain their previous benefits. While legislation should not be retroactive, the legal system should also benefit citizens equally, or the system's legal legitimacy will erode.

The attempt to redress all the problems caused by segregation was yet more difficult because many discriminatory acts were in the domain of activities long regarded as private and beyond the legitimate scope of government activity. Given their past benefits, citizens could rely on the constitutional and legal structure to resist integration. The Supreme Court could strike down statutes and state constitutional provisions one after the other, but once it had rendered the legal system presumably neutral, schools would still be largely segregated because of private decisions made by citizens without any overt governmental support. This became especially clear in the pattern of segregation in northern schools, which proved to be based on residential housing patterns. When the Court could find deliberate decisions made by local authorities to bring about the segregation of schools, it could strike them down; it could do far less, however, when discrimination was not the result of deliberate governmental action.

Yet this is what the notion of civil rights entails—affirmative guarantees that the government will act to provide fairness for all individuals. Moreover, other groups besides African Americans claim to have suffered discrimination in the past (no group more obviously so than women) and were not granted equal protection of the laws in the late 1800's, despite their pressing claims at that time. For some such groups the case for relief from past discrimination is not so clear. They will need to advance their claims carefully and persuasively if they are to win the support of a broad segment of fellow Americans.   — *Richard L. Wilson*

See also Affirmative action; *Brown v. Board of Education*; Civil liberties; Civil Rights Act of 1957; Civil Rights Act of 1960; Civil Rights Act of 1964; *Civil Rights Cases*; Civil Rights movement; Commission on Civil Rights; Equal Employment Opportunity Commission (EEOC); Jim Crow laws; National Association for the Advancement of Colored People (NAACP); Racial and ethnic discrimination; Segregation, *de facto* and *de jure*; Voting Rights Act of 1965.

BIBLIOGRAPHY

An excellent book of general scholarship in this field is Henry J. Abraham and Barbara A. Perry, *Freedom and the Court* (6th ed. New York: Oxford University Press, 1994). A cogent statement of the case against the Court's current understanding of civil rights is made by Raoul Berger in *The Fourteenth Amendment and the Bill of Rights* (Oklahoma City: University of Oklahoma Press, 1989). Ronald J. Fiscus, *The Constitutional Logic of Affirmative Action* (Durham, N.C.: Duke University Press, 1992), presents a tightly logical argument in support of the concept of affirmative action as a part of the package of rights known as "civil rights." An opposing view can be found in Kent Greenwalt, *Discrimination and Reverse Discrimination* (New York: Alfred A. Knopf, 1983). See also Milton R. Konvitz, *Century of Civil Rights* (New York: Columbia University Press, 1961), and Richard Kluger, *Simple Justice: The History of Brown v. Board of Education and Black America's Struggle for Equality* (New York: Alfred A. Knopf, 1975).

Civil Rights Act of 1957

DATE: Became law September 9, 1957

DEFINITION: A law creating the Civil Rights Commission to monitor violations of civil rights and making it a federal crime to harass voters in federal elections

SIGNIFICANCE: The 1957 Civil Rights Act was the first civil rights law passed by Congress since Reconstruction and provided a first step toward federal protection of voting rights

During the mid-1950's, the Civil Rights movement gathered momentum as it challenged racial segregation and discrimination in many areas of southern life. One area where progress proved slow was voting rights. Intimidation and irregular registration procedures limited electoral participation by African Americans. By 1957, support for legislation to protect voting rights was growing among Northern Republicans and Democrats in Congress. Yet Congress had not passed a civil rights bill since 1875, and there was strong Southern opposition to any change in the status quo. It was, however, Senator Lyndon Johnson of Texas, the Senate majority leader, who took the lead. Not known at this point in his career as an advocate of civil rights, Johnson used his considerable legislative ability to shepherd the new bill through Congress. It passed just as the Little Rock school integration crisis was breaking.

The bill had several major provisions. It created a new body, the Civil Rights Commission, to investigate complaints of violations of civil rights. It raised the Civil Rights Section of the Department of Justice to the status of a division, to be headed by an assistant attorney general. It also made it a federal crime to harass those attempting to vote and allowed the attorney general to initiate proceedings against those violating the law.

The law's short-term effects were modest. Though the number of black voters did grow, many impediments to voting remained, especially in the rural South. Many criticized the act's weak enforcement procedures: The Civil Rights Commission could gather information and investigate complaints, but it could take no action to protect those trying to vote. Not until the Voting Rights Act of 1965 would effective machinery for ensuring voting rights be established.

On the other hand, the act was not without impact or importance. In the early 1960's, the administration of President John F. Kennedy did use its provisions (which were strengthened by the 1960 Civil Rights Act) to proceed against some of the worst cases of harassment. More important perhaps was the fact that the act broke a psychological barrier by putting the first national civil rights law in eighty-two years on the books. It also highlighted the importance of voting rights to the overall civil rights struggle.

See also Civil rights; Civil Rights Act of 1960; Civil Rights Act of 1964; Civil Rights Act of 1968; Civil Rights Act of 1991; Civil Rights Acts of 1866-1875; *Civil Rights Cases*; Civil War Amendments; Little Rock school integration crisis.

Civil Rights Act of 1960

DATE: Became law May 6, 1960; first invoked May 9, 1960
DEFINITION: A follow-up to the Civil Rights Act of 1957; also known as the Voting Rights Act of 1960
SIGNIFICANCE: The law provided remedies for denial of civil rights, especially the right to vote, and it was a step toward the sweeping Civil Rights Act of 1964

As the Civil Rights movement advanced in the 1950's, efforts to desegregate led to a "backlash" in the form of bombings and burnings of black churches, homes, and other property. African Americans, otherwise fully qualified, were still denied the right to vote by many local officials, often under implicit threat of violent reprisals.

During 1959 the U.S. Commission on Civil Rights made its first report, minutely documenting a massive denial of the right to vote in the South and recommending that the president appoint federal voting registrars in response to citizen complaints. Attorney General William P. Rogers proposed instead that complaints should be filed with federal courts, which would appoint voting referees. In the House, a bill favoring the referee plan passed. Majority Leader Lyndon Johnson and Minority Leader Everett Dirksen then maneuvered passage of the bill in the Senate. Southern conservatives were pleased that the bill was so weak that no major change occurred; civil rights proponents had to accept half-a-loaf in order to advance their cause.

According to section 6 of the act, the procedure for those deprived of the right to register or to vote is to complain to the U.S. attorney general to file suit in a federal court, which has ten days to respond. If the court finds that a pattern or practice of exclusion has existed in a voting jurisdiction for at least one year, the judge appoints one or more voting referees. Within a second ten-day period, the voting referees then screen applicants to determine whether they meet statutory requirements for voting; if an applicant is found qualified to vote, the judge then issues a voting certificate to the applicant, who can vote in the next election, provided that the initial application was filed twenty days before the election.

To ensure enforcement of the right to vote, section 6 provides that election officials who refuse to honor the federal voting certificate can be found in contempt of court. The U.S. attorney general, in filing a motion to find an election official in contempt of court, can also sue the state in which the voter resides in case the voting official is later fired.

Since voting records were often destroyed in cases of this sort, section 3 requires all election officials to keep records of votes cast in federal elections for twenty-two months.

The law did not challenge voting requirements, such as the literacy test, only the unequal application of voting requirements to blacks and whites. Later voting rights acts repealed various artificial voting requirements. Other provisions of the 1960 Civil Rights Act empower the U.S. Commission on Civil Rights to administer oaths and permit U.S. government property to be used for desegregated schools when facilities for locally desegregated schools are unavailable.

See also Civil rights; Civil Rights Act of 1957; Civil Rights Act of 1964; Civil Rights Act of 1968; Civil Rights Act of 1991; Civil Rights Acts of 1866-1875; Commission on Civil Rights; Vote, right to; Voting Rights Act of 1965.

Civil Rights Act of 1964

DATE: Became law July 2, 1964
DEFINITION: The most sweeping and forceful civil rights legislation in U.S. history
SIGNIFICANCE: The Civil Rights Act of 1964 outlawed the exclusion of African Americans from hotels, theaters, restaurants, and other public accommodations; barred federal funds to any activity that involved racial discrimination;

warranted the Justice Department to initiate school desegregation suits; and forbade racial discrimination in employment and union membership policies

The legislation that became the Civil Rights Act of 1964 was originally proposed by President John F. Kennedy on June 19, 1963, following a confrontation with Alabama governor George Wallace over the admission of black students to the University of Alabama. Kennedy declared that the bill should be passed "not merely for reasons of economic efficiency, world diplomacy and domestic tranquility—but above all because it is right." The act was forcefully advocated by President Lyndon B. Johnson after Kennedy's assassination. Its passage was facilitated both by pressure from civil rights advocates and by segregationist responses to those pressures. Events that helped rouse the public to support civil rights included the March on Washington in August, 1963, the bombing of black churches, the "battle of Oxford" that ensued when James Meredith sought to enter the University of Mississippi, the mistreatment of freedom marchers and freedom riders, and the murder in Mississippi of three civil rights workers.

Passage of the act, termed by President Johnson the foundation of the "just society," came only after senators voted to end

a filibuster on June 19, 1964, exactly one year after Kennedy had proposed the bill. This was the first time the Senate had applied cloture (a parliamentary technique for ending debate and bringing a matter to a vote) to a civil rights measure since adoption of the cloture rule in 1917. Republican senator Everett M. Dirksen, the Senate minority leader, shared credit for passage of the act. Traditionally an opponent of civil rights legislation, Dirksen implored Republicans to support the bill as "an idea whose time has come."

Major Provisions of the Act. Unlike the first two civil rights acts of the modern period—those of 1957 and 1960, which were limited principally to ensuring the right to vote—the 1964 act attacked segregation on a broad front. The final bill was stronger than President Kennedy's proposal to Congress. Its main provisions are found in the first seven of the act's ten titles. Title I, concerned with voting, was intended to create more effective enforcement of the right to vote in federal elections without consideration of color or race. It expedites the procedure for settling voting rights suits and mandates that uniform standards be applied to all individuals seeking to register and vote. To diminish the discriminatory use of literacy and comprehension tests, it equates completion

The 1963 March on Washington was instrumental in increasing support for the Civil Rights Act of 1964. (AP/Wide World Photos)

of the sixth grade with literacy. Finally, it empowers the U.S. attorney general to bring suit if there is a "pattern or practice" of voting discrimination.

Title II forbids discrimination on the basis of race, color, religion, or national origin in places of public accommodation. Privately owned or operated facilities, such as country clubs, are exempted from the Title II prohibition. Title III deals with public facilities such as municipally owned or state-owned or operated hospitals, libraries, and parks. It authorizes the attorney general to bring a civil suit to order desegregation of any such facility whenever the attorney general receives a written complaint of discrimination from an individual or individuals unable to take the necessary legal actions themselves.

Title IV's concern is public education. Its main provision authorizes the U.S. Office of Education to organize training institutes to prepare school personnel to deal with desegregation; to assist school districts, states, and other political subdivisions in implementing school desegregation plans; and to offer financial assistance to school boards to facilitate their hiring of specialists for in-service training.

Title V reauthorized the U.S. Commission on Civil Rights, created by the Civil Rights Act of 1957, for four years and gave it the additional responsibilities of serving as a national clearinghouse for civil rights information and investigating allegations of fraud in voting. Under Title VI, any federal body that offers contracts, grants, or loans is required to bar discrimination on the grounds of race, color, or national origin from programs it supports financially.

Title VII established a federal right to equal opportunity in employment and created the Equal Employment Opportunity Commission (EEOC) to assist in implementing this right. Under Title VII, employers, employment agencies, and labor unions are required to treat all persons without regard to their color, race, religion, sex, or national origin. Equality or nondiscrimination was mandated in all phases of employment, including hiring, firing, promotion, job assignments, and apprenticeship and training. (President Kennedy's proposal had not addressed employment issues.) Gender was inserted into the bill at the insistence of Senator James Eastland, a Democrat from Mississippi, in the vain hope that its inclusion would weaken support for the entire bill. The final three sections of the act confer no rights. They provide structures for federal authorities to operate while mitigating possible conflicts with communities under pressure to comply with other provisions of the act.

The 1875 and 1964 Civil Rights Acts. The Civil Rights Act of 1964 significantly resembled the Civil Rights Act of 1875, which had provided that:

> [A]ll persons within the jurisdiction of the United States shall be entitled to the full and equal enjoyment of the accommodations, advantages, facilities, and privileges of inns, public conveyances on land or water, theaters, and other places of public amusements.

The 1875 law was rendered ineffectual by the Supreme Court in 1883, when, in the *Civil Rights Cases*, it ruled that Congress did not have power under the Fourteenth Amendment to enact such a law, that the Fourteenth Amendment did not "authorize Congress to create a code of municipal law for the regulation of private rights," and that the denial of full and equal access to public accommodations was not a "badge of slavery" forbidden by the Thirteenth Amendment. Subjected to judicial scrutiny, the 1964 legislation survived several challenges to each of its main sections. Many of its provisions were later strengthened by subsequent legislation, including the Voting Rights Act of 1965 and the Civil Rights Act of 1968.

—Ashton Wesley Welch

See also Civil rights; Civil Rights Act of 1957; Civil Rights Act of 1960; Civil Rights Act of 1968; Civil Rights Act of 1991; Civil Rights Acts of 1866-1875; Civil Rights movement; Johnson, Lyndon B.; Kennedy, John F.; Voting Rights Act of 1965.

BIBLIOGRAPHY

Among the many fine sources for information on the Civil Rights movement and the 1964 Civil Rights Act are Derrick A. Bell, Jr., *Race, Racism, and American Law* (2d ed. Boston: Little, Brown, 1980); Charles S. Bullock III and Charles M. Lamb, *Implementation of Civil Rights Policy* (Monterey, Calif.: Brooks-Cole, 1984); Anthony Lewis, *Portrait of a Decade* (New York: Bantam Books, 1965); Sig Synnestvedt, *The White Response to Black Emancipation* (New York: Macmillan, 1972).

Civil Rights Act of 1968

DATE: Became law April 11, 1968

DEFINITION: Also known as the Fair Housing Act, the Civil Rights Act of 1968 was the last of the major civil rights acts of the 1960's

SIGNIFICANCE: The Civil Rights Act of 1968 banned racial discrimination in the sale or rental of most types of housing; it also extended most of the protections of the Bill of Rights to Native Americans

After 1965 the Civil Rights movement devoted increasing attention to conditions in the North. It found much segregation there, a condition that was rooted in residential patterns rather than in Jim Crow laws. The prevalence of segregated housing determined the composition of schools and other aspects of urban life. Martin Luther King, Jr.'s Chicago campaign in 1966 focused national attention on the housing issue. His lack of success showed that white resistance to opening neighborhoods to minority residents was strong and would be difficult to overcome. Urban riots in northern and western cities provoked a "white backlash," as many northern whites ceased their support for further civil rights reform. In 1966 and 1967, President Lyndon Johnson tried and failed to persuade Congress to pass civil rights bills outlawing discrimination in housing.

Passing the Act. In 1968, liberal Democrats in the Senate brought forward a new civil rights bill containing a fair housing provision. Heavy lobbying by Clarence Mitchell, of the National Association for the Advancement of Colored People (NAACP), helped to marshal a majority of senators in support of the bill. As with earlier civil rights measures, southern senators attempted to talk the bill to death with a filibuster. The key figure in defeating this tactic was the leader of the Republican minority, Senator Everett M. Dirksen of Illinois. In return for some relatively minor modifications in the bill, Dirksen agreed to support an attempt to cut off the filibuster. This succeeded, and the bill passed the Senate on March 11, 1968.

The scene now shifted to the House of Representatives, where passage was far from sure. The assassination of Martin Luther King, Jr., on April 4, however, shocked the country and dramatically altered the political landscape. Support for the bill grew; it passed easily and was signed by President Johnson on April 11.

Fair Housing. The main thrust of the 1968 Civil Rights Act was to outlaw discrimination on the basis of race, religion, or national origin in the sale and rental of most forms of housing in the United States, as well as in the advertising, listing, and financing of housing. Exempted from the act's coverage were single-family houses not listed with realtors and small apartment buildings lived in by the owner. (About a month after the act became law, the Supreme Court ruled, in the case of *Jones v. Alfred H. Mayer Co.*, that the Civil Rights Act of 1866 prohibited racial discrimination in housing and other property transactions.) Two other provisions of the act also grew out of the racial turmoil of the 1960's. One enumerated specific civil rights whose violations were punishable under federal law. Another sought to make the act more acceptable to the growing number of Americans concerned about urban riots by specifying stiff penalties for inciting or engaging in riots.

As an open-housing measure, the act proved disappointing. Its enforcement provisions were weak. Those with complaints of discrimination were directed to file them with the Department of Housing and Urban Development (HUD), which would then attempt to negotiate a voluntary settlement. If this failed, complainants would have to file their own lawsuits; the federal government would intervene only in cases where there was a clear pattern of past discrimination. In addition, white resentment at attempts to integrate neighborhoods remained high. Banks often found ways to avoid the law's provisions, making it difficult for many African American families to secure necessary financing. By the late twentieth century, it was clear that the act had not ended the country's dominant pattern of racial segregation in housing.

The Indian Bill of Rights. The Civil Rights Act of 1968 contained another provision unrelated to concerns over fair housing: the Indian Bill of Rights. This was grounded in the fact that Indians on reservations, as members of tribal communities, were not considered to be covered by the Bill of Rights. (Nonreservation Indians were held to be subject to state or federal law.) In 1896, the Supreme Court had ruled, in the case of *Talton v. Mayes*, that the Bill of Rights did not apply to Indian tribes or to their courts. In 1961, Senator Sam Ervin, a North Carolina Democrat, was surprised to discover the fact. Over the next several years he held hearings on the subject. These raised the level of awareness of the Indians' constitutional position. In 1968 he was able to amend the civil rights

The 1968 Civil Rights Act banned racially segregated housing. Shown is a Washington D.C., rooming house around 1960. (Library of Congress)

bill then moving through the Senate to include coverage of Indian rights.

The Indian Bill of Rights extended a variety of constitutional protections to Native Americans with regard to the authority of their tribal governments. Among these were freedom of speech and religion, as well as protections for those suspected or accused of crimes. In fact, all or part of the First, Fourth, Fifth, Six, and Eighth Amendments were held to apply to reservation Indians, as was the Fourteenth Amendment's guarantee of due process. Some parts of the Bill of Rights were not included, however; the First Amendment's ban of religious establishments was not included, in deference to tribal customs, nor were the Second Amendment's right to bear arms or the Third's prohibition against the quartering of troops. Most important to most Indians was a provision that required tribal permission before states could further extend jurisdiction over tribal land. — *William C. Lowe*

See also American Indians; Civil rights; Civil Rights Act of 1957; Civil Rights Act of 1960; Civil Rights Act of 1964; Civil Rights Act of 1991; Civil Rights Acts of 1866-1875; Civil Rights movement; *Jones v. Alfred H. Mayer Co.*

BIBLIOGRAPHY

Useful views of the 1968 Civil Rights Act may be found in James A. Kushner, *Fair Housing: Discrimination in Real Estate, Community Development, and Revitalization* (New York: McGraw-Hill, 1983); Lyndon Baines Johnson, *The Vantage Point: Perspectives of the Presidency 1963-1969* (New York: Holt, Rinehart and Winston, 1971); Donald G. Nieman, *Promises to Keep: African-Americans and the Constitutional Order, 1776 to the Present* (New York: Oxford University Press, 1991); Robert Weisbrot, *Freedom Bound: A History of America's Civil Rights Movement* (New York: Plume, 1991); John R. Wunder, *"Retained by the People": A History of the American Indians and the Bill of Rights* (New York: Oxford University Press, 1994).

Civil Rights Act of 1991

DATE: Became law November 21, 1991

DEFINITION: A law amending the Civil Rights Act of 1964 to provide greater protection against employment discrimination

SIGNIFICANCE: The 1991 Civil Rights Act limited the impact of a number of Supreme Court decisions that had made it difficult for victims of employment discrimination to sue

To many supporters of the Civil Rights movement, the 1980's was a decade of disappointment, when earlier gains seemed threatened by unsympathetic presidents and a conservative political atmosphere. Especially troubling from this viewpoint was the direction taken by the U.S. Supreme Court. In 1989 the Court issued a number of decisions that seemed to endanger past protections against employment discrimination by making the position of voluntary affirmative action programs less secure (*Richmond v. J. A. Croson Co.*), making it more difficult for women and minorities to sue for job discrimination (*Wards Cove Packing Co. v. Atonio*), and reducing protection against racial harassment on the job (*Patterson v. McLean Credit Union*).

Reaction against these decisions, especially the last two, made it easier for liberal Democrats to create a bipartisan coalition in Congress in support of an effort to pass a new civil rights bill. Though the administration of President George Bush did not initially support the bill, the president did sign the bill when it finally passed after two years of congressional consideration and debate.

The Civil Rights Act of 1991 took the form of a series of amendments to Title VII of the Civil Rights Act of 1964. Among its many sections were three important provisions. One sought to overturn the *Wards Cove* decision, which had required those claiming employment discrimination to prove that a specific employer practice had created a discriminatory effect and allowed employers to justify such a practice as a "business necessity." The act eliminated the latter claim as a defense against a charge of intentional discrimination. Another provision counteracted the *Patterson* decision by extending the 1875 Civil Rights Act's ban on racial discrimination in contracts to cover protection from harassment on the job.

Finally, the act allowed victims of discrimination to sue for larger monetary damages in cases brought under the 1964 Civil Rights Act and the 1990 Americans with Disabilities Act.

Though rather technical and legalistic in character, the 1991 Civil Rights Act did make it easier for those who considered themselves victims of various types of discrimination to bring their cases to court.

See also Americans with Disabilities Act (ADA); Civil rights; Civil Rights Act of 1957; Civil Rights Act of 1960; Civil Rights Act of 1964; Civil Rights Act of 1968; Civil Rights Acts of 1866-1875; *Griggs v. Duke Power Co.*; Rehnquist, William; *Richmond v. J. A. Croson Co.*; *Wards Cove Packing Co. v. Atonio*.

Civil Rights Acts of 1866-1875

DATES: 1866, 1867, 1870, 1871, and 1875

DEFINITION: Statutes designed to give legal protection for the fundamental rights of African Americans in the South

SIGNIFICANCE: These statutes generally failed to provide long-term, effective protection because of Supreme Court decisions and public disenchantment with the issue

After the Thirteenth Amendment abolished slavery throughout the United States in 1865, almost all freed blacks were without property or education, and most white southerners bitterly opposed any fundamental improvement in their political and social status. In 1865-1866 southern legislatures enacted the highly discriminatory black codes, and proponents of racial equality responded by calling for new federal laws.

Congress, using its new authority under the Thirteenth Amendment, overrode President Andrew Johnson's veto to pass the first Civil Rights Act on April 9, 1866. This law conferred citizenship on African Americans, a measure necessitated by the Supreme Court's Dred Scott decision (*Scott v. Sandford*, 1857). The law included a list of enumerated rights, including the right to make and enforce contracts, to sue and give evidence in court, and to purchase and inherit all forms of property. It also punished public officials if they used their legal powers to deny equality to blacks. Since the law's constitutionality was questionable, many of its major provisions were incorporated into the Fourteenth Amendment.

On July 16, 1866, Congress again overrode President Johnson's veto, this time to enlarge the scope of the Freedmen's Bureau. Among other items, this law authorized the bureau to use military commissions to try persons accused of violating the civil rights of freedmen.

Again voting to override a presidential veto on March 2, 1867, Congress passed the First Reconstruction Act. Dividing the South into five military districts, the act required southern states to call new constitutional conventions elected by universal manhood suffrage and to ratify the Fourteenth Amendment. Under the act, 703,000 blacks and 627,000 whites were registered as voters, with black majorities in five states.

As the Ku Klux Klan conducted a wave of terrorism against African Americans and Republicans in the South, Congress responded with the Ku Klux Klan Acts of 1870 and 1871, which provided police protection to enforce the rights guaranteed in the Fourteenth and Fifteenth Amendments. In several decisions, such as *United States v. Cruikshank* (1876), the Supreme Court ruled that key parts of the statutes exceeded the constitutional powers of Congress.

Finally, on March 1, 1875, President Ulysses S. Grant signed into law the Civil Rights Act of 1875. This far-reaching act, largely the work of Senator Charles Sumner, outlawed discrimination based on race in public accommodations (inns, businesses, theaters, and the like) and made it illegal to exclude blacks from jury trials. In the *Civil Rights Cases* (1883), however, the Supreme Court struck down most of the 1875 law, holding that the Fourteenth Amendment did not authorize Congress to prohibit discrimination by private individuals. This decision ended almost all federal attempts to protect African Americans from private discrimination until the passage of the Civil Rights Act of 1964.

Although the Civil Rights Acts of the Reconstruction era failed to guarantee any long-lasting equality for blacks, they did provide points of reference for the Civil Rights movement of the 1950's and 1960's. The Civil Rights Act of 1866 was resurrected in *Jones v. Alfred H. Mayer Co.* (1968), when the Supreme Court upheld its use to outlaw private racial discrimination in economic transactions as a "badge of slavery."

See also Black codes; Civil rights; Civil Rights Act of 1957; Civil Rights Act of 1960; Civil Rights Act of 1964; Civil Rights Act of 1968; Civil Rights Act of 1991; *Civil Rights Cases*; *Heart of Atlanta Motel v. United States*; *Jones v. Alfred H. Mayer Co.*; *Moose Lodge No. 107 v. Irvis*; Reconstruction.

Civil Rights Cases

COURT: U.S. Supreme Court

DATE: Opinions released October 15, 1883

SIGNIFICANCE: The Supreme Court ruled that the Thirteenth and Fourteenth Amendments did not give Congress the authority to outlaw racial discrimination in public accommodations by private individuals

In the aftermath of the Civil War, the Constitution was amended three times in five years. The three amendments, taken as a whole, were designed not only to end slavery but also to eliminate its "badges and incidents." Each of the amendments contained a clause empowering Congress to pass implementing legislation. In 1875 Congress passed a Civil Rights Act which made it illegal for anyone to deny access to places of public accommodation—including inns, public transportation, and theaters—on account of race, color, or previous condition of servitude. Five cases claiming violations of the public accommodations provisions were consolidated for decision by the Supreme Court.

The Court ruled that Congress did not have the authority to prohibit discrimination by private individuals. Justice Joseph P. Bradley's majority opinion analyzed the congressional authority granted by two of the Civil War Amendments. The Fourteenth Amendment, he said, gave Congress authority to provide relief from state action which interfered with a person's rights to due process of law and to equal protection of the laws. The amendment did not allow Congress to legislate against an invasion of rights by private individuals. Such power belonged to the state alone. Since the Civil Rights Act purported to provide a remedy for private discrimination, it exercised a congressional power not granted by the Constitution.

In regard to the Thirteenth Amendment, the Supreme Court conceded that Congress had been empowered to abolish "all badges and incidents of slavery"; however, the "badges and incidents" included only legal disabilities, such as the inability to make contracts, hold property, and have standing in court. They did not include the "social rights of men and races in the community." The Court concluded that it was time for the former slave to "take the rank of a mere citizen, and cease to be the special favorite of the laws."

In his dissent, Justice John Marshall Harlan argued that since state governments established and maintained the roads, highways, and harbors used by public conveyances, and since the states licensed theaters, inns, and other places of public accommodation, state tolerance of discrimination amounted to state action that furthered discrimination in violation of the Fourteenth Amendment.

The significance of the *Civil Rights Cases* is twofold. First, the Court ruled that Congress could not outlaw discrimination by private parties under the authority of the Civil War Amendments. Therefore, the victims of racial discrimination could expect relief only from state governments, which, in the South, had by 1883 reverted to the control of white supremacists. Second, the *Civil Rights Cases* prevented Congress from legislating against private discrimination in public accommodations for nearly one hundred years. In 1964 Congress passed a Civil Rights Act that drew its authority not from the Civil War Amendments but from the "commerce clause" in the U.S. Constitution.

See also Civil rights; Civil Rights Act of 1964; Civil Rights Acts of 1866-1875; Civil War Amendments; Commerce clause; *Heart of Atlanta Motel v. United States*; *Moose Lodge No. 107 v. Irvis*; Reconstruction; *Shelley v. Kraemer*; *Slaughterhouse Cases*.

Civil Rights Commission. *See* **Commission on Civil Rights**

Civil Rights movement

DEFINITION: The twentieth century movement, which reached its peak effectiveness between the mid-1950's and mid-1960's, that sought to bring equality under the law to African Americans

SIGNIFICANCE: The quest for political equality in the second half of the twentieth century transformed the face of American politics; the pursuit of economic equality has met with greater opposition and had less success

Although the modern Civil Rights movement began with the Montgomery bus boycott in 1955, the struggle for civil rights has been an ongoing battle. The founding of the National Association for the Advancement of Colored People (NAACP) in

Birmingham, Alabama, police used dogs and firehoses against civil rights demonstrators in the spring and summer of 1963.
(AP/Wide World Photos)

1909 was one of the first attempts to organize in the pursuit of civil rights. With the exception of some legal victories under the leadership of the NAACP, there was little progress in the field of civil rights until the end of World War II.

Voting Rights. With the end of Reconstruction after the Civil War, all the southern states developed devices to eliminate black voters. Each of the southern states adopted new state constitutions between 1890 and 1910 and employed devices such as the grandfather clause, the white primary, the poll tax, and the literacy test to strip blacks of their right to vote. These devices were enormously successful. There were more than 130,000 black voters in Louisiana in 1896. By 1900, only two years after Louisiana adopted a new constitution containing many discriminating features, there were only 5,320 black voters left on the rolls.

For several reasons, African Americans made securing the right to vote their number one objective. First, the U.S. Constitution, particularly the Fifteenth Amendment, contains specific guarantees against voter discrimination. Second, blacks believed there was less social stigma involved in granting the right to vote than in integration. Integration meant race mixing, which was feared by white southerners. Giving blacks the right to vote did not mean that whites would have to intermingle with blacks. Finally, African Americans believed that securing the right to vote would bring about other changes. Black voting would result in the election of black politicians, and it would force white politicians to moderate their racial views.

The grandfather clause was the first major barrier to fall. Grandfather clauses said that if a person had a relative who voted prior to the Civil War, then the person was exempt from other voter qualifications. Since blacks were not allowed to vote prior to the Civil War, they had to meet voter qualifications such as poll taxes and literacy tests. The U.S. Supreme Court unanimously struck down grandfather clauses in *Guinn v. United States* (1915).

The next major barrier to fall was the white primary election. As the term implies, only whites were permitted to vote in primaries. Since southern politics was dominated by the Democratic Party, whoever won the Democratic primary would win the general election. If blacks could not participate in the primary selection process, then they had no real input into the selection of political candidates.

In 1924, the Texas legislature passed a law prohibiting blacks from participating in that state's primary election. A unanimous U.S. Supreme Court struck down the Texas law in *Nixon v. Herndon* (1927). Immediately, the Texas legislature passed another law delegating authority to the executive committee of each party to determine who could participate in the primaries. As expected, they excluded blacks from participation. In a 5-4 decision, the U.S. Supreme Court once again threw out Texas' white primary in *Nixon v. Condon* (1932). Undaunted, Texas made a third effort to ban blacks from the primaries. In 1932 the state convention of the Texas Democratic Party, without any authorization from the state legislature, limited primaries to white voters. A unanimous U.S. Supreme Court, in *Grovey v.*

Townsend (1935), upheld the action of the state convention, concluding that there was no state discrimination involved. Political parties were voluntary associations that had the right to determine their membership. It was not until *Smith v. Allwright* (1944), some twenty years after the first Texas white primary law was passed, that the U.S. Supreme Court finally declared white primaries to be unconstitutional. The NAACP had brought most of the white primary cases, including the *Smith* case, to the U.S. Supreme Court.

The third major voting barrier to fall was the poll tax, which was the payment of a fee in order to vote. Blacks were less able to afford the tax, and poor whites could always find someone to pay or waive their tax. Opponents of the poll tax tried to get Congress to abolish the fee. Five times the House of Representatives passed legislation to ban poll taxes, but each time the legislation was filibustered by southern senators. In 1964, the Twenty-fourth Amendment, which eliminated poll taxes in federal elections, was approved. Two years later, in *Harper v. Virginia Board of Elections*, the U.S. Supreme Court abolished poll taxes in state and local elections.

The last barrier to fall was also the most significant barrier in keeping blacks from voting: the literacy test. Most literacy tests required the voter to be able to read, write, and understand sections of the state or federal constitution. While many blacks could pass the reading and writing portion of the test, almost all failed the understanding portion, primarily because white voter registrars had the sole authority to determine if a person understood a section of the constitution.

Attempts to get the courts to ban literacy tests were unsuccessful. The U.S. Congress passed the Voting Rights Act of 1965, which prohibited literacy tests in areas that were covered by the law. In 1970 an amendment to the Voting Rights Act banned literacy tests in all fifty states, and another amendment in 1975 permanently banned literacy tests.

School Desegregation. Prior to the Civil War, most states prohibited blacks from getting an education. After the Civil War, schools were established for black education, but on a segregated basis. In many areas, education for blacks ended at the sixth grade. High schools, vocational schools, and colleges and universities were often unavailable for black students.

In 1890 the Louisiana legislature passed a Jim Crow law requiring "separate but equal" accommodations for white and black passengers on the railroads. The railroads backed a challenge to the law because of the additional expense they would encounter. Homer Plessy, one-eighth black, was selected to test the law; he sat in the whites-only coach and was arrested. In *Plessy v. Ferguson* (1896), in a 7-1 decision, the U.S. Supreme Court upheld the Louisiana law. The Court found no violation of the "equal protection clause" of the Fourteenth Amendment because whites were as separated from blacks as blacks were from whites. Although the *Plessy* decision had nothing to do with education, the doctrine of "separate but equal" was quickly adopted to justify segregated schools.

The NAACP led the legal attack against segregated schools. The first strategy of the organization was not to seek to overturn *Plessy* but, on the contrary, to seek enforcement of *Plessy*. African American schools were indeed "separate," but were they "equal"? Black schools received far fewer dollars per student to operate, and black teachers were paid a fraction of what white teachers received. Black schools had a limited curriculum, few textbooks, no transportation for students, and often the buildings were no more than one-room shacks. In a series of Supreme Court cases involving higher education in the South, the NAACP time and again demonstrated that black schools were not equal. In fact, in many of the cases, there were no law schools or professional schools available to blacks. The Supreme Court consistently ordered the enrollment of black students where "separate but equal" was not being met.

By the late 1940's, the NAACP was ready to mount a direct challenge to *Plessy v. Ferguson*. Cases were brought in South Carolina, Delaware, Virginia, Kansas, and the District of Columbia. In 1954 the U.S. Supreme Court overturned *Plessy* and the "separate but equal" doctrine in *Brown v. Board of Education*. Chief Justice Earl Warren, speaking for a unanimous Court, wrote: "We conclude that in the field of public education the doctrine of 'separate but equal' has no place. Separate educational facilities are inherently unequal."

Many southern states invoked the doctrine of states' rights and argued that the federal government was usurping the power of states to control education. Massive resistance to the court's decision became the standard policy throughout the South. Some school districts closed their schools rather than integrate, while other communities exploded in violence. When a large, unruly mob prevented the integration of Central High School in Little Rock, Arkansas, President Dwight D. Eisenhower was forced to send in federal troops to protect the nine black students.

Token integration was the policy during the 1960's, but in 1969 the U.S. Supreme Court finally declared that the time for delay was over. Fifteen years after *Brown*, the Court declared that school districts were ordered to comply "at once" with the *Brown* decision. School districts increasingly relied upon busing as the means to desegregate the schools, and opponents of busing in both the north and south argued that it was leading to the destruction of neighborhood schools.

Public Accommodations. On December 1, 1955, a racial incident in Montgomery, Alabama, transformed the face of the Civil Rights movement. On that day, Rosa Parks, a black seamstress, refused to give up her seat on a Montgomery bus to a white passenger. Parks was arrested, and her arrest ushered in the contemporary Civil Rights movement. Blacks, led by a new resident to the community, the Reverend Martin Luther King, Jr., organized one of the most effective mass movements and boycotts in the nation's history, a boycott of the city's bus system. Almost a year after the boycott began, Montgomery officials reluctantly desegregated the bus system after a decision from the Supreme Court.

King emerged from the bus boycott as a national political figure, and in 1957 he and his supporters established the Southern Christian Leadership Conference (SCLC). Combining his Christian beliefs with the precepts of nonviolent resistance, King led several mass protest movements against what he perceived to be the moral injustices of a segregated society. In 1963 King wrote his famous "Letter from a Birmingham Jail," in which he outlined his views on just and unjust laws. That same year King led more than 200,000 civil rights supporters on a march on Washington, D.C. In 1965 King led one of the last major protests of the Civil Rights movement when he and his supporters marched from Selma to Montgomery, Alabama, to pressure Congress to pass a voting rights bill.

Another significant phase of the Civil Rights movement was the "sit-ins." Triggered by four black college students seeking service at the "white" lunch counter of the local Woolworth's in Greensboro, North Carolina, within days similar sit-ins took place in more than sixty communities. Two months after the sit-in started in Greensboro, the lunch counters were integrated.

Many of the student leaders in the sit-in movement came together in 1960 and established the Student Nonviolent Coordinating Committee (SNCC). SNCC played a major role in voter registration drives throughout the South. By the mid-1960's, tired of the violence against them and the slow pace of change, SNCC became one of the most militant of the civil rights organizations and a key exponent of "black power."

In 1960 the Congress of Racial Equality (CORE) initiated the "Freedom Rides." Thirteen riders—some white, some black—boarded buses in Washington, D.C., on a trip through the heart of the deep South. Attacked and viciously beaten by white mobs outside Anniston, Alabama, and in Birmingham, the Freedom Riders focused the attention of the nation on the failure of southern states to protect passengers in interstate travel.

Realizing the difficulties blacks experienced in seeking service in public accommodations such as hotels, restaurants, and theaters, Congress passed the landmark Civil Rights Act of 1964, which made it illegal to discriminate in public accommodations on grounds of "race, color, religion or national origin." Another section of the law banned discrimination in employment and established the Equal Employment Opportunity Commission (EEOC) to enforce the law. The section on employment discrimination established "affirmative action," an approach that has been blamed by some for eroding white support for the Civil Rights movement.

The Collapse of the Civil Rights Movement. After 1965, the Civil Rights movement fell into disarray and decline. There were numerous reasons for the decline of the movement. To begin with, the broad base of public support for civil rights began to erode. Many Americans believed that Congress had passed enough legislation to deal with the problem of discrimination (most notably the sweeping 1964 Civil Rights Act) and that now it was time to let those laws work. Another factor was the nationalization of the push for civil rights. Until the mid-1960's the civil rights issue was widely viewed as a southern problem. When the movement moved northward, some white northerners abandoned their support. With the

More than 200,000 people participated in the March on Washington in August, 1963, to lobby Congress to pass civil rights legislation. (AP/Wide World Photos)

institution of busing for school desegregation and the attempt to integrate housing, many white Americans felt threatened.

The controversy over affirmative action policies also divided support for the movement. To many Americans, affirmative action meant quotas and programs that unfairly threatened their own job security. Another factor was the diffusion of the movement as it was broadened to include discrimination based on age, gender, physical disability, and sexual orientation. Fewer Americans were willing to support what they viewed as special privileges for women, the disabled, and homosexuals than to support civil rights, particularly voting rights, for African Americans.

The urban riots of the 1960's shattered white support for civil rights. White voters and politicians—President Lyndon Johnson among them—felt betrayed by the riots. They thought that the nation was trying to deal with the problems of racism and discrimination. Congress had passed three civil rights laws and one voting rights law within an eight-year period.

When the Watts riot in Los Angeles broke out within a week after passage of the Voting Rights Act of 1965, the "white backlash" against civil rights essentially brought the movement to a halt. The riots represented the chasm that still existed between black and white, and they frightened many whites into thinking of "law and order" first and civil rights gains second. On the national scene, the escalating war in Vietnam drew attention away from the Civil Rights movement. When Martin Luther King, Jr., openly opposed the war, he was widely criticized by many Civil Rights leaders, as well as by President Johnson. In the late 1960's, the Vietnam War displaced the issue of civil rights.

Ideological disputes among black leaders of the movement also led to its collapse. Major disputes arose among civil rights organizations such as the NAACP, SCLC, CORE, and SNCC with respect to tactics and objectives. Younger blacks, particularly those in SNCC, were dismayed by the slow pace of change and, as a result, favored more militant tactics. The emergence of the Black Power movement in 1966, led by young leaders such as Stokely Carmichael of SNCC, was a direct assault on the approach of King and other moderates.

Accomplishments. The Civil Rights movement forever altered the political landscape of the United States. Perhaps the greatest accomplishment of the movement can be seen in the thousands of African Americans who hold elective office. The number of black members of Congress was at a record high in the mid-1990's. Blacks have been elected to virtually every political office in all areas of the country. The Civil Rights movement also ended the humiliating practice of segregation and abolished the laws which attempted to create two classes of citizens. Finally, the Civil Rights movement created a sense of pride and self-esteem among those who participated in the movement. — *Darryl Paulson*

See also Affirmative action; Black Power movement; Brown, John; Busing; Civil Rights Act of 1964; Congress of Racial Equality (CORE); King, Martin Luther, Jr.; Little Rock school integration crisis; Montgomery bus boycott; National Association for the Advancement of Colored People (NAACP); Racial and ethnic discrimination; Segregation, *de facto* and *de jure*; Southern Christian Leadership Conference (SCLC); Student Nonviolent Coordinating Committee (SNCC); Voting Rights Act of 1965.

BIBLIOGRAPHY

Good overviews of the Civil Rights movement include Fred Powledge, *Free at Last?: The Civil Rights Movement and the People Who Made It* (Boston: Little, Brown, 1991), and Robert Weisbrot, *Freedom Bound: A History of America's Civil Rights Movement* (New York: Plume, 1991). An excellent source on the major barriers to black voting and the struggle to overturn those barriers is Steven Lawson, *Black Ballots: Voting Rights in the South, 1944-1969* (New York: Columbia University Press, 1976). On school desegregation, the best single source is Richard Kluger, *Simple Justice: The History of Brown v. Board of Education and Black America's Struggle for Equality* (New York: Alfred A. Knopf, 1976). The legislative battle over the Civil Rights Act of 1964 is splendidly told by Charles and Barbara Whalen, *The Longest Debate* (Washington, D.C.: Seven Locks Press, 1985). On the major civil rights organizations, see Clayborne Carson, *In Struggle: SNCC and the Black Awakening of the 1960's* (Cambridge, Mass.: Harvard University Press, 1981), and Taylor Branch, *Parting the Waters: America in the King Years, 1954-63* (New York: Simon & Schuster, 1988).

Civil service system

DEFINITION: The civil service is the government's civilian personnel system, including the descriptions and classifications of jobs, a scheme for paying employees according to job classification, and rules governing recruitment, selection, training, promotion, disciplinary actions, firing, and other personnel actions

SIGNIFICANCE: Government personnel systems are generally governed by civil service regulations that encourage decisions to be made on the basis of merit principles, protect public employees from abuses of political and administrative power, and encourage fairness and equality of opportunity

Government civilian workforces can be organized in many different ways, and those variations generally reflect the culture and politics of the community or the interests of the dominant political elite. In most nations, the government is one of the largest employers, and employment is generally based on rules and regulations, although personal or class biases still may influence who is hired, what workers are paid, and how quickly or far they may rise in the government bureaucracy. Hiring may be based upon ascriptive criteria, such as social class or wealth, or upon merit criteria, such as education and job experience. In less-developed nations and even in poorer regions of the United States, positions with government agencies are often highly prized because they offer stable employment in unstable economies. Government jobs can offer an opportunity for personal power or influence.

History. During the early years of the republic, the federal civil service system based hiring decisions on "fitness of character." Government officials were frequently chosen because of their service to the nation during the American Revolution. Recruiting former military officers with proven loyalty assured support for the new government and its leaders during a time when many in the new nation were not supporters. It also increased the likelihood of recruiting educated men. By the early 1800's, as factionalism and partisan competition in national politics increased, a "spoils system" developed: Government jobs were given out as rewards to friends and political supporters. The administration of Andrew Jackson is generally identified with the birth of the spoils system. Competence was less valued than partisan loyalties. The Reconstruction period following the Civil War saw major national scandals involving elected and appointed officials, a series of economic recessions, and mounting public dissatisfaction with the poor quality of government services. That dissatisfaction, along with the assassination of President William McKinley by an angry job-seeker in 1882 and the fear among Republican officials that their supporters would be forced out of federal jobs after the next election, encouraged passage of the Pendleton Act (or Civil Service Act) of 1883. The Pendleton Act created the Civil Service Commission to oversee a federal personnel system based on merit. Initially only a small percentage of federal jobs were covered under civil service regulations, but the percentage expanded in the decades to follow and the adoption of merit principles was encouraged in state and local personnel systems. While there are still many vestiges of the spoils system, such as the 2,500 to 5,000 federal officials appointed by each new president and the political appointments still made by state governors, mayors, and other officials, the vast majority of civil service systems in the United States are merit based.

Because of abuses of power during the Nixon Administration and widespread sentiment that the civil service system had become inflexible and unresponsive to executive direction, Congress passed the Civil Service Reform Act of 1978. This act created the Senior Executive Service, the Merit Systems Protection Board, and the Office of Personnel Management. The Senior Executive Service permits the president greater flexibility to move executive-level administrators from one agency to another and to provide monetary rewards based on performance. The Merit Systems Protection Board oversees the application of merit principles, and the Office of Personnel Management acts as the executive personnel office in administering the civil service.

Functions of Merit-Based Personnel Systems. Most American civil service systems are based on merit principles. Hiring is based on competitive examinations, with some requiring demonstrations of job-related skills and others consisting primarily of graded application forms with points given for educational attainment, experience, and other qualifications. The names of the applicants demonstrating the necessary skills and competencies are placed on a register or list based on the examination scores. Agency managers are given the names of the top three or five or ten applicants on the register, depending upon the regulations governing the selection process, and make their selection after interviewing some or all of the approved candidates. Promotions and other personnel actions are based upon the same merit principles.

Equity Issues. Civil service systems also are expected to reflect other important social and political values. Equal opportunity regulations help assure that the system represents the population as a whole in terms of the number of women and minorities hired and does not discriminate against those groups or others, such as older workers and workers with disabilities. Equal employment opportunity guidelines assure that recruitment, selection or hiring, promotion, and other personnel actions do not discriminate against anyone because of their race, ethnic background, gender, age, or religion. Equal employment opportunity protections are increasingly being broadened to include sexual orientation.

Civil service systems also typically give special preference to military veterans by adding extra points to their examination scores during hiring and promotion processes and giving them preference during reductions-in-force. Veterans' preference has often been criticized because it tends to give advantage to men in public employment and may be contrary to merit principles. In some civil service systems, veterans' preference is limited to the initial employment or a fixed period of time after leaving military service.

Separate civilian personnel systems are operated by the Federal Bureau of Investigation, the Central Intelligence Agency, and other national security agencies, the Foreign Service in the U.S. Department of State, and the Foreign Commercial Service in the U.S. Department of Commerce. Typically, state and local governments have separate personnel systems for law enforcement and corrections personnel, health workers, and teachers. — *William L. Waugh, Jr.*

See also Affirmative action; Americans with Disabilities Act (ADA); Ethics in Government Act; Hatch Act; Pendleton Act; Spoils system and patronage.

BIBLIOGRAPHY

For general information, see Lloyd G. Nigro and Felix A. Nigro, *The New Public Personnel Administration* (4th ed. Itasca, Ill.: F. E. Peacock, 1994), and Donald E. Klingner and John Nalbandian, *Public Personnel Management: Contexts and Strategies* (3d ed. Englewood Cliffs, N.J.: Prentice-Hall, 1993). Major contemporary civil service issues are covered in Carolyn Ban and Norma M. Riccucci, eds., *Public Personnel Management: Current Concerns, Future Challenges* (White Plains, N.Y.: Longman, 1991). The issue of political patronage in the civil service is examined in Anne Freedman, *Patronage: An American Tradition* (Chicago: Nelson-Hall, 1994), and proposed reforms of the federal civil service are examined in John J. DiIulio, Jr., ed., *Deregulating the Public Service: Can Government Be Improved?*, with an introduction by Paul A. Volcker and William F. Winter (Washington, D.C.: Brookings Institution, 1994). Current scholarly analyses of civil service issues can be found in *Public Personnel Management*, the journal of the International Personnel Management Association, and the *Review of Public Personnel Administration*, the journal of the American Society for Public Administration's Section on Personnel and Labor Relations, as well as in more general public administration and personnel administration texts and journals.

Civil War

DATE: April 12, 1861-May 26, 1865
SIGNIFICANCE: The Civil War established the primacy of the federal government over the states in the administration of justice, and it elevated the ethical system of free-labor capitalism as the national standard

The Civil War redefined both the relationship between U.S. government and the individual and between the central and state governments. During the course of the conflict, the Union and Confederate governments pursued aggressively nationalistic policies that undermined states' rights, civil liberties, and property rights.

The Slavery Issue. By the mid-nineteenth century, the free-labor ideal had taken hold in the states of the North. It was believed that economic opportunity should be open to all. To many in the North, the slave system in the South appeared to be the antithesis of the free-labor ideal. Northerners believed that slavery was inefficient, that it degraded labor as a whole, and that it created economic stagnation. Though most were willing to tolerate slavery where it existed, they wanted the western territories reserved for free white labor. They interpreted the Constitution as a document that made freedom national and slavery local.

Southerners shared a belief in the positive benefits of economic opportunity, but they identified it with the acquisition of land and slaves. Slavery was thus seen as a positive good, and Southerners dreamed of extending the slave system into the territories. Southerners argued that the territories were the common property of all Americans; to prohibit slavery within them deprived Southern people of their right to share in the nation's bounty.

The Confederate Army's attack on Fort Sumter on April 12, 1861, ignited the Civil War. (Library of Congress)

The Republican victory in 1860 brought to power an administration pledged to restrict slavery in the territories. Fearing that the new administration would undermine slavery, seven Southern states asserted their right to secede from the federal union and form a new government. Abraham Lincoln's administration denied the right of secession and refused to relinquish federal property in the South to the new Confederacy. When the state of South Carolina fired on a federal fort in Charleston harbor, President Lincoln called upon the states to supply troops to suppress the rebellion and preserve the federal union. Four additional states believed Lincoln's action to be an unjust usurpation of federal power and joined the Confederacy.

For the Lincoln Administration, the highest good was the preservation of the Union. All issues of justice were considered in relation to that objective. The Confederacy was dedicated to the proposition that human property was an unalienable right and must be preserved. For the first year of fighting, the Lincoln Administration took no action to destroy slavery. It enforced the provisions of the Fugitive Slave Law, and Lincoln rebuked Union general John C. Fremont when he issued a proclamation freeing the slaves of Confederate sympathizers in Missouri. Lincoln's Emancipation Proclamation did not take effect until January 1, 1863. When he issued the proclamation, Lincoln justified his action in terms of military neces-

sity. The proclamation freed only the slaves behind Confederate lines, but after the Emancipation Proclamation was issued, the Union Army became a force for liberation.

Civil Liberties. Both the Union and Confederate governments restricted traditional civil liberties during the conflict. In early 1862, the Confederate Congress authorized President Jefferson Davis to suspend the writ of *habeas corpus* and to declare martial law in areas in danger of attack. That same year President Davis ordered the first military draft in North America and established a Conscription Bureau to carry it out. Even more striking, the Confederacy never established a Supreme Court and allowed the attorney general to judge the constitutionality of laws. That omission seriously undermined the notion of judicial independence and gave the executive branch unprecedented powers over the administration of justice.

Thousands of civilians were arrested by the Union government during the war, and many were tried by military courts. In response to civil disturbances in Baltimore, Lincoln suspended the privilege of *habeas corpus* on April 27, 1861, along the rail line from Philadelphia to Washington. The suspension was later extended to other areas of the North and gradually became general in certain types of cases.

Most military arrests by the Union government were not political. The vast majority of civilian prisoners were blockade-runners, residents of Confederate states, army deserters, draft dodgers, foreign nationals, people who dealt in contraband goods, or fraudulent war contractors. A loyal opposition continued to function in the North throughout the war and actually won control of several state legislatures.

Among those arrests early in the war was John Merryman. Merryman was a member of a pro-Confederate Maryland cavalry unit that had damaged railroad bridges in April, 1861. Merryman's attorney successfully petitioned a federal circuit court for a writ of *habeas corpus* to show just cause for his arrest. The commander of Fort McHenry, where Merryman was being held, refused to honor the writ on the grounds that President Lincoln had suspended the privilege in Maryland. Judge Roger B. Taney responded by issuing a circuit court ruling stating that only the Congress had the power to exercise such a suspension (*Ex parte Merryman*, 1861). In spite of the ruling, Lincoln continued to maintain his right to suspend the writ as an essential power necessary to suppress the rebellion.

For purposes of election propaganda, unscrupulous Republican politicians and military officers attempted to exploit fears that traitorous secret organizations existed in the Midwest. Recent scholarship has demonstrated that the major "Copperhead" societies, such as the Knights of the Golden Circle and the Sons of Liberty, were little more than paper tigers. In the wake of Democratic victories in the state elections of 1862, Republican newspaper editors frequently printed tales of treasonable Democratic activities.

When Ohio Democrat Clement L. Vallandigham declared that the war was being fought to free blacks and enslave whites, General Ambrose Burnside ordered his arrest. A military commission convicted Vallandigham of attempting to hamper the government's efforts to suppress the rebellion and recommended imprisonment. President Lincoln altered the sentence to banishment, and Vallandigham was escorted to Confederate lines. Lincoln justified his action by arguing that it made no sense to shoot a simple-minded deserter and do nothing to the man who induced him to desert.

Later in the war, Democratic activist H. H. Dodd of Indiana organized the Sons of Liberty to protect the civil liberties of those opposed to the Republican Administration. Acting on rumors that the Sons of Liberty had aided Confederates, Union general Henry Carrington arrested Indiana Democrats linked to the Sons of Liberty, including editor Lambdin Milligan. A military commission sentenced three of the defendants to death. Others received prison terms. The death sentences were never carried out, but it is clear that the men were tried on questionable evidence by military commissions in areas where civil courts were functioning. After the war, the Supreme Court ruled in *Ex parte Milligan* (1866) that such trials were illegal.

Treatment of Black Troops. When the conflict began, neither the Union nor Confederate governments would sanction the use of African American soldiers. As the Union government moved toward an acceptance of emancipation, however, it also began to organize African American regiments.

In spite of the large-scale recruitment of black soldiers during the last two years of the war, the Union army discriminated against African Americans in a wide variety of ways including pay, chance of promotion, and the amount of fatigue duty black units were expected to perform. While a few blacks did receive commissions, the vast majority of officers in the United States Colored Troops (USCT) were white combat veterans. The men of the USCT proved their courage at the battles of Port Hudson, Milliken's Bend, and Fort Wagner,

President Lincoln meeting with his cabinet and one of his generals to discuss the war. (James L. Shaffer)

where they took heavy casualties. Generally, however, the prejudice of many commanding officers led to the use of USCT regiments for fatigue or guard duty while saving white units for combat.

The Confederacy reacted harshly to the use of black troops by the Union army. President Davis approved of the execution of black prisoners of war in South Carolina in November, 1862. Later, Davis ordered that all former slaves captured while serving in the Union army be returned to the states for trial. The massacre of black prisoners by Confederate troops on several occasions forced Union authorities to threaten retaliation in order to stem the injustice.

The use of large numbers of black troops by the Union war effort helped pave the way for universal emancipation. Throughout his political career, Lincoln consistently asserted that slavery was morally wrong. Though emancipation began as a military tactic, it became a war aim. The courage of black soldiers allowed Lincoln to secure passage of the Thirteenth Amendment, providing for an end to slavery throughout the country.

Military Justice. The system of military justice employed within the army was seriously flawed. At least 267 soldiers were executed by the Union army during the Civil War era. More than half of those executed were either foreigners or African Americans. A number of black soldiers were convicted of mutiny for protesting unequal pay in the Union army. Racial tensions accelerated during the final months of the conflict. A high number of black soldiers were executed for alleged sexual offenses against white women. The Confederacy had an incomplete record of military justice. Since many Southern officers had received their training in the prewar U.S. army, the procedural flaws of courts-martial were similar in both armies.

The Civil War moved the United States toward a more perfect application of its ideals of equality and justice. The United States entered the war as a federal union with contrasting standards of justice, one based on free-labor ideals, the other on the slave system of the Southern states. Property rights took precedent over human rights, and equal justice was denied African Americans in virtually every section of the country. The Union government, through its policy of emancipation and the enlistment of African Americans into its armed forces, transformed the war from a crusade to preserve the Union into a war of liberation. In doing so, it expanded the nation's concept of justice to include equality for African Americans. — *Thomas D. Matijasic*

See also Abolitionist movement; Civil War Amendments; Conscription; Emancipation Proclamation; *Habeas corpus*; Kansas-Nebraska Act; Lincoln, Abraham; Lincoln-Douglas debates; Martial law; *Merryman, Ex parte*; *Milligan, Ex parte*; Missouri Compromise of 1820; Reconstruction; Slavery; Taney, Roger Brooke.

BIBLIOGRAPHY

The most comprehensive source for military records on the Civil War is the U.S. War Department, *The War of the Rebellion: A Compilation of the Official Records of the Union and Confederate Armies* (130 vol. Washington, D.C.: U.S. Government Printing Office, 1880-1901). An excellent overview of all aspects of the war condensed into readable form is James M. McPherson, *Battle Cry of Freedom: The Civil War Era* (New York: Oxford University Press, 1988). Robert I. Alotta, *Civil War Justice: Union Army Executions Under Lincoln* (Shippensburg, Pa.: White Mane, 1989), argues that the military justice system was hopelessly flawed. Joseph T. Glatthaar, *Forged in Battle: The Civil War Alliance of Black Soldiers and White Officers* (New York: The Free Press, 1990), chronicles discrimination within the Union army. Frank L. Klement, *Dark Lanterns: Secret Political Societies, Conspiracies, and Treason Trials in the Civil War* (Baton Rouge: Louisiana State University Press, 1984), explodes the myth of vast treasonable societies operating in the North during the war. Mark E. Neely, Jr., *The Fate of Liberty: Abraham Lincoln and Civil Liberties* (New York: Oxford University Press, 1991), defends Lincoln's record on civil liberties and disputes the notion that arbitrary arrests were common. James G. Randall, *Constitutional Problems Under Lincoln* (rev. ed. Urbana: University of Illinois Press, 1951), blames Lincoln's subordinates for violations of civil liberties. Emory M. Thomas, *The Confederate Nation: 1861-1865* (New York: Harper & Row, 1979), is a brief, readable overview of the functioning of the Confederate government.

Civil War Amendments

DATE: Declared in force December 18, 1865 (Thirteenth Amendment); July 28, 1868 (Fourteenth Amendment); and March 30, 1870 (Fifteenth Amendment)

DEFINITION: The Thirteenth, Fourteenth, and Fifteenth Amendments are collectively known as the Civil War Amendments

SIGNIFICANCE: The Civil War Amendments ended slavery, established the principle of equality before the law for American citizens, and prohibited racial discrimination in voting

The Civil War and its aftermath made up one of the greatest periods of change in American history. The end of slavery and the need to define the legal position of former slaves led to three constitutional amendments that introduced the concept of equality to the Constitution and permanently altered the face of American justice and the constitutional order.

Thirteenth Amendment. During the Civil War, the abolition of slavery became a war aim of the U.S. government. President Abraham Lincoln's Emancipation Proclamation (1863) declared slaves in areas still in rebellion against the United States to be free and signaled that a Union victory would mean the end of slavery. The proclamation was a wartime measure, grounded in the president's authority as commander in chief. As the war drew to a close, concern over the proclamation's constitutionality grew, as did concern about the continued existence of slavery in the border states and areas of the South not covered by the proclamation. Congressional Republicans determined to seek a constitutional amendment that would abolish slavery everywhere in the country. The amendment cleared Congress in the spring of 1865 and was ratified by the end of the year.

The major impact of the Thirteenth Amendment was to end American slavery forever. The Supreme Court subsequently ruled that it might also provide grounds for congressional action against the "badges and incidents" of slavery. Use of the amendment in this regard has been relatively uncommon.

Fourteenth Amendment. Concern over the status and treatment of former slaves soon led to another amendment. Despite the Civil Rights Act of 1866, many former slaves found their freedom limited by "black codes" passed by southern state legislatures. Republicans of abolitionist background determined to define the status of African Americans in terms of legal equality: As they saw it, the Constitution needed to be brought into line with the Declaration of Independence. After a stiff battle in Congress, the Fourteenth Amendment emerged in 1866. Its ratification was made a condition of readmission for former Confederate states, and it completed the ratification process in 1868.

The Fourteenth Amendment's first section provided—for the first time—a constitutional definition of American citizenship: all persons born or naturalized in the United States and subject to its jurisdiction. This was especially important in defining the status of former slaves, because it overturned the Supreme Court decision in *Scott v. Sandford* (1857), which held that African Americans were not citizens even if free. It further provided that states might not abridge the "privileges and immunities" of citizens, deprive them of life, liberty, or property without due process of law, or deny them the "equal protection of the laws." The last clause marked the first time that equality before the law was written into the Constitution. Most of the rest of the amendment dealt with particular concerns growing out of the Civil War that gradually faded in importance: Certain former Confederates were barred from holding office, the U.S. war debt was guaranteed, and funding of the Confederate war debt was prohibited. A provision permitting a state's congressional representation to be reduced if the state did not allow a segment of its adult male population to vote was never used and was soon overtaken by the Fifteenth Amendment.

Interpreting the Fourteenth Amendment. Defining and implementing the apparently simple language of the amendment proved to be a complicated and lengthy process. In the short term, the amendment disappointed those who hoped that they had set the rights of African Americans on a firm basis of equality. One reason for this was the Supreme Court's lack of sympathy. As early as 1873 (in the *Slaughterhouse Cases*), the Court drastically limited the amendment's scope by ruling that most of the important "privileges and immunities" were those bestowed by state—rather than federal—citizenship. This opened the door for states and individuals to discriminate against African Americans (and others). By 1896, when the Court decided the case of *Plessy v. Ferguson*, it found nothing wrong with states requiring the separation of the races, as long

as some token effort at "equal" treatment was made. Under the "separate but equal" rule, racial segregation increasingly became a hallmark of American life.

At the same time that the Fourteenth Amendment was being limited in its impact on civil rights, the Court employed it to protect the operations of big business. A corporation was declared to be a "person" within the meaning of the amendment, and states were increasingly limited as to what steps they might take to regulate them.

It was only in the mid-twentieth century that the amendment was revived to fulfill something like its original purpose. The National Association for the Advancement of Colored People (NAACP) was an important factor in this. For decades it fought in the courts to challenge racial discrimination and make the Fourteenth Amendment a force in American life. At first, it succeeded only in minor challenges and in improving facilities given blacks under the "separate but equal" doctrine. In 1954 the NAACP finally scored a stunning victory in *Brown v. Board of Education*, when the Supreme Court used the equal protection clause of the Fourteenth Amendment to rule that segregated schools—and by implication other institutions and facilities—were inherently inferior and thus unconstitutional. Similar interpretations of the Fourteenth Amendment would underpin other important civil rights decisions in the second half of the twentieth century.

Incorporation Doctrine. By the time of the *Brown* decision, the Fourteenth Amendment had become vitally important to American justice in another way: as a means of utilizing the Bill of Rights as a restraint on the states. Scholars have never agreed whether the amendment's limitations on state action were originally intended to include the protections that the Bill of Rights provides against federal action. Some argued for such an interpretation, and beginning in the early twentieth century their ideas began to have an impact. A major breakthrough came in the 1925 case of *Gitlow v. New York*. Here the Supreme Court decided that the Fourteenth Amendment did "incorporate" the First Amendment's protection of free speech against violation by state government. Though the court held back from endorsing the idea that the entire Bill of Rights was "incorporated" in the Fourteenth Amendment, it did begin the gradual incorporation of specific rights. The process gathered speed during the era of Chief Justice Earl Warren's leadership (1953-1969). By this time, the recognition of individual rights protected against state action by the Fourteenth Amendment, especially those accused or suspected of committing crimes, was having a major impact on the administration of American justice. The well-known warning to one arrested for committing a crime—that a person has the right to remain silent, that anything the accused says can be used against him or her in court, and that the accused has the right to have an attorney present during questioning—derives from the case of *Miranda v. Arizona* (1966), in which the Supreme Court applied the Fifth Amendment's protection against self-incrimination to state and local government through the Fourteenth Amendment's due process clause.

Fifteenth Amendment. The question of whether African Americans should be allowed to vote on the same basis as whites was approached indirectly by the section of the Fourteenth Amendment that provided for a state's congressional representation to be reduced proportionately if it denied the vote to any segment of its adult males. By the late 1860's, many congressional Republicans favored more forceful protection for black voters. While the former Confederate states were required to write black suffrage into their state constitutions as a condition of readmittance to the Union, there was always the possibility that such provisions could be altered in the future. There were also pressing political considerations. Democratic strength was reviving, and seventeen states still denied African Americans the vote. Enfranchising blacks in the border, midwestern, and western states became a matter of crucial importance to Republicans. The means to this end was the Fifteenth Amendment. The amendment was originally proposed as a positive statement of manhood suffrage, with protections against states requiring property qualifications or literacy tests. In order to secure passage by the necessary two-thirds majority in the House of Representatives, however, the amendment's sponsors had to compromise. The amendment emerged with negative wording: States could not deny the right to vote based on race. In this form, the amendment was ratified in 1870.

The history of the Fifteenth Amendment ran generally parallel to that of the Fourteenth: short-term disappointment followed by mid-twentieth century revival. By the 1890's, southern and border states were finding ways around the amendment. Its wording implied that the right to vote could be denied on a basis other than race, and such pretexts were developed with a decidedly negative effect on black voting rights. Literacy tests, poll taxes, and—most effective of all—all-white primaries were used to deny African Americans the vote. Not until 1944 did the Supreme Court rule the white primary a violation of the Fifteenth Amendment in the case of *Smith v. Allwright*. In 1964, the Twenty-fourth Amendment prohibited the poll tax in federal elections. The most effective revitalization of the Fifteenth Amendment's original purpose came in 1965 with the passage of the Voting Rights Act.

Taken together, the Civil War Amendments have had a major impact on the Constitution; some scholars have even seen them as creating a "second constitution" because of the extent of their impact over time. These amendments introduced a new type of right in that they offered the possibility of intervention by the federal government to protect a citizen from unconstitutional abuse by a state or even private individuals. Moreover, the Fourteenth Amendment expressly incorporated the concept of equality into the Constitution. Without it, the words inscribed on the Supreme Court Building

An African American parade in New York City celebrating the adoption of the Fifteenth Amendment. (Library of Congress)

(EQUAL JUSTICE UNDER LAW) would have no literal basis in the nation's fundamental law. — *William C. Lowe*

See also Abolitionist movement; Bill of Rights, U.S.; Black codes; Citizenship; Civil War; Due process of law; Equal protection of the law; Incorporation doctrine; Reconstruction; *Slaughterhouse Cases*; Slavery; Vote, right to.

BIBLIOGRAPHY

Raoul Berger, *Government by Judiciary: The Transformation of the Fourteenth Amendment* (Cambridge, Mass.: Harvard University Press, 1977), argues that the courts have used the Fourteenth Amendment in such a way as to assume vast legislative powers that properly belong to Congress and state legislatures. Richard C. Cortner, *The Supreme Court and the Second Bill of Rights: The Fourteenth Amendment and the Nationalization of Civil Liberties* (Madison: University of Wisconsin Press, 1981), is the best overview of the incorporation of the Bill of Rights into the Fourteenth Amendment; Michael Kent Curtis, *No State Shall Abridge: The Fourteenth Amendment and the Bill of Rights* (Durham, N.C.: Duke University Press, 1986), stresses the abolitionist origins of the Fourteenth Amendment and argues that its framers did intend to incorporate the Bill of Rights; Eric Foner, *Reconstruction: America's Unfinished Revolution, 1863-1877* (New York: Harper & Row, 1988), provides invaluable context for understanding the era and includes good treatments of the three amendments. William Gillette, *The Right to Vote: Politics and the Passage of the Fifteenth Amendment* (Baltimore: The Johns Hopkins University Press, 1969), stresses the importance of partisan political factors in the Fifteenth Amendment's genesis; Harold Hyman and William C. Wiecek, *Equal Justice Under Law: Constitutional Development, 1835-1875* (New York: Harper & Row, 1982), places the amendments within the overall context of the period's constitutional history. Earl M. Maltz, *Civil Rights, the Constitution, and Congress, 1863-1869* (Lawrence: University Press of Kansas, 1990), finds little evidence to support the view that Congress intended to incorporate the Bill of Rights in the Fourteenth Amendment; William E. Nelson, *The Fourteenth Amendment: From Political Principle to Judicial Doctrine* (Cambridge, Mass.: Harvard University Press, 1988), provides the best general account of the Fourteenth Amendment's complex and controversial history; and Donald G. Nieman, *Promises to Keep: African-Americans and the Constitutional Order, 1776 to the Present* (New York: Oxford University Press, 1991), provides a handy brief account of the amendments and their role in defining the place of blacks under the Constitution.

Civilian review boards

DEFINITION: Official groups of citizens that examine the merits of complaints against police officers

SIGNIFICANCE: Civilian review boards have been instituted in various cities as a way to restore public confidence in police departments, some of which had been tainted by corruption scandals and charges of brutality

One of the greatest potential threats to justice is corruption within law enforcement organizations. Police corruption has been addressed historically through a variety of mechanisms, including internal affairs divisions, police commissions, political oversight agencies, and special investigatory bodies. Despite these mechanisms, complaints have persisted that charges of police corruption are sometimes ignored by governmental authorities. In the 1960's, experiments were conducted with civilian review boards (CRBs), groups of citizens from the community who would examine complaints against police officers and recommend further action. Police departments strongly opposed the establishment of these boards as a threat to police professionalism and morale. In the 1980's and 1990's, however, enthusiasm for CRBs increased, particularly in larger cities. A series of notorious cases of alleged police abuse of power, particularly against persons belonging to racial minority groups, fueled calls for civilian oversight.

CRBs seldom are empowered to make ultimate determinations on citizen complaints. Instead, their findings and recommendations are passed on to other authorities as well as made available to the general public. CRBs can be seen as a logical complement to the trend toward community-oriented policing, which was gaining popularity at the same time.

See also Chief of police; Community-oriented policing; Deadly force, police use of; King, Rodney, case and aftermath; Knapp Commission; Miami riots; Police; Police brutality; Police corruption and misconduct.

Class action

DEFINITION: A lawsuit brought by or against many individuals or organizations with common interests

SIGNIFICANCE: Class action suits give individuals with similar small claims a greater chance for justice

The modern class action originated in the English court of chancery in a procedure known as the bill of peace, which allowed persons with a common complaint to gain justice against a larger group or a more powerful wrongdoer. In the United States, prior to the nineteenth century, these ideas were embodied in the Federal Equity Rules, regulations outside the state and federal codes. In the nineteenth century, state codes made class actions legal actions at the state level. In 1938, federal courts followed.

Groups that want to initiate a class action must convince a judge that the complaints of individual members bringing the suit are sufficiently similar that justice is better served by processing the group action rather than individual actions. In addition, the judge must be convinced that absent class members will be fairly represented. Once the class action is under way, those bringing the action must try to find others who will be bound by the findings of the court, so that they may participate in or voice their objections to the representation.

Class actions are most commonly used in cases involving the environment, securities, antitrust regulation, racial or sexual discrimination, unfair employment practices, and governmental benefits. Class actions have also been used by prisoners who believe the conditions of their confinement are unlawful and by consumers who can show a systematic pattern of misrepresentation of a product.

Since the early 1970's, the number of class action suits has greatly increased. Much of the increase probably reflects changes in the legal profession, specifically in fields of substantive law, and in the rising fees from class action suits. The class action also provides a way to bring important social issues to light, and such issues received increasing attention. Despite the increase in class actions in general, the trend has been to eliminate class actions from federal courts and get them into state courts.

Class actions have their drawbacks. Leaders of a class action can be bought off by an opponent to the detriment of others in the group. Members of the group may lose heart during the time-consuming legal process. The results represent an anomaly to the general rule that everyone has the right to a day in court because those results are ultimately binding on all class members, regardless of whether they participated in the case.

See also Affirmative action; Age discrimination; *Amicus curiae* brief; Civil procedure; Gay rights; Injunction; Litigation; Nader, Ralph; Racial and ethnic discrimination; Sex discrimination; Suit.

Classic, United States v.

COURT: U.S. Supreme Court
DATE: Decided May 26, 1941
SIGNIFICANCE: This case overturned an earlier decision and brought primary elections under constitutional protection

Two decisions of the U.S. Supreme Court, in 1921 and 1935, gave southern states the authority to exclude African Americans from voting in primary elections. These decisions were important because the South was dominated by the Democratic Party from the end of Reconstruction until the middle of the twentieth century. If blacks could not vote in the Democratic primary, they were denied any real choice in the selection of elected officials.

In 1921, the Supreme Court ruled in *Newberry v. United States* that Congress did not have the authority to regulate primary elections. At issue was a Michigan senatorial primary race between Henry Ford and Truman Newberry in which Newberry alleged that he was the victim of vote fraud. The *Newberry* case provided the opportunity for southern states to pass white primary laws, since the Court declared that such elections fell outside of constitutional protection. In *Grovey v. Townsend* (1935), the Court ruled that state party conventions could exclude blacks from primaries without violating the Constitution. In the battle to eliminate the white primary, the U.S. Justice Department had to persuade the Supreme Court to overturn the *Newberry* decision. *United States v. Classic* provided the opportunity to reverse *Newberry*. Although the *Classic* case did not involve racial discrimination or the white primary, it did involve the relationship of the primary to the election process.

Vote fraud was a common feature of Louisiana elections. While investigating charges of fraud by the heirs of former governor and senator Huey Long, the Justice Department discovered that Patrick Classic, an opponent of the Long faction,

had engaged in altering and falsely counting votes. Classic, invoking the *Newberry* decision, argued that primaries were beyond federal control.

Reversing *Newberry*, the U.S. Supreme Court declared that the Constitution protected the right to vote in primaries as well as general elections. This was certainly true in Louisiana, the Court stated, "where the state law has made the primary an integral part of the procedure of choice, or where in fact the primary effectively controls the choice."

The reversal of *Newberry* by the *Classic* decision provided the framework for the final attack on white primaries. It was evident that in the one-party South, whoever won the Democratic primary won the general election. Only three years after the *Classic* decision, the National Association for the Advancement of Colored People (NAACP) successfully challenged the white primaries in *Smith v. Allwright*. Without the *Classic* decision, the assault on the white primaries would have been delayed for years.

See also *Grovey v. Townsend*; National Association for the Advancement of Colored People (NAACP); *Newberry v. United States*; *Smith v. Allwright*; Vote, right to.

Clay, Henry (Apr. 12, 1777, Hanover County, Va.—June 29, 1852, Washington, D.C.)

IDENTIFICATION: United States senator and political leader
SIGNIFICANCE: Clay persistently brought compromise to the regional conflicts that ultimately led to the Civil War

Henry Clay moved to Richmond, Virginia, in 1791, becoming a clerk in the High Court of Chancery and reading law in the attorney general's office. After being licensed to practice, Clay moved to Kentucky in 1797; there he was elected to the state assembly in 1803. In 1806 he was appointed to an unexpired term in the U.S. Senate, after which he was reelected to the state assembly, becoming speaker in 1807. He was elected U.S. representative in 1811 and became known as a "war hawk" regarding the War of 1812. He later served on the peace commission ending the war in 1814. He returned to the House of Representatives in 1815, where, in 1820, he led in developing the Missouri Compromise, resolving the sectional dispute over extending slavery in the territories.

Clay ran for president in 1824, ultimately throwing his support to John Quincy Adams, who appointed him secretary of state. In 1831 he was elected senator and led opposition to Andrew Jackson. He again ran for president in 1832. Losing, he and John C. Calhoun secured passage of the compromise tariff of 1832. In response, South Carolina retracted its ordinance of nullification. Clay continued opposing Jackson's economic policies, leading a coalition that became the Whig Party. Clay ran for president a third time in 1844 but lost to James K. Polk, largely because he failed to take a strong stand regarding annexation of Texas as a slave state. Clay returned to the senate in 1849, where he was pivotal in persuading Congress to accept the Compromise of 1850.

See also Constitution, U.S.; Fugitive Slave Laws; Jacksonian democracy; Missouri Compromise of 1820; Whig Party.

Clayton Antitrust Act

DATE: Enacted October 15, 1914

DEFINITION: A law that outlawed a number of business practices limiting competition and strengthened the legal position of labor unions

SIGNIFICANCE: While providing a symbolic victory for those seeking to halt the dominance of American industry by large corporations, the Clayton Act proved disappointing in its impact

The growing power of great corporations, or "trusts," was a major concern in the early twentieth century. How best to deal with the problem was a major issue in the 1912 presidential campaign. Woodrow Wilson, the Democratic candidate, advocated a "New Freedom" platform that promised to cut trusts down to size and encourage a more competitive business environment. After Wilson's election, one approach of his administration was to remedy what was thought to be too general language of the Sherman Antitrust Act (1890), the nation's primary antitrust law. In 1914, under the leadership of Congressman Henry D. Clayton, chairman of the House Judiciary Committee, Congress proceeded to pass a new antitrust measure whose main thrust was to foil would-be monopolists by outlawing tactics that in the past had fostered the growth of large corporations.

The Clayton Act attacked a range of business practices: acquisition of stock of a competitor, interlocking directorates (the same directors sitting on the boards of supposedly competing companies), price discrimination (giving some customers an advantage by charging them lower prices than their competitors), and exclusive or tying contracts. All these practices were outlawed "where the effect may be to substantially lessen competition or tend to create monopoly." The act also made corporate officials personally liable for the actions of their companies. Individuals or heads of firms who believed that they had been harmed by such tactics could seek an injunction to stop the objectionable practice, and they could sue for triple damages.

The act also sought to improve the legal position of organized labor. It declared that labor was not a commodity and that antitrust laws could not be used against legitimate union activities, such as peaceful strikes or boycotts. It also prohibited the use of injunctions in labor disputes unless danger threatened persons or property.

The Clayton Act proved disappointing to many of those who had supported it. President Wilson switched his emphasis, trying to encourage greater competition in the economy through regulation provided by the Federal Trade Commission, also created in 1914. Corporate lawyers soon found ways to get around the act's provisions, especially since the courts found latitude in the act's wording that made violations difficult to prove. Though strengthened in 1936 and 1950, the act has been less important in antitrust law than the Sherman Act. Although labor leader Samuel Gompers had hailed the act as "labor's Magna Carta," it did not meet the hopes of its supporters in this arena either, for it failed to end the use of injunctions in labor disputes.

See also Antitrust law; Capitalism; Federal Trade Commission (FTC); Injunction; Labor law; Sherman Antitrust Act; Wilson, Woodrow.

Clear and present danger test

DEFINITION: The principle, articulated by Oliver Wendell Holmes, Jr., that political speech is protected unless it creates a "clear and present danger that [it] will bring about the substantive evils that Congress has a right to prevent"

SIGNIFICANCE: This was the first principle used by the Supreme Court to distinguish unprotected from protected political speech; the principle is no longer used to suppress political speech but has been used to prohibit hate speech and disruptive speech

In 1798, Congress passed the Alien and Sedition Act, which prohibited false, scandalous, and malicious publications against the United States government, the Congress, and the president. The act was particularly designed to punish newspapers which opposed President John Adams and supported Thomas Jefferson. Punishment was a fine of up to two thousand dollars and a jail sentence of up to two years. Similar prohibitions occurred in the Espionage Act of 1917, the Sedition Act of 1918, and the Smith Act of 1940, which were designed to suppress opposition to the war efforts of those times.

The first Supreme Court case to test whether a prosecution for seditious libel constituted a violation of the First Amendment occurred in 1919. Charles Schenck, the general secretary of the Philadelphia Socialist Party, published fifteen thousand leaflets protesting U.S. involvement in World War I. Schenck and several others in the party were convicted of violation of the Espionage Act; the conviction was appealed to the Supreme Court in 1919.

Justice Oliver Wendell Holmes, Jr., wrote the opinion of the Court and formulated the test which could justify suppression of speech. In ordinary times, such pamphlets might be permissible, he wrote, but the character of every act depends upon the circumstances in which it is done. "The most stringent protection of free speech would not protect a man in falsely shouting fire in a theater and causing a panic." "The question in every case," Holmes stated, "is whether the words are used in such circumstances and are of such a nature as to create a clear and present danger that they will bring about the substantive evils that Congress has a right to prevent" (*Schenck v. United States*, 1919).

The principle was used to support the conviction of more than two thousand protesters during World War I in spite of the fact that Justice Holmes dissented from these later convictions. Later, in *Whitney v. California* (1927), Justice Louis D. Brandeis formulated what was intended to be a more permissive version of the principle. Brandeis wrote that the wide difference between advocacy and incitement, between preparation and attempt, between assembling and conspiracy must be borne in mind.

This is the formulation that was adopted in *Brandenburg v. Ohio* (1969). In this case the Supreme Court overturned a conviction based on the clear and present danger test for the first time. Defendants have not been convicted of seditious libel since.

See also *Abrams v. United States*; Brandeis, Louis D.; *Brandenburg v. Ohio*; Censorship; *Gitlow v. New York*; Holmes, Oliver Wendell, Jr.; *Schenck v. United States*; Seditious libel; Speech and press, freedom of.

Coast Guard, U.S.

DATE: Established 1789

SIGNIFICANCE: The United States Coast Guard helps protect the shores of the United States and has made American coastal waters safer; the Coast Guard also helps to prevent smuggling and enforces customs laws

One of the first acts of the new United States government begun under its new constitution in 1789 was to provide for the organization of the United States Coast Guard. Under the first Tariff Act of 1789, the first secretary of the treasury, Alexander Hamilton, was given authority to construct ten boats (approximately forty feet long and armed with swivel guns) to patrol the coastal waters of the United States. The original name given to the Coast Guard was United States Revenue Marine.

The Revenue Marine was to prevent smuggling in order to increase government revenues from import duties. The organization was also to cooperate with the United States Navy (which was not created until 1798). During the undeclared naval war with France in 1798-1799, the Revenue Marine fought alongside the U.S. Navy in the West Indies, capturing sixteen French ships. That tradition has been followed in every war in United States history.

In the War of 1812 the Coast Guard had sixteen ships, averaging 125 tons apiece, with crews of fifteen to thirty men. They were armed with a half dozen or more light guns. In this period these ships fought pirates on the Gulf Coast. The Coast Guard took an active role in the Mexican War (1846-1848) and in the American Civil War (1861-1865). When the United States purchased Alaska from Russia in 1867, the cutter *Lincoln* was the first American vessel sent to patrol Alaskan waters. By then the Coast Guard was called the Revenue Cutter Service.

After the accidental sinking of the *Titanic* in 1912, the Coast Guard began regular patrols of the North Atlantic. From there it operated against German U-boats in World War I. During World War II and subsequent wars, the Coast Guard has often aided the Navy in combat zones but has been particularly important in maintaining the defense of the United States while the Navy was preoccupied with foreign wars.

In time of peace the Coast Guard is under the authority of the Treasury Department, but in time of war it is under orders from the United States Navy. An important function of the Coast Guard is to give assistance to vessels in distress, especially in severe weather. Hundreds of people have been rescued and thousands of tons of cargo have been saved in storms at sea by the Coast Guard.

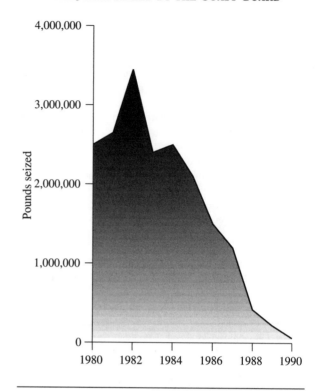

MARIJUANA SEIZED BY THE COAST GUARD

Source: U.S. Department of Justice, Bureau of Justice Statistics, *Drugs, Crime, and the Justice System.* Washington, D.C.: U.S. Government Printing Office, 1992.

Note: In 1990, the largest amount of marijuana was seized in the southeastern U.S. and the Caribbean. Less than 62,000 pounds of marijuana was seized in 1990.

See also Admiralty law; Immigration laws; International law; Prohibition; Treasury, U.S. Department of the.

COINTELPRO

DATE: Primarily important for operations in the late 1960's and early 1970's

SIGNIFICANCE: This secret FBI campaign to neutralize political dissidents in the United States employed a number of illegal means in its efforts

COINTELPRO, an abbreviation of "counter-intelligence program," refers to a program of legal and extralegal activities by the Federal Bureau of Investigation (FBI) intended to control political dissent in the United States. Details of COINTELPRO activities remained secret before March, 1971, when a citizens' committee investigating the FBI removed previously secret FBI files from an agency office. Gradually more files were obtained through the Freedom of Information Act. A few agents and informers have also substantiated COINTELPRO's existence. Congressional hearings describing COINTELPRO have also been published. The full story may never be known, but the program engaged in harassment, misinformation, persecution, imprisonment, and perhaps even assassination in its efforts to discredit and destroy dissident and radical groups.

The primary targets of COINTELPRO were antiwar dissidents and black, American Indian, and Puerto Rican militants. Targeted groups included the American Indian Movement (AIM), Students for a Democratic Society (SDS), the Nation of Islam, and the Black Panther Party. The Black Panthers were apparently a particular target of FBI director J. Edgar Hoover; he ordered agents to "exploit all avenues of creating dissent" within the party.

See also Black Panther Party; Federal Bureau of Investigation (FBI); Hoover, J. Edgar.

Coker v. Georgia

COURT: U.S. Supreme Court
DATE: Decided June 29, 1977
SIGNIFICANCE: The Court ruled that capital punishment for the crime of rape is an excessive and disproportionate penalty that violates the Eighth Amendment

While serving sentences for murder, rape, kidnapping, and other crimes, Erlich Anthony Coker escaped from a Georgia prison in 1974. That same evening he entered the private home of a couple, tied up the husband in the bathroom, raped the wife, and then forced her to leave with him in the car belonging to the couple. Apprehended by the police, Coker was tried and convicted on charges of rape, armed robbery, and kidnapping. Based on procedures that had been approved by the U.S. Supreme Court in *Gregg v. Georgia* (1976), the jury found Coker guilty of rape with aggravating circumstances and sentenced him to death. After the Georgia Supreme Court upheld the conviction and sentence, the U.S. Supreme Court accepted the case for review.

The Supreme Court limited its review to the single question whether capital punishment for rape is a cruel and unusual punishment that violates the Eighth and Fourteenth Amendments. Ruling 7 to 2 in the affirmative, the Court reversed Coker's death sentence and remanded the case to the Georgia courts for a new sentencing.

Writing the majority opinion, Justice Byron R. White argued that the sentence of death for the crime of rape is unconstitutional because it is an excessive and disproportionate punishment. As evidence that the public judgment agreed with this conclusion, White pointed to the fact that Georgia was the only state to authorize the death penalty for the rape of an adult woman. Although the crime of rape deserved serious punishment, it was disproportionate to inflict the defendant with a more severe punishment than he inflicted on his victim. Although rape was not equivalent to the unjustifiable taking of a human life, the crime of deliberate murder in Georgia was not a basis for the death penalty except where there were aggravating circumstances. White wrote that it was disproportionate to punish a rapist more severely than a deliberate killer.

As in other cases dealing with capital punishment, the justices expressed a variety of views. Two concurring justices opposed all use of capital punishment, while two dissenters would have allowed it for rape. One justice, Lewis F. Powell, Jr., joined the majority because the rapist did not inflict great brutality or serious injury on the victim.

The *Coker* decision underscored the extent to which the Court had accepted the view that the Eighth Amendment prohibited excessive and disproportionate punishments. It appeared that the Court would not approve the use of the death penalty for any crime other than deliberate murder, but it was not certain how the Court would react to capital punishment for rape with excessive brutality or when the victim sustained serious injury. Some observers noted that *Coker* appeared to indicate that the Court was becoming more reliant upon the doctrine of substantive due process.

See also Capital punishment; Cruel and unusual punishment; *Furman v. Georgia*; *Gregg v. Georgia*; *Robinson v. California*; *Rummel v. Estelle*.

Colegrove v. Green

COURT: U.S. Supreme Court
DATE: Decided June 10, 1946
SIGNIFICANCE: In this case, which remained as a precedent until the 1960's, the Supreme Court decided that it could not decide whether congressional districts were properly drawn because this issue constituted a "political question" that had to be decided by elected officials

Three voters who resided in Illinois districts with much larger populations than other congressional districts in the state filed an action to challenge the unequal sizes of Illinois legislative districts. In Illinois and other states, state legislatures had marked out legislative districts of unequal size or else had failed to draw new district boundaries when population patterns changed. One congressional district in Illinois, for example, contained 914,000 people while another district contained only 112,000. The effect of such maldistribution was to dilute the voting strength of voters in larger districts and enhance the power of voters in smaller districts. In Congress, two representatives from districts containing fewer than 150,000 people could outvote a representative from a district containing more than 900,000. Thus government was more responsive to and controlled by people from smaller districts rather than representative of the wishes of the majority of voters, whose votes would be diluted in larger districts. Rural interests in many states controlled political power and the development of public policy, despite the fact that a majority of citizens lived in urban and suburban areas.

In an opinion by Justice Felix Frankfurter, the Supreme Court declined to decide whether unequal legislative districts violated the equal protection rights of voters in larger districts. On behalf of a five-member majority, Frankfurter declared that issues concerning legislative districting were "beyond [the] competence" of courts because such issues were "of a peculiarly political nature and therefore not meant for judicial determination." By labeling legislative districting a "political question" unsuited for judicial resolution, the majority of justices avoided any examination of questions about discrimination and voting rights that were raised by the existence of unequal districts.

Three dissenting justices, Hugo Black, William O. Douglas, and Frank Murphy, complained that the Court was improperly permitting state legislatures to violate the rights of voters in larger districts. One justice, Robert H. Jackson, did not take part in the case.

The Court's decision left districting temporarily in the hands of state legislatures. Justices Black and Douglas were still on the Court two decades later, however, when a new set of justices revisited the issue and decided that districts must be designed with comparable populations in order to avoid violating citizens' equal protection rights. In *Baker v. Carr* (1962), the Supreme Court decided that such legislative districting questions were not reserved for the legislative branch alone but could also be examined by the judiciary. In the subsequent cases of *Wesberry v. Sanders* (1964) and *Reynolds v. Sims* (1964), the *Colegrove* precedent was completely eliminated when the Court mandated that federal and state legislative districts be of equivalent sizes.

See also *Baker v. Carr*; Frankfurter, Felix; Representation: gerrymandering, malapportionment, and reapportionment; *Reynolds v. Sims*; *Wesberry v. Sanders*.

Color of law

DEFINITION: An action performed under color of law has the appearance of authority and legality but is actually unauthorized and illegal

SIGNIFICANCE: The color of law provision in the U.S. Code has been important in civil rights cases, particularly in enforcement of the rights guaranteed by the Fourteenth Amendment

"Color," in the phrase "color of law," means having the appearance but not the reality; it means pretense, semblance, or disguise. Acting under color of law therefore means maintaining a position of legal authority when in fact a person, usually a government official, does not have that authority (for example, performing an illegal act as though it were legal). Acting under color of law is an abuse of power.

Color of law is a powerful civil rights provision in the U.S. Code. Section 1983, Title 42, grants a cause of action to every person who, "under color of any statute," is deprived of any rights, privileges, or immunities guaranteed by the Constitution or by law. Section 1983 has been called the Fourteenth Amendment's legislative "sword": It provides that state law cannot be enforced to work against the privileges and immunities provided by the Fourteenth Amendment.

Two notable civil rights cases that involved the color of law provision were *Monroe v. Pape* (1961) and *United States v. Price* (1966). In *Monroe*, thirteen police officers were accused of misusing their authority by entering a home without warning, ransacking it, and using their authority in a manner inconsistent with state law. Justice William O. Douglas held that the alleged action occurred under color of law and that the victim

had recourse to the courts. Color of law was held to apply to all rights guaranteed by the Fourteenth Amendment. In *Price*, eighteen people were implicated in the Mississippi murder of three civil rights workers. Justice Abe Fortas' opinion stated that even private citizens (as opposed to state officials) can be said to be acting under color of law when they are working in concert with state officials.

See also Civil rights; Civil War Amendments; Malfeasance, misfeasance, and nonfeasance; *Neagle, In re*; *Posse comitatus*; United States Code.

Commerce clause

DEFINITION: The clause in the U.S. Constitution giving Congress the power to regulate trade among the states

SIGNIFICANCE: The Supreme Court has upheld Congress' use of the commerce clause as justification for a broad range of federal legislation

Article I, section 8 of the U.S. Constitution states that Congress "shall have the power . . . to regulate commerce with foreign nations, and among the several states, and with the Indian tribes." The part of this clause dealing with the states was extremely important in enabling the United States to develop an effective, integrated economic system, but its influence reaches far beyond the realm of a narrow definition of commerce. The first Supreme Court case involving the commerce clause, *Gibbons v. Ogden* (1824), established that it applies to interstate commerce but not to commerce within one state. Chief Justice John Marshall's opinion in the case broadly defined commerce to include all commercial "intercourse," not only the traffic of goods. In the late nineteenth century, the commerce clause was cited as justification for congressional establishment of the Interstate Commerce Commission and for the Sherman Antitrust Act (1890).

In the early twentieth century the federal government began using the commerce clause as the basis for national legislation involving crime, public safety, and morality, as in the Mann Act (1910) and the Automobile Theft Act of 1915. Until the 1930's, the Supreme Court maintained a distinction between manufacturing and commerce, but in 1937 it began to interpret the commerce clause broadly enough to allow regulating the manufacture of goods intended for interstate transportation and sale. In the years since World War II, there has been considerable federal legislation based on the commerce clause. One of its most remarkable uses was in justifying civil rights legislation in the 1960's. In cases such as *Heart of Atlanta Motel v. United States* (1964), the Supreme Court held that, because racial discrimination has a harmful effect on interstate commerce, Congress can pass and enforce antidiscrimination laws.

See also *Carter v. Carter Coal Co.*; Civil Rights Act of 1964; *Darby Lumber Co., United States v.*; *Heart of Atlanta Motel v. United States*; Interstate Commerce Commission (ICC); *Lopez, United States v.*; Mann Act; National Labor Relations Act (NLRA); Sherman Antitrust Act; Transportation law; *Wickard v. Filburn*.

Commercial law

DEFINITION: The area of law that covers commercial transactions, generally guided by the Uniform Commercial Code (UCC)

SIGNIFICANCE: Consistent regulation of commercial transactions is essential for the smooth functioning of an economy based on capitalism and a free market

U.S. commercial law—law governing such things as the transfer of goods and funds—has its historical basis in the English legal system called the "law merchant," which was integrated into English common law in the eighteenth century. The English system was brought to America by the English colonists. For a number of reasons, including the fact that the states all passed their own individual commerce laws, the system did not work as well in the United States as it had in England. Eventually, in 1892, the National Conference of Commissioners on Uniform State Laws was established to deal with the problem. A variety of commercial legislation drafted by the ongoing National Conference was passed in the early twentieth century.

By 1940 the National Conference had recognized a need to consolidate the various laws into a more consistent, comprehensive code. In 1944 the conference undertook an agreement with the American Law Institute to work jointly on the project. The completed Uniform Commercial Code (UCC) was published in 1952. States enacted the code at different times; Pennsylvania was the first. Because of debates over the code in some states and because of Pennsylvania's practical experience with it, modifications were made in 1957 and 1958. The code continues to evolve, and new versions are published periodically. The UCC has nine articles, each covering a different aspect of commercial transactions.

Article 1 consists of "general provisions" and states the purpose and intent of the UCC. It states that parties to a contract can vary the rules of the UCC if both parties agree, and it provides guidelines by which the appropriate standards of conduct for a given situation may be determined. It states that the UCC does not displace other laws, such as those covering bankruptcy or fraud, and that they supplement the UCC. Article 2 covers sales, defining what is meant by the term "sale" (sales agreements of less than $500 need not necessarily be in writing, for example), and what is to be done when one party does not fulfill the terms of a sales agreement. It also discusses warranties, both express and implied. Article 3 governs "commercial paper," a term that applies to checks, drafts, promissory notes, and certificates of deposit. These items, called "negotiable instruments," must be signed and must contain an unconditional promise to pay a certain sum at a certain time.

Article 4 covers bank deposits and collections, detailing banks' role in dealing with the commercial paper of Article 3. This article has been updated extensively to cover electronic fund transfers (also addressed in the Electronic Fund Transfers Act of 1978) and automatic teller machines (ATMs). Article 5 deals with letters of credit, Article 6 with bulk transfers, Article 7 with "documents of title" (or stocks), and Article 8 with

investment securities. Article 9 covers what are called secured transactions: situations in which a seller sells goods on credit on the condition that, if the buyer refuses to pay, the seller has a right to some property of the buyer in order to recoup losses. This property may include either "personal property" or "fixtures" but not real estate or wages.

See also Banking law; Bankruptcy; Capitalism; Contract, freedom of; Contract law; Copyrights, patents, and trademarks; Fraud; Interstate Commerce Commission (ICC); Property rights; Real estate law; Securities and Exchange Commission (SEC); Truth in Lending Act.

Commercialized vice

DEFINITION: A business enterprise catering to various human desires which are often considered immoral and frequently are crimes, whether felonies or misdemeanors

SIGNIFICANCE: Commercialized vice is a controversial area in American justice involving mostly voluntary, consensual activity widely regarded as not directly harming anyone and thus frequently designated "victimless crimes"

Commercialized vice is often described in textbooks as crimes against public morality. Among other tabulations, the *Uniform Crime Reports* for the United States, published yearly by the Federal Bureau of Investigation, lists the total number of arrests for various "vice" crimes. One should be cautioned that the local police departments that report these figures are often inconsistent in their classifications and that, since the conduct involved is consensual, many victimless crimes are unreported. For all that, a sense of the magnitude of these activities is conveyed by the arrest statistics for 1993, shown in the accompanying figure. These numbers include all reporting agencies and estimates for unreported communities.

Prostitution and Related Offenses. Most commonly, prostitution is the indiscriminate exchange of a woman's sexual services for money or other consideration. Less frequently, it involves the sexual services of a male or a minor. At first, prostitution was not an offense per se under either English or American law. It was only in 1914 that an Indiana statute defined the trade and only in 1917 that Massachusetts became the first state to make prostitution directly punishable. Before that time, prostitutes were charged with such offenses as solicitation, vagrancy, and disorderly conduct. Starting around 1920, most states enacted laws against prostitution. There are variations, and state and local criminal statutes may apply to the prostitute, panderer, pimp, customer, economic beneficiary of the prostitute's activity (if it is someone other than a pimp), and trafficker in prostitutes. In Nevada, criminalization of prostitution is left to the individual county.

The federal government, using the commerce clause of the U.S. Constitution as its authority, has also taken part in regulating these offenses, beginning with the Mann Act of 1910, which bars the interstate transportation of girls or women for purposes of prostitution and persuasion or coercion of women or girls into prostitution. Under its war powers, the U.S. Congress banned prostitution around military bases during World War I.

Prostitution is one of the most widespread forms of commercialized vice. (AP/Wide World Photo)

As of the mid-1990's, in every state but Nevada, prostitution was illegal. The constitutional justification for such restraint is the state's police powers to protect the health, safety, welfare, and morals of citizens. The enforcement of antiprostitution statutes and ordinances across the United States has been extremely variable and discriminatory. Antiloitering and disorderly conduct provisions are still frequently used by local law enforcement officers because they are so open to interpretation (some, in fact, have been disallowed by the courts for being unconstitutionally vague). Streetwalkers, making up an estimated 10 to 20 percent of all prostitutes, account for some 85 percent or more of arrests because they are far more visible than other categories such as call girls, in-house sex workers, and those in massage parlors, photo studios, and the like. There is little empirical evidence that arrests are effective in curbing prostitution. Pimps often pay fines or hire lawyers to get their "working girls" out of jail, and the police often argue that they have more serious priorities than victimless crimes. Still, there are some notable examples of police vice squads strictly enforcing the laws relating to crimes against morality.

There are also male prostitutes, primarily in the gay sex market, although a few males are hired by older women. As in the case of their female counterparts, male prostitutes fall into different categories, such as street hustlers, bar hustlers, call boys, kept boys, and escorts. Homosexual prostitution tends to fall even more afoul of the law than heterosexual prostitution. In the 1990's, homosexual behavior was still criminalized in nearly half the states, and at the federal level the U.S. Immigration and Naturalization Service denied aliens either entry into the country or citizenship if they were proved to be gay.

Morality laws and their applications have been inconsistent. The musical revue *Oh! Calcutta*, containing considerable nudity, played on Broadway for years in the 1970's, and the courts have upheld the freedom of individuals to advertise live sex shows and sex-related services such as escort services. People can also view pornographic materials in the privacy of homes. Nevertheless, prostitution remains illegal. In the last decade of the twentieth century, the ideological shift to political (if not moral) conservatism and the public's fears about the spread of acquired immune deficiency syndrome (AIDS) made it unlikely that there would soon be any serious political movement toward the protection of prostitutes' rights despite political pressure by such interest groups as COYOTE (Call Off Your Old Tired Ethics) and, much more reluctantly and ambivalently, the National Organization for Women (NOW).

Obscenity and Pornography. The crime of obscenity or pornography (the nonlegal term for obscenity) involves the selling, delivering, airing, or supplying in any form any sex-related materials considered offensive according to certain standards. Generally, these materials or acts have to go beyond the customary lines of candor in description or representation. The U.S. Supreme Court has struggled to define just what the benchmarks of acceptability should be. As Justice Potter Stewart stated in *Jacobellis v. Ohio* (1964), he could not describe pornography, but he said, "I know it when I see it." Justice John Marshall Harlan opined in *Cohen v. California* (1971) that "one man's vulgarity is another man's lyric."

Over the years, beginning with the case of *Roth v. United States* (1957), the Court has held that once it is ascertained, obscenity falls outside the First Amendment's guarantee of freedom of speech, actual and symbolic. The justices also made it clear, however, that nudity and sex are not by definition obscene; they are only obscene in cases of "hard-core pornography." (Certain types of pornography, therefore, are not legally obscene.) The landmark ruling in *Miller v. California* (1973), applicable in subsequent decades, decided that, to be obscene, a work, taken as a whole, must be deemed by "the average person applying contemporary community standards" to appeal to the "prurient interest" or to depict "in a patently offensive way, sexual conduct specifically defined by applicable state law." The work must lack "serious literary, artistic, political, or scientific value."

In 1990, a Cincinnati court applied the Miller obscenity test to seven homosexual and sadomasochistic photographs by Robert Mapplethorpe being exhibited in that city's Contemporary Arts Center. Two other Mapplethorpe photographs showed totally and partially nude toddlers. The jury concluded that while the photographs appealed to prurient interest in sex and were patently offensive (thereby meeting two Miller criteria for obscenity), the work nevertheless had artistic merit; thus, the penalties sought against the museum and its director were not applicable. The acquittal verdict was unanimous.

The case epitomizes the difficulty the courts face in walking the fine line between, on the one hand, the right of citizens to read, see, and hear what they wish and, on the other hand, the right of others to protect the community from moral "degradation." Accordingly, recognizing that in a pluralistic society differing values will be in evidence, by the late twentieth century the Supreme Court, in referring to artistic, literary, scientific, or political merit and in deferring to community standards, had shown wide fluctuations of opinion in the decisions it handed down in this area.

Indecent Sexual Liberties and Indecent Solicitation of Minors. The crime of indecent liberties generally consists of acts of sexual misconduct committed upon the person of a juvenile member of either sex. It also involves contributing to the sexual delinquency of a child. Generally, this kind of criminal behavior involves as objects those below the age of consent in exchange for money or other consideration but consists of acts falling short of sexual intercourse. Getting a minor to play a role in a pornographic film is an example. Severe federal child pornography laws and state child endangerment laws have helped curtail child pornography since the 1980's.

The crime of indecent solicitation applies to the propositioning of a child under a state's statutory age to perform an act of deviant misconduct. Such solicitation may also involve performing or submitting to any lewd act in the presence of a child or soliciting another person to commit such an act in front of a minor.

Drug-Related Crimes. Of relatively recent origin, the so-called drug crisis in the United States relating to the abuse of narcotics is not a single problem but a broad range of problems. In the largest sense, it is part of a global situation involving a vast network of growers, smugglers, wholesale dealers, street retailers, and even criminal justice officers who cannot resist the money involved in bribes or in extortion of the dealers themselves.

Historically, the substance most frequently abused in the United States has been marijuana, which at one time was widely used (as cocaine was) in popular elixirs. By the 1970's, cocaine had again become a preferred narcotic, with an estimated four million to five million regular users. The invention of newer and more powerful drugs such as crack cocaine has reportedly popularized drug use even more and led to higher rates of addiction. For example, the National Institute of Justice's Drug Use Forecasting Program reported the percentage of arrestees who tested positive for drugs in twenty-three American cities in 1990. In Atlanta, Georgia, the figures were 71 percent for females and 62 percent for males; in Cleveland, the respective percentages were 73 and 56; in Detroit, 74 and 51; in Kansas City, 64 and 45; in the borough of Manhattan, New York City, 71 and 76; in San Diego, 75 and 78; and in San Jose, 57 and 55. Surveys of prison populations have identified similar drug-use levels.

Beginning in 1906, with the Pure Food and Drug Act, and in 1914, with the Harrison Narcotic Drug Act, the federal government has imposed gradually greater control over drug use. In 1919, two U.S. Supreme Court cases (*United States v. Doremus* and *Webb v. United States*) declared almost all forms of drug addiction illegal. Federal control was tightened in the

1930's as heroin use spread and as organized crime became more involved in the distribution and sale of illegal drugs. State control was not far behind.

In 1970, the Comprehensive Drug Abuse Prevention and Control Act went even further, consolidating all existing measures in the U.S. Code. Stricter penalty schedules for drug abuse and trafficking went into force in the wake of the Vietnam War-era drug epidemic. Most states began to follow the uniform code recommended by the U.S. Department of Justice, updated by the Uniform Controlled Dangerous Substances Act of 1974.

Since then, some states have either relaxed or are considering easing the rules, including decriminalizing some drugs. In 1973, New York State's Republican Governor Nelson A. Rockefeller enacted the toughest drug laws in the country, mandating prison sentences in certain classes of felony involving possession of even relatively small amounts of controlled substances. By the mid-1990's, however, the state's prison system was overwhelmed by the number of nonviolent inmates mandatorily confined for drug offenses. New York was therefore considering amending the harsh "Rockefeller laws" to free several thousand prison cells for more serious violent criminals. Indeed, by the 1990's, inmates incarcerated for drug crimes in the state had quintupled, with corresponding increases across the country. Furthermore, the cost of building one prison cell at about $100,000 and of confining an inmate at a cost of more than $25,000 a year was adding to the budget crises in New York State and elsewhere. The government's "war on drugs" is far from being won. Some 75 percent of new federal prisoners since 1987 have been drug offenders. The burden of the antidrug campaign has been heavy on taxpayers, with important political consequences. Yet because of the fairly wide agreement that it is morally right to continue the antidrug drive—and because of the lack of viable alternative solutions—it seems destined to continue.

Gambling. Gambling is the staking of money or something else of value on an uncertain future event. The element of luck is the controlling factor in gambling. Wagers are made on the outcome of a game of chance or skill. The range of games, devices used, and places where bets are made is very wide.

English common law was not concerned with gambling in private; however, if gambling took place in a gaming house open to all and the activity was common knowledge, then the parties concerned could be charged with being a public nuisance. This was not only because of possible breaches of the peace but also because of gambling's tendency to encourage idleness and greed, the breakdown of family life, and the corruption of public morals.

Since 1948, after a half-century of gambling regulation by the states, the federal role was expanded. In the 1970's, the federal government passed statutes controlling, among other things, interstate and foreign transportation of gambling paraphernalia, the transmission of wagering information through wire facilities, and state-conducted lotteries. By the end of the twentieth century, the federal government was extensively involved in regulating gambling and in applying sanctions against violators.

At the same time, however, a number of gambling activities—church raffles and bingo games, state lotteries, and even gambling casinos—were being legalized. As in the case of other victimless crimes such as drug use, arguments were made that legalizing certain games would reduce the profits of illegal ones, especially those run by organized crime. In turn, this would curtail the corruption of officials and law enforcement agents who apply gambling laws in a discriminatory manner. It was also argued that decriminalization of something that is widely regarded as a harmless form of entertainment is appropriate. Yet there is disagreement on most of these points. There is also a fear (one that is also voiced in connection with decriminalizing other victimless crimes) that ancillary criminality—for example, prostitution—may flourish and increase at gambling casinos and other gaming locations. In this connection, the experiences of Las Vegas and Atlantic City have not been encouraging.

In *Marchetti v. United States* (1968), the U.S. Supreme Court ruled on whether requiring gamblers to register with the Internal Revenue Service (IRS) and pay an occupational tax on their gambling earnings violates the U.S. Constitution's Fifth Amendment privilege against self-incrimination. Until then, by registering with the IRS, a gambler was open to federal and state prosecution for engaging in illegal gambling and was thus incriminating himself or herself. In *Marchetti*, the Court struck down the IRS regulation requiring gamblers to register and to submit monthly information concerning their wagering activities on the grounds that such information was not customarily kept, that the reports had no public records aspects, and that the requirements were directed at a "select group inherently suspect of criminal activities."

Alcoholism. In the United States on average, the annual consumption of alcoholic beverages—beer, wine, and liquors—by individuals over fourteen years of age exceeds the consumption of milk and coffee. Like drug abuse, alcoholism—defined as excessive use of these beverages—is closely linked to violent crime, driving while intoxicated, problems in the workplace, disorderly conduct of various sorts, family abuse, and other problems.

Criminal law has attempted to check alcohol abuse and its consequences by raising the minimum drinking age in public places, limiting bar hours, and curtailing secondary criminality relating to this national addiction, such as operating after-hours bars. Yet the dismal experience of the Prohibition era (1919-1933), when the Eighteenth Amendment to the U.S. Constitution unsuccessfully attempted to bar the manufacture, sale, transportation, import, and export of intoxicating liquors, stands as a reminder of the difficulty of controlling such a widespread and widely accepted activity as drinking.

Controlling Vice. Law is always evolving, just as the cultural mores that influence the law evolve. An activity once widely considered reprehensible may no longer seem so at a later time. The development of a better-educated and more

ARRESTS FOR VICTIMLESS CRIMES, 1993	
Prostitution and commercialized vice	97,800
Sex offenses (except forcible rape and prostitution)	104,100
Drug abuse violations	1,126,300
Gambling	17,300
Liquor law violations	518,500
Disorderly conduct	727,000
Vagrancy	28,200
Total	**2,619,200**

Source: U.S. Department of Justice, Federal Bureau of Investigation, *Crime in the United States* (Uniform Crime Reports). Washington, D.C.: U.S. Government Printing Office, 1994.

sophisticated public desiring freedom, equality, and diversity has tended to broaden mainstream values somewhat. The drug legalization debate, to take one example, has taken place within that context. To be effective, laws must have a broad community consensus; some would say that they also should be in keeping with advances in the social sciences which attempt to define and explain "normal" human behavior. The divergences in U.S. Supreme Court opinions in its constitutional adjudication of questions relating to commercialized vice probably reflect the wide differences in viewpoint on these matters. Accordingly, the debate—launched decades ago by the American Law Institute's Model Penal Code of 1959—concerning which criminalized behaviors should be legalized and which should not continues. —*Peter B. Heller*

See also *Barnes v. Glen Theatre, Inc.*; Disorderly conduct; Drug legalization debate; Gambling law; Organized crime; Pandering; Prohibition; Vagrancy laws; Victimless crimes.

BIBLIOGRAPHY

Daniel S. Campagna and Donald L. Poffenberger, *The Sexual Trafficking in Children: An Investigation of the Child Sex Trade* (Dover, Mass.: Auburn House, 1988), looks at the problems of child pornography and prostitution. Nanette J. Davis, ed., *Prostitution: An International Handbook on Trends, Problems, and Policies* (Westport, Conn.: Greenwood Press, 1993), includes an excellent chapter on the United States. Edward de Grazia, *Girls Lean Back Everywhere: The Law of Obscenity and the Assault on Genius* (New York: Random House, 1992), is an authoritative treatise against government censorship by a practicing law professor involved in some landmark cases. Other valuable perspectives are presented by Paul J. Goldstein, *Prostitution and Drugs* (Lexington, Mass.: Lexington Books, 1979); John R. Goodwin, *Gaming Control Law: The Nevada Model* (Columbus, Ohio: Publishing Horizons, 1985); Richard Green, *Sexual Science and the Law* (Cambridge, Mass.: Harvard University Press, 1992); David Musto, *The American Disease: Origins of Narcotics Control* (rev. ed. New York: Oxford University Press, 1987); David M. O'Brien, *Civil Rights and Civil Liberties*, vol. 2 of *Constitutional Law and Politics* (New York: W. W. Norton, 1991); David A. J. Richards, *Sex, Drugs, Death and the Law: An Essay on Human Rights and Overcriminalization* (Totowa, N.J.: Rowman

& Littlefield, 1982); Edwin M. Schur, *Victimless Crimes* (Englewood Cliffs, N.J.: Prentice Hall, 1974); and National Institute of Law Enforcement and Criminal Justice, *The Development of the Law of Gambling: 1776-1976* (Washington, D.C.: U.S. Government Printing Office, 1977).

Commission on Civil Rights

DATE: Established 1957

SIGNIFICANCE: The reports and studies of the Commission on Civil Rights have been an important factor in the passage of major civil rights legislation

The U.S. Commission on Civil Rights was created in 1957 by Congress as part of the Civil Rights Act of 1957. It consisted of six members, appointed by the president and approved by Congress. The original purpose of the agency was to monitor civil rights (particularly violations of voting rights in the South), issue reports, and then disband, but Congress has continuously renewed its mandate. The Commission on Civil Rights (abbreviated as CRC, for Civil Rights Commission) was created in the wake of the 1954 Supreme Court decision of *Brown v. Board of Education*. In this case, the Court decided that separate facilities for black and white students in public education were unconstitutional. A year later, in *Brown II*, the Court ruled that schools must integrate with "all deliberate speed." No specific timetable was given, however, for fear of further alienating southern whites.

The CRC helped lay the foundation for the civil rights legislation of the 1960's. The commission's mandate involved investigating voting rights violations, collecting and studying voting data related to denials of equal protection under the law, and appraising federal laws and policies as they related to equal protection. In addition to creating the CRC, the 1957 Civil Rights Act made the civil rights component in the Justice Department a division, and empowered the U.S. attorney general to initiate civil court proceedings to enforce voting rights. The 1957 statute gave the attorney general the power to intervene only on a case-by-case basis, which was tedious, as there were thousands of cases of voting rights violations.

Civil Rights Legislation. During Dwight D. Eisenhower's administration, the Commission on Civil Rights investigated voting rights violations in eight southern states and found no less than a hundred counties using discriminatory measures against African Americans. The Civil Rights Act of 1960 was passed as a result of the CRC's 1959 report. Although the CRC had recommended that Congress pass legislation authorizing federal registrars in obstructionist districts, the act only provided court-appointed referees to oversee and resolve alleged voting rights abuses. Continuing studies by the CRC would assist in more powerful legislation in 1964 and 1965.

The 1964 Civil Rights Act was instrumental in the desegregation of public facilities in a still-segregated South. Based on ongoing concerns and studies by the CRC in education, voting, and employment, and influenced by the intensifying Civil Rights movement and the March on Washington in 1963, the 1964 act forbade racial discrimination in public facilities, voting registration procedures, and employment. The act empowered the attorney general to intervene and take civil action in cases of racial discrimination in public accommodations. It also cut federal funds to school districts that discriminated and created the Equal Employment Opportunity Commission to oversee discrimination complaints in the workplace.

The 1965 Voting Rights Act is the most powerful legislation in the area of suffrage, and it eliminated virtually all remaining loopholes. The act effectively took the process of voter registration out of the hands of states and localities, providing federal machinery for this process. The legislation also forbade literacy tests in most instances. In addition, a preclearance mechanism (often called Section 5) was put in place that required political districts to submit proposed changes in elections or districts to the federal government for approval. A "clean record" provision was instituted, allowing political districts to be removed from coverage of the preclearance provision if no discrimination or voting irregularities have been found for the previous ten years.

The CRC has played a vital role in the extension of the 1965 Voting Rights Act and thus in continued suffrage among African Americans in the Deep South. One of the most controversial areas of the act, the preclearance provision, was challenged by southerners. Testimony by the CRC revealed that southern states, and particularly Mississippi, were seeking to subvert the intent of the act and dilute the black vote and black political victories. Legislatures did this by racial gerrymandering of political districts, going to at-large systems of municipal elections, developing multimember districts, and consolidating black and white counties. The CRC was instrumental in the extension of Section 5 and the drafting of other provisions of the 1970 Voting Rights Act. Reports by the commission would play an important role in the 1975 and 1982 extensions of the act as well.

Challenges and Impact. A major challenge to the commission came in the early 1980's, after it issued a 1981 statement entitled *Affirmative Action in the 1980's*, which advocated quotas to ensure the hiring of minorities. President Ronald Reagan strongly opposed the recommendations and removed three of the CRC's commissioners, appointing more conservative commissioners. A lawsuit ensued, and in 1983 Reagan was ordered by the courts to reinstate the commissioners he had fired. Also in 1983, the commission was reorganized by a compromise congressional act (Reagan had vowed to veto an act routinely renewing the commission) to consist of eight members chosen by the president and Congress. The commission was criticized from many quarters in the 1980's, partly for appearing to succumb to various political pressures, and many of its leaders, including Clarence Pendleton, were controversial. In the early 1990's, it began to resume the more active role it had played in the past.

Originally intended as a watchdog agency, the Commission on Civil Rights has been essential as a bipartisan fact-finding body and a resource for both Congress and the president in developing legislation. While its early charge was in the area of voting rights, it has conducted numerous studies and provided congressional testimony in education, housing, racial segregation, employment discrimination, and denial of civil rights based on race, creed, color, religion, national origin, sex, age, or disability. —*Mfanya D. Tryman*

See also *Brown v. Board of Education*; Civil Rights Act of 1957; Civil Rights Act of 1960; Civil Rights Act of 1964; Civil Rights Act of 1968; Civil Rights Act of 1991; Civil Rights Acts of 1866-1875; Civil Rights movement; Eisenhower, Dwight D.; Reagan, Ronald; Voting Rights Act of 1965.

BIBLIOGRAPHY

Among the best sources for information on the CRC are Gerald David Jaynes and Robin M. Williams, Jr., eds., *A Common Destiny: Blacks and American Society* (Washington, D.C.: National Academy Press, 1989); Theodore Eisenberg's article "Civil Rights Commission," in *Civil Rights and Equality: Selections from the Encyclopedia of the American Constitution* (New York: Macmillan, 1989); Frank R. Parker, *Black Votes Count* (Chapel Hill: University of North Carolina Press, 1990); Steven F. Lawson, *Running for Freedom* (New York: McGraw-Hill, 1991); Hugh Davis Graham, *Civil Rights and the Presidency* (New York: Oxford University Press, 1992); Charles S. Bullock III and Charles M. Lamb, *Implementation of Civil Rights Policy* (Monterey, Calif.: Brooks/Cole, 1984); and Gertrude Ezorsky, *Racism and Justice* (Ithaca, N.Y.: Cornell University Press, 1991).

Common law

DEFINITION: Principles of law long established in customary behavior and based on previous court decisions

SIGNIFICANCE: American law, with its roots in English law, is based as much on common-law practice and previous court decisions as on statutory law

The American common law originated in the ancient unwritten law of England, so to understand American law one must consult the English common law. The original American "common law" was all the case-law background of England and the American colonies before the American war for independence from England. The authority for the common law is the customary and accepted practices of the English courts and political institutions from centuries ago, sometimes referred to as the "English constitution." In other words, the courts, in the Anglo-American political system, have been more significant in establishing law than in countries using the "Roman law" system of completely codified law.

Sources of the Common Law. Early English history was Anglo-Saxon, and the early Anglo-Saxons had a legal system very similar to that of ancient Israel. It was decentralized and related to extended families. The legal code of Alfred the Great was biblical in nature, beginning with the Ten Commandments and other parts of the Mosaic law. The Danes and the Norwegians also held part of England and thus influenced the English common law with Viking law, or "Danelaw" as it was sometimes called. The highly individualistic nature of Danelaw is reflected in the Magna Carta and later in American institutions. In the common law, justice comes before power. The king or queen had the power to control and rule but did not have the right to do so without justice. That was the basis of the English common law.

Though even they professed a belief in the English common law, the ancient Tudor rulers of England believed in unlimited royal power under the concept of *Rex Lex*, meaning "The King is Law." The Protestant Reformation in England changed that concept to *Lex Rex*, meaning "The Law is King." After the English Revolution of 1642, the rulers also had to be subject to, and limited by, statutory law. The Glorious Revolution of 1688 further limited royal powers by insisting that the king's powers be shared with elected parliaments.

Common Law in the United States. The American Revolution built on this foundation, and the concept of popular-based, shared, representative government was taken a step further in the U.S. Constitution. The basic ideas of the Constitution are that government is limited in its powers, and authority must be shared among various parts of the political system. In the American system, law consists of constitutional law, statutory law, and the common law based on judicial precedent. It is a shared power system: shared between the states and the national government, shared within each level of government, and even shared within the types of law argued at various levels of the judiciary.

The American common law recognizes this heritage. The California Civil Code, for example (section 22.2), states that the "common law of England, so far as it is not repugnant to or inconsistent with the Constitution of the United States, or the Constitution or laws of this State, is the rule of decision in all the courts of this State."

The two law works most widely read by American attorneys in the colonial and early national periods were William Blackstone's *Commentaries on the Laws of England* (1765-1769) and Sir Edward Coke's *Reports*. Emphasis on the importance of the common law was put into American form in the 1830's in Joseph Story's *Commentaries on the Constitution of the United States* and James Kent's *Commentaries on American Law*.

Americans have looked to the common law as well as to the Bill of Rights for protection of their basic rights, but they modified tradition for American use. The land laws in England, for example, were feudal in nature and origin. In the United States, land was much more plentiful, and title was made much easier to change. American emphasis was on the freedom to enter contracts and on the sanctity of contracts. The common law was influenced by the Old Testament, especially by the legal code in the Pentateuch. Its assumption of individual responsibility for one's own actions was consonant with the individualism of early American life. It also recognized the importance of individual conscience, even in the wording of oaths or "affirmations" in court.

Uses of the Common Law. An example of the use of the common law is in the concept of relationships. Domestic relations appear often in the common law, as do various pairs of relationships involving financial arrangements: landlord and tenant, principal and agent, principal and surety, vendor and purchaser. Common-law courts have always sought to solve legal problems in relational terms. With relationships as a starting point, deductive logic brings in others not involved in the relationship. The courts seek to enforce the duties and liabilities implied or explicitly stated in the relationship.

Importance of the Common Law. The sense of justice—what is considered right, just, and fair by the ordinary citizens of the land—is reflected in the common law. Sometimes the common law is referred to as "unwritten law" because of its roots in the customs and traditions of the people. In reality, however, it is written in the court records of hundreds of cases. A better name for it, therefore, is "case law."

To rule on a present case, judges must consult the body of established legal precedents that apply to the current case before the court. Often both litigants in a case will cite judicial precedents and earlier cases in order to make a strong case for their client. The lawyer who can show more convincingly that precedent and tradition is on his or her side will frequently win the case. The intent of following precedents, or *stare decisis*, is to assure continuity, or evenhanded justice from year to year and century to century. Its authority is reinforced in the popular mind by the perception of fairness that goes with such consistency. Judges are seen in the popular mind, not as arbitrarily governed by their own idiosyncrasies, but as bound by the accumulated experiences of legal custom. Justice is not capricious.

The common law is also distinguished by the use of a jury in determining facts of law and judgment. Guilt or innocence is determined in open court by free citizens whose findings cannot be reversed by the judge. Decisions regarding life, liberty, and property are made by unanimous verdicts of one's peers.

The U.S. Bill of Rights is essentially a reassertion of the fundamental liberties of American citizens under the common law, an additional safeguard to long-standing tradition. Individual liberties that American citizens have long come to expect owe more to the practice of following common-law traditions than many people realize.

The grounds of decision in common law cases are more based on judicial experience than on written legislative texts. The common-law judge seeks to ascertain exactly how predecessors in earlier cases arrived at their decisions and on what principles. Adjudicated cases rather than law codes are the research areas of the common law. Universal ideas are applied in real-life situations within the court's inquiries.

— *William H. Burnside*

See also Bill of Rights, U.S.; Case law; Civil liberties; Constitutional law; Contract law; Equity; *Habeas corpus*; Jurisprudence; Jury system; Law; Magna Carta; *Mala in se* and *mala prohibita*; *Stare decisis*.

BIBLIOGRAPHY

A classic work on the common law is Oliver Wendell Holmes, Jr., *The Common Law* (Boston: Little, Brown, 1909, reprint 1963). Another is Roscoe Pound's lecture, "What Is the Common Law?," in *The Future of the Common Law*, first published in 1937 and reprinted in 1965 (Gloucester, Mass.: Peter Smith). Colonial history of the common law in the American colonies is recounted in Paul Reinsch, *The English Common Law in the Early American Colonies* (New York: Da Capo Press, 1970), and in David T. Konig, *Law and Society in Puritan Massachusetts* (Chapel Hill: University of North Carolina Press, 1979). The search for a distinctly American approach to the English legal system is discussed in George Lee Haskins, *Law and Authority in Early Massachusetts: A Study in Tradition and Design* (New York: Archon Books, 1968). The history of the common-law tradition and its place in the American legal system is described in Bernard Schwartz, *The Law in America: A History* (New York: McGraw-Hill, 1974), and in Donald Fleming and Bernard Bailyn, eds., *Law in American History* (Cambridge, Mass.: Harvard University, 1971). A valuable study analyzing the significance of the common law in preserving American liberties is in Russell Kirk, *The Roots of American Order* (3d ed. Washington, D.C.: Regnery Gateway, 1991). A lengthy discussion comparing the common law with statutory law is found in Alexander H. Pekelis (Milton R. Konvitz, ed.), *Law and Social Action: Selected Essays of Alexander H. Pekelis* (New York: Da Capo Press, 1970).

Communist Party, American

DATE: Founded 1919

SIGNIFICANCE: The party, the American member of the Communist International loyal to the Soviet Communist Party, was subjected to unofficial and judicial harassment and persecution by government agencies

The American Communist Party, or Communist Party, USA, is a minor political party and organization founded in 1919. It has never played a significant role in American politics. For example, it has never elected anyone at the national or state level and very rarely won even local elections. Its greatest support in terms of both membership and electoral strength came during the Great Depression. Nevertheless, it suffered considerable harassment and criminal prosecution from the United States government and local and state authorities and thus has played a key role in American jurisprudence. Prominent Americans such as the labor leader Elizabeth Gurley Flynn, the novelist Howard Fast, and the scholars W. E. B. Du Bois and Angela Davis have been members.

From its beginning, the Communist Party, USA, suffered from factionalism. It was composed of dissident socialists, members of the International Workers of the World (IWW), leftists of all sorts enamored of the Russian Revolution, immigrants, veterans of European socialism and anarchism, and many other diverse individuals and organizations. From its beginning, its single unifying factor was loyalty to the Russian, then Soviet, Communist Party and the Communist International. This allegiance created further splits as factions opposed to Moscow's doctrines or policies dropped out.

The Communist Party was the center of a number of court cases involving civil and legal rights and even police actions without trial. In the early 1920's, U.S. attorney general James Palmer imprisoned or deported thousands of legal aliens and hundreds of naturalized citizens on the grounds that they were Communists, even though most were not party members. These punishments were meted out on flimsy evidence and sometimes entirely without due process of law. The party's unswerving loyalty to Moscow, the United States' antagonist in the post-World War II era, not only limited its significance and membership but also subjected it to further harassment by the government. The Communist Party was outlawed by the Smith Act of 1940 (the Alien Registration Act). The government placed it on the list of prohibited organizations, allegedly for security reasons. Several individual Communists were charged with espionage and tried in controversial, well-publicized trials. Alger Hiss, a state department employee from a well-connected Boston family, was convicted of perjury before a Senate hearing in 1948 on the evidence of Whitaker Chambers, himself an admitted former Communist. In 1952 Julius and Ethel Rosenberg were convicted on controversial evidence and executed for passing atomic secrets to Soviet agents. The impression of many observers was that both Hiss and the Rosenbergs were convicted mainly because they were Communists. A number of prominent American politicians rode to power in part (or entirely) on the anti-Communist bandwagon, including Richard Nixon, Ronald Reagan, and, most notably, the notorious senator Joseph McCarthy.

See also House Committee on Un-American Activities (HUAC); McCarthyism; Marxism; Palmer raids and the "red scare"; Rosenberg trial and executions; *Scales v. United States*; Smith Act; Socialist Party, American.

Community-oriented policing

DEFINITION: A strategy of policing in which police officers work with members of a community in order to reduce crime

SIGNIFICANCE: This strategy focuses on bringing members of the community back into crime control, and it was a significant emphasis of President Bill Clinton's 1994 crime bill

Historically it has been believed, both by the citizenry and by the police themselves, that the police are solely responsible for reducing and fighting crime. Community-oriented policing stresses the importance of members of the community in the fight against crime and emphasizes ways citizens can work with police to make their communities safer. It has been argued that the growth of urban areas and the growth in population in the United States in general have contributed to a lack of community. People often seem to be isolated from the communities in which they live. Community-oriented policing attempts to bring individuals together and urges them to help police the areas around their homes themselves.

A major goal of community policing is to reduce the reactive side of policing and increase the proactive side of policing. In a reactive policing strategy, police fight crime mainly by responding to citizen calls for help. On the other hand, a proactive strategy emphasizes police work that actively fights

Community-oriented policing emphasizes personal interaction between police officers and members of the community. (James L. Shaffer)

crime by going out and looking for it. In addition, community-oriented policing seeks to reintegrate "wayward" members of society. That is, it attempts to rehabilitate offenders by using community-based punishments (such as community service) rather than to isolate them in the form of incarceration.

Community policing has not been clearly defined by those individuals who study police behavior and organization. Thus, it is unclear how police officers should enlist the help of the community in the fight against crime. Indeed, officers can have varying views of community policing, depending on their own beliefs and the beliefs of the department in which they work. Community policing can involve increased foot patrols, police involvement in community watch groups, and in some areas, "storefront" precincts. All these measures are expected to increase dialogue and interaction with members of the community. While this list is not exhaustive, it includes some of the more prominent methods of increased citizen involvement. How police interact with the citizenry will also affect the workings and effectiveness of community policing.

Whether community-oriented policing is effective had yet to be determined in the mid-1990's. Because of the vagueness inherent in the definition of community-oriented policing, this strategy can mean different things to different police officers and different police departments. Several studies of communities utilizing increased foot patrols have been conducted. Overall, research findings indicate that increased foot patrols do not necessarily reduce crime but can significantly reduce the fear of crime for citizens living in these neighborhoods. This leads some to believe that other community-oriented policing efforts will have a similar effect.

See also Arrest; Civilian review boards; Neighborhood watch programs; Police; Violent Crime Control and Law Enforcement Act of 1994.

Community service as punishment for crime

DEFINITION: Punishment that involves unpaid work in the community rather than incarceration

SIGNIFICANCE: This type of punishment is commonly used as an alternative to incarceration; it helps alleviate jail overcrowding and avoids the costs of incarceration

When an individual commits a crime, a judge has many options as to punishment. Community service is one option that allows the offender to be punished without the state having to pay the high costs of imprisonment. An offender is typically sentenced to a certain number of hours (anywhere from forty to two hundred) of community service instead of being incarcerated. Some jurisdictions use community service in combination with other punishments, such as monetary fines.

Community service is viewed as restitution, or a punishment that makes an offender "pay back" society for the crime committed. The types of community service available to a judge are too great to mention, but typically include some kind of work to better the community, such as cleaning litter off the streets or lecturing about the dangers of certain criminal behaviors. For example, individuals convicted of driving under the influence of alcohol sometimes lecture to high school students about the possible effects of committing this particular crime.

See also Diversion; Punishment; Reparations; Sentencing.

Comparable worth

DEFINITION: The payment of employees based on the relative importance (worth) of their jobs to their employer

SIGNIFICANCE: The concept of comparable worth was put forth as a way to rectify the widespread inequities in pay between men and women in different but "comparable" occupations

According to the Equal Pay Act of 1963, employers must give equal pay to all workers in the same establishment if they perform work with equal skill, effort, and responsibility under similar working conditions. In principle, the law applies only to men and women working together in identical jobs.

The concept of comparable worth goes beyond this law and the idea of equal pay for equal work. It argues that many women work at occupations that have historically been considered "women's work" and have systematically been paid less than men doing "men's" jobs. The women's movement was in the forefront of the push for comparable worth, and it has become a significant social issue. Under a comparable worth policy, the values of different jobs to an employer are compared—for example, the "worth" of a librarian might be compared with that of an electrician. Differing types of jobs determined to be of comparable worth would pay the same salary. Comparable worth is a significant departure from traditional market approaches to setting wages.

In *AFSCME v. Washington* (1983, 1985), an employee union, the American Federation of State, County, and Municipal Employees, challenged the policy of establishing workers' pay on the basis of prevailing market wages for each job. Based on a study that assessed "job points" for knowledge and skills, mental demands, accountability, and working conditions, women were receiving 20 percent less than men in jobs with equal points. Although the district court found for AFSCME in 1983, the appeals court reversed the decision in 1985, arguing that there was no intentional discrimination and that pay calculated on the basis of market rates did not violate the Equal Employment Opportunity Act of 1972. The state of Washington, however, upgraded the pay of women, so the case never reached the Supreme Court.

By 1995, twenty-three states and dozens of local governments had voluntary comparable worth plans. From 1982, the state of Minnesota has equivalenced such job pairs as (male) delivery drivers and (female) clerk typists, auto parts technicians and dining hall coordinators, and prison guards and registered nurses.

See also Equal Employment Opportunity Act; Equal Employment Opportunity Commission (EEOC); Equal Pay Act; Feminism; National Organization for Women (NOW); Sex discrimination.

Compensatory damages

DEFINITION: Monetary awards to a plaintiff that compensate for injury or loss

SIGNIFICANCE: There are two general types of compensatory damages, general damages and special damages; both are distinct from punitive damages

Compensatory damages, sometimes called actual damages, are intended to compensate a plaintiff in a civil case for an injury or loss caused by the wrongful action or misconduct of another person (the defendant). The purpose is to return the plaintiff to the position he or she was in before the loss occurred. For example, car A does not stop at a stop sign and hits car B in the intersection. The driver of car B is injured, and she is taken to the hospital. Compensatory damages, paid by the driver of car A (or his insurance company) will pay her medical and hospital expenses. Compensatory damages are distinct from punitive damages, which are awards beyond compensatory damages that are intended to punish and make an example of the wrongdoer.

Two subdivisions of compensatory damages are general damages and special (or consequential) damages. General damages require a causal relationship between the wrongful act and the loss. The loss is something that can normally be foreseen to occur as a consequence of the defendant's act. An injured driver, for example, would be expected to have medical bills.

Special damages are those which stand separately from expected damages. They may be payable for an indirect loss, yet the wrongdoing of the defendant must be the proximate cause of the loss. In the example given, the injured driver may also collect amounts for "pain and suffering" and for lost income during the period she is unable to work.

See also Civil law; Civil procedure; Litigation; Medical malpractice; Punitive damages; Restitution; Suit.

Competency to stand trial

DEFINITION: The determination whether a person is mentally able to understand the charges against him or her and to understand trial proceedings

SIGNIFICANCE: It is a long-standing American and English legal tradition that a mentally incompetent person should not be subjected to a criminal trial

The idea that a person judged to be incompetent should not be forced to stand trial on criminal charges has its basis in English common law. In the United States it has been considered a constitutional principle as well since the Supreme Court case *Drope v. Missouri* (1975). Part of the rationale is that if an accused party does not have the capacity to participate in the trial, then the American adversarial system of justice cannot be fairly applied, and the accused will therefore not receive due process of law.

Dusky v. United States (1960) established that the standard of incompetency for federal trials was to be whether the accused has "sufficient present ability to consult with his lawyer with a reasonable degree of rational understanding" and could have a rational and factual understanding of court proceedings. To be "competent," a person must be able to confer with a lawyer, testify coherently, and follow evidence that is presented. State courts generally follow this standard as well, although the wording of state statutes varies. Although the federal incompetency statute refers to mental incapacitation, some cases of severe physical incapacitation have been held to constitute incompetency.

Determining competency involves three stages: initiating an inquiry, making a preliminary determination as to competency, and, if there is sufficient evidence, holding a competency hearing. An inquiry is usually initiated by counsel, either prosecution or defense. Generally a psychiatric examination is then mandatory. If the examination indicates that the defendant may be incompetent, a competency hearing is mandatory. The hearing is adversarial in nature; the main witness is usually the psychiatrist who gave the psychiatric examination, but other witnesses may also be called. The trial judge usually rules on the defendant's competency, and the judge may consider the defendant's appearance and demeanor as well as the witness' testimony. A finding of incompetency does not mean that the person has been judged not guilty. Traditionally, a person found incompetent would be committed to a psychiatric institution, and there were no restrictions on how long such confinement could be. In 1972, however, in *Jackson v. Indiana*, the Supreme Court held that commitment could not exceed a "reasonable period of time" for determining whether the person could be expected to regain competency.

See also Arraignment; Common law; Criminal intent; Insanity defense; Insanity Defense Reform Act; Psychopath and sociopath.

Comprehensive Crime Control Act of 1984

DATE: Became law October 19, 1984
DEFINITION: A selective but fundamental overhaul of the federal criminal code
SIGNIFICANCE: This act expanded the government's law enforcement power and emphasized the rights of the public over those of the criminal or accused criminal

Work on this legislation began in the 1970's in a Democratic-controlled Senate. Passage of the bill (by a vote of 94 to 1) reflected close cooperation between Democrat Edward Kennedy and Republican Strom Thurmond. Democrats in the House of Representatives were less cooperative because they wanted a more piecemeal approach to the revision of the

federal criminal code than the major recodification supported in the Senate. Thus a collection of procedural and substantive crime proposals were made instead of a systematic overhaul.

Fearing that the Democratic House leadership would block passage of the proposals, Republican Dan Lungren moved to add the crime proposals to an unrelated resolution on continuing appropriations, which would require urgent consideration on the House floor in order to keep the government in operation. Facing reelection in November, 1984, congressional Democrats voted in favor of law and order rather than explain a recorded "no" vote to their constituents. When the joint appropriations resolution emerged from the House, it had tacked to it a Title XI: the Comprehensive Crime Control Act of 1984.

For the first time federal judges could detain repeat offenders in preventive detention, without bail, before trial. They could also detain individuals accused of certain major crimes if they were deemed dangerous to the community. In the past, bail was granted unless there was reason to believe the defendant would flee. Moreover, if the detained defendant were later acquitted or the charges dismissed, no recompense would be given for the time spent in jail awaiting trial.

Under the act, federal judges follow a system of guidelines in imposing sentences. The guidelines, established by a presidentially appointed sentencing commission, eliminate disparities in sentences for the same crimes and dismantle the early-release parole system. Under the guidelines, federal prosecutors are able to select charges that carry the likelihood of the longest sentence. Judges are required to explain in writing any departure from the guidelines, while both prosecutors and defendants are entitled to appeal sentences that depart from the standard.

The act also restricts the use of insanity as a defense to individuals who are unable to understand the nature and wrongfulness of their acts. The law prevents expert testimony on the ultimate issue of whether the defendant has a particular mental state or condition. It shifts the burden of proof from the prosecutor, who formerly had to prove that the defendant was not insane, to the defendant, who must prove that he or she is. This change in the insanity defense was a direct response to the John Hinckley case. Hinckley's lawyer proved that Hinckley was psychotic and depressed. The jury found him not guilty because of insanity in the attempted assassination of President Ronald Reagan on March 30, 1981.

Finally, the legislation allows the government to seize profits and assets, including real estate, that are used in organized crime enterprises such as drug trafficking.

See also Crime; Forfeiture, civil and criminal; Insanity defense; Insanity Defense Reform Act; Omnibus Crime Control and Safe Streets Act of 1968; Organized Crime Control Act; United States Sentencing Commission.

Comprehensive Drug Abuse Prevention and Control Act of 1970

DATE: Became law October 27, 1970
DEFINITION: A law that consolidated previous drug-control legislation

SIGNIFICANCE: This 1970 act enlarged the scope of federal jurisdiction over drug laws; it was "comprehensive" in that it contained provisions for treatment, control, and enforcement in a single law

Legislation to control the use of drugs has existed in various forms in the twentieth century. By 1970, public opinion polls indicated that the American public cited use of illegal drugs as one of the most important public concerns. The federal government estimated that between 800,000 and 1.2 million Americans were using marijuana on a daily basis. The availability of other drugs, particularly heroin, had increased public anxiety about drug use. Federal law-enforcement officials and the Nixon Administration sought to strengthen and clarify the large number of federal laws that governed controlled substances.

The 1970 act distinguished among several categories of drugs based on the potential for abuse and medicinal uses. Heroin, lysergic acid diethylamide (LSD) and other hallucinogens, and marijuana were outlawed, and any medicinal uses were subject to approval by federal officials. Title I of the act clarified the definition of a "drug dependent person" and provided structures for rehabilitation treatment.

The main effect of the act on the structure of law enforcement was the expansion of federal jurisdiction over drug laws. Prior to the 1970 act, the federal role had been confined primarily to enforcing prohibitions of the interstate transport of drugs, enforcing laws against tax violations, and prohibiting illegal imports. The act granted federal officials greater search powers and permitted the attorney general to utilize paid informants. Many states have used the 1970 federal act as a model for state drug laws.   — *Lawrence Clark III*

See also Drug Enforcement Administration (DEA); Drug legalization debate; Drug use and sale, illegal; Search and seizure.

Computer crime

DEFINITION: The illegal use of computers either for its own sake or to further other criminal activities

SIGNIFICANCE: Computer crime imposes significant economic costs on victims and undercuts societal confidence in records and information maintained by computers

As individuals, businesses, organizations, and governments have increasingly relied on computers for critical activities, computer crime has grown in frequency and significance. Computers have been used in diverse types of crimes, including fraud, theft, larceny, embezzlement, bribery, burglary, sabotage, espionage, conspiracy, extortion, and kidnapping. In addition, computers themselves have been the objects of crime: unauthorized computer access, theft of computer services, and malicious destruction of data and records. Computers can also play passive parts in offenses when usable evidence of illegal acts reside in computer records. The complex processes that are sometimes necessary to identify, collect, and understand these records can make the detection and investigation of computer crimes extremely difficult.

Victims. A wide range of victims are affected by computer crimes. Potential victims include all persons or institutions that use or are affected by computers. People about whom data and records are stored in computers are also potential computer crime victims. Unlike victims of older forms of crime, the victims of computer crimes are not necessarily located in proximity to offenders. For example, one series of computer crimes involved computer users in Australia who utilized international communication networks to gain unauthorized access to several computer systems in the United States and to destroy data on those systems.

Persons affected by processes controlled by computers can also be computer crime victims. For example, hospital patients who are given improper medications because of improper alterations of computerized medical records are indirect victims of computer crimes. Additional victims include persons who—because of doubts raised by an illegal breach in the integrity of computer-controlled processes—forgo beneficial activities to avoid being harmed by similar crimes. An example of this type of harm would be a decision to forgo useful business transactions conducted by computers because past incidents of computer fraud raise doubts about the integrity of computer-based communication and record-keeping systems.

Types of Computer Crimes. A study conducted on behalf of the U.S. Department of Justice found that all known and reported cases of computer-related crime involved computers in one or more of the following capacities: object, subject, instrument, and symbol.

A computer can be the object of an offense though criminal activity aimed at the destruction or alteration of computers, data, or programs, or aimed at causing damage to supportive facilities and resources such as air conditioning equipment and electrical power that allow computer facilities to operate. In some cases, the computers involved in these offenses may be intermediate objects along the path to some other criminal end. This would be the case, for example, if a computer facility were sabotaged to interrupt the operation of a bank and cause it financial injury.

A computer can also be the subject—the site or environment in which a crime is undertaken. This is the case when computer systems are used to assemble or maintain valuable forms of intellectual property such as programs or data and a crime targets the theft of that property.

Some types of sophisticated crimes require the manipulation of computer programs or data. In these offenses, computers are used as instruments or tools, much as a criminal might use a lock pick or a crowbar as a preliminary to theft. Some computer criminals are sufficiently clever to accomplish criminal ends by relying on the normal operation of computer systems. For example, one offender was able to divert depositors' funds to his account by leaving deposit slips with his computer-readable account number on a table in a bank branch. Persons making deposits and lacking their own deposit slips would pick up the forms, thinking that they were blank slips, enter their own account numbers (which were ignored by the computer), make a deposit, and have their funds automatically deposited in the offender's account.

A computer can also be used as a symbol for intimidation or deception. For example, this would be the case in an offense involving false advertising of nonexistent computer services, such as a nonexistent computer dating service.

Prohibited Conduct. Federal law and the laws of many states include statutes specifically addressing computer crime. Federal statutes prohibit unauthorized computer access to obtain classified information, data in the records of a bank or other financial institution, or information in a computer system operated by a government agency or department. Additional provisions bar the use of multiple computers in two or more states for fraudulent purposes. The knowing transmission of a program, information, code, or command to a computer via interstate commerce or communications systems with an intent to cause harm to a computer system or with reckless disregard for the likelihood of such harm also is forbidden. Separate provisions prohibit trafficking in illegitimately obtained computer passwords or financial access codes such as credit card numbers.

Furthermore, federal copyright laws include criminal provisions punishing the intentional copying or distribution of copyrighted materials without the permission of the copyright holders. In addition to limiting computer users' potential abuses of copyrighted materials, this legislation also prohibits contributory assistance to such abuses by computer bulletin board operators who know that their systems are being used for copyright infringement.

State laws aimed at computer crime generally prohibit thefts of data or programs from confidentially maintained systems. In addition, some states have laws separately criminalizing the tampering with computerized bank teller machines (ATMs) and unauthorized access to computer systems for the purpose of obtaining credit card numbers or otherwise furthering fraudulent credit card use. More recent state statutes prohibit unauthorized access to computer systems, with especially serious penalties for intentional misappropriation, alteration, or destruction of computer programs or data.

Even in states that do not have criminal standards specifically addressing computer crimes, offenses accomplished through computer misuse will often be prosecutable under more broadly applicable crime statutes. Computer misuse may be a part of such state offenses as theft, forgery, fraud, trade secret misappropriation, and invasions of privacy, including improper disclosures of private information by public officials.

— *Richard S. Gruner*

See also Bank robbery; Banking law; Embezzlement; Fraud; Theft; White-collar crime.

BIBLIOGRAPHY

Further information on computer crime can be obtained from the following texts describing common computer crime techniques, the prevalence of computer crime in modern society, and efforts to develop and enforce criminal laws related to computer crime. A comprehensive survey of computer crime methods is presented in Donn B. Parker, *Computer Crime:*

Criminal Justice Resource Manual (2d ed. Washington, D.C.: National Institute of Justice, 1989). Other detailed descriptions of incidents of computer crime are contained in Buck Bloombecker, *Spectacular Computer Crimes: What They Are and How They Cost American Business Half a Million Dollars a Year* (Homewood, Ill.: Dow Jones-Irwin, 1990); Donn B. Parker, *Crime by Computer* (New York: Scribner, 1976); and Thomas Whiteside, *Computer Capers* (New York: Crowell, 1978). The prohibitions of federal and state computer crime statutes are examined in Jay Bloombecker, *Computer Crime Laws* (Deerfield, Ill.: Clark Boardman Callaghan, 1993); Raymond T. Nimmer, *The Law of Computer Technology* (2d ed. Boston, Mass.: Warren, Gorham, and Lamont, 1992); Michael D. Scott, *Scott on Computer Law* (2d ed. Englewood Cliffs, N.J.: Prentice Hall, 1991).

Comstock Law

DATE: Became law March 3, 1873

DEFINITION: A law amending postal legislation to enforce the prohibition against using the mails to send sexually suggestive material

SIGNIFICANCE: The most restrictive obscenity statute ever passed by Congress, the Comstock Law limited the availability of even mild forms of pornography until the courts expanded First Amendment protection in the 1950's

In 1865, Congress passed the Postal Act, making it a crime to use the mails for sending any "publication of a vulgar or indecent character." Anthony Comstock, a tireless crusader against pornography, successfully lobbied Congress to make the postal regulations more restrictive. The resulting 1873 legislation created special agents with wide discretion to seize obscene matter and provided for criminal penalties of up to five years' imprisonment for the first offense. Books and magazines, including serious novels such as Theodore Dreiser's *Sister Carrie* (1900), were proscribed if they contained any sexual references considered "lewd" or "lascivious" by Victorian standards.

By the 1930's, the Comstock Law had been amended to become less restrictive, but much of its language, while reinterpreted, continued into the 1990's. The Supreme Court affirmed the constitutionality of the law's principles in numerous cases after 1877, but beginning with the landmark case *Roth v. United States* (1957), the Court liberalized the law by insisting on a narrow definition of obscenity.

See also Birth control, right to; Censorship; *Miller v. California*; *Roth v. United States*; Sanger, Margaret; Speech and press, freedom of.

Congress of Racial Equality (CORE)

DATE: Established 1942

SIGNIFICANCE: CORE, a civil rights organization, helped to eliminate discrimination in interstate travel on buses and trains; it also helped to end discrimination in both the public and private sectors of society, especially in housing and employment

The Congress of Racial Equality (CORE) was founded in Chicago in the spring of 1942 by fifty young people who were committed to nonviolent direct action in their opposition to segregation and racial discrimination. Although James Farmer, the first national director of CORE, is often given credit for the founding of CORE, George Houser, Bernice Fisher, Homer Jack, Joe Guinn, and James Robinson also played substantial roles.

Initially, CORE was a volunteer organization. Along with the Fellowship of Reconciliation, CORE actually began the Freedom Rides in 1947. These early rides were called "journeys of reconciliation." They consisted of integrated teams of young adults traveling throughout the upper South on interstate buses testing the 1946 Supreme Court ruling that outlawed segregation in interstate travel.

CORE gained much of its reputation for its participation in the student sit-ins and (in particular) the Freedom Rides of the early 1960's. The Freedom Rides were a response to the 1960 Supreme Court ruling expanding its 1946 decision. The Court decreed that train and bus terminals used by passengers engaged in interstate travel must also be desegregated. Arrests and violence followed the two integrated CORE teams in 1960 as they sought to force the hand of the federal government. With the assistance of the Student Nonviolent Coordinating Committee (SNCC) and the Southern Christian Leadership Conference (SCLC), they were successful in forcing the Interstate Commerce Commission to institute new penalties for noncompliance with the decreed desegregation.

During the first half of the 1960's, CORE carried on a number of concurrent campaigns around the country. While the national office focused on voter registration, local CORE chapters concentrated on desegregating lunch counters and roadside restaurants and fighting for fair housing practices, equal employment opportunities, and school integration. CORE participated in demonstrations, boycotts, and marches with the SCLC, SNCC, and the National Association for the Advancement of Colored People (NAACP). CORE took a leadership role in the 1963 March on Washington and was one of the ten civil rights organizations that met with President John F. Kennedy prior to the march.

In 1964 CORE began to move away from nonviolent direct action and political neutrality, and by 1966 it had developed a political action program and was active in community organizing. CORE eventually broke with the nonviolent integrationist philosophy and joined the ranks of the more radical activist groups. CORE embraced "black power" and replaced James Farmer with Floyd B. McKissick as its national director.

The anti-integration posture assumed by CORE tended to push it more and more to the fringe of the Civil Rights movement. Membership in CORE dwindled during the 1970's and 1980's, and by the 1990's it had experienced such a drop in membership and support that it was only a shell of its former self. Many attribute its decline to a change in philosophy and to the black nationalist position it took in the 1960's.

See also Black Power movement; Civil Rights movement; National Association for the Advancement of Colored People (NAACP); Southern Christian Leadership Conference (SCLC); Student Nonviolent Coordinating Committee (SNCC).

Conscientious objection

DEFINITION: Refusal to participate in a war or military training on the grounds of moral objection

SIGNIFICANCE: Conscientious objection involves a moral rejection of mandatory military service, a tradition in the United States which began with colonial militias and was reinstituted during the Civil War, World War I, World War II, and the Vietnam War

Conscientious objection (CO) traces its roots to pacifism, the complete rejection of war on moral grounds. Leaders of the Catholic church in the third century, such as Tertullian and Origen, stated that war was the antithesis of Christ's teachings. Later, splinter groups in the Protestant Reformation such as the Anabaptists and Hutterites interpreted pacifism as the rejection not only of war but also of governments themselves; they withdrew into self-contained colonies.

Immigrant Conscientious Objectors. The first instances of conscientious objection in the United States came from immigrant groups such as the Quakers and Mennonites, who had embraced pacifism in Europe. Followed by the Shakers, Brethren, Christadelphians, and Rogerenes, these groups refused the universal obligation of all male citizens to serve in the colonial militia. Because these religious groups were regarded as moral, hard-working, and otherwise law-abiding citizens, refusal to serve was regarded with tolerance by their fellow citizens. Responding to the surge of conscientious objection claims by Civil War draftees, Abraham Lincoln stated that the Union needed good farmers as well as good soldiers. When Civil War conscientious objectors were drafted into service far from their homes, they were treated harshly, even tortured, by fellow conscripts who had no sympathy for their claims for noncombatant status.

As the nation grew, so did the number of groups claiming conscientious objector status. Jehovah's Witnesses allowed that their individual status as ministers exempted them from any draft. The Molokans and Dukhobors immigrated to America in order to escape mandatory service under the Russian czar. Generally, in times of conscription, COs were allowed to perform alternative duties to fulfill their service obligation. Those who refused alternative service or refused to register for the draft (absolute objectors) faced the possibility of prison sentence.

With the Korean War, the nature of conscientious objection began to change from objection on the basis of religious beliefs to objection on the grounds of personal philosophy. The two new variants on conscientious objection were nonreligious or secular objection and selective objections.

Nonreligious Objection. A nonreligious or secular objector removes himself from the umbrella protection against mandated service offered by an established, pacifist religion. A secular objector resists war and military service on the grounds of personal beliefs independent of any organized religion. Such dissidence has been supported by the Supreme

Court's liberal interpretation of what can constitute an individual's personal credo (religion).

Selective Objection. A selective conscientious objector (SCO) is not a religious or philosophical pacifist. An SCO may view some wars (and the need for obligatory service) as just and some wars as unjust. The underlying SCO philosophy is that the right to determine the rectitude of any war belongs to the individual. Having rationalized that a particular war is wrong, the individual has no obligation to further the purpose of that war. The primacy of individual independence in SCO philosophy challenges the sovereignty of government and, taken to the extreme, threatens anarchy.

One of the first selective conscientious objectors was Henry David Thoreau. He regarded the Mexican War (1846) as U.S. imperialism at its worst and refused to pay that portion of a tax earmarked to finance the war. Thoreau subsequently popularized the phrase "civil disobedience" by affixing it to an essay which celebrated his night in jail as the result of not paying the war tax. On the other hand, Thoreau was a fervent abolitionist and saw the Civil War as a holy war. When John Brown was hanged after his abortive raid on the Harpers Ferry arsenal to acquire arms for a slave revolt, Thoreau compared his fate to the crucifixion of Christ.

The Vietnam War. As the conflict in Southeast Asia deepened and American casualties worsened in the 1960's, U.S. authorities moved to make the burden of the draft more equal by limiting exemptions. Consequently, levels of protest rose, and draft evasion and draft avoidance increased. An estimated 500,000 young men failed to answer their draft notices, while perhaps 50,000 more emigrated to escape conscription. At the same time the Supreme Court redefined conscientious objector status in a broader, more inclusive manner, allowing exemptions for "beliefs that are purely ethical or moral in source." At the peak of the Vietnam conflict, from 1965 to 1970, 170,000 registrants were granted draft exemptions for CO status.

In 1968, newly elected President Richard Nixon convened the Gates Commission to study the feasibility of an all-volunteer service (AVS). The commission found the draft to be an unfair and costly burden on selected young men and recommended it be replaced by the AVS. Conscription was abandoned in the United States in 1973, and while young men are still required to register at age eighteen for a potential draft, no draft calls have occurred since the end of the Vietnam War. As a result, the issue of conscientious objection and its ramifications for society remains on the back burner. — *John A. Sondey*

See also Civil disobedience; Civil liberties; Conscription; Religion, free exercise of; Students for a Democratic Society (SDS); Vietnam War.

BIBLIOGRAPHY

Two seminal texts, written twenty-five years apart, provide excellent insight into the issue of conscientious objection in all of its permutations: Lillian Schlissel, comp., *Conscience in America* (New York: E. P. Dutton, 1968), and Charles Moskos and John W. Chambers II, eds. and authors of "The Secularization of Conscience," in *The New Conscientious Objection* (New York: Oxford University Press, 1993). Two other texts which make meaningful contributions to the subject are Caroline Moorehead, *Troublesome People* (Bethesda, Md.: Adler & Adler, 1987), and John A. Rohr, *Prophets Without Honor* (Nashville, Tenn.: Abingdon Press, 1971).

Conscription

DEFINITION: The power of a government to require its citizenry to serve in its armed forces

SIGNIFICANCE: Military conscription, or "the draft," has caused tension in the United States because the concept of compulsory service may be argued to conflict with the American ideal of personal liberty; nevertheless, it was generally accepted from the Civil War to 1973, at which time the armed forces adopted an all-volunteer policy

Concepts of conscription stem from the idea that it is the obligation of all able-bodied men to bear arms on behalf of their country. It evolved from the city-states of Greece through the professional militaries of the Middle Ages and the rise of European military modernization with the French Revolution.

Conscription Through World War I. The first European nation to adopt a modern military draft was France in 1688. Subsequently, with the entrenchment of the draft as a military institution, a committee reporting to the French National Assembly in 1789 stated: "Every citizen must be a soldier and every soldier a citizen or we shall never have a constitution."

America formed militias shortly after colonization. All able-bodied men aged sixteen through fifty were required to enroll with the militia. The outbreak of the Revolution found no colonial standing army ready to fight against the British forces. Initial battles on behalf of the newly formed republic were undertaken by the lumbermen of Massachusetts. The First Continental Army, an outgrowth of this voluntary militia, resulted from a solicitation from the Second Continental Congress for additional volunteers. The Congress then established a system of bounties with monetary and land-based inducements intended to persuade military trainees to remain in the militia following their initiation and training periods. This system failed to maintain an adequately trained militia to defend the nation.

The first attempt at conscription in the United States was during the Civil War. The Confederacy passed a law mandating military service for all white men ages eighteen through thirty-five for a period of three years. As the tides of war turned against the Confederacy, the law was changed to include all white men between the ages of seventeen and fifty, and finally the Confederacy included slaves.

The federal government under President Abraham Lincoln initially called for seventy-five thousand men to serve for a three-month period. When it became evident that the war would not soon be over, additional troops were requested to serve a three-year period. Then a bounty system was attempted. This culminated in the first real military draft on American soil. Lincoln was empowered by a congressional act to draft men ages twenty through forty-five. In addition to exemptions, though, this act provided for the substitution by another for the individual drafted or a payment of a $300 commutation fee as replacements for military service. The Union drafted 255,000 men, of whom 204,000 either supplied a substitute or paid the commutation fee. This was the first example of the federal government subsuming individual rights in favor of perceived national interests. The inequities of this system led to dissension and to the first widespread rioting over draft issues on American soil.

The Selective Service Act of May 18, 1917, was a response to American entry into World War I. This draft law, as the one that predated it in Civil War times, recognized certain exemptions as well as the status of the conscientious objector (CO). This legislative recognition, rather than any constitutional right, provides for classification as a conscientious objector. The 1917 act met with little resistance. The argument that the draft represents compulsory bodily service antithetical to American concepts of liberty and justice was rebutted by the Supreme Court, which upheld congressional power to conscript in *Selective Draft Law Cases* (1918). This power, the Court said, evolved from constitutional power to build armies and was not in conflict with the Thirteenth Amendment's prohibition against involuntary servitude. Further, the drafters of the 1917 act learned well from the problems with previous conscription laws, and neither substitutions nor bounties were part of the legislation.

After World War II. Shortly after the expiration of the 1917 act, Congress passed the first peacetime draft. That draft expired in 1947, but a new draft law was passed in 1948 in response to the increasing tensions of the Cold War with the Soviet Union.

The draft laws have changed form and increased or decreased in notoriety according to the political and social mores of the times. The very name of the bureaucracy, the Selective Service System, denotes its prime inequity prior to 1973: By definition, it was selective. The dramatic protests against the draft in the 1960's and early 1970's must be viewed in the social and political context of the times. Throughout the years, various deferments and exemptions have existed, but they were never met with the level of incendiary reaction that the Vietnam War years brought. The violent antimilitarism of the era is best understood as a reaction against a very unpopular war. While July 1, 1973, was the official date of the inception of the all-volunteer armed forces, the federal government had stopped drafting men six months prior to the expiration of the president's power to do so under the Selective Service Act.

Conscientious Objector Status. Conscientious objector status is based on a showing of deeply and sincerely held religious, moral, or ethical beliefs in opposition to taking part in all wars no matter what form they take (*Clay v. United States*, 1971). Those who believe that they can neither morally nor ethically participate in any war are required to register for the draft under one of two classifications. These classifications distinguish between those willing to serve in noncombatant roles in the military and those who believe that even noncom-

batant roles would intolerably compromise them. Conscientious objectors need neither prove that they are pacifists nor that there are no circumstances under which they would harm another (such as self-defense or defense of a loved one). They need only show that their beliefs are sincerely held. Those conscientious objectors who register for the draft are subject to being called up in the same manner as their peers. Upon the requisite showing, however, conscientious objectors will either be subject to serving in noncombatant roles or performing some type of alternative national service. — *Murray Henner*

See also Civil liberties; Civil War; Conscientious objection; Military justice; Vietnam War.

BIBLIOGRAPHY

Overviews of volunteer and conscripted military service include Bruce Bliven, Jr., *Volunteers: One and All* (New York: Reader's Digest Press, 1976); Marion Bressler and Leo Bressler, *Country, Conscience, and Conscription: Can They Be Reconciled?* (Englewood Cliffs, N.J.: Prentice-Hall, 1970); and Raymond Aron, *Politics and History: Selected Essays* (New York: Free Press, 1978). In-depth discussions of the draft, the Selective Service System, and the need for the Selective Service System in the United States are found in George Q. Flynn, *The Draft 1940-1973* (Lawrence: University Press of Kansas, 1993); R. Charles Johnson, *Draft, Registration, and the Law* (2d ed. Occidental, Calif.: Nolo Press, 1991); Brent Scowcroft, ed., *Military Service in the United States* (Englewood Cliffs, N.J.: Prentice-Hall, 1982); and L. B. Taylor, Jr., *The Draft: A Necessary Evil?* (New York: Franklin Watts, 1981).

Consent decree

DEFINITION: A formal agreement entered into by two or more parties that specifies certain conditions under which the parties must operate

SIGNIFICANCE: Private companies sometimes enter into consent decrees to avoid prosecution or civil suits for improper practices

Consent decrees are used in order to ensure correct practices in corporate behavior, but they are also sometimes used in criminal and juvenile courts to keep individuals from engaging in criminal behavior. Companies that have been taken to court for inappropriate corporate behavior may enter into a consent decree. When this occurs, the company (or individual) agrees to change its practices as outlined in the consent decree. For example, a corporation that is manufacturing unsafe automobiles may agree to a consent decree and change the method of auto production rather than face prosecution by the government for its practices.

If a consent decree is accepted by the court, the parties named in the decree must conform to the requirements. If they do not, they face punitive measures by the court that approved the decree. These punitive measures are most often fines, but they can sometimes take the form of injunctions that forbid continuation of behavior or production of materials named in the consent decree.

See also Civil procedure; Criminal procedure; Injunction.

Conservatism, modern American

DEFINITION: The concern to limit the authority of the state to regulate the economy and to support the traditional institutions of society

SIGNIFICANCE: As an ideology and state of mind, conservatism has challenged and sought to replace, with some degree of success in the 1980's and 1990's, the liberal ideology that had dominated American political life since the 1930's

Since the late 1960's, the United States has witnessed a resurgence of conservatism as a social and political movement. Modern American conservatism is primarily a reaction to the progovernment public philosophy and welfare liberalism that had dominated the country's political life since the New Deal era in the 1930's.

Historically, the American political tradition, which is antistatist and antimonarchical, is liberal. It had few conservative authors and leaders. In its political culture and tradition, its government roots and ideals—as enshrined in patriotic emblems such as the Declaration of Independence, the Pledge of Allegiance, and the Gettysburg Address—the United States reflects deeply established liberal and progressive values. Beginning in the late 1960's, however, overt conservative views have been expressed by southern Democrats and (especially) the Barry Goldwater wing of the Republican Party, which later supported Ronald Reagan in the 1970's and 1980's.

The rise of conservatism has been closely associated with the general perception of the cause of the economic and social malaise in the country. In the economic sphere, conservatives have identified the problem of a stagnant economy coupled with inflation—"stagflation"—with the "big government" of "tax-and-spend" Democrats, who have been taking away taxpayers' hard-earned money and spending it on questionable social welfare programs for the undeserving poor. A few major events in the 1970's—New York City's fiscal crisis in the mid-1970's and the tax revolt embodied in Proposition 13 passed in California in 1978, for example—helped the conservatives in making an antigovernment case and in advancing the argument, which quickly became popular, that big govern-

The "contract with America" unveiled by Speaker of the House Newt Gingrich in 1995 was emblematic of 1990's conservatism. (AP/Wide World Photos)

ment is responsible for the country's economic woes. In the cultural and social domain, conservatives criticize liberals on issues such as race, family, "permissiveness," and crime and argue in favor of supporting the traditional institutions of society such as family, church, and neighborhood schools.

Varieties of Conservatism. The meaning and substance of conservatism in the United States are different from those in Europe, where conservatism originated to defend the alliance between monarchy, church, and aristocracy. European conservatives, following the basic principles of traditional conservatism as outlined by Edmund Burke in the eighteenth century, believe in tradition, custom, a hierarchical manorial society, a strong state, mercantilism, and natural leaders. Since they are pessimistic about people's ability to improve their lot through the use of reason, they resist change, especially drastic change.

American conservatism, on the other hand, is individualistic in conception and antistatist in orientation. Taking inspiration from the Constitution and European philosophers such as Burke, American conservatives essentially believe in a limited government. The welfare state is their main target of attack, and they ask for the dismantling of much of the New Deal legislation. Conservatives differ, however, on the specifics of economic and social policy.

Neoconservatism and the New Right. Two distinct traditions, Neoconservatism and the New Right, can be identified in modern American conservatism. The dominant theme of neoconservatism—as articulated by outspoken critics of "big government" such as Irving Kristol and Norman Podhoretz and political leaders such as Ronald Reagan—is the economic ideology of free market capitalism, first articulated by Adam Smith in *The Wealth of Nations* (1776), and of antistatism, which has been summed up as "private, good; public, bad." In particular, neoconservatives advocate deregulation of the economy; complete elimination of some national programs and decentralization of the administration of others; privatization of public functions; nationalist foreign policy; and support of traditional institutions in society.

The emphasis of the Radical or New Right, which is closely associated with the New Christian Right movement and is the extreme right group within the Republican Party, is on social and cultural issues. Leaders of the New Right movement such as Jerry Falwell and Pat Robertson are mainly concerned with the decline in traditional values. In particular, they are opposed to abortion, sex on television and in film, and forced busing to integrate public schools. The New Right leaders advocate a return to morality—defined in terms of the moral code of Christian fundamentalism—in government and society. In the 1980's and 1990's they succeeded in generating a national debate on moral issues central to the movement. The New Right failed, however, in its effort to become the voice of the Republican Party.

The Future of Conservatism. The conservative majority has dominated presidential politics since 1968, and it has taken control of the Republican Party. Reagan's election in 1980, followed by George Bush's in 1988, symbolized the end of the

liberal era in modern American politics. In 1992, even the Democratic Party platform and presidential candidate Bill Clinton accepted a number of conservative ideas in order to win the election.

The "Republican Revolution" in the 1994 elections—the party's greatest sweep since 1946—led to a conservative majority in both houses of the Congress. The Republicans thereupon launched a full-scale attack on the notion that the federal government should play a central role in the life of a nation. Under the leadership of Newt Gingrich, the Republican who became Speaker of the House, the party promised in its "Contract with America" to dismantle the welfare state and the "welfare-state bureaucracy" brick by brick. The conservatives succeeded in discrediting liberalism by building strong public opposition to the welfare state and state regulation. In the 1990's, liberals were on the defensive regardless of the outcome of specific conservative policy initiatives.   — *Sunil K. Sahu*

See also Democracy; Democratic Party; Liberalism, modern American; New Deal; Reagan, Ronald; Republican Party; States' rights; Welfare state.

BIBLIOGRAPHY

The most influential works in American Conservative thought since World War II include Friedrich Havek, *The Road to Serfdom* (Chicago: University of Chicago Press, 1976); Russell Kirk, *The Conservative Mind from Burke to Eliot* (7th ed. Chicago: Regnery Books, 1986); Whittaker Chambers, *Witness* (New York: Random House, 1952); Irving Kristol, *Two Cheers for Capitalism* (New York: Basic Books, 1978); and Robert Nisbet, *Conservatism* (Minneapolis: University of Minnesota Press, 1986). More recent books on the subject are J. David Hoeveler, Jr., *Watch on the Right: Conservative Intellectuals in the Reagan Era* (Madison: University of Wisconsin Press, 1991); E. J. Dionne, Jr., *Why Americans Hate Politics* (New York: Simon & Schuster, 1991); Paul Gottfried, *The Conservative Movement* (rev. ed. New York: Twayne, 1993); and Andrew Adonis and Tim Hames, eds., *A Conservative Revolution? The Thatcher-Reagan Decade in Perspective* (New York: Manchester University Press, 1994). *National Review*, established in 1955, is the premier conservative magazine; its editor, William F. Buckley, is the most important individual figure in the rise of conservatism in postwar American political thought.

Conspiracy

DEFINITION: Two or more persons planning to commit an unlawful act or to use unlawful means

SIGNIFICANCE: The criminality of conspiracy is the justification for a number of laws, including antiracketeering and antitrust legislation

The common-law definition of "conspiracy" is a combination of two or more persons formed for the purpose of committing some unlawful or criminal act or for the purpose of using unlawful or criminal means to commit an act which is not in itself unlawful. In most jurisdictions, the crime of conspiracy focuses on the agreement of the parties to work together to commit an unlawful act or exploit lawful means. In these jurisdictions, a conspiracy exists at the moment the parties agree to either the unlawful act or purpose. Because of the difficulty of proving the state of mind of the persons involved, however, some jurisdictions require an agreement accompanied by either acts or the taking of steps to effect the plan to show the existence of a conspiracy.

The terms "conspiracy" and "collusion" are often used interchangeably, although there are distinctions between the two. A collusion is a secret agreement between two or more persons for a deceitful or fraudulent purpose. It implies the use of fraudulent means or the use of lawful means for an unlawful purpose. Unlike conspiracy, collusion is not usually considered a crime in itself, but it may be an element in other offenses such as perjury, contempt, or fraudulent representation. For example, an individual may be charged with conspiracy to commit murder as a separate crime, regardless of whether the murder was committed, if there is sufficient evidence of the existence of the conspiracy. A man and woman who agree to misrepresent the grounds for a divorce, however, are engaging in collusive activity. They might be charged with perjury for lying under oath in a court of law, but they are not likely to be charged with collusion or conspiracy to get a divorce. In addition to receiving a criminal sentence, conspirators can be liable to their victims for monetary damages.

Historically, conspiracy charges have been used as a tool for squelching political activity. For example, in the nineteenth century, labor unions were frequently charged with conspiracy in connection with strikes and other protests. Courts often upheld these conspiracy charges on the theory that while individual protest might be a lawful purpose, an agreement to protest could be viewed as an agreement to use unlawful means to achieve a lawful purpose. In more recent years, as labor unions have gained power and acceptance in American society, striking is no longer considered conspiratorial or collusive activity.

Conspiracy is the backbone of federal statutes such as the Racketeer Influenced and Corrupt Organizations Act (RICO), the Sherman Antitrust Act, the Clayton Antitrust Act, and the Robinson-Patman Act. RICO focuses primarily on conspiracies related to organized crime. The Sherman Antitrust Act, Clayton Antitrust Act, and Robinson-Patman Act work together to attack business engaged in collusive price fixing, monopolization, and other limits on competition or restraint of trade. Other federal statutes make it unlawful to conspire to commit an offense against the federal government or to conspire to harm, threaten, or intimidate a federal officer.

See also Accessory, accomplice, and aiding and abetting; Anti-Racketeering Act; Antitrust law; Attempt to commit a crime; Organized crime; Racketeer Influenced and Corrupt Organizations Act (RICO).

Constitution, U.S.

DEFINITION: The fundamental document establishing the national government of the United States of America

SIGNIFICANCE: This document describes the nature and limits of political power within the national government; it also describes how the different branches of government will be structured

The Constitution of the United States is an extraordinary document, both theoretically and historically. Knowing how this document was developed is important to understanding both its purpose and its success.

Development. The Constitution of the United States was not the first—and some would argue that it is not the most important—of the United States' founding documents. The Constitution was developed eleven years after the approval of the Declaration of Independence. After declaring and then winning independence from Great Britain, the new nation spent a number of years governed by the Articles of Confederation. The Articles created a loose federation of states which eventually proved too weak to serve the needs of the young nation. In 1787 delegates from twelve of the states (all but Rhode Island) met to discuss ways of revising the Articles of Confederation to create a more adequate government. The Constitutional Convention of 1787 quickly decided that the basic premise behind the Articles of Confederation rendered them inadequate for governing the nation. The Convention began discussing a far more centralized form of government than was possible under the Articles of Confederation. James Madison and Edmund Randolph, two Virginia delegates who had anticipated this possibility, arrived at the Convention with the rough outlines of a totally new form of government. After considerable debate and numerous compromises, the Convention approved the Constitution of the United States and sent it to the states for their ratification. After further debate and much political maneuvering, the Constitution was eventually ratified by all thirteen states.

Basic Principles of the Constitution. One of the most unique aspects of the Constitution was that it was (and is) firmly based on a clear set of theoretical principles. To describe the Constitution as a document of the Enlightenment—an eighteenth century movement in European thought that celebrated the capacity of reason to solve human problems—would be to tell the truth but not necessarily the whole truth. Alexander Hamilton, a delegate to the Constitutional Convention from New York, claimed that the U.S. Constitution reflected what he described as a "new science of politics." According to Hamilton, this new science was based on principles either unknown to or not fully understood by previous generations. It is generally acknowledged that the most fundamental principles of the Constitution are separation of powers, federalism, and republicanism.

Each of these principles is critical to a clear understanding of the American system of government, but each was developed because of the founders' commitment to a prior principle—the principle of limited governmental power. A government founded on the principle of limited powers must develop safeguards to ensure that the people who wield the powers of government do not go beyond the limits. Within the American constitutional system this is accomplished by the three principles cited above.

Article I of the U.S. Constitution. (National Archives)

Separation of Powers. Separation of powers was a political principle advocated by English philosopher John Locke and French philosopher Baron de Montesquieu. The Constitution of the United States was the first national political document to apply this concept of government. Distinct governmental powers had long been recognized, but the Constitution of the United States was the first to place these powers in separate branches of government. The first three articles of the Constitution describe the location and authority of the legislative, executive, and judicial powers of government.

Article I, section 1 of the Constitution begins by stating: "All legislative Powers herein granted shall be vested in a Congress of the United States, which shall consist of a Senate and House of Representatives." In addition to establishing the location of the legislative powers, this statement declares that those powers will be shared by two separate legislative chambers. Bicameralism (the term used to describe a two-chambered legislature) permits the two legislative chambers to provide internal checks on each other.

The notes taken at the Constitutional Convention reveal that disagreements over how the representatives to Congress would be apportioned and selected were the most difficult for the delegates to settle. At one point, delegates threatened to withdraw from the convention over this issue. The solution to this dispute produced one legislative chamber that represents states equally (the Senate) and another that represents states according to their population (the House of Representatives).

The Senate consists of two senators from each state in the Union. Senators are elected for six-year terms; the long term was intended to give them relative freedom from the passing whims of the electorate. One of the rationales for such long terms was that the Senate would be freer to speak to the long-term needs of the nation. The Constitution requires staggered terms for the senators so that a third of the Senate seats are up for election every two years. This requirement provides a degree of stability and continuity in the national government.

In contrast, the members of the House of Representatives hold two-year terms. These shorter terms keep House members in much closer contact with the American voters. By requiring that House members seek reelection every two years, the Constitution provides the voting public with regular access to national lawmakers.

Legislators who desire new laws or want to alter old ones must be able to persuade a majority of the lawmakers in both legislative chambers of Congress. By design, this process was not intended to be quick or easy. The legislature was meant to be a deliberative group that carefully examines all proposed laws. In a bicameral legislature, proposals that might be rushed through one chamber may be examined carefully in the second chamber. The framers of the Constitution believed that it was more important that laws be carefully and thoughtfully examined than that they be approved quickly.

Article II, section 1 of the Constitution places the executive powers of the United States government in the hands of "a President." The Constitutional Convention had considerable difficulties developing the executive branch of government. In part, this was attributable to their basic suspicion of executive power. They also realized, however, that one of the greatest shortcomings of the Articles of Confederation was the absence of a clearly defined executive branch. The first question was whether the executive authority should be placed in a single executive or multiple executives. The second question, and one of the last to be settled at the Convention, concerned the method for selecting the executive.

After much debate, the Convention settled on a single executive. In the words of Alexander Hamilton, only a single executive would provide the "unity and dispatch" modern governments required. This sentiment prevailed, and the Convention then had to determine how "the President of the United States" would be selected. The electoral college was the method upon which they eventually settled. This system utilizes the states as electoral units and follows the representative principle devised for Congress to distribute the votes among the states.

The president's basic responsibilities are to see that national laws are faithfully executed, to serve as the commander in chief of the national armed forces, to appoint the executive officers of the different federal agencies, and to recommend judges to serve on the Supreme Court and the lesser courts established by Congress. In addition to these responsibilities, the president has a limited veto over the acts of Congress.

Article III of the Constitution describes the judicial branch of government. More specifically, it establishes the Supreme Court and any additional courts Congress may establish. One of the more unusual aspects of the Constitution is its establishment of an independent judiciary. Judges receive lifelong appointments, so they are as free from political influences as is humanly possible. The only qualification to this independence is that Congress has the power to impeach and remove judges if they behave in a manner that would warrant such removal. In this respect, judges are subjected to the same kind of scrutiny as are members of the executive branch of government.

One aspect of the separation of powers that is often given particular consideration is the concept of checks and balances. The Constitution provides that each of the three branches of government has certain "checks" on its power that are under the control of another branch. Congress, for example, controls the budget of the president and the judiciary. The president, on the other hand, can veto acts of Congress (Congress, in turn, can override a veto with a two-thirds vote in both houses). The president also appoints justices to the Supreme Court (with congressional approval). Finally, the Supreme Court can rule that the laws of Congress or the actions of the president are unconstitutional.

Federalism. This aspect of the Constitution is one of the more ingenious creations to grow out of the Constitutional Convention. Historically, national governments had been either unitary governments or confederal governments. Unitary governments place all power in the hands of a centralized authority. The British government is an example of such a

The U.S. Constitution is exhibited in the rotunda of the National Archives building in Washington, D.C. (National Archives)

system. In a confederal system, the ultimate power is decentralized among member states. Some responsibility may be given over to a centralized authority, but the real power remains with the decentralized units of government. This was the case under the Articles of Confederation. The federal system established by the Constitution was unique in that it created a governmental system in which the real powers of the political system were truly divided between the centralized and decentralized units of government.

The distribution of powers between the states and the national government has created considerable political tensions during the course of American history. It is important to realize that these tensions were largely intended by the founders. Federalism, like the separation of powers, was built into the constitutional system as a check on governmental powers. Article VI establishes the Constitution, acts of Congress, and treaties as the "supreme Law of the Land," but the Tenth Amendment to the Constitution declares the limits of that supremacy: The states and the people possess all powers not delegated to the United States by the Constitution.

Republicanism. Article IV of the Constitution guarantees that every state in the union will have a republican form of government. The Federalist Papers, a collection of essays writ-

ten by Alexander Hamilton, James Madison, and John Jay in 1787 and 1788, explain why a republican system of government was considered preferable to a democratic system. The tenth essay of this collection provides a detailed comparison of these two popular systems of government. The first advantage of republicanism is that governmental authority is delegated to a small group of citizens. The second is that republican governments can cover a much larger geographical area than a direct democracy can.

When a smaller group has the responsibility of representing a larger group, each of the representatives must speak for a variety of interests. By learning the interests and needs of a diverse number of groups, representatives approach governmental decision making with a broader perspective than they would if they were simply advocating their own interests and needs. Public opinion is thereby filtered through a select group of representatives who must keep the many needs of their district in mind.

The advantage of a large geographical area is that it produces a great diversity of interests. This diversity decreases the likelihood that a single interest will constitute a majority on any given issue. For example, while chicken processors may hold a majority interest in Arkansas or oil producers may be a major political force in Texas, neither of these groups can dominate a large geographical area such as the entire United States. Together, these factors increase the likelihood that governmental decisions will serve the general interests of the nation instead of one or a few dominant groups.

The existence of these basic principles within the Constitution creates a significant barrier to government guided by passion as opposed to government guided by reason. The many checks within the system provide numerous obstacles to laws that are not in the interest of a fairly wide and diverse group of citizens. The system also places a substantial burden of proof on those who want to change existing laws or develop new laws. The cumbersome nature of the political process exposes any legislative initiative to a series of examinations before a number of different bodies.

Amendments. The Constitution has been a remarkably stable political document. The method described in Article V for amending the Constitution has not been utilized very often. By 1995 there were only twenty-seven amendments to the Constitution. The first ten amendments, known as the Bill of Rights, were passed within three years of the Constitution's ratification.

Three amendments (thirteen through fifteen) were passed at the end of the Civil War to make the institution of slavery unconstitutional and to extend certain citizenship rights to African Americans liberated by the Civil War. One of these, the Fourteenth Amendment, through its requirements of "due process" and "equal protection of the laws," has been instrumental in expanding basic civil rights to a number of other groups as well. The Seventeenth Amendment instituted the direct election of senators, the Twenty-second Amendment limited presidents to two terms, and the Twenty-fifth Amendment provided for the transfer of power in cases of presidential disability. A number of amendments (fifteen, nineteen, twenty-three, twenty-four, and twenty-six) have expanded the electorate.

One of the reasons often cited for the Constitution not having gathered more amendments through the years is the role the federal courts have played in determining questions of constitutionality. This process, known as judicial review, has permitted the courts to clarify and fine tune aspects of the Constitution. At times the courts have been accused of taking undue advantage of this authority. President Woodrow Wilson, for example, once referred to the Supreme Court as an ongoing constitutional convention.

The Constitution has proved to be one of the most durable political documents of all time. One of the key reasons for this durability is the document's brevity. The founders had a sense of what a constitution needed to specify and what it did not. Leaving many details unsettled, the founders recognized that statutory laws, administrative law, and precedents could handle the more specific and transient details of government.

—*Donald V. Weatherman*

See also Assembly and association, freedom of; Bill of Rights, U.S.; Civil liberties; Civil rights; Civil War Amendments; Constitutional interpretation; Constitutional law; Declaration of Independence; Due process of law; Equal protection of the law; Federalism; Incorporation doctrine; Jeffersonian democracy; President of the United States; Supremacy clause; Supreme Court of the United States.

BIBLIOGRAPHY

The most important work describing the Constitution is the collection of essays written by Alexander Hamilton, James Madison, and John Jay, *The Federalist Papers*. The Clinton Rossiter edition (New York: New American Library, 1961) is probably the most readily available. One of the most thorough recent volumes is edited by the late Allan Bloom, *Confronting the Constitution* (Washington, D.C.: AEI Press, 1990). A clearly written and thoughtful examination of some of the theoretical aspects of the Constitution can be found in Harvey C. Mansfield, *America's Constitutional Soul* (Baltimore: The Johns Hopkins University Press, 1991). The most readable constitutional history available is probably Alfred H. Kelly, Winfred A. Harbison, and Herman Belz, *The American Constitution: Its Origin and Development* (6th ed. New York: W. W. Norton, 1983). For a well-reasoned and well-written intellectual history, see Forrest McDonald, *Novus Ordo Seclorum: The Intellectual Origins of the Constitution* (Lawrence: University Press of Kansas, 1979).

Constitutional interpretation

DEFINITION: The process by which general principles of a constitution are applied by officials to individual laws or actions

SIGNIFICANCE: Arguments over the "correct" reading of constitutional principles may easily become political issues, and their resolution can affect the scope of citizens' rights and the powers of government in modern societies

Almost all modern societies operate under constitutional principles and provisions contained in one or more documents. Even the so-called "unwritten" British constitution has written parts and is more concrete than a set of norms accepted by the population. Constitutions usually are initially written when a country adopts a new and different form of government as the result of breaks in continuity. Such breaks include revolution (for example, the American Revolution), replacement of one regime by another as the result of military defeat (as when Nazism was destroyed in Germany at the end of World War II), or the ending of colonial rule (as when India and Pakistan gained their independence from Britain in 1947). Because constitutions are framed in the hope that they will last a long time and that their provisions can be effectively applied to new and diverse situations, they tend to include considerable general language, some of it vague and thus capable of being interpreted in more than a single way.

It is inevitable, then, that constitutions will need to be interpreted by somebody or some institution if they are to continue to serve as guidelines for the conduct of government and to be capable of application to specific situations many years after their original formulation. The proper way a constitution should be interpreted, as well as who has the legitimate power to do so, often becomes a major national controversy. Thus it is not surprising that justice issues involving individual rights and liberties, the power of the state to define criminal acts, whether due process of law is being observed, or what constitutes appropriate punishment often center on disputes about how the language of the constitution should be interpreted.

Varieties of Interpretation. Constitutional interpretation in the United States falls mainly to the courts, especially the U.S. Supreme Court. Resort to the courts to settle controversial issues arising under the constitution happens in many other nations that have written constitutions. Unlike the United States, however, countries such as France, Germany, and Italy have separate constitutional courts whose sole job is to render decisions on the constitutionality of laws and the actions of government officials. There are countries with especially strong parliamentary systems that tend to regard this power of the courts as undemocratic because courts are not directly elected by the people or easily answerable to them. Such countries often prefer to have constitutional issues interpreted by officials closer to the people. Great Britain is one of those countries. There, although as in the United States the courts may have power to interpret laws of the elected Parliament in individual cases, they lack the power to overrule Parliament on constitutional grounds.

Even in countries such as the United States, where constitutional interpretation is largely done by the courts, such power

is not absolute. U.S. courts are not involved in the process by which the Constitution itself can be amended; that is up to Congress and the state legislatures. Amendment can be viewed as an extreme form of interpretation. Furthermore, courts normally do not render judgments unless cases come before them challenging existing laws or practices on constitutional grounds. For that reason, it might be argued that political actors such as the president, Congress, or state and local officials also are involved in interpreting the Constitution when they apply general principles to particular cases without being challenged on the grounds of unconstitutionality. For example, the Supreme Court has issued opinions prohibiting certain religious practices in the public schools, but in some small communities these rulings are disregarded, especially when no citizen is bold enough to buck local opinion by bringing a court challenge to the practices.

The Centrality of the U.S. Judiciary. Apart from providing for amendment, the original U.S. Constitution of 1787 did not make it clear by what process it was to be interpreted in later years. It was only after disputes arose in the early years of the republic that the Supreme Court, under the leadership of Chief Justice John Marshall, justified its role as the principal interpreter of the Constitution. Two leading court cases firmed up this power in the early nineteenth century. In the case of *Marbury v. Madison* (1803), the Court assumed the power of

Constitutional interpretation is primarily the job of the courts; pictured is the U.S. Supreme Court in 1866 under the leadership of Chief Justice Salmon P. Chase. (M. P. Rice, collection of the Supreme Court of the United States)

judicial review—that is, the power to review and, if necessary, negate laws of Congress and actions of the executive on the ground that they violate provisions of the Constitution. Later, in *McCulloch v. Maryland* (1819), the Marshall Court asserted the doctrine of implied powers, justifying the exercise by the federal government of powers not specifically stated in the Constitution with the argument that the powers which were set out in the original document logically implied others, even if they are not spelled out in so many words. In the chief justice's words in the *McCulloch* case, the Constitution is "intended to endure for ages to come and, consequently, to be adapted to the various crises of human affairs." As the result of these and other decisions, the courts at every level of the American system took on increased powers of constitutional interpretation, and people came to look to them as having virtually the last word in such matters.

Through American history, the courts have, consciously or unconsciously, shaped public policy, especially in key areas such as economic regulation, equality of rights and opportunity, and criminal justice. They have done so partly as enforcers of norms but also as interpreters of the Constitution and the laws made under it. From the time of the Civil War to the New Deal, the courts interpreted the Constitution largely in ways favorable to business and corporations. Since the New Deal, the courts have been more tolerant of government regulation of business and have shifted their attention increasingly to the areas of civil rights, equality of treatment, and criminal justice. The Earl Warren Court (1953-1969) supported the powers of the federal government to legislate in the civil rights arena. The Court gave a strong boost to racial desegregation in the South, for example, in a series of decisions beginning with *Brown v. Board of Education* (1954). The rights of persons accused of crimes were reinforced by such decisions as *Miranda v. Arizona* (1966), which required that persons arrested by the police be told of their rights, and *Gideon v. Wainwright* (1963), which guaranteed the right to counsel in all criminal cases. Courts in the 1980's and 1990's showed a more conservative bent; for example, they approved a freer role for the police and chipped away at the rights of the accused advanced by the Warren Court.

Disagreement and Disputes. The Constitution does not interpret itself, and every time the courts issue decisions invoking their view of what it means, there are winners and losers. As new and different members are appointed to the courts, there is always the possibility that new decisions will overrule previous ones—hence the keen political interest paid to who is nominated to the higher courts and what they believe. In the wake of decisions in the areas of desegregation, abortion, and the drawing of electoral districts, for example, criticism has mounted (usually from those on the losing end of decisions) that instead of "finding" the law, judges are really "making" it, taking to themselves powers that rightly belong to legislatures and elected officials.

Jurists believe that the behavior of judges today can be seen as reflecting the interplay of two different philosophies: judicial activism and judicial restraint. Judicial activists take the position that the judicial branch should play an active, creative role in shaping the development of the country, a role at least equal to those of the other branches of government. They take a more aggressive view of the judiciary's role in making policy and are ready to say no to actions of the other branches of the federal government, and the states, that they believe violate the Constitution. Judicial self-restrainers, on the other hand, believe that it is the job of the courts to uphold the actions of the elected branches of government unless they clearly violate a specific section of the Constitution. Their "strict constructionist" views are opposed to the idea that the courts are justified in intervening broadly in controversies coming before them, especially when they consider the issues of a case to be political.

There have been few examples of Supreme Courts made up purely of judicial activists or judicial self-restrainers. Most Supreme Courts have some judges with each tendency, but there usually is a center of gravity in one direction or the other. The court of Chief Justice John Marshall in the early 1800's was of an activist bent, as was the one in the 1930's that negated several legislative pillars of the New Deal. Those courts were ideologically conservative. The Warren Court was also dominated by the activist view, but its political bent was liberal. More recently, the Warren Burger (1969-1986) and William Rehnquist (beginning in 1986) Courts have tended toward judicial self-restraint and have favored more conservative outcomes in their decisions.

History shows that it is difficult simply to equate judicial activism with liberal decisions and self-restraint with conservative ones. Liberals and conservatives in the country at large have been alternately happy and unhappy with courts dominated by both perspectives. How elected politicians and the public at large are likely to respond to the latest constitutional interpretation by the courts depends less on their belief in the virtues of activism or restraint than on whether their own interests have been served or have suffered as a result.

One particular manifestation of the judicial restraint perspective is the concept of "original intent." Its advocates argue that the sole duty of the courts should be to ensure that laws adhere to what the framers of the Constitution themselves intended it to mean. Determining exactly what the framers meant by their words and phrases in 1789 is not necessarily an easy matter, however; it involves intensive historical and political study. Conclusions concerning original intent are open to debate. Supporters of original intent (Robert Bork and Edwin Meese are among the most prominent) insist that adhering to the framers' intent is the only way to prevent the courts from overstepping their bounds and "legislating from the bench." Critics often argue that the framers themselves did not intend the Constitution to be interpreted rigidly but wanted it to be adaptable to changing times. Indeed, many important passages of the Constitution are written in language so open-ended that literal interpretation is extremely difficult if not impossible.

Consequences for Justice Issues. In the United States, most of the provisions of the Constitution concerned with issues of justice are found not in the body of the document but in amendments to it that were adopted subsequently. Almost all of them have required extensive interpretation before they could be applied to real-life situations. The bulk of these provisions occur in two sections, the Bill of Rights (1791) and the Fourteenth Amendment (1868). The Bill of Rights contains the following slippery phrases: "[T]he right of the people to keep and bear arms, shall not be infringed" (Second Amendment); people have a right "to be secure . . . against unreasonable searches and seizures" (Fourth Amendment); no person shall be "deprived of life, liberty, or property, without due process of law" (Fifth Amendment); "In all criminal prosecutions, the accused shall enjoy the right to a speedy and public trial" (Sixth Amendment); "Excessive bail shall not be required, nor excessive fines imposed, nor cruel and unusual punishments inflicted" (Eighth Amendment). The Fourteenth Amendment forbids the states to "make or enforce any law which shall abridge the privileges or immunities of citizens of the United States, . . . deprive any person of life, liberty, or property, without due process of law; nor deny to any person . . . the equal protection of the laws."

On each of these phrases in the U.S. Constitution rides enormous consequences for individuals and groups. None of them is self-evident or automatically enforceable. Their proper interpretation has given rise to strong controversy and political activity and to resort to courts, legislatures, and executives in the hope that the newest interpretation of the Constitution will favor oneself or one's favored institution or cause. The process began almost before the ink had dried on the Constitution, and it shows no sign of slowing today.   — *James B. Christoph*

See also Bill of Rights, U.S.; Cardozo, Benjamin Nathan; Constitution, U.S.; Constitutional law; *Gideon v. Wainwright*; Judicial review; *Marbury v. Madison*; Marshall, John; *Miranda v. Arizona*; Supreme Court of the United States; Warren, Earl.

BIBLIOGRAPHY

Early classics on this subject include Benjamin Cardozo, *The Nature of the Judicial Process* (New Haven: Yale University Press, 1921), and Charles A. Beard, *The Supreme Court and the Constitution* (Englewood Cliffs, N.J.: Prentice-Hall, 1962). More recent coverage is given in Archibald Cox, *The Court and the Constitution* (Boston: Houghton Mifflin, 1987), and Walter Murphy, *American Constitutional Interpretation* (Mineola, N.Y.: Foundation Press, 1985). The strict constructionist case is made by Alexander Bickel in *The Supreme Court and the Idea of Progress* (New Haven: Yale University Press, 1978). A vivid case study of the hammering out of a new judicial doctrine can be found in Anthony Lewis, *Gideon's Trumpet* (New York: Random House, 1970).

Constitutional law

DEFINITION: The dynamic body of law that defines and limits the powers of government and sets out its organizational framework

SIGNIFICANCE: Constitutional law is the fundamental law embodied in the Constitution and in court decisions interpreting that document; it blends vital legal decisions with elements of politics, history, economics, public policy, and ethics

The body of law known as American constitutional law rests first on the U.S. Constitution and second on the thousands of federal court decisions through the years that have defined, interpreted, and sometimes reinterpreted the Constitution. The ninety-four U.S. district courts, the thirteen U.S. courts of appeals, and the U.S. Supreme Court are all involved in defining constitutional law as it evolves over time.

A resilient document, the U.S. Constitution has endured with only twenty-seven amendments since its formulation in 1787 because of its sweeping language and vague generalities, which allow change and interpretation as situations arise which necessitate them. There are few rules contained in the Constitution, nor is it self-explanatory. That lack of specificity, however, was intentional. The framers of the Constitution outlined their general intent to stick to fundamentals: creating a national government, prescribing how it should operate, and limiting the scope of its power. The ongoing interpretive process by the Supreme Court allows the provisions of the Constitution to change and adapt over time. The general nature of the language contained in the Constitution allows interpretation to conform to necessity, political and social climate of the times, and the composition of the Court. The constitutions of the fifty states are patterned after the U.S. Constitution.

Constitutional protections are considered fundamental in nature—they are rights which belong to citizens of free governments. The focus is popular rather than parliamentary; the initial phrase in the preamble—"We the people"—provides evidence that the central purpose of the Constitution was to create a limited national government devoted to the rule of law with fairness and justice for all. It should be noted that "we the people" was somewhat less inclusive in 1787 than it is today. Throughout American history, in a series of legal decisions from the post-Civil War era through the Civil Rights movement and beyond, that phrase came to include all citizens regardless of race, class, or gender.

Separation of Powers. Constitutional law also covers the structure of the federal government itself. It is helpful to note the basic provisions the Constitution makes for the form of the federal government and, particularly, the role of the judiciary within that framework.

The authority of government is divided among several branches to prevent the concentration of excessive power. The American system created three separate branches of government—legislative, executive, and judicial—with overlapping responsibilities making them interdependent. Each branch has separate duties but also the obligation to cooperate with and monitor the others. That system of checks and balances augments the separation of powers by specifying the controls of each part of government over the others. Because of this decentralization of governmental power, no branch can dominate for a significant period of time. The system, however, has been criticized as creating potential fragmentation or disunity if conflicts exist between branches.

Duties of the legislative, or lawmaking, branch are set out in Article I of the Constitution. Congress has certain expressly enumerated powers: to tax, borrow money, regulate commerce, coin money, establish post offices, declare war, raise and support armies and navies, and regulate naturalization and bankruptcy. Under the "necessary and proper" clause, the Constitution also gives Congress the power to adopt any means convenient and useful for implementing the foregoing powers.

The second branch of government is the executive branch (Article II), headed by the president at the national level and the governor on each state level. The president has the power to approve or reject acts of Congress by means of a veto, which can be overridden by a two-thirds congressional majority.

The third branch is the judiciary, or courts (Article III), having the power to interpret the laws and mediate disputes. The Constitution specifies only the establishment of a supreme court, with inferior courts "as the Congress may from time to time ordain and establish." As the role of the Supreme Court expanded in the twentieth century, because of the diverse body of cases before it, the Court increasingly played a role in determining the extent of the powers of the other branches.

Judicial Review. A unique contribution to the political theory of the United States, judicial review is the means by which courts participate in the development of constitutional law. In the landmark case *Marbury v. Madison* in 1803, considered the point at which constitutional law begins, the Supreme Court held that Article III of the Constitution empowers courts to review government actions and invalidate those found to be repugnant to the Constitution by declaring them "unconstitutional." The "supremacy clause" contained in Article VI states that no provision of state law and no legislative enactment may conflict with the national Constitution, which is the supreme law of the land. Courts safeguard the integrity of constitutions from improper action through judicial review. That power was later held to extend to acts of Congress as well as to state government activities.

Federalism. Considered to be one of the most important contributions to government, federalism was the main method used by the framers of the Constitution to decentralize control. It is a dual system in which powers are distributed between central (national) and local (state) authorities. The American Constitution is structured in a way that permits power to be shared by the national government and the states. Interaction between state and federal courts is called "judicial federalism," one aspect of which involves Supreme Court review of state court decisions, which arguably rest on the state, not the national, constitution.

U.S. Supreme Court. Virtually all cases before the Supreme Court are seeking review of a decision by a federal court of appeals or a state supreme court. The final authority on federal matters and questions dealing with the Constitution and treaties, the Supreme Court exercises appellate jurisdiction (appeals) and functions as a trial court (original jurisdiction) only in certain limited situations involving ambassadors or instances in which a state is a party. The bulk of the cases

reach the Supreme Court for review by means of a writ of *certiorari*, or through the exercise of the Court's discretion. This means that the Court has almost complete control of its docket. More than five thousand petitions for a writ of *certiorari* are filed annually, but only 2 percent are granted. Cases are accepted for review according to the "rule of four": If four of the nine sitting justices decide that resolution of a particular case would serve the interests of justice, it is accepted. The Court does not have to explain its refusal.

Decisions of the Supreme Court are final because there is no higher court to which to appeal. Its interpretation of statutes can be reversed only by congressional legislation, and its constitutional rulings overturned only by constitutional amendment or subsequent reinterpretation by the Court itself. Absent these remedies, therefore, all courts are obliged to follow the Supreme Court in matters of federal law. In its decisions the Court attempts to adhere to precedent (the doctrine of *stare decisis*), thereby providing a uniform interpretation of the law. Nevertheless, there have been well-known instances of the Court overturning its own earlier rulings which have outlived their usefulness or have been proven to have been wrongly decided. One of these was its 1954 school

The Supreme Court building in Washington, D.C. The Supreme Court has the power to declare government actions or laws "unconstitutional" through judicial review. (McCrea Adams)

desegregation ruling in *Brown v. Board of Education*, which overturned the 1896 *Plessy v. Ferguson* decision that had allowed segregated public facilities for nearly sixty years.

The Court has imposed certain limitations or barriers before accepting a case for review. "Standing to sue" requires that the litigants have a personal stake in the outcome of the case, having suffered an injury in fact, in order to assure concrete adverseness. The case must present a live dispute involving a real conflict of interests or rights between parties. Accordingly, there must be an ongoing case or controversy at all stages of the proceedings including appeal. The case, therefore, cannot be moot or already resolved, settled, feigned, collusive, or hypothetical. An exception to the mootness doctrine was carved out for abortion cases. In *Roe v. Wade* (1973), in which the plaintiff was pregnant when the suit was initiated but not when the decision was rendered, the Court refused to dismiss the case on mootness grounds. Justice Harry A. Blackmun wrote, "Pregnancy provides a classic justification for a conclusion of nonmootness. It truly could be 'capable of repetition, yet evading review.'" Ripeness requires the issues in the case to be clearly delineated and sharply outlined, not premature, in flux, or abstract. Furthermore, the Court will not engage in speculation, contingencies, or predictions. It will not consider hypothetical cases or political questions—matters which it believes should be decided by another branch of government (*Baker v. Carr*, 1962)—and will not issue advisory opinions or extrajudicial advice. The absence of an actual controversy, ripeness, standing, or jurisdiction makes a case nonjusticiable, or inappropriate for settlement by a court.

The Bill of Rights. The framers of the U.S. Constitution believed that protecting the fundamental rights of individuals was of the utmost importance, and many believed that explicit enumeration of those rights would make them more secure. Fulfilling a promise made by the advocates of the proposed Constitution during the ratification struggle of 1788, Congress in 1789 proposed ten amendments to the Constitution that became known as the Bill of Rights. The states ratified the amendments in 1791. While the main body of the Constitution concerns government, the Bill of Rights represents the popular perception of constitutional guarantees. Today the Bill of Rights protects individuals from state governments as well as the federal government, but until the twentieth century the Bill of Rights applied only to actions of the federal government.

Basic to American identity is the First Amendment and its central guarantees of freedom of speech, press, religion, assembly, and right to petition for redress of grievances. Despite language to the contrary, the rights contained in the Bill of Rights are not absolute. In the speech area, for example, certain categories of expression can be regulated, and others are not protected at all. "Pure" speech (communication that does not create any substantial danger to the public) is protected. If imminent unlawful action that presents a "clear and present danger" is advocated, the speech loses its protection (*Schenck v. United States*, 1919). Symbolic speech, or the use of actions as a substitute for words, is generally protected. In that context,

flag burning has been upheld as a valid, if controversial or offensive, expression of political views (*Texas v. Johnson*, 1989). The type of offensive speech that has been labeled "hate speech" has also been held to be protected. Examples of hate speech upheld as content neutral are racial slurs, hateful religious propaganda, and cross burning. Speech codes on college and university campuses in the late 1980's and 1990's were struck down as unduly restrictive.

Obscenity is unprotected speech. Material may be deemed to offend accepted standards of decency and therefore be obscene if, taken as a whole, the material lacks serious literary, artistic, political, or scientific value, and appeals to the prurient interest in sex (*Miller v. California*, 1973). Regulation of obscene material does not reach an individual's home (*Stanley v. Georgia*, 1969), except in cases of child pornography; states can outlaw even private possession of child pornography (*Osborne v. Ohio*, 1990). Freedom of the press prohibits prior or previous restraint, a restriction on publication before it takes place or before published material is circulated, in nearly all situations. Prior restraint may be justified only when publication threatens national security, incites overthrow of the government, is obscene, or substantially interferes with others' private rights. Freedom of the press may conflict with the right of a criminal defendant to a fair trial, for example, leading to the imposition of limitations on the press to minimize pretrial publicity. Libel and slander are also unprotected forms of expression.

The Fourth, Fifth, Sixth, and Eighth Amendments apply to criminal procedure and law enforcement. The Fourth Amendment safeguards citizens from unreasonable searches and seizures by government officials absent probable cause and the issuance of a warrant. To resolve legal issues presented in this area, a court balances the citizen's right of personal privacy against the government's interest in law enforcement. Exceptions to the warrant requirement exist in cases of emergency or exigent circumstances, drug screening, searches incident to a lawful arrest, and consent searches. The exclusionary rule prohibits the use in criminal trials of items obtained as a result of an unreasonable search.

The Fifth Amendment contains the due process clause and prohibitions against self-incrimination and double jeopardy. Those guarantees are applicable in any legal proceeding, including grand jury hearings. The Sixth Amendment mandates a fair trial in criminal cases and contains specific guarantees: a speedy and public trial, an impartial jury, a right to confront one's accuser, and assistance of counsel. *Gideon v. Wainwright* (1963) added the guarantee of court-appointed counsel for indigent defendants in felony trials (later extended to misdemeanors). The Eighth Amendment prohibits imposition of excessive bail and proscribes cruel and unusual punishment (punishment generally considered "barbaric" in nature).

The Fourteenth Amendment. Ratified in 1868, this amendment prohibits any state from depriving any persons of "life, liberty, or property, without due process of law" or from denying any person within its jurisdiction "the equal protection of the laws." In the twentieth century the Supreme Court began to interpret the "due process" clause as requiring the states to respect important rights listed in the federal Bill of Rights deemed "implicit in the concept of ordered liberty." This "incorporation" of the Bill of Rights against the states involved numerous court decisions that occurred over several decades. It has resulted in a large role for the Supreme Court in policy areas previously outside federal control, such as school prayer, control of pornography, and abortion rights. The "equal protection" clause has had a major impact on racial discrimination, civil rights, and civil liberties cases. Holding that people similarly situated must be treated the same, the equal protection clause requires classifications that impinge on fundamental rights to withstand strict judicial scrutiny, or close examination. The same standard applies if the classification affects a "suspect" class, or a group of people who are powerless or saddled with disabilities, having received unequal treatment over time. In this regard, some race-conscious affirmative action policies have been upheld; others have been overturned.

Right of Privacy. Not explicitly mentioned in the Constitution, the right of privacy emanates from "penumbras" of several constitutional provisions that protect life from government interference: the First, Fourth, Fifth, Ninth, and Fourteenth Amendments. Among the most significant privacy cases are *Griswold v. Connecticut* (contraception, 1965), *Roe v. Wade* (abortion, 1973), and *Cruzan v. Director, Missouri Department of Health* (the "right to die," 1990).   —*Marcia J. Weiss*

See also Bill of Rights, U.S.; Civil liberties; Civil rights; Constitution, U.S.; Constitutional interpretation; Due process of law; Equal protection of the law; Federalism; Incorporation doctrine; Judicial review; Natural law and natural rights; Speech and press, freedom of; Supreme Court of the United States.

BIBLIOGRAPHY

Peter G. Renstrom, *Constitutional Law and Young Adults* (Santa Barbara, Calif.: ABC-Clio, 1992), is a guide to the Constitution, the court system, and key provisions of the Bill of Rights and Fourteenth Amendment with case references. It is comprehensive in scope and comprehensible to the general reader. Edward Samuel Corwin and J. W. Peltason, *Corwin and Peltason's Understanding the Constitution* (11th ed. New York: Holt, Rinehart and Winston, 1988), is a general overview. G. Alan Tarr, *Judicial Process and Judicial Policymaking* (St. Paul, Minn.: West, 1994), contains valuable information for those with some legal or political science background, as does Jerome A. Barron and C. Thomas Dienes, *Constitutional Law in a Nutshell* (2d ed. St. Paul, Minn.: West, 1994). Samuel Walker, *Hate Speech: The History of an American Controversy* (Lincoln: University of Nebraska Press, 1994), is a well-documented history of offensive speech as developed in case law and of First Amendment issues generally.

Consumer fraud

DEFINITION: Selling goods or services in a manner that is deliberately misleading or false

SIGNIFICANCE: Consumers have frequently been misled by false or confusing information and been sold products and services that do not perform as advertised

The buying and selling of goods and services have historically been characterized by the principle of *caveat emptor* ("let the buyer beware"). It has been assumed that it is the responsibility of the buyer to know what he or she is purchasing. That principle may work in a small economic system, such as a small town or a particular region of the country, and in many circumstances, because there may be strong social pressures on sellers to act responsibly; moreover, those who sell inferior or faulty products or services cannot long stay in business. Having the consumer assume full responsibility for faulty products or services can present problems, however, when they present dangers to public health or safety or unduly victimize buyers. For example, hundreds or even thousands of people across the country or the world could be poisoned or injured before a product such as a medicine could be withdrawn from the market.

The Nature of Consumer Fraud. Legally, "fraud" is selling a product or service under false pretenses. That is, fraud occurs when consumers do not understand what they are buying, know that they are getting an inferior or faulty product but have been induced to sign anyway, do not know about defects or problems with the product, are sold a product that might injure or kill them, are misled by someone who has a fiduciary responsibility to protect them from financial harm, are sold a product without benefit of disclosures required by law, or are sold a product in violation of the law by a professional who should know better. The key is that consumers are given incomplete, misleading, or false information about a product and do not fully understand what they are buying.

Concerns about consumer fraud are not new, although the rights of consumers have expanded in recent decades. Early attempts to regulate consumer fraud focused on medical equipment and medicines, financial institutions, foodstuffs, and a variety of other products and services. Legal restrictions on consumer fraud and product safety have expanded tremendously over the last half century and are enforced by federal and state regulatory agencies.

Product Safety and Information. The Food, Drug, and Cosmetic Act of 1938 (and amendments), for example, gave the Food and Drug Administration (FDA) the power to regulate food, drugs, food additives, medical devices, cosmetics, and other products sold to the public in the United States as well as to monitor and regulate the use of pesticides, food and color additives, animal drugs, biological material, and radiation. For such products or services to be sold in the United States, application must be made to the FDA (application must include results of scientific testing), and the agency must give its approval. FDA regulation reduces the potential danger to public health and increases the information available to the public about the products it uses. Similarly, the U.S. Department of Agriculture regulates and grades meats and other foodstuffs, and the Consumer Product Safety Commission

(CPSC) monitors and collects data on product safety and can force unsafe products to be removed from the market. The CPSC is also concerned with fair packaging, poison prevention, flammable fabrics, toy safety, refrigerator safety, and wool and fur products safety. The Truth in Packaging Act of 1966, for example, requires accurate information on product packaging to assure that consumers understand the contents and appropriate use and to minimize the potential for injuries or death.

Truth in Advertising and Selling. In addition to agencies that protect the public against faulty products and services, there are those with responsibility for assuring that consumers know what they are getting. For example, the Federal Trade Commission (FTC) enforces restrictions on unfair and deceptive practices, such as false advertising, consumer fraud, and abusive sales tactics. The FTC is concerned with sellers using misinformation designed to mislead consumers, including making unsubstantiated claims about a product's safety or effectiveness. For example, in the case of *Federal Trade Commission v. Colgate Palmolive Co.* in 1965, the Supreme Court ruled that the company had engaged in false and deceptive advertising because its advertisement claimed that the product Rapid Shave could shave sandpaper, but its television commercial actually used plexiglas onto which sand had been glued. The claim was not borne out by the test, in other words, and the Court required that the claim be withdrawn. The FTC also has responsibility for fraudulent "bait and switch" marketing, in which consumers are lured into a store by the prospect of purchasing a high value product and find that they can only get a lesser product, the seller actively discourages purchase of the less expensive product in favor of a more expensive one, or the seller does not have or only has a few of the advertised product available for purchase. Prohibited practices also include aggressive door-to-door selling that may coerce consumers into purchasing a product and sending unsolicited merchandise through the mails.

Product Quality and Warranties. The Magnuson-Moss Warranty Act of 1975 prohibits deceptive product warranties. It requires that sellers of products costing more than fifteen

Telemarketing is one area in which significant consumer fraud has occurred. (James L. Shaffer)

MAJOR CONSUMER PROTECTION LEGISLATION		
Date	*Legislation*	*Issue*
1906	Pure Food and Drug Act	Adulterated food and drugs
1914	Federal Trade Commission Act	Deceptive food, drug, and cosmetic advertising
1938	Food, Drug and Cosmetics Act	Safety of drugs
1958	Food, Drug and Cosmetics Act amendments	Safety of food additives; banning of carcinogenic additives
1962	Food, Drug and Cosmetics Act amendments	Effectiveness of drugs
1966	Fair Packaging and Labeling Act	Deceptive packaging and labeling
1966	National Traffic and Motor Vehicle Safety Act	Safety standards for tires and motor vehicles
1968	Truth in Lending Act	Informing consumers of total loan costs
1970	Highway Safety Act	Creation of National Highway Traffic Safety Administration
1972	Consumer Product Safety Act	Creation of Consumer Product Safety Commission

dollars provide a warranty in simple and clear language, disclosing information required by law and restricting disclaimers or modification of the warranty that may mislead consumers. Several states have also passed "lemon laws" to require disclosure of defects in automobiles that may lead to injuries or death and have set up arbitration processes to assist consumers in dealing with automobile dealers. Similar legislation has been suggested for disputes between homeowners and homebuilders.

Truth in Lending and Credit. The Truth-in-Lending Act of 1968 (with amendments) requires disclosure of information to those seeking credit. Regulation Z specifies the information that must be disclosed, including the cash or base price of the product being purchased, finance charge, annual percentage rate (APR) of the finance charge, payment procedures, and other charges. Regulations to reduce credit fraud have received attention because of the victimization of elderly homeowners by home mortgage and home improvement companies, causing them to lose their homes. Consumers who use their homes as security for credit have three business days to "rescind" the credit and back out of the deal. Creditors are required to let consumers know of that right and must refund any payments within twenty days of receiving the notice of rescission. If a creditor does not let the consumer know of that right, the consumer has up to three years to seek the refund.

Consumer fraud laws are often hotly debated. The extent to which government should protect buyers from sellers and what constitutes deceptive or fraudulent practices are major issues. While consumers can file suit when they feel misled about a product, legal action can be very expensive. Government regulation provides broader legal protection and a consistent national policy. — *William L. Waugh, Jr.*

See also Consumer rights movement; Criminal intent; Federal Trade Commission (FTC); Food and Drug Administration (FDA); Fraud; Mail fraud; Nader, Ralph; Price fixing; Products liability; Regulatory crime; Truth in Lending Act.

BIBLIOGRAPHY

Consumer fraud, a broad topic in business law, can be examined from a variety of perspectives. A good general text will cover the major types of fraud, ranging from product safety to warranty and disclosure issues. A recommended text is Henry R. Cheeseman, *Contemporary Business Law* (Englewood Cliffs, N.J.: Prentice Hall, 1994). The roles of government agencies in protecting consumers against fraud and assuring product safety are described in books on specific agencies and in some broader texts. Excellent descriptions of the roles and functions of the Consumer Product Safety Commission and the Food and Drug Administration can be found in Gary C. Bryner, *Bureaucratic Discretion: Law and Policy in Federal Regulatory Agencies* (New York: Pergamon Press, 1987).

Consumer rights movement

DEFINITION: The movement to assist consumers in selecting products and purchasing products less expensively and to regulate sellers of goods more effectively to assure product safety and quality

SIGNIFICANCE: The consumer rights movement, a social and political movement that began in the 1960's, increased consumer demand for product information, product quality, government regulation of product safety, and clarity in language and truthfulness in advertising and packaging

The consumer rights movement was born in the social and political activism of the 1960's, although some consumer rights have been protected for many years as a result of major public health disasters and financial scandals. For example, as a result of the Great Depression, the U.S. government developed comprehensive programs to monitor and regulate the operations of banks and other financial institutions. The objectives included protecting depositors from corrupt and inept bankers.

Often cited as inspiring the consumer rights movement was the publication of Ralph Nader's *Unsafe at Any Speed* in 1965. Nader's book led to passage of the National Traffic and Motor

Vehicle Safety Act of 1966, which mandated federal standards for vehicle safety. The success of Nader and his staff of "raiders" in getting Congress to address consumer issues encouraged activism by many other groups and encouraged lobbying for reform in many areas. For example, Maggie Kuhn, founder of the Gray Panthers, an advocacy group for older Americans, worked with Nader in pushing for a national health program and in lobbying for better regulation of nursing homes. The extent of consumer activism is apparent in the activities of the Consumer Federation of America, which was founded in 1967. It provides technical and political support to more than two hundred member organizations.

By the 1970's, consumer activism had encouraged the development of consumer affairs agencies in many state governments and had resulted in stronger consumer protection efforts by federal agencies. Many of the administrators drawn into the federal service came from consumer organizations such as Nader's Public Citizen group. One of the targets of Nader's criticism in the late 1960's was the Federal Trade Commission (FTC), which Nader and other consumer advocates believed was too business-oriented and generally uninterested in protecting consumers. A number of consumer rights leaders were appointed to positions with the FTC, the Environmental Protection Agency, the National Highway Traffic Safety Administration, and other agencies during the Jimmy Carter Administration, and the effect was more federal attention to consumers' rights and interests. President Carter's proposal for a department-level "consumer affairs agency," however, failed in Congress in February of 1978. By the 1980's, support for consumer rights was losing momentum. Presidents Ronald Reagan and George Bush were actively opposed to strong regulatory action, and consumer rights advocates shifted much of their lobbying to state legislatures.

The consumer rights movement is also a social phenomenon. Purchasing cooperatives are one aspect of the movement. People join "co-ops" in order to take advantage of economies of scale. Food, clothing, and other items are purchased at wholesale prices and sold to members with minimal charge. In many cases, the cooperatives provide access to organic foods and other goods that are not easily found. Private cooperatives still operate in some communities, but commercial "cooperatives" or buying clubs are becoming more popular in larger urban areas. Consumer information cooperatives, such as Consumers Union, provide consumers with information on product quality and safety. Purchasing services that, for example, negotiate automobile purchases are a newer manifestation of the consumer movement.

See also Consumer fraud; Nader, Ralph; Products liability; Regulatory crime; Truth in Lending Act.

Contempt of court

DEFINITION: Conduct that obstructs a court's administration of justice or undermines its dignity

SIGNIFICANCE: A court's power to punish contempt helps to safeguard the efficient administration of justice by assuring

that its orders are complied with and its basic dignity preserved

Contempt of court has its origins in the period when all English courts were part of the Curia Regia, or court of the sovereign. Disparagement of either the sovereign or his courts was punishable as contempt. Today, contempt of court includes disregard for, or disobedience of, a court's order as well as misbehavior in the presence of the court which tends to bring the authority and administration of the law into disrespect. Contempts are usually classified as being either civil or criminal in nature. A civil contempt is one involving disobedience of an order of the court rendered on behalf of one party. Criminal contempt involves disrespect of the court itself or conduct which undermines the court's dignity. Civil contempts are remedied by a fine intended to recompense the party for whose benefit an order was made. Criminal contempts are subject to punishment in the form of a fine or imprisonment.

See also Bailiff; Bench warrant; Chicago seven trial; Civil procedure; Criminal procedure; Judicial system, U.S.; Subpoena power.

Contingency fee

DEFINITION: A method of payment to an attorney in civil lawsuits in which payment is based on a percentage of the recovery if the case is won

SIGNIFICANCE: This type of payment has enabled many injured people who could not otherwise afford the services of an attorney to file lawsuits

An attorney working on a contingency basis does not collect a retainer from the client. The percentage of recovery to be paid must be fair to the client and is sometimes regulated by statute or court rule. The figure ranges from 20 percent to 60 percent depending on many factors, such as the amount of expected awards, time involved, and whether the case is settled out of court.

If the attorney does not win the case, the client pays no fee: The fee is contingent on winning the case. A lawyer therefore will not take a case on a contingency basis unless the plaintiff has a strong case for a favorable outcome against the defendant.

See also Civil procedure; Compensatory damages; Punitive damages; Suit; Tort reform.

Contraception. *See* Birth control, right to

Contract, freedom of

DEFINITION: The freedom of individuals to make voluntary and informed choices as to the terms and type of a legally enforceable private agreement

SIGNIFICANCE: Freedom of contract is the central feature of classical contract law and has been described as the fundamental and indispensable requisite of economic progress

Freedom of contract allows individuals to agree privately and voluntarily as to the type of terms of a contractual relationship. The principle of freedom of contract is sometimes called "liberty to contract" or "autonomy of contract." Freedom of contract is based on the concept of self-determination and the freedom of individuals to choose their own destiny without restrictions. It recognizes that every citizen has a right to contract freely for the price of labor, services, or property. The principle includes two important elements; the actual power to agree to the type and terms of the agreement, and the ability to enforce of the contract.

History. The law of the United States is founded on the common law as developed in England. Prior to the eighteenth century, freedom of contract was not generally recognized in England. During the eighteenth century, however, England became a center of international commerce and trade, and freedom of contract became important to commerce. Freedom of contract was liberally construed in the late nineteenth century as commerce and trade expanded. In the twentieth century, limitations and restrictions have been imposed on the freedom of contract both in England and in the United States. The era of limitations has been labeled by some academics as the "decline of contract."

The United States Constitution does not specifically state that individuals have the freedom to make contracts; however, the freedom to make contracts is embraced in the conception of liberty that is guaranteed by the Constitution and applied to the states by the Fourteenth Amendment. The United States Supreme Court has recognized that the freedom of contract is a qualified right as opposed to an absolute right. In other words, there is no absolute freedom to do as one desires or to contract as one chooses.

Limitations. Limitations on the freedom of contract can arise from the unequal bargaining power of the parties to the contract. The ability of individuals to contract freely is dependent on their relative social and economic status. The social and economic status of the parties can affect their relative bargaining strength, which in turn affects the parties' ability to choose freely the terms or type of agreement that will govern their relationship. In a large number of modern contracts there is little or no freedom of contract because the parties do not have equal bargaining power or the terms of the contract are fixed by one of the parties and are not open to negotiation.

Limitations on the freedom to contract can also arise through governmental or legislative actions. The government has the power to restrain some individuals from all contracts, as well as all individuals from some contracts. Generally, freedom of contract is limited on the basis of public and government policy considerations. Public policy limits contractual choices based on considerations of the health, welfare, morals, and safety of society. Government policy limits contractual choices based on the promotion of certain goals or objectives. Contracts that are contrary to public or government policy will not be upheld or enforced.

The legislature, through administrative regulations and laws, also restricts the parties' right to make choices in private agreements. Such restrictions are justified as being in the best interest of the public. For example, antidiscrimination laws prohibit many contracts and contract provisions that might discriminate against protected groups. Consumer protection laws prohibit certain types of contracts and terms that would be unfair to consumers. Antitrust and unfair business practice laws prohibit certain agreements that would have detrimental impacts on business competition and commerce. Minimum wage laws and maximum interest rate laws apply to limit contractual relationships. Sales, loans, and the prices for many goods and services are also regulated.

The courts limit the freedom to contract by applying legal principles and doctrines that relate to the enforcement and formation of contracts. Historically, the courts gave great deference to private agreements and were reluctant to interfere with the terms on which the parties had agreed. When contracts or contract terms are contrary to public policy, however, the courts will not enforce them. For example, contract law is based on the principle that the parties have entered into an agreement and participated in good faith. The courts are reluctant to enforce a contract in which a party attempts to take advantage of a lack of good faith. Further, the freedom of contract will not be upheld if the subject matter of the contract is illegal. For example, a wagering agreement may not be enforced in a state where gambling is illegal.

Freedom to contract is based on the parties having the capacity to choose and make voluntary and informed choices. Therefore, freedom of contract may not be enforced where a party has not been properly informed as to the material terms or provisions of the contract. Failure to be informed often occurs where there have been misrepresentation, fraud, mistake, or nondisclosure of material information in the contract or during contract negotiations. Generally, the courts will not allow the contract or its provisions to operate to the detriment of the innocent party. Additionally, the parties' choice may not be upheld where one of the parties did not have the capacity to make an informed choice because of a mental incapacity such as intoxication, mental incompetency, or being too young to understand. Finally, an agreement may not be upheld if it was not voluntary, as in cases where an individual entered into a contract because of undue influence or duress. — *Bruce E. May*

See also Arbitration and mediation; Capitalism; *Charles River Bridge v. Warren Bridge Co.*; Commercial law; Common law; Contract law; *Dartmouth College v. Woodward*.

BIBLIOGRAPHY

Patrick S. Atiyah, *The Rise and Fall of Freedom of Contract* (Oxford: Clarendon Press, 1979); Michael J. Trebilcock, *The Limits of Freedom of Contract* (Cambridge, Mass.: Harvard University Press, 1993); E. Allen Farnsworth, *Contracts* (2d ed. Boston: Little, Brown, 1990); John D. Calamari and Joseph M. Perillo, *The Law of Contracts* (3d ed. St. Paul, Minn.: West, 1987).

Contract law

DEFINITION: A contract is a promise or set of promises that the law will enforce

SIGNIFICANCE: Contracts allow parties to shape legal obligations to fit their specific needs and to create obligations that support planned endeavors and long-term activities

Contracts involve promises of future action that the government will help benefited parties enforce. Contract law defines the means for making legally enforceable promises, standards for measuring breaches of those promises, and remedies for such breaches.

Typically, a contract is formed through an exchange of promises. For example, one person might promise to pay for a car tomorrow if a second person promises to deliver the car to the first person's house. Should either of the persons refuse to perform their respective promises at the appointed time, the person who was to receive the benefit of the breached promise can seek a legal remedy. The objective of that remedy will be to put the party in as good a position (at lease economically) as if the promise had been performed. Hence, contract law confirms one's ability to count on the benefit of promises by others because those persons will either perform as they promised or the law will provide a substitute remedy that is economically as good as performance.

History. English common law is the source of many features of American contract law. English courts developed a general basis for enforcing promises by adopting certain doctrines from the law of torts. As of the beginning of the fifteenth century, English tort law recognized an action of "trespass on the case" or *assumpsit* (from Latin, meaning that the defendant undertook something). This type of action arose in cases where a defendant undertook to perform a duty and then performed it in a way that caused harm to the person to whom the duty was owed. For example, a case in 1436 explained this type of liability as follows:

> If a carpenter makes a [promise to] me to make me a house good and strong and of a certain form, and he makes me a house which is weak and bad and of another form, I shall have an action of trespass on my case.

Liability under these circumstances extended to amounts necessary to place promisees in the position they would have been if they had never relied on the promises involved. In the case of the defective construction described above, this equaled the amount paid for the construction less any amount the defective construction had benefited the promisee. While this type of liability still had severe limitations, it tended to promote transactions involving delayed performance by reassuring parties relying on such performance of a restorative remedy if the performance was defective.

Eventually, this type of liability was expanded in two important respects to form the basis for modern contract law. First, from cases involving affirmative misconduct by promisors (such as the construction case described above), common-law courts at the end of the sixteenth century expanded the action of *assumpsit* to include cases of promisors' inaction leading to harm. Second, the remedies in these sorts of actions were expanded not only to serve restorative ends in the sense of returning promisees to their positions prior to the making of promises but also to protect their expectations by placing promisees in the positions they would have reasonably ex-

pected to be in had promises been carried out. For example, in the case described above, this sort of expectancy remedy would equal the difference between the value of the house as promised and the value of house as defectively constructed. This type of remedy improved the confidence of promisees in promised performance by ensuring that promisees could count on reaching the economic position implied by the promises.

American contract law incorporated these principles and added several further rules that made contract standards more flexible and useful in the country's expanding free enterprise system. Lawmakers augmented common-law rules with standards that clarified the means to form enforceable agreements and the breadth of enforceable contract terms that private parties could adopt. "Freedom of contract" reached its peak in the late 1800's, when parties were given great latitude to define (and limit) their rights through contracts. At the same time, severe limitations were placed on governmental authority to restrict contracting processes.

Following this peak in unrestricted contracting, standards have increasingly constrained contracting through two mechanisms. First, consumer protection standards have been enacted to combat contracts formed under conditions of poor consumer information or extreme contracting pressures. Some such standards give consumers several days to reconsider contracts free of contracting pressures. Other such standards nullify particularly onerous terms of consumer contracts or add protective terms that cannot be eliminated from contracts. Second, the power of the state to enact regulatory or protective legislation that impinges on the freedom of contract of particular individuals has been recognized in many contexts. This reflects the view, prevalent particularly since the late 1930's, that in some spheres (such as labor negotiations or environmental protection) government action is necessary to protect key interests because private bargaining to protect those interests will be ineffective. Private protection through contracts and other privately initiated mechanisms is still the primary means for individuals to safeguard their interests, however, and government officials designing regulatory and protective legislation are increasingly attentive to the need to minimize impacts of regulation on free contracting.

Underlying Policies. Contract law serves important societal and individual goals. From the perspective of society as a whole, the law of contracts furthers general economic welfare by encouraging parties to enter into productive transactions that involve planning for and reliance on future performance. Given the scale of many modern business transactions and the need for coordinated actions by multiple parties to accomplish those transactions, the certainty engendered by contracts promotes important business activities. Contracts provide similar support to other types of individual and group activities that require certainty about group action or long-term behavior.

From an individual perspective, contracts aid in personal fulfillment and success by better allowing people to plan for future activities and to carry out their expectations. In everyday living, contract laws assist individuals in having confidence about the meaning of promises arising in such common contexts as mail order transactions, product warranties, service contracts, and life insurance agreements. Without contract laws, the value of these types of promises and one's willingness to count on their fulfillment would be severely undercut.

Overall, contract law lies at an unusual juncture of utilitarian and libertarian policies. From a utilitarian perspective, the freedom to contract maximizes the welfare of contracting parties and therefore the good of society as a whole. From a libertarian perspective, such freedom gives individuals a sphere of influence in which they can act freely and pursue their interests.

Features of Contract Law. Two fundamental themes permeate contract law. First, not all promises lead to contracts. The law will not stand behind all promises, but will instead only enforce promises made under certain circumstances, involving limited types of valuable exchanges, and capable of reasonably precise understanding and enforcement.

In part, these limitations on the legal enforceability of promises reflect an unwillingness of courts and governments to invoke judicial machinery and expense in support of insignificant or uncertain promises. Some limitations also protect parties from being held responsible for promises made in circumstances where their free choice to enter into the promises is in doubt, such as promises obtained through fraud or duress or from a minor. Restrictions on the enforceability of promises also stem from the limited capacity of courts and juries to evaluate and enforce vague promises.

Second, the law of contracts is forward looking. That is, it is primarily concerned with future performances, rather than past exchanges of things of value. If A promises to sell his car to B and then does so, but a week later it is determined that the car was stolen from C, the question of whether B is entitled to the car will be resolved as a matter of property law rather than contract law. This is a property law question because it relates to which party's continued control over the car will best serve society's interests—B because she bought the car with no notice of the theft or C because the car was stolen from him.

Assuming that B must give back the car, however, contract law will bear on whether A fully performed his obligations at the time of the sale. This last question raises contract law issues since it relates to the future performance obligations created when the parties made their contract. In this case, A may have implicitly promised that he would convey good title to the car and, since he did not, he would be deemed to have breached his part of the contract. Alternatively, if A was a participant in the theft of the car from C, the contract to sell the car might simply be unenforceable as an illegal contract to dispose of stolen goods or as a contract induced by fraud.

Contract Formation. A contract between two parties is formed through an offer and an acceptance. An offer is created through a statement or conduct that indicates a person is willing to be bound to a contract if the terms of the offer are accepted. Usually, an offer will specify a promise to do or refrain from doing something. For example, if A points to his car and says to B, "I will sell you this car if you will pay me $1,000," this will generally be taken as an offer in which A promises to take the steps necessary to transfer title to the car if B pays the indicated amount. This promise will ripen into a contract if it is accepted by B. The offer itself implies the steps that B must take to form the contract—she must pay A the $1,000 within a reasonable time.

Beyond requiring that the formation of a contract involve an offer and an acceptance, contract laws require that the promises of the parties have certain characteristics in order to create an enforceable agreement. Generally, a party to a contract must promise to do something that the party is not already legally required or obligated to do. This can involve a promise to refrain from doing something an individual is otherwise entitled to do, such as a promise to refrain from smoking. A promise must also be part of a bargain. This requirement is reflected in two tests. First, a promise must be made for the purpose of inducing another party to restrict their conduct under a contract. Second, the return promise or conduct of the other party must be prompted by the first party's promise.

The formation of contracts is also subject to limitations related to the capacity of individuals to decide to enter into contracts. Certain individuals, such as minors or mentally incompetent persons, are deemed unable to form enforceable contracts because they lack the capacity to make responsible independent judgments. Similarly, contracts formed on the basis of fraud or duress are unenforceable because the individuals involved have not had a fair opportunity to evaluate the surrounding facts and decide to enter into contracts.

To deter persons from using contracts to gain rewards for illegal conduct, contracts are unenforceable if they are either formed through illegal means (for example, a contract formed as the result of a bribe) or to be carried out through illegal conduct (such as a contract to engage in fraudulent activities).

In order to combat fraud and promote certainty in measuring later performance, some contracts must be in writing (or at least evidenced by a written document) to be enforceable. The nature of contracts subject to this requirement varies from state to state. In many jurisdictions, the requirement that a contract be in writing applies to the following types of agreements: (1) a promise to answer for the debts of another, (2) a contract to transfer an interest in real property, (3) a promise which by its terms will not be fully performed within one year from its making, (4) a promise made in consideration of marriage such as a prenuptial agreement, and (5) a contract for the sale of goods with a price of $500 or more.

Performance Under Contracts. The performance required under a contract is determined by interpreting the terms of the parties' agreement. The parties are free to define the required performance in detailed terms and to redefine the requirements of the contract by mutual consent during the life of the contract.

Where the parties to a contract have used general or ambiguous terms to describe the obligations of the parties, several rules of interpretation are used to give meaning to those terms. In most contexts, contract terms are interpreted in the light of the prior course of performance of the contract at hand, the course of prior dealings between the parties before their entry into the present contract, and customary usages of trade in the field addressed by the contract.

For example, if a contract called for the delivery of one thousand "chickens" with no definition given for the latter term, the type of fowl that would be acceptable would be determined in the light of these rules. If the parties had established standards for accepting fowl in earlier deliveries under the present contract or in dealings under prior contracts, these standards would be applied once again. If there were no prior understanding among these parties but the term "chicken" had a standard meaning among tradespersons such as the parties to this agreement, then that standard meaning would be presumed to be what the parties probably meant.

A number of other interpretational rules are widely used. Specific contract terms are given meaning over conflicting terms in the same agreement that are more general. In choosing among reasonable alternative meanings, contract terms are construed to have the meaning that is least favorable to the party that drafted them, since that party had the best opportunity to include language to avoid this onerous interpretation if it was not intended. Where parties have attempted to form an agreement, they are presumed to have intended that their contract terms be given effect. Hence, where only one of several available interpretations will lead to an enforceable agreement, courts will tend to construe an agreement in the manner that will make it lawful and enforceable.

Remedies for Contract Breaches. Contract laws provide for a number of remedies following a failure of one or more parties to provide promised performance. In certain circumstances, breaches of contracts are excused. Where performance of a contract is rendered impossible or highly impractical for unexpected reasons through no fault of the parties, the failure to render that performance will usually be excused. Thus, if A contracts to rent B's theater on July 1, and on June 1 the theater burns down without any fault on the part of B, B's obligation to rent the theater space is deemed discharged by the destruction of the subject matter of the contract.

Similarly, if the purpose for which performance is sought becomes unattainable, a related contract may become unenforceable. For example, if a person contracts to rent a hotel room at an elevated charge for the purpose of watching a parade from a hotel window and the parade is cancelled, the contract for the room may be unenforceable because its underlying purpose (to see the parade) has been frustrated.

Another basis on which performance may be excused is the illegality of performance. In some instances, performance that is lawful when a contract is made is prohibited by the time performance is due. Under these circumstances, the prohibition is given effect and the failure to render the performance is excused. Thus, if A contracts on January 1 to buy B's handgun on February 1, but on January 15 the local supervisors ban the sale of such weapons, the contract will be deemed unenforceable because of the supervening illegality of performance.

Where a party materially breaches a contract—that is, fails to meet the terms of an agreement in a manner that is significantly prejudicial to the interests of the other party—the party who has not breached can generally suspend his or her future performance and seek a remedy for the breach. Where a party's breach is minor and the party has substantially performed, however, the other party will still need to render his or her performance while seeking a remedy for the breach.

In most instances, the remedy available for a contract breach is an award of a dollar amount sufficient to place the nonbreaching party to the contract in the same economic position that the party would have been in had the breach not occurred. This rule is tempered somewhat by the limitation that types of losses that were not reasonably foreseeable by the breaching party are not recoverable. For example, assume that a factory operator takes a key machinery part to a repair shop and the repairperson at the shop fails to repair and return the part to the party by the date agreed upon. The repairperson's liability for the extra expense of keeping the plant idle after the agreed return date will be recoverable only if the repairperson had some reason to know that the failure to meet the agreed return date would have these types of consequences.

Where the loss to a nonbreaching party cannot be accurately measured in dollar terms (such as when a contract calls for the sale of a unique painting), courts may be willing to order specific performance of contract terms. This type of remedy will be carried out through the issuance of a judicial injunction compelling adherence to the contract terms, coupled with contempt sanctions for failure to comply with the injunction.

— *Richard S. Gruner*

See also Banking law; *Charles River Bridge v. Warren Bridge Co.*; Commercial law; Common law; Consent decree; Contract, freedom of; *Dartmouth College v. Woodward*; Fraud; Injunction; Property rights.

BIBLIOGRAPHY

The historical development of contract law is described in Kevin M. Teeven, *A History of the Anglo-American Common Law of Contract* (New York: Greenwood Press, 1990), and Grant Gilmore, *The Death of Contract* (Columbus: Ohio State University Press, 1974). Present contract law standards are summarized in John D. Calamari and Joseph M. Perillo, *The Law of Contracts* (3d ed. St. Paul, Minn.: West, 1987); E. Allan Farnsworth, *Contracts* (2d ed. Boston: Little, Brown, 1990); and James J. White and Robert S. Summers, *Uniform Commercial Code* (3d ed. St. Paul, Minn.: West, 1988). Policy issues affecting the possible future development of contract law are evaluated in Richard Craswell and Alan Schwartz, eds., *Foundations of Contract Law* (New York: Oxford University Press, 1994), and Peter Linzer, ed., *A Contracts Anthology* (Cincinnati, Ohio: Anderson, 1989).

Contributing to the delinquency of a minor

DEFINITION: Assisting or encouraging a minor to commit a crime or otherwise engage in unruly behavior

SIGNIFICANCE: The notion of "contributing" to a minor's delinquency recognizes the relative vulnerability of children and the special responsibilities of adults

Contributing to the delinquency of a minor can take many forms. It can be as blatant as helping a minor to commit a theft or any other crime. Helping a minor to obtain controlled substances such as drugs or alcohol also can be considered contributing to delinquency. Exposing a minor to obscene material and engaging in sexual relations with a minor can fall under this category as well. In all these and other cases of contributing to the delinquency of a minor, there is an assumption that the perpetrator is fostering a tendency toward crime or unruly conduct. Whether the minor has truly become "delinquent" is a secondary point.

There is significant variation across jurisdictions in the age of majority, the definition of "contributing," and the interpretation of delinquency. The crime is defined as either a misdemeanor or a felony, depending on the state and the circumstances. In some states the crime falls under "endangering the welfare of a minor." Many states authorize juvenile courts to hear cases of contributing to the delinquency of a minor.

See also Juvenile delinquency; Juvenile justice system; Majority, age of; Status offense.

Cooley, Thomas (Jan. 6, 1824, near Attica, N.Y.—Sept. 12, 1898, Ann Arbor, Mich.)

IDENTIFICATION: American jurist

SIGNIFICANCE: Cooley was the author of influential books about law, a judge on the Michigan Supreme Court, a distinguished law teacher, and the first chairman of the Interstate Commerce Commission

After working as compiler of Michigan laws, Thomas McIntyre Cooley was appointed to the newly opened University of Michigan Law Department in 1859. Six years later he was elected to the Michigan Supreme Court, remaining on the court twenty-one years. A recognized authority on the history of American constitutional law and the common law, Cooley in 1868 published his most influential book, *Treatise on the Constitutional Limitations Which Rest upon the Legislative Power of the States of the American Union*. Going through six editions by 1890, the book had greater sales and was quoted more often than any other work of law written in the second half of the nineteenth century. Cooley's works emphasized a structural analysis of constitutional power and presented a substantive definition of "due process," based on the "established principles" and "settled usages" of property rights. His views on due process have been somewhat distorted so as to support a conservative "freedom of contract" doctrine. Actually, Cooley was a critic of excessive corporate power, and he defended Jeffersonian values, protection for labor, individual liberties, rights of local government, and judicial self-restraint.

See also Common law; Contract, freedom of; Due process of law; Jeffersonian democracy; Jurisprudence; Property rights.

Cooper v. Aaron

COURT: U.S. Supreme Court

DATE: Ruling issued September 12, 1958

SIGNIFICANCE: The Supreme Court ruled that the threat of violence or racial unrest was not sufficient grounds for postponing school integration and that governors and state legislators were bound by the decisions of the U.S. Supreme Court

In *Brown v. Board of Education* (1954) the Supreme Court ordered an end to segregated schools and overturned the "separate but equal" doctrine established in *Plessy v. Ferguson* (1896). The ambiguity about how to implement school desegregation, however, created the opportunity for school boards to delay and defy the court's order.

After the *Brown* decision, the Little Rock, Arkansas, school board approved a plan calling for the desegregation of grades ten through twelve in 1957, to be followed by the desegregation of junior high schools and, finally, the elementary schools. The plan was to be completed by the 1963 school year.

Nine black students, carefully selected by the National Association for the Advancement of Colored People (NAACP), were to begin integration of Central High School on September 3, 1957. The day before desegregation was to begin, Governor Orval Faubus ordered the Arkansas National Guard to prevent the black students from enrolling. Governor Faubus claimed that he acted to prevent violence from occurring. After three weeks, a federal court injunction forced the National Guard to withdraw. On September 23, the nine black students entered Central High School and were met by an unruly mob. President Dwight D. Eisenhower was forced to dispatch federal troops to Little Rock to enforce the Court's desegregation order. In the face of the civil unrest, the school board asked for and received a two-and-a-half-year delay in their desegregation plan. The NAACP appealed the delay in *Cooper v. Aaron*.

There were two primary issues confronting the U.S. Supreme Court. First, could the desegregation plan be postponed because of the fear of civil unrest? A unanimous Supreme Court emphatically said no: "The law and order are not here to be preserved by depriving the Negro children of their constitutional rights." Second, were the governor and legislature bound by decisions of the federal court? Invoking the supremacy clause of the Constitution, the Court said: "No state legislative, executive or judicial officer can War against the Constitution without violating his undertaking to support it."

Although Governor Faubus lost the legal battle, he became a political folk hero in Arkansas and was elected to six consecutive terms (1955-1967). President Eisenhower was both praised and condemned for his actions. He was praised for sending in federal troops to enforce the Court's decision and condemned for failing to endorse personally the *Brown* decision and lend the weight and prestige of the White House to the Court's ruling. The *Cooper* case was the first legal confrontation over the enforcement of *Brown v. Board of Education*. The courts stood alone in this enforcement effort until Congress passed the 1964 Civil Rights Act. The Civil Rights Act endorsed the

Brown decision and cut off federal funds to school districts refusing to comply with the Court's desegregation decision.

See also *Brown v. Board of Education*; Civil Rights Act of 1964; Eisenhower, Dwight D.; Little Rock school integration crisis; *Plessy v. Ferguson*; Racial and ethnic discrimination; Segregation, *de facto* and *de jure*; Supremacy clause.

Copyrights, patents, and trademarks

Definition: Copyrights, patents, and trademarks protect what is collectively referred to as "intellectual property"

Significance: Owners of intellectual property have the right to prevent unauthorized use, but what amounts to unauthorized use of intellectual property varies widely depending on the type—as do ways of obtaining such rights initially

Information is often regarded as the essential raw material of commerce. Information that cannot be literally locked up is protected by intellectual property laws. For many years, strong intellectual property rights were thought to be against the public interest, but since the mid-1980's such rights have come to be widely regarded as important to a strong national economy.

Historical Background. Federal patent and copyright laws are based on Article I, section 8, clause 8 of the U.S. Constitution. It provides that "Congress shall have power . . . to promote the progress of science and useful arts, by securing for limited times to authors and inventors the exclusive right to their respective writings and discoveries." That clause is, in turn, based on two independent English laws passed many years apart: the statute of monopolies (1625, applicable to patents) and the statute of Anne (1710, regarding copyright). States are not permitted to make patent laws. State copyright laws can govern only works that have not yet been "fixed in a tangible medium"—for example, songs that have not been recorded.

U.S. trademark law also comes from England, but from the courts rather than Parliament. The U.S. Constitution makes no provision for trademarks, and in 1879 the Supreme Court declared the first federal trademark statute to be unconstitutional. Since then, however, the Court has dramatically expanded congressional power over commerce affecting interstate transactions. Thus the federal law, reflected in the 1946 Lanham Act (as amended), is important, as are the laws of the various states.

Copyrights. Copyright can protect a wide variety of works. Besides books, motion pictures, photographs, and music, it can protect such things as architecture, sculpture, and computer software. With copyright often extending fifty years beyond the lifetime of the longest-living author, qualifying works are protected under provisions in Title 17 of the U.S. Code as soon as they are recorded in some form. Also, because the United States has signed several international copyright treaties, most notably the Berne Convention, copyrights automatically extend throughout much of the world. This is not true for any other kind of intellectual property.

Copyright notice and the depositing of copies of works with the Copyright Office are no longer needed for protection within the United States. The first is important because, until recently, works published without a notice that they were indeed copyrighted materials could be copied by anyone for any purpose. Because of that, many publishers still provide notice. Copyright registration is needed only if owners of works created in the United States wish to sue. Registering before infringement occurs allows substantial statutory damages and attorney fees. Registration cost twenty dollars as of 1995, and it rarely requires professional help. Many works of a single "author" can be included in one registration.

Although obtained more easily and cheaply than patents, copyrights offer less protection. Independently created works (such as independent photographs of the same object from the same angle) do not infringe on a copyright, even if they are identical, but defendants have difficulty convincing courts that they did not copy published works. Also, copyrights do not protect ideas. Someone who devises a new way of doing something and writes a book about it can only prevent others from copying the book—not from using the idea or even from writing another book about it.

The biggest problem many copyright owners face is practical. Computer programs are the best example. Much software retailing for hundreds of dollars can be duplicated for pennies. Such duplication is illegal, but owners have great difficulty enforcing their rights. The best they can do is tell those who copy illegally that this increases prices for people who pay and sometimes puts software publishers out of business.

Copyright Fair Use. Copying, or otherwise using, protected works is sometimes permitted under the doctrine of fair use. Fair use was invented by the courts, but teachers, librarians, and others demanded that it be addressed in the copyright statute. Publishers, too, were concerned. As a result, it was included in the last major revision of the statute in 1976.

The basic fair use provision cites four factors that affect whether otherwise illegal use is fair: the user's purpose, the nature of the work used, the fraction used, and the effect on the owner's (copyright holder's) income. Specific fair uses occupy about half of the statute. Some focus on the work; for example, anyone can back up software. Other sections focus on users (for example, teachers and librarians). Fair use is complicated, and even most law professors have no idea what they can or cannot do as teachers. A 1994 Supreme Court ruling in a dispute over a rap version of the song "Pretty Woman" (*Campbell v. Acuff-Rose Music*) clarified only one or two major issues. For most people, the best approach is to ask copyright owners for permission.

Patents. Of the several forms of intellectual property, patents offer the strongest protection because they can be used to prevent independent inventors from practicing protected technology. They are also the most expensive to get, however, rarely costing less than five thousand dollars, and they are the most expensive to preserve and enforce. The basic patent statute appears in Title 35 of the U.S. Code. It provides for three distinct kinds of patent: utility, design, and plant. Design patents cover only ornamentation, and plant patents cover only certain asexually propagated plants. Utility patents are concerned with how a wide range of subject matter works, and they can even cover genetically engineered plants or animals. Because utility patents are far more numerous and are what people generally mean when they refer to "patents," design and plant patents will not be further considered.

To obtain a patent, one must file an application with the U.S. Patent and Trademark Office. After receipt, applications are assigned to patent examiners to ensure that they cover proper subject matter and otherwise meet statutory requirements such as utility, novelty, and unobviousness. Examination usually takes eighteen months or longer and involves at least two negotiations over "claims" appearing at the end of each patent. Claims set forth, as the metes and bounds in a deed, what is protected. Few people appreciate that claims may be very specific or very general—they may cover the intellectual equivalent of a square inch of Arctic tundra or a square mile of Manhattan. Securing proper patent protection requires considerable skill, because patent owners need the broadest possible protection. If claims cover too much territory, however, a court will find them invalid.

Patent law is very complex, but the most important thing for inventors to know is that anything offered for sale instantly loses potential patent protection throughout most of the world and, after a year, loses possible protection in the United States. Another important point is that it is often much easier to patent inventions than to find people who will pay money for them. Many patents do not make it to market because independent inventors fail to consider such factors as whether their inventions might cost more to make than consumers would be willing to pay for them. Finally, many people do not understand that "patent pending" provides little useful information. No rights exist until the patent is issued, and even then they amount to no more than the claims specifically provide.

Trademarks. Everyone is familiar with trademarks such as Coca-Cola, Chevrolet, and H&R Block. (The last is technically a "service mark," because the firm sells tax services rather than goods, but this distinction is rarely important.) Owners of trademarks can prevent others from using "confusingly similar" marks on goods or services without their permission. Yet trademark rights are very different from patents and copyrights: They cannot be used to stop others from copying the goods or services themselves as long as consumers can recognize them as having a different commercial source.

As the distance between manufacturers and consumers increases, trademarks become more important to people on both ends of the chain. Without trademark rights, any restaurant could sell a "Big Mac," and consumers would have no more idea of what they might get than when they ordered a generic hamburger. Consumers could not seek products with which they or their friends have had happy experiences. Worse, they would have considerable difficulty in avoiding low-quality or overpriced goods. Even with trademarks, consumers must be alert to counterfeit merchandise. Conversely, if people were not willing to pay a premium for such things as superior quality or a no-questions-asked return policy, manufacturers would have no way to recover extra costs.

The longer trademarks or service marks are used, the more valuable they become. Often a firm's trademarks are its most valuable assets. Companies that avoid marks confusingly similar to others' marks, for example, have legal rights as soon as consumers can identify their trademarks as indicating a specific commercial source. Nevertheless, because some kinds of marks are stronger than others, companies usually seek expert professional advice. They also usually find it worthwhile to register their marks. Trademarks can be registered cheaply at the state level, but this confers few advantages. Federal registration under the Lanham Act at the U.S. Patent and Trademark Office (PTO) is much better. Although this can easily cost more than a thousand dollars, even smaller firms find that federal registration is worth much more.

Without federal registration, rights in a mark exist only in locations where a firm's products or services have been sold. Thus, smaller firms may encounter prior users with superior rights when they try to expand. Federal registration does not cut off prior users' rights, but it gives rights in unused territory throughout the United States. Thus, if a firm searches to avoid marks being used anywhere in the country, registers its mark with the PTO, and is reasonably diligent in protecting its rights, the risk of being excluded from a new market is very small. Also, rights involved in federally registered marks are generally stronger.

Trade Secrets. A trade secret is any commercially valuable information that is kept secret. In all states, sometimes under a statute such as the Uniform Trade Secrets Act, firms can be prevented from using certain information acquired from other firms (for example, from new employees who used to work for a competitor).

In 1964, the U.S. Supreme Court suggested that such state law might discourage people from seeking patents and might therefore be federally preempted. When faced squarely with the issue in 1976, the Court, in *Kewanee Oil Co. v. Bicron Corp.*, found state trade secret law constitutional. Perhaps emboldened by that decision, some states passed statutes forbidding copying, or "reverse engineering," boats bought in the open market. In 1989, in *Bonito Boat Inc. v. Thunder Craft Boats*, the Court found those statutes unconstitutional, making it clear that states cannot forbid the copying of anything found in the marketplace. Those two cases are crucial for an understanding of trade secret law.   —*Thomas G. Field, Jr.*

See also Commercial law; Constitution, U.S.; Property rights.

BIBLIOGRAPHY

Advice on protecting intellectual property may be found in Thomas Field, Jr., *Avoiding Patent, Trademark, and Copyright Problems* (Washington, D.C.: U.S. Small Business Administration, 1992). The Copyright Office, Washington, D.C., offers a variety of informative publications on registration as well as a fair use guide (*Circular 21*). The Patent and Trademark Office in Washington, D.C., publishes booklets about patents and trademarks. See also Frank H. Andorka, *A Practical Guide to Copyrights and Trademarks* (New York: World Almanac,

1989), and David A. Burge, *Patent and Trademark Tactics and Practice* (New York: John Wiley and Sons, 1984), but keep in mind that copyright, patent, and trademark law is always evolving, so the older the work, the more out of date it will be.

Coroner

Definition: An official of a municipal corporation who is responsible for determining the cause of death in violent or suspicious deaths

Significance: The coroner provides evidence to aid the police in their investigation

The office of coroner is based in English common law. As early as the sixteenth century, investigations into suspicious deaths were made by the king's officer, the Custos Placitorum Coronae (guardian of the decrees of the crown), who not only investigated unexplained deaths but also disposed of the deceased person's property after a suicide or homicide. William Pitt is believed to have been the first coroner in the American colonies.

The office of coroner is usually an elective one and may include the office of sheriff or magistrate. The coroner does not have to be a doctor. The administrative duties of a coroner may overlap those of police, but only the coroner may subpoena witnesses for an inquest.

Before an inquest is held, there must be an autopsy. An autopsy is the medical examination of the corpse of someone who died under violent or suspicious circumstances or as a result of suicide. It is a medical procedure and must be conducted by a qualified doctor. If the coroner is not qualified, the municipality may have a medical examiner, a doctor qualified in pathology and forensic pathology, who can conduct the autopsy. If there is no medical examiner, the coroner must hire a qualified doctor to perform the autopsy. The hired doctor does not need the same medical qualifications as a medical examiner. The coroner also decides who will be present during the autopsy. Neither the coroner's jury nor any accused persons have the right to be present.

The inquest is the presentation of the evidence gathered by the autopsy, and it is held even if there is only a possibility of a criminal charge. An inquest is not a trial. It is a public hearing open to all who choose to attend. Questioning of witnesses is done by the coroner, and any witness may refuse to answer any question. The coroner's jury then renders a formal verdict as to cause of death.

The coroner accepts the verdict from the jury and submits it to the prosecutor. The evidence from the inquest is used in police investigations. If there is sufficient evidence for prosecution for murder or manslaughter, the coroner may request a warrant to arrest a suspect. Coroners who have magisterial duties may issue the warrant themselves.

The coroner's inquest is not part of a criminal prosecution. It is used by police as a guide in finding the person or persons responsible for the death and in investigating the crime committed. Inquest evidence may also be used in civil cases, such as speeding, if death is involved.

In the normal course of duties, the coroner is not held liable for error, mistake, or misconduct while exercising judicial authority. There may be liability, however, for an abuse of magisterial duties, and if an autopsy is ordered when no real reason exists, the coroner may be sued by the next of kin.

See also Autopsy; Forensic science and medicine; Medical examiner; Murder and homicide.

Corporal punishment

Definition: The infliction of physical pain or discomfort as the means to punish behavior that violates established rules, including criminal laws

Significance: Although corporal punishments were once commonly applied, they were eliminated from the American justice system as the United States moved toward exclusive reliance on fines and restrictions on freedom, such as probation and incarceration, as methods of criminal punishment

In seventeenth and eighteenth century Europe and colonial America, people routinely received physical punishments for violating society's rules. These corporal punishments included branding, whipping, cutting off ears, fingers, hands, or tongues, and placing people in stocks—wooden structures in a town square into which a person's head, arms, or legs could be locked. These corporal punishments were legacies of religious beliefs that had also encouraged torture, burning people at the stake, and public executions for a variety of offenses, both serious and minor. A basic belief that underlay these physical punishments of people's bodies was an assumption that people who misbehaved were possessed by the devil and therefore unable to conform their behavior to God's rules for society.

During the Enlightenment period of the late eighteenth century, the emphasis on corporal punishment in Europe began to be displaced by reforms intended to rehabilitate offenders. Instead of branding or whipping them, various localities began to incarcerate them with a Bible or make them work in prison shops in the hope that they would discover God and self-discipline and thereby become good people.

Punishment in the United States. During the colonial and postrevolutionary periods, the United States employed many of the corporal punishments that had been brought from Europe, including whipping, branding, and stocks. The movement away from corporal punishments in favor of incarceration occurred during the nineteenth century.

In the southern United States, corporal punishments of the most vicious kinds, particularly whipping, branding, and dismemberment, were applied against African American slaves as punishment for escapes or any other infractions as defined by slave owners. Local law enforcement officials and courts reinforced the institution of slavery by actively supporting these forms of punishment.

After the Civil War, corporal punishments began disappearing as formal punishments for crimes, but their use still flourished on an informal basis. Police in many localities throughout the country utilized beatings and even torture as a means to punish people informally and to obtain confessions. While corporal punishment was used successfully to obtain many confessions, these confessions often came from innocent people who had simply been selected for victimization by unethical police officers. Such abusive behavior by police officers became less common in the twentieth century as the police began to become a profession with training, and as judges scrutinized the activities of police.

Corporal punishment was used in prisons and jails until the 1960's. Prisoners in some states were beaten, locked in small compartments, and otherwise physically coerced into obeying orders. Officials sometimes permitted inmates to abuse other inmates in order to force prisoners to perform labor under harsh conditions. These practices were outlawed by federal judges as a result of lawsuits in the 1960's and 1970's.

Corporal Punishment and the Law. By 1969, all but two states had abolished whipping as a punishment for prison inmates. The final two states were effectively barred from further use of corporal punishment when a U.S. court of appeals decision said that Arkansas' continuing use on prisoners of the "strap"—a leather whip attached to a wooden handle—violated the prohibition on cruel and unusual punishments (*Jackson v. Bishop*, 1969).

Beginning in the 1970's, prison officials, like police officers, could not use corporal punishments. They could, however, use physical force for self-defense and for gaining control over people who were fighting, threatening, or disruptive. Despite the prohibition on corporal punishments, occasional lawsuits are still filed against police officers and corrections officials who have beaten criminal defendants and inmates.

The formal abolition of corporal punishment in the criminal justice system did not mean that corporal punishment no longer existed in the United States. Parents are permitted to apply corporal punishment to their children as long as that punishment does not cause injuries or break laws against child abuse. In addition, corporal punishment is permitted in schools in many states. In 1978, the Supreme Court decided that the Eighth Amendment's prohibition of cruel and unusual punishments did not apply to disciplinary corporal punishments in schools (*Ingraham v. Wright*, 1978). Thus many schools continued to use corporal punishments, most frequently paddling with a wooden paddle, as a means to punish misbehaving students. By 1992, twenty states and the District of Columbia had banned the use of corporal punishment in schools, and many individual school districts in the remaining states had done the same.

In 1994, public debates resumed concerning the desirability of corporal punishment when Singapore sentenced Michael Fay, an American teenager, to six lashes with a bamboo cane for committing acts of vandalism. Although the U.S. government protested on Fay's behalf that the punishment ("caning") was barbaric, leaders in many American local communities seized on the issue to advocate the reintroduction of corporal punishment as a cheaper and more effective punishment for juvenile offenders. Corporal punishment was not reinitiated, but the debate demonstrated that many Americans still con-sider corporal punishment to be an effective deterrent to mis-behavior by young people.　　　　—*Christopher E. Smith*

See also Bill of Rights, U.S.; *Brown v. Mississippi*; Child abuse; Cruel and unusual punishment; Police brutality; Punishment; Slavery.

BIBLIOGRAPHY

The decline of corporal punishment in the eighteenth century is discussed in Michel Foucault, *Discipline and Punish: The Birth of the Prison* (New York: Pantheon, 1977), and David Garland, *Punishment and Modern Society* (Chicago: University of Chicago Press, 1990). For a history of punishment in the United States, see David J. Rothman, *The Discovery of the Asylum: Social Order and Disorder in the New Republic* (Boston: Little, Brown, 1971). The use of whipping and other corporal punishments during American slavery is discussed in Eugene D. Genovese, *Roll, Jordan, Roll: The World the Slaves Made* (New York: Pantheon Books, 1974). The legal aspects of corporal punishment and other punishments are discussed in Larry Berkson, *The Concept of Cruel and Unusual Punishment* (Lexington, Mass.: Lexington Books, 1975). An examination of the debates concerning the use of corporal punishment in schools is contained in Irwin A. Hyman and James H. Wise, eds., *Corporal Punishment in American Education: Readings in History, Practice, and Alternatives* (Philadelphia: Temple University Press, 1979).

Counsel, right to

DEFINITION: Entitlement provided for criminal defendants by the U.S. Constitution to receive representation by an attorney during criminal proceedings

SIGNIFICANCE: In the adversary system of justice employed in the United States, it is considered essential that criminal defendants receive professional representation in order to protect their constitutional rights and prevent the conviction of innocent people

American legal proceedings employ an adversary system of justice which assumes that the truth will emerge through the clash of professional advocates who oppose each other in the courtroom. In criminal cases, the permanent advocate for the government is the prosecutor. If individuals accused of crimes did not have professional advocates to represent them, there would be grave risks that the prosecution would automatically overwhelm the average citizen-defendant in the courtroom and thereby obtain convictions, whether justified or not. Defendants who have sufficient funds can hire their own attorneys, but poor people who are accused of crimes cannot afford to secure their own professional representation. In order to increase the fairness of legal proceedings and provide protection for criminal defendants' rights, the U.S. Supreme Court gradually interpreted the words of the U.S. Constitution to provide a broad right to counsel for people who otherwise could not afford to hire an attorney on their own.

Constitutional Law. The Sixth Amendment to the U.S Constitution includes various rights intended to ensure that criminal defendants receive fair trials. One of those rights is

Attorneys conferring with a trial judge. Because of the complexities of law and the American legal system, the Supreme Court has held that felony defendants have a right to be represented by an attorney. (James L. Shaffer)

the right "to have the Assistance of Counsel for his defense." For most of American history, the application of this right to counsel was limited for two reasons. First, until the middle of the twentieth century, the Bill of Rights was regarded as protecting people only against the federal government. Thus the Sixth Amendment applied only to federal criminal cases, which are a tiny proportion of the total criminal cases processed each year. Second, the right to counsel was interpreted to mean that people could not be prevented from having an attorney if they could afford to hire one. It did not mean that an attorney would be provided for people who could not afford to hire their own.

The Supreme Court began to alter its interpretations of the Sixth Amendment in the 1930's. In a case concerning several unrepresented African American youths convicted of rape and sentenced to death in a lynch-mob atmosphere in Alabama (*Powell v. Alabama*, 1932), the Supreme Court declared that poor defendants facing the death penalty must be provided with attorneys. In *Johnson v. Zerbst* (1938), the Supreme Court said that all defendants facing felony charges in federal court must be provided with attorneys if they are too poor to hire their own. In the 1940's, the right to appointed counsel was expanded to cover poor state felony defendants who needed professional representation because of "special circumstances" such as illiteracy or mental retardation.

In the 1950's and early 1960's, state legislatures, state supreme courts, and local state judges began to require that poor defendants be supplied with attorneys in criminal cases. By

1963, seven states still did not ensure that defense attorneys were provided for all felony defendants. The Supreme Court brought the entire country into line in 1963 with its decision in *Gideon v. Wainwright* (1963), which applied the Sixth Amendment to all state courts by requiring that poor defendants be given attorneys in felony cases. In subsequent decisions, the Supreme Court expanded the right to counsel to cover initial appeals after conviction (*Douglas v. California*, 1963) and misdemeanor cases in which the defendant faces the possibility of incarceration for less than one year in jail (*Argersinger v. Hamlin*, 1972). The Supreme Court also applied the right to counsel to pretrial processes by declaring that the Sixth Amendment required that defense attorneys be made available during police questioning of suspects, during preliminary hearings, and at identification line-ups after a defendant has been charged with a crime.

Limitations on the Right to Counsel. Under the Supreme Court's interpretations of the Sixth Amendment, the right to counsel applies only when a criminal defendant faces a charge that might result in incarceration. If a defendant faces only a small fine, then the county or state government is not required to supply a defense attorney unless mandated by that state's laws.

The right to counsel does not apply at all to civil cases. Poor people who want to file lawsuits usually must obtain their own attorneys, unless they qualify for free representation through the Legal Services Corporation, a federal government agency.

The right to counsel for criminal defendants does not guarantee that the defense attorney supplied by the state will take the case all the way to trial or will do an outstanding job in representing the defendant. Whether the state chooses to supply defense attorneys for poor people through state-salaried public defenders or through assignments to private attorneys who receive a small sum for each case, most attorneys work to obtain plea bargains for their clients. If the defendants are unhappy with their court-appointed attorney or public defender, there is little that they can do about it. It is difficult to prove that an attorney's performance was so bad that it violated the Sixth Amendment by providing "ineffective assistance of counsel." Thus there is often distrust and dissatisfaction evident in the relationships between poor defendants and the attorneys provided for them by the state.

—*Christopher E. Smith*

See also *Argersinger v. Hamlin*; Arrest; Assigned counsel system; Bill of Rights, U.S.; *Escobedo v. Illinois*; *Gideon v. Wainwright*; *In forma pauperis* petition; Legal Services Corporation; *Minnick v. Mississippi*; *Miranda v. Arizona*; *Powell v. Alabama*; Public defender; Scottsboro cases.

BIBLIOGRAPHY

The history of the right to counsel is presented in Anthony Lewis' classic account of the *Gideon v. Wainwright* case that expanded the right to all state courts, *Gideon's Trumpet* (New York: Random House, 1964). A first-person account of the work of a criminal defense attorney is presented in Seymour Wishman, *Confessions of a Criminal Lawyer* (New York: Penguin, 1982). Other discussions of the development and extent of the right to counsel can be found in Henry J. Abraham, *Freedom and the Court* (New York: Oxford University Press, 1982); Rolando V. del Carmen, *Criminal Procedure: Law and Practice* (3d ed. Belmont, Calif.: Wadsworth, 1995); and Christopher E. Smith, *Courts and the Poor* (Chicago: Nelson-Hall, 1991).

Counterfeiting and forgery

DEFINITION: Counterfeiting is producing copies of valuable items with intent to defraud; forgery is the illegal alteration of existing documents

SIGNIFICANCE: Counterfeit and forged items, especially documents, money, and related items, cheat individuals, corporations, and nations in a number of ways, including major losses of personal property

Forgery is often defined as any deliberate tampering with a written legal paper for the purpose of deceit or fraud. It may start with a blank piece of paper and involve the production of an entire forged document, but in most cases forgery involves the signing of another person's name to a check or to some other legal document (such as a contract or a will). In other cases, it entails altering the language or the monetary values on such a document. Forgery is a close cousin of counterfeiting, wherein an imitation of an article—most often money or related items (artworks will not be considered here)—is made. Both are viewed as serious crimes.

In the United States, forgery is punished by fines or by imprisonment, the extent of which depends on local and federal laws. Intent to defraud must be proved before a sentence can be passed. In contrast, the federal courts try the majority of counterfeiters (those who imitate legal tender), and prison sentences often range from five to twenty years, accompanied by large fines. Counterfeiting and forgery are so close—though different—that the Comprehensive Act of June, 1864 (first reenacted in 1873), combined them into a single area of federal statutory law, where they have stayed. Not all sources agree on exactly what items other than false money and false or changed legal documents are considered to be forged or counterfeited.

History and Context. Every world currency has been counterfeited since the Chinese and the Ionian Greeks invented money. The modern counterfeits of currency are defined as being fraudulent items that so closely resemble the money, obligations, or securities issued under the authority of a nation that they defraud an honest and sensible person of normal caution, dealing with others presumed to be honest. Laws against counterfeiting are quite uniform among the world's major nations, because of a 1932 diplomatic conference in Geneva, Switzerland. This conference produced an agreement, honored by all the signatory nations, to punish counterfeiters of their own and other currencies. It was also agreed that offenders would be extradited from these nations to prevent their escaping punishment.

Laws against forgery are reported to date back to the Rome of the first century B.C.E. More recent attempts to codify such law arose in Elizabethan England. By the middle of the eighteenth century, William Blackstone had declared that all forgery in England was a capital crime. In the United States, although federal law codifies forgery, it may be handled by the state courts or the federal courts, depending on its substance.

Perpetrators and Defenses. Counterfeit or forged items are not illegal until their possessors attempt to use them. In forgery cases, perpetrators may invoke any of several lines of defense against the accusation. The first is that authority was granted to them to be the signatory for another person; another is that the alteration performed was a genuine effort to correct a perceived error in the document. Another argument frequently brought forth is that the accused person did not forge the item in question. Finally, forgers have been known to insist that the writing or document is genuine and to attempt to impeach the experts brought in to verify forgery. This sometimes will work, for even the most current techniques of scientific document examination by forensic scientists are not infallible.

In cases of the counterfeiting of money and related items, the falseness of an item is usually clear, as is the intent of the perpetrator to defraud others. Only a nation has the right to issue legal tender of any sort. Complex precautions are taken to produce items that are clearly identifiable upon close inspection by experts. Average persons, and even fiduciary institutions, however, may be much more fallible. Hence, the only loophole for counterfeiters is pleading a lack of knowledge of false currency. Possession of the paraphernalia used in counterfeiting operations is also against the law.

Producing and Recognizing Counterfeit Money. In most counterfeiting operations, the bills are made by offset printing, although modern color xerography is increasingly common. The identification of counterfeit bills requires thorough examination. Embedded in the U.S. currency design that came into use in 1929 is a vertical strip which reads USA and the denomination (for example, USA TWENTY) repeated over and over, with every other rendition of the words upside down. This may be seen when the bills are held up to the light. Another characteristic is the paper used. A special paper is produced exclusively for U.S. currency. The red and blue silk fibers running through it are quite distinctive and very difficult to counterfeit. In addition, the identification of counterfeits is aided by laying them next to real bills in good light and examining both the front and back for the clarity of printing seen in real banknotes, which are made by line-intaglio printing. Especially important is a close look at the portrait on the front, which on genuine bills is clear and lifelike, at the treasury seal, and at the serial number. The backs of suspect bills should also be examined, because counterfeiters often take less care in preparing them. The presumption is that most people never look carefully at the back of currency. The redesigned U.S. currency that was unveiled in 1995 contains further anticounterfeit measures.

Apprehending Counterfeiters and Forgers. Reportedly, the U.S. Secret Service seizes the vast majority of counterfeits before they are ever placed in circulation. This federal agency was created in 1865 by Treasury Secretary Hugh McCullough. Its mandate was to combat the then-extensive counterfeiting of the first U.S. currency, authorized in 1863. Over the next fifty years the Secret Service evolved into an organization widely believed to do an excellent job at the prevention of extensive circulation of counterfeit currency. The Secret Service's primary technique reputedly is getting leads on fake currency before it has been distributed. Their methodology relies on a number of approaches, including informers, checking up on all purchasers of currency-grade bond paper, and scouting printing shops which are in financial difficulty.

The operation of the Secret Service is facilitated by the way counterfeiting operations usually operate—in a series of steps beginning with production of the fake bills by the counterfeiting ring. Suppliers of counterfeit money often sell them in large lots to "criminal wholesalers" at about twenty cents on the dollar. The wholesalers in turn sell the bills at thirty-five to forty-five cents per dollar to others who "pass" them. In some cases, currency counterfeiting is done by a single individual who is also the wholesaler and passer. These people are much more difficult to apprehend, and some such individuals have actually persisted successfully for up to twenty years.

Countermeasures. Counterfeiting has become a serious problem regarding money, credit cards, and other fiduciary documents. In addition, nearly everything imaginable is being

COUNTERFEITING CONVICTIONS IN U.S. DISTRICT COURTS

Source: U.S. Department of Justice, Bureau of Justice Statistics, *Sourcebook of Criminal Justice Statistics—1993.* Washington, D.C.: U.S. Government Printing Office, 1994.

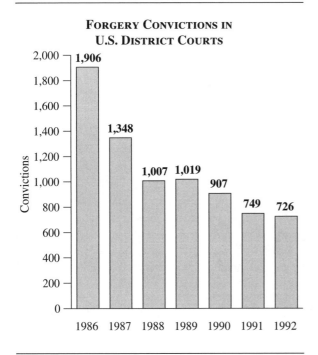

FORGERY CONVICTIONS IN U.S. DISTRICT COURTS

Source: U.S. Department of Justice, Bureau of Justice Statistics, *Sourcebook of Criminal Justice Statistics—1993*. Washington, D.C.: U.S. Government Printing Office, 1994.

counterfeited today, including auto parts, clothing, medicines, postage stamps, and cosmetics. The counterfeiting epidemic causes huge damage to many individual companies and to entire nations.

Unduplicability and easy recognition of fakes are the key countermeasures available. Hence, an industry is springing up to provide these capabilities. Solutions for nondocument items include the installation of tags, disks, or other identifiers into manufactures items. In many cases these hard-to-spot identifiers require special instruments that enable purchasers (primarily wholesalers and retailers) to recognize the bona fide item. In other cases special printing processes are used to produce tags and other components of bona-fide items identifiable with the naked eye.

Concerning money, it is particularly important that a useful system be designed so that individual consumers, as well as banks and companies, can easily recognize fraudulent items. This requires education of the public, an approach long pushed by the Secret Service and its equivalents in many other nations. In addition, and more basic, is the need to produce identifiers that are easy to recognize and very difficult to counterfeit. The advent of nearly perfect color document copiers has made this task more difficult. To fight this problem, the Treasury Department experimented with many ways to redesign U.S. currency; once it settled on a design, it began introducing new bills in 1996, beginning with the $100 bill. The bills contain a polymer thread that glows red under ultraviolet light, microprinted words, larger presidential portraits, con-

centric fine-line printing in the portrait background, and a watermark that will not reproduce on color copiers or computer scanners. —*Sanford S. Singer*

See also Banking law; Criminal law; Fraud; Organized crime; Secret Service; Treasury, U.S. Department of the.

BIBLIOGRAPHY

The American Law Institute's *Model Penal Code and Commentaries: Official Draft and Revised Comments* (Philadelphia: Author, 1980) and Francis Wharton's *Wharton's Criminal Law* (14th ed., by Charles E. Torcia. Rochester, N.Y.: Lawyers Co-operative, 1978) both describe the legalities associated with counterfeiting and forgery. As its title implies, *Counterfeiter: Story of a Master Forger* by Charles Black and Michael Horsnell (New York: St. Martin's Press, 1989) gives a look into the mind of a successful counterfeiter/forger and describes aspects of the business. Doug Stewart's "The Buck Starts Here and May Stop Here, at the Nation's Money Mills," *Smithsonian* 20 (May, 1989) tells about making money and the many precautions involved in its production. Lynn Glaser's *Counterfeiting in America: The History of an American Way to Wealth* (New York: C. N. Potter, 1968) is a useful older book on counterfeiting and forgery. A detailed 1986 article by Michael Neubarth, "Fakebusters: How Technology Spots Counterfeits," *Popular Science* 228 (April, 1986), helps to identify a number of means used to render items unduplicatable and individualized so as to protect them against being counterfeited easily.

Court-packing plan of Franklin D. Roosevelt

DATE: February 5-August 24, 1937

PLACE: Washington, D.C.

SIGNIFICANCE: This plan to increase the membership of the Supreme Court was a major challenge to the fundamental constitutional principle of separation of powers

By 1936, President Franklin D. Roosevelt was increasingly unhappy with Supreme Court declarations of his New Deal legislation, including the National Recovery Act, as unconstitutional. After rejecting a possible constitutional amendment to curb the Court's power, he and Attorney General Homer Cummings decided upon a plan based on one first proposed in 1913.

Their bill went to Congress February 5, 1937. Roosevelt declared that the courts were inefficient because of insufficient and physically unable personnel. He wanted to appoint up to six additional Supreme Court justices for each justice who had served at least ten years and who failed to resign within six months after his seventieth birthday. Forty-four similar lower-court judges could also be appointed.

Many in Congress saw the proposal as an attack on the Constitution's system of checks and balances. Liberals feared that it could destroy defense of civil rights. Chief Justice Charles Evans Hughes argued that the Supreme Court was efficient as it was. The public worried that weaker courts would lead to greater labor unrest.

Support for the plan diminished further when Justice Willis Van Devanter retired, and the Supreme Court began to uphold

The Second Lesson for Congress!

A contemporary cartoonist's view of Roosevelt's plan to expand the Supreme Court. (Franklin D. Roosevelt Library)

New Deal legislation such as the National Labor Relations Act. This "switch in time that saved nine" resulted from Justices Owen Roberts and Hughes rethinking their legal positions. After earlier rejecting the president's plan, Congress, on August 24, 1937, finally passed the moderate Judiciary Reform Act.

See also Hughes, Charles Evans; New Deal; Roosevelt, Franklin D.; Supreme Court of the United States.

Crime

DEFINITION: Any behavior that violates the law and makes the offender subject to punishment; the term is generally applied to adult behavior, while juvenile criminal behavior is called "delinquency"

SIGNIFICANCE: Definitions of what constitutes adult criminal behavior are at the core of the American justice system and have much to do with how members of the society categorize certain individuals and classes of people as outlaws

The term "crime" is popularly associated with violent or patently unacceptable adult behavior, such as murder, rape, treason, theft, or housebreaking. In strict legal terms, a crime is any behavior that contravenes laws; however, this narrow definition does not match broader social definitions of crime which are shaped by customs, cultural value systems, and other factors. For example, while jaywalking, double-parking, spitting in public, and flying kites in parks are technically crimes in some communities, few members of those communities would regard offenders as criminals. Conversely, some members of society regard certain behaviors—such as extramarital sex acts, drinking alcohol, and swearing—as morally criminal, although such behaviors are legal.

Traditional Concepts of Crime. Within all human societies, the essence of criminal behavior is misconduct that threatens the security, welfare, or sense of propriety of the community as a whole. Acts such as murder, arson, theft, rape, assault, sabotage, and treason are thus almost universally regarded as criminal and virtually all societies have statutory or tacit laws against them. Actions such as these violate the most deeply felt needs of human communities. They are thought to be more than mere wrongs against individual victims; rather, they are wrongs so outrageous that all members of the society must collectively act to prevent them and to punish their perpetrators.

While certain behaviors that are regarded as dangerous to society as a whole are almost universally regarded as unacceptable, definitions of specific crimes can and do vary widely among communities. The severity of punishments for criminal behavior has always tended to reflect the egregiousness of the crime against the community as a whole. For example, before the creation of modern fire departments, many societies regarded arson as a more serious crime than murder because deliberately set fires could potentially destroy entire communities, while a murderer might kill one or a few people.

Categories of Crime. A variety of criteria are used to classify crimes by their fundamental nature, by their association with violent behavior, by their seriousness, and by whether they are committed by individuals or by organized criminal groups. In modern societies, criminal acts fall into three fundamental categories: crimes against the government, crimes against "common morality," and crimes against persons. Tax fraud, sabotage, and treason are examples of crimes against government; certain sex behaviors—such as homosexuality or adultery—may be considered examples of crimes against common morality; and murder, assault, and theft are examples of crimes against persons.

Crimes Against Persons. Although crimes such as assault, theft, and murder are committed against individual persons, governments regard them as offenses against the community as a whole. When such a crime occurs, the government steps in and acts as if the offense were against it, relieving the victims of the burden of filing suits in their own behalf against the offenders. Criminal wrongs are distinguished from civil wrongs, another type of wrong done to a person. A common example of a civil wrong is the failure of a person or corporate body to fulfill a legal contract. Another type of civil wrong is a tort—an act that involves negligence or malice that harms another person but is neither covered by the criminal code nor the subject of a contract.

A further distinction between crimes and civil wrongs is that criminal behavior requires that the crime be committed with willful intent. In modern society, the determination that an act constitutes criminal behavior requires the intent to commit the crime. For example, acts such as arson and murder that are normally regarded as crimes may not be considered criminal if they are committed by persons who are found to be mentally ill and therefore cannot form criminal intent. Exempting the mentally ill and incompetent from criminal prosecution is a long-standing modern commitment, but it has had challenges within the fields of psychology and psychiatry.

Violent and Nonviolent Crimes. Distinctions between violent and nonviolent crime are widespread in Western societies. Violent crimes are those that involve physically harming, or threatening to harm, human beings. Such crimes, which include murder, rape, assault, and armed robbery, attract the most serious attention by law enforcement agencies as well as the most severe punishments for those who are convicted.

Nonviolent crimes include drug dealing, gambling, theft, housebreaking, vandalism, computer fraud, and a host of other activities. A broad category of nonviolent criminal behaviors has become popularly known as "white-collar" crimes. Drawing their nickname from the clothing traditionally associated with executive and management-level job holders, these crimes are typically characterized by subtlety and secrecy. Such crimes include fraud and embezzlement—both of which can be difficult to detect and even more difficult to prosecute and punish.

Distinctions between violent and nonviolent crimes are not always sharp, partly because some nonviolent crimes can generate unexpected violence. For example, burglary is normally considered a nonviolent crime because it usually involves breaking into a business or home when the proprietors or residents are absent; however, if a burglar unexpectedly encounters someone at the scene of the crime, the nonviolent

Most reported crimes are property crimes, not violent crimes. Burglary—such as the safe burglary being investigated here—accounted for 20 percent of reported crime in 1993. (James L. Shaffer)

burglary can quickly turn into a violent assault. Other supposedly nonviolent crimes can have violent results depending the emotional content of the situation.

Felonies and Misdemeanors. Another basic distinction used to separate crimes is their seriousness. For example, petty shoplifting and grand theft are both considered crimes, but the latter is regarded as much more serious. Most legal codes in the United States use the terms "felonies" and "misdemeanors" to separate crimes by their seriousness, with felonies being the more serious and misdemeanors being the less serious.

American criminal statutes generally classify as felonies those crimes for which punishments carry the possibility of incarceration for periods longer than one year. Felony convictions may also carry such additional penalties as loss of professional licenses and loss of certain political rights, such as the right to vote or hold public office.

Misdemeanors are typically lesser offenses for which maximum periods of incarceration are less than a year. This distinction is not exact, however, as persons convicted of felonies can receive suspended sentences, probation, parole, or continuations of previous sentences which may require their serving less time than persons convicted of misdemeanor offenses. Distinctions between felonies and misdemeanors cut across distinctions between violent and nonviolent crimes. Misdemeanors are typically nonviolent crimes, but such nonviolent activities as usury, gambling, and drug dealing are often classified as felony offenses. In contrast, minor cases of violent assault may in certain circumstances be treated as misdemeanors.

Certain crimes, such as murder, rape, and armed robbery, are regarded as inherently so serious that they are always treated as felonies. Other crimes, such as petty theft, parking offenses, and smoking in elevators, are virtually always regarded as misdemeanors or infractions. For many crimes, however, distinctions between misdemeanor and felony offenses are matters of degree. For example, distinctions between misdemeanor and felony theft are typically defined by the amounts of money or the values of goods that are stolen. Likewise, distinctions between misdemeanor and felony drug possession may be defined by the quantities of illegal drugs that offenders possess. Many criminal codes leave distinctions between misdemeanor and felony criminal behavior sufficiently flexible to allow district attorneys to choose between preferring misdemeanor and felony charges against suspects in individual cases.

Individual Versus Organized Crime. A further classification of crimes is between acts committed by individual persons and those committed by organized groups. Such distinctions do not necessarily have anything to do with the seriousness of the crimes. For example, an individual crime can be exceptionally violent, as when one person murders many people. The distinction is of importance primarily to law enforcement agencies, which regard individual crimes as generally simpler to control than those committed by organized groups. Once an individual criminal is apprehended and incarcerated, that person's criminal behavior can usually be stopped, at least for a time. By contrast, stopping the criminal activities of a group does not necessarily end when individual members of the group are arrested and convicted.

Organized crime can present special challenges to law enforcement when criminal networks are too large for individual law enforcement agencies, such as local police departments, to monitor and control. Organized crime networks often extend beyond the jurisdictions of individual municipalities or even states, presenting local law enforcement agencies with the additional problems of being restrained by their jurisdictional boundaries. The rapid mobility made possible by modern society allows agents of organized crime to commit offenses in one jurisdiction and quickly flee to another. Historically, this fact has helped promote the development of police forces on the federal and state levels.

Organized crime occasionally involves such violent crimes as murder, armed robbery, and assault; more typically, however, it involves nonviolent crimes, which generally elicit less vigorous law enforcement responses. Organized crime often tends to mimic legitimate businesses by building elaborate infrastructures and responding to market forces. Many organized criminal groups engage in buying and selling commodities and services—such as drugs, stolen goods, and prostitution—which require procuring, reselling, distribution, and delivery. Like ordinary business, organized crime can benefit from economies of scale.

Victimless Crime and Decriminalization. A special category of crime popularly known as "victimless" comprises illegal activities in which all parties participate willingly. These crimes typically involve the exchange of contraband goods (such as drugs) or services (such as gambling, usury, prostitution, or certain sexual activities among consenting adults). It can be difficult to place the dividing line between victimless crimes and crimes with victims, and the distinction is not without its problems. For example, persons who voluntarily buy illegal narcotics for their own use are not victims in the usual sense—the sellers are necessarily trying to harm them—but they may be regarded by society as victims of a larger evil. Further, willing participants in so-called victimless crimes who repent their initial decisions and elect to withdraw from the illegal activity may provoke violent responses from the persons with whom they are dealing.

As fears of violent crime have grown in the United States, there has been a growing public acceptance of the idea of decriminalizing victimless crimes. A primary motivation behind this trend has been the desire to see the nation's limited law enforcement resources respond more effectively to violent crimes. There has not, however, been anything resembling a consensus on this issue. Many Americans have such strong moral objections to such activities as prostitution and drug use that they regard them as inherently criminal. Further, there have been many critics of decriminalization proposals who, rather than resting their arguments on moral grounds, have argued that activities such as drug use, gambling, and prostitution will foster other types of criminal behavior even if they themselves are legalized.

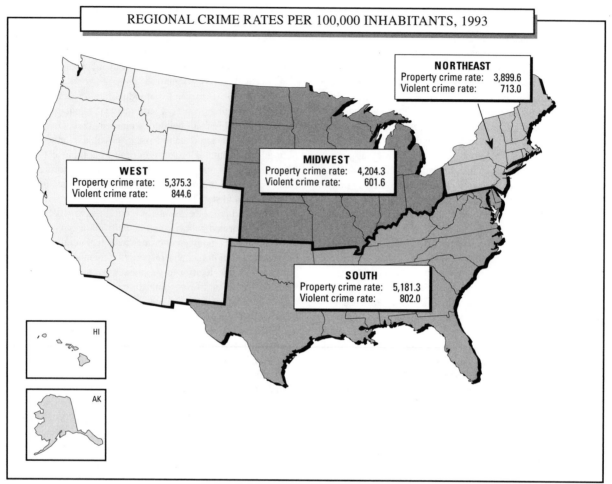

REGIONAL CRIME RATES PER 100,000 INHABITANTS, 1993

NORTHEAST
Property crime rate: 3,899.6
Violent crime rate: 713.0

WEST
Property crime rate: 5,375.3
Violent crime rate: 844.6

MIDWEST
Property crime rate: 4,204.3
Violent crime rate: 601.6

SOUTH
Property crime rate: 5,181.3
Violent crime rate: 802.0

Source: U.S. Department of Justice, Federal Bureau of Investigation, *Crime in the United States* (Uniform Crime Reports). Washington, D.C.: U.S. Government Printing Office, 1994.

The best-known example of decriminalization of a victimless crime was the repeal of Prohibition in 1933. During the dozen years that federal law banned the sale of alcoholic beverages, violations were so widespread that a new constitutional amendment was passed to end Prohibition. Gambling is another pervasive form of criminal activity that is gradually being decriminalized. Legalized casino gambling was once limited to the state of Nevada, and betting on horse and dog races was limited to a comparatively small number of jurisdictions. By the 1990's, state-run lotteries for revenue enhancement were commonplace, and other forms of gambling were increasingly being legalized.

Crime Statistics. Public perceptions of the incidence of crime have shifted over time, with different criminal behaviors occupying the public's attention. Public perceptions are, however, strongly molded by the media and may have little connection with local realities. Each year the U.S. Federal Bureau of Investigation (FBI) publishes the Uniform Crime Reports (UCR) under the title *Crime in the United States*, which pro-

vides the most objective available picture of the incidence of crime reported to law enforcement agencies. Voluntarily submitted by almost all American law enforcement agencies, the information in the UCR is divided into violent crimes against persons (such as murder, rape, robbery, and aggravated assault) and crimes against property (such as burglary, larceny-theft, and motor vehicle theft).

It is important to recognize the limitations of UCR data. UCR figures are based solely on reported crimes and can be distorted in two ways. First, not all crimes are reported to the police. Other studies, which have been cross-checked against the UCR, have shown, for example, that violent crimes are more likely to be reported than property crimes. Further, murder and aggravated assault are more likely to be reported than rape, which many victims hesitate to report because of the stigma that attaches to victims. Among property crimes, automobile theft is far more likely to be reported than other kinds of theft, largely because automobile owners must report thefts in order to collect on their insurance. For these reasons, the

CRIME INDEX / 221

data in the UCR should be compared with that in the annual National Crime Victimization Survey, published annually by the U.S. Bureau of Justice Statistics; this survey collects crime data by polling households directly and therefore is able to measure crime that is never reported to police.

Second, figures in the UCR are distorted by the tendency of some jurisdictions to underreport crimes out of concern that high crime rates will reflect negatively on their communities. A well-known example of this was found by an audit showing

TOTAL ESTIMATED ARRESTS, UNITED STATES, 1993	
Total	**14,036,300**
Arrests for FBI "Index Crimes"	
Murder and nonnegligent manslaughter	23,400
Forcible rape	38,420
Robbery	173,620
Aggravated assault	518,670
Burglary	402,700
Larceny-theft	1,476,300
Motor vehicle theft	195,900
Arson	19,400
Arrests for Other Crimes	
Other assaults	1,144,900
Forgery and counterfeiting	106,900
Fraud	410,700
Embezzlement	12,900
Stolen property; buying, receiving, possessing	158,100
Vandalism	313,000
Weapons; carrying, possessing, etc.	262,300
Prostitution and commercialized vice	97,800
Sex offenses (except forcible rape and prostitution)	104,100
Drug abuse violations	1,126,300
Gambling	17,300
Offenses against family and children	109,100
Driving under the influence	1,524,800
Liquor laws	518,500
Drunkenness	726,600
Disorderly conduct	727,000
Vagrancy	28,200
All other offenses	3,518,700
Suspicion (not included in totals)	14,100
Curfew and loitering law violations	100,200
Runaways	180,500

Source: U.S. Department of Justice, Federal Bureau of Investigation, *Crime in the United States* (Uniform Crime Reports). Washington, D.C.: U.S. Government Printing Office, 1994.

Note: Arrest totals are based on data from all agencies reporting to the Uniform Crime Reporting Program and estimates for unreported areas. Because of rounding, figures may not add to total.

that Washington, D.C., was downgrading almost a third of all grand larcenies to simple larceny in order to keep them out of the crime report. Finally, some categories of crimes, such as misdemeanor assaults and consumer fraud, are not included in the UCR.

Keeping the limitations of the UCR in mind, some generalizations can be made about crime in the modern United States. During the early 1970's, the nation's annual overall crime rate stood at about four criminal offenses per one thousand persons; by the mid-1990's, this figure had risen to about six offenses per one thousand persons. Among property crimes, the incidence of burglary historically rose until the early 1980's, when it began to recede. However, other larcenies—particularly auto theft—began increasing substantially. Murder figures have fluctuated annually, but generally have ranged between 8.5 and 10 murders per 100,000 persons from the early 1970's through the mid-1990's. Meanwhile, robberies climbed substantially, while figures for rape nearly doubled. *—Richard L. Wilson*

See also Arson; Burglary; Crime Index; Criminal; Criminal justice system; Felony; Juvenile delinquency; Misdemeanor; Motor vehicle theft; Murder and homicide; National Crime Victimization Survey; Regulatory crime; Robbery; Uniform Crime Reports (UCR); Victimless crimes; White-collar crime.

BIBLIOGRAPHY

One of the best surveys of the crime in the United States is Lawrence M. Friedman's *Crime and Punishment in American History* (New York: Basic Books, 1993). A panoramic history of criminal justice going back to early colonial times, this book attempts to explain the origins of purely American ideas about crime and punishment. Another good historical survey is *Law and Justice* by Howard Abadinsky (Chicago: Nelson-Hall, 1988). Herbert Jacob's *Justice in America* (4th ed. Boston: Little, Brown, 1984) has become a standard work in the study of criminal justice generally. The Federal Bureau of Investigation's annual Uniform Crime Reports details the level of reported crime in the United States and is usually cited as *Crime in the United States: Uniform Crime Reports* (Washington, D.C.: U.S. Government Printing Office); the Bureau of Justice Statistics' National Crime Victimization Survey is published annually as *Criminal Victimization in the United States* (Washington, D.C.: U.S. Government Printing Office). Other studies include Robert F. Meier, ed., *Major Forms of Crime* (Beverly Hills, Calif.: Sage Publications, 1984); James Q. Wilson and Richard J. Herrnstein, *Crime and Human Nature* (New York: Simon & Schuster, 1985); and Doris MacKenzie et al., eds., *Measuring Crime: Large-Scale, Long-Range Efforts* (Albany: State University of New York Press, 1990).

Crime Index

DEFINITION: Part of the Federal Bureau of Investigation's annual Uniform Crime Reports (*Crime in the United States*)

SIGNIFICANCE: The Crime Index is the most complete compilation of national reported crime statistics for the eight most serious types of crime, as determined by the Federal Bureau of Investigation

CRIME INDEX OFFENSES, 1993

Percent Distribution

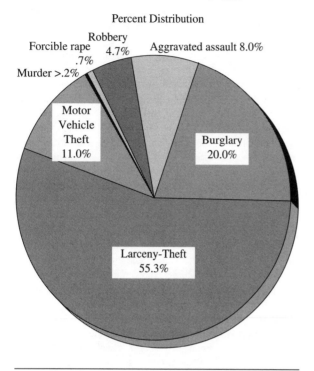

Source: U.S. Department of Justice, Federal Bureau of Investigation, *Crime in the United States* (Uniform Crime Reports). Washington, D.C.: U.S. Government Printing Office, 1994.

The Federal Bureau of Investigation (FBI) Crime Index is part of the FBI's annual Uniform Crime Reports (UCR), which is a compilation of crime statistics reported monthly to the FBI by more than sixteen thousand police agencies. These agencies, taken together, have jurisdiction over 98 percent of the United States, making the index the best single source of information concerning national crime levels. The Crime Index consists of arrests and reported crimes of the eight types ("index crimes") deemed most serious by the FBI: murder and non-negligent homicide, forcible rape, robbery, aggravated assault, burglary, larceny, motor vehicle theft, and arson. This last category, the most recent addition to the index, has been included since 1981. National estimates of the volume and rate of Crime Index incidents for every 100,000 people over the past two decades are included as well as the number of reported crimes cleared by arrest or other means. Information for the entire United States is broken down into various geographic divisions, including individual states, metropolitan areas, cities, towns, counties, and college and university campuses. Crimes are also classified according to types of weapons used and the value of property stolen or recovered, as well as by the sex, race, and age of victims and perpetrators. The Crime Index does not attempt to explain the reasons for an increase or decrease in crime. It is used by law enforcement

agencies and others to identify long-term trends and assess police effectiveness.

Several factors should be borne in mind by the reader when interpreting data from the Crime Index. First, although most major cities report crime statistics, not all police agencies do, so while the Crime Index is the most inclusive compilation of national crime statistics that is available, it is not 100 percent complete. Second, while the FBI issues definitions for the eight major crimes tabulated in the crime index, each of the reporting agencies independently interprets those definitions, causing considerable potential variation in the meaning of the reported statistics. Third, the number of crimes actually occurring is unknown and may or may not be proportional to the number of crimes reported to the various law enforcement agencies who then report to the FBI. Also, when assessing the geographic distribution of crimes, the reader is cautioned to consider the size of the region's population as well. Finally, the FBI warns that crime can vary dramatically from year to year and advises against drawing sweeping conclusions about long-term trends on the basis of a few years' data.

See also Crime; Federal Bureau of Investigation (FBI); National Crime Victimization Survey; Uniform Crime Reports (UCR).

Criminal

DEFINITION: A person who breaks the codified rules of a society, especially one who breaks them repeatedly

SIGNIFICANCE: A society's values and ethical code strongly affect its views on who is considered a criminal and how criminals should be treated; there is no consensus among social scientists on what makes a person commit crimes

Without laws there can be no crime (lawbreaking) and no criminals; a criminal is, in the simplest sense, one who breaks the law. Beyond this inadequate definition, however, are numerous questions about crime and criminals that have intrigued sociologists and criminologists since the late nineteenth century.

Most typically it is those people whose actions create significant fear, unease, or revulsion who are thought of as criminals. People who commit violent acts such as murder and armed robbery are high on this list. Those who commit crimes such as murder, robbery, rape, assault, burglary, theft, and arson are sometimes characterized as "street criminals." Statistics indicate that they are predominantly male and young; compared with the general population, they are also disproportionately black, urban, and unmarried. (The fears of white suburbanites notwithstanding, their victims are usually other young inner-city dwellers, many of them unemployed.) Combating street crime accounts for much of the efforts of law enforcement.

Through the years, many theories have been put forth regarding what makes a person commit criminal acts. One of the first was that criminals are biologically or mentally inferior to most people. In the nineteenth century, Cesare Lombroso theorized that biological factors lead to criminality. He believed that criminals could be identified by their skull shapes and could be divided into four categories: born criminals, insane criminals, "passion" criminals, and occasional criminals.

In the twentieth century, many tests and labels have been applied in attempts to measure and predict criminality. Intelligence quotient (IQ) tests were used (and misused) in this regard. A variety of psychological tests have also been tried. Some studies using the Minnesota Multiphasic Personality Inventory have indicated that that testing instrument can identify burglars and drug offenders. Among psychiatrists and people working in the criminal justice system, terms such as "psychopath," "sociopath," and "antisocial personality" have been used to describe people who, for various theorized reasons, have criminal tendencies. Sociology has produced a number of theories regarding criminality. Among the suggested causes of crime have been social disorganization ("anomie"), poverty and unemployment, frustration at reaching one's goals, and "differential association," which attempts to

explain why some people facing harsh conditions turn to crime while others facing the same conditions do not. No sociological theory, however, has been able to explain or predict the breadth of criminal behaviors adequately.

One difficulty in identifying and describing criminals is the fact that there is no neat dividing line between "us" (supposedly law-abiding citizens) and "them" (criminals). Millions of Americans from all levels of society break laws every day and are therefore, in some sense, criminals. People gamble, drive over the speed limit and under the influence of alcohol, smoke marijuana, and cheat on their taxes. Husbands beat their wives; parents abuse their children. White-collar crime, ranging from bribery to consumer fraud to embezzlement, flourishes.

Nevertheless, many people who engage in such behaviors think of themselves as normal and consider certain other types of people criminals. Most likely to be labeled "criminal" are people who commit crimes with obvious victims (versus those engaging in "victimless crimes"), people who have committed

For a variety of reasons, producing a useful definition of "criminal" has proved nearly impossible. This man is being arrested for having outstanding traffic warrants. (James L. Shaffer)

crimes repeatedly and have been in jail (versus one-time offenders), and people who commit violent crimes. This last holds true in spite of the fact that nonviolent, white-collar crimes can have devastating effects on large numbers of people. The role of prison in fighting or encouraging crime has been debated: Does incarceration act as a deterrent or does exposure to other offenders in prison encourage a person to become a habitual or "career criminal"? Recidivism (returning to crime after being released from prison) is especially high among burglars and robbers.

Radical or critical criminologists look at the stratification of society and point out that those in power write the laws and therefore define who is a criminal. In the criminal justice system itself, the police and judiciary practice discretion, applying the force of the law differentially: Minorities and members of what sociologists sometimes call "out-groups" are more likely to be criminalized than members of society's dominant group. For all these reasons, although numerous government agencies attempt to track, punish, and reduce crime, producing a consistent and useful definition of "criminal" has proved extremely difficult.

See also Crime; Crime Index; Criminal intent; Criminal justice system; Criminal law; Criminal procedure; Criminology; Organized crime; Prison and jail systems; Psychopath and sociopath; Ten most wanted criminals; Victimless crimes; White-collar crime.

Criminal intent

DEFINITION: The mental state involved in deliberately committing a criminal act

SIGNIFICANCE: Criminal intent, in addition to a criminal act, is one of the defining elements of committing a crime

A crime is committed only if there is an act or omission accompanied by a certain mental state. An act alone does not equal guilt. For example, bumping into someone as a crowded subway takes a curve is not considered a criminal act if the person who causes the jostle does not intend the act. If, on the other hand, the jostler either deliberately sticks out an elbow to jab a fellow rider, or if a reasonable person would expect that there is a risk that another might be hurt by the movement in question, then the act might be considered a crime because it is accompanied by the necessary mental state. This mental state is called *mens rea* (Latin for "guilty mind"), scienter, or criminal intent.

Criminal intent has been incorporated into modern criminal codes by such words as "knowingly," "intentionally," "deliberately," and "with malice." These words illustrate criminal intent by prohibiting only conduct that is voluntary and therefore suggests a guilty mind.

While it is traditional to think of words such as "knowingly" as a part of the definition of most criminal behavior, modern statutes also require criminal intent through phrases such as "recklessly" or "negligently." Criminal recklessness is determined if people, in their own minds, realize the risk their conduct involves. Criminal negligence is found when a reasonable person in the same circumstances would have realized the risk, but the actor need not realize it at the time the act or omission occurs. Consequently, the subway jostler could become liable for a criminal assault either if he realized in his own mind the risk of raising his elbow or if a reasonable person in the same circumstances would have realized the risk. Criminal intent inferred from the reckless or negligent conduct of the actor is called constructive intent. The intention to injure a fellow subway rider might be inferred by such things as the number of people on the train, the proximity of the injured person, and whether the jostler raised an arm or the point of his umbrella.

In some jurisdictions, criminal intent includes deliberation, knowledge, intention, or purpose. In others, criminal intent includes recklessness and negligence, even though the actor may not have either knowledge or intent to cause the act in question.

Criminal intent can be general or specific. General intent in some instances refers to *mens rea* in the broadest sense: a guilty mind or a mind to commit some criminal activity. It can also refer to all the designations of intent a criminal code or statute might require, such as acting intentionally, knowingly, recklessly, or negligently. Under this definition of general intent, an actor with any of these states of mind might be guilty of committing the act. On the other hand, specific intent refers to the specific kind of mental state one must have to be guilty of a specific crime. For example, prosecution for larceny typically requires a taking with "intent to steal."

See also Crime; Insanity defense; Malice; *Mens rea*; Negligence.

Criminal justice system

DEFINITION: The total complex of local, state, and federal laws, policing forces, prosecuting offices, court systems, and correctional facilities and programs in the United States

SIGNIFICANCE: The operation of the various agencies and institutions that investigate, prosecute, and punish violators of criminal laws advances justice by promoting public safety and punishing offenders

The American criminal justice system encompasses all the laws, procedures, and institutions that communities employ to apprehend, prosecute, and punish those who violate the property or persons of others.

State and Local Systems. Within the United States, criminal justice is primarily a state and local concern. More than nine-tenths of all crimes are dealt with at the state and local levels. Similar proportions apply to the personnel who work in criminal justice and to the expenditures that go to combat crime. The crimes that most concern average citizens—property crimes such as burglary and violent crimes such as robbery and assault—are typically violations of state, not federal, laws. The criminal justice systems of other countries contrast sharply with the American system in this regard. Outside the United States, most criminal offenses are defined by national laws; in most other countries, national, not local, institutions respond to violations of criminal codes.

The American system commonly designates the most serious crimes as felonies; in most jurisdictions, these are crimes that can be punished by prison sentences of at least a year. Lesser offenses are designated as misdemeanors—crimes for which punishments cannot exceed a year in jail. Felonies include most violent crimes, such as murder, rape, and robbery; some of the most serious property crimes, such as burglary; and drug trafficking. Misdemeanors typically include less serious crimes, such as simple thefts, vandalism, and disorderly conduct. In some cases repeated commission of a misdemeanor can elevate the crime to a felony.

Police. County sheriffs and city and town police bear the chief responsibility for responding to most property and violent crimes. In 1992 such agencies employed more than half a million sworn officers and another 200,000 civilians throughout the United States. Nationally, more than two-fifths of all criminal justice expenditures go toward police protection. In the vast majority of cases the police learn about crimes through calls from victims or witnesses; the police are rarely the first to learn about them. According to the National Crime Victimization Survey, which began in 1973, as many as three-fifths of crimes that are committed are never reported to the police, ranging from three-quarters of

Apprehension by a police officer is a suspected offender's entrance into the criminal justice system. (James L. Shaffer)

all thefts to about two-fifths of all aggravated assaults. Overall, only about half of violent crimes are reported to police. In 1992, more than fourteen million crimes of seven major types were reported to police; these included murder and non-negligent manslaughter, rape, robbery, aggravated assault, burglary, theft, and motor vehicle theft.

The sheer number of criminal acts limits most police activity to simply responding to crimes after they are committed. Police work thus consists mostly of tasks such as going to the scenes of crimes, interviewing witnesses, gathering physical evidence, searching for suspects, and preparing investigative reports. In the past—especially in the nineteenth century, when municipal police forces were first established—most police activity involved maintaining order within communities rather than responding to crimes. This activity included preventing unruly—but not necessarily illegal—behaviors, prohibiting loitering or vagrancy, and checking on shops and

businesses after closing hours. In recent years, many Americans have called for the police to involve themselves more actively in the communities they serve by engaging in what is usually called "community policing": walking beats instead of cruising randomly in squad cars, establishing storefront offices to increase police visibility, meeting with community groups to identify problems, and other such proactive measures. Pilot projects of community policing in American cities provide evidence that such programs increase citizens' feelings of personal security and confidence in the police. Whether such programs actually reduce crime, however, is less certain.

A major impediment to adopting community policing more widely is the enormous demand that merely responding to present crime levels places on police resources. In 1992 local police were able to make arrests in only a fifth of the major crimes brought to their attention, including 65 percent of the

CRIMINAL JUSTICE PROCESS

| Entry into the system | Prosecution and pretrial services | Adjudication | Sentencing and sanctions | Corrections |

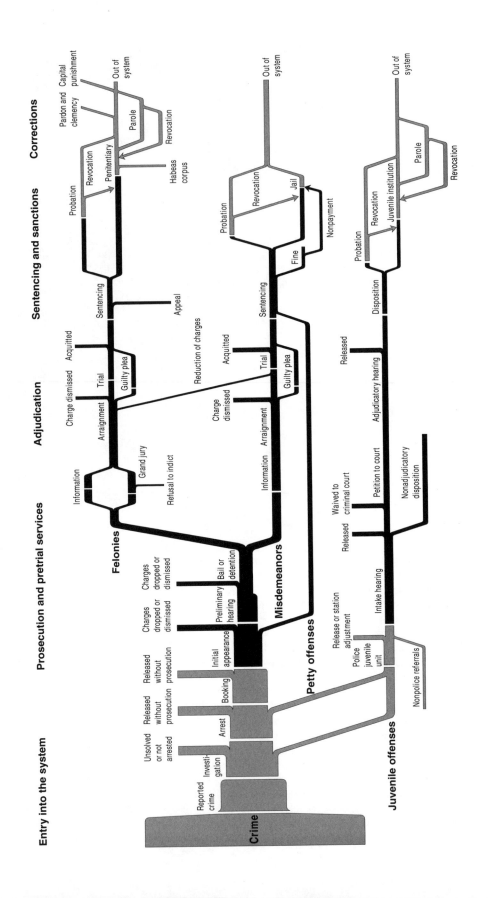

Graphic by Deborah Cowder; adapted from U.S. Bureau of Justice Statistics, *Drugs, Crime, and the Justice System.* Washington D.C.: U.S. Government Printing Office, 1992.

murders, 52 percent of the rapes, 24 percent of the robberies, 13 percent of the burglaries, and 20 percent of the thefts. For all crime types, arrests totaled just over fourteen million. The largest categories of arrests were for driving under the influence of alcohol (1.6 million), assaults (1.6 million), theft (1.5 million), and drug law violations (1 million).

Prosecutors and Courts. Once an arrest is made, the case is turned over to a prosecutor, a public official who is charged with representing the people in the action against the defendant. Typically, most serious property and violent crimes are handled by the office of the county prosecutor, usually called the district, or state's, attorney. In most jurisdictions district attorneys are elected officials; they are often assisted by dozens or even hundreds of assistant district attorneys. Lesser offenses may be prosecuted by municipal attorneys, and specialized offenses—such as consumer fraud and commercial law violations—may be handled by prosecutors in the offices of state attorneys general.

Prosecutors perform several distinct functions: screening cases before charges are filed in court, interviewing victims and witnesses in preparing for trials, presenting evidence before grand juries, trying cases in court, and handling appeals. Although defendants cannot be convicted without proof "beyond a reasonable doubt," a lesser standard—"probable cause"—determines whether defendants should stand trial. Either before a grand jury or in a preliminary hearing, the prosecutor must show that a crime probably occurred and that the defendant under arrest probably did it. Although most states allow either a preliminary hearing or grand jury in felony cases, some states require a grand jury proceeding before an accused felon can go to trial. Unlike trial juries, which usually comprise twelve members, grand juries typically have up to twice that number. They meet secretly and do not follow most of the standard rules of evidence that apply in courtroom trials. Also in contrast to trials, defendants typically have no right to counsel in grand jury proceedings. Although in British and American legal history grand juries were originally instituted to protect citizens from overzealous prosecutors, modern critics contend that they have developed into agents serving the state.

Courtroom Procedures. Trials are adversarial proceedings between prosecutors, who have the burden of proving guilt, and defendants, who are represented either by private attorneys or by public defenders (or other attorneys appointed by the courts) if they cannot afford private counsel. All trials are presided over by judges, who may be appointed or elected. Under American law all persons charged with serious crimes have the right to trial by jury. Juries serve as the triers of fact; they determine whether defendants committed the acts with which they are charged in violation of the criminal law. The judges are responsible for all legal rulings, particularly in applying the rules of evidence to the actual proceedings. When defendants choose not to exercise their right to trial by jury, the judges become the triers of fact. In some jurisdictions prosecutors can request jury trials even when defendants do not.

Pleas. Although every defendant has the right to go to trial for the determination of guilt or innocence, most defendants in most jurisdictions plead guilty rather than contest their cases at trial. Nationally, about 90 percent of felony convictions result from guilty pleas; 6 percent result from jury trials and 4 percent from bench trials (in which judges determine guilt or innocence). Critics have charged that the high rate of guilty

REPORTED CRIMES SOLVED ("CLEARED") BY ARREST, 1993

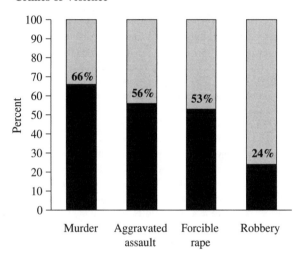

Crimes of Violence

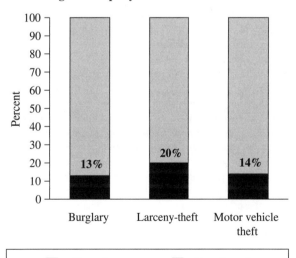

Crimes Against Property

Source: U.S. Department of Justice, Federal Bureau of Investigation, *Crime in the United States* (Uniform Crime Reports). Washington, D.C.: U.S. Government Printing Office, 1994.

pleas indicates two dangerous flaws in the system. On the one hand, it may imperil public safety when prosecutors reduce charges and potential punishments in exchange for guaranteed convictions; on the other hand, it may be unfair to innocent defendants who may be tempted to plead guilty in return for substantially reduced punishments rather than take chances on being convicted in a trial.

Sentencing. In 1990, 830,000 persons were convicted of felonies in state courts in the United States, up from 667,000 in 1988 and 583,000 in 1986 (there are no national data on misdemeanor convictions, but these are almost certainly several times more common than felony convictions). Just under a fifth of the 1990 felony convictions were for violent crimes; a third were for property crimes; another third were for drug offenses; and the balance were for other crimes. Among the felony convictions were 11,000 for murder or non-negligent manslaughter, 18,000 for rape, 47,000 for robbery, 54,000 for aggravated assault, 110,000 for burglary, and 168,000 for drug trafficking. Of all the persons convicted of felonies in 1990, 29 percent were sentenced to probation (a period of supervision in the community as an alternative to incarceration), 25 percent were sentenced to local jails for less than a year, and 46 percent were sentenced to state prisons.

Sentencing systems throughout the United States are of two main types: determinate and indeterminate. In determinate sentencing systems a judge who sentences a convicted felon to prison designates a specific number of years, and the offender must serve this time, minus credits for behaving well in prison ("good time") or for involvement in educational or job training programs. Such sentence reduction credits can reach as high as half the formal sentence, depending on individual state laws. In indeterminate sentencing systems, the judge designates a range of years, such as ten to twenty years in prison, and the actual time served is determined by a parole board once the inmate becomes eligible for release. The result of these sentencing systems is that inmates of state prisons in the United States serve an average of only 35 percent of their maximum sentences.

Judges have traditionally had three basic options available when sentencing convicted felons: probation, several weeks or months in local jails, or a year or more in state prison. As expansion of the nation's prison population accelerated in the 1980's, a growing number of jurisdictions began experimenting with "intermediate sanctions." Punishments that are more severe than normal probation but less severe than incarceration, these include more intensive probation supervision, house arrest (sometimes monitored electronically with ankle bracelets), community service, and restitution to victims. Some proponents of such sanctions defend them as appropriate and less expensive alternatives to incarceration. Others support their use as alternatives to probation but regard them as insufficiently severe to use in place of incarceration.

Death Penalty. By the mid-1990's, the federal government and about three-fourths of the states had authorized the death penalty for certain specified offenses, principally murder. In 1990 there were 23,440 reported murders in the United States, about 11,000 murder convictions, 265 murderers sentenced to death, and 23 executions. Another 108 persons convicted of murder were removed from death rows through successful appeals of their convictions or sentences during that same year. Between 1976—when the U.S. Supreme Court reinstated the death penalty—and 1992, state courts sentenced a total of 3,979 persons to death and executed 188. Inmates who were actually executed spent an average of seven and a half years on death row. By the end of 1992, 2,575 prisoners were on death rows throughout the nation.

One of the most controversial justice issues relating to the administering of capital punishment is the question of whether the race of convicted murderers or their victims affects courtroom decisions to impose the death penalty. While blacks are disproportionately represented on death row, compared to their share of the American population, whites arrested for murder are more likely to be sentenced to death than blacks arrested for murder. Of the inmates on death row at the end of 1992, for example, just over half were white non-Hispanics, two-fifths were black, and 8 percent were Hispanics.

Correctional System Populations. By the end of 1993, 859,000 persons were inmates in state prisons; another 90,000 were in federal prisons, and 450,000 more were in local jails. About half of the latter were serving sentences; the rest were awaiting trial. These figures for state and federal prisoners are almost three times greater than those for 1980. Despite the amount that prison populations increased, nearly three-fourths of the 4.9 million offenders under correctional supervision in 1993 were not incarcerated, but were under supervision in the community. Of those under supervision, 2.8 million were on probation and 909,000 were on parole (a period of supervision after release from prison).

According to surveys of state prison inmate populations, typically about 11 percent are serving time for murder and non-negligent manslaughter, 9 percent for rape or other sexual assault, 15 percent for robbery, 8 percent for assault, 4 percent for other violent crimes, 12 percent for burglary, 13 percent for drug trafficking, and 28 percent for other crimes. Many state prison inmates have extensive prior records: Four-fifths have at least one prior conviction, three-fifths have at least two, more than half have at least three, and almost a fifth have at least six prior convictions. Sixty percent of those sent to state prisons are return prisoners; 25 percent are beginning at least their fourth terms. Altogether, 93 percent of state prison inmates are either convicted violent offenders or convicted recidivists (repeat offenders).

Federal Criminal Justice System. Although the federal criminal justice system accounts for less than 5 percent of all felony convictions in the country and less than 10 percent of all prison inmates, the federal government enforces hundreds of criminal laws covering such offenses as counterfeiting, interstate drug trafficking, immigration violations, assaults on federal officials, terrorism, espionage, and violations of federal regulations concerning such matters as environmental pollution and commercial transactions. There are more than fifty separate federal law enforcement agencies. The principal bodies include the Federal Bureau of Investigation, which investigates a wide variety of federal offenses; the Drug Enforcement Administration (DEA), which concentrates on drug law violations; the Bureau of Alcohol, Tobacco, and Firearms (ATF), which is especially important in monitoring weapons violations; the Secret Service, which investigates counterfeiting and threats to the safety of the president; and the Immigration and Naturalization Service (INS), which investigates immigration law violations.

Responsibility for prosecution of federal offenses falls on the Department of Justice; it is headed by the attorney general, who is appointed by the president and confirmed by the U.S. Senate. Federal trials are conducted in federal district courts. Appeals of their decisions are made to federal appeals, or circuit, courts. The small fraction of such appeals that reach the Supreme Court usually raise basic constitutional questions or involve contradictory rulings from federal appeals courts in different parts of the country.

The compositions of prison populations reveal the differences in focus between state and federal criminal justice systems. For example, nearly half of all state prison inmates serve time for committing violent crimes, compared with under a fifth of federal prisoners. Conversely, while about a fifth of state prisoners serve sentences for drug offenses, almost three-fifths of federal prisoners serve time for such crimes; three-quarters of them are incarcerated for drug trafficking.

Resources Devoted to Criminal Justice. In 1990, federal, state, and local governments in the United States spent $74 billion for civil and criminal justice. This figure, which includes police protection, prosecution and courts, and corrections (prisons, jails, probation, and parole), accounted for 3.3 percent of all government spending in the nation that year. State and local governments devoted between 6 and 7 percent of their budgets to criminal justice, the federal government less than 1 percent. Nationally, criminal justice agencies employ about 1.6 million persons full-time. Nearly half work for police or investigative agencies; about a third work in corrections.

—*Joseph M. Bessette*

See also Bail system; Crime; Criminal law; Criminal procedure; Judicial system, U.S.; Justice; Model Penal Code; Police; Prison and jail systems; Punishment.

BIBLIOGRAPHY

Perhaps the most readable and informative book on the criminal justice system is the Bureau of Justice Statistics' *Report to the Nation on Crime and Justice* (2d ed. Washington, D.C.: U.S. Government Printing Office, 1988), which presents a wealth of reports on specific crime rates and trends, felony sentencing, prison populations, and recidivism. The Bureau of Justice Statistics also publishes the annual *Sourcebook of Criminal Justice Statistics* (Washington, D.C.: Bureau of Justice Statistics). As its title implies, Samuel Walker's *Popular Justice: A History of American Criminal Justice* (New York: Oxford University Press, 1980) surveys the history of the

subject. Other overviews include Geoffrey P. Alpert, *The American System of Criminal Justice* (Beverly Hills, Calif.: Sage, 1984); H. Frank Way, *Criminal Justice and the American Constitution* (North Scituate, Mass.: Duxbury Press, 1980); George F. Cole, *The American System of Criminal Justice* (Belmont, Calif.: Wadsworth, 1992); and Howard Abadinsky, *Law and Justice: An Introduction to the American Legal System* (2d ed. Chicago: Nelson-Hall, 1991). An excellent survey of key issues is James Q. Wilson's *Thinking About Crime* (Rev. ed. New York: Basic Books, 1983). Richard C. Monk has edited a useful collection of nineteen essays on criminal justice controversies: *Taking Sides: Clashing Views on Controversial Issues in Crime and Criminology* (2d ed. Guilford, Conn.: Dushkin, 1991).

Criminal law

DEFINITION: That branch of law which defines, prosecutes, and punishes conduct that society deems harmful

SIGNIFICANCE: As an instrument of social control, criminal law seeks to punish wrongdoers and to deter similar conduct by others

A crime is often defined as an offense against society. As such, crimes are prosecuted on behalf of the public by the district attorney and punished by the state according to its laws. The United States does not have a single set of criminal laws. Instead, each of the fifty states has its own criminal law, and the federal government has a separate criminal code. The general terms are similar, but the definitions of specific crimes as well as the penalties or punishments attached vary from state to state.

Elements of a Crime. General principles of liability are contained in every criminal code. They include *actus reus*, or "evil act"; *mens rea*, or "evil mind" (also termed intent); concurrence; and causation of harmful result. Proof of each element is required beyond a reasonable doubt for conviction. That standard has been defined as follows: "A reasonable doubt is one that arises from the evidence and its character, or from the absence of satisfactory evidence, and is such a doubt that a reasonable man has a right to entertain after a fair review and consideration of all the evidence" (*People v. Friedland*, an 1896 New York case).

Actus reus requires an overt voluntary act. It also helps to prove *mens rea*, or intent, which can be inferred from actions. Failure to act in situations where the law imposes a duty to act by statute, contract, or special relationship will also satisfy the *actus reus* requirement, as in failure to file an income tax return or to report child abuse.

Mens rea may be divided into four mental states: general intent, or an intent to commit the act required in the definition of the crime, as breaking and entering in burglary; specific intent, or an intent to cause a particular result, as the intent to cause death in homicide; transferred intent, sometimes called "bad aim intent," where the actor intends to harm one individual but instead harms another (the law transfers the intent to harm the intended victim to the actual victim); and constructive intent, where actual harm is unintended but the actor should have known that the behavior would create a high risk of injury. For example, speeding on an icy street and killing a pedestrian may be construed as an intent to kill. Most states follow the premise that people intend the natural and probable consequences of their acts.

Mens rea constitutes the mental element of crime and deals with the state of mind of the actor at the time of the act. The Model Penal Code (MPC), compiled by the American Law Institute, an advisory committee on criminal justice, as a model guide to legislation on the criminal law, includes four levels of culpability: purposely, or with conscious intention to engage in forbidden conduct or produce a forbidden result; knowingly, with an awareness that a particular forbidden result will follow; recklessly, with a conscious disregard of a substantial and unjustifiable risk of harm; and negligently, with an unconscious disregard of a substantial and unjustifiable risk of harm.

Motive does not equate with intent, but it may explain the reason for committing a criminal act and may influence punishment or even the likelihood of conviction. To illustrate, euthanasia or mercy killing is generally accomplished to ease the victim's suffering. Although the premeditated and purposeful nature of causing another's death is demonstrated, a jury might refuse to convict or a judge might reduce the sentence because of mitigating factors such as beneficent motive.

Concurrence requires that the *mens rea* set the criminal act in motion and merge with it to produce a harmful result. The *mens rea* generally must precede the *actus reus*; one without the other produces no crime, except in strict liability offenses, which impose liability without fault in certain limited circumstances (as with noxious gases, unsafe workplaces, or impure foods). Actual harm that differs from intended harm only in degree will satisfy the requirement of concurrence.

Causation requires the conduct to be the actual or factual cause as well as the legal or proximate cause of the harm. In factual cause ("but for" or *sine qua non* causation), the conduct sets in motion a chain of events that leads to the harmful result: "But for the actor's conduct, the harm would not have occurred. Legal cause, also termed proximate, direct, or substantial cause, requires nearness in time and place. If the connection between act and subsequent harm is sufficiently remote, or if unforeseeable intervening circumstances produce the harm, the act will not satisfy the requirement of proximate cause. Generally, the criminal law will not punish persons whose actions produce results that are accidental or could not reasonably have been anticipated.

A traditional standard of proximate causation that may be applied to homicide cases is the "year-and-a-day rule," which holds that a person cannot be charged with causing the death or another if death occurs more than a year and a day after the harm was inflicted. This ancient rule was created prior to the advent of modern medicine because it was difficult to determine the precise cause of death. If death occurred shortly after infliction of an injury, it was presumably attributable to the injury. If it occurred later, it was attributable to "natural causes." Today, the rule is still retained in many states despite the fact that the cause of death can be ascertained with great precision and artificial life supports can keep people alive for lengthy periods because of advances in medical science and technology.

Classifications. Only one crime is mentioned in the U.S. Constitution: treason. All other crimes are statutory: felonies, offenses punishable by death or imprisonment for more than one year, and misdemeanors, offenses punishable by incarceration for less than one year. Summary or petty offenses are minor infractions for which a fine is imposed. The common law, derived from the British legal system and brought to the United States in the colonial period, classified crimes as *mala in se*, or those inherently evil and posing a threat to society (murder, manslaughter, rape, arson, and theft), and *mala prohibita*, those made criminal by definition because they offend public sensibilities and morals.

Crimes Against the Person. Homicide, or intentional killing, is divided into murder and manslaughter; "malice aforethought" distinguishes the two. First-degree murder commonly is premeditated, purposeful, and deliberate. Courts have held that premeditation does not require advance planning but can be formulated instantaneously with the killing. Some states (Massachusetts and Oklahoma, for example) have an additional category of first-degree murder called "atrocious murder," characterized by extreme brutality. In most states, deaths that occur during the commission of a felony constitute felony murder. Although the intent to kill is not required specifically in felony murder, any killing occurring during the perpetration of the underlying felony will be sufficient. Thus, the actor will be held liable for even an unintentional killing. In Pennsylvania, for example, felony murder constitutes second-degree murder, and "all other" murders fall into a catchall category called third-degree murder, including murders not premeditated or deliberate and those resulting from the intent to inflict great bodily harm. Some other states' statutes contain only two degrees of murder.

Manslaughter is divided into voluntary and involuntary. A third type, called negligent homicide, includes, for example, vehicular homicide and negligent use of firearms and explosives. Voluntary manslaughter requires adequate provocation, acting in the heat of passion with no time to cool, and a causal link. Certain circumstances will reduce murder to voluntary manslaughter: mistaken use of deadly force in self-defense, mutual combat, battery, assault, trespass, and insulting words. At common law, a man who caught his wife in the act of adultery had adequate provocation to kill his wife, her paramour, or both in the first heat of passion. Those states retaining the paramour rule consider paramour killings justifiable homicide.

Involuntary manslaughter is criminal homicide in which death is unintentional, resulting from either reckless or negligent actions or occurring during illegal conduct. The misdemeanor manslaughter rule is the counterpart to the felony murder doctrine.

Another crime against the person is rape, or carnal knowledge by a man of a woman not his wife, forcibly and without consent. The amount of resistance required by the victim has changed over time, from utmost resistance to reasonable resistance, measured by that amount required by the totality of the circumstances. During the 1970's and 1980's, many states no longer required corroboration to prove rape, and most enacted rape shield statutes that prohibited inquiry into the victim's sexual past. Rape law has become gender-neutral and comprehensive in scope; marital rape has also been recognized as a criminal act. The crime of statutory rape, or carnal knowledge of a woman under the age of consent, exists in all states. Several states recognize reasonable mistake of age as a defense.

Other crimes against the person are battery, a harmful or offensive touching; assault, the reasonable apprehension of an imminent battery; false imprisonment, or forcible detention or confinement of a victim's liberty; and kidnapping, or detention and aspiration (moving or carrying away) by force or threat of force.

Crimes Against Property. The common-law designation of burglary and arson as crimes was designed to protect one's habitation. Burglary, or entering another's property without privilege, has been expanded to include other occupied structures such as hotel rooms, garages, and even vehicles. Some statutes and the Model Penal Code substitute for the entry requirement a standard called "surreptitious remaining," or entering lawfully with the intention of remaining until unlawful in order to commit a crime. Arson, a willful and malicious burning or setting on fire of the property of another, also includes explosions.

"Theft" is a modern term that consolidates the common-law crimes of larceny, larceny by trick, embezzlement, and false pretenses. At early common law, larceny (encompassing robbery) was the only theft crime and was punishable by death. Developed to protect the valued Anglo-Saxon possession of livestock, larceny law on the American frontier protected cattle and horses. Judges were reluctant to expand the crime to include other similar offenses; therefore, certain kinds of thefts similar to larceny were punished differently. The MPC and subsequent legislation altered the common-law scheme and filled in gaps.

Larceny, a taking and carrying away of the property of another with intent to deprive the owner of its possession permanently, is distinguished from larceny by trick, in which the owner transfers possession because of another's misrepresentations, and false pretenses, in which ownership or title is transferred through reliance on the deception of another. Embezzlement, or fraudulent conversion, is a statutory offense created in response to a case in which a bank teller pocketed money given to him for deposit by a customer. The would-be embezzler is a fiduciary entitled to possess the property temporarily and for a specific purpose. When, however, a person retains it for personal use, he or she has converted or embezzled the property. Theft statutes modeled after the 1962 MPC group larceny, embezzlement, and false pretenses together and

eliminate the necessity to distinguish the manner in which the property has been misappropriated.

Robbery is larceny from a person by present force or immediate threat of force with intent to permanently deprive the owner of possession. Most states have divided robbery into degrees according to injury and force used or threatened. Extortion or blackmail threatens future harm.

Defenses. Certain circumstances may mitigate or totally eliminate criminal responsibility. These defenses are grouped into justifications and excuses. In justifications, defendants admit criminal responsibility but claim that under the circumstances what they did was correct. In excuses, defendants admit that their behavior was wrong but argue that under the circumstances they were not responsible for their actions. The defenses and their uses differ widely from state to state. At trial the defendants bear the burden of affirmatively proving a defense to justify, excuse, or mitigate their behavior.

The most common justification is self-defense, which permits citizens to use reasonable force when necessary to protect themselves against imminent attack or serious bodily injury. Only that amount of force necessary to repel the attack may be used; excessive force cannot be used. When one is attacked in one's home, deadly force may be used to repel an unprovoked attack if life or serious bodily injury is threatened. Defense of others generally requires a special relationship, but some states have broadened use of that defense to include all third persons. The defense of necessity justifies otherwise criminal conduct when it avoids a greater harm and the actor chooses the lesser of two evils (such as exceeding the speed limit to rush a dying person to the hospital, or destroying property to prevent the spreading of a fire). Consent of a victim will absolve the defendant of criminal responsibility even though the conduct was intentional and wrong.

Common excuses to criminal responsibility include duress (when defendants are in immediate danger of death or serious injury), intoxication (voluntary intoxication never excuses crime, but involuntary intoxication excuses crime if it impairs formulation of intent), age (either old or young excuses if it impairs *mens rea*), mistake, entrapment, and insanity. Entrapment will excuse criminal conduct if an agent of the government induces law-abiding citizens to commit a crime they would not have otherwise committed. If one is predisposed to criminal behavior, however, the entrapment defense is inapplicable.

The insanity defense has undergone extensive evolution and modification. A legal and not a medical concept, insanity excuses criminal liability because it impairs *mens rea*. The standard applied in approximately one-third of the states is the M'Naghten rule, or right-wrong test, dating from 1843. It specifies that a defendant is not guilty if he or she had a disease of the mind at the time of the act and could not distinguish right from wrong or was unaware of the nature and quality of the act because of a disease of the mind. Several states supplement the M'Naghten test with the irresistible impulse test, which requires capacity to understand the nature and quality of the act coupled with an uncontrollable capacity to commit the wrongful act. The MPC's "substantial capacity" approach is followed by most states, requiring that defendants lack "substantial," not total, mental capacity to appreciate the criminality of their conduct or comply with legal requirements. The Durham rule, or product test, was formulated in 1871 and exists only in New Hampshire. It provides that mental disease or defect excuses criminal responsibility. Certain states (such as Pennsylvania and Michigan) also use an optional "guilty but mentally ill" standard, under which defendants are sentenced and imprisoned but also require and receive treatment for mental illness during their incarceration.

Inchoate Offenses. Certain conduct which is preparatory to the completion of criminal activity is punishable, regardless of whether the substantive crime occurs. The inchoate or incomplete offenses are attempt, conspiracy, and solicitation. Criminal attempt is composed of an intent to commit a crime, some overt act or acts in furtherance of the intent, and a failure to consummate the crime. Mere preparation does not constitute criminal attempt. States are divided as to what degree of completion beyond preparation is necessary.

Conspiracy is an agreement or combination between two or more persons formed for the purpose of doing an unlawful act or a lawful act by unlawful means. In certain states (such as Texas and Arkansas), only agreements to commit felonies constitute conspiracy; others (Colorado, Arizona, and Hawaii, for example) include both felonies and misdemeanors. Alabama includes any act injurious to public health and morals. The MPC and Connecticut, Georgia, and Illinois include all agreements with criminal objectives.

Solicitation is a request or command to a third person to commit a crime. Some states restrict solicitation to felonies, others to violent felonies. The MPC allows conviction and punishment of one who solicits any criminal offense, no matter how minor, regardless of whether the substantive crime is committed.

Complicity. Under certain circumstances, criminal activity may involve cooperation or assistance before, during, or after commission of the crime. The common law recognized four parties to crime: principals in the first degree, who actually commit the crime; principals in the second degree, who assist in commission of the crime or are present during its commission; accessories before the fact, those who facilitate crime but are not present during commission; and accessories after the fact, those who give aid and comfort to persons known to have committed crimes, or who assist in escape or concealment. The MPC and statutes in all states have removed the common-law distinctions by making "principals" those who were accessories before and during the crime. The common-law "accessory after the fact" has been retained.   *—Marcia J. Weiss*

See also Accessory, accomplice, and aiding and abetting; Assault; Conspiracy; Crime; Criminal intent; Criminal justice system; Criminal procedure; Felony; Misdemeanor; Murder and homicide; Rape and sex offenses; Robbery; White-collar crime.

BIBLIOGRAPHY
Charles W. Thomas and Donna M. Bishop, *Criminal Law: Understanding Basic Principles* (Newbury Park, Calif.: Sage Publications, 1987) traces the history and development of the common law and the nature of criminal law. Arnold H. Loewy, *Criminal Law in a Nutshell* (2d ed. St. Paul, Minn.: West, 1987) is a basic text written for law students and those interested in a detailed explanation of the subject. A complete general overview with cases is Joel Samaha, *Criminal Law* (4th ed. St. Paul, Minn.: West, 1993). Chapters on criminal law are contained in Harold J. Grilliot and Frank A. Schubert, *Introduction to Law and the Legal System* (5th ed. Boston: Houghton Mifflin, 1992) and Beth Walston-Dunham, *Introduction to Law* (2d ed. Minneapolis, Minn.: West, 1994).

Criminal procedure

DEFINITION: The stages and points at which particular decisions are made in the criminal justice process that are mandated by statutes and constitutional judicial decisions

SIGNIFICANCE: The procedural steps in the processing of criminal cases are designed to ensure that correct decisions are made about guilt and innocence and that authorities respect the rights of criminal defendants

Every country has the authority to decide how it will determine which individuals will be punished for committing crimes. In some systems, the police or the army may have complete authority to identify and punish wrongdoers. The individual suspect may have no ability to question the law enforcement officers' decisions or swift imposition of punishment. In the United States, however, criminal procedure has been established to ensure that only guilty defendants receive punishment and to protect the public from abusive practices that police and prosecutors might employ in investigating, convicting, and punishing suspected criminals.

Historical Background. American criminal procedure, like other aspects of law, traces its roots to legal practices in England. The practice of using trials as a procedural mechanism to determine guilt and innocence began in England. Originally, England used physical trials to identify guilty offenders. Suspects were forced to place their hands in boiling oil, for example, or fight in a public duel with the assumption that God would protect the innocent but injure the guilty during such events. Eventually, the church discontinued its sponsorship of such events and England gradually shifted to the use of trials involving the presentation of testimony and the use of witnesses and jurors. Juries assumed an important role by protecting the public against abusive decisions by prosecutors. If there was insufficient evidence of guilt presented by the prosecutor, then the jury could acquit the defendant and the defendant would go free. The American jury trial, a key component of criminal procedure, developed from these English origins.

The U.S. Constitution. The first ten amendments to the Constitution, commonly known as the Bill of Rights, contain several provisions that mandate procedures to be followed in the investigation, prosecution, and punishment of criminal offenders. The Fourth Amendment protects people against "unreasonable searches and seizures." It also requires that search warrants and arrest warrants be supported by probable cause and that they specifically describe places to be searched and persons or things to be seized. The Fifth Amendment requires indictment by a grand jury before serious charges are prosecuted. The amendment also provides protection against compelled self-incrimination and the possibility of being tried twice for the same offense. The Sixth Amendment provides rights to speedy and public trials by impartial juries, as well as the right to be informed of charges, to obtain relevant documents and witnesses, to be confronted by adverse witnesses, and to have the assistance of a defense attorney. The Eighth Amendment prohibits excessive bail and fines and bans cruel and unusual punishments. The Fourteenth Amendment, which was added to the Constitution in 1868, provides additional rights to due process and equal protection of the laws. All of these provisions help to shape the procedures used in criminal cases by defining suspects' rights, limiting the authority of police, prosecutors, and judges, and mandating elements that must be incorporated into the legal process.

The provisions of the Bill of Rights originally applied only in federal court cases concerning defendants accused of violating criminal laws enacted by Congress. From the 1920's through the 1960's, the U.S. Supreme Court made many decisions that incorporated individual provisions of the Bill of Rights into the due process clause of the Fourteenth Amendment and made them applicable in state criminal cases. The only federal constitutional right concerning criminal procedure that has not been incorporated is the Fifth Amendment right to be indicted by a grand jury. State courts are not required by the Supreme Court to use grand juries, but many use such proceedings on their own. States are required to abide by all of the other provisions of the Bill of Rights concerning criminal procedure.

State and Federal Criminal Justice System. The legislatures for each state have the authority to design procedures that will be used within their state courts to process the cases of criminal defendants. Congress possesses this authority with respect to the federal courts. In addition, all court systems must obey the U.S. Supreme Court's decisions that apply to them and mandate the use of certain procedures or respect for specific rights. State court systems must also obey the decisions of their own state supreme courts. The highest court in each state has the authority to interpret its state constitution and apply those decisions to the procedures used in processing criminal cases within that state. If legislatures want to change the kinds of procedures used within their own state's courts, they can enact reforms as long as those reforms respect the relevant provisions of the state and federal constitutions as interpreted by the state supreme court and the U.S. Supreme Court.

Because each state legislature and Congress possess the power to design procedures for the courts under their authority, there are differences in the criminal procedures used in different court systems. Although certain requirements of the U.S. Constitution which apply to all court systems, such as the use of defense attorneys and the availability of jury trials, provide common elements to all systems, other aspects of states' criminal procedure are quite different, especially with respect to preliminary proceedings.

Pretrial Proceedings. Immediately after an arrest is made by police officers, the individual arrested by the police is processed through the various steps of the state or federal court's criminal procedure. Two issues are decided shortly after arrest: first, whether the defendant will be released from custody on bail while the case is being processed; second, whether there is enough evidence to justify pursuing charges against the person arrested.

The process for setting bail varies from state to state and from county to county within states. If the suspect is arrested for a minor charge, the police may have the authority to release the suspect after fingerprinting, photographing, and obtaining relevant personal information. The person may be released on his or her "own recognizance," which means that the suspect does not have to post any amount of money with the police or court in order to gain release. The person merely signs a promise to appear at scheduled court dates. The person may also be required to post a set amount of money which will be forfeited if he or she fails to appear in court. It is more common for bail to be set by judges in an initial court hearing, and judges will always handle bail decisions when a person is charged with a very serious crime.

In some state constitutions, there is a right granted for each defendant to have bail set. Judges, however, will set a very high bail, perhaps even in the millions of dollars, if they do not want the person released while the case is being processed. In the federal courts and some states, the judge can deny bail by finding that the person would endanger the community if released or by deciding that no amount of money would guarantee that the person would return to court. In other states, suspects arrested for the most serious crimes, such as first-degree murder, may not be eligible for bail at all.

If a suspect was arrested through a decision by a police officer rather than through an arrest warrant issued by a judge upon the presentation of evidence, then the suspect is entitled to an initial hearing to make sure that evidence exists to support the arrest. The U.S. Supreme Court has interpreted the Fourth Amendment's prohibition on unreasonable seizures to require that initial hearings be held within forty-eight hours after a warrantless arrest (*County of Riverside v. McLaughlin*, 1991).

People who are arrested have a right to have an attorney represent them in court. The police must inform them of this right before any questioning takes place (*Miranda v. Arizona*, 1966), and defendants who are too poor to hire an attorney have a right to have an attorney provided for them by the government (*Gideon v. Wainwright*, 1963; *Argersinger v. Hamlin*, 1972). Attorneys need not be provided immediately after arrest if the police do not intend to question the suspect or if the suspect agrees to answer questions without an attorney present. Attorneys must be made available, however, to represent defendants at arraignments in which an initial plea is entered and at preliminary hearings in which a judge determines whether there is enough evidence to proceed with the case. Attorneys can also seek to have bail set or the amount of bail reduced by presenting arguments at a bail hearing.

At the arraignment, the court officially informs the suspect of the charges against him or her and gives the suspect the opportunity to plead "guilty" or "not guilty." Very few suspects plead guilty at felony arraignments, because their attorneys have just begun to work for them, and even if they will plead guilty eventually, as most defendants do, their attorneys need time to develop plea bargain proposals. It is more common for guilty pleas to be entered immediately in traffic courts or in misdemeanor cases, because defendants usually face only fines or probation and are anxious to get the cases resolved quickly. At preliminary hearings, prosecutors must present enough evidence to persuade a judge that sufficient grounds exist to proceed in a case against the defendant. In some states, arraignments and preliminary hearings take place in lower level courts, often called municipal courts or district courts. After these initial proceedings, felony cases will be transferred to upper-level courts, often called superior courts, circuit courts, or courts of common pleas. Defendants frequently waive formal proceedings for arraignments and preliminary hearings because they are aware of the charges and they already know that enough evidence exists to move the cases forward.

Some states and the federal government use grand jury proceedings to make the final determination about whether sufficient evidence exists to prosecute a defendant on serious charges. Grand juries are composed of citizens drawn from the community who meet in secret proceedings to hear witness testimony and examine the prosecutor's other evidence to determine whether charges should be pursued. The suspect has no right to be present in the grand jury proceedings. Defense attorneys are barred from the courtroom when grand juries meet. If the grand jury believes that charges are justified, it issues an indictment against the defendant.

Defense Attorneys and Criminal Procedure. Beginning with the preliminary hearing, defense attorneys file motions in an effort to have evidence excluded or to learn more about the evidence possessed by the prosecutor. Motions provide the basis to protect the defendant's rights against unreasonable searches and seizures. The defense attorney often argues during the preliminary hearing and subsequent pretrial motion hearings that specific evidence should be excluded from trial because it was obtained in violation of the defendant's rights.

The defense attorney also often initiates plea negotiations with the prosecutor. More than 90 percent of defendants whose cases are carried forward past grand jury indictments or preliminary hearings eventually enter guilty pleas in exchange for agreements about what punishment will be imposed. Although felony defendants have a right to have their cases decided at trial under constitutional rules for criminal procedure, most defendants prefer to make a plea agreement. Such agreements frequently produce lighter punishments than those

that might have been imposed after a trial. Defendants' guilty pleas may be entered at any point in the process, from the arraignment through the middle of a jury trial.

The Trial Process. Defendants who face felony charges are entitled to a jury trial. Many defendants choose to have a bench trial before a judge alone rather than a jury if their case is controversial or if they believe that a judge will be fairer or more understanding. Misdemeanor defendants are entitled to jury trials under some states' laws, but they may have only bench trials under the laws of other states. The U.S. Supreme Court has said that the Sixth Amendment's right to trial by jury applies only to serious charges (*Blanton v. North Las Vegas*, 1989).

Under the Supreme Court's interpretations of the Sixth Amendment right to an impartial jury and the Fourteenth Amendment right to equal protection, jurors must be drawn from a fair cross-section of the community, and jurors cannot be excluded because of their race or gender. Through a process called *voir dire*, the prosecutor and defense attorney question potential witnesses and ask the judge to exclude those who might be biased because of their attitudes or personal experiences.

Although the federal government and most states use twelve-member juries in criminal cases, many states use six- to eight-member juries for misdemeanor cases. Six states use six- or eight-member juries for felony cases. The Supreme Court has declared that six-member juries must reach unanimous verdicts (*Burch v. Louisiana*, 1979), but non-unanimous verdicts are permissible for convicting defendants before twelve-member juries if permitted under a state's laws (*Apodaca v. Oregon*, 1972).

At the trial stage of criminal procedure, the prosecutor and defense attorney present evidence, question witnesses, and raise objections to each other's evidence and arguments. Each attorney attempts to persuade the jury or judge (in a bench trial) about the defendant's guilt or innocence. A conviction requires a finding of guilt beyond a reasonable doubt. In considering whether the evidence presented by the prosecutor achieves that standard, jurors must follow the judge's instructions about how to interpret the relevant law and evidence. Throughout the trial, the judge must follow the relevant laws of procedure and evidence that govern the state or federal court in which the trial is being conducted. The relevant laws are created by the state legislature for state courts and by Congress for the federal courts, and then they are refined and clarified by decisions of appellate courts, such as the state supreme court and U.S. Supreme Court. Decisions by the U.S. Supreme Court guide trial judges with respect to constitutional rights, such as those concerning double jeopardy, compelled self-incrimination, and confrontation of adverse witnesses, that can arise in the context of a trial.

Post-trial Procedures. After the jury or judge reaches a verdict, a defendant who is found guilty will be sentenced by the trial judge. In some states, juries determine the sentence in death penalty cases. Death penalty cases have special hearings

Individuals accused of felonies are entitled to a trial by an impartial jury that will weigh the evidence against the accused. (James L. Shaffer)

in which the judge or jury must consider aggravating and mitigating circumstances, which are any circumstances making the crime or criminal especially deserving or not deserving of execution. Every sentence imposed for a crime must follow the punishments established by the legislature for that crime. The sentence must not violate the Eighth Amendment's prohibitions against excessive fines and cruel and unusual punishments.

Convicted defendants have a right to appeal their convictions by filing legal actions in appellate courts. These legal actions allege that the trial judge made specific errors which violated relevant laws or the defendant's constitutional rights. In most states, such appeals go first to an intermediate appellate court, usually called the state court of appeals, and then may be pursued in the state supreme court. In twelve states, however, there is no intermediate appellate court, so appeals go directly to the state supreme court. A few states have special appellate courts that hear only criminal appeals. There is a right to counsel only for the first appeal (*Douglas v. California*, 1963). Any subsequent appeals may have to be prepared and presented by the convicted offender unless he or she can hire an attorney or unless the relevant state law provides assigned counsel for convicts beyond the first appeal. Unsuc-

cessful appeals to state supreme courts can subsequently be filed in the U.S. Supreme Court, but the nation's highest court accepts very few cases for hearing.

Convicted offenders can also file writs of *habeas corpus*, a traditional legal action from English history that permits a person to seek release or a new trial through a claim of wrongful detention. In the American system, prisoners must be able to show that their federal constitutional rights were violated in the course of the case and conviction. Very few prisoners prevail in such actions, but several thousand *habeas corpus* petitions are filed in the federal courts each year.

—Christopher E. Smith

See also Appellate process; *Argersinger v. Hamlin*; Arraignment; Bail system; Bill of Rights, U.S.; Capital punishment; Criminal justice system; Due process of law; *Duncan v. Louisiana*; *Escobedo v. Illinois*; *Gideon v. Wainwright*; Grand jury; *Habeas corpus*; Jury system; *Miranda v. Arizona*; Prosecutor, public; Public defender; Reversible error; *Sheppard v. Maxwell*; *Voir dire*.

BIBLIOGRAPHY

A comprehensive and readable review of criminal procedure, including constitutional rights, is contained in Rolando V. del

Carmen, *Criminal Procedure: Law and Practice* (3d ed. Belmont, Calif.: Wadsworth, 1995). This volume covers each stage of criminal procedure, with special attention given to relevant U.S. Supreme Court cases. More in-depth coverage of legal cases is provided by Yale Kamisar, Wayne R. LaFave, and Jerold H. Israel, *Modern Criminal Procedure: Cases, Comments, and Questions* (6th ed. St. Paul, Minn.: West, 1986). Reviews of the Supreme Court's criminal procedure decisions in the 1970's and 1980's are presented in John Decker, *Revolution to the Right: Criminal Procedure Jurisprudence During the Burger-Rehnquist Court Era* (New York: Garland, 1992), and Alfredo Garcia, *The Sixth Amendment in Modern American Jurisprudence* (New York: Greenwood Press, 1992). The history of criminal procedure is reviewed in David Bodenhamer, *Fair Trial* (New York: Oxford University Press, 1992), and Henry Abraham, *Freedom and the Court* (5th ed. New York: Oxford University Press, 1988). Bodenhamer's book in particular provides a brief, readable perspective on the development of criminal procedure.

Criminology

DEFINITION: The systematic study of the nature, extent, etiology, and control of law-breaking behavior

SIGNIFICANCE: Criminology seeks to establish empirical knowledge about crime and its control as a basis for explanation, prediction, prevention, and criminal justice policy

Ever since the term "criminology" was coined by Raffaele Garofalo in 1885, its content and scope have been controversial. Questions have been raised over whether criminology is scientific, whether it is an autonomous discipline, which of its several theories offers the best explanation for crime, and whether its applied approach—driven by the desire to control crime—is sufficiently value neutral. Such controversies have been exacerbated by criminology's disciplinary fragmentation, relative failure to recommend policy that reduces crime, and reliance on government funding.

Criminology's substantive focus is somewhat elastic. Unquestionable core components include discussions of the definition and nature of crime as harm-causing behavior; descriptions and classification of the different types of criminal activity, from spontaneous individual offenses to collective, organized criminal enterprises; statistical analysis of the extent, incidence, patterning, and cost of crimes; profiles of typical victims and offenders, including organizational and corporate law violators; and analysis of the causes of crime. There is less agreement about whether criminology should also include victimology, criminal justice, penology, and the sociology of law. In the United States the inclusive term "criminal justice" generally refers to theories about and studies of the crime control practices, philosophies, and policies of police, courts, and corrections.

Criminology as a Multidisciplinary Social Science. A restrictive view of criminology demands adherence to the "scientific method." The scientific method requires that knowledge be built on logically interrelated, theoretically grounded, and empirically tested hypotheses that are subject to retesting and subsequent verification. A twenty-eight-year survey conducted in 1992, however, revealed that only 27 percent of the articles in criminology's main professional journal actually tested theory. A more expansive view of criminology includes knowledge based on systematic ethnographic methods of study, acknowledging that these have produced some of its richest studies in the field.

Although most strongly influenced by sociology, American criminology comprises several disciplines, including economics, biology, anthropology, psychiatry, psychology, philosophy, political science, history, and geography. Each contributes its own assumptions, theories, and methods to the study of crime. This variety, however, raises questions of disciplinary integrity: Does this combination of diverse theoretical perspectives constitute an independent academic discipline, is criminology interdisciplinary, or are these different aspects merely subfields or special applications of other established disciplines? If "interdisciplinary" is understood to imply the integration of knowledge into a distinct whole, then criminology is not yet interdisciplinary. On the other hand, there is sufficient independence of the subject from its constituent disciplines to prevent criminology being subsumed under any one of them. For this reason criminology is best defined as "multidisciplinary." This definition can be illustrated by looking at its component theories.

Criminological Theories. Criminology has shifted its emphasis from the search for a single cause of crime, common in the nineteenth century, to a recognition that crime is the result of a number of causes. Less settled is the question of whether criminology should be based on one general theory of human behavior or on several theories. Since its beginnings, criminology has been characterized by both theoretical dominance and disciplinary diversity. Its origins are rooted in the seventeenth century Enlightenment philosophies of Cesare Beccaria and Jeremy Bentham. It developed through the early anthropological and biopsychiatric formulations of Italian School foundationalists Cesare Lombroso, Raffaele Garofalo, and Enrico Ferri and then entered an early twentieth century psychoanalytical period heavily influenced by Sigmund Freud. Early American hereditary and constitutional theorists such as Ernest Hooton and William Sheldon were displaced in the mid-twentieth century by the sociological approach, heralded by the Chicago School's concept of "cultural ecology," which was reflected in the 1940's studies of Clifford Shaw and Henry McKay. Chicago School sociologists, inspired by nineteenth century statisticians Lambert Adolphe Quételet and Andre Guerry, showed that biological explanations alone could not account for crime: For example, why did certain geographical areas of a city show consistent patterns of crime even when their populations changed?

By the 1940's and 1950's a variety of sociological theories of criminal behavior emerged. The structural sociology of Robert Merton's "strain" or "anomie" theory saw crime as an illegitimate response to the unequal distribution of resources.

Other theories ranged from Edwin Sutherland and Donald Cressey's learning theory of "differential association" to Thorsten Sellin's culture conflict theory to the many subcultural theories of delinquency, such as those by Albert Cohen, Richard Cloward, and Lloyd Ohlin. These sociological explanations demonstrated that crime involves more than individual choices governed by the pain-pleasure principle, as early classicists had asserted. They also showed that crime cannot be explained adequately by individual differences in biology or personality, as the early positivists had claimed; rather, it was shown to be shaped by sociocultural, structural, and organizational forces.

The predominance of structural and cultural explanations in American criminology began to be challenged in the 1960's by sociopsychological concepts emphasizing active social processes over both deterministic structures and internal forces. Albert Bandura established "social learning" as a major explanatory framework for violence. With roots in Gabriel Tarde's "imitation theory," this explanation went beyond the mechanistic "operant conditioning" model of B. F. Skinner. It superseded the criminal personality theory of Hans Eysenck and Samuel Yochelson as well as Stanton Samenow's "criminal thinking patterns" theory. The rejection of "faulty mind theories" (which tended to locate the cause of crime in a lack of intelligence or in a form of insanity) as a major explanation for crime was further encouraged by the neutralization and control theories of David Matza and Travis Hirschi. They convinced criminologists that socialization processes—or their negation—could be powerful enough to free any ordinary citizen from moral and legal conformity. Extensions of control theory have been the most empirically tested in the discipline.

Less proven but no less influential on 1970's American criminology was the labeling theorists' idea that crime is actually made worse by criminal justice agencies' attempts to control it. They contended that this worsening effect occurs through the dramatic negative effect the system can have on individual self-identities. The "new deviancy theory," as the labeling perspectives of Howard Becker, Edwin Schur, Erving Goffman, and Thomas Scheff were called, showed how criminal and deviant careers are shaped progressively over time. It was not long before conflict, radical, and critical criminology, reflected in the works of William Chambliss, Richard Quinney, Ian Taylor, and Jock Young, were building on the early Marxist ideas of Dutch criminologist Willem Bonger to suggest that it is not only the agents of government that cause additional crime: The whole capitalist system, they theorized, is "criminogenic." This "new criminology" argued that powerful social classes, and even the capitalist state itself, commit more and worse crimes than individual offenders through corporate pollution, faulty product manufacture, bribery, fraud, and corruption while punishing the less powerful for expressing their resistance to the system through property and violent crimes.

By the 1980's and early 1990's, it had become clear that the merit or applicability of many of these ideas was limited; more important, however, criminology had become uncertain about any and all of its particular theories. The result was new research, new theoretical developments, and new empirical studies testing the whole range of theories and resurrecting and revising some of those previously discarded. Radical theories were no longer uniformly radical; they became more self-critical, separating under the weight of feminist, anarchist, realist, and postmodernist criticism into a variety of "constitutive criminologies." Leading feminist criminologists such as Carol Smart and humanist criminologists such as Hal Pepinsky and Stan Cohen even questioned the value of academic criminology as a professional enterprise.

The Profession of Criminology. A criminologist is someone whose professional training and occupation focus on the study of crime and its control, and whose primary income derives from that activity. Criminologists should be distinguished from criminalists and forensic scientists, who are employed by police departments to investigate crime scenes. Criminologists use a variety of qualitative and quantitative methods of research to study crime, including documentary and historical records, surveys, interviews, direct observation, ethnography, and experimentation.

In the United States there are more than a thousand academic programs in criminology or criminal justice, more than one hundred graduate programs, and ten doctoral programs in criminology. Criminology is also one of several key courses in professional police training programs. More than two thousand professional criminologists are employed by universities, research institutes, government, and private agencies. Academic criminology is served by two professional societies. The American Society of Criminology has more than two thousand members, two-thirds of whom are also members of the Academy of Criminal Justice Sciences. Their two journals, *Criminology* and *Justice Quarterly*, reflect the interwoven interests and concerns of criminologists regarding crime and justice issues.   —*Stuart Henry*

See also Capitalism; Crime; Criminal; Criminal justice system; Forensic science and medicine.

BIBLIOGRAPHY

One of the best of numerous introductory criminology texts is Piers Beirne and James Messerschmidt, *Criminology* (2d ed. Fort Worth, Tex.: Harcourt Brace College, 1995). Excellent analyses and overviews of criminological theories include George B. Vold and Thomas J. Bernard, *Theoretical Criminology* (3d ed. New York: Oxford University Press, 1986), and Werner Einstadter and Stuart Henry, *Criminological Theory: An Analysis of Its Underlying Assumptions* (Fort Worth, Tex.: Harcourt Brace College, 1995). For a focus on the works of selected criminologists, see Randy Martin, Robert J. Mutchnick, and W. Timothy Austin, *Criminological Thought: Pioneers Past and Present* (New York: Macmillan, 1990), and Piers Beirne, *Inventing Criminology: Essays on the Rise of 'Homo Criminalis'* (Albany, N.Y.: State University of New York Press, 1993). A sampling of original classic criminological statements can be found in Joseph E. Jacoby, *Classics of Criminology* (2d ed. Prospect Heights, Ill.: Waveland Press,

1994). Feminist theory and postmodernism are exemplified, respectively, by Loraine Gelsthorpe and Allison Morris, eds., *Feminist Perspectives in Criminology* (Philadelphia: Open University Press, 1990), and Stuart Henry and Dragan Milovanovic, *Constitutive Criminology: Beyond Postmodernism* (London: Sage, 1995). For lively discussions of key issues and future prospects for the discipline, see Don C. Gibbons, *Talking About Crime and Criminals: Problems and Issues in Theory Development in Criminology* (Englewood Cliffs, N.J.: Prentice-Hall, 1994) and David Nelken, ed., *The Futures of Criminology* (London: Sage, 1994).

Cruel and unusual punishment

DEFINITION: A punishment of a degrading, torturous, or barbaric nature, or punishment so disproportionate to the crime or offense as to shock the moral sense of a community

SIGNIFICANCE: The prohibition of cruel and unusual punishments not only has become a common part of the legal processes of all developed democracies but also has become a general barometer of a society's civil evolution

In the Eighth Amendment to the U.S. Constitution, the prohibition against cruel and unusual punishment is joined to the prohibition against excessive bails and fines. To the founders of the United States, these practices represented uses of the state's criminal justice machinery that ranged from inappropriate to inhuman. Both sets of practices had sordid histories in England, and the founders believed that the prohibition against both needed to be written into the Constitution in general terms so that the determination of what constitutes a cruel or unusual punishment or excessive bail could be made by each generation in the context of the changing circumstances of life and the evolving norms of civilized societies.

Development. The prohibitions against both cruel and unusual punishment and excessive bail and fines have their roots in English history as far back as the Magna Carta. Curiously, most of the battles between king and countrymen over these matters focused not on cruel and unusual punishments but on the right-to-bail issue. The decisive battles ensued during the seventeenth century, when—as America was being settled on the opposite side of the Atlantic—a 1627 ruling by English judges upholding the king's right to imprison anyone without bail before trial led to a battle between the Crown and Parliament. The latter decisively won with the inclusion in the 1689 British Bill of Rights of a provision outlawing "excessive bail."

One hundred years later the "excessive bail" clause of the British Bill of Rights was linked with the prohibition of cruel and unusual punishments and included, otherwise essentially unaltered, in the Eighth Amendment of the United States Bill of Rights. There was a small degree of controversy over its inclusion. When the Congress considered the Bill of Rights in 1789, two members objected to the Eighth Amendment because of the subjective and indefinite nature of the terms being employed with respect to both fines and bails ("excessive") and punishments ("cruel," "unusual"). One of these members of Congress also objected more generally to the "cruel and unusual" provision, explaining to his colleagues that "it is sometimes necessary to hang a man, villains often deserve whipping, and perhaps having their ears cut off." Most of those present, however, not only held reasonably definite notions of what constituted cruel and unusual punishments but also were willing to proscribe such punishments even if they were likely to be more effective in dissuading villainy than less cruel, alternative measures.

Throughout the nineteenth century, the Supreme Court limited its interpretation of the cruel and unusual clause essentially to the historic punishments obviously intended to be banned by the framers of the Constitution—for example, burning at the stake, crucifixion, use of the thumbscrew, drawing and quartering, and the breaking of a body on the rack. Not until the landmark 1910 case *Weems v. United States* (1910) was the provision given the liberal construction of having an "expansive and vital character" which alters with the changing sensitivities of modern societies. Since that time, most of the significant cases revolving around the cruel and unusual clause have involved either proportionality issues centering on the form of punishment compared with the nature of the crime or issues pertaining to the constitutionality of capital punishment and its means of implementation.

The argument that the Eighth Amendment can be violated by penalties which "shock" the sense of justice in their severity or by a sentence whose length is "greatly disproportioned to the offenses charged" was first voiced by Justice Stephen J. Field in his dissenting opinion in the 1892 case *O'Neil v. Vermont* (1892). Eighteen years later, the disproportionate test was applied for the first time by a majority in *Weems v. United States*, a case involving a Philippine law prescribing twelve to twenty years of hard labor imprisonment for knowingly entering a false statement in a public record. Subsequently, the proportionality test has been applied in cases involving such matters as court-martial proceedings leading to the revocation of citizenship for desertion in the armed forces in time of war (*Trop v. Dulles*, 1958); the infliction of punishment for being a drug addict (*Robinson v. California*, 1962); and the imposition of life imprisonment without parole for minor, nonviolent crimes (*Solem v. Helm*, 1983).

Capital Punishment. The issue of capital punishment first significantly came before the Supreme Court in 1879 in the case of *Wilkerson v. Utah*, in which the Court upheld execution by firing squad over the objection that it was cruel and unusual punishment. Likewise, the Supreme Court tacitly upheld the constitutionality of capital punishment itself eleven years later when it sustained, in *In re Kemmler* (1890), the use of the electric chair for carrying out executions. At the time, capital punishment was not a controversial issue in American society. Public hangings were still routine, and both the *Kemmler* and *Wilkerson* cases were unanimous decisions. Four generations later, however, the issue of whether capital punishment itself is a cruel and unusual punishment became one of the principal issues confronting—and to a degree dividing—the Supreme Court.

In *Witherspoon v. Illinois*, decided in 1968, the Supreme Court gave its first indication that the death penalty might be in trouble as a part of the United States' criminal justice machinery. *Witherspoon* did not involve the Eighth Amendment. Rather it was a "fair trial" case arising under the Sixth Amendment, in which the Supreme Court invalidated the death sentence imposed on the accused by a "hanging" jury (one from which opponents of the death penalty had been excluded). Noting the divided nature of public opinion on the death sentence throughout the United States, the Supreme Court decided that the jury in the case "fell woefully short of that impartiality to which the petitioner was entitled under the Sixth and Fourteenth Amendments."

The *Witherspoon* ruling emboldened the opponents of capital punishment to mount a judicial assault on the death penalty under the cruel and unusual test of the Eighth Amendment.

Their timing proved to be bad, though, for *Witherspoon* was one of the last important, rights-of-the-criminally-accused cases decided during the Warren Court era. By the time the cases challenging the constitutionality of capital punishment under the Eighth Amendment began to reach the Supreme Court, President Richard Nixon had not only replaced a retiring Earl Warren with Chief Justice Warren Burger but also appointed a majority of the nine justices on the Supreme Court with an eye to tilting it in a more conservative, law-and-order direction. Thus, in several 1970's cases involving the constitutionality of capital punishment, the Supreme Court affirmed that, per se, capital punishment is not a cruel or unusual punishment for certain categories of crimes. At the same time it also ruled, in a series of split decisions, that the administration of capital punishment must conform to specific and strict guidelines to ensure that it is not imposed by juries in such a

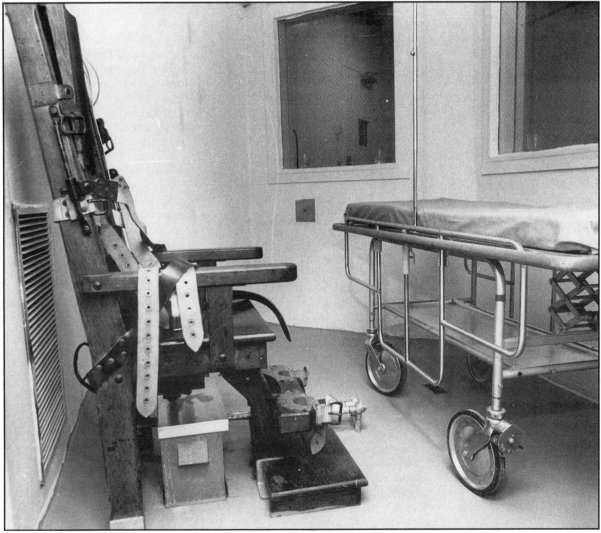

The Supreme Court has held that capital punishment is not by definition cruel and unusual punishment; pictured is the electric chair at the Florida State Prison. (AP/Wide World Photos)

capricious, arbitrary, and/or "freakish" manner as to become cruel or unusual. In *Furman v. Georgia* in 1972, the Court essentially threw out capital punishment as it was then being administered in the United States; four years later, in *Gregg v. Georgia*, it approved the first state statute written after *Furman* that satisfied the Supreme Court's requirements for the constitutional imposition of capital punishment, including a review process designed to compare "each death sentence with the sentences imposed on similarly situated defendants to ensure that the sentence of death in a particular case is not disproportionate" (*Gregg v. Georgia*, 1976). Other judicially mandated requirements involved limiting the discretion of juries in imposing the death sentence and making the right to appeal automatic in capital punishment cases. Still later cases further elaborated the rules for imposing the death sentence in terms of such matters as the relevance in sentencing proceedings of information pertaining to the character of the crime and the character and record of the criminally accused. Mandatory death sentences have routinely been struck down as unconstitutional (*Woodson v. North Carolina, Roberts v. Louisiana*, 1976).

Excessive Bail and Fines. Although the Supreme Court has never specifically addressed the issue of what constitutes an "excessive fine" within the meaning of the Eighth Amendment, except to indicate that the clause applies only to fines levied in criminal proceedings (*Browning Ferris Industries v. Kelco Disposal*, 1989), an evolutionary approach has characterized the judiciary's consideration of the Eighth Amendment's excessive bail clause.

For nearly two hundred years, the prevailing view was that bail existed only to prevent flight and that there is a reasonable amount of bail for any category of crime to ensure that the criminally accused will appear at his or her trial. The right to bail was seen as a basic constitutional right by the founding fathers, to whom the debtors prisons of Britain and the Crown's willingness to incarcerate political enemies without trial were comparatively recent history. Hence, although it was generally agreed that what constituted "excessive bail" must be determined on a case-by-case basis, the Supreme Court generally adhered to the view that at no point may bail be set at an amount which has either the intent or effect of depriving the accused of the full opportunity to prepare for his or her defense (*Stack v. Boyle*, 1951). Like the cruel and unusual clause, this protection did not necessarily apply to all legal proceedings. Deportation proceedings against alien communists, for example, were exempted from the bail requirement in 1952 (*Carlson v. Landon*), as were juvenile court proceedings some thirty years later (*Shall v. Martin*, 1984). In criminal proceedings, though, the right to bail was basic. Without it, the Supreme Court explained in *Stack v. Boyle*, the accused would be hampered from preparing a defense, punishment could be inflicted without conviction, and "the presumption of innocence, secured only after centuries of struggle, would lose its meaning."

In 1987, however, in the watershed case of *United States v. Salerno*, the Supreme Court created two significant exceptions to this rule. The pretrial detention of "arrestees charged with serious felonies" was to be permitted when the accused are deemed either to pose a threat to the safety of the community if released or likely to flee regardless of the amount of bail posted because of the gravity of the charges against them. Most states have subsequently rewritten their bail statutes to deny bail in certain classes of crime—for example, in cases involving multiple counts of first-degree murder.

The Still-Expanding Eighth Amendment. Like the evolving meanings attached to the concept of equality, which each new generation has had to define for itself since the inception of the Republic, the definitions attached to excessive fines and especially those given to cruel and unusual punishments have been one of the measures by which Americans—as well as citizens in other democracies—have assessed their level of civility. As Chief Justice Earl Warren wrote in *Trop v. Dulles*, the content of the Eighth Amendment "must draw its meaning from the evolving standards of decency that mark the progress of a maturing society." By this test, the citizens of the United States traveled a great distance in the half century following World War II.

As late as 1947, in *Louisiana ex rel. Francis v. Resweber*, the Supreme Court was unwilling to rule that the execution of an individual twice for the same crime (Louisiana's electric chair having failed to discharge a lethal dose of electricity on the first occasion) was a cruel or unusual punishment within the meaning of the Constitution. As late as the 1950's, the whipping post was still being employed as punishment for a variety of petty offenses by the state of Delaware. "The penology of a state," Justice Felix Frankfurter wrote for the majority in *Resweber*, "is not to be tested by the scope of the Eighth Amendment," even though the Supreme Court had at least implicitly assumed that the Eighth Amendment limited state action when it reviewed the early cases involving the constitutionality of capital punishment by firing squad and electrocution.

By the 1990's, not only had the provisions of the Eighth Amendment been made implicitly applicable to the states through incorporation into the due process clause of the Fourteenth Amendment in *Robinson v. California*, but also the prohibition against cruel and unusual punishments had been extended from courtroom sentences to the nature of the confinement in prison cells (which must meet certain minimally decent standards) and to the treatment of prisoners serving sentences. These developments marked substantial departures from existing precedents. As late as 1977, a 5-4 majority on the Supreme Court had upheld the use of "reasonable corporal punishment" in schools in *Ingraham v. Wright*, at least in part by adhering to the traditional view that the cruel and unusual punishments clause only applies to the penalties given to those convicted in state or federal courts. The other side of the coin has traditionally been that the clause does not limit the penalties inflicted on people by the government in such other arenas as school systems, deportation proceedings (*Harisiades v. Shaughnessy*, 1952), the treatment of those in jail awaiting trial (*Bell v. Wolfish*, 1979), and hearings involving committal to mental institutions (*Youngberg v. Romeo*, 1982). By the

1990's, however, federal appellate courts were routinely reviewing the treatment of prisoners before and after trial on the basis of the 8-1 ruling in *Hutto v. Finney* (1978) to the effect that "confinement in prison . . . is a form of punishment subject to scrutiny under the Eighth Amendment standards."

Even more revealingly, by the late twentieth century, litigation involving the cruel and unusual clause had begun to revolve around topics which in the recent past would have been regarded as esoteric but scarcely cruel and unusual. Appeals under the Eighth Amendment have thus been made in cases involving such issues as mandatory life sentences without parole for those convicted of possessing more than 650 grams of cocaine (*Harmelin v. Michigan*, 1991), the sentencing of defendants suffering from acquired immune deficiency syndrome, "unreasonable" exposure to second-hand environmental tobacco smoke in prison (*Helling v. McKinney*, 1993), society's obligation to protect from physical harm those being involuntarily retained in custody, including those in mental hospitals and orphanages, the prosecution of pregnant addicts, the arrest of the homeless, and death sentences for juvenile offenders.

The same expansive philosophy can be seen in cases involving the excessive fines portion of the Eighth Amendment. Although the Supreme Court continues to adhere to the position that the size of a fine does not make it excessive no matter how great the fine may be and that the Eighth Amendment's injunction against excessive fines applies only to criminal cases, in a civil case arising in Oregon in the 1990's the Supreme Court did adopt an "excessive" test involving the size of a punitive damages award.

Perhaps because of the broadening construction given to the Eighth Amendment as a restraint on state action, cases involving this amendment became among the most controversial of those arising from the Bill of Rights during the late twentieth century. Many states, for example, have proscribed corporal punishment in their school systems, even though the Supreme Court has refused to invalidate it under the Eighth Amendment. Likewise, cases involving the proportionality test have been highly controversial, especially when tied to capital punishment cases. Sometimes the Supreme Court's rulings have even provoked a short-term national outrage, as in 1977, when a narrow majority in *Coker v. Georgia* ruled that the death penalty for the crime of raping an adult woman, in the absence of such aggravating circumstances as the commission of another crime, constituted a "grossly disproportional, excessive penalty" which violated the Eighth Amendment.

The United States has not necessarily moved in tandem with the remainder of the world in its perception of the rules of ordered decency in the domain of cruel and unusual punishments. In condoning the continued use of capital punishment, the Supreme Court has left the United States nearly alone among developed democratic states, virtually all of which eliminated capital punishment from their criminal justice systems during the latter half of the twentieth century. Moreover, although the federal judiciary's decisions designed to correct the substandard nature of prison conditions in the United States have often exposed it to domestic criticism for "coddling criminals," several European states have persistently refused to extradite criminals to the United States because of what they perceive to be the unsafe and intolerable nature of American penitentiaries, and European courts of justice have routinely sustained such action. On the other hand, if the definition of cruel and unusual punishments in the United States has not yet become as exacting as that of the European Court of Human Rights, it remains an expanding one, far removed not only from the rack and iron-maiden meanings attached to it by the founding fathers but also from the proportionality and physical discomfort tests by which the amendment was being interpreted as late as the 1960's. —*Joseph R. Rudolph, Jr.*

See also Capital punishment; Corporal punishment; *Furman v. Georgia*; *Gregg v. Georgia*; *Harmelin v. Michigan*; Punishment; Scottsboro cases.

BIBLIOGRAPHY

Particularly good sections on the evolving meaning of cruel and unusual punishment can be found in David J. Bodenhamer and James W. Ely, Jr., eds., *The Bill of Rights in Modern America: After 200 Years* (Bloomington: Indiana University Press, 1993), and Jethro K. Lieberman, *The Evolving Constitution: How the Supreme Court Has Ruled on Issues from Abortion to Zoning* (New York: Random House, 1992). Among the many older, more detailed examinations of the amendment, see Larry Charles Berkson, *The Concept of Cruel and Unusual Punishment* (Lexington, Mass.: Lexington Books, 1975), and, on capital punishment, Frank Carrington, *Neither Cruel nor Unusual* (New Rochelle, N.Y.: Arlington House, 1978).

Cruzan v. Director, Missouri Department of Health

COURT: U.S. Supreme Court

DATE: Decided June 25, 1990

SIGNIFICANCE: Although allowing states much discretion for requiring rigorous evidence of an individual's wishes, the Court affirmed that the due process clause protects one's substantive liberty to refuse medical intervention even if the consequence is death

Nancy Cruzan, at the age of twenty-five, had a serious automobile accident on January 11, 1983, and as a result her brain was deprived of oxygen for about fourteen minutes. Her parents approved the insertion of a feeding tube to keep her alive, but it soon became apparent that Cruzan would never regain consciousness and had entered an "irreversible persistent vegetative state." After several years the parents sought permission to have the feeding tube removed. Although a state trial judge approved, the Missouri Supreme Court denied permission based on the state's living will statute which required "clear and convincing evidence" that Cruzan would have wanted the tube removed. Not possessing such evidence, the Cruzans, supported by the American Civil Liberties Union (ACLU), took their case to the U.S. Supreme Court.

The Court decided by a 5-4 vote to uphold the constitutionality of the Missouri law. In the majority opinion, Chief Justice

William Rehnquist acknowledged a common-law doctrine of informed consent which includes the right of a competent adult to refuse medical treatment, but he pointed to *Jacobson v. Massachusetts* (1905) as a precedent for balancing the state's interest in preserving life with the individual's "liberty interest in refusing unwanted medical treatment." The Constitution allowed states wide discretion to establish strict procedures to assure that the decisions of surrogates would conform to the wishes of a person before becoming incompetent. The minority agreed with much of Rehnquist's analysis but argued that Missouri's procedures, which required evidence for declining but not for accepting treatment, failed to provide a reliable determination of which choice the person would have preferred.

Although the Cruzans did not prevail at the Supreme Court, thereafter friends of their daughter came forward to testify that she had earlier expressed views consistent with her parents'

wishes, and a state court determined the new evidence to be sufficient. Eleven days after the tube was removed, Nancy Cruzan died on December 26, 1990.

The true importance of *Cruzan* was its affirmation of broad "liberty interests" based on a "substantive due process" reading of the Fourteenth Amendment. All members of the Court accepted that the due process clause gave competent adults the right to refuse unwanted medical intervention. Justice Antonin Scalia was the only member of the Court to emphasize the limits of this right and explicitly to reject a constitutional "right to die." At the same time, however, the Court insisted that the right to refuse medical intervention must be exercised personally by a competent adult, and it allowed states much latitude in the formation of living will legislation.

See also *Bolling v. Sharpe*; *Bowers v. Hardwick*; Due process of law; Medical and health law; Privacy, right of; Suicide and euthanasia.

Dandridge v. Williams

COURT: U.S. Supreme Court

DATE: Decided April 6, 1970

SIGNIFICANCE: In this case, the Supreme Court held that legislation involving social and economic matters such as the distribution of welfare benefits would be accorded deferential review and would not generally be found to violate the equal protection requirement of the Fourteenth Amendment

The state of Maryland's Aid to Families with Dependent Children (AFDC) program made most of its grants on the basis of a computed standard of need. The program, however, imposed a maximum monthly grant of $250 per month regardless of a family's size or computed need. Plaintiffs with large families challenged the program, claiming that it violated the equal protection clause of the Fourteenth Amendment and the provisions of the federal Social Security Act. A majority of the Supreme Court rejected both claims.

Justice Potter Stewart delivered the Court's opinion. He emphasized that the case did not involve any of the rights guaranteed by the Bill of Rights. Instead, it was a form of social or economic legislation that the Court resolved should be accorded substantial deference. Justice Stewart argued that the benefit cap served valid purposes. It encouraged employment and avoided discrimination between welfare families and the families of the "working poor." It was enough, he said, that the statute was rationally based and free from "invidious discrimination."

Justices Thurgood Marshall, William Brennan, and William O. Douglas dissented—Douglas because he believed that Maryland's program violated federal law, and Marshall and Brennan because they believed the program violated both federal law and the equal protection clause of the Fourteenth Amendment. The latter argued that Maryland's program discriminated between small and large families by giving small families enough to survive but withholding the same benefit from large families. For Marshall and Brennan, the case was about children having enough to eat. Viewing the matter in this light, they argued that the state should have had to do more to justify its discrimination.

During the 1960's the Supreme Court protected a variety of rights through the equal protection clause of the Fourteenth Amendment and the equal protection component of the Fifth Amendment's due process clause. In *Dandridge v. Williams*, however, the Court refused to recognize a fundamental right to welfare benefits and signaled instead that the steady proliferation of rights guarded by the equal protection doctrine was ending. Especially in the area of social and economic legislation, such as the distribution of welfare benefits and other governmental benefits, *Dandridge* established a pattern of deferential review that usually upheld such legislation against constitutional challenge. This pattern would be reinforced within a few years when the Court held in *San Antonio Independent School District v. Rodriguez* (1973) that the Constitution did not guarantee a fundamental right to a public education.

See also Aid to Families with Dependent Children (AFDC); Constitution, U.S.; *San Antonio Independent School District v. Rodriguez*; Welfare state.

Darby Lumber Co., United States v.

COURT: U.S. Supreme Court

DATE: Decided February 3, 1941

SIGNIFICANCE: In upholding the right of Congress to enact minimum wage-maximum hour legislation, the Supreme Court returned to a broad interpretation of the commerce clause, laying the constitutional foundation for the federal government's control over the economy

In the first case to interpret Congress' constitutional power to "regulate commerce . . . among the several States," *Gibbons v. Ogden* (1824), Chief Justice John Marshall etched the power of Congress expansively. In what is widely regarded as his finest opinion, Marshall defined commerce as "intercourse," not merely traffic or trade, and held that the power to regulate it "is complete in itself, may be exercised to the utmost extent, and acknowledges no limitations other than are prescribed in the Constitution."

During the next hundred years, however, a brace of arguments converged to limit Congress' control over commerce. First, an inflexible line was drawn between interstate and intrastate commerce (transactions inside a state). Congress could regulate the former; however, local economic activities such as manufacturing were often ruled to lie beyond the reach of the commerce clause. Second, in *Hammer v. Dagenhart* (1918), the Supreme Court ruled that the Tenth Amendment limits the authority of the federal government to those powers "expressly" delegated to it, and hence precludes federal control of such matters as child labor because the Constitution does not explicitly give Congress the power to regulate it.

Despite the *Hammer* decision, constitutional law pertaining to Congress' influence over intrastate matters was often confused between the *Hammer* and *Darby* cases. In *Carter v. Carter Coal Co.*, in 1936, for example, the Court ruled that Congress' power over interstate commerce extends to those intrastate activities having a direct impact on interstate commerce. The following term, the Court expanded this stance by holding that the power to regulate interstate commerce extends to intrastate matters substantially affecting interstate commerce, even if they only indirectly do so (*National Labor Relations Board v. Jones & Laughlin Steel Corp.*, 1937).

Nevertheless, it was *United States v. Darby* in 1941 that ended the debate concerning Congress' authority over local matters. The case involved a challenge to the constitutionality of the Fair Labor Standards Act, passed by Congress in 1938. Fred Darby was paying the employees of his lumber company between twelve and eighteen cents an hour (these were not unusual wages in the lumber industry at the time), and the act set the minimum wage at twenty-five cents an hour for workers engaging in interstate commerce or producing goods whose sale involved interstate commerce. When Darby continued to pay low wages after the act was passed, he was indicted. When the case reached the Supreme Court, the Court voted unanimously to uphold the act. Explicitly overruling *Hammer v. Dagenhart*, the *Darby* decision returned to Marshall's broad interpretation of the commerce clause to sustain the minimum wage-maximum hours of employment provisions of the Fair Labor Standards Act. To the majority, Congress' power to regulate interstate commerce included the power to regulate intrastate matters whenever their regulation may be considered a reasonable means of achieving the legitimate end of regulating interstate commerce.

So construed, the commerce clause has become the constitutional foundation for federal policies aimed at controlling the economy and the basis for exercising a federal police power. The Federal Bureau of Investigation (FBI) may investigate local crimes if the channels of interstate commerce may be used to commit the crime (as with drug smuggling) or to enable the perpetrator to elude local law enforcement agencies. Indeed, so well established had Congress' power to regulate local matters under the commerce clause become by the 1960's that Congress chose to base the provisions of the 1964 Civil Rights Act outlawing racial discrimination in privately owned enterprises of public accommodation (hotels, restaurants) on the commerce clause.

See also *Carter v. Carter Coal Co.*; Commerce clause; *Hammer v. Dagenhart*; *Heart of Atlanta Motel v. United States*; *Muller v. Oregon*.

Dartmouth College v. Woodward

Court: U.S. Supreme Court

Date: Decided February 2, 1819

Significance: By deciding that a charter issued to a private corporation constituted a contract protected by the contract clause of the Constitution against impairment by a state legislature, the U.S. Supreme Court for the first time placed private contracts beyond state control

In 1769, King George III granted a charter to Dartmouth College, empowering a twelve-person board of trustees to govern college affairs "forever." Throughout the revolutionary era, the charter remained unchanged. In the early nineteenth century, however, bitter conflicts between the trustees and Dartmouth's second president, John Wheelock, whom the trustees eventually removed, attracted such notoriety that it brought the state's political parties into the affair. The Federalist Party, proponents of strong national government and of

federal policies aiding private economic expansion, supported the trustees, while New Hampshire's Republican Party, generally favoring states' rights and relatively weak federal power, supported Wheelock.

Dominated by a Republican majority, the state legislature in 1816 enacted three laws that amended Dartmouth's charter, created a new body of trustees, and changed the institution's name. Ignoring the new laws, the old trustees, backed by a majority of faculty and students, continued to run the college. The new trustees appointed under the amended charter removed the old trustees and reelected John Wheelock as president.

Alleging that the Republicans' 1816 legislation impaired the obligation of contract contained in Dartmouth's charter of 1769, the old board of trustees sued in the state courts to recover the college charter, records, seal, and accounts from one Woodward, secretary of the new board of trustees. After New Hampshire's courts decided against them, the old trustees carried their case to the U.S. Supreme Court on a writ of error. Their case was argued in 1818 by Daniel Webster and Joseph Hopkinson, two of the country's ablest lawyers, before Chief Justice John Marshall, who has since been recognized as a seminal figure in the creation of the American judiciary and as a major force in giving direction to constitutional interpretation. Two justices delayed the Supreme Court's decision, their doubts being resolved by the conservative legal arguments of New York's Chancellor James Kent.

On February 2, 1819, Chief Justice Marshall, his colleagues voting with him 5 to 1, delivered the opinion that New Hampshire's laws were an unconstitutional violation of the obligation of contracts. While Marshall was at pains to indicate that the Constitution did not envision restraint of the states in regulating their civil institutions, Dartmouth College was private and not subject to state control. The Dartmouth ruling was the first in which the Court held that a charter was a contract protected by the Constitution.

Representing an assertion of federal judicial power and an expansion of the contract clause, the *Dartmouth* decision contributed little to the growth of corporations and was modified subsequently by *Ogden v. Saunders* (1827), by *Charles River Bridge v. Warren Bridge Co.* (1837), by *Home Building and Loan Association v. Blaisdell* (1934) as well as by other decisions expanding the states' police power.

See also *Charles River Bridge v. Warren Bridge Co.*; Contract, freedom of; Contract law; *Fletcher v. Peck*; Marshall, John; *Ogden v. Saunders*; *Sturges v. Crowninshield*.

Daugherty, Harry M. (Jan. 26, 1860, Washington Court House, Ohio—Oct. 12, 1941, Columbus, Ohio)

Identification: President Warren G. Harding's attorney general

Significance: Daugherty curtailed rail union power and banned branch banking

In 1882, Harry M. Daugherty was elected town clerk of Washington Court House, Ohio. Subsequently he was a city councilman and a state legislator. He unsuccessfully sought nomination for attorney general of Ohio (1895), Congress (1896), governor (1897), and senator (1902, 1908, and 1916), and he campaigned for William McKinley, Warren G. Harding, and William Howard Taft. Appointed U.S. attorney general in 1921, Daugherty undertook the investigation of World War I contract fraud. Ten million dollars were recovered, but he was accused of laxity. He opened the first federal prison for first offenders, brought J. Edgar Hoover into the Justice Department, and successfully recommended freeing Eugene V. Debs.

Daugherty obtained an injunction against the railroad shopmen's union on September 1, 1922, that established the preeminence of public interests in industrial controversy. A congressional resolution on September 11, 1922, calling for his impeachment failed in the House Judiciary Committee. Further attacks arising from the Teapot Dome scandal caused leading Republican senators to call for Daugherty's resignation. Daugherty refused to resign until the charges were proved, but after he denied Senate committee requests for departmental papers, President Calvin Coolidge demanded his resignation. Daugherty resigned March 24, 1924. Investigators then unsuccessfully attempted to subpoena officers and records of the Midland National Bank of Washington Court House. Daugherty refused to appear before the committee, and the investigation ended without charges or reported findings. Daugherty was prosecuted in 1927 for fraudulent dealings, but the trial ended in a hung jury. In 1932, he published *The Inside Story of the Harding Tragedy*.

See also Attorney general of the United States; Debs, Eugene V.; Hoover, J. Edgar; Taft, William Howard; Teapot Dome scandal.

Deadly force, police use of

DEFINITION: The killing of people by police officers through the use of choke holds, firearms, or other methods of physical control

SIGNIFICANCE: Because of controversies about excessive, inappropriate, and discriminatory applications of force to citizens by police officers, fatalities caused by the police have been reduced through training programs, regulations, and court decisions

In order to control crime and maintain order in society, law enforcement officers have traditionally been granted the authority to use physical force to capture or gain control of people who violate the law. American police officers, unlike those in some other countries, carry firearms, and police throughout the country have used their guns to kill people in the course of seeking to enforce the law and maintain order. Police officers have also caused people's deaths through the use of choke holds around people's necks and blows to the head administered with nightsticks, flashlights, or pistols.

The Context of Police Deadly Force. Deaths caused by the police were not randomly distributed throughout the broad spectrum of society, but instead occurred most frequently among poor people and members of racial minority groups who lacked the political power to complain effectively about improper police behavior. Because criminal offenders have easy access to firearms in the United States, American police officers know that they risk being shot; therefore they sometimes overreact to persons whom they suspect of being armed and dangerous. The problem has been compounded throughout American history because of negative attitudes toward poor people and members of minority groups. Officers have used guns, nightsticks, and choke holds more frequently in seeking to capture or gain control over people in inner-city neighborhoods. Lethal physical force was applied not only to people suspected of committing felonies but sometimes also to people who argued with officers about parking tickets or failed to cooperate with the police about other relatively minor matters.

During the 1960's and 1970's, as African Americans became more assertive about gaining equal rights and American society became less tolerant of discrimination, many police departments came under sharp criticism for their harsh behavior toward members of minority groups. In the urban riots of the late 1960's, for example, most of the fatalities were caused by police officers' shooting of suspected looters and rioters. The actual nature and extent of police deadly force varied by city, depending on the training provided to officers and the guidelines developed by police departments for the use of firearms and other physical interventions. Deadly force was more likely to be applied by officers whose police chiefs saw their job as attacking criminal segments of society as opposed to serving the entire public in a professional manner.

Control of Police Deadly Force. Controversies over highly publicized killings by the police led many police departments to develop stricter rules about the use of force. Greater attention was given to the precise situations in which officers would be justified in firing their guns or hitting someone with a nightstick. Officers also received more training in crowd-control techniques and immobilizing holds that would not threaten the lives of resisting civilians. Most important, courts and juries increasingly found police officers and their departments liable for needlessly causing the deaths of citizens. The threat that a city might have to pay millions of dollars in damages to the family of a person killed by police created even greater incentives for police chiefs to address the deadly-force issue through stricter guidelines, better supervision, and increased training. Such guidelines still permit officers to use their weapons against armed offenders who pose an immediate threat, but they significantly narrow the circumstances in which it is reasonable for potentially lethal force to be applied.

As a result of these changes, the number of people killed annually by police officers in major U.S. cities dropped from approximately 350 in 1971 to 170 in 1984. Yet the guidelines for officers had developed unevenly, and some states still permitted officers to shoot unarmed suspects if they were suspected of fleeing from the scene of a felony. In 1985, in *Tennessee v. Garner*, the U.S. Supreme Court provided a common national rule regarding the use of deadly force on fleeing felons. The Court declared that it was an unconstitutional violation of a person's rights to shoot at an unarmed suspect who is fleeing from the scene of a crime. Under Fourth Amendment rules, such actions constituted an unreasonable use of force to seize people.

This ruling helped to clarify and standardize the application of deadly firearms force, but it could not solve the problem completely. Some police departments, including that of Los Angeles, faced further controversy and lawsuits over deaths that resulted from the use of choke holds—especially given that the holds appeared to be applied most frequently to members of minority groups.

Although police use of deadly force will inevitably remain an issue, particularly because of the need for American police to confront armed criminals, developments since the 1970's have reduced the scope of this problem.   —*Christopher E. Smith*

See also Arrest; Civilian review boards; Discretion; Kent State student killings; Miami riots; Police; Police brutality; Reasonable force; *Tennessee v. Garner*.

BIBLIOGRAPHY

Various aspects of police use of deadly force are discussed in detail in James J. Fyfe, *Readings on Police Use of Deadly Force* (Washington, D.C.: Police Foundation, 1982), and Catherine H. Milton et al., *Police Use of Deadly Force* (Washington, D.C.: Police Foundation, 1977). Deadly force is discussed in the larger contexts of police brutality in Jerome H. Skolnick and James J. Fyfe, *Above the Law: Police and the Excessive Use of Force* (New York: Free Press, 1993). Legal rules and consequences affecting police use of deadly force are presented in Victor E. Kappeler, *Critical Issues in Police Civil Liability* (Prospect Heights, Ill.: Waveland Press, 1993), and Rolando V. del Carmen, *Civil Liabilities in American Policing* (Englewood Cliffs, N.J.: Prentice-Hall, 1991).

Debs, Eugene V. (Nov. 5, 1855, Terre Haute, Ind.—Oct. 20, 1926, Elmhurst, Ill.)

IDENTIFICATION: Labor leader and social justice advocate

SIGNIFICANCE: Debs was the Socialist Party candidate for president five times as well as a labor organizer and leading radical economic and social critic

Born to a family of immigrants, Debs left school at the age of fourteen to work on the railroad. He quit his job in 1874 to become an officer in the local Brotherhood of Locomotive Firemen. In 1880, Debs became secretary-treasurer of the national brotherhood and editor of the *Locomotive Firemen's Magazine*. During this time he was also active in politics, serving as a Democratic representative on the Terre Haute City Council and in the Indiana State Legislature.

In 1893 Debs began to organize all railroad employees into one organization, the American Railway Union. It became the nation's largest industrial union, but after several successful labor actions it was destroyed as a result of the 1894 Pullman strike. Arrested for his activities during the strike, Debs served six months in prison. This experience led him to become a socialist, and he became the Socialist Party candidate for president in the elections of 1900, 1904, 1908, and 1912. In

the last of these contests he received more than 900,000 votes, 6 percent of the total.

Debs opposed U.S. involvement in World War I and was convicted for violating the Espionage Act. In 1918 he was sentenced to serve ten years in prison. While an inmate in the Atlanta Federal Penitentiary in 1920 he ran for president and again received more than 900,000 votes. President Warren G. Harding commuted his sentence in 1921, and Debs spent his declining years giving speeches and supporting various radical causes. Many of his ideas are expounded in his published speeches and editorials and in a book on prison conditions, *Walls and Bars* (1927). Debs was an eloquent socialist spokesperson who advocated woman suffrage, social security legislation, industrial unionism, and the extension of civil liberties.

See also Conscientious objection; *Debs, In re*; Espionage Act; Labor unions; Palmer raids and the "red scare"; Pullman strike; Socialism; Socialist Party, American.

Debs, In re

COURT: U.S. Supreme Court

DATE: Decided May 27, 1895

SIGNIFICANCE: The Supreme Court for the first time upheld the authority of the federal government to use an injunction against striking union members

In re Debs was a by-product of the 1894 strike against George Pullman's Palace Car Company. The strike began in May as a response to wage cuts and high rents at the company town of Pullman, located near Chicago, Illinois. The American Railway Union, headed by Eugene V. Debs, supported the striking Pullman workers by refusing to handle trains with Pullman cars. By the end of June, nearly all the railroads west of Chicago had been paralyzed by the strike.

Railroad owners, alleging that the strike was hampering the movement of the mails, petitioned President Grover Cleveland to send federal troops to Illinois. In July, Cleveland complied by dispatching two thousand troops to the strike scene. At the same time, Cleveland's attorney general, Richard Olney, secured an injunction prohibiting the strikers from interfering with the mails or with railroads engaged in interstate commerce. Olney found authority for this legal device in the Sherman Antitrust Act, enacted by Congress in 1890 to control corporate monopolies. The statute outlawed combinations or conspiracies in restraint of trade. When Debs and other leaders of the American Railway Union ignored the injunction, they were arrested. The strike subsequently collapsed.

Debs and his associates were arraigned in the Federal Circuit Court for Northern Illinois, convicted for contempt of court, and sentenced to imprisonment. In sentencing Debs to six months in jail, Judge William Woods upheld the right of the federal government to secure an injunction, under the Sherman Act, against strikers. The activities of Debs and his cohorts, according to Woods, constituted a conspiracy in restraint of interstate commerce.

In an attempt to test the constitutional propriety of the labor injunction, Debs petitioned the U.S. Supreme Court for a writ of habeas corpus. In 1895, Justice David Brewer read the unanimous opinion of the Court. Brewer made no judgment on the constitutional propriety of using the Sherman Act against unions. Instead, he based his decision on the broader grounds that the relationship of the federal government to interstate commerce and the delivery of the mails justified the use of the injunction to prevent forcible obstruction by Debs and his fellow strikers. "The strong arm of the national government," he asserted, "may be put forth to brush away all obstructions to the freedom of interstate commerce or the transportation of the mails." Debs's petition was denied.

In legalizing the federal injunction against the railway strikers, the Court gave to employers a powerful new weapon in their wars against unions. The injunction subsequently became a regular feature of labor-management struggles. Over the next thirty-seven years, the labor injunction was used more than two hundred times against strikers. Management continued to seek injunctions from federal courts until Congress passed the Norris-LaGuardia Anti-Injunction Act in 1932.

See also Debs, Eugene V.; *Habeas corpus*; Injunction; Labor law; Pullman strike; Sherman Antitrust Act.

Declaration of Independence

DEFINITION: The document in which a group of colonial American leaders declared themselves independent of England and George III

SIGNIFICANCE: The Declaration of Independence was the legal basis for the formation of the United States; it has significantly influenced American political thought, as well as that of other emerging nations, through the years

When in the Course of human events, it becomes necessary for one people to dissolve the political bands which have connected them with another, and to assume among the powers of the earth, the separate and equal station to which the Laws of nature and of Nature's God entitle them, a decent respect to the opinions of mankind requires that they should declare the causes which impel them to the separation.

So begins one of the most famous documents in political history. The American Declaration of Independence has had broad and sweeping historical effects. Believing in self-government, the signers of the declaration also believed they were providing the legal basis for organizing a new government—provided that the new republic, with the help of its allies, could win control of the field in battle. The endeavor marked the origins of what eventually became the most powerful nation in the world. In the twentieth century the United States has had great significance in world history, and the origins of that historical effect can be traced back to Philadelphia, Pennsylvania, and July 4, 1776.

The Declaration and the Revolution. Many nations have found in the Declaration of Independence inspiration and ideological support for their own revolutions. Some of the wording and many of the ideas have found their way into later, more modern declarations of independence in various parts of the world. The American Revolution was not really a revolution in

the modern sense of the word, but was a separatist war seeking independence rather than seeking to overthrow an existing government. In that sense the war could more accurately be called the American war for independence from Great Britain.

The colonists claimed they were fighting a defensive war for the preservation of English liberties in the American colonies. There was indeed a continuity with the past, and many of the prewar political leaders in America continued as leaders in the new republic, but major changes also took place, including the writing of the Constitution of the United States in 1787. English customs, traditions, and the continuity of the English common law in the United States helped to preserve stability and minimize the upheaval of such momentous change. In several states the colonial charters were kept largely intact, changing only terms to meet the new political realities.

The Declaration of Independence was not entered into lightly, as the preamble and first paragraph explicitly state: "Prudence, indeed, will dictate that Governments long established should not be changed for light and transient causes." The Americans, though, were convinced that there was a design on the part of King George III of Great Britain to "reduce" the American colonies to rule under "absolute Despotism." For that reason they decided to declare independence and risk their lives, fortunes, and "sacred Honor" in the pursuit of freedom and independence. They stood on principle and they stood together, for as Benjamin Franklin so aptly put it, "We must all hang together or surely we will all hang separately." Obviously the British did not consider the Declaration of Independence to be a legal document. The risks were great and so was the courage of the Patriots. In the end the British had no choice but reluctantly to acknowledge American Independence as declared.

The Americans declared that they were fighting for certain things besides independence. Thomas Jefferson, the author of the Declaration of Independence, penned the views of the assembled Continental Congress. His famous words expressed their views on the purpose for, and basis of, government:

We hold these truths to be self-evident, that all men are created equal, that they are endowed by their Creator with certain unalienable Rights, that among these are Life, Liberty, and the pursuit of Happiness. That to secure these rights, Governments are instituted among Men, deriving their just powers from the consent of the governed; That whenever any Form of Government becomes destructive of these ends it is the Right of the People to alter or to abolish it, and to institute new Government, laying its foundation on such principles and organizing its powers in such form, as to them shall seem most likely to effect their Safety and Happiness.

"Unalienable Rights." All Americans (indeed all people, according to the implication of these words) have "certain unalienable Rights." Where did those rights come from? Certainly not from the state—or else the state could change and take them away, and they would not be "unalienable." They came from "their Creator," from "the Laws of nature and of

Nature's God." The Declaration of Independence then acknowledges a higher law, or natural law, to which government and human laws must conform. Jefferson was a leader of the American Enlightenment and so used "natural law" terminology. Many of the other leaders were orthodox Christians and so used biblical terminology. John Dickinson, a leader of the Stamp Act Congress, for example, wrote that "Our liberties do not come from charters; for these are only the declaration of preexisting rights. They do not depend on parchments or seals; but come from the King of Kings and Lord of all the earth." Enlightenment or traditional Christian, both groups agreed that Americans are born with certain God-given rights, including life and liberty.

The concept of inalienable rights for the individual presupposes limitations on the power of the state, and that idea is the basic assumption involved in writing a constitution. During the American Revolution the main constitutional authority in the United States rested in the thirteen state constitutions. The Continental Congress acted as the extralegal representative assembly that attempted to hold the states together and to conduct the war and diplomatic relations. It was not until 1781 that the first "constitution" of the United States was adopted, the Articles of Confederation. Both the Continental Congress and the Confederation Congress lacked sufficient authority to act as a central government, however, and in due time the United States Constitution was written, adopted, and put into effect in 1789.

Thomas Jefferson did not claim originality in writing the Declaration. "All American whigs [Patriots]," he wrote, "thought alike on these subjects." He wrote the declaration "to place before mankind the common sense of the subject, in terms so plain and firm as to command their assent, and to justify ourselves in the independent stand we are compelled to take. . . . It was intended to be an expression of the American mind, and to give to that expression the proper tone and spirit called for by the occasion. All its authority rests then on the harmonizing sentiments of the day, whether expressed in conversation, in letters, printed essays, or in the elementary books of public right, as Aristotle, Cicero, Locke, etc."

The Declaration of Independence is not a constitution. It was partially designed to attract international support to the American cause. Yet if its basic presuppositions are correct and "the people" have a right to change their form of government, then the declaration is extremely important as a representative expression of the collective will of the people.

—*William H. Burnside*

See also American Revolution; Bill of Rights, U.S.; Common law; Constitution, U.S.; Magna Carta; Natural law and natural rights.

BIBLIOGRAPHY

A good starting point for further reading on the Declaration of Independence is a collection of essays on the subject (and related matters), Earl Latham, *The Declaration of Independence and the Constitution* (3d ed. Lexington, Mass.: D.C. Heath, 1976). The ideas leading to the signing of the Declara-

tion of Independence are brilliantly discussed in Bernard Bailyn, *The Ideological Origins of the American Revolution* (Cambridge, Mass.: Belknap Press of Harvard University Press, 1967), and in Gordon S. Wood, *The Creation of the American Republic, 1776-1787* (Chapel Hill: University of North Carolina Press, 1969). Dumas Malone, *The Story of the Declaration of Independence* (New York: Oxford University Press, 1975) is a pictorial book prepared for the bicentennial of the signing of the Declaration of Independence and is useful not only for the story but also for its sketches of the lives of the signers of the declaration. Those are given in more detail in C. Edward Quinn, *The Signers of the Declaration of Independence* (2d ed. The Bronx, N.Y.: The Bronx County Historical Society, 1988). Carl L. Becker's classic account, *The Declaration of Independence: A Study in the History of Political Ideas* (New York: Vintage Books, 1922, reprint 1960), is still useful. Russell Kirk has a chapter on the ideas implied in the Declaration of Independence in his *The Roots of American Order* (3d ed. Washington, D.C.: Regnery Gateway, 1991). Many biographies of Thomas Jefferson are available, including Merrill D. Peterson, *The Jefferson Image in the American Mind* (New York: Oxford University Press, 1960).

Declaratory judgment

DEFINITION: An action to determine the rights of parties to a contract

SIGNIFICANCE: This action is available before or after breach of contract and serves to resolve controversy over the terms of a contract

All states have statutes allowing declaratory judgments. Under these statutes, a party to a contract may bring an action for declaratory judgment, asking the court to determine the rights and obligations of either party under the contract. A declaratory judgment action may be brought before breach of the contract, so that legal rights and duties are determined (and damages, if any, minimized) before a breach has completely destroyed the relationship between the parties.

In order to obtain a declaratory judgment, the plaintiff generally must plead and prove that (1) a written contract exists (although a minority of states allow an oral contract to support a declaratory judgment); (2) the declaratory judgment will resolve the entire dispute; (3) no other relief is available; (4) there is an actual controversy; (5) there is no other action pending that involves this contractual duty; and (6) the matter can be resolved as a matter of law. A declaratory judgment is a final judgment and can involve the award of damages, injunctive relief, and any other supplemental relief available from the court.

See also Commercial law; Compensatory damages; Contract law; Injunction.

Defamation

DEFINITION: Any false communication that lowers another person's reputation

SIGNIFICANCE: A person who believes that he or she has been defamed may sue the person or publication that spreads the defamation for libel or slander; to win the suit, identification, publication, actual injury, falsity, and fault must be shown

Defamation, or an attack on an individual's reputation, can occur in either oral or written form. Oral attacks, called slander, are generally regarded as more spontaneous and as less likely to do harm because fewer people are aware of a spoken attack than a written one. Written attacks, or libel, are more likely to be prepared with ill intent, and they reach more people. They are therefore considered more serious. Attacks on an individual's reputation which are broadcast are considered libelous rather than slanderous even though, strictly speaking, they are spoken rather than written. Compensation (damages) for libel is considerably greater than for slander.

Defamation law in the United States has developed over several centuries. Today the process of gaining retribution for an attack on one's reputation is highly institutionalized. In earlier times, disputes over questions of honor were settled out of court, sometimes by dueling. The most famous duel in the United States involved Aaron Burr, vice president under Thomas Jefferson, who fatally shot Alexander Hamilton, the first secretary of the treasury, in 1804.

Defamation disputes are sometimes settled in court, but most are settled out of court. Taking a dispute to court has its disadvantages—the litigation costs can be very high, often more than the cost of a settlement, and the person bringing the lawsuit runs the risk that the defamatory statements will be spread to even more people. The advantages of a lawsuit are that the individual can recover damages, restore his or her reputation, receive vindication in court, and perhaps receive substantial monetary damages. The majority of defamation suits are initially won by the plaintiff (the person who has been defamed); of these verdicts, however, a majority—70 percent—are overturned in favor of the defense when appealed to a higher court. The reasons for this are that the public generally does not understand the complexity of American libel law and that people are generally dissatisfied with the prevalence of negative coverage by the press. Individual reporters are seldom sued, because the media they work for are responsible for what is published and because damages against the media can be much higher than damages against an individual. Although each of the states has developed its own defamation law, there are significant elements of defamation suits required by the supreme courts of all the states.

Defining Elements. A number of elements must be present before there is the possibility of winning a defamation suit. First, the reputation of the individual bringing the suit must have been threatened in some way. Most often the plaintiff has been accused of committing a crime, of sexual impropriety, of having a disease (particularly a sexually transmitted disease), of immoral or loathsome personal habits, of corruptness, or of incompetence or lack of qualifications in occupation or business.

Defamation often involves carelessness on the part of the media. Most notably, a person may be wrongly identified in a news story. A headline may mistakenly say that a doctor has killed a child in an automobile accident (particularly damaging, perhaps, if the doctor happens to be a pediatrician); a woman who is opposed to alcoholism may be falsely accused of being tipsy. What specifically constitutes a statement that would lead others to think less of a person is determined by the judge.

The defamation must also be "published" to the extent that at least one other person has access to it. The person must be identified to the extent that at least one other person could know who is being talked about. Again, this is in the judgment of the judge. Identification can take place by naming the individual, or through a physical or personality description that is considered identifying; defamation can occur even in a work of fiction. In most states defamation must involve a person who is still alive. The dead generally can not be defamed and can "suffer no wrongs." A group of individuals can be libeled only if there is a small number and it is believed that everyone in the group is defamed.

Next, in most states, the defamation must be shown to be false. If the statement is true, there is no defamation suit possible, although a suit for an invasion of privacy might be possible. In *Philadelphia Newspapers v. Hepps* (1986), the Supreme Court ruled that if the defamation involves an issue of public importance (as, in that case, whether a beer distributor has ties to organized crime), then the plaintiff must prove the statement is false before the defamation suit can proceed. Evidence that the defamation is false must relate to the general gist of the charge. Minor errors in a story will not establish falsity. Even if plaintiffs succeed in the burden of proof to establish falsity, they still might not win the suit. They still must show fault on the part of the defendant.

Fault is perhaps the most difficult element for a plaintiff to establish. The nature of fault required depends on the type of individual claiming defamation. If the individual is a public official, such as a congressman or mayor, or holds a significant elective or appointed office, or if the person is a public figure (someone who is in the public eye, such as a celebrity), then that person must establish malice on the part of the defendant. The burden of proof is on the plaintiff. Defendants do not have to defend themselves until plaintiffs establish fault. Malice, as a type of fault, was defined by the Supreme Court in *New York Times v. Sullivan* (1964) as knowledge that a statement is false or "reckless disregard" as to whether it is false

Malice is very difficult for a plaintiff to prove, although it is possible. Actress and comedian Carol Burnett was able to show malice, for example, when the publication did not verify the account of her being tipsy in a restaurant. The report was submitted by an individual who was known to be unreliable in the past, and therefore the publication had an obligation to check the accuracy of the report more carefully (*Burnett v. National Enquirer*, 1981).

Because malice is so difficult to establish, the Court ruled in *Gertz v. Welch* (1974) that the states could use a standard of negligence if the defendant is a private individual—a person who is in the public limelight through no desire on his or her part and is not someone in whom the media have shown general interest. Different states define negligence somewhat differently, but it generally connotes carelessness, a standard of journalism that responsible outlets do not practice. Generally it means not being careful and not properly attempting to check the facts in the account. Key factors are whether there was time to check a charge and whether the source was a reliable and trustworthy one.

Defenses. Many countries allow a defamed person a "right of reply" in the publication where the defamation occurred. This has the advantage of allowing the plaintiff to reach the original audience and allows robust debate in the media, but it has the disadvantage of requiring publishers to give up space (or air time). It also takes the editorial decision-making process out of their hands by requiring that particular content be published. For these reasons, right of reply is not generally granted in the United States. Instead, the individual or organization accused of defamation presents a defense in court. Several defenses are possible.

The best defense, perhaps, is evidence that the statements are true; however, that is often a difficult defense. Sources relied on for support may not be willing or able to come forward. Accurate quotation is not considered proof; quoting someone else who made the charge does not make the charge true. If the person quoted is a legislator, however, or if the quotation was part of a court record or part of a report presented at a public meeting, the quotation may constitute a privileged communication, which may be a sufficient defense even if the charge turns out to be false. Meetings of all public bodies, all aspects of the legal process, and reports or statements made by members of the executive branch of government are privileged and therefore protected from defamation suits.

Statements of opinion are also protected from defamation suits. People are allowed to express their own opinion, but the court must agree that the statement in question is indeed a statement of opinion and not a statement of fact. Calling someone a member of the Communist Party is not protected, because that is a statement of fact. On the other hand, calling someone a "fascist" is protected, because that is a statement of opinion. This is the defense of fair comment. Exaggeration, satire, and humor also tend to be protected.

Additional defenses include the statute of limitations, which is usually two to three years; reliance on a usually reliable source; and retraction and correction. The last one is called a mitigating defense, meaning that it can lessen the damages but does not completely remove them.

Damages. Since *Garrison v. Louisiana* (1964), defamation has not been considered a criminal offense. A person who is convicted of defamation does not go to jail but is subject to a civil fine. The fine can be considerable when administered against a media outlet. As of 1994, the largest damage amount was awarded to Brown & Williamson, a cigarette manufacturing company, when they successfully argued that Walter Ja-

cobson, a television commentator for CBS News in Chicago, had falsely accused them of hiring an advertising agency to prepare cigarette ads targeting children. Malice was established when the records that supposedly showed this was done could not be produced. CBS had to pay punitive damages of $3.05 million, and Jacobson had to pay damages of $50,000 (*Brown & Williamson v. Jacobson*, 1987).

To collect damages in a defamation suit, plaintiffs must demonstrate that there was actual harm to their reputations. Evidence that the plaintiff suffered mental anguish, humiliation, or loss of standing in the community must be established. These are called actual damages. Whether such damages exist, and the monetary amount that should be awarded if they do exist, is the decision of the jury. Loss of business income or the incurring of medical bills resulting from mental anguish caused by the defamation constitute special damages. General, compensatory, or presumed damages can be awarded when fault is established. They do not require actual harm to be established. The most serious type of damages, because the largest monetary awards are associated with them, are punitive damages. In most states, malice must be established before punitive damages will be awarded. Because amounts awarded under punitive damages can be large enough to bankrupt a media outlet and force it out of business, there have been some efforts to limit the amount of punitive damages that can be awarded.

—*Roger D. Haney*

See also *New York Times Co. v. Sullivan*; News media; Privacy, right of; Seditious libel; Speech and press, freedom of.

BIBLIOGRAPHY

Readable overviews of defamation include Anthony Lewis, *Make No Law* (New York: Random House, 1991), written from the perspective of a political commentator, and Randall P. Bezanson, Gilbert Cranberg, and John Soloski, *Libel Law and the Press* (New York: Free Press, 1987). Textbooks with useful sections include Don R. Pember, *Mass Media Law* (6th ed. Madison, Wis.: Brown and Benchmark, 1993), and Donald M. Gillmor, Jerome A. Barron, Todd F. Simon, and Herbert A. Terry, *Mass Communication Law: Cases and Comment* (5th ed. St. Paul, Minn.: West, 1990). A useful law review article is Marc A. Franklin and Daniel Bussel, "The Libel Tort Today," *Washington and Lee Law Review* 45 (1988).

Defense attorney

DEFINITION: Attorneys who are engaged to represent criminal defendants and are paid by the clients

SIGNIFICANCE: Private attorneys are essential to a fair defense in criminal cases

Private defense attorneys engage in the representation of persons charged with crimes in local, state, federal, or tribal courts. Unlike public defenders, private defense attorneys are engaged and paid by their clients, rather than by the state.

Criminal defense lawyers must be members of the bar in good standing in the jurisdiction in which they practice. A law student wishing to become a criminal defense lawyer will usually take (in addition to the courses in criminal law gener-

A defense attorney (center) and his client (right), who is on trial for murder. Criminal defense attorneys are essential to the American judicial system. (James L. Shaffer)

ally required in law school) specialized courses preparing them for criminal trial work, including advanced criminal law, trial practice, criminal procedure, and negotiation. Many defense lawyers begin their career as prosecutors in the local district attorney's office and go into private practice after receiving some criminal trial experience.

The defense lawyer's task is to represent the client zealously, regardless of any personal feelings about the defendant or the crime. If the client has not yet been charged, the defense attorney's job is to advise the client on communicating with the grand jury, to accompany the client to meetings with police and prosecutors, and to advise the client as to evidence. Once the client is arrested, the defense attorney will represent the client at bail hearings and arraignment. The defense attorney will often try to "build a Chinese wall" around the client, denying the police and prosecution access to the client and regulating the prosecution's access to evidence to the extent possible. The defense attorney is entitled to any information

the prosecution has on the crime and defendant prior to trial, and the defense attorney will often use a private investigator to evaluate this information and discover new information. At trial, the criminal defense lawyer will seek to exclude damaging evidence, or at least minimize its impact, and will present evidence to introduce a "reasonable doubt" in the jury's mind as to guilt. If a defendant is convicted, a criminal defense attorney may participate in filing an appeal, but a different attorney will usually represent the defendant on appeal.

While criminal defense lawyers often take cases to trial, they also spend considerable time negotiating plea bargains for their clients. A plea bargain is an agreement between the prosecutor's office and the defendant for the latter to plead guilty to a particular charge in exchange for a predetermined sentence. A defense lawyer must be prepared to offer a plea bargain to a prosecutor, evaluate any offer of a plea bargain by the prosecuting attorney, make sure that the client understands any offer, and help the client decide either to take the offer or to go to trial. It is, however, ultimately the client's responsibility (not the lawyer's) to decide whether to make or accept a plea bargain offer.

See also Attorney; Bar, the; Counsel, right to; Criminal justice system; District attorney; Prosecutor, public; Public defender.

Democracy

DEFINITION: A concept according to which citizens participate equally in the process of choosing political leaders and by which official policy is made to respond to the public's preferences

SIGNIFICANCE: Although there is no perfect agreement on what constitutes democracy, the concept has served as both an inspirational ideal and a rough yardstick by which people have tried to measure political institutions and processes such as government structure, elections, civil rights, and access of groups to power

The concept of democracy has been a powerful force in the development of modern society. It has been invoked time and again to justify regimes and actions as well as to criticize them. Most people believe that they have a reasonably good sense of what democracy is (or should be), but it is difficult to get complete agreement on an exact definition or a fixed set of basic characteristics. Historically, democracy has meant different things to different people. It is not surprising, therefore, that it is often found modified by adjectives, such as liberal, direct, participatory, representative, majoritarian, and industrial, each giving a special twist to the concept.

Political systems around the world call themselves democratic almost as a matter of form. Even palpably authoritarian systems often claim to be the "true" democracies. For that reason one must be explicit about which version of democracy one is employing when trying to determine whether democracy exists in a particular place. These distinctions are necessary when discussing the relationship between democracy and issues of law and justice in modern society. Like many general ideas in our political vocabulary, democracy can be used in two related but distinct ways: descriptively, emphasizing what the concept means and how to determine when it exists, and normatively, emphasizing what needs to be done to bring the ideal into reality.

History. Although it did not take on institutional form until at least the end of the eighteenth century, democracy as a concept has a pedigree that stretches much farther back, even if only in pieces of the whole. The word itself is Greek, meaning rule (*kratia*) by the people (*demos*). While the Greeks named it, they were not especially fond of democracy, equating it with unconstrained rule by the masses. Some ancient and medieval philosophers described the psychological conditions for democracy and were not wholly averse to limited forms of popular participation, but they believed in largely authoritarian societies having no real democratic institutions.

It was not until the seventeenth and eighteenth centuries that some of the building blocks of democracy began to be formed, initially in England, and later in the American colonies. The struggle between the English monarchs and Parliament gave rise to the concept that central executive power should and could be limited by a legislature, even if not one based on democratic representation. Later, the works of influential seventeenth and eighteenth century political thinkers such as the Englishman John Locke and the Frenchman Baron de Montesquieu spread the idea of balanced government and popular sovereignty beyond Europe to the American colonies, as shown in the Declaration of Independence of 1776. The American (1775-1783) and French (1789-1793) revolutions created actual governments based on many of these ideas for the first time, guaranteed rights to their citizens, and stimulated the movements toward greater democracy which flowered gradually in the nineteenth and twentieth centuries.

By the end of World War I a fairly large number of countries in North America and Europe had accepted the norms of modern democracy and had constitutions guaranteeing civil and political rights, universal suffrage, and representative but limited government. The aftermath of World War II saw the extension of democratic institutions to the formerly fascist countries of Europe and to much of the rest of the world, although with only partial success. In the late 1980's, the collapse of authoritarian communist systems in Eastern Europe was followed by experiments with democratization, the results of which are still far from clear.

Institutions of Democracy. Students of the process by which democracies emerge emphasize the importance of the development and acceptance of core institutions. Whether viewed mainly as process or as substance, democracy seems to need a set of appropriate institutions for its values to be put into practice. Democratic institutions are intended to permit a free choice of ends and means, and of the persons who implement them, by those subject to the power of government. Although there is not complete agreement on a single list of necessary political institutions, the following are generally considered basic to democracy and distinguish it from authoritarian systems.

Freedom of speech and freedom of association are essential. In a democracy, individual citizens must be free to speak without hindrance, to express their views and criticize the government and its operation if they choose. (It is a hallmark of antidemocratic systems that the state fears and habitually interferes with unfettered speech by its subjects.) Related to this freedom is freedom of the media, such as newspapers, radio, and television, from censorship or government control of their content. Citizens must also be allowed to join with like-minded people to form groups to further causes and interests freely. Without these freedoms, citizens are unable to perform the tasks asked of them in a democracy.

Those tasks include choosing the most important policy makers and influencing the choices of policy made by those in power. Democracy requires that people have the right to vote in free and periodic elections, the results of which are normally decided by the principle of majority rule, with every

This city council meeting represents democracy at the local level. For democracies to be successful, citizens must be willing to learn about matters affecting them and participate in the political process. (James L. Shaffer)

person's vote being equal to every other's. A key institution in making this power real is the political party, and the genuine competition of two or more political parties is strongly associated with the rise and maintenance of modern democracy.

When direct democracy is feasible, as in very small groups such as New England town meetings, the voters could be said to represent themselves. In large-scale and specialized modern societies, the principle of representation is called upon to link voters with government. Whether they are called parliaments, legislatures, or Congress, these representative institutions exist to attempt to convert the preferences of the electorate into policy.

Constitutionalism is another basic element of modern democracy. Constitutionalism implies that government institutions must be limited in their powers and must be made to respect citizens' rights, that government officials are bound by the rule of law and must follow fair processes in exercising their authority, and that the majority of the moment will be prevented from becoming so powerful as to trample the rights and opportunities of those in the minority at that time. In a democracy, constitutionalism means more than literal adherence to a historic document: It relies on adherence to a larger group of agreed values.

Democratic Values. The elements described in the previous section are generally agreed to be essential components of a political democracy. Many observers believe that a viable democracy also depends on the widespread acceptance of certain values. Four values seem to be associated with successful democratic systems. The first is a belief in the essential worth of the individual. In a democracy, government and politics are to rest on the needs and rights of individuals rather than on abstract groupings such as the state or classes. A second, related value underlying democracy is the premise that people are essentially equal and should be treated as such in the political system. Therefore, self-governing citizens need to have equal rights and equal votes.

A third value associated with democracy is toleration of the views of others. In contrast to authoritarian societies, where people are required to adhere to a single line, democracy assumes that getting to the truth is a difficult process requiring that minds be kept open and even skeptical. Democratic citizens and their institutions need to be open to new information and a wide diversity of views. A fourth value assumption is that democracy asks for a high level of responsibility from its citizens. Democrats must be willing to educate themselves about public matters and take the time to participate in the political process. In addition, citizens and those holding government power are expected to follow the rules of the democratic process, accepting defeat and abstaining from violence when legitimate procedures are followed. The democratic value system is a demanding ideal and is not always easy to follow.

Problems of Democracy. Achieving genuine democracy is a daunting task. Many elements of democracy pose problems that societies have not always been able to solve to everyone's satisfaction. There is, for example, continuing tension between the norm of majority rule and the assurance of minority rights. Representative institutions, such as legislatures, seldom reflect perfectly the preferences of all or even a majority of citizens. Freedom of speech, when carried beyond certain points, bothers many people. Freedom of association sometimes justifies uncontrolled pressure group activity; in some countries a profusion of political parties has made majority rule difficult to assert and stable government hard to sustain.

The guarantee of a trial by a jury of one's peers in criminal cases in the United States would seem to stem from populist democratic values. Yet the existence of a federal bench composed of judges appointed for life—and capable of negating laws of an elected Congress as well as presidential actions—reflects the view of the makers of the Constitution that there should be limits to the will of the populace. Given its emphasis on the essential equality of individuals, democracy would seem to require at least the equal treatment of persons before the law and as political participants. It was a sense of democratic shortfall that led to civil rights legislation after the Civil War, to the extension of the vote to women in the early twentieth century, and to the movements to assure equal rights to racial minorities in the 1960's.

Democratic ideals also were invoked in the various efforts to advance equality of opportunity and of treatment after 1970. The latter demands remain controversial and far from secured. Other efforts to extend democracy into the workplace and to reduce inequalities of wealth and income have met with greater success in democratic socialist governments in Europe than in the United States, where democracy is viewed as centered on individual rights, political participation, and limited government. As an ideal, democracy has been a powerful influence in modern societies, even if in practice its institutions have varied considerably from society to society, its full acceptance has been marked by difficulties, and its fragile health has been dependent on a citizenry not always up to its challenges.

—*James B. Christoph*

See also Bill of Rights, U.S.; Citizenship; Civil liberties; Civil rights; Constitution, U.S.; Federalism; Jacksonian democracy; Jeffersonian democracy; Natural law and natural rights; Vote, right to.

BIBLIOGRAPHY

Carl Cohen's *Democracy* (Athens: University of Georgia Press, 1971) discusses basic issues, as does Robert A. Dahl, *A Preface to Democratic Theory* (Chicago: University of Chicago Press, 1973). An influential work that relates democracy to justice issues is John Rawls, *A Theory of Justice* (Cambridge, Mass.: Harvard University Press, 1971). Theodore Lowi's *The End of Liberalism* (New York: W. W. Norton, 1969) examines critically the traditional American commitment to pluralism. For a comparative worldwide treatment, see Arend Lijphart, *Democracies* (New Haven, Conn.: Yale University Press, 1984).

Democratic Party

DATE: Emerged in the 1820's from Jeffersonian Democratic-Republican Party

SIGNIFICANCE: The Democratic Party views itself as the party of the lower and middle classes and racial minorities and pursues a liberal agenda on issues of racial, social, and criminal justice

The Democratic Party traces its origins to Thomas Jefferson's Democratic-Republican Party in 1800. President Andrew Jackson, the other patron saint of the party, shortened its name to "Democratic Party" during the 1820's. It remains the oldest major party organization in the United States. Beginning with the election of President Abraham Lincoln in 1860, the Democrats were dominated by the Republicans until the 1932 election. The election of President Franklin D. Roosevelt in 1932, however, signaled six decades of Democratic dominance, especially in congressional politics.

Racial Justice. The Democratic Party has viewed itself as the party of civil rights and racial equality, but the party's record is not altogether positive. During the 1800's, the bulk of Democrats were either proslavery or neutral on the issue. The party's failure to take a stand against slavery provided the opportunity for the Republican Party to form.

After the Civil War, the Democratic Party was split into two separate factions—northern Democrats and southern Democrats. Northern Democrats were supportive of civil rights and racial equality, while southern Democrats supported racial segregation and states' rights. Since most Democratic presidents realized that they could not pass their political agenda without the support of southern Democrats, they refused to deal with racial issues out of fear that they would alienate southern Democrats in Congress. The Civil Rights movement of the 1950's and 1960's tore the Democratic Party apart. Most southern Democrats vigorously opposed extending political and social equality to African Americans. While Democratic presidents John F. Kennedy (president from 1961 to 1963) and Lyndon B. Johnson (1963-1969) were introducing major civil rights bills in Congress, southern Democrats engaged in filibusters and other techniques in their attempt to defeat such legislation. Their efforts proved futile, however, and the political mobilization of the black electorate forced southern Democrats to moderate their racial views.

As the issues of racial equality moved from concerns over civil rights to efforts to achieve economic equality, further divisions occurred in the party. Affirmative action, more than any other issue, created divisions between white and black Democrats. The racial division allowed the Republicans to woo conservative white Democrats over to the Republican Party.

The Democratic national convention in July, 1992, which nominated Bill Clinton as its presidential candidate. (AP/Wide World Photos)

Social Justice. While both the Democratic and Republican parties originally envisioned a limited role for government in assisting the needy, the situation changed dramatically with the Great Depression. When the stock market collapsed in 1929 and millions of Americans lost their jobs, the nation demanded political and economic changes. President Franklin D. Roosevelt quickly introduced legislation to deal with the economic crisis. His New Deal legislation created agencies such as the Works Progress Administration and Civilian Conservation Corps, which put hundreds of thousands of Americans to work building roads, dams, libraries, parks, and other public works projects. For the first time, government was viewed as having responsibility for providing jobs and income assistance to individuals in need. Social security, minimum wages, and public assistance all had their origins in Roosevelt's New Deal.

In the 1960's, Democratic presidents Kennedy and Johnson introduced a new round of social programs. Kennedy, profoundly influenced by Michael Harrington's book *The Other America: Poverty in the United States* (1962), was determined to introduce legislation to alleviate poverty in the country. After Kennedy's assassination in 1963, Johnson continued the "war on poverty" with the introduction of his Great Society legislation. New social legislation was passed, the most impor-

tant of which established Medicare and Medicaid. Medicare provided subsidized health care for the elderly, while Medicaid provided medical care for the needy.

In the 1990's, a growing number of Democrats, including President Bill Clinton (who took office in 1992), came to support programs requiring welfare recipients to receive job training and work for their benefits. Though Clinton advocated a two-year limit on benefits, many members of the president's own party believed that such a standard was unrealistic and would unduly punish children living in impoverished families.

Criminal Justice. The Democratic position on crime emphasizes the role of society in causing crime. Poverty, racial and class discrimination, and other social conditions are viewed as primary causes of crime. To reduce crime, most Democrats support policies designed to curb poverty and discrimination.

In the 1980's and 1990's, Republicans exploited the crime issue and attacked Democrats as being "soft" on crime. To reverse such public perceptions, Democratic legislators advocated policies designed to prove that they were just as tough as Republicans on the crime issue. President Clinton introduced an anticrime proposal in August, 1993. The core elements of the package included money to hire 100,000 new police officers, expanded the death penalty for numerous federal crimes, and banned nineteen types of assault weapons. The final bill, signed into law on September 13, 1994, provided $8.8 billion to hire more police, $7.9 billion in grants for the construction of state prisons, and $6.9 billion for crime prevention programs.

Advocating Activist Government. The Democratic Party has consistently supported an activist role for government in the pursuit of racial, social, and criminal justice. Unlike Republicans, who see government as playing a negative role in the pursuit of justice, Democrats see government as a positive force. Government must eliminate the causes of crime, especially poverty and discrimination. Until that is done, Democrats believe, little progress can be made in reducing the nation's crime rate. —*Darryl Paulson*

See also Carter, Jimmy; Jackson, Jesse; Jacksonian democracy; Jeffersonian Republican Party; Johnson, Lyndon B.; Kennedy, John F.; Liberalism, modern American; New Deal; Republican Party; Roosevelt, Franklin D.; States' Rights Party; Truman, Harry S; Welfare state.

BIBLIOGRAPHY

Excellent sources on racial justice include Derrick Bell, *Faces at the Bottom of the Well: The Permanence of Racism* (New York: Basic Books, 1992); Thomas Edsall and Mary Edsall, *Chain Reaction: The Impact of Race, Rights, and Taxes on American Politics* (New York: W. W. Norton, 1991); and Andrew Hacker, *Two Nations: Black and White, Separate, Hostile, Unequal* (New York: Charles Scribner's Sons, 1992). On poverty and social justice, see Richard Cloward and Frances Fox Piven, *Regulating the Poor: The Functions of Public Welfare* (New York: Vintage Books, 1971), and Michael Harrington, *The Other America: Poverty in the United States* (New York: Macmillan, 1962).

Dennis v. United States

COURT: U.S. Supreme Court
DATE: Decided June 4, 1951
SIGNIFICANCE: The Court's decision in the Dennis case upheld the constitutionality of the Smith Act and significantly modified the clear and present danger test in relation to limits on subversive expression

As the Cold War settled in during the second half of the 1940's, the threat of internal subversion became a major concern. When the administration of President Harry S Truman was criticized for failing to safeguard the nation from communist subversion, the American Communist Party became an obvious target for government action. In 1948, the government obtained indictments against Eugene Dennis and ten other leaders of the American Communist Party under the Smith Act, a measure passed in 1940. The Smith Act made it a crime to advocate, enter a conspiracy to advocate, or become a knowing member of a group that advocated the overthrow of an American government by force or violence.

Convicted in federal district court, Dennis and the others appealed their convictions, contending not only that there had been irregularities in the original trial but also that the Smith

Act itself imposed unconstitutional limitations on free expression. The federal appeals court upheld the convictions. Writing for the court, Judge Learned Hand put aside his own preference for broad protection for political speech in deference to congressional action. He acknowledged that since *Schenck v. United States* in 1919, limitation on expression had been governed by the clear and present danger test: Speech that posed a clear and present danger of provoking illegal actions was not protected by the First Amendment. In the current situation, the danger of a communist rebellion might not be present, but the seriousness of the threat had to be considered along with its probability of inciting illegal action. By this test, Hand argued, the Smith Act was constitutional, and the convictions were upheld.

The case was then appealed to the U.S. Supreme Court, being argued in 1950. The Court upheld the convictions and the constitutionality of the Smith Act by a 6-2 vote. In the majority opinion, Chief Justice Fred M. Vinson leaned heavily on Hand's earlier opinion. The clear and present danger test was thus substantially modified, with greater emphasis on the seriousness of the threat represented by expression and the probability that it would provoke illegal action. This cleared the way for the Smith Act to be used in further prosecutions against domestic communists. Eventually more than 140 were prosecuted.

As the country became more accustomed to the Cold War and fears of domestic subversion abated, the Court refined its interpretation. In *Yates v. United States* (1957), it distinguished between the mere advocacy of doctrine that included the overthrow of the government (which it found protected by the First Amendment) and the advocacy of action (even in the indefinite future) defined as illegal.

See also *Brandenburg v. Ohio*; Civil liberties; Clear and present danger test; Communist Party, American; Hand, Learned; *Scales v. United States*; *Schenck v. United States*; Vinson, Fred M.; *Yates v. United States*.

Departments, U.S. *See name of department*

Deposition

DEFINITION: A statement taken under oath, out of court, by a lawyer
SIGNIFICANCE: Depositions are the only oral method by which witnesses who are not parties to an action may be questioned prior to trial

The right to confront one's accusers is granted by the Seventh Amendment to the Constitution. It is reaffirmed by the Fourteenth Amendment, which forbids states from depriving accused persons of life or property without due process of law.

Depositions are a significant part of the process of confronting one's accusers and are a useful tool in the pretrial process. The deposition is the only pretrial procedure in which lawyers may orally question and cross-examine witnesses who are not direct parties to the underlying litigation. Notice must be given of the intention to take a deposition to all parties to the litigation or their lawyers, and all parties and their lawyers have the right to be present. Unless a party is not represented by a lawyer, only the lawyers may question the witness.

A deposition generally is given before a court reporter or notary public authorized to administer oaths. A transcript, a written record of what is said in the deposition, may be prepared after the deposition. The deponent, the person being deposed, has the right, unless waived, to read the transcript for accuracy and make minor contextual changes. No major changes may be made.

The deposition gives lawyers an opportunity to assess a deponent's appearance, presentation, and effectiveness as a possible trial witness. The recorded proceedings commit a witness to the statements recorded. Substantially changing these statements while testifying in court requires full and serious explanation by the witness to the court about the discrepancies and could lead to charges of perjury, or lying under oath. Depositions usually are taken in the county in which the witness lives, works, or conducts business. If a witness lives at a great distance from the place in which the litigation occurs, the lawyers may travel to the witness or the witness may be brought in to testify.

The widespread availability of recording equipment permits the videotaping of a deposition when it is known beforehand that a witness will not be available at the time of trial. Not only is the jury able to hear the testimony, but also it may visually assess the reliability of the witness, almost as though that witness were present.

There are other forms of deposition in addition to oral testimony. A deposition *duces tecum* ("under penalty you shall take it with you") requires the witness to bring a list of documents to the deposition, about which the witness may be questioned. The deposition *de bene esse* ("provisional") is a conditional arrangement permitting the transcript of the witness' statement to be read in court when it is suspected that the witness may be unavoidably absent at the time of trial (as a witness who is terminally ill).

See also Civil procedure; Criminal procedure; Due process of law; Expert witness; Litigation.

Detectives, police

DEFINITION: Sworn police officers with specific, highly specialized investigative duties who are normally assigned to units specializing in criminal investigations

SIGNIFICANCE: The complexities of criminal activities require highly qualified and well-trained police personnel capable of independent action; police detectives are assumed to have the ability to investigate serious crimes free of bias and prejudice

The origin of the concept of police detective is generally considered to be tied to Henry Fielding and his Bow Street Runners in England in 1750. The concept spread throughout Europe and eventually to the United States. By 1789, the United States government had established a special investigative unit known as the Revenue Cutters to thwart smuggling.

By the mid 1850's, the concept of assigning specialized investigative (detective) units to municipal police departments was growing in popularity. In most medium and large police departments, investigating the more serious crimes is normally a joint responsibility between officers assigned to patrol activities and those assigned to a detective (or investigations) division. Patrol officers normally handle the preliminary phase of any investigation, and the detectives (investigators) handle the more detailed follow-up phase of the investigative process. Essential qualities of the police detective include objectivity, a thorough knowledge of the criminal justice system and the fundamental laws upon which it is based, the proper method of case preparation, a high degree of self-discipline, and expert knowledge of legally acceptable methods of collecting and preserving evidence.

See also Crime; Deterrence; Entrapment; Evidence, rules of; Forensic science and medicine; Incapacitation; Just deserts; Police; Prison and jail systems; Punishment; State police; Sting operation.

Deterrence

DEFINITION: In the arena of criminal justice, "deterrence" refers to the idea that punishment will discourage individuals from involvement in criminal conduct

SIGNIFICANCE: The prevention of crime is a major public issue; if punishments could indeed be shown to deter crime, the finding would be of considerable importance to numerous public policy questions

There are two categories of deterrence, specific (or simple) and general. Both involve the idea that the threat of punishment will influence individuals not to commit crimes. Specific deterrence focuses on the individual and rests on the assumption that if the punishment imposed on a specific offender is severe enough for a crime, the offender will not commit crimes in the future. General deterrence focuses on society and is based on the idea that potential offenders will be deterred by the fear of being punished. Both categories of deterrence are based on the assumptions that potential offenders are rational and will perceive the possible punishment for crime as painful.

Does punishment, in fact, deter? Although many people would intuitively argue that it does, scholarly studies have not proven with certainty that punishment, or the fear of it, deters. There are several problems with the notion that punishment or fear of punishment will prevent crimes in the future.

A major assumption of deterrence theory is that people are rational and will consider the costs of committing a crime before committing the act. While this may be true in some cases, many crimes are unplanned events resulting from chance and opportunity.

Another assumption of deterrence theory is that swift punishment proportional to the seriousness of an offense will deter. In the American criminal justice system, however, many offenders are provided with the opportunity for numerous delays prior to trial. Moreover, many cases end in plea bargains that call for punishment for less than the actual offense.

Both specific and general deterrence theories rest on the notion that most offenders fear being caught. Critics of deterrence policies, however, note that many potential offenders do not believe that they will be caught and prosecuted. Victimization surveys reveal that fewer than half the crimes committed in the United States are known to law-enforcement authorities. Violent crimes are the crimes most frequently reported to the police, yet studies reveal that fewer than 47 percent of all violent crimes are reported. Fear of punishment is further mitigated by the fact that fewer than 5 percent of all crimes reported to police are ultimately prosecuted.

A final argument used to bolster deterrence theory is the assertion that potential offenders will avoid criminal activity because they fear the pain associated with punishment. Yet some studies have shown that although substantial portions of the offender population in prisons acknowledge that prison is recognized as a cost of criminal activity, many offenders do not consider it an especially painful experience. Even with regard to crimes that carry the potential for the death penalty, most studies reveal, few criminals fear the pain of punishment prior to the crime because they do not believe that they will ever receive such a punishment. Although politicians and the public often clamor for stiffer penalties as a solution to rising crime rates, few scholars would argue that such remedies are likely to prove very effective.

See also Capital punishment; Crime; Incapacitation; Just deserts; Prison and jail systems; Punishment.

Dictum

DEFINITION: A statement that is included in a judicial opinion but is not necessary to deciding the case

SIGNIFICANCE: Since a *dictum* is not formally a part of a judicial decision, it is not considered binding as precedent; however, it is not unusual for a *dictum* to influence outcomes in subsequent cases

As judges write complex judicial decisions, they sometimes express personal opinions that have only incidental bearing on the particular case before the court. Such an opinion, or *dictum*, should be distinguished from the rationale necessary to deciding the case (called the *ratio decidendi*). The term *obiter dictum*, which emphasizes that the statement goes beyond the case, is commonly used as a synonym for *dictum*.

While a *dictum* is not binding precedent, the reader of a judicial opinion sometimes will find it difficult to separate a *dictum* from the rationale of the decision. Judges themselves occasionally will quote *dicta* as if they were authoritative pronouncements. An example of an influential *dictum* is Chief Justice Earl Warren's comment that the phrase "cruel and unusual punishment" should be interpreted according to "evolving standards of decency that mark the progress of a maturing society" (in *Trop v. Dulles*, 1958).

See also *Amicus curiae* brief; Common law; Constitutional interpretation; Cruel and unusual punishment; *Furman v. Georgia*; *Stare decisis*.

Discretion

DEFINITION: The flexibility allowed to the police and the courts to make decisions such as whether to arrest and prosecute an individual and how severe a sentence to impose

SIGNIFICANCE: A public official may employ conscience and good sense, not only the letter of the law, in the reasonable exercise of power; however, discretion, particularly judicial discretion, has its critics

Discretion is the ability of a public official to decide whether and how a law will be enforced. It allows a range of judgments to be made to fit particular circumstances while still maintaining the spirit of the law. Discretion exists in many areas of the criminal justice system, from the actions of the police to the sentencing of a criminal by a judge. Discretion is therefore a very important aspect of the system, and it is one reason that the law as written often differs from the law in practice. Regarding police actions, for example, a law may prohibit all incidents of public drunkenness, but police officers may arrest only certain violators of the law who are particularly disorderly or appear disheveled. Officers always have

Police are allowed to exercise discretion in deciding whether to arrest a suspect. (Lou Dematteis)

the power to decide whether or not to arrest a person at the scene of a disturbance or suspected crime. In addition, administrative discretion exists within the police department: The administration decides where and how to deploy what numbers of officers and, particularly in the case of large-scale disturbances, how much force officers should be instructed to use.

Various aspects of discretion in the courts apply to the prosecution, defense, and judge. Prosecutorial discretion comprises deciding whether to prosecute, what charges to bring, the method of conducting the trial, and the type of sentence requested. In defense of a matter, discretion permits counsel to choose to present a case under one of several equal provisions of the law. The discretion of the judge at the time of sentencing has been the most criticized aspect of discretion in the system. The judge typically weighs a number of factors, such as the convicted person's criminal history and character, in deciding how severe a sentence to pass within the guidelines of the law. A first-time offender may receive a suspended sentence or probation, while a person with many past convictions may receive the maximum sentence allowable. Reforms such as strict sentencing guidelines and mandatory sentencing laws (including "three-strikes" laws) have attempted to reduce the allowable amount of judicial discretion. Discretion exists even after sentencing, in the corrections system. For example, corrections officers have discretion in determining who will be eligible for parole and when.

See also Arrest; Diversion; Judicial system, U.S.; Mandatory sentencing laws; Model Penal Code; Parole; Plea bargaining; Probation; Sentencing; Sentencing guidelines, U.S.; United States Sentencing Commission.

Discrimination. *See* Age discrimination; Racial and ethnic discrimination; Sex discrimination

Disorderly conduct
DEFINITION: Criminal conduct which generally includes acts that tend to disturb public peace and good order, that disturb others who hear or see the conduct, or that endanger the morals, safety, or health of the community
SIGNIFICANCE: Disorderly conduct statutes are widely applied by states and municipalities to ensure public tranquility

A general and unusually elastic category, disorderly conduct can include public intoxication, public swearing, crimes such as harassment and loitering, and even crimes such as larceny. Because disorderly conduct is often used as a charge against unruly protesters, some constitutional challenges to disorderly conduct statutes have focused on whether these statutes unreasonably inhibit public speech.

A disorderly conduct charge is generally a misdemeanor punishable by a fine or by a short imprisonment in the county jail. State statutes proscribing disorderly conduct generally fall into two categories. The first type specifically enumerates acts that constitute the prohibited conduct. The second type describes the conduct only generally as disturbing the public peace. The latter type of statute is subject to challenge as unconstitutional on the grounds that it is too vague to give the defendant adequate notice of what conduct is prohibited.

See also Assembly and association, freedom of; Breach of the peace; Moral turpitude; Public order offenses; Vagrancy laws.

District attorney
DEFINITION: An official who institutes criminal proceedings on behalf of a jurisdiction
SIGNIFICANCE: The district attorney has the expertise and resources necessary to conduct a criminal prosecution

Unlike much of American law, which originated in England (where private prosecution was the rule), the idea of the public district attorney originated in Dutch-speaking areas of the American colonies. The tradition of private prosecution of criminals continued, however, until the mid-nineteenth century.

The terms "state's attorney" and "district attorney" are often used interchangeably, but there is a difference. A district attorney may be an officer of a municipality, a district, or a state. A state's attorney represents only a state. Both "state's attorney" and "district attorney," however, are synonymous with "prosecuting attorney."

A district attorney for a particular federal district is known as a United States attorney. Special prosecutors, or United States attorneys, may be appointed to investigate possible criminal activities of the executive branch of the federal government.

A district attorney is elected or appointed as the legal representative of a particular area with the primary responsibility of instituting proceedings against the violators of laws. The district attorney must be an attorney, usually with a specified minimum number of years in practice. The legislative body of the particular district may prescribe certain other requirements for the office, such as place of residence and minimum age.

The jurisdiction that the district attorney represents may provide assistant district attorneys to assist in the conduct of cases. Many new lawyers gain valuable litigation experience by serving as assistant district attorneys. In addition, the courts may appoint extra prosecuting attorneys, as needed, to help in times of particularly heavy caseloads.

Duties of the District Attorney. Once a person is indicted by a grand jury, the district attorney is responsible for seeing that due diligence—complete attention to the matter at hand, investigation, and prosecution—is exercised. This includes the study of evidence provided by an inquest, evidence gathered by the police in their investigation of a crime, and statements made by witnesses and others.

A district attorney bases the decision on whether to prosecute a crime on a number of criteria. There must be enough evidence to overcome the higher burden of proof which exists in criminal, as opposed to civil, proceedings. The accused comes into court innocent; the prosecution must prove clear and convincing guilt. Because a decision to prosecute is subjective, one defendant may be dismissed while another indicted for the same crime is tried. The decision is made based on the chances of securing a conviction. While a defendant may feel singled out for prosecution, if there exists a genuine basis for the prosecution, due process has been observed.

If the district attorney believes that a case may not be strong enough to ensure conviction, the prosecution may offer the defendant a plea bargain. A plea bargain guarantees conviction on at least a lesser charge and avoids the risk that the accused would be acquitted by a jury. A plea bargain also avoids the expense of time, money, and manpower on a case that may be difficult to win, and it secures a certain conviction.

Responsibility and Liability. The district attorney bears responsibility for how a particular prosecution is conducted, even though the actual courtroom work may be done by assistants. Because of heavy caseloads and administrative duties, a district attorney may personally conduct only a few trials—often those that are "high profile." The district attorney may not attempt to control a grand jury by announcing ahead of time which crimes will or will not be prosecuted, nor can any criminal charges pending before a grand jury be dismissed.

In general, district attorneys cannot be held liable for damages when they are acting within the scope of official duties, but they may be liable for statutory misconduct, official misconduct, neglect of duty, or exceeding the official scope of their duties. District attorneys may be removed by impeachment for official misconduct, failure to disclose evidence that might be favorable to the accused, or failure to observe due process (see *Brady v. Maryland*, 1963).   —*Elizabeth Algren Shaw*

See also Attorney general, state; Criminal justice system; Criminal procedure; Prosecutor, public.

BIBLIOGRAPHY

For a good overview of the office of district attorney, consult a legal encyclopedia such as *The Guide to American Law* (St. Paul, Minn.: West, 1983-1985), or a basic dictionary such as Henry Campbell Black, *Black's Law Dictionary* (rev. 4th ed. St. Paul, Minn.: West, 1968). Also valuable are general legal guides such as Melvin M. Belli, Sr., and Allen P. Wilkinson, *Everybody's Guide to the Law* (San Diego, Calif.: Harcourt Brace Jovanovich, 1986), and Lewis Mayers, *The American Legal System* (New York: Harper & Row, 1964).

Diversion

DEFINITION: The procedure by which juveniles are referred from the formal juvenile justice system to informal adjustment or community-based programs

SIGNIFICANCE: Diversion reduces the number of juveniles who are under the control of the juvenile justice system, and it spares some juveniles the harsh experience of the system

The main goal of diversion is to redirect juveniles who otherwise would have received a formal adjudicatory hearing into alternative programs. Proponents of diversion argue that diversion is necessary to keep juveniles from being labeled delinquent. They contend that there is a stigma associated with being processed through the juvenile justice system and that juveniles who avoid that stigma are less likely to commit criminal acts in the future. Alternatives for diverted juveniles include drug treatment centers, community-based programs,

and family or individual counseling. Critics of diversion have argued that diversion serves to "widen the net" of social control by the juvenile justice system. That is, instead of diverting juveniles who would have been formally adjudicated, diversion may focus on juveniles who would *not* have otherwise received a formal hearing. Those juveniles, critics say, mostly consist of less serious offenders who would probably have had their cases dismissed or been informally disposed.

See also Boot camps; Community service as punishment for crime; Discretion; House arrest; Juvenile delinquency; Juvenile Justice and Delinquency Prevention, Office of; Juvenile Justice and Delinquency Prevention Act; Juvenile justice system; Sentencing.

Divorce. *See* Family law

Dix, Dorothea Lynde (Apr. 4, 1802, Hampden, Maine—July 17, 1887, Trenton, N.J.)

IDENTIFICATION: Reformer of mental health system, prisons, and jails

SIGNIFICANCE: Dix established thirty-two mental hospitals in the United States, Canada, Europe, and Japan, and she revolutionized the treatment of the mentally ill

Dorothea Dix was a teacher, reformer, writer of children's books, and administrator of nurses during the Civil War. Her greatest accomplishments were in reforming the way the mentally ill were treated. In 1841, while teaching a Sunday school class to a group of women inmates at the Cambridge, Massachusetts, House of Corrections, she discovered mentally ill inmates who were chained naked in unlit, unheated rooms. She prepared a report to the legislature of Massachusetts, which resulted in the expansion of the Worcester Insane Asylum. She left her teaching career to work full-time toward improving the conditions and treatment of the mentally ill. At that time, a common belief was that mental illness was a moral disease and that moral training was the appropriate treatment. Wealthy individuals had been successfully treated in hospitals; adequate facilities did not exist for the poor, however, who were often simply sent to prison. Dix believed that mental illness could be cured if treated early and that the brutality of life for the poor caused mental illness.

See also Civil War; Medical and health law; Prison and jail systems.

DNA testing

DEFINITION: A laboratory procedure for comparing two samples of genetic material to determine whether they came from the same individual

SIGNIFICANCE: DNA tests can be used to confirm whether a suspect was present at the scene of a crime, to confirm or refute claims of paternity, and to confirm or refute the identity of a sex offender

Deoxyribonucleic acid (DNA) is the chemical which codes the genetic blueprint for every living thing. Although all humans have basically the same blueprint and the same DNA, only genetically identical individuals (such as identical twins) will have exactly the same DNA. Since DNA is a component of almost every cell in the body, it can be extracted from flakes of skin, hair follicles, blood, or other body tissues or fluids left at the scene of a crime. By comparing the DNA from such a sample to DNA taken from a suspect, one can confirm or deny, with great accuracy, whether the two samples came from the same person. Because this technique is based on the same idea as the matching of fingerprints from a crime scene to those of a suspect, it is often referred to as "DNA fingerprinting."

See also Autopsy; Expert witness; Fingerprint identification; Forensic science and medicine; Rape and sex offenses.

Doe v. Bolton

COURT: U.S. Supreme Court
DATE: Decided January 22, 1973
SIGNIFICANCE: A companion case to *Roe v. Wade*, it established a woman's legal right to abortion and helped to define the limits of that right by limiting state requirements which make access difficult

This case, brought by a pregnant Georgia woman, challenged the constitutionality of a Georgia law which prohibited all but medically necessary abortions. Additionally, the Georgia law included strict procedural requirements for obtaining even medically necessary abortions. A second doctor was required to approve the abortion, abortions could be performed only in state-certified hospitals, and a committee from that hospital had to review the case and give its approval. Finally, the law restricted medically necessary abortions to state residents.

"Mary Doe" challenged the law in a district court on the grounds that it infringed on her right to privacy and that the procedural requirements violated constitutional guarantees of due process of law and equal protection of the law. The district court did rule that the restriction of abortion only to cases in which the mother's life or health was threatened, in which there was serious risk of severe fetal abnormality, or in which pregnancy was a result of rape was an infringement on a woman's constitutional "right to privacy." The district court, however, upheld the procedural requirements on the grounds that the state has a proper interest in protecting the health and life of a potential person, the fetus.

The case was appealed to the Supreme Court, where it was heard as a companion case to *Roe v. Wade*. The Court affirmed a woman's right to abortion without restriction during the first trimester of pregnancy. Using guidelines established in *Roe v. Wade*, it held invalid the requirement that abortion could be performed only in state-accredited hospitals. The court argued that clinics and other facilities could provide trained personnel and equipment for performing abortions. To limit where abortions could be performed during the first trimester infringed on a woman's right to abortion. It also held that requiring approval by a second physician and a hospital committee was unacceptable, infringing unnecessarily on a woman's rights and imposing requirements that were not applied to other surgical procedures. Requiring a second physician's approval

was also viewed as infringing on a doctor's freedom to practice medicine. Finally, the Court ruled that restricting abortion to state residents was not allowed because a state is required to provide services for all persons who enter a state and need or seek medical services. Coupled with *Roe v. Wade*, the decision strongly affirmed a woman's right to abortion and firmly established a doctrine of trimesters in which no restrictions on abortion are allowed during the first trimester of pregnancy (the first three months) and only restrictions pertaining to the safety of the mother during the second. It prohibited states from enacting requirements that would make abortion unduly difficult to obtain during this time period.

See also Abortion; Birth control, right to; Feminism; *Roe v. Wade*.

Domestic violence

DEFINITION: A pattern of physical, sexual, or psychological abuse between persons involved, or formerly involved, in an intimate relationship
SIGNIFICANCE: Domestic violence is the most significant cause of injury to women in the United States, and it endangers children as well

According to Federal Bureau of Investigation statistics, a woman is beaten every fifteen seconds in the United States. Three out of four women murdered are killed by their husbands, and 22 percent to 35 percent of women visiting hospital emergency rooms are there because of domestic violence. In fact, battery is the most significant cause of injury to women in the United States, according to former U.S. Surgeon General C. Everett Koop. Moreover, this type of violence threatens children as well as women. Researchers estimate at 3.3 million the number of children ages three to seventeen who are exposed to violence in the home. These children are at serious risk of perpetrating domestic violence or being abused themselves in their adult relationships. The legal system's response to assault and battery among intimates has historically been very different from its response to crimes between strangers. The behavioral context of domestic violence is different from stranger crime, and the criminal justice system has struggled to respond adequately to the special challenges posed by domestic violence.

Defining Domestic Violence. Domestic violence is defined by two parameters: the conduct and the relationship. Domestic violence includes hitting, choking, kicking, assault with a weapon, shoving, scratching, biting, unwanted sexual touching, rape, threats of violence, harassment, destruction of property, and stalking—all of which may constitute a crime. Other types of conduct do not constitute criminal conduct but nevertheless are classified as domestic violence because of their contribution to the overall context of the abuse. These include degrading comments, suicide attempts or threats, not allowing access to family resources, and isolation and control of the abused party.

In domestic violence, this conduct occurs within an intimate relationship. The relationship may be husband and wife (or former spouses), boyfriend/girlfriend (or former boyfriend/girlfriend), gay and lesbian relationships, or any people who live together, or have lived together, in an intimate relationship. Moreover, the conduct is a part of a pattern of controlling and assaultive behavior rather than an isolated incident. The conduct may escalate over time, moving from psychological abuse to physical and sexual abuse, even murder. Taken in context, the conduct creates a pervasive atmosphere of fear and control.

The Dynamics of Domestic Violence. Domestic violence is not the exclusive domain of a particular class, race, or ethnic background; it crosses all walks of life. The overwhelming number of victims are women, and their attackers are men. Although researchers have discovered that in many American families both spouses are violent to each other, this does not suggest that women are as violent as men. The consequences of men's violence to women are vastly more severe in terms of physical injury than those of women against men. Moreover, research suggests that in many cases women's violence is defensive, while men's is offensive in nature. Finally, the context of control in which violence occurs (discussed below) makes men's violence qualitatively different than women's violence. This is not to say that there are no battered men; it is simply to recognize that the problem is gender oriented, reflecting the norms of a society in which, traditionally, men have exerted power and control over women.

Domestic violence is not, as many people suppose, motivated by anger or stress or caused by alcohol or drugs. It is purposeful and instrumental behavior, designed to control the victim and to ensure that the victim is available exclusively for the purposes of the batterer. The dynamic usually begins with efforts to isolate the victim from the usual support systems of family, friends, and work. Isolation is important in order to prevent the victim from leaving and to create a situation in which the victim is dependent on the batterer. Thus, the creation of financial dependency and expression of extreme jealousy may be part of this strategy. Physical force and sexual abuse ensure that the victim will obey the batterer, and psychological abuse reminds the victim that the batterer may back up threats with violence. The goal of the batterer is control over and exclusive access to the victim (and, at times, her children).

An often-asked question is "Why don't battered women leave?" In fact, many do leave. Populations at shelters across the United States are increasingly young, are leaving relationships of shorter duration, and report leaving after fewer violent incidents than was the case in the mid-1970's to mid-1980's. Those that do not leave generally have very rational reasons for staying. The primary reason is that they fear escalation of the violence. This fear is justified: National crime statistics suggest that 75 percent of reported spousal assaults occur while the parties are divorced or separated. For many victims, isolation and financial dependency make realistic alternatives scarce. Furthermore, as many crime victims know, trauma can immobilize a victim, impairing the ability to plan. This is even more accentuated for victims of domestic violence than for victims of stranger crimes because the perpetrator has continued access to the victim, knows her daily routine, and potentially controls her children.

The Legal Response to Domestic Violence. Historically, formal legal systems have not only failed to recognize domestic violence as a crime but also granted husbands specific rights to control, chastise, and even beat their wives. These traditions carried over to early American justice, and only in the mid- to late 1800's did courts and legislatures begin to recognize wife beating as a crime. For example, in 1882, Maryland was the first state to pass a law punishing brutal wife beating with a whipping at the whipping post. In 1871, an Alabama court was the first in the United States to hold that the husband had no legal right to beat his wife (*Fulgham v. State*, 1871).

These early developments were not extended during the first half of the twentieth century. Marital immunity laws were enacted, specifically precluding any action by one spouse against another for damages for assault or rape. Divorce laws permitted divorce only for specific conduct, and violence in the home was rarely considered sufficient to warrant a divorce. In addition, the formal legal gains of the previous century were not accompanied by changes in the actual practice of the legal system. Wife beating remained a shameful secret in most cases, and in the unusual instance when the police became involved, they rarely treated the incident as a crime.

In the 1970's the women's movement began to advocate change. Change began with the establishment of "shelters" for battered women—safe places for women in danger and their children. Lawsuits against police and local government established a new standard: Police were required to respond to domestic violence calls in the same manner as they would a stranger crime. Research suggesting that batterers could be deterred by arrest led to the enactment of mandatory arrest laws, in which police are required to arrest the batterer if they have probable cause to believe that a crime has been committed. Although in many situations this led to an arrest of both parties, many states responded with legislation requiring the police to determine, and arrest, the "primary aggressor" in the incident.

The crimes of domestic violence are often prosecuted as harassment or battery (typically misdemeanors) or as assault, rape, or attempted murder (typically felonies). Some jurisdictions offer diversion or deferred sentencing programs. In these programs, the defendant pleads guilty or *nolo contendere* (no contest) to the charge. Sentence will not be imposed if the defendant completes certain requirements, typically evaluation for alcohol and drug abuse, a batterers' treatment program, and supervised probation. The design of batterers' treatment programs is a matter of lively debate. Some programs focus on techniques to manage anger. Others focus on having the batterer take responsibility for his actions and change his views on controlling his partner. These programs are generally regarded as suitable only for misdemeanors and first-time offenders. When the injury to the victim is great or the defendant is a repeat offender, the criminal justice system approaches the crime as a stranger crime, but with special care to ensure the participation of the major witness, the victim.

The criminal justice system is not the only part of the legal system to address issues of domestic violence. Repeal of the marital immunity laws mentioned earlier has led to tort suits by an abused spouse against the abuser for damages incurred by the victim. Very few victims, however, wish to pursue a lengthy court battle for tort damages. Instead, most prefer divorce. With the enactment of no-fault divorce laws, the conduct of either party during the marriage is largely irrelevant in the divorce proceeding. Thus, the division of property upon divorce will typically not be affected by a history of battering. This history may be relevant to spousal support (alimony), however, if the battering has impaired the health and earning capacity of the victim. An open question is the relevance of domestic violence when the custody of children is an issue. Courts are undecided on whether a history of spousal abuse is relevant to determining the best interests of the child in custody decisions. Although some research suggests that many men who batter women also batter their children, and thus would not make good custodial parents, courts sometimes take the view that the divorce will end the spousal abuse and therefore disregard the abuse.

All fifty states and the District of Columbia have laws that provide for domestic violence restraining orders. These laws allow a victim of domestic violence to petition the court for an order that requires the perpetrator to stay away from the victim and to leave the home; it may also grant other protection and relief to the victim. If the victim can show that she is or was in danger of domestic violence, the order will be granted *ex parte* (that is, to the victim without a hearing to the respondent), but the respondent is allowed a hearing to dispute the order within a short time (such as twenty-one days) after the order is entered. The order typically lasts for a year, and violation is either a crime or a contempt of court, depending on the jurisdiction.

A restraining order offers the victim a period of time in which she can be free from threat and during which she can make plans in relative safety. It also impresses upon the perpetrator that the court takes domestic violence seriously and will not tolerate further violence. Although the domestic violence restraining order is successful in achieving these goals in many cases, a court order alone cannot ensure the safety of a victim of domestic violence. Thus, an important aspect of this process is safety planning for the victim, which can occur as an adjunct to the court process with the participation of victim's advocates.

The increase in domestic violence cases often threatens to overwhelm the legal resources of communities large and small. Some participants in the legal system—judges, prosecutors, police—recognize that a reactive approach to this problem is inadequate. Instead, they are engaging in collaborative efforts to join educational, social service, and legal resources to devise a proactive approach to prevention of domestic violence through education and community awareness.

—*Gwendolyn Griffith*

See also Assault; Battered child and battered wife syndromes; Child abuse; Child molestation; Family law; National Organization for Victim Assistance (NOVA); Rape and sex offenses; Restraining order.

BIBLIOGRAPHY

A classic study on the incidence of violence in American families is discussed in Murray Straus, R. J. Gelles, and S. K. Steinmetz, *Behind Closed Doors: Violence in the American Family* (Garden City, N.Y.: Anchor Press/Doubleday, 1980). The "cycle of violence" is discussed in Suzanne Steinmetz, *The Cycle of Violence: Assertive, Aggressive, and Abusive Family Interaction* (New York: Praeger, 1977). Research on interventions in domestic violence is discussed in Eve S. Buzawa and Carl G. Buzawa, eds., *Domestic Violence: The Changing Criminal Justice Response* (Westport, Conn.: Greenwood Press, 1992). Theory about the history of intervention is found in Martha Fineman and Roxanne Mykitiuk, eds., *The Public Nature of Private Violence: The Discovery of Domestic Abuse* (New York: Routledge, 1994). Recommended reforms of the court system in dealing with domestic violence are discussed in National Council of Juvenile and Family Court Judges, *Family Violence: Improving Court Practice (Recommendations from the National Council of Juvenile and Family Court Judges' Family Violence Project* (Reno, Nev.: Author, 1990). Stories of women who successfully leave their partners are collected in Ginny NiCarthy, *The Ones Who Got Away: Women Who Left Abusive Partners* (Seattle: Seal Press, 1987). An excellent bibliography has been prepared by the Urban Institute, *Family Violence: A Guide to Research* (San Francisco: Courts and Communities: Confronting Violence in the Family, 1993).

Double jeopardy

DEFINITION: Being tried a second time for the same crime

SIGNIFICANCE: The Fifth Amendment prohibits the state from trying and retrying a case until it gets the conviction it is seeking; there are exceptions, however—a retrial is allowable in certain types of mistrials, for example

The Fifth Amendment to the U.S. Constitution states that no one shall "be subject for the same offense to be twice put in jeopardy of life or limb." Being put "in jeopardy" means being put in a situation where one may be subject to punishment for a crime. This protection against being tried more than once applies to both state and federal criminal proceedings; the Supreme Court decision in *Benton v. Maryland* (1969) held that the prohibition applies to the states as well as to the federal government. It also applies both to situations in which a trial has been completed and the defendant found innocent and to situations in which a trial has been halted in the middle after a jury has been sworn in and evidence has been introduced.

There are a number of exceptions to the protection against double jeopardy. It does not apply in cases in which a mistrial has been requested by, or declared with the consent of, the defense. It does not apply if a jury is deadlocked or if certain conditions, such as illness or death, hinder the completion of a trial. If an appellate court overturns a lower court's guilty verdict, a new trial is permissible. Moreover, as the Supreme

Court held in *Bartkus v. Illinois* (1958) and reaffirmed in *Heath v. Alabama* (1985), the protection against double jeopardy does not apply in cases where federal and state jurisdictions overlap (that is, when conduct violates both federal and state laws).

A unique situation may arise in cases where an individual is accused of committing several crimes—for example, robbing a convenience store and shooting the attendant. Because attempted murder carries the higher penalty, the state might not pursue the robbery charges but attempt to convict the suspect of attempted murder. If the state fails to prove its case, it cannot recharge the suspect with felonious assault, based on the same crime of shooting the attendant. The state could, however, bring robbery charges against the suspect without violating this concept, because it is a different crime. Another possibility also exists: Although the state cannot retry the crime of attempted murder, it could file civil charges. The charge in this case would be violating the attendant's civil rights. An example of this approach was the trial of the four Los Angeles police officers accused of beating Rodney King. A jury acquitted the four officers in 1992, but because of the public outcry the government tried the officers on charges of violating King's civil rights; two of the officers were convicted in the civil trial. The drawbacks to such civil trials are that the penalties that can be given are usually less, and there is the danger that the state may appear to be carrying out a vendetta against the suspects.

See also Bill of Rights, U.S.; Constitution, U.S.; Constitutional law; Criminal procedure; King, Rodney, case and aftermath; Mistrial; *Palko v. Connecticut*.

Douglas, Stephen A. (Apr. 23, 1813, Brandon, Vt.— June 3, 1861, Chicago, Ill.)

IDENTIFICATION: United States senator

SIGNIFICANCE: Douglas supported the principle of popular sovereignty regarding the issue of slavery in the territories

Stephen Douglas grew up on a Vermont farm and in Canandaigua, New York, where he began reading law. In 1833 he wandered westward, eventually finding work in Winchester, Illinois. He read law at night and appeared in peace court on Saturdays. Licensed in 1834, he began practice in Jacksonville, Illinois. Within a year he was elected attorney general of the state, which also made him a circuit judge. He was elected state legislator in 1835. In 1837 President Martin Van Buren appointed him registrar in the Springfield Land Office. In 1837, although legally too young to serve, he narrowly lost a congressional election. On December 2, 1840, he was appointed Illinois secretary of state, and in February, 1841, he was elected a judge of the state Supreme Court.

He was elected to Congress in 1842 and to the United States Senate in 1847. There he opposed compromise on the Oregon boundary and supported the Mexican War. He opposed the Wilmot Proviso of 1846 (excluding slavery and involuntary servitude from annexed Mexican territory), but he urged application of the Missouri Compromise to annexed Mexican terri-

tory. Douglas supported the Fugitive Slave Law of 1850, allowing arrest of fugitive slaves without warrant. In 1853, he introduced the Kansas-Nebraska bill (it was passed in 1854), embodying his doctrine of popular sovereignty under which territorial settlers were allowed to decide the slavery issue after statehood. In 1858 Douglas defeated Abraham Lincoln for the Senate in the campaign that featured the Lincoln-Douglas debates. Douglas ran for president in 1860 and lost.

See also Fugitive Slave Laws; Kansas-Nebraska Act; Lincoln, Abraham; Lincoln-Douglas debates; Missouri Compromise of 1820.

Stephen Douglas introduced the Kansas-Nebraska bill into the Senate and engaged in a series of famous debates with Abraham Lincoln. (James L. Shaffer)

Douglas, William O. (Oct. 16, 1898, Maine, Minn.—Jan. 19, 1980, Washington, D.C.)

IDENTIFICATION: U.S. Supreme Court justice, 1939-1975

SIGNIFICANCE: Douglas, who was the longest-serving justice the Court has ever known, is remembered primarily as an exemplar of American individualism and an advocate for the underprivileged

William O. Douglas was born into a poor family headed by a Presbyterian missionary. The family became poorer still when Douglas' father died. Douglas, only six years old at the time, suffered further childhood trauma when he was stricken with polio, which he combated with a program of rigorous outdoor exercise in the foothills near his home in Yakima, Washington.

After working his way through college, Douglas taught for two years, saving money to go east to continue his education. Nevertheless, when he traveled to New York to attend Columbia Law School, he did so by hopping a freight train and by hitchhiking. He was graduated near the top of his class, despite having tutored nearly full time throughout law school.

Two unhappy years in private practice led Douglas to accept a teaching post at Columbia Law School, then one at Yale Law School. He flourished at Yale, specializing in corporate law and becoming one of the school's youngest holders of an endowed chair. His restlessness led him next to Washington, D.C., where he went to work on the New Deal as a member of, then as chairman of, the Securities and Exchange Commission. He became a confidant of President Franklin D. Roosevelt, who in 1939 nominated him to the Supreme Court.

At forty-one, Douglas was the second-youngest appointee to the Court (only Joseph Story, who took his seat 128 years earlier, was younger). Roosevelt had named him largely because of his ultraliberal political orientation, and Douglas quickly allied himself with Justice Hugo L. Black in upholding the constitutionality of the New Deal and, later, of civil rights legislation that came before the Court. Even so, Douglas' most significant contribution as a justice arguably came in a series of opinions concerning business regulation that he wrote in the 1940's. In the later years of Black's tenure, the two justices' views diverged, Black's outlook growing more conservative while Douglas maintained a liberal course. Douglas never seemed concerned about standing alone as a dissenter; indeed, in his later years he cultivated the image of a maverick, both on the Court and in his personal life.

In the 1950's he divorced his wife of twenty-nine years, then married three more times in quick succession. Unlike most modern justices, he flirted with politics. When his political ambitions came to an end, he embarked on a series of highly visible world travels to promote his many books on travel, other cultures, and the environment. His nonconformist behavior led to two attempts to impeach him, first in 1953, and again in 1970. The latter attempt was more serious, but Douglas defended himself ably, and the call for impeachment was dropped.

In December, 1974, Douglas suffered a paralyzing stroke that kept him away from the Court for most of the remainder of that term. He returned the following October, but he was still disabled, and in November, 1975, he retired as the longest-serving justice in history.

See also Black, Hugo L.; Civil rights; Liberalism, modern American; Roosevelt, Franklin D.; Supreme Court of the United States.

Douglass, Frederick (Feb., 1817?, Tuckahoe, Talbot County, Md.—Feb. 20, 1895, Washington, D.C.)

IDENTIFICATION: Abolitionist, autobiographer, journalist, and statesman

SIGNIFICANCE: A famed writer and orator for the cause of abolition, Douglass inflamed public opinion against the institution of slavery with his speeches and his *Narrative of the Life of Frederick Douglass*

Born a slave in Maryland, Frederick Douglass grew to manhood struggling against the physical and intellectual restrictions placed upon him by that institution. Escaping to freedom in the North in 1838, he took the name Douglass from a character in Sir Walter Scott's *Lady of the Lake*. After meeting William Lloyd Garrison in 1841, he was hired as a speaker by the Massachusetts Anti-Slavery Society, for which he delivered antislavery lectures throughout the North and East. His success as an orator was immense; he often peppered his speeches, which sometimes lasted for nearly two hours, with dramatic or humorous stories and asides.

Feeling the need for a wider audience, greater artistic freedom, and a medium capable of accommodating greater depth of detail, Douglass wrote the first of his autobiographies, *Narrative of the Life of Frederick Douglass, an American Slave: Written by Himself* (1845). It was the most popular of the hundred or so contemporary slave narratives, primarily because it was a first-hand account written by Douglass himself rather than a mere transcription of oral narratives, but also because it was an extremely powerful account of his personal struggle for identity, which he sought through intellectual as well as physical freedom. The book provides insights into the troubled lives of slave owners as well, from the complex strategies required to defend slavery against the criticism it drew to the religious hypocrisy the institution engendered.

Fearing capture as a fugitive slave, Douglass spent several years lecturing in England and Ireland, returning in 1847 after English friends purchased his freedom. Upon his return to Rochester, New York, he established the *North Star*, an abolitionist newspaper in which he advocated the use of political methods to bring about the end of slavery, and which he edited until the end of the Civil War. His *Narrative* was also followed by two expansions, *My Bondage and My Freedom* (1855) and *Life and Times of Frederick Douglass* (1881, 1892), but the 1845 text remained by far the most influential, selling more than eleven thousand copies in its first three years, with substantial sales in England, France, and The Netherlands as well. Douglass also wrote *The Heroic Slave* (1851), a fictional story of a mutiny aboard a slave ship and the continuing struggle for freedom by the slaves. During the Civil War, Douglass helped organize two regiments of Massachusetts Negroes and urged other blacks to join the Union ranks. After the war, he held a number of appointed posts, including secretary of the Santo Domingo Commission (1871), marshal of the District of Columbia (1877-1881), recorder of deeds for the same district (1881-1886), and minister to the Republic of Haiti (1889-1891). Douglass died of a heart attack in Washington, D.C.

See also Abolitionist movement; Civil War; Garrison, William Lloyd; Slavery.

Dred Scott decision. *See Scott v. Sandford*

Drive-by shooting

DEFINITION: Firing weapons at persons or property from a moving vehicle, frequently with intent to kill

SIGNIFICANCE: Most often drive-by shootings are precipitated by gang disputes; the crime has received considerable attention because of the danger it poses for innocent bystanders

Drive-by shooting is not a new crime. Its roots go back to the 1930's. The term itself was not in use then, but the "gangland hits" of the era sometimes involved firing guns from automobiles and speeding away. Drive-by shootings began in large midwestern and western cities. Because these cities were less densely populated and larger geographically than those of the Northeast, motor vehicles quickly became the primary mode of transportation. In gang disputes, gang members found it convenient to drive by a site, stop, shoot, and leave quickly. Eastern American cities tend to be more densely populated and to have less well developed road systems, making the logistics of a drive-by shooting much more difficult.

With the marked increase in drive-by shootings during the 1980's and 1990's, attempts to combat the crime began to take on greater urgency. As the incidence of the crime grew, so did the number of innocent bystanders killed or wounded in the attacks. Because drive-bys often involve firing into a house, family members of the intended target, including children, are the most frequent innocent victims. The city of San Diego provides one example of the growth of drive-by shootings. As a percentage of all gang-related assaults, drive-by shootings there increased from 23.7 in 1981 to 40.8 in 1988. Nationally, drive-by shootings increased by a factor of 20 between 1983 and 1992.

In *Gangbangs and Drive-bys: Grounded Culture and Juvenile Gang Violence* (1994), William Sanders identifies several situations, not necessarily mutually exclusive, during which drive-by shootings occur. During "emergent arguments," the shooting occurs spontaneously or even accidentally. In other cases, a victim may simply be "hanging out," while the perpetrator is seeking a member of an opposing gang to victimize. One gang, for example, may believe that someone has acted disrespectfully toward them. The gang members seek the most opportune target from the other gang, regardless of whether that person has done anything personally to them. The victim has little or no time to react to the shooting. Drive-by shootings can also occur at parties. In this situation the perpetrator knows of the party (presumably attended by rival gang mem-

bers) and wants to impress fellow gang members. Business competition between gangs is an explanation for an increasing number of drive-by shootings. With the growth in strength and organization of urban African American gangs, competition among these gangs (and with other organized crime groups) has intensified. Particularly with the competition for the crack cocaine business, drive-by shootings have become a tool for retribution. Finally, shootings of inanimate targets (homes, automobiles, and businesses) have become more common. This activity is generally intended to "send a message" rather than to inflict grave harm.

See also Gangs, youth; Murder and homicide; Saint Valentine's Day massacre.

Driving under the influence

DEFINITION: Driving a motor vehicle while impaired by the effects of alcohol or another drug

SIGNIFICANCE: Driving under the influence is one of the leading causes of traffic accidents and deaths in the United States

Driving under the influence (DUI) is a pervasive social problem and legal dilemma. The behavior has proved very difficult to change, partly because the act of drinking, in and of itself, is legal and socially accepted, and partly because law enforcement resources are inadequate for dealing with the problem of drunk drivers. In most states, driving under the influence is defined by driving with a blood-alcohol level of more than 0.08 percent; no similar standards for driving under the influence of other drugs have been established.

Police estimate that more than one-half the drivers involved in automobile accidents after drinking are likely to have consumed large amounts of alcohol. Research has shown that blood-alcohol concentrations higher than 0.08 percent are dangerous and that on most weekend nights about 10 percent of all drivers have concentrations of more than 0.10 percent. (Blood-alcohol levels measure the amount of alcohol, in milligrams, found in one hundred milliliters of blood.) Research has indicated that excessive drinking plays a role in one-third to two-thirds of all fatal accidents. Accidents in which alcohol plays a role tend to be far more deadly and to result in far more serious injuries than those that are not alcohol related.

Early efforts to deal with drunk driving were ineffective because intoxication proved difficult to define. The first efforts to detect the level of alcohol in the blood that makes a person incapable of driving safely took place in Sweden and Norway in the 1930's. This research led to a 1936 law that defined driving while intoxicated as operating a vehicle while having a blood-alcohol level of fifty milligrams of alcohol per one hundred milliliters of blood (0.05 percent). To deal with the problem, Sweden instituted heavy penalties for a violation: One month in prison, a heavy fine, and license suspension were mandatory. At least for a time, this harsh treatment led to greatly reduced levels of drunken driving.

In 1937 Indiana became the first American state to enact a law defining intoxication; Indiana adopted a blood-alcohol level of 0.10 percent for its law. By 1963 thirty-nine states and

In most states, driving with a blood-alcohol level of 0.08 percent or more constitutes driving under the influence. (James L. Shaffer)

the District of Columbia had laws modeled after the Indiana statute, but a majority set the legal concentration level at a higher level, 0.15 percent. In 1967, the National Highway Safety Traffic Administration set a recommended standard of 0.10 percent and initiated a program to persuade all the states to accept that level. It threatened to withhold highway construction funds from states with higher limits, but not until 1981 did every state adopt the 0.10 percent level.

The Offenders. Researchers have discovered that a small percentage of the population, the "problem drinkers," causes a disproportionately high percentage of alcohol-related accidents. Strict laws outlining severe penalties for driving under the influence have not been found to deter these drivers. They have learned through experience that the risk of being stopped is very small: Typically, only one in two thousand intoxicated drivers is arrested. Moreover, of those stopped by the police,

fewer than half receive any significant punishment. Thus, only a small risk of punishment is involved in driving after having a few drinks, though even moderate drinking strongly increases the risk of an accident.

Increasing the probability of arrest for driving under the influence from one in two thousand to one in a hundred would require the arrest of twenty times more drunk drivers, and there simply are not enough police officers to arrest that many people on the highways. The drunk driver's statistical probability of having an accident is only 0.00045 on any trip; for sober drivers that figure is 0.00016.

Punishment. The Uniform Vehicle Code adopted by the Department of Transportation has served as a model for state laws. It prohibits driving with a blood-alcohol level of 0.10 percent and mandates chemical testing for suspects. According to the code, refusal to provide a breath sample can be used

Arrests for Driving Under the Influence, 1993

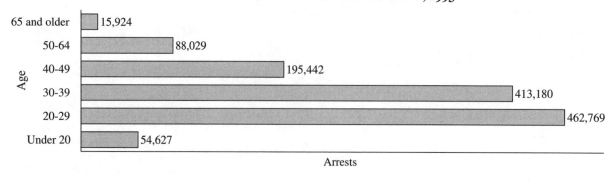

Source: U.S. Department of Justice, Federal Bureau of Investigation, *Crime in the United States* (Uniform Crime Reports). Washington, D.C.: U.S. Government Printing Office, 1994.

Note: Total 1993 driving under the influence arrests: 1,229,971.

against a person in a trial, resulting in license suspension. The code calls for a mandatory prison term or participation in a treatment program after the first conviction. In the United States, judges are generally reluctant to impose heavy penalties on first offenders. Most offenders go to treatment programs instead, and the success levels of these programs are very low. Fewer than two out of ten people who attend such programs refrain from drunk driving even after lengthy behavior-modification efforts.

The Victims. Automobile accidents cause the death of more Americans between the ages of one and thirty-five than anything else, and they are second only to cancer-caused deaths in their economic burden on society. More than fifty-two thousand Americans die in accidents every year, and driving under the influence is a factor in one-half of these deaths. A majority of cases of total disability, including paraplegia and quadriplegia, result from accidents involving alcohol, and accidents caused by drunk driving are the leading cause of facial lacerations and head fractures. Billions of dollars are spent treating victims of alcohol-related automobile accidents every year.

—*Leslie V. Tischauser*

See also Deterrence; Drug use and sale, illegal; Mothers Against Drunk Driving (MADD); Negligence; Prohibition.

BIBLIOGRAPHY

A variety of aspects of the drunk-driving problem are examined in H. Laurence Ross, *Deterring the Drinking Driver* (Lexington, Mass.: Lexington Books, 1982); Ralph K. Jones and Kent B. Joscelyn, *Alcohol and Highway Safety in 1978: A Review of the State of Knowledge* (Washington, D.C.: National Highway Traffic Safety Administration, 1978); R. F. Borkenstein, *The Role of the Drinking Driver in Traffic Accidents* (Bloomington: Indiana University Press, 1969); George A. Beitel, "Probability of Arrest While Driving Under the Influence of Alcohol," *Journal of Studies on Alcohol* 36 (January, 1975); and Jack P. Gibbs, *Crime, Punishment, and Deterrence* (New York: Elsevier, 1975).

Drug Enforcement Administration (DEA)

DATE: Established July 1, 1973

SIGNIFICANCE: With the establishment of the DEA, federal drug enforcement was unified under a single administrative structure for the first time in United States history

The Drug Enforcement Administration's establishment in 1973 as the sole federal drug enforcement agency within the Department of Justice was eclipsed by the Watergate scandal that was then erupting in Washington, preoccupying most of the media. President Richard Nixon had long wished to consolidate drug enforcement activities. Under a reorganization act, such a move was subject only to the disapproval of Congress. When this disapproval was not expressed by the June 11 deadline, the way was clear for the DEA, as authorized by Nixon, to start operations on July 1, 1973.

On June 29, John R. Bartels, Jr., son of a New York federal judge, was appointed acting head of the agency that would come into being two days later. On September 12, Bartels was made permanent director, being confirmed by the Senate on October 4. Six weeks later, the agency was funded for the next fiscal year at $107,230,000.

Drug Enforcement Before the DEA. Drug enforcement had become a high priority of the Department of Justice, largely because of the connections between the drug trade and organized crime. The Central Intelligence Agency (CIA) was much involved in monitoring drug traffic from Central America and from Asia's Golden Triangle, which was centered in Bangkok, Thailand, while the Federal Bureau of Investigation (FBI) monitored drug trade within the United States. The Bureau of Narcotics and Dangerous Drugs (BNDD), the Office of Drug Abuse Law Enforcement (ODALE), and the Office of National Narcotics Intelligence (ONNI) were also involved.

BNDD, ODALE, and ONNI were absorbed into the new Drug Enforcement Administration, whose ranks were increased by the addition of five hundred special agents transferred from the Customs Service to the Justice Department. Initially, nine hundred agents from the Immigration and Naturalization Service were to be transferred to the Customs Service, but that plan failed because of opposition from labor unions.

The Beginnings of the DEA. As in any consolidation of this sort, some top administrators lost the high-level jobs they previously held. John E. Ingersoll, who had headed BNDD, resigned on June 29, consoled in thinking that drug enforcement would be managed at the highest levels by narcotics agents rather than customs agents. The following day, Myles J. Ambrose, former director of ODALE, resigned to take a job in the private sector.

Following Bartels' confirmation as permanent director, the DEA, already drawing congressional criticism, went through a difficult period, partly because of the suspicion that the Watergate debacle had cast upon all federal activities but also because Bartels appointed friends to high offices within the agency. It was also charged that Bartels made promotions on the basis of friendship rather than performance and was lax in enforcing agency rules. His biggest mistake, however, was appointing Vincent Promuto public affairs director despite Promuto's widely reported links to organized crime.

The agency had already drawn fire when, under the "no-knock" provision of the 1970 crime bill, a group of DEA agents in April, 1973, burst into six Collinsville, Illinois, homes in the middle of the night, roughed up the inhabitants, tore apart the furniture, and detained some of the occupants for up to three days only to discover that the agents had gone to the wrong addresses. Subsequent trials vindicated the officers involved.

The Functions of the DEA. The major function of the DEA is to control drug traffic in the United States. An important part of this job involves the interdiction of drug shipments from other parts of the world and, in some cases, the destruction of drug crops both abroad and domestically. The Customs Service is much involved in the interdiction of drugs being shipped clandestinely into the United States, with the DEA coordinating some of its efforts with information obtained through the CIA, the FBI, and other cooperating agencies.

Although the DEA makes raids on homes, clubs, bars, and other places where drug use is suspected, this is a minor part of its operation. Its major thrusts are to cut off the flow of drugs into the United States, to control the distribution of drugs that slip through customs, and to work strenuously to educate United States citizens about the dangers of drug use, a danger that has intensified with the spread of acquired immune deficiency syndrome (AIDS) through the use of contaminated hypodermic needles.

Attempts to Disband the DEA. In 1993, Vice President Al Gore's proposals for streamlining federal government listed the DEA under the heading, "Eliminating Obsolete Programs." His proposal was to consolidate the DEA and the Bureau of

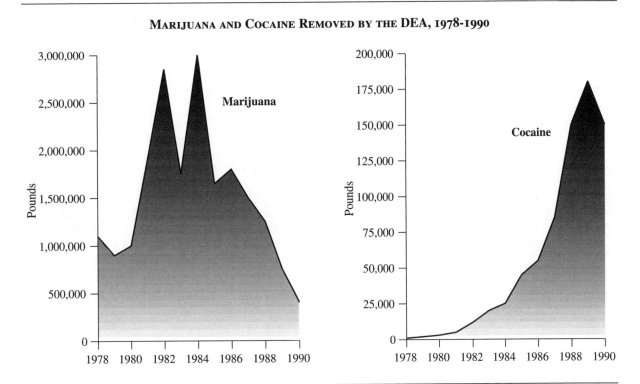

MARIJUANA AND COCAINE REMOVED BY THE DEA, 1978-1990

Source: U.S. Department of Justice, Bureau of Justice Statistics, *Drugs, Crime, and the Justice System.* Washington, D.C.: U.S. Government Printing Office, 1992.

Alcohol, Tobacco, and Firearms with the FBI, a move that FBI director Louis Freeh supported. On October 21, 1993, however, Attorney General Janet Reno announced that the plan had been scrapped despite support from many critics of national law enforcement who believed that the merger would reduce interagency bickering. DEA officials had argued convincingly that Gore's plan would cripple federal enforcement of antidrug laws.   —*R. Baird Shuman*

See also Alcohol, Tobacco, and Firearms (ATF), Bureau of; Comprehensive Drug Abuse Prevention and Control Act of 1970; Drug legalization debate; Drug use and sale, illegal; Forfeiture, civil and criminal; Harrison Narcotic Drug Act; Justice, U.S. Department of; National Narcotics Act; Search and seizure.

Bibliography

Useful books on the Drug Enforcement Administration and the enforcement of drug laws are James B. Bakalar and Lester Grinspoon, *Drug Abuse in a Free Society* (New York: Cambridge University Press, 1988); Gilda Berger, *Drug Abuse: The Impact on Society* (New York: Franklin Watts, 1988); national issues forum staff, Public Agenda Foundation, *The Drug Crisis: Public Strategies for Breaking the Habit* (Dubuque, Iowa: Kendall-Hunt, 1989); Rebecca Stefoff, *The Drug Enforcement Administration* (New York: Chelsea House, 1989); Robert M. Stutman and Richard Esposito, *Dead on Delivery: Inside the Drug Wars, Straight from the Street* (New York: Warner Books, 1992); William O. Walker III, *Drug Control in the Americas* (rev. ed. Albuquerque: University of New Mexico Press, 1989).

Drug legalization debate

Definition: The issue of whether drug use, possession, and sale should be addressed through the criminal justice system

Significance: In the 1980's and 1990's the government tried to control drug use by criminalizing acts associated with it; however, because criminalization has not significantly reduced the amount of drugs in society and the costs of enforcement are high, some argue for reevaluating criminalization of drug use

The crux of the drug legalization debate centers on the tension between individual freedom and societal responsibility. Generally, Americans believe that they should have the freedom to do what they please to themselves and that this freedom should only be regulated when the costs to the others in society become too high. If one agrees with this line of reasoning, the central aspect of the debate over legalizing drug use is determining what the costs to society would be if drugs were legalized. Among the costs to consider are the loss of productivity and health of individual members of society and increased crime (either because of lack of control or the need for

One aspect of the legalization debate concerns the impracticality of policing activities that millions of people pursue in their own homes. (James L. Shaffer)

PERCENTAGE OF NATIONAL OPINION RESEARCH CENTER RESPONDENTS WHO THINK MARIJUANA SHOULD REMAIN ILLEGAL

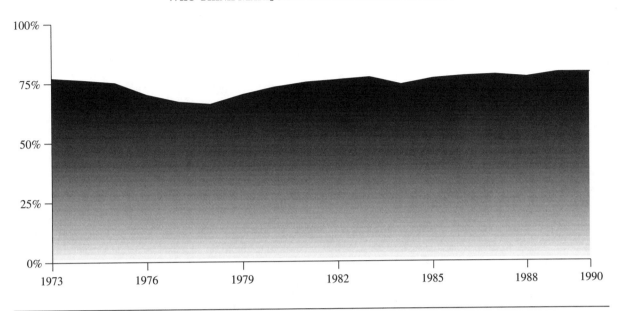

Source: U.S. Department of Justice, Bureau of Justice Statistics, *Drugs, Crime, and the Justice System.* Washington, D.C.: U.S. Government Printing Office, 1992.
Note: Based on interpolated NORC data from a number of sources.

cash). These costs must be balanced against the expense of continuing to fund the "war on drugs."

On one side of the debate, "zero tolerance" advocates (those who believe that no amount of illegal drug use is acceptable) want to continue the war on drug sales and use and to abolish drugs in the United States. On the other side of the debate is a movement to decriminalize drugs—to stop their regulation through the criminal justice system except for specialized cases such as sale to, or use by, children. Others want the government to take an active role and permit, but regulate, their sale through purity checks and taxation.

Arguments for Criminalization. Proponents of the restriction of drugs cite the high numbers of people lost to society through drug use or addiction. They believe that if more people have legal access to drugs, more people will experiment with them. The more people who experiment with drugs, the more who will become addicted, and the costs to society will increase.

Second, they argue that drug use increases crime because people under the influence of drugs have less self-control and therefore are more willing to commit crime. In addition, they argue that when people suffer from a dependence on drugs they become more desperate and are willing to steal to get drugs or the cash to purchase them.

Third, supporters of continued criminalization argue that if the government continues using the criminal justice system to keep the sale and use of drugs difficult, then it can stop children and previous nonusers from starting. Even if society can never "win," in the sense of a complete drug ban, it is worth the fight even to protect a few.

Arguments for Legalization. On the other side of the debate, proponents of legalization argue that drug use is a victimless crime. People are allowed to smoke cigarettes, drink alcohol, and eat butter, all of which have been deemed harmful. Drawing the line at marijuana or cocaine is unjust when weighed against the loss of liberty and privacy involved. Supporters of legalization argue that legalized drug use would, in general, remain casual and recreational and would not seriously affect the productivity or health of the user.

Second, supporters of legalization say that only those persons who are predisposed to crime will commit crime. They believe that there is no pharmacological incentive to commit crime. People who are desperate for drugs and commit property crime for cash, they argue, do so because drug costs are exorbitantly high. Legalization could actually reduce crime because it will reduce the costs of the drugs by taking the uncontrollable black market out of the picture.

Finally, proponents of legalization suggest that there is no way that the "war on drugs" can be won. They look to the banning of alcohol during Prohibition as the model of failure: One cannot stop a nation of people dedicated to personal choice from participating in the recreational activities they choose. The resources dedicated to large police forces, crowded courtrooms, and increased prison capacity are enormous. Most important, they argue, the war on drugs (particularly if adhering to the zero tolerance philosophy) is an assault on justice in that Americans are sacrificing their constitutional right to be protected from search and seizure in the name of zealous law enforcement. People are losing personal property through confiscations without a trial, and punishments are excessive when weighed against the relatively minor harm personal drug use presents to society. Governmental regulation, taxation, and rehabilitation would be effective ways to deal with any negative repercussions of the decriminalized use of drugs. —*Megali S. D. B. Havens*

See also Civil liberties; Commercialized vice; Drug Enforcement Administration (DEA); Drug use and sale, illegal; Privacy, right of; Victimless crimes.

Bibliography

Various aspects of the debate are addressed in Richard Lawrence Miller, *The Case for Legalizing Drugs* (New York: Praeger, 1991); William J. Olson, *Why Americans Should Resist the Legalization of Drugs* (Washington, D.C.: Heritage Foundation, 1994); Ronald Bayer, "The Great Drug Policy Debate—What Means This Thing Called Decriminalization?," *The Milbank Quarterly* 69 (no. 3, 1991); James A. Inciardi, ed., *The Drug Legalization Debate* (Newbury Park, Calif.: Sage Publications, 1991); Griffith Edwards, et al., eds., *Drugs, Alcohol, and Tobacco: Making the Science and Policy Connections* (New York: Oxford University Press, 1993).

Drug use and sale, illegal

Definition: Consuming or selling drugs whose nonprescription use is prohibited by law

Significance: The question of how to combat illegal drug use is a major law enforcement issue in the United States

Since the 1960's, the use of illegal drugs (as well as the abuse of legal drugs such as prescription tranquilizers) has pervaded American society. Few crime issues have elicited as much controversy in the United States as the problem of illegal drug use. On one side of the issue are those who advocate a full-fledged "war on drugs," as proclaimed by the Ronald Reagan Administration in the 1980's; President Reagan went so far as to appoint William Bennett the federal "drug czar" to address the issue. The concept of "zero tolerance"—the idea that no illegal drug use should be tolerated—gained popularity, and the possession of even very small amounts of drugs made individuals in some jurisdictions subject to extremely severe penalties, including long prison terms and possible forfeiture of property, such as loss of their house. Lending weight to this type of approach are statistics that demonstrate a correlation between drug use and increases in other types of crime.

On the other side of the debate are those who argue that a war on drugs is unwinnable and that pursuing such a drug policy is a waste of time and money. They tend to refer to drug use as a victimless crime and point to Prohibition in the 1920's as an example of the failure of attempts to "legislate morality" and to prevent millions of people from doing something they want to do. Some advocate decriminalization, even legaliza-

tion of drugs. They also argue that penalties for some drug offenses have become so severe as to be out of proportion to the crime. Drug users, for example, may get harsher punishments than people convicted of violent crimes or white-collar criminals who may have bilked innocent victims out of millions of dollars.

The use and sale of illegal drugs undeniably affects many facets of American life, from the economy to violent crime to education. Apprehending and prosecuting offenders has placed an unprecedented burden on the criminal justice system and on the taxpayers who support it. Federal and state laws define the restrictions and penalties assigned to illegal substances, and these statutes are enforced by municipal and state police forces as well as federal agencies such as the Drug Enforcement Agency (DEA) and the Federal Bureau of Investigation (FBI).

History of Drug Use and Regulation. Legislation designed to control the use and sale of certain drugs began in the mid-1800's with the passage of the Pharmacy Act of 1868, which required the registration of individuals dispensing drugs. It was not until the early twentieth century that federal, state, and local governments began regulating drug use and sale aggressively. Distinctions were made between drugs which could be used freely, those which could be used under certain conditions, and those that were banned altogether. As legislative acts became more numerous and complex, agencies were established for the specific purpose of governing the enforcement of drug policies.

Legal drugs include proprietary, or "over-the-counter," drugs and ethical, or prescription, drugs. Legal drugs are legal only so long as their manufacture, use, and sale fulfill the

PEOPLE REPORTING THEY USED ILLICIT DRUGS, 1991		
	Number of Users	
Drug	*In Lifetime*	*In Past Month*
Any illicit drug	75.4 million	12.6 million
Marijuana/hashish	67.7	9.7
Cocaine	23.7	1.9
Crack	3.9	.5
Inhalants	11.3	1.2
Hallucinogens	16.7	.7
PCP	7.3	.4
Heroin	2.9	*
Nonmedical psycho- therapeutics	25.5	3.1
Stimulants	14.2	.7
Sedatives	8.7	.8
Tranquilizers	11.3	.9
Analgesics	12.3	1.4

Source: U.S. Department of Justice, Bureau of Justice Statistics, *Drugs, Crime, and the Justice System.* Washington, D.C.: U.S. Government Printing Office, 1992. Data are from National Institute on Drug Abuse (NIDA).

Note: Asterisk (*) indicates no estimate reported.

PERCENTAGE OF TOTAL STATE AND LOCAL ARRESTS THAT WERE FOR DRUG OFFENSES, 1965-1990

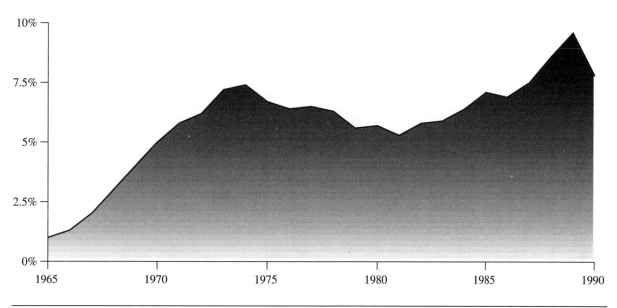

Source: U.S. Department of Justice, Bureau of Justice Statistics, *Drugs, Crime, and the Justice System*. Washington, D.C.: U.S. Government Printing Office, 1992. Data are from Federal Bureau of Investigation, *Crime in the United States*, 1965-1990.

requirements of state and federal law. Legal standards for drug manufacture are published in the *United States Pharmacopeia*. Drugs found to be addictive became subject to control under the Harrison Narcotic Drug Act of 1914 and the Narcotics Control Act of 1957, which set parameters for the administration, use, and sale of these substances. The 1938 Food, Drug, and Cosmetic Act, as amended in 1962, grants the Food and Drug Administration (FDA) authority to determine the safety and efficacy of all new drugs.

The regulation of illegal drugs was standardized in 1932 with the Uniform State Narcotics Act, which was adopted by a majority of states. This act made the possession or sale of any narcotic drug illegal. The Comprehensive Drug Abuse Prevention and Control Act of 1970 served as the model for statutes that would replace the Uniform State Narcotics Act. Most states repealed the latter act in favor of legislation based on the Uniform State Controlled Dangerous Substances Act (1970), which list drugs by type and designates controls and penalties for each type. Schedule I includes heroin, marijuana, and hallucinogens. Opiates and cocaine are listed on schedule II. Schedule III contains most depressants and stimulants. Many of the mild tranquilizers are listed on schedule IV, and schedule V includes drugs which are considered to be medically useful and less harmful, such as cold medications containing codeine.

In 1973, the Drug Enforcement Administration was established, merging the functions of four previously separate law enforcement agencies that dealt with the use and sale of illegal and legal drugs. The administration's focus is to reduce the supply of illicit drugs that are either domestically created or imported. The administration also manages an intelligence system that tracks nationwide use and sale of narcotics, regulates the legal trade of narcotics and other dangerous drugs, and works with other agencies to prevent illicit drug trade. In 1982, the FBI and the DEA were given shared responsibilities on the illegal drug front.

Issues of Constitutionality. The guarantees of the U.S. Constitution limit the ways in which drug control can be practiced. The Constitution's implied right to privacy limits the government's ability to interfere with individuals' actions within the privacy of their homes. The Supreme Court has also ruled that any law which attempts to punish someone for being a drug addict is unconstitutional. Punishment for addiction is considered cruel and unusual; it is not, however, unconstitutional to punish an addict for possession of an illegal substance. Prison sentences also cannot violate the constitutional stipulation outlawing cruel and unusual punishment. The courts have not overruled state laws imposing extremely long prison terms for possession or sale of relatively small amounts of drugs, however, holding that even life terms (which some states mandated during the 1980's) do not constitute cruel and unusual punishment. The Supreme Court has held that the right of companies to test their employees for drug use, especially if such use endangers public safety, outweighs the individual's right to privacy (*Skinner v. Railway Labor Executives Association*, 1989, and *National Treasury Employees Union v. Von Raab*, 1989).

A number of common defense techniques are used by defendants charged with drug offenses. Individuals charged with selling drugs to an undercover agent often suggest that they

Boys at an antidrug march in Detroit; endemic drug use can have devastating effects on neighborhoods and communities.
(Jim West)

are victims of entrapment. Others attempt to prove that an illegal search and seizure was used to discover their drug possession.

Drugs and Crime. Drug crimes are divided into several levels: sale and/or possession of drug paraphernalia, possession of a controlled substance, importation, transportation, distribution, falsification of a medical prescription, possession with an intent to sell, and sale. The statutes guiding these crimes vary from state to state. Moreover, federal and state jurisdiction of drug crimes overlaps. Offenses that violate both state and federal law may be settled through plea bargaining and cooperation between the agents of the involved organizations.

A strong correlation has been found between drug abuse and other crimes. Effects of substance abuse can include increased aggression and violence, paranoia, a diminishing of cognitive control, and impaired pain sensations, all of which can help contribute to crime and acts of violence. The Drug Use Forecasting Program has reported that urine tests of arrested persons in custody who voluntarily agreed to drug testing revealed that more than 50 percent of the prisoners had recently used drugs. Of individuals entering treatment facilities, studies indicate that 60 percent or more had committed a crime for economic gain prior to entering treatment. Surveys of violent offenders in state prisons revealed that more than two-thirds of manslaughter offenders or victims were using drugs, alcohol, or both at the time of the incident. Additionally, research by the National Research Council involving tracking national trends and individual rehabilitation cases has shown that the incidence of crime rises and falls with the incidence of drug abuse.

Social Issues. Use of illicit drugs occurs throughout all levels of society, and it has been found to have profound effects on consumer economics, family and community stability, crime prevalence, education, national productivity, and state and federal tax burdens. The 1991 National Household Survey on Drug Abuse indicated that more than 75 million individuals had used illicit drugs. The survey revealed that 44 percent of high school seniors, 80 percent of state prison inmates, and 37 percent of the general population had used illegal drugs. Mid-1990's estimates of the Office of National Drug Control Policy stated that Americans spent approximately 41 billion dollars annually for illegal drugs. Eighteen billion dollars was spent on cocaine, 12 billion dollars on heroin, 9 billion dollars on marijuana, and 2 million dollars on various other illicit substances.

Widespread drug use damages communities by destabilizing group cohesiveness and causing an increase in the crime rate. When sale and use of drugs becomes endemic to a neighborhood, the population becomes segmented as users and nonusers grow increasingly alienated from each other. This decline in informal community structure makes an area vulnerable to more serious crime problems. Increases in theft, violence, prostitution, and criminal gang activity are all common results of the atrophy of the local community.

Families may be similarly damaged by drug abuse. Adult drug users often fail to provide economic support to their partners and children because of their drug expenditures. They also exhibit a lack of emotional support of partner and children, decreased participation in household and family activities, a failure to provide a positive role model for children, and an inability to accumulate the money necessary for a house, a car, and funding for children's schooling. These problems disrupt the family, leaving children more likely to turn to crime or drug abuse themselves.

Drug use has had a impact on the educational system, affecting the student user, fellow students, and the educational system as a whole. Teenage users tend to suffer cognitive and behavioral difficulties which interfere with their school work. Nonusers may find that their classes are disrupted or slowed by the learning and behavioral problems of drug-using classmates. At schools where drug use and drug-related crime are prevalent, non-using students face an increased risk of theft. Drug use also affects the workplace, as does the problem of employee alcoholism. The use of illegal drugs and alcohol can seriously impair coordination, concentration, and other attributes vital to a productive workforce. Employers' primary concerns regarding drug use on the job are employee and customer safety, but they also see drugs as counter to business productivity, citing poor decisions, shoddy workmanship, absenteeism, and a high employee turnover rate. Health care costs and employee benefit expenses also figured as a significant concern, as drug users generally require more sick days and medical treatment than non-users.

Law enforcement efforts to combat drug use and funding for medical treatment of drug users cost the taxpayers approximately 20 billion dollars annually, with 11 billion dollars going to federal drug expenditures, 6 billion dollars going to state and local expenditures, and 3 million dollars going to pay for the health care costs of illegal drug users.

Law Enforcement and Prevention. Between the antidrug hysteria of the 1920's and the emergence of extensive drug use—notably hallucinogens—in the late 1960's, illegal drug use was not a primary concern of law enforcement at the federal level. Since the 1960's, drug trafficking, sale, and use have been viewed as serious problems, and the highest levels of government as well as the criminal justice system have tried to decide how best to deal with the problem. Since the 1980's the federal government has been attempting to combat drug crimes with a multijurisdictional approach that overlaps the boundaries of various law enforcement agencies. This approach is being pursued through the Office of National Drug Control Policy. Created in 1989, the agency produces an annual strategy recommendation. Its strategic reports generally focus on state, local, and private resources, on measuring progress in drug use behaviors, and on emphasizing personal accountability among users and sellers. Also considered are the criminal justice system's role in drug enforcement and the need for more treatment resources and increased international cooperation.

Effective preventive methods are also being sought. Federal, state, and local drug education and self-esteem enhancement programs have been implemented in elementary and secondary schools with the hope of increasing awareness of the dangers of illegal drugs and of building the independence necessary to resist peer pressure. Crime control legislation in 1990 and 1994 provided increased funding to police departments and drug education programs and strengthened antidrug laws. Additionally, the federal "Weed and Seed" program assists communities with the criminal, economic, and social problems that are both contributory to and indicative of drug trafficking. The program aims at eliminating violent criminal behavior, illegal gang activities, and drug sales by using coordinated federal, state, and local law enforcement resources. The program then establishes social, economic, and criminal justice programs and services in order to establish the stability necessary to maintain a drug-free environment. —*H. C. Aubrey*

See also Alcohol, Tobacco, and Firearms (ATF), Bureau of; Commercialized vice; Comprehensive Drug Abuse Prevention and Control Act of 1970; Drug Enforcement Administration (DEA); Drug legalization debate; Forfeiture, civil and criminal; Gangs, youth; Harrison Narcotic Drug Act; Justice, U.S. Department of; Marijuana Tax Act; National Narcotics Act; Opium Exclusion Act; Search and seizure.

BIBLIOGRAPHY

A thorough analysis of illicit drug use, sale, and import and of corollary law enforcement regulations and practices is presented in the Bureau of Justice Statistics' *Drugs, Crime, and the Justice System: A National Report* (Washington, D.C.: U.S. Government Printing Office, 1992). Additional discussions on the various facets of drug use, sale, legislation, and related law enforcement issues include Patrick Anderson, *High in America* (New York: Viking Press, 1981); Vincent T. Bugliosi, *Drugs in America* (New York: Knightsbridge, 1991); Magie Mahar, "Dirty Money," *Barron's*, June, 1989; and Wesley G. Skogan, *Disorder and Decline: Crime and the Spiral of Decay in American Neighborhoods* (New York: Free Press, 1990).

Du Bois, W. E. B. (Feb. 23, 1868, Great Barrington, Mass.—Aug. 27, 1963, Accra, Ghana)

IDENTIFICATION: African American essayist and educator

SIGNIFICANCE: Du Bois was one of the founders of the National Association for the Advancement of Colored People

The first African American to earn a doctorate from Harvard University, W. E. B. Du Bois argued for equal rights for blacks, not only in the United States but all over the world as well. Du Bois' works include *The Souls of Black Folk* (1903), a series of essays on blacks in America. In 1905, he founded the Niagara movement, an organization of black intellectuals, professionals, and businessmen who opposed the conservative views of Booker T. Washington (founder of Tuskeegee Institute), the preeminent African American leader of the time. In 1909-1910, Du Bois cofounded the National Association for the Advancement of Colored People (NAACP), and he served as the editor of its publication *The Crisis* for twenty-four years. Through *The Crisis*, Du Bois called for an end to segregation and demanded full participation for blacks in American life, placing the obligation for leadership and improvement on

the "talented tenth," educated African Americans. Du Bois' writings on the rights of self-government for African nations earned him the appellation "father of pan-Africanism."

See also Civil Rights movement; Garvey, Marcus; National Association for the Advancement of Colored People (NAACP); Washington, Booker T.

Due process of law

DEFINITION: There are two aspects to due process; procedural due process refers to fair and established procedures, while substantive due process refers to protecting the substance of liberty and property

SIGNIFICANCE: Used in both criminal and civil law, "due process of law" is probably the most influential and controversial phrase in American constitutional law

The Fifth and Fourteenth Amendments to the U.S. Constitution both contain due process clauses; together they forbid federal and state governments from depriving a person of "life, liberty, or property without due process of law." The U.S. Supreme Court has refused to give a single, comprehensive definition of due process; rather, the Court has relied on the case-by-case approach of deciding specific issues as they appear. State rules for due process vary considerably from one state to another.

Origins. Developing from the English common law, the concept of due process was originally limited to judicial proceedings. Chapter 29 of the Magna Carta of 1215 stipulated that the state could not punish a "free man" except by "the law of the land," and a parliamentary statute of 1354 used the term "due process of law" to mean the same thing, a usage established by the Petition of Right of 1628. American colonial documents tended to use the two terms interchangeably.

During the ratification of the American Constitution, four states urged an amendment based on chapter 29 of the Magna Carta, with New York using the term "due process of law." James Madison followed this recommendation by including the due process clause in the Fifth Amendment. Unfortunately, there were no discussions at the time to illuminate the meaning of the clause. In *Murray's Lessee v. Hoboken Land & Improvement Co.* (1856), the Supreme Court interpreted the clause to include the procedures of the Constitution as well as the settled proceedings of English law at the time the Constitution was written (as they were adapted to American conditions).

Fourteenth Amendment Incorporation. The first nine amendments originally did not apply to the states, but some of the framers of the Fourteenth Amendment argued that the new amendment, which did apply to the states, would incorporate the Bill of Rights and make them binding on the states as well as on the federal government. After the *Slaughterhouse Cases* (1873) made this impossible to do through the privileges and immunities clause, the Supreme Court gradually began to use the due process clause as the means of incorporation. During the twentieth century, most of the Bill of Rights was applied to state governments.

The first incorporation case occurred in 1897, when the Court interpreted the due process clause to require states to honor the Fifth Amendment requirement for "just compensation" in the taking of private property. Twenty-eight years later, in *Gitlow v. New York* (1925), the Court ruled that the due process clause included the free expression components of the First Amendment. After *Wolf v. Colorado* (1949), states were required to follow the Fourth Amendment prohibition against "unreasonable searches and seizures," and in *Mapp v. Ohio* (1961), the Court applied this exclusionary rule to the states.

The major incorporation issue of the Sixth Amendment was whether states had the obligation to provide a lawyer for indigent defendants. In the case of the "Scottsboro boys" (*Powell v. Alabama*, 1932), the Supreme Court announced that the concept of due process included the right to counsel when uneducated defendants in a capital case had no chance to present a meaningful defense. In the landmark case of *Gideon v. Wainwright* (1963), the Court announced the right to counsel in all felony cases, and nine years later the Court required states to provide counsel in all cases involving a jail sentence. By this time, the only unincorporated provisions of the Bill of Rights were the Second and Third Amendments, the right to indictment by a grand jury, the right to a jury trial in a civil suit, and the prohibition against excessive fines and bail.

As the Court applied most of the Bill of Rights to the states, justices disagreed about the meaning of the due process clause of the Fourteenth Amendment. Justice Hugo Black argued that the clause referred only to the actual provisions of the Constitution, while Justice Felix Frankfurter gave the clause the subjective meaning of fundamental fairness. The majority of the Court, however, followed Justice Benjamin Nathan Cardozo's view that the clause referred to rights in the Constitution which are fundamental and "implicit in the concept of ordered liberty."

Procedural Due Process. Many of the first eight amendments are concerned with issues of civil and criminal procedure. In addition to explicit provisions in the Constitution, there are many ways that a law may violate procedural due process. It is well established, for example, that due process means that statutes can be found invalid because of vagueness. This principle requires that laws be sufficiently clear so that people of common intelligence will not have to guess about possible meanings and that the police will not be given excessive discretion about when they can arrest and charge a person.

One of the major issues of procedural due process is the proper burden of proof for various kinds of cases. In criminal trials, the defendant enjoys the presumption of innocence, and the government must prove guilt beyond a reasonable doubt. For most civil proceedings, in contrast, the standard is the preponderance of evidence, meaning that the side with the most evidence wins. In some proceedings, due process is satisfied by the intermediate standard of "clear and convincing evidence." In different kinds of proceedings, moreover, there are different rules for procedural matters such as the use of evidence, the choice of a jury, the need for a unanimous jury, and so on.

Since the 1970's, the Supreme Court has generally ruled that the due process clauses require government agents to provide a notice and a hearing whenever a person is deprived of liberty or property. The nature of the hearing, however, depends upon circumstances and the extent of deprivation. In the case of *Goldberg v. Kelly* (1970), the Court declared that there must be a trial-type hearing before the termination of welfare benefits. In contrast, when students are suspended from the public schools for disciplinary reasons, the courts usually accept a notice combined with an informal hearing.

Substantive Due Process. The doctrine of substantive due process means that the government may not arbitrarily deprive a person of liberty or property and that all such deprivations must be justified by a satisfactory state interest. The Supreme Court in *Scott v. Sandford* (1857) first used the doctrine in ruling that the Fifth Amendment protected the property rights of slaveowners.

From 1897 to 1937, the Supreme Court interpreted the due process clause of the Fourteenth Amendment as giving substantive protection to economic liberty, especially the "freedom of contract." In cases such as *Lochner v. New York* (1905), the Court overturned numerous economic regulations, including laws for minimum wages and maximum hours. This so-called *Lochner* era continued until *West Coast Hotel v. Parrish* announced the "judicial revolution of 1937." During the *Lochner* years, the court occasionally used substantive due process to protect noneconomic liberties, as in the incorporation of the First Amendment and in *Pierce v. Society of Sisters* (1925), which defended parental rights in the choice of schools.

Although the Court after 1937 no longer used substantive due process to give special protection to economic liberties, it extended the doctrine to protect a variety of other liberty interests. Two watershed cases were *Griswold v. Connecticut* (1965), which ruled anticontraceptive laws to be unconstitutional, and *Roe v. Wade* (1973), which recognized a woman's right to choose to have an abortion. The Court has found it difficult to be consistent in cases involving substantive due process. While the Court in *Cruzan v. Director, Missouri Department of Health* (1990) recognized a constitutional right to refuse medical treatment, it refused to recognize a constitutional right to engage in homosexual practices in *Bowers v. Hardwick* (1986).

In practice, it is often difficult to separate the substantive aspects from the procedural aspects of due process of law. Both refer to a normative legal process which is not arbitrary or oppressive, a process which seeks an accommodation between individual rights and legitimate state interests.

—Thomas T. Lewis

See also *Adamson v. California*; *Arizona v. Fulminante*; Bill of Rights, U.S.; *Bolling v. Sharpe*; Civil procedure; Criminal procedure; Evidence, rules of; *Gideon v. Wainwright*; *Gitlow v. New York*; Incorporation doctrine; Jury system; *Mapp v. Ohio*; Privacy, right of; Search and seizure; Standards of proof.

BIBLIOGRAPHY

Useful introductions include Edward Corwin and J. W. Peltason, *Corwin & Peltason's Understanding the Constitution* (San Diego: Harcourt Brace Jovanovich, 1991); and Joel Gora, *Due Process* (Skokie, Ill.: National Textbook, 1977). For history, see

A. E. Dick Howard, *The Road from Runnymede: Magna Carta and Constitutionalism in America* (Charlottesville: University of Virginia Press, 1968). For incorporation, see Richard Cortner, *The Supreme Court and the Second Bill of Rights: The Fourteenth Amendment and the Nationalization of Civil Liberties* (Madison: University of Wisconsin Press, 1981). For issues of criminal due process, see Charles Whitebread and Christopher Slobogin, *Criminal Procedure* (3d ed. Westbury, N.Y.: Foundation Press, 1993). Substantive due process is discussed in Henry Abraham and Barbara Perry, *Freedom and the Court* (6th ed. New York: Oxford University Press, 1994), and Gerald Gunther, *Constitutional Law* (12th ed. Westbury, N.Y.: Foundation Press, 1991). For philosophical essays, see J. Roland Pennock and John Chapman, eds., *Due Process* (New York: New York University Press, 1977).

Dueling

DEFINITION: Combat with deadly weapons between two people

SIGNIFICANCE: Dueling, once accepted as a way to resolve a grievance between two people, is now considered a crime

Dueling originated in medieval Europe, where it became an alternative to the grim trial by ordeal. Strict honor codes

In the most famous duel in American history, Aaron Burr killed Alexander Hamilton. (National Portrait Gallery)

evolved that governed the practice of dueling. From the fifteenth century onward, dueling was officially discouraged, but prohibitions and punishments—including the death sentence in France in the late seventeenth century—had little effect. In England, dueling was abolished in 1819.

In the United States, dueling revived after the Revolution, especially in the antebellum South. The honor code of the duel afforded a means to skirt state laws prohibiting assault, battery, and wrongful death. Insults such as defamation were difficult to prove in court, and dueling gave participants an alternative remedy. Nevertheless, state legislatures enacted laws requiring lawyers and those seeking public office to swear that they would not participate in duels. Undoubtedly the most famous duel in American history occurred on July 11, 1804, when Aaron Burr shot and killed longtime enemy and political opponent Alexander Hamilton. Burr demanded "satisfaction" after Hamilton had apparently made remarks denigrating him at a dinner party. Today a death from dueling is legally murder, although some states have specific statutory provisions under which the crime falls so that it is not covered by the general homicide statute.

See also Arms, right to keep and bear; Assault; Criminal intent; Murder and homicide; Self-defense.

Duncan v. Louisiana

COURT: U.S. Supreme Court

DATE: Decided May 20, 1968

SIGNIFICANCE: Overruling several earlier decisions, the Supreme Court held that the due process clause of the Fourteenth Amendment required states to apply the Sixth Amendment right to a jury trial in a serious criminal case

Gary Duncan, a nineteen-year-old African American, defended his younger cousins who were having an exchange with four Caucasian boys, and apparently Duncan slapped the arm of one of the boys. Duncan was arrested and tried on charges of assault and battery, with a possible maximum sentence of two years in prison. Duncan and his lawyer requested a trial by jury, but the request was denied, since Louisiana law mandated a jury only when capital punishment or imprisonment at hard labor might be imposed. Duncan was found guilty, fined $150, and sentenced to sixty days in prison. After the Louisiana Supreme Court upheld the sentence, Duncan appealed to the U.S. Supreme Court.

Originally the Bill of Rights had applied only to the federal government, but by 1968 many of those rights had been applied to the states ("incorporated") through the due process clause of the Fourteenth Amendment. The precedents of the Supreme Court, however, had endorsed the approach of *Palko v. Connecticut* (1937), which interpreted due process as referring to "fundamental fairness" and recognized that jury trials were not essential to fairness or to a "scheme of ordered liberty."

In *Duncan v. Louisiana*, nevertheless, the Court held by a 7-2 vote that the states must recognize a defendant's "fundamental" right to a trial by jury in every serious criminal case. In the majority opinion, Justice Byron R. White wrote that the question was not simply whether a procedure was consistent with fairness, but whether it was "necessary to an Anglo-American regime of ordered liberty." He conceded that petty offenses carrying maximum penalties of less than six months were not subject to the Sixth and Fourteenth Amendments, but he insisted that any crime carrying a *possible* prison term of two years was sufficiently serious to entitle a defendant to a trial by jury.

In the *Duncan* opinions, the justices defended different theoretical views concerning the relationship between the Bill of Rights and the Fourteenth Amendment. Justice White endorsed a variant of the "selective incorporation" approach. Justice Hugo Black, in his concurring opinion, defended the "total incorporation" doctrine of applying all of the first eight amendments to the states. Finally, Justice John M. Harlan's dissent argued that the Fourteenth Amendment was not designed to incorporate, or to be limited to, the specific guarantees of those amendments and insisted that states should have the discretion to adopt alternative practices consistent with fundamental fairness.

The immediate impact of *Duncan* was somewhat limited, because all the states were already using juries in almost all serious criminal cases. The decision was important, however, because it was one of the last in a series of "incorporation" cases which required the states to follow most principles in the Bill of Rights. Later decisions softened the impact of *Duncan* by not requiring states to imitate all the requirements of federal jury trials.

See also *Adamson v. California*; *Batson v. Kentucky*; Due process of law; Incorporation doctrine; Jury system; *Palko v. Connecticut*.

Dunn v. Blumstein

COURT: U.S. Supreme Court
DATE: Decided March 21, 1972
SIGNIFICANCE: The Supreme Court limited the ability of the states to impose residency requirements on voters

James Blumstein moved to Tennessee on June 12, 1970, and attempted to register to vote on July 1, 1970. The county regis-trar refused to register him because Tennessee law allowed people to register only if they had been residents of the state for at least one year and residents of the county for three months. On constitutional grounds, Blumstein challenged the Tennessee durational residency requirement before a three-judge federal court. The court held the Tennessee law unconstitutional because it interfered with the right to vote and penalized some residents for exercising their right to interstate travel.

The Supreme Court framed the issue as whether the equal protection clause of the Fourteenth Amendment to the Constitution allowed a state to discriminate among its citizens based on how long they have been citizens. Equal protection analysis begins by asking whether a law or regulation impinges on a fundamental right or freedom. If it does, then the state must show a substantial or compelling interest before it may impose the regulation. In addition, the state must show that it has used the least drastic means to further its interest. The Court found that the Tennessee residency requirement impinged on two fundamental rights: voting and interstate travel. As a result, Tennessee had to show a compelling interest for its residency requirement and had to demonstrate that the requirement was the least drastic means that could be used to further its purposes.

Tennessee alleged that a one-year residency requirement could protect against voter fraud and give some assurance that voters were knowledgeable. Rejecting both arguments, the Court found that voter fraud could be prevented by other, less drastic means such as criminal penalties, which Tennessee had already passed. Furthermore, the Court could find no evidence that living in Tennessee for one year made a person into a more informed voter. The concept of an intelligent voter was found to be elusive and susceptible to abuse.

The importance of *Dunn v. Blumstein* lies in its assertion that states and other governmental agencies cannot impose more than minimal burdens on the right to vote and other similar rights. Subsequent Supreme Court cases have, however, accepted fifty-day residency requirements.

See also Equal protection of the law; *Harper v. Virginia Board of Elections*; *Reynolds v. Sims*; *Shapiro v. Thompson*; Vote, right to.

Edwards v. Aguillard

COURT: U.S. Supreme Court

DATE: Decided June 19, 1987

SIGNIFICANCE: In this case the Supreme Court dealt a major blow to proponents of "creation science" by finding that a Louisiana statute forbidding public school instruction in evolution without corresponding instruction in "creation science" violated the establishment clause

Edwards v. Aguillard involved a Louisiana statute called the Balanced Treatment for Creation-Science and Evolution-Science in Public School Instruction Act, which prohibited public schools from teaching only the theory of evolution, requiring them—if they taught about evolution—to teach also scientific evidence in support of creation as it is described in the Bible. A group of parents, teachers, and religious leaders subsequently challenged the act, claiming that it violated the establishment clause (the clause in the First Amendment stating that Congress shall "make no law respecting an establishment of religion"). The Supreme Court, in a 6-2 decision, agreed.

Applying the three-part test of *Lemon v. Kurtzman* (1971), which required a statute to have a secular purpose, a predominantly secular effect, and no excessive entanglement between government and religion to survive an establishment clause challenge, the Court in *Edwards* determined that Louisiana's act violated this test because it lacked a secular purpose. Although the act stated that its purpose was to protect academic freedom, the Court, in an opinion by Justice William Brennan, found this purpose a sham. The act, according to the majority opinion, gave teachers no more freedom than they already possessed to discuss varying theories of the world's origins. Furthermore, the act unfairly forced creation science in several ways—for example, by providing for the development of curriculum guides and the provision of resource materials for creation science but not for instruction concerning evolution. The Court sensed a religious purpose at the heart of the Louisiana act and, having done so, declared it an unconstitutional establishment of religion. Justice Antonin Scalia, in an opinion joined by Chief Justice Rehnquist, disagreed with the majority on precisely this point. He argued that the majority had misconstrued the act's purposes. According to Scalia, that purpose was simply to protect students from being indoctrinated with respect to the theory of evolution without exposure to other theories concerning the world's origin. This purpose, he believed, was a permissible one and should have satisfied the demands of the establishment clause.

The decision in *Edwards v. Aguillard* is significant for reaffirming the Court's vigilant watchfulness over the public schools against what it views as attempts to smuggle religious teaching into the classrooms. For the majority in the case,

Louisiana's "Balanced Treatment Act" was in some ways a rerun of the famous Scopes "monkey" trial that pitted Clarence Darrow against Williams Jennings Bryan in a debate between the Bible and evolution. The Supreme Court had previously ruled in *Epperson v. Arkansas* (1968) that the establishment clause barred state attempts to forbid the teaching of evolution. Here the Court went a step further and prohibited Louisiana from attempting to stage a debate between creationism and evolution.

See also *Abington School District v. Schempp*; Bryan, William Jennings; Establishment of religion; *Lemon v. Kurtzman*; Scopes "monkey" trial.

Eichman, United States v.

COURT: U.S. Supreme Court

DATE: Decided June 11, 1990

SIGNIFICANCE: The Flag Protection Act of 1989 violates freedom of speech as guaranteed by the First Amendment

Burning an American flag arouses strong emotional responses. This fact is what makes the action so appealing to political protestors: It is an ordinary person's way of attracting attention. The Supreme Court's decision in *Texas v. Johnson* (1989) that the First Amendment protects flag burning as a symbolic form of expression generated considerable controversy. Politicians, recalling how effectively President George Bush had used patriotic themes in his 1988 campaign, rushed to support the flag. The House and Senate overwhelmingly passed resolutions pledging to seek ways to penalize flag burners. President Bush urged that a constitutional amendment be enacted to this end. Others advocated legislation to restrain flag desecration. The Flag Protection Act was approved by both houses. President Bush, preferring a constitutional amendment, allowed the bill to become law without his signature.

The new law was immediately challenged by demonstrators in Seattle and in the District of Columbia. The federal government initiated prosecutions in these two cases. Both the U.S. District Court for the Western District of Washington and the U.S. District Court for the District of Columbia found the act unconstitutional. The government appealed both cases directly to the U.S. Supreme Court, where they were consolidated as *United States v. Eichman*.

In a 5-4 vote, the Supreme Court affirmed the decisions of the lower courts. As in *Texas v. Johnson*, Justice William Brennan, joined by Justices Thurgood Marshall, Harry Blackmun, Antonin Scalia, and Anthony Kennedy, wrote the majority opinion. Brennan held that the defendants' burning of the flag was expressive conduct and that the act, like the state law in *Texas v. Johnson*, improperly suppressed expression out of concern for its communicative impact. Even assuming that a national consensus favoring prohibition of flag burning existed, he said, "any suggestion that the Government's interest in suppressing speech becomes more weighty as popular opposition to that speech grows is foreign to the First Amendment." Further, punishing flag desecration "dilutes the very freedom that makes this emblem so revered."

Justice John Paul Stevens, joined by Chief Justice William Rehnquist and Justices Byron White and Sandra Day O'Connor, dissented. Stevens conceded that the government may not prohibit expression simply because it finds the idea itself offensive; however, certain modes of expression can be restricted if such restrictions are supported by legitimate societal interests and if the speaker is free to express his or her ideas by other means. The decision in this case reinforced the principle that the First Amendment protects flag burning as a symbolic form of expression.

Subsequently, a constitutional amendment was introduced in Congress that would permit the states and the national government to restrict flag burning. The amendment fell short of the two-thirds majority required in both houses.

See also Civil disobedience; *O'Brien, United States v.*; Speech and press, freedom of; *Texas v. Johnson*; *Tinker v. Des Moines Independent Community School District.*

Eisenhower, Dwight D. (Oct. 14, 1890, Denison, Tex.— Mar. 28, 1969, Washington, D.C.)

IDENTIFICATION: President of the United States, 1953-1961

President Eisenhower found it necessary to order the National Guard to Little Rock, Arkansas, to protect the safety of black schoolchildren. (Library of Congress)

SIGNIFICANCE: As president, Eisenhower influenced events concerning social and political justice, including McCarthyism and civil rights

President Dwight D. Eisenhower perceived his own function as that of a leader serving national integration and standing above political controversies. During his two terms as president, he was confronted with the anticommunist crusade of Wisconsin senator Joseph McCarthy and with the early years of the Civil Rights movement and school desegregation. Holding strong anticommunist convictions himself and concerned with maintaining his shaky alliance with Republican conservatives, Eisenhower only subtly distanced himself from McCarthy and his agenda. Only when McCarthy publicly began to attack the Army did Eisenhower distance himself more firmly from the politics of the Republican right.

A Texan by birth, Eisenhower sympathized with white southern concerns on the issue of race relations. When the Supreme Court in *Brown v. Board of Education* (1954) struck down racial segregation in public schools in an opinion authored by his own appointee, Earl Warren, Eisenhower, as historian Stephen Ambrose puts it, "missed an historic opportunity to provide moral leadership." During a press conference in 1956, he explicitly refused to endorse the *Brown* decision. It was not until 1957, after violence at Little Rock, Arkansas, directed at nine black students selected to attend Central High School, that Eisenhower ordered the National Guard to restore order in a situation involving civil rights.

See also *Brown v. Board of Education*; Civil Rights Act of 1957; Little Rock school integration crisis; McCarthyism; President of the United States; Warren, Earl.

Eisenstadt v. Baird

COURT: U.S. Supreme Court
DATE: Decided March 22, 1972
SIGNIFICANCE: Overturning a state ban on the distribution of contraceptives to unmarried persons, the Court employed a broad right to privacy and insisted that classifications of persons be rationally related to legitimate objectives

While concluding a lecture on contraception at Boston University, William Baird exhibited contraceptive articles and gave a young woman a package of vaginal foam. Based on a ninety-year-old Massachusetts statute making it a felony to dispense contraceptives to unmarried persons, Baird was tried and convicted at a bench trial in the Massachusetts Superior Court. After his conviction was upheld by the Massachusetts Supreme Judicial Court, he was successful in his petition for a writ of *habeas corpus* in the federal court of appeals. The sheriff of Suffolk County, Thomas Eisenstadt, appealed the case to the Supreme Court.

A few years earlier, in *Griswold v. Connecticut* (1965), the Court had recognized a "right of privacy" which included the liberty for married persons to acquire contraceptives and contraceptive information. Based on the reading of this case, it was not clear how the Court would decide regarding the Massachusetts law.

The Court voted 6 to 1 that Massachusetts could not outlaw the distribution of contraceptives to single persons when they were legally available to married persons. Delivering the opinion for the Court, Justice William Brennan interpreted *Griswold* to mean that procreational decisions were constitutionally protected under the right to privacy, and he added the idea that the right to privacy inheres in the individual rather than the marital couple. All fundamental freedoms, moreover, were under the umbrella of the equal protection clause of the Fourteenth Amendment. This clause did not prohibit states from treating different classes of persons in different ways, but the amendment did mean that all classifications must be reasonable and bear a substantial relation to a legitimate concern of the state. Brennan could find no legislative purpose that would justify limiting contraceptives to married persons.

The *Eisenstadt* decision was important for three reasons. First, the Court presented a broad conception of procreational freedom as an element of the right to privacy, with the latter reaffirmed as a fundamental right. Second, the Court explicitly recognized that the right to privacy inheres in the individual rather than in a more narrow relationship or place. Third, by attaching the right to privacy with the application of the equal protection clause to distinctions between the married and the unmarried, the Court was clearly extending the strict scrutiny test to broader issues and categories. One year after *Eisenstadt*, the implications of the decision would become apparent in the famous case of *Roe v. Wade* (1972).

See also Birth control, right to; Civil liberties; *Griswold v. Connecticut*; *Pierce v. Society of Sisters*; Privacy, right of; *Roe v. Wade*; *Shapiro v. Thompson*.

Electronic surveillance

DEFINITION: The use of wiretaps or remote sensing equipment to obtain evidence

SIGNIFICANCE: Issues surrounding electronic surveillance have been important in clarifying the scope of Fourth Amendment restrictions governing search and seizure

The U.S. Supreme Court ruled in *Olmstead v. United States* (1928) that electronic surveillance by the use of a telephone wiretap did not require a warrant if the wiretap did not involve entrance to the premises. The decision was close (5 to 4), and Justice Louis Brandeis wrote a vigorous dissent. He suggested that this interpretation would spell the end of the Fourth Amendment as scientific advances made remote sensing possible. Nevertheless, the rule stood until the case of *Katz v. United States* (1967).

In *Katz*, the Supreme Court reversed its *Olmstead* decision and held that the Fourth Amendment protected people rather than places. The *Katz* decision meant that warrants would be necessary for electronic surveillance regardless of whether it took place inside or outside the suspect's premises. After the decision in *Katz*, the U.S. Congress passed the Omnibus Crime Control and Safe Streets Act of 1968, which established guidelines for obtaining warrants for electronic surveillance. Court decisions have held, however, that conversations held over

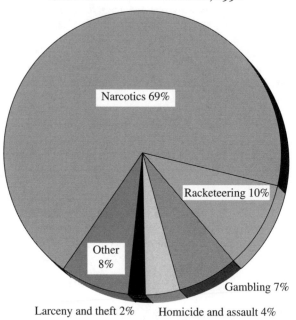

OFFENSES INVOLVED IN COURT-AUTHORIZED ELECTRONIC SURVEILLANCE, 1992

Narcotics 69%
Racketeering 10%
Other 8%
Gambling 7%
Larceny and theft 2%
Homicide and assault 4%

Source: U.S. Department of Justice, Bureau of Justice Statistics, *Sourcebook of Criminal Justice Statistics—1993*. Washington, D.C.: U.S. Government Printing Office, 1994. Data are from the Administrative Office of the U.S. Courts.

Note: Includes state-authorized and federal-authorized interception of wire, oral, and electronic communications. Total number of authorizations was 919 (340 federal and 579 state).

cordless telephones, if intercepted via radio waves, can be used as evidence even if no warrant was involved. At issue is whether a person could have a reasonable expectation of privacy regarding a given means of communication.

See also Evidence, rules of; *Katz v. United States*; *Olmstead v. United States*; Omnibus Crime Control and Safe Streets Act of 1968; Privacy, right of; Search and seizure; Telecommunications law.

Ellsworth, Oliver (Apr. 29, 1745, Windsor, Conn.— Nov. 26, 1807, Windsor, Conn.)

IDENTIFICATION: Chief justice of the United States, 1796-1800

SIGNIFICANCE: Ellsworth, one of the United States' founders and an originator of the Great Compromise, was also the main author of the Judiciary Act of 1789, which developed the federal judiciary

As a member of the Connecticut Assembly in the early 1770's, Oliver Ellsworth was inevitably drawn into the American Revolution. During the war, he acted as his state's delegate to the Continental Congress, where he served on the Committee

Oliver Ellsworth, the third chief justice of the United States. (Painting by William Wheeler, collection of the Supreme Court of the United States)

of Appeals, a precursor of the Supreme Court. In 1787, he was selected one of Connecticut's representatives to the Constitutional Convention, where he played a prominent role in the adoption of the Connecticut Compromise, or Great Compromise, which gave the nation a bicameral legislature. He also participated in the creation of the judicial branch, and it is clear that even from this early stage, he regarded the Supreme Court as having the power to interpret the Constitution and overrule state and federal statutes not in accord with it. In 1796, President George Washington named Ellsworth the nation's third chief justice. In the four years Ellsworth held this office, he had little direct impact on the Court's decisions, as illness and diplomatic missions abroad kept him away much of the time. After successfully negotiating a treaty ending the Quasi-War with France in 1800, he tendered his resignation.

See also Judiciary Acts; Supreme Court of the United States.

Elrod v. Burns

COURT: U.S. Supreme Court
DATE: Decided June 28, 1976
SIGNIFICANCE: In this case, the Supreme Court acted to protect government employees from being fired simply because they were not affiliated with the same political party as a newly elected local official

In December 1970, Richard Elrod, a Democrat, replaced a Republican predecessor and became sheriff of Cook County, Illinois. John Burns, the chief deputy of the Process Division in the sheriff's office, and other Republican employees were discharged because they were not political supporters of the new Democratic leaders who had gained control of the sheriff's office. The termination of their employment was consistent with established practices in Cook County, where employees who were not part of the civil service system were routinely replaced if they did not belong to the same political party as newly elected leaders. Burns and the other discharged Republican employees challenged their terminations, however, on the grounds that the firings violated their First Amendment right to free association. They believed that they should be free to act on their beliefs by joining and supporting the Republican Party without placing their jobs at risk when Democrats gained control of local governmental offices.

Five justices on the Supreme Court agreed with Burns that the firings violated his constitutional rights. Justice William J. Brennan's opinion concluded that "patronage dismissals severely restrict political belief and association." The dissenting justices asserted that patronage hiring and firing were essential to maintaining the stability and accountability of political parties in the American democratic system.

The five justices who found fault with Burns's firing could not agree about how far their decision should go toward limiting traditional political patronage employment practices in local government. They all agreed, however, that politically motivated firings of nonpolicymaking personnel were improper. The Supreme Court distinguished between policymak-

ing personnel, who could be replaced because they needed to make discretionary decisions in accordance with the wishes of new governmental leaders, and nonpolicymaking personnel, who simply follow orders in processing forms and administering the programs initiated by leaders.

The *Elrod* decision was especially important because it laid the groundwork for the Supreme Court's subsequent examinations of patronage employment practices in government. In subsequent decisions in *Branti v. Finkel et al.* (1980) and *Rutan v. Republican Party of Illinois* (1990), the Court further limited the ability of newly elected officials to make employment decisions based on employees' political party affiliations. Eventually the justices placed limitations on the firings of some kinds of policy-making personnel as well as on the use of political party affiliation in hiring decisions. Although the Supreme Court's decisions did not eliminate the use of political considerations in governmental employment decisions, they limited the decision-making power enjoyed by newly elected political officials. By permitting lower-level government employees to win lawsuits, the justices made government officials more cautious about explicitly applying political criteria in hiring and firing any but the highest-level employees.

See also Assembly and association, freedom of; Democracy; Machine politics; Spoils system and patronage.

Emancipation Proclamation

DATE: Issued January 1, 1863
DEFINITION: A military order to the Union Army to free all slaves held in regions of the Confederacy still in rebellion against the Union
SIGNIFICANCE: The Emancipation Proclamation provided the means by which the majority of American slaves became free

During the Civil War, 600,000 slaves freed themselves by escaping to Union Army lines, presenting military commanders with the question of what to do with the fugitives. In time, most commanders accepted the slaves into their lines because the Confederate war effort would be injured by denying it the use of slave labor. Although initially hesitant to turn the Civil War into a crusade against slavery, President Abraham Lincoln, too, embraced the idea that destroying slavery would weaken the Confederacy. Lincoln's Emancipation Proclamation of January 1, 1863, was a military order which freed all slaves in areas still in rebellion against the United States.

Lincoln's critics claimed that the Emancipation Proclamation had little real meaning because the Confederate slaves were beyond Lincoln's control. Critics also charged that Lincoln was not fully committed to emancipation, because the Emancipation Proclamation did not free the slaves in the loyal slave states or in parts of the Confederacy conquered before 1863. Such criticisms fail to note the real meaning of the Emancipation Proclamation. Lincoln's action turned the Union Army into an army of liberation which henceforward freed slaves in the parts of the South it occupied. Thus, the vast

The Emancipation Proclamation, issued in January of 1863, declared that the slaves in the Confederacy were free.
(Library of Congress)

majority of American slaves obtained their freedom from the military actions of the Union Army operating under the orders of the Emancipation Proclamation. Lincoln's power to free the slaves came from his power, as commander in chief, to seize enemy property. Lincoln could not constitutionally use this power against loyal citizens of the Union or against defeated areas of the Confederacy which were no longer waging war against the United States. The sincerity of Lincoln's commitment to emancipation can be seen in the fact that both before and after he issued the Emancipation Proclamation, Lincoln urged Congress to pass a constitutional amendment which would free all American slaves.

The Emancipation Proclamation ensured that slavery would be a casualty of the Civil War. Subsequently, most of the loyal slave states and conquered areas of the Confederacy bowed to the inevitable and abolished slavery by the actions of state legislatures during the Civil War: West Virginia (1863), Maryland (1864), Louisiana (1864), Tennessee (1865), and Missouri (1865). Only two loyal slave states, Kentucky and Delaware, refused to abolish slavery by state law. Slavery was abolished in these states and other scattered parts of the South by the Thirteenth Amendment to the U.S. Constitution (1865), which freed all remaining slaves owned by American citizens. The last black slaves on American soil to be emancipated were the property of American Indian nations. These slaves were freed by treaty between the Indians and the United States government in 1866.

See also Abolitionist movement; Civil War; Civil War Amendments; Lincoln, Abraham; Slavery.

Embezzlement

DEFINITION: A violation of trust wherein offenders misappropriate or convert to their advantage other people's money or property that has been entrusted to their care or control

SIGNIFICANCE: Embezzlement is a nonviolent crime whose economic cost far exceeds that of burglary and robbery combined

Embezzlement was first identified as a crime under English common law in the 1473 Carrier's case, in which someone who was contracted to transport wool absconded with it. It became a statutory offense in 1529 under the master-servant laws of Henry VIII, and by 1589 it was applied by Elizabeth I to "persons who embezzled munitions of war entrusted to them."

The offense is distinguished from fraud in that intention is not present prior to the formal relationship of trust but emerges subsequently, although for many of those convicted the timing of intent is difficult to establish. Strict interpretations of embezzlement limit it to the illegal use of a legitimate occupational position affording temporary control over entrusted money or property. Wider interpretations accept that the broad legitimacy of an occupation or position makes available several opportunities for employees or office holders to pilfer property or make money for themselves using the resource afforded by the position. Here embezzlement includes employee theft (which in Britain is often referred to as "fiddling,"

to convey the sleight of hand typically accompanying this type of offense). A broader definition also includes computer crimes. An extension to the concept is "collective embezzlement," which refers to the siphoning off of funds from an organization by those entrusted to manage it.

Research based on convicted embezzlers shows that there are at least four major typical motives for the individual financial embezzler. The embezzler has a pressing financial need or problem, such as excessive debt, whether or not this has been self-generated by a drug or gambling problem or by demanding social/family roles. The embezzler also has a perception that the problem is nonshareable; this aspect varies with gender, however, such that for women, in contrast to men, it may be seen as shareable. The embezzler has the means, the knowledge, and the legitimate opportunity to make the transfer of ownership. The embezzler is able to find words and phrases to neutralize (or rationalize) any perceived guilt, thereby rendering the offender morally free to commit the crime while denying responsibility for it or denying the seriousness of any harm to the victim.

In 1992 there were 10,522 reported arrests for embezzlement, a 51.8 percent increase over 1983. Of those arrested, 94.4 percent were over eighteen. Of these, 61 percent were male and 68.6 percent were white. In 1992, 1,743 defendants were convicted in U.S. district court, down 11.6 percent from 1982 and the lowest number in that period. In 1992, 41.2 percent of convicted embezzlers received prison sentences, compared with fewer than 30 percent in the previous ten years. The average sentence was 15.2 months, but the average time served was only ten months. Criminologists have questioned the justice of such sentencing, given that the typical bank robber nets approximately one-third less than the average embezzler yet serves an average of sixty months.

See also Bank robbery; Computer crime; Fraud; Mail fraud; Theft; White-collar crime.

Eminent domain

DEFINITION: The taking by government of private property for a public purpose with fair compensation and with due process of law

SIGNIFICANCE: The power of eminent domain is a fundamental mechanism by which the needs of the public may be balanced against the rights associated with private property

The Fifth Amendment of the U.S. Constitution sets the criteria of public purpose and just compensation for the taking of private property. This stipulation (the "takings clause") was meant to provide for the protection of property rights from government actions and applies to state actions as well. The fundamental legal issues center on the definitions of a "taking" and "public purpose." For example, it is not a "taking" to impose requirements on private property designated a historic landmark, yet some government actions that interfere with the original use of private property may require compensation. Likewise, a private landholder might be prevented from developing land if such development is not in keeping with public goals. While eminent domain ultimately is a protection of private property rights, it has been used as a mechanism to further government regulation, especially in environmental, zoning, and land use matters.

See also Due process of law; Environmental law; Property rights; Takings clause.

Employee Retirement Income Security Act (ERISA)

DATE: Became law September 2, 1974

DEFINITION: A technical regulation of the private pension system

SIGNIFICANCE: ERISA protects the assets of employee benefit plans and makes plans fairer

The Employee Retirement Income Security Act applies to benefit plans in which wages are invested in a trust administered by a fiduciary (such as the employer or other person). Benefit plans include pension plans, money purchase plans, profit-sharing plans, employee stock ownership plans, thrift plans, and welfare plans. Most provide retirement income. Welfare plans are different because they can pay for disability, training, legal services, and other items.

Minimum participation standards require that most employees (rather than only highly paid employees) be covered by a plan. Vesting standards allow employees to keep benefits even if they lose their jobs. Funding standards, which apply only to some pension plans, require the employer to make sufficient contributions to the plan to pay the promised retirement benefit.

Fiduciaries have a duty of disclosure and reporting. Employees receive a plan description and annual financial report. All documents are filed with the United States Secretary of Labor. Fiduciaries must operate plans solely in the interest of employees for the exclusive purpose of providing benefits and with the care and skill of a prudent person. Fiduciaries must normally diversify investments to prevent large losses. Fiduciaries cannot engage in prohibited transactions, such as the borrowing of trust funds by an employer. Breach of an ERISA duty can lead to civil and criminal penalties, including payment of money damages by a fiduciary.

See also Fiduciary trust; Social Security system; Welfare state.

Employment Act of 1946

DATE: Became law February 20, 1946

DEFINITION: Committed the federal government to economic stabilization

SIGNIFICANCE: This act, sometimes called the Full Employment Act, created agencies in Congress and the executive branch to focus on problems of depression and inflation

During the 1930's, the United States experienced the worst economic depression in its history. Under the influence of John Maynard Keynes, many economists came to believe that depressions could be remedied by government actions to influence the aggregate spending for goods and services. During World War II, federal expenditures skyrocketed, and unemployment was reduced to record low levels; however, there was widespread fear that, with the end of the war, the economy would again lapse into depression.

A campaign to commit the federal government to the maintenance of full employment enlisted the support of economists such as Harvard University's Alvin Hansen, private organizations such as the National Planning Association and the National Farmers Union, and government agencies such as the Bureau of the Budget and the National Resources Planning Board. On January 22, 1945, Senator James E. Murray of Montana introduced the full employment bill. The bill asserted that "[a]ll Americans able to work and seeking work have the right to useful, remunerative, regular, and full-time employment." Further, it was the government's responsibility "to provide such volume of Federal investment and expenditure as may be needed to assure continuing full employment." The president was directed to present a forecast of aggregate demand, compare it with the level needed for full employment, and recommend changes in federal spending to remedy any shortfall or excess.

The Full Employment Bill passed the Senate (with amendments) on September 28, 1945, by a vote of 71 to 10 and was endorsed by President Harry S Truman; however, the House of Representatives removed from the bill the statement involving the "right" to employment and greatly reduced the force of the government's commitment to forecasting and remedying any shortfall of aggregate demand. The ultimate result was the Employment Act, signed into law by President Truman on February 20, 1946.

The final law contained two main provisions. The first committed the government to "promote maximum employment, production and purchasing power." In practice, this came to be seen as a mandate to avoid significant depression or inflation. The second provided for two agencies to focus attention on the problems of economic stabilization: a three-person Council of Economic Advisors (CEA), who would help prepare a required annual economic report from the president, and within Congress, a Joint Committee on the Economic Report (later renamed the Joint Economic Committee, or JEC), expected to analyze the president's proposals and present its own.

The CEA has involved many prominent professional economists, such as James Tobin, Herbert Stein, Walter Heller, and Martin Feldstein, and has been a useful producer of research, but the agency has not been a powerful policy influence. Nor has the JEC, which does not initiate legislation. Nevertheless, the government's record regarding economic stability has been far better than before 1940. The Employment Act was extended by the Full Employment and Balanced Growth Act (Humphrey-Hawkins Act) of 1978, which set nonbinding targets of 4 percent unemployment and 3 percent inflation to be achieved by 1983.

See also Equal Employment Opportunity Act; Equal Employment Opportunity Commission (EEOC); Liberalism, modern American; War on Poverty; Welfare state.

Employment Division, Department of Human Resources of Oregon v. Smith

COURT: U.S. Supreme Court

DATE: Decided April 17, 1990

SIGNIFICANCE: Narrowly interpreting the free exercise clause, the Supreme Court allowed Oregon to apply its drug laws to prohibit Native Americans from using peyote in religious ceremonies

Alfred Smith and Galen Black, two members of the Native American Church, were fired from their jobs in a drug rehabilitation clinic after their employer discovered that they used the hallucinogenic drug peyote during religious rituals. They applied for unemployment compensation, but Oregon's Department of Human Resources denied their claims based on a state law that disqualified employees who were discharged for work-related "misconduct." A state appellate court and the Oregon Supreme Court ruled that the denial of benefits was a violation of the free exercise clause of the First Amendment. Oregon appealed to the U.S. Supreme Court, contending that Smith's free exercise of religion had to be balanced by the state's interest in preventing the use of harmful drugs. The Supreme Court's first judgment was to remand the case to the Oregon Supreme Court to decide whether state law made an exception for the religious use of peyote. Oregon's court responded that state law provided no exception and that the only issue was the religious freedom of the First Amendment. The Supreme Court accepted the case for a second time.

The Supreme Court's major precedent, *Sherbert v. Verner* (1963), suggested that Oregon could prevail only if it could defend its policy with the "compelling state interest" test combined with the "least restrictive alternative" test. From this perspective, it appeared difficult for Oregon to justify the refusal of unemployment benefits to Smith and Black. The Court had upheld the *Sherbert* tests in at least seven cases since 1963.

In the *Smith* case, however, the Court voted 6 to 3 that Oregon had no constitutional obligation to make a religious exception for illegal drugs, provided that the law was reasonable, neutral, and generally applicable to all persons. Writing for the majority, Justice Antonin Scalia argued that in enforcing valid criminal laws not specifically directed at religious acts, government had no obligation to make a religious exemption. Such matters were generally left to the legislature's discretion, even if an "unfortunate consequence" was an incidental burden on unpopular religious practices.

In a concurring opinion, Justice Sandra Day O'Connor insisted that the Oregon policy could and should be justified according to *Sherbert*'s compelling interest test. The three dissenters agreed with O'Connor concerning the appropriate test, but they maintained that Oregon had not shown a compelling state interest to refuse to allow peyote for religious usage.

The *Smith* decision appeared to limit the extent to which religious minorities might claim constitutional protection for unpopular practices. Religious leaders and civil libertarians were outraged at the ruling, and Congress responded to the anti-*Smith* movement by passing the Religious Freedom Restoration Act (RFRA) of 1993. The RFRA was designed to restore both the compelling state interest test and the least restrictive means test against any incidental burden on religious practice.

See also American Indians; *Church of the Lukumi Babalu Aye v. Hialeah*; Religion, free exercise of; *Reynolds v. United States*; *Sherbert v. Verner*; *Wisconsin v. Yoder*.

Enforcement Acts

DATES: Enacted May 31, 1870; February 28, 1871; April 20, 1871; repealed 1894

DEFINITION: Congress passed the Enforcement Acts as an attempt to enforce the Fourteenth and Fifteenth Amendments and to end Ku Klux Klan violence

SIGNIFICANCE: Sponsored by Radical Republicans, the Enforcement Acts for the first time designated specific individual actions as crimes punishable under federal law; the acts expanded federal authority, creating debates about the jurisdiction of the federal government

The Enforcement Acts made conspiracies to deprive citizens of their rights under the Fourteenth and Fifteenth Amendments punishable under federal law. If a state failed to enforce the laws, federal district attorneys could prosecute directly. A state's failure to comply with the law could result in a military intervention and the suspension of *habeas corpus*. Opposed by the Democrats and some Republicans, the acts raised questions about the scope of federal jurisdiction over a class of cases over which the states previously had sole jurisdiction. The Supreme Court struck down key provisions of the acts in *United States v. Cruikshank* (1876) and *United States v. Reese* (1876). Congress repealed the acts in 1894.

See also Black codes; Civil rights; Civil Rights Acts of 1866-1875; *Civil Rights Cases*; Civil War Amendments; Ku Klux Klan (KKK); Reconstruction; *Slaughterhouse Cases*; States' rights.

Engel v. Vitale

COURT: U.S. Supreme Court

DATE: Decided June 25, 1962

SIGNIFICANCE: In this controversial ruling, the Supreme Court found that the reading of a nondenominational prayer in public school classrooms violates the establishment clause of the First Amendment, as applied to the states through the Fourteenth Amendment

In 1958, the New York State Board of Regents composed a twenty-two-word nondenominational prayer, for adoption by local school districts. The prayer, which was to be recited at the beginning of the school day, read as follows: "Almighty God, we acknowledge our dependence upon Thee, and we beg Thy blessings upon us, our parents, our teachers, and our country."

The Board of Education of Union Free School District #9 adopted the prayer as part of the opening activities of schools in the district. Lawrence Roth, a parent in the district, believed that the Regents' Prayer violated the rights of those children who would otherwise choose not to take part. Even though the prayer was not compulsory, Roth believed that young children would feel pressured to participate and that the school district, as a state agency, had no right to impose religious perspectives on students. Roth was joined in a class action suit by nine other parents, including Steven Engel, whose name (alphabetically first) became a part of the case's title.

The case was brought before the New York Supreme Court (a trial court in New York), which ruled in favor of the school district. The trial court pointed out that the prayer was not compulsory. Parents opposing the prayer argued that the practice of reciting the school prayer, authorized by the school district and state Board of Regents, violated the establishment clause of the First Amendment. The establishment clause states that "Congress shall make no law respecting an establishment of religion." The New York State appellate division and New York State Court of Appeals both upheld the practice of reciting the prayer. The U.S. Supreme Court reversed the decision.

In a 7-1 decision written by Justice Hugo L. Black, the majority declared that encouraging recitation of the prayer was "wholly inconsistent" with constitutional dictates. Black wrote that "neither the fact that the prayer may be denominationally neutral, nor the fact that its observance on the part of the students is voluntary can serve to free it from the limitations of the Establishment Clause." Black argued that the Court's decision was not hostile to religion. Historically, he pointed out, the Constitution's framers supported separation of church and state because they knew "that one of the greatest dangers to the freedom of the individual to worship in his own way lay in the Government's placing its official stamp of approval upon one particular kind of prayer or one particular form of religious services."

The sole dissenter, Justice Potter Stewart, disagreed with the reasoning and conclusions of his colleagues: "I cannot see how an 'official religion' is established by letting those who want to say a prayer say it." He further asserted that to deny the wishes of schoolchildren to recite the prayer "is to deny them the opportunity of sharing in the spiritual heritage of our Nation." Stewart pointed out that many governmental bodies make reference to God, for example, in the opening of Supreme Court sessions, daily congressional sessions, and in the swearing in of the president of the United States.

Reaction to *Engel v. Vitale* was vociferous and often angry. The Supreme Court justices received thousands of telegrams. While some public officials, such as President John F. Kennedy, supported the Court's decision, many others spoke out against it. Numerous constitutional amendments were introduced in Congress in attempts to overturn the decision. One such amendment, the Becker Amendment, passed in the House but could not muster the two-thirds vote necessary for a constitutional amendment in the Senate. While prayer in the schools became less common as a result of the ruling in *Engel v. Vitale*, many school districts at first refused to comply with the decision and prayer continued. By 1965, protests over the decision had waned.

See also *Abington School District v. Schempp*; *Edwards v. Aguillard*; Ethics in Government Act; *Everson v. Board of Education*; *Lemon v. Kurtzman*; School prayer; *Wallace v. Jaffree*; *Wisconsin v. Yoder*.

Entrapment
DEFINITION: The unlawful inducement of a person to commit a crime

SIGNIFICANCE: No one may be trapped into the commission of a crime and then subjected to prosecution

Entrapment is the unlawful inducement, offered by a person in an official capacity, of a person to commit a crime. It assumes that the person does not already have a predisposition to commit the crime. Should this predisposition exist, then entrapment cannot occur. The test of entrapment is often whether an ordinary person, when presented with such an opportunity, would commit the crime offered. In judging entrapment, the type of inducement is balanced against the person's predisposition.

If a defendant is found not guilty because he or she was entrapped, the prosecution can then be condemned for that crime. Entrapment becomes a new matter for prosecution and, if proven, may result in a judgment against the person bringing the original complaint—even if all the allegations contained in the original complaint are true.

See also Detectives, police; Evidence, rules of; Self-incrimination, privilege against; Solicitation to commit a crime; Sting operation.

Environmental law
DEFINITION: The body of law that deals with issues of environmental regulation when public and private interests are in conflict

SIGNIFICANCE: Environmental protection laws have had strong public support since the 1970's, and although conflicts between economic interests and regulations are frequent, the courts have supported government regulation of land use, wildlife, pollution, water quality, and hazardous and toxic materials

The beginnings of the environmental movement in the United States are generally traced to the publication of Rachel Carson's *Silent Spring* in 1962. That volume dramatically introduced the public to the effects of pesticides on wildlife and people as well as on agricultural and various pests. When leaking oil from a rig off the coast of California in 1969 turned beaches around Santa Barbara black and killed sea birds and mammals, public attention was further sensitized to environmental issues. When the heavily polluted Cuyahoga River caught fire near Cleveland, Ohio, in 1969 there were more public demands for action. The growing pressure for federal action to protect the environment compelled the president and Congress to act in the early 1970's.

Legislation from 1970 to 1980. In 1970, Congress passed the National Environmental Policy Act, and environmental regulation became a major part of the federal agenda. Under the act, federal agencies were given the broad mandate to

Oil and other pollutants caused the Cuyahoga River to catch fire in 1969, prompting calls for legislation to protect the environment. (AP/Wide World Photos)

create a more harmonious relationship between humans and the environment. Environmental impact statements were required for federal projects, the Council on Environmental Quality was formed to monitor environmental quality, and the president was required to make an annual Environmental Quality Report to Congress. Agencies were encouraged to work together to assure that environmental issues were being recognized and addressed. Following passage of the National Environmental Policy Act, the president and Congress addressed more specific problems.

As well as signing the National Environmental Policy Act into law, President Richard Nixon created the Environmental Protection Agency (EPA) by executive order to be the federal government's lead agency for environmental regulation. The EPA was created as an independent regulatory agency, report-

ing directly to the president, and given responsibility for air pollution, water pollution, pesticides, nuclear hazards, hazardous material disposal, drinking water, and other toxic substances. Given the environmental activism of the time, the EPA attracted an enthusiastic and committed cadre of analysts and administrators.

Other legislation followed, particularly as the president's Council on Environmental Quality identified major environmental problems. Some of the major acts during the 1970's included the Resource Recovery Act of 1970, the Clean Air Act Amendments of 1972, the Federal Water Pollution Control Act of 1972, the Safe Drinking Water Act of 1974, the Toxic Substances Control Act of 1976, the Resource Conservation and Recovery Act of 1976, and the Clean Water Act of 1977. The general regulatory pattern was to mandate the setting of national standards, require organizations and/or individuals to use the "best available technology" to reduce pollutants or hazards, set a timetable to implement the standards, and provide an enforcement strategy. For example, the Clean Air Act Amendments were passed to broaden the regulatory role of the federal government. The Clean Air Act had been passed in 1955, but it primarily provided assistance to state governments. The 1972 amendments charged the EPA with developing and enforcing national air quality standards. States were required to develop implementation plans that would meet the standards by the late 1980's. Sources of pollution were to use the "best available technology" to reduce specific emissions. Similarly, the Clean Water Act of 1977 (amended in 1981 and 1987) set standards and forced local governments to monitor and clean water supplies more effectively.

Environmental protection legislation culminated with the passage of the Comprehensive Environmental Response, Compensation, and Liability Act (also called CERCLA, or "Superfund") in 1980. CERCLA was mandated to identify major hazardous materials sites and provide an implementation plan to clean up the site. Responsible parties, such as the firms that produced the hazardous materials or improperly disposed of them, were to be identified and their liability determined. The impetus behind the passage of CERCLA was the tragedy at the Love Canal community near Niagara Falls, New York. Chemicals buried beneath the community were causing severe health problems among the residents in the 1970's. Many people could not afford to abandon their homes and find new places to live. CERCLA was designed to address the issues of liability for the hazard and compensation for the residents and to provide financing for the clean-up.

Legislation from 1981 to 1995. During the Reagan Administration, environmental programs were delayed and weakened. The administration's hostility to government regulation in general and regulations that interfered with economic activity in particular resulted in a policy of environmental deregulation. Scandals at the EPA and other agencies resulted from mismanagement and unethical behavior by political appointees. One approach taken in the 1980's was to weaken environmental regulations by requiring cost-benefit analyses when new regulations were proposed. The analyses delayed action and, because decisions were often based primarily on economic impact rather than on social and ecological impact, changed the nature of the regulations. Deadlines on automobile emissions standards, air quality standards, and other standards were delayed. Attempts to overturn legislation more directly, however, were met with strong public opposition. Even large corporations expressed concern, because weakened federal regulations meant that they had to deal with as many as fifty different sets of state environmental regulations. Because

Protesters in 1978 demanding that the state help relocate families living near the Love Canal toxic dump site. (AP/Wide World Photos)

of the weakened federal enforcement and strong public pressure, many states strengthened their own environmental protection laws. Despite the opposition of the Reagan Administration, environmental regulation expanded with the 1986 reauthorization of CERCLA through the Superfund Amendment and Reauthorization Act (SARA). SARA provided a "community right to know" about hazardous materials, sensitizing communities and companies to the amounts of, and potential risks from, hazardous materials. Further legislation has resulted from communities' concerns about hazardous materials that may be affecting their residents.

The Bush Administration's record was better than the Reagan record on environmental protection. The passage of the Clean Air Act Amendments of 1990 expanded the focus to include acid rain, chlorofluorocarbons, and other airborne toxic materials that may affect community air quality. The amendments require firms to obtain operating permits, and they improve enforcement of the national standards. The amendments also provide for civil and criminal liability for "knowingly endangering" the public. Pressure to increase environmental regulation mounted in the early 1990's. The environmental movement was energized by the *Exxon Valdez* tanker disaster in Prince William Sound in 1989. Expectations for the Clinton Administration were high, partly because of Vice President Al Gore's strong expressions of concerns about the environment in his book *Earth in the Balance: Ecology and the Human Spirit* (1992), but action proceeded slowly. On the other hand, attempts by Congress to weaken the Endangered Species Act and other environmental regulations met stiff public opposition.

The Practice of Environmental Law. Courts have generally taken a broad view of "standing" in environmental cases. ("Standing" refers to the doctrine stating that only a person or group with a personal stake in a matter can file a lawsuit.) Part of the reason may be the strong public opinion in favor of environmental protection. The comparatively liberal Supreme Court of the 1960's and 1970's may also have had an effect. In addition, environmental issues have traditionally found support in common law. One basis of standing in environmental law is "nuisance," or impairing the right of another person. Actions that cause damage to another or deprive another individual of a right can generally find standing in the courts.

There are private and public nuisances. That is, an individual may be hurt and can seek remedy in the courts, or the public at large may be hurt.

In terms of the impact of law on those people exercising their rights to use their property as they wish, there is generally more freedom in use of property in rural areas, where few if any are affected, than there is in urban, particularly residential, areas. The issue is whether an action damages or hurts someone else, so the more crowded the community, the greater the likelihood that someone else will be hurt. For example, hunting is difficult in urban areas because someone or someone's property may be damaged by errant shotgun pellets. There are also trade-offs between economic benefits and nuisance effects, such as when a factory creates noise that disturbs neighbors or smells that are unpleasant. The "balancing of equities" doctrine is firmly rooted in our common-law heritage.

Environmental law also covers land-use regulation and zoning, which frequently conflict with property rights. The regulation of land use is most common and most necessary in urban communities, where some land uses may damage the property values of residents or may cause real or potential damage to the community as a whole. Unregulated building on flood plains, for example, may increase flood levels and damage other property in or near the flood plain. A common notion of economics is the "tragedy of the commons," the idea that shared resources may be destroyed by overuse. There are some things that individuals and small groups can do without harm that cannot be done by large groups without causing great harm. Because of the relationship between land-use regulation and the size and density of the population, there is generally greater support for strong land-use regulation in the Northeast and Midwest and in urban and suburban areas. Westerners, particularly those who do not live in major urban areas, often dislike such regulations.

The principle of eminent domain is also central to environmental law. Eminent domain, or the taking of private real property (land and buildings) by the government for public purposes, is permitted under the Fifth Amendment of the U.S. Constitution. The Fifth Amendment requires that the property owner be given "due process" before the property is taken and must be paid "just compensation" for the property. "Just compensation" usually means fair market value, or how much a

CRIMINAL ENFORCEMENT ACTIVITIES OF THE ENVIRONMENTAL PROTECTION AGENCY									
Enforcement and Penalties	*1984*	*1985*	*1986*	*1987*	*1988*	*1989*	*1990*	*1991*	*1992*
Referrals to the U.S. Department of Justice	31	40	41	41	59	60	65	81	107
Cases successfully prosecuted	14	15	26	27	24	43	32	48	61
Defendants charged	36	40	98	66	97	95	100	104	150
Defendants convicted	26	40	66	58	50	72	55	82	99
Penalties for convicted defendants									
Months sentenced to prison	6	78	279	456	278	325	745	963	1,135
Months served in prison	6	44	203	100	185	208	222	610	744
Months sentenced to probation	552	882	828	1,410	1,284	1,045	1,176	1,713	2,478

Source: U.S. Department of Justice, Bureau of Justice Statistics, *Sourcebook of Criminal Justice Statistics—1993*. Washington, D.C.: U.S. Government Printing Office, 1994.

property owner might reasonably be offered if he or she were selling the land, although it may be argued that compensation should reflect the most profitable uses for property. The Fourteenth Amendment has been interpreted as guaranteeing the same rights to due process and just compensation when land is taken by state governments. Zoning laws have similarly been upheld by the courts when cities and counties are acting as agents for or subunits of state government.

One widely debated issue is what should happen when government regulation reduces the value of property. For example, when coastal zone regulations forbid construction of homes on a beach to prevent destruction of sand dunes (which are natural barriers to storm surges and protect other property along the beach), should governments be required to compensate owners for the loss of value of their property? This issue is critical to government protection of wetlands for migratory birds, flood plain regulations, and other land-use regulations. Without the power to regulate such land uses, governments cannot protect waterways from development, prevent beach and other shoreline erosion, or assure that individuals do not cause serious damage to their own communities. There is also a "public trust doctrine," or requirement that governments act in the "public interest" in allocating resources.

Regulation of wildlife poses particular problems. The "state ownership" doctrine holds that governments can regulate the taking of wildlife, but wildlife on private property is still difficult to protect. Federal wildlife regulation is based on the government's treaty power, "ownership" of wildlife on property, and regulatory power over interstate commerce. The protection of migratory birds and regulation of commercial fishing, for which there are international treaties, have been accepted by the courts, but wildlife regulation is very limited.

—*William L. Waugh, Jr.*

See also Administrative law; Eminent domain; International law; Nuisance; Occupational Safety and Health Administration (OSHA); Property rights; Standing; White-collar crime; Zoning.

BIBLIOGRAPHY

A broad and detailed discussion of environmental law can be found in Susan J. Buck (foreword by R. W. Behan), *Understanding Environmental Administration and Law* (Washington, D.C.: Island Press, 1991). The issues around which law is built are discussed in a variety of public policy books. For example, see Allan Schnaiberg and Kenneth Alan Gould, *Environment and Society: The Enduring Conflict* (New York: St. Martin's Press, 1994), and Jacqueline Vaughn Switzer, *Environmental Politics: Domestic and Global Dimensions* (New York: St. Martin's Press, 1994).

Equal Employment Opportunity Act

DATE: Became law March 24, 1972

DEFINITION: Legislation that expanded Title VII of the Civil Rights Act of 1964

SIGNIFICANCE: This act, significant to minorities and women, stipulated that government agencies and educational institu-

tion could not discriminate in hiring, firing, promotion, compensation, and admission to training programs; it also allowed the Equal Employment Opportunity Commission (EEOC) to bring discrimination lawsuits directly rather than referring them to the attorney general

Equal employment opportunity issues emerged in the 1960's as a result of changes in societal values, the changing economic status of women and minorities, and the emerging role of government regulation in the area of civil rights. The enactment of the 1964 Civil Rights Act occurred at a time when African Americans were fighting for equal treatment and protection under the law with respect to voting rights, employment, fair housing, and better educational facilities. A provision of this act was the prohibition of discriminatory hiring practices on the basis of race, color, religion, sex, or national origin. The 1964 act, however, lacked major enforcement and punishment provisions. It also failed to include all aspects of employment within government, labor, and the private sector. Almost ten years after the passage of the Civil Rights Act of 1964, Congress was lobbied to provide amendments to the act which would enhance employment opportunities for minorities.

The passage of the Equal Employment Opportunity (EEO) Act of 1972 amended Title VII of the Civil Rights Act of 1964 by expanding the protection of individuals with regard to hiring, firing, promoting, and other human resource functions to all persons without regard to race, color, religion, sex, or national origin. The EEO Act strengthened the enforcement powers of the 1964 Civil Rights Act by allowing individuals who believed that they were being discriminated against to file suit in court for legal recourse to remedy the discriminatory employment practices.

The EEO Act of 1972 tied previous employment legislation (the Civil Rights Act of 1964, Executive Order 11246 of 1964, and the Intergovernmental Personnel Act of 1970) together and required federal and state agencies, government subcontractors, small businesses with more than fifteen employees, and labor organizations to establish affirmative action programs to remedy past discriminatory practices and to prevent future discriminatory employment problems.

See also Affirmative action; Civil Rights Act of 1964; Comparable worth; Employment Act of 1946; Equal Employment Opportunity Commission (EEOC); Equality of opportunity; *Griggs v. Duke Power Co.*; Labor law.

Equal Employment Opportunity Commission (EEOC)

DATE: Established 1964

SIGNIFICANCE: Created by the Civil Rights Act of 1964, the EEOC took a very active role in monitoring workplace compliance with civil rights legislation; it investigates complaints of discrimination based on race, ethnicity, sex, age, religion, national origin, or disability

Increasing numbers of cases being brought under the Civil Rights Acts of 1866 and 1871 and the Fourteenth Amendment in the 1950's and 1960's encouraged passage of the Civil

Rights Act of 1964 to provide protection for workers against discrimination in the workplace. The Equal Employment Opportunity Commission (EEOC) was created to investigate complaints and to provide legal remedy to those victimized.

Initially, the EEOC focused on cases of racial discrimination in the private sector. The landmark Supreme Court decision in *Griggs v. Duke Power Co.* (1971) forced employers to show the job-relatedness of employment requirements. In 1972, the Civil Rights Act of 1964 was amended to include the public sector as well as the private. Affirmative action programs were created during the 1960's and 1970's, and the EEOC monitored their implementation and operation. EEOC regulatory efforts were very broadly focused and, through consolidation of complaints into class actions, the agency was able to address broad categories of discrimination.

Judicial interpretation of the Civil Rights Act of 1964 expanded the focus of the commission to include sex discrimination and sexual harassment cases. EEOC guidelines addressed issues such as sex-based job classifications ("pink collar" occupations) that limited employment opportunities for women. The concept of comparable worth was addressed by the EEOC in the 1970's. A lack of presidential support for equal employment opportunity during the 1980's, however, slowed the process of reducing sex discrimination and addressing issues of sexual harassment. In 1979, the *Regents of the University of California v. Bakke* case challenged the validity of affirmative action programs, and the status of such programs was being hotly debated as the decade ended.

Under Presidents Ronald Reagan and George Bush, the EEOC was much less active than it had been during the 1960's and 1970's. Under the direction of Clarence Thomas, who was appointed chairman by President Reagan, the commission was much less aggressive in investigating complaints and declined to pursue sex discrimination complaints based on the concept of comparable worth. The imposition of quotas to rectify cases of long-term discrimination and the consolidation of broad classes of discrimination were effectively ended. The handling of cases one by one severely limited the effectiveness of the EEOC. The Civil Rights Act of 1991 reaffirmed the principles of equal employment opportunity and affirmative action, although the use of quotas was discontinued.   —*William L. Waugh, Jr.*

See also Affirmative action; Age discrimination; Civil rights; Civil Rights Act of 1964; Civil Rights Act of 1991; Comparable worth; Equal Employment Opportunity Act; Equality of opportunity; Gay rights; *Griggs v. Duke Power Co.*; Racial and ethnic discrimination; *Regents of the University of California v. Bakke*; Sex discrimination.

Equal Pay Act

Date: 1963

Definition: The Equal Pay Act (EPA) barred the practice of paying women less than men for doing the same job under equal conditions

Significance: A major step in the struggle for equality for women, the EPA inaugurated a series of court decisions which for the next thirty years increasingly guaranteed women equal pay in employment

The culmination of numerous historical forces, including feminist agitation in the late nineteenth and early twentieth centuries, labor unions desiring to protect men's jobs from alleged unfair competition by low-paid women, and women's employment experiences during World Wars I and II, the Equal Pay Act helped lessen wage discrimination against American women.

By the early 1960's, with women (many of whom were heads of households because of rising divorce rates) accounting for more than 30 percent of the American workforce, renewed impetus was lent to agitation for equity of pay. The EPA's passage was viewed by many feminists as a major step toward equality, particularly after the EPA was tested and upheld in the Civil Rights Act of 1964. That act, prohibiting discrimination in employment, incorporated gender as a criterion for discrimination. While the EPA guaranteed equal pay for men and women performing identical jobs, it also afforded momentum to the continuing debate regarding the concept of "comparable worth."

See also Civil Rights Act of 1964; Comparable worth; Equal Employment Opportunity Commission (EEOC); Equal Rights Amendment (ERA); Sex discrimination.

Equal protection of the law

Definition: The provision of the Fourteenth Amendment which prevents states from denying to any individual or group the rights and privileges accorded others

Significance: Although not significant until the 1930's, cases involving the equal protection clause profoundly altered the nature of political authority and society in the postwar United States

Although the founders' commitment to equality found expression in the Declaration of Independence, references to "equality" were not incorporated into the Constitution until after the Civil War, when the Fourteenth Amendment prohibited any state from denying "to any person within its jurisdiction the equal protection of the laws." Nor did the Fourteenth Amendment's ratification in 1869 immediately advance the cause of equality. In two landmark nineteenth century decisions, the Supreme Court significantly undercut the amendment. In the *Slaughterhouse Cases* (1873), the equal protection clause was interpreted as applying only to cases involving race. A generation later, in *Plessy v. Ferguson* (1896), the Supreme Court limited even this protection by ruling that segregation laws could satisfy the equal protection clause if they provided "separate but equal" facilities for the races.

Plessy provided the constitutional justification for four decades of segregation during which the Supreme Court routinely upheld segregation schemes whenever any facilities were provided to African Americans, however inferior they were to those given white Americans. Only during the late 1930's did the Court begin to require equality in segregated facilities, and it was not until after World War II that decisions based on the equal protection clause began to transform the country.

The first judicial battleground remained race. In 1950 the Court elevated the test of equality in higher education to levels that could not be realized under the separate but equal doctrine. It stressed the intangibles (such as reputation) involved in measuring institutions (*Sweatt v. Painter*, 1950). Then, in *Brown v. Board of Education* in 1954, the Supreme Court unanimously ruled that racially segregated public school facilities are inherently unequal. For the next decade the Court was overwhelmed by cases involving state efforts to avoid compliance with court-ordered desegregation of schools and other public facilities. In time these decisions led to a more integrated United States containing a better educated, politically empowered, African American middle class.

During the 1960's, the equal protection clause was applied to the debasement of a person's vote based on residency. The American population had moved to cities throughout the early twentieth century; however, rural-dominated state legislatures had refrained from redistricting. Urban Americans were consequently woefully underrepresented in state legislatures, and they frequently suffered from that situation. Beginning with *Reynolds v. Simms* (1964), the Supreme Court ordered the states to equalize the weight attached to a citizen's vote regardless of where he or she might live. Virtually overnight, political power shifted in state legislatures in favor of the cities.

In the 1970's, women's rights profited from decisions applying the equal protection clause to gender-based legal distinctions; in the 1980's and 1990's, battles were fought over the constitutionality of affirmative action programs and laws discriminating against citizens because of their choice of sexual partners. Equality is a concept which each generation must define for itself. Since the 1930's, the equal protection clause has been the primary vehicle for defining that term in the United States, and the Supreme Court the primary arena in which that process has occurred.

See also *Baker v. Carr*; Bill of Rights, U.S.; *Brown v. Board of Education*; Civil War Amendments; Incorporation doctrine; *Plessy v. Ferguson*; *Reed v. Reed*; Representation: gerrymandering, malapportionment, and reapportionment; *Reynolds v. Sims*; *Sweatt v. Painter*; *Wesberry v. Sanders*.

Equal Rights Amendment (ERA)

DATE: 1923-1983

DEFINITION: A proposed amendment to the United States Constitution which would have guaranteed equality of rights regardless of sex

SIGNIFICANCE: Though the amendment did not secure enough states for its ratification, the Equal Rights Amendment (ERA) focused debate on issues of gender equity

After the Nineteenth Amendment, which awarded women the vote, was ratified in 1920, demand grew for legislation providing other rights for women. The first equal rights amendment, introduced in 1923, failed mainly because of the strong opposition of organized labor. Labor opposed it because it would have invalidated protective legislation for women workers such as mandatory rest periods or limits on hours to be worked or weight to be lifted.

A 1977 march in Washington in support of the Equal Rights Amendment. (AP/Wide World Photos)

The ERA Passes in Congress. Through the efforts of two Democratic congresswomen, Martha Griffiths of Michigan and Edith Green of Oregon, the ERA passed the House of Representatives in 1970. Previous obstructions were bypassed through a discharge petition which received bipartisan support, especially from President Richard Nixon. When the ERA was reintroduced in 1971, it easily passed with overwhelmingly favorable votes in the House and in the Senate the following year.

The text of the Equal Rights Amendment was extremely simple:

Section 1. Equality of rights under the law shall not be denied or abridged by the United States or by any State on account of sex.
Section 2. The Congress shall have the power to enforce, by appropriate legislation, the provisions of this article.
Section 3. The Amendment shall take effect two years after the date of ratification.

Some members of Congress proposed amendments which would have retained protective legislation or exempted women from the draft. Supporters of the ERA viewed these amendments as permitting inequalities in pay, hiring, and advancement. Although these amendments were defeated, their arguments later surfaced in further debates.

Supporters of the ERA. Groups of middle-class women such as the Business and Professional Women's Clubs and League of Women Voters were among the earliest supporters of the ERA, and they were joined by the National Education Association and reform groups such as Common Cause. The National Organization for Women (NOW), founded in 1966, was a more militant group that sought to apply the tactics of civil rights groups to women's causes and aggressively supported the ERA. Between 1970 and 1973 organized labor changed its position from opposition to support.

The principal rationale for the ERA was that it was a statement of principle that women were entitled to equal status with men. It would set a national standard to prevent discrimination on local or state levels. The Fifth and Fourteenth amendments, ERA supporters argued, were not designed to deal with sex-related discrimination; moreover, stereotypes regarding

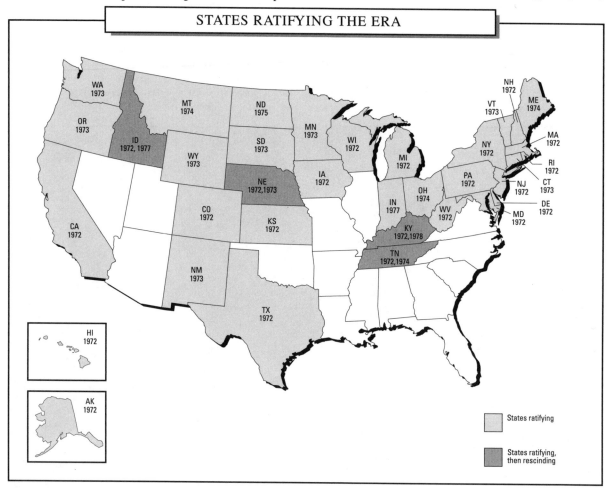

STATES RATIFYING THE ERA

Source: Data are from Janet K. Boles, *The Politics of the Equal Rights Amendment.* New York: Longman, 1979.

gender roles were perpetuated in common law, and women were underrepresented in legislative bodies and courts.

Opponents of the ERA. Several religious denominations opposed the ERA: Mormons because it could interfere with the traditional family, Catholics because it might require ordaining women despite the church's insistence on a male priesthood, and fundamentalist Protestants because of biblical prohibitions against women clergy. Among other objections was the idea that the ERA was unnecessary because of the equal protection clause of the Fourteenth Amendment and such legislation as Title VII of the Civil Rights Act of 1964 (extending the same protection to sex as to race) and the Equal Pay Act of 1963. Under the ERA, its opponents feared, even women with small children could not only be drafted but also assigned to combat duty. Homosexuals would gain the right to marry and to adopt children. Abortion would be protected through the amendment, and state regulations thereof would be preempted. Unisex dormitories, prisons, and restrooms could not be prohibited.

Philosophically, the ERA would shift state policy powers from the legislature to the judiciary, and from the states to the federal government. Some worried that the vague wording of the ERA could lead to unpredictable court decisions, and previous decisions on school integration, criminal rights, and abortion had led to a profound distrust of the federal courts, especially in the South.

The Decline of the ERA. Twenty-two states ratified the Equal Rights Amendment in 1972, and eight more did so in 1973. Yet only five more states ratified: The last, Indiana, did so in 1977. The holdout states were mainly in the South and West; Illinois was the only northern industrial state among them.

The ERA failed for several reasons. Nixon was the only president to give it his personal support, whereas Ronald Reagan actively opposed it. The Republican party platforms had included the ERA for several decades, but it did not in 1980 or thereafter. Conservative activist Phyllis Schlafly became a highly articulate and effective opponent of the ERA, raising arguments that it would force women to support idle husbands and would deprive them of preference in divorce and child custody cases. Some members of minority groups perceived the ERA as providing gains for middle-class white women at the expense of men and women of color. Male government workers feared that the ERA would undermine laws that gave war veterans preference in employment. The Soviet invasion of Afghanistan in 1979 brought about draft registration for men in 1980 and raised concerns about women in combat.

The ERA's supporters were unprepared for the intensity of the debate which arose in the late 1970's. Their last victory was getting Congress to vote a three-year extension of the ratification deadline in 1978, which proved fruitless: No additional states ratified despite boycotts, demonstrations, and even hunger strikes by the more radical ERA supporters. In 1983 the ERA was reintroduced in Congress, but it did not receive enough votes in the House to pass. —*R. M. Longyear*

See also Civil Rights Act of 1964; Equal Pay Act; Equal protection of the law; Feminism; Gay rights; *Lochner v. New York*; *Muller v. Oregon*; National Organization for Women (NOW); *Roe v. Wade*; Sex discrimination.

BIBLIOGRAPHY

A view of the controversy raised by the ERA can be found in Mary Frances Berry, *Why ERA Failed* (Bloomington: Indiana University Press, 1986). Views of the ERA from a variety of perspectives include Mary Delsman, *Everything You Need to Know About ERA* (Riverside, Calif.: Meranza Press, 1975); Rex Lee, *A Lawyer Looks at the Equal Rights Amendment* (Provo, Utah: Brigham Young University Press, 1980); Phyllis Schlafly, *The Power of Positive Woman* (New Rochelle, N.Y.: Arlington House, 1977); and Gilbert Steiner, *Constitutional Inequality* (Washington, D.C.: Brookings Institution, 1985).

Equality of opportunity

DEFINITION: The ideology that one's chance for economic success should depend on one's abilities and effort rather than on one's sex, race, socioeconomic background, or other such accidents of birth

SIGNIFICANCE: The U.S. government and courts since the 1950's have implemented numerous policies to promote equality of opportunity

American society is characterized by large job-related inequalities in income, prestige, and influence. These inequalities are commonly found to be acceptable provided that there is equality of opportunity. In other words, the competition for desirable positions should be fair so that individuals who are similarly qualified and motivated have similar chances to obtain these positions. It does not mean that individuals who are equally qualified and dedicated must equally succeed in economic life. Desirable positions are scarce; not everyone can win the race for these positions (equality of outcome), but the race can be made fair (equality of opportunity).

Minimally, equality of opportunity involves a situation in which one is not excluded from competing for desirable positions because of one's race, sex, or class background. More broadly, this ideal of justice requires that one's race, sex, and socioeconomic background do not negatively influence one's chances for economic success. Thus equality of opportunity calls for hiring processes, including recruitment and screening practices, free of discrimination against minorities and women. To make the competitive race for desirable positions fair, it is also necessary that men and women, people of different races, and the economically advantaged and disadvantaged all have equal educational opportunities for developing their abilities. The same applies to groups such as visually impaired individuals and people with physical disabilities.

During the 1950's and 1960's it became widely acknowledged that American society did not offer equal opportunity to all its citizens, and judicial and legislative action was undertaken to correct this situation. In *Brown v. Board of Education* (1954), the Supreme Court mandated racial integration in public schools, arguing that segregated schools deprive minority children of equal educational opportunity. Title VII of the Civil Rights Act of 1964 prohibits discrimination in employment. During the 1970's the federal government initiated affirmative action programs, requiring that employers not only refrain from intentional discrimination but also actively recruit women and minorities for underrepresented positions and eliminate bias in job criteria. These programs might involve that qualified minorities or women are hired or promoted instead of equally or seemingly more qualified white males. Critics view these programs as violating the equality of opportunity of white males, whereas their defenders maintain that they only eliminate the undeserved competitive advantage that white males have acquired because they are not subject to institutional discrimination as minorities and women are. Critics succeeded during the 1980's in curtailing but not eliminating affirmative action programs. Since the 1960's, various laws have been adopted that improve the educational and job opportunities of individuals who are physically impaired. Much less political attention has been given to addressing inequality of opportunity caused by economic poverty as such.

See also Affirmative action; *Brown v. Board of Education*; Civil Rights Act of 1964; Equal Employment Opportunity Act; Equal Employment Opportunity Commission (EEOC); Great Society; Racial and ethnic discrimination; *Regents of the University of California v. Bakke*; Sex discrimination.

Equitable remedies

Definition: Remedies granted by a court using its equity jurisdiction as opposed to its legal jurisdiction

Significance: Courts have power to expand the usual remedies available to compensate for a wrong; equity courts can fashion such remedies as they see fit in the name of substantial justice

Equitable remedies are those remedies originally granted by an equity court, as distinguished from a court of law. In the English common-law tradition, a court of law could give a plaintiff money, land, or some other property if the plaintiff won a lawsuit. These remedies were often inadequate, however, and did not give people substantial justice. As a result, the courts of equity were developed to expand the relief available. The number of equitable remedies expanded over time; the more traditional ones include injunction, specific performance, reformation, contribution, and estoppel.

An injunction is a legal writ issued by a court of equity directing someone to do or refrain from doing an act that threatens injury to someone else. It is issued only if the legal remedy is inadequate to prevent or pay for the damage threatened. Because injunctions limit the freedom of the person enjoined and often themselves cause damage or inconvenience, a court will grant an injunction only if the harm threatened outweighs the harm that may be caused by the injunction.

Specific performance is an order directed to parties to a contract, compelling them to perform their obligations under the contract. It is most often granted when the subject matter of the contract involves unique goods or land. In such cases, money damages are not sufficient to compensate the injured party; for example, the money cannot be used to purchase an identical item when there is no identical item.

Reformation is an equitable remedy granted when a written instrument does not express the real agreement of the parties. A court will reform or rewrite the instrument to protect an innocent party. Deeds, contracts, and other instruments will be reformed where there has been fraud, error, mistake, or inadvertence. Normally, however, reformation will not be granted if a person had the opportunity to read a contract but failed to do so.

Contribution is the sharing of loss among several people. Two or more people may be liable on the same contract or may have committed a tort together. If one of these people has paid the whole debt or suffered the entire liability, the other parties must reimburse him or her for a proportionate share.

Estoppel is used in contract and similar contexts to prevent a person from denying certain facts. For example, one person may promise something to another. Though there is no legally enforceable contract to verify the promise, the second person may take action based on the promise. If the first person reneges on the promise, insisting that there was no contract, and the second person is harmed as a result, the first person can be estopped on the basis of equity.

Trust law has given rise to many equity issues. A constructive trust is imposed by a court when a person is wrongfully in possession of property belonging to someone else. The person in possession is said to hold the property in trust for the true owner.

See also Civil law; Civil remedies; Common law; Equity; Fiduciary trust; Nuisance; Restitution.

Equity

Definition: A part of the justice system which seeks to do justice when legal remedies are inadequate

Significance: Courts have the power to vary from strict legal rules in order to create substantial justice, and such "equity powers" have been used to transform law

Equity is an area of law that attempts to do substantial justice where the normal remedies and procedures of law are inadequate. Equity developed at an early date in England and was brought to America as part of the common-law tradition. The English courts of law were limited in their jurisdiction and the kinds of relief they could grant. They were also not responsive to changing conditions in society. As a result, people took their petitions to the king's chancellor, who had discretion to grant new forms of relief. Eventually an entire legal system known as equity developed from the chancellor's office. Today, however, most courts can grant both legal and equitable remedies.

Equity will not grant a remedy where the parties have an adequate remedy at law. Equity follows the law, so it will rarely undo rights created by law. Under the doctrine of laches, parties can lose their remedies if they wait too long to file their case in court. Under the clean hands doctrine, a party who seeks equity must not have acted unfairly.

See also Civil law; Common law; Equitable remedies; Injunction.

Escobedo v. Illinois

Court: U.S. Supreme Court

Date: Decided June 22, 1964

Significance: The Supreme Court barred the use of confessions in criminal cases when they are obtained after the police have refused a suspect's request for an attorney and have failed to warn the suspect that any admissions can be used against him or her

Viewed historically, *Escobedo v. Illinois* was a transition case, bridging the right-to-counsel rulings in *Gideon v. Wainwright* (1963) and the capstone case of *Miranda v. Arizona* (1966).

In *Gideon*, the Supreme Court ruled that a criminal defendant is entitled to an attorney in his or her trial. *Gideon* thus definitely answered the question of the applicability of the Sixth Amendment's right-to-counsel guarantee to state action which had been pending since the 1932 case of *Powell v. Alabama*, in which a coincidence of factors had prompted the Supreme Court to set aside a guilty verdict on the grounds that the defendants had not enjoyed adequate counsel. In *Miranda*, decided two years after *Escobedo*, the Supreme Court wove together several threads of developing judicial thought to rule that a person also has a right to counsel during pretrial questioning once the process moves to the (accusatory) stage of eliciting evidence to be used to convict the suspect being questioned. In between, *Escobedo v. Illinois* suggested the need to move the right to counsel from the courtroom to the precinct house because of the constitutionally objectionable nature of the questioning techniques used to elicit Escobedo's confession.

In a nutshell, Danny Escobedo was tricked into confession (he was falsely informed that his co-accused had fingered him for the crime) after requesting an attorney. Indeed, accounts of Escobedo's interrogation indicated that his lawyer was, at the time of Escobedo's confession, in an adjacent room being physically restrained by the police from seeing his client. This image was too much for the Supreme Court majority. In a 5-4 opinion, the Court ruled that the state's unwillingness to grant Escobedo's request for counsel rendered his confession inadmissible.

Escobedo v. Illinois is thus analogous to such cases as *Rochin v. California* (1952) in the Fourth Amendment area involving the admissibility of illegally seized evidence. In *Wolf v. Colorado* (1949), the Supreme Court absorbed the Fourth Amendment's protection against illegal searches and seizures into the due process clause of the Fourteenth Amendment, but it did not go so far as to exclude illegally seized evidence from being admitted in court. In a number of cases that followed, the zeal of the police to obtain conviction with minimal attention to a suspect's rights (as in *Rochin*, where the accused's stomach was illegally and involuntarily pumped to obtain damning evidence) prompted the Supreme Court to apply to state actors the exclusionary rule which already precluded federal law enforcement agencies from introducing illegally obtained evidence (*Mapp v. Ohio*, 1961).

So it was with the *Escobedo* case. The case achieved instant notoriety; Danny Escobedo's face even graced the cover of one week's edition of *Time* magazine. In constitutional law, however, *Miranda v. Arizona* remains the major case involving both the pretrial right to an attorney and the admissibility of evidence and confessions obtained in pretrial interrogations.

See also *Arizona v. Fulminante*; Counsel, right to; *Gideon v. Wainwright*; Incorporation doctrine; *Mapp v. Ohio*; *Miranda v. Arizona*; *Powell v. Alabama*; Public defender; *Wolf v. Colorado*.

Espionage

Definition: The use of information interception to discover the economic, military, political, or scientific secrets of other countries

Significance: Espionage and its corollary, counterespionage, necessarily involve special and unusually secret activities and powers that, if abused by governments, may threaten civil liberties and stifle political and social dissent

Espionage is more commonly called "intelligence" by the professionals who undertake this activity, though it is generally known as "spying" by the general public. It mostly involves interception and analysis by government agents, using a variety of means, of any and all possible information about real or potential enemies of the state. This information may be public, in which case the emphasis is on appraisal; or it may be secret and well guarded, in which case the emphasis is necessarily on acquisition before analysis can take place. Espionage incorporates all activities required to gather such information and all conclusions ("intelligence product") drawn from its systematic study ("analysis").

Espionage, Counterespionage, and Justice. The central purpose of gathering and closely analyzing intelligence is to accumulate accurate knowledge of the real state of affairs in the outside world and thereby to gain some foreknowledge of the plans and intentions of adversaries and competitors. Most governments regard analysis of the information gathered through espionage as an essential part of the prelude to any major foreign policy decision. In practice, however, such information is often unreliable and suspect, because it may be partial in nature or thought to be deliberately distorted by foreign agents. More simply, it may be ignored by decision makers overconfident of their own talents and insights or suspicious of the political agendas of their underlings in the intelligence services.

The term "espionage" also covers covert action, which is the concealed use of agents to influence foreign governments or to misdirect or expose terrorist groups or other enemies, or, more rarely, the use of limited force to deter or eliminate opponents. Such "active measures" go beyond mere information gathering and can include assassination, bribery, funding foreign political parties or guerrillas, and spreading propaganda and disinformation.

Originally, espionage was a function of diplomats and was so valued for the information it provided to both sides in a given conflict that it was often openly tolerated. Most modern governments regard spying on foreign opponents as an entirely legitimate, if secret, business. To a degree, they also regard espionage against themselves by the agents and agencies of other states as an inescapable reality of world affairs.

All states engage in spying to the extent that their human resources and technical talents permit, at least on an ad hoc basis. The most wealthy and powerful states maintain elaborate, secret intelligence services and installations specifically dedicated to gathering information abroad.

Technological advances have changed some of the methods, though not the aims, of espionage. Electronic intelligence, or "elint," is information gathered in secret by electronic means. Its advocates regard it as highly reliable compared to human or signals sources of information. Its main drawbacks are that it is extremely expensive to gather information this way and that one can be lulled into a possibly misleading sense of information security by overreliance on high technology. Signals intelligence, or "sigint," is information obtained by intercepting and listening to signals, which are messages sent to foreign governments by its diplomats or spies. Human intelligence, or "humint," is any and all information garnered by people, whether agents or informers.

It is generally easier to provide disinformation through humint than through elint or sigint. Disinformation is the deliberate provision of misleading or false information as part of an operation to confuse an opponent's political strategy, military intelligence, or counterintelligence. It is different from propaganda in that it is done in secret and is not usually intended for a mass audience. Because of this vulnerability, there is commonly a division within the intelligence community over humint. At the extremes, it is seen either as unreliable to the point of being useless or, when it is accurate, as the most vital and incisive form of intelligence.

Governments expend considerable resources on trying to block other states from spying and on working to expose the secret plots of terrorist organizations. Such counterintelligence, or counterespionage, involves detection and blocking of the activities of foreign agents or saboteurs, or turning them into double agents, and deliberate deception through provision of disinformation to an adversary's spies. States usually will not maim or kill a foreign agent in peacetime, but instead accept the presence of foreign agents as the necessary price for the safety of one's own operatives abroad. Spying on enemies in wartime, however, constitutes a special case. Although wartime spying is not prohibited under international law, it is so threatening to the nations being spied upon that spies are denied the legal status of prisoners of war. Instead, they are summarily executed, to provide a deterrent example to others. Many of the basic techniques of counterintelligence are used against terrorists. Less happily, the inherent and necessary secrecy of intelligence capabilities means that they also may be used illegally in a domestic context, against legitimate political dissenters or unpopular social groups.

The most important questions of justice pertaining to espionage arise for democratic states at the intersection of their unquestionable need to defend national security from foreign threats and the temptation to use intelligence resources against domestic social or political opponents. For example, a common counterintelligence ploy is to plant an "agent provocateur" in an opponent's inner circle. This intelligence operative pretends to belong to the group but actually incites selected persons to actions that make them liable to arrest, prosecution, or political defeat. When used properly, this can be a highly effective way to expose terrorist or other plots before they lead to tragedy. Still, the practice raises questions of entrapment: Would the targeted group have carried out its plans if the government agent had not been there to provoke and encourage its members?

The secrecy of intelligence operations also raises the more general problem of when, if ever, it is morally and legally acceptable for a democratic government to lie to the public. Are some issues of foreign policy so important, are some external threats so severe and overriding, that constitutional liberties may be legitimately set aside in the name of national security? A third problem area concerns treason, or the betrayal of a state by one of its citizens. What constitutes betrayal is a slippery idea. The United States defines it narrowly, limiting it to mean making war against one's own country, aiding and abetting the enemy in wartime, or committing peacetime espionage. Other states do not count peacetime espionage as treasonable, merely criminal. Yet some define treason so broadly that it becomes indistinguishable from dissent. The usual penalty for treason is death, although in recent American history this retribution has rarely been exacted. Finally, issues of justice may arise if an intelligence agency becomes involved in activities abroad that would be criminal if carried out at home, such as murder or otherwise breaking U.S. law.

Espionage in the United States. A major development was the Espionage Act of 1917, passed in response to United States entry into World War I. It aimed at countering German spies but was applied mainly against American communists, labor leaders, pacifists, and southern blacks. This act severely limited free speech in wartime. It led to the important decision in *Schenck v. United States* (1919), which enunciated the "clear and present danger" doctrine. This principle was upheld in the related case *Dennis v. United States* (1951), but its scope was limited by *Yates v. United States* (1957). Before World War II most intelligence activity by the U.S. government was tightly circumscribed, confined mainly to counterespionage and antisubversion measures. Most field work was carried out by the Federal Bureau of Investigation (FBI), which is primarily responsible for counterintelligence within the borders of the United States. The House Committee on Un-American Activities (HUAC) was set up in May 1938 to monitor the activity of both Nazi and Soviet agents and sympathizers. Yet it, too, soon also targeted labor and civil rights activists, particularly among southern blacks. In 1942, the Office of Strategic Services (OSS) was created to conduct espionage and covert action against Nazi Germany. It was dissolved in October, 1945. With the coming of the Cold War, the United States finally established permanent intelligence agencies, much later than most other major powers.

In the 1940's and 1950's, a series of spectacular espionage cases dramatically affected the legal and political climate of the day, though they had few lasting effects on American jurisprudence. The most important of these cases came in 1948, when Alger Hiss, a top-level official in the State Department who had been present at the Yalta Conference in 1945, was accused of being a communist agent. The charges against Hiss played an important role in elevating the profile of the HUAC, in the early development of McCarthyism, and more generally in a temporary erosion of respect for civil rights and liberties in the climate of fear surrounding the early Cold War.

In 1949 a political officer in the Justice Department, Judith Coplon, was charged with being a Soviet spy. In contrast with the Hiss case, her original conviction for espionage was overturned because evidence used against her was obtained without a warrant or through illegal wiretapping. She was reconvicted in 1951, but her case showed that U.S. courts did not regard even national security against espionage as valid grounds for suspending all rules of evidence.

The most bitterly divisive case of this period concerned the Rosenbergs, Ethel and Julius. Tried under the Espionage Act of 1917, they were convicted in 1951 and executed in 1953. There were numerous other espionage charges and trials after that, but no other convicted spies were executed in the United States.

In 1947, U.S. intelligence was subdivided into military and civilian agencies, with the latter concentrating on economic and political intelligence. The Central Intelligence Agency (CIA) is the civilian agency. The CIA is forbidden by law from involvement in any internal police or security functions. Even the monitoring of foreign spies operating within the United States is handled by the FBI. Instead, the CIA is the main clearinghouse for U.S. intelligence, though it is not the largest of the main agencies. It was created to adapt to peacetime the World War II work of the disbanded OSS, especially to undertake analysis and provide covert political support for U.S. containment of communist states. Its budget is secret ("black") but certainly reaches the multibillions. The CIA's main function is information gathering and analysis, including "humint" but also spy plane and satellite surveillance. It is best known to the public for covert operations that failed, such as the 1961 Bay of Pigs invasion of Cuba and the Phoenix assassination program in Vietnam. It is also known for interventions in the internal affairs of several nations, most famously including Chile, where it was involved in destabilizing an elected Marxist government in the early 1970's. Its covert successes, by definition, remain mostly unknown and unheralded. Best known was aid to the *mujahadeen* during the Afghan-Soviet War. Yet to concentrate on such activities is largely to miss the point about the CIA, for its main task is analysis of economic, social, and political information, not covert action.

In 1975 Democratic Senator Frank Church of Idaho headed a Senate select committee investigating CIA abuses; this became a permanent committee (SSCI) in 1976. The House of Representatives also established a select committee, which became permanent in 1977 (HPSCI). Between 1978 and 1982, Presidents Jimmy Carter and Ronald Reagan instituted a series of reforms aimed at producing more conformity with domestic

Alger Hiss (seated) being questioned by the House Committee on Un-American Activities in 1948. Hiss was later convicted of perjury. (AP/Wide World Photos)

law and providing additional oversight by congressional committees relating to defense and foreign affairs. For example, Presidential Order 12333, issued by Reagan on December 4, 1981, prohibits the CIA from participating in assassinations. The CIA operates under various other directives and controls by the president and the National Security Council. It has been most strongly criticized in official circles for failing in its main role during the Cold War: to analyze information about the capabilities and intentions of the Soviet Union and other hostile states. CIA estimates of the Soviet economy were often grossly wrong. It also failed to predict the collapse of the Soviet bloc and the Soviet Union between 1989 and 1991. In the mid-1990's the CIA faced budget cuts and then revelations that it was badly penetrated by spies working for the KGB. The CIA then sought a post-Cold War role in countering terrorism, protecting against economic espionage, tracking arms proliferation, and monitoring the worldwide rise of fundamentalism.

—Cathal J. Nolan

See also Espionage Act; Federal Bureau of Investigation (FBI); House Committee on Un-American Activities (HUAC); McCarthyism; Rosenberg trial and executions; Smith Act; Treason.

BIBLIOGRAPHY

The best single-volume history of American espionage is John Ranelagh, *The Agency: The Rise and Decline of the CIA*

(New York: Simon & Schuster/Touchstone, 1987). A more detailed look at a critical period in CIA history, the 1970's, is Thomas Powers, *The Man Who Kept the Secrets: Richard Helms and the CIA* (New York: Alfred A. Knopf, 1987). These books should be read in tandem with a revealing exposé of the KGB by Christopher Andrew and Oleg Gordievsky, *KGB: The Inside Story of Its Foreign Operations from Lenin to Gorbachev* (London: Hodder & Stoughton, 1990). A landmark study of private espionage, which is a growing phenomenon, is Jacques Bergier, *Secret Armies: The Growth of Corporate and Industrial Espionage*, translated by Harold J. Salemson (Indianapolis: Bobbs-Merrill, 1975).

Espionage Act

DATE: Became law June 15, 1917; amended May 16, 1918

DEFINITION: The Espionage Act sought to limit subversive activity during wartime by providing for censorship of speech and of the press

SIGNIFICANCE: Following a decade-long debate over the nature of freedom of speech during wartime, the Espionage Act sought to censure speech intended to elicit actions that would hinder the war effort

Under provisions of the Espionage Act, attempts to incite military insubordination, obstruct military enlistment, or otherwise interfere with military operations became felonies. Furthermore, treasonous materials were banned from the mails. The amendment sometimes known as the Sedition Act (1918) made the Espionage Act more comprehensive by providing for the indictment and prosecution of anyone obstructing the sale of liberty bonds, interfering with factory production, or speaking or writing anything deemed "disloyal, profane, scurrilous, or abusive."

Implementation of the Espionage Act was problematical since it was designed to punish intent—always difficult, if not impossible, to determine. Nevertheless, more than fifteen thousand indictments and ten thousand convictions have occurred under the act. The Espionage Act's constitutionality was upheld in the Supreme Court decision *Schenck v. United States* (1919), in which the clear and present danger doctrine—directed at speech in wartime causing actions which Congress is empowered to prevent—was first delineated.

See also Alien and Sedition Acts; Clear and present danger test; Federal Bureau of Investigation (FBI); Smith Act; Treason.

Establishment of religion

DEFINITION: Originally referring to the establishment by law of a national church, this phrase eventually became part of the American debate on separation of church and state

SIGNIFICANCE: The establishment of religion clause of the First Amendment to the U.S. Constitution ignited a long period of political debate and judicial confusion concerning issues related to governmental participation in matters of religion

The first ten words of the First Amendment state that "Congress shall make no law respecting an establishment of religion." Freedom from a state-established church is one of the most cherished freedoms of the American people, as is the right to worship according to the dictates of individual conscience. Finding and maintaining the correct balance between these concepts have presented the courts with considerable difficulties.

Historical Development. In 596, when Pope Gregory I sent missionaries to England, the result was the Established Church, later to become the national Church of England. Statutory law required membership in the Established Church and regulated its operation. The early English settlers in America, whether they agreed or disagreed, brought this long-standing concept of established religion with them. As a consequence, nine of the thirteen English colonies had some degree of statutory religious establishment; six established the Church of England, and three established the Puritans' Congregational church.

One of those early settlers was Roger Williams, who opposed established religion but declared that God had erected a wall to protect the church from the world. Thomas Jefferson later applied this idea to government regulation of religion. In his "Address to Danbury Baptists, 1802," as quoted in *Reynolds v. United States* (1879), Jefferson proclaimed:

> Believing with you that religion is a matter which lies solely between man and his God; . . . I contemplate with sovereign reverence that act of the whole American people which declares that their legislature should "make no law respecting an establishment of religion or prohibiting the free exercise thereof," thus building a wall of separation between church and state.

Both Williams and Jefferson obviously intended to protect the church from the government but not the government from the church.

The original meaning of "establishment," and the likelihood that the First Amendment clause applied only to a national establishment, is further clarified by the fact that five of the colonies with established churches retained their establishment when they became states. The final state disestablishment, that of the Congregational church in Massachusetts, took place in 1833. After the signing of the Constitution in 1787, an intense ratification debate began. Several states ratified only with assurance that a bill of rights would be immediately added. In the first Congress, Representative James Madison of Virginia urged his colleagues to fulfill this promise. In his original wording of what became the First Amendment, Madison wrote, "nor shall any national religion be established." The later compromise wording did not change the original intent.

Judicial Interpretations. All judicial decisions concerning the establishment of religion clause of the First Amendment must by necessity meet the requirements of the due process of law phrase of the Fifth Amendment and the application of due process to the states by the Fourteenth Amendment. Far from being consistent, these decisions support at least three distinct theories of what establishment really means.

The first theory is that of strict separation. Although based on Jefferson's "wall of separation," this theory goes beyond

In this nineteenth century drawing, the separation between church and state is being strictly maintained. (James L. Shaffer)

Jefferson not only to protect the church from the government but also to protect the government from the influence of the church. The *Reynolds v. United States* decision by the Supreme Court first advocated this interpretation. The most dogmatic declaration was in *Everson v. Board of Education* (1947), in which Justice Hugo Black declared that neither any state nor the federal government could use tax money to support even the most general and impartial religious activity.

The second discernible interpretation, defined by Supreme Court justice Tom Clark in *Abington School District v. Schempp* (1963), is that of complete neutrality. This means that all government laws and programs must be written so that they neither advance nor inhibit religion. Even a secular goal, such as good citizenship, cannot be supported by essentially religious exercises, such as prayer and Bible reading. A variation of this theory is that the First Amendment bans preferential treatment of a particular religion but that the government could still support religion in general. The third article of the Northwest Ordinance of 1787 supports this view by declaring, "Religion, morality, and knowledge being necessary to good government and the happiness of mankind, schools and the means of education shall forever be encouraged."

The final major interpretation is referred to as accommodation, which means that government can support the availability of religion. Supreme Court justice William O. Douglas, in *Zorach v. Clauson* (1952), approved a program in which public schools in New York City released students for religious instruction as long as it took place off the school grounds. Douglas stated, "We are a religious people whose institutions presuppose a Supreme Being. . . . We make room for as wide a variety of beliefs and creeds as the spiritual needs of man deem necessary."

The issue of religious establishment has been the subject of many Supreme Court decisions. Yet no decision by the Court has ever been completely reversed by a later decision following a difficult interpretation. Instead, many decisions, although they differ from earlier decisions, have quoted from the language of previous Courts. Therefore, this vital part of the U.S. Constitution remains without a firm judicial interpretation.

—Glenn L. Swygart

See also *Abington School District v. Schempp*; Bill of Rights, U.S.; Black, Hugo L.; Blue laws; Douglas, William O.; *Engel v. Vitale*; *Everson v. Board of Education*; *Lemon v. Kurtzman*; Religion, free exercise of; School prayer.

BIBLIOGRAPHY

Part of any study of the establishment clause of the First Amendment should begin with an understanding of the historical context, including the views of the men responsible for its writing. Among sources available are Robert Cord, *Separation of Church and State* (New York: Lambeth Press, 1982); Edward Corwin, *The Constitution and What It Means Today* (Princeton, N.J.: Princeton University Press, 1972); John Eidsmoe, *Christianity and the Constitution: The Faith of Our Founding Fathers* (Grand Rapids, Mich.: Baker Book House, 1987); Alvin Johnson, *Separation of Church and State in the United States* (New York: Greenwood Press, 1934); Stanley Kutler, *The Supreme Court and the Constitution* (New York: W. W. Norton, 1977).

Ethics in Government Act

DATE: Became law October 26, 1978

DEFINITION: The Ethics in Government Act requires nominees for positions requiring Senate confirmation to make financial disclosure reports; it also established the Office of Government Ethics to oversee the administration of ethics policies in the executive branch

SIGNIFICANCE: The Ethics in Government Act was passed in the aftermath of the scandals during the Nixon Administration to lessen the likelihood that presidential nominees for government positions will have conflicts of interest that may result in personal or financial gain

The Ethics in Government Act of 1978 requires that presidential nominees for positions requiring Senate confirmation file financial disclosure reports. The required report lists sources of income, assets and liabilities, and affiliations with organizations that may lead to conflicts of interest. The act also created the Office of Government Ethics, which reviews the disclosure reports of presidential nominees and issues opinion letters concerning possible conflicts of interest.

Possible Conflicts of Interest. The principal concerns that guide the reviews of financial disclosure reports are the potentials for officials to (1) participate in matters in which they have personal financial interests, (2) receive income from nongovernment sources for government service, (3) participate in outside activities that may involve the government, and (4) experience conflicts following their government employment because of restrictions on dealings with former agencies. The latter issue primarily affects former officials, but it is frequently a concern for officials entering government service because it can affect their future employment prospects.

The Review Process. The Office of Counsel to the President typically solicits complete financial records to anticipate problems before nominations are announced and explains reporting requirements to potential nominees. The Office of Counsel provides forms to potential nominees and gives the completed reports to designated agency ethics officials and to the Office of Government Ethics. Agency heads are responsible for compliance with the ethics program, and they appoint the agency's ethics official. The financial disclosure reports are also reviewed by the employing agency's representative, and the agency's evaluation is included in the Office of Government Ethics' opinion letter. The opinion letters are reviewed by the president before the nomination is sent forward.

The members of the Senate involved in the confirmation process review the letters and generally include their own assessment of possible conflicts of interest.

The identification of possible conflicts may result in nominees being asked to disqualify or recuse themselves from participation in decisions regarding firms or industries in which they may have personal or financial interests, divest themselves of financial interests in particular firms or industries which may cause conflicts of interest, or put their financial holdings into "blind trusts" so that they will have no knowledge of their financial interests in particular firms or industries. A waiver may also be granted if it is determined that a nominee's interests in a particular firm or industry are so slight or peripheral as to assure that any conflict of interest will be very minor.

Restrictions on Future Employment. President George Bush appointed a Commission on Federal Ethics Law Reform, which in 1989 recommended strengthening the provisions dealing with "influence peddling" as well as broadening the provisions dealing with conflicts of interest when officials may gain personally or financially. Subsequent amendment of the Ethics in Government Act expanded its scope to include influence peddling by former officials. The act restricts what former government officials may do upon leaving office, principally in terms of a two-year prohibition against representing private interests before their former agencies. These provisions were designed to lessen conflicts of interest that may arise during an official's tenure with an agency, when he or she may be anticipating future employment outside government, and to help stop the "revolving door" pattern of employment in which individuals move from government agencies to the industries they were responsible for regulating and vice versa. The provisions also include a one-year prohibition on former officials representing private interests before their former government employer when the individual had no responsibilities relating to his or her current employer.

Impact of the Act. Critics of the Ethics in Government Act have charged that it makes it very difficult to recruit potential officials from the private sector. This criticism was expressed numerous times during the Reagan Administration. At issue are whether the financial disclosure requirements themselves are impediments to recruitment because individuals do not want to make their finances public or whether other restrictions on employment discourage individuals from accepting nominations. In addition to financial disclosure and limitations on relationships with former and future employers, the act restricts the freedom of officials to manage their own financial affairs.

Supporters of the act argue that it focuses attention on the issue of ethics and, in particular, reinforces the principle that even the appearance of impropriety is to be avoided in public-sector employment. The Ethics in Government Act also reaffirms the principles that government officials should not use their positions for personal gain and that government business should be conducted "in the sunshine." Moreover, the act serves to protect appointing officials from inadvertently selecting someone who might be motivated to seek public employment for personal gain or who might later be charged with bias in making decisions.

The standards set in the Ethics in Government Act have had a broad impact in government. States and municipalities are increasingly requiring financial disclosure by political appointees and elected officials to lessen the potential for conflicts of interest. Conflicts that may arise because of dual employment, financial interests in businesses that deal with government agencies, and the use of public positions to benefit private interests are examined closely. Conflicts arising from the employment of law enforcement officers in private security during their off-duty hours are cases in point.—*William L. Waugh, Jr.*

See also Bribery; Civil service system; Discretion; Freedom of Information Act; Legal ethics; Malfeasance, misfeasance, and nonfeasance; Police corruption and misconduct; Political corruption.

BIBLIOGRAPHY

Two good sources are William L. Richter, Frances Burke, and Jameson Doig, eds., *Combating Corruption: Encouraging Ethics, a Sourcebook for Public Service Ethics* (2d ed. Washington, D.C.: American Society for Public Administration, 1995), and Robert B. Denhardt, *Public Administration: An Action Orientation* (2d ed. Belmont, Calif.: Wadsworth, 1995).

Everson v. Board of Education

COURT: U.S. Supreme Court
DATE: Decided February 10, 1947
SIGNIFICANCE: The Supreme Court for the first time held that the Fourteenth Amendment incorporated the establishment clause of the First Amendment

A New Jersey statute provided for local school districts to reimburse parents for transportation of their children to and from schools, both public and private. The board of education of the Township of Ewing authorized such reimbursement. Arch R. Everson, a taxpayer, challenged the statute on the grounds that such aid to parents of parochial school students was subsidizing religion, thereby violating the First Amendment prohibition against the establishment of religion.

Writing for the 5-4 majority opinion, Justice Hugo L. Black stated that Everson contended that the state statute and the board of education's authorization violated the federal Constitution in two aspects. First, they authorized the state to take by taxation the private property of some and bestow it upon others, to be used for their own private purposes. This, Black said, allegedly violated the due process clause of the Fourteenth Amendment. Citing two earlier cases, *Cochran v. Louisiana State Board of Education* (1930) and *Interstate Railway v. Massachusetts* (1907), Black said that the Court had allowed parents to send their children to a religious rather than a public school if the school meets with secular educational requirements of the state. The New Jersey parochial schools, he stated, met the requirements.

In the second aspect of the violation of the Constitution, the New Jersey statute, wrote Black, was challenged as a "law respecting an establishment of religion." He emphasized that the First Amendment was made applicable to the states by the Fourteenth Amendment and therefore commanded that a state "shall make no law respecting an establishment of religion, or prohibiting the free exercise thereof." While the First Amendment prohibits states from consistently contributing to religious schools, he said, the same amendment prohibits states from hampering their citizens in the free exercise of their own religion. It cannot exclude individual Catholics, Lutherans, Jews, or members of other groups, or either believers or nonbelievers, from receiving the benefits of public welfare legislation.

Such legislation could include the requirement that a local transit company provide reduced fares to schoolchildren, including those attending parochial schools. If general government services as police and fire protection, and public highways and sidewalks, were cut off from church schools, it would make it difficult for them to operate. This was not the purpose of the First Amendment. State power cannot be used to favor or to handicap religions. In describing state power as being neutral in its relation with religious believers and nonbelievers, Black quoted Thomas Jefferson, who said that "a wall of separation [exists] between church and state."

The importance of *Everson v. Board of Education* is twofold. On the one hand, it prohibits state-supported churches, while on the other hand it does not prohibit a state from extending state benefits to all its citizens without regard to their religious belief.

See also *Abington School District v. Schempp*; Black, Hugo L.; Establishment of religion; Religion, free exercise of.

Evidence, rules of

DEFINITION: Rules that govern the facts presented to support a legal position or allegation
SIGNIFICANCE: The rules of evidence establish the weight to be given to facts in court cases and provide reasons that certain facts must be excluded from presentation in court

Evidence to support a position is an important part of the legal system. Originally, the rules governing evidence were not codified but grew out of the common laws of a jurisdiction and traditions regarding what evidence was acceptable to assure reliability. This loose set of rules and traditions was refined through the years and found acceptance in most courts, but it became increasingly obvious that some codification was necessary.

In 1975, the U.S. Supreme Court adopted the Federal Rules of Evidence under a special authorization of Congress. The rules became effective July 1, 1975, and shortly thereafter, basic precepts similar to the federal rules were adopted in all states. Although the federal rules focus on what may be excluded as evidence, these exclusions indicate what may be included as well. The rules provide a framework for a routine and orderly presentation of evidence so that the truth may emerge.

Evidence must be something that tends to prove or disprove an allegation. Evidence is judged on its admissibility, its addition to the burden of proof, its relevancy and weight, and its sufficiency of facts. These principles determine what may be offered as proof and how much credibility it has. Admissible

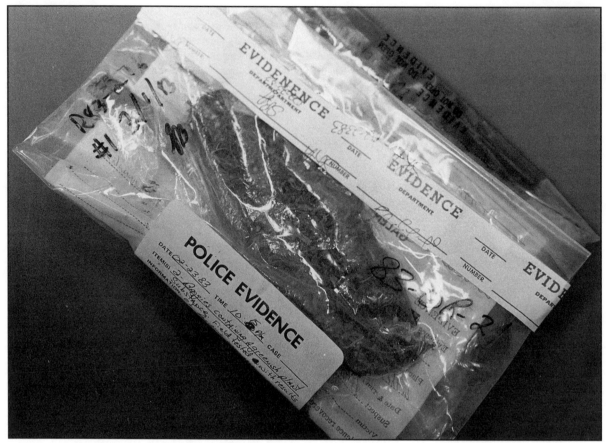

To be admissible in court, evidence must be relevant and must have "probative value." (James L. Shaffer)

evidence in a criminal matter may include eyewitness testimony, documents, or properly identified weapons.

In accordance with the "exclusionary rule," a judge may exclude certain evidence if it is believed to have been gathered in violation of statutes. The question of whether constitutional rights were violated in the gathering of evidence is raised on appeal only, and the appellate court may order a new trial to be held without the questionable evidence. Two Supreme Court cases were particularly important in establishing the exclusionary rule: *Weeks v. United States* (1914) applied to federal trials, and *Mapp v. Ohio* (1961) to state trials.

If no objection is made to the admissibility of evidence, then all later claims to its inadmissibility are waived. Objections to evidence should be specific; blanket objections, such as incompetence or irrelevance, are considered outdated.

Admissible Evidence. To be admissible and of worth to the matter in court, evidence must have probative value, tending to prove some point in the case. It must be relevant, bolstering the probative value.

In most instances, evidence may not be hearsay, facts that are not directly stated but are reported by a third party. In such cases the original speaker is not available for cross-examination, which is deemed a serious disadvantage to the party trying to refute the hearsay evidence. There are exceptions. Hearsay evidence may be admissible if it is an out-of-court statement made by a litigant, if it consists of business records kept in the normal course of business and the custodian of the records testifies to their authenticity, or if the hearsay can be termed *res gestae*, words closely connected to an occurrence or spoken in the excitement of the moment. In the latter case, the assumption is that the spontaneity of a comment testifies to its truthfulness.

Excluded from evidence are conversations that are termed "privileged." These include conversations between attorney and client, doctor and patient, member of the clergy and congregant, and husband and wife.

Witnesses are also evidence and may be of two types. The nonexpert or factual witness testifies only to what is personally known. The expert witness has special knowledge that may lead to a clearer understanding of the facts.

The "best evidence" rule calls for the most reliable available proof of the fact. A contract that proves the facts presented by one of the litigants is best evidence, the highest degree of proof available. Direct evidence is proof without the need for other facts leading to it.

Rules for Use of Evidence. The amount of evidence needed depends on the legal standard of proof (the degree of persuasiveness needed) and the burden of proof (the responsibility to establish the existence of a fact) that have been established for a particular matter.

The court itself helps in the presentation of evidence by allowing certain shortcuts, notably inference, presumption, and judicial notice. Inference is a logical and reasonable conclusion from the facts presented: From a piece of foreign matter in a canned product, for example, one may infer carelessness in the canning process. Presumption is a conclusion directed by law: A person may be presumed dead, for example, if not heard from in seven years. Judicial notice is the act of the court recognizing a fact without its being put in evidence: Expert testimony is not needed to prove that the earth is round.

Under certain circumstances the court may accept a motion to strike evidence already presented and accepted. The evidence may have been proper when received but was later shown to be objectionable. When the evidence was admitted, agreement may have been made as to a later ruling on its admissibility. The admitted evidence may have been always subject to a motion to strike. A witness may have made a statement without a question being asked or a statement that was voluntary. An answer may not have been responsive to the question asked.

In a civil suit, written admissions may be accepted as evidence. These are out-of-court written statements conceding facts that are relevant to the adversary's case. Admissions permit a trial to move more quickly without the presentation of evidence to prove facts that are already known by all parties.

—*Elizabeth Algren Shaw*

See also Detectives, police; DNA testing; Due process of law; Electronic surveillance; Entrapment; Expert witness; Fingerprint identification; Hearsay rule; *Illinois v. Krull*; *Leon, United States v.*; *Mapp v. Ohio*; Search and seizure; Simpson, O. J., trial; *Weeks v. United States*.

BIBLIOGRAPHY

Legal dictionaries provide exhaustive descriptions of the many types of evidence. Two of the easiest to read are Steven H. Gifis, *Law Dictionary* (2d ed. Woodbury, N.Y.: Barron's Educational Series, 1984), and *Reader's Digest Family Legal Guide* (Pleasantville, N.Y.: Reader's Digest Association, 1981). For a frequently amusing account of personal experiences in court, including skirmishes over evidence, see Charles Rembar, *The Law of the Land* (New York: Simon & Schuster, 1980). More in-depth studies of evidence include Edmund M. Morgan, *Basic Problems of Evidence* (Philadelphia: American Bar Association, 1961), and John Henry Wigmore, *Evidence in Trials at Common Law* (rev. by John T. Naughton. Boston: Little, Brown, 1961).

Ex parte cases. *See name of party*

Ex post facto law

DEFINITION: A law enacted "after the fact" of some action or occurrence which retrospectively alters the legal consequences of the action or occurrence

SIGNIFICANCE: The United States Constitution prohibits both federal and state governments from enacting *ex post facto* laws and thus protects individuals from suffering punishment for actions which were innocent at the time they occurred

Ex post facto laws rewrite legal history to change retroactively the legal significance of a past event. The most obvious example of an *ex post facto* law would be one that subjected an individual to criminal punishment for an act performed before the law's enactment which was innocent at the time of performance. *Ex post facto* laws violate elementary notions of fairness and justice. According to William Blackstone, the great eighteenth century legal commentator, individuals have no cause to abstain from engaging in actions which are innocent at the time performed and only later classified as criminal. To punish individuals on the basis of such retroactive determinations is, he insisted, "cruel and unjust."

Article I of the United States Constitution prohibits *ex post facto* laws, both those enacted by the federal government and those adopted by state governments. Many state constitutions also contain prohibitions against such laws. The Supreme Court, however, early interpreted the Constitution's prohibition against *ex post facto* laws as applying only to criminal or penal laws. The Court adopted this construction of the clause in 1798 in *Calder v. Bull* and has continued to maintain this view. Accordingly, civil statutes may be given retroactive effect without violating the prohibition against *ex post facto* law. Federal or state governments, for example, may generally pass statutes taxing income earned or limiting rights acquired before the statutes' enactment.

The Constitution's *ex post facto* clause embraces three kinds of prohibitions. First, it bars government from punishing as a crime an act which was innocent at the time it was committed. Second, it prohibits government from retroactively increasing the seriousness of the punishment for an act already defined as a crime. Finally, it restrains federal and state governments from eliminating criminal defenses that existed at the time the allegedly criminal act was performed. The *ex post facto* clause does not, however, completely foreclose retroactive legislation relating to criminal law or procedure. Government may, for example, retroactively vary the type of punishment imposed for a crime. It may substitute the electric chair for the hangman's noose without violating the prohibition against *ex post facto* laws. Government may also reduce the degree of punishment meted out for a particular crime. Finally, state and federal governments are free to punish individuals for continuing to engage in conduct that was once not subject to the criminal sanction but was subsequently made illegal. Thus, a person could not be punished for violating Prohibition laws for purchasing liquor before such laws went into effect but could be punished for continuing to possess liquor after possession had been outlawed.

See also Blackstone, William; Constitution, U.S.; Crime; Criminal law; Prohibition; Retroactivity of Supreme Court decisions.

Expert witness

DEFINITION: A person called to testify at a trial because he or she has specialized knowledge that has a bearing on the case

SIGNIFICANCE: Expert witnesses can provide valuable information and opinions in a number of types of cases, but they cannot render opinions as to guilt or innocence in a criminal case

An expert witness is a witness qualified by knowledge, skill, experience, training, or education whom a court may permit to testify in the form of an opinion or otherwise. Typically an expert witness is allowed to testify if scientific, technical, or other specialized knowledge will assist a judge or jury in understanding the facts or evidence at issue. In most civil cases, experts may testify not only to the facts but also to their opinions respecting the facts, so far as necessary to enlighten the judge or jury to enable it to reach the appropriate verdict. In a criminal case, however, expert witnesses may not testify as to their opinions with regard to the guilt or innocence of the defendant. Expert witnesses have been offered in a variety of areas of expertise which were unheard of or rarely used before the 1970's. There are, for example, safety and defective product experts. Further, as there are continuous advances in scientific knowledge, experts in new areas of technology have emerged, such as deoxyribonucleic acid (DNA) experts and computer software intellectual property experts.

See also Civil procedure; Criminal procedure; DNA testing; Evidence, rules of.

Extradition

DEFINITION: The transfer of a person from one territorial jurisdiction to another for the purpose of trial for a criminal offense under the second jurisdiction's laws

SIGNIFICANCE: Extradition, in essence, closes off an escape route, preventing an accused criminal from avoiding prosecution by leaving the jurisdiction under which the crime was committed

The U.S. Constitution (Article IV, section 2) provides for the extradition of a fugitive criminal to the state in which the crime was committed upon demand of that state's governor. Although extradition is a common practice, the U.S. Supreme Court has found the clause to be discretionary. A governor may refuse to extradite a person for any reason, including a fear that the person would not receive a fair trial.

More problematic is extradition between sovereign countries. Many countries have signed extradition treaties, which provide for the mutual granting of extradition requests. Nevertheless, political and diplomatic considerations often color extradition decisions. Persons suspected of espionage, terrorism, and other crimes sometimes are protected by the governments to which they flee. Sometimes such cases have led to extradition by force.

See also *Alvarez-Machain, United States v.*; Fugitive Slave Laws; International law; Interpol; Skyjacking; Terrorism.

Family law

DEFINITION: The body of law devoted to the rights and duties among family members, including husband and wife in intact marriages and in divorce, parents and children, and the extended family

SIGNIFICANCE: Family law touches almost every person in modern life, whether through marriage, divorce, or the rearing of children

Since colonial times, the various states have claimed responsibility for overseeing the creation or dissolution of the "legal" family. State law defines the conditions for marriage and for divorce. In addition, state law defines the rights of parents and children, the rights of grandparents with respect to their grandchildren, and the division of property and income upon divorce.

Marriage and Divorce. Most states place minimal conditions on marriage. Typically, marriage must be between a man and a woman not already married to someone else, and there are various licensing, solemnization, and blood testing requirements. Because the right to marry is a fundamental right, the state cannot make it unreasonably hard for persons to marry (*Zablocki v. Redhail*, 1978).

A person can be legally married to only one person at a time. If a person entering marriage is already married to another, the later marriage is void (not a marriage at all), although the spouse of the void marriage may have some claims to property or income if he or she did not know of the prior marriage. In some states, "common-law marriage" still exists. This form of marriage recognizes a couple as married if they present themselves to the world as married, even if they do not fulfill the technical legal requirements for marriage.

More difficult legal issues arise around divorce than around marriage. Before about 1970, a person seeking divorce in the United States had to assert "grounds" for doing so. Grounds such as adultery, insanity, and extreme cruelty served as the only basis for obtaining a divorce. Rather than keeping couples together, however, grounds instead often encouraged perjury and falsification of evidence. In about 1970, states began to enact "no-fault" divorce laws, in which a divorce was available to anyone who simply asserted that his or her marriage was irretrievably broken. By 1990, all fifty states had enacted no-fault divorce laws, although some states allowed the former laws to remain on the books. The proponents of no-fault divorce laws recognized that forcing a spouse to continue in a marriage would not improve the marriage and that most failed marriages can be blamed on both sides. Airing the parties' "dirty laundry" in fact hurts both the spouses and their children.

Property Division and Spousal Support. There are two very different state marital-property regimes in the United States. Most states base their marital property laws on English common law, in which title to property determined the ownership and management of that property. Thus, in "title" states, the person holding title to property is the owner and manager of that property during the marriage. The other system is called "community property" and is based on Continental Europe's civil law system. In this system, the husband and wife jointly own all the "community property"—that is, property acquired during the marriage. Although historically the husband managed community property during the marriage, today either the husband or the wife may manage the property. Only eight states have the community property system: Arizona, California, Idaho, Louisiana, Nevada, New Mexico, Texas, and Washington.

Historically, the effects of these systems upon divorce were very different. Community property systems resulted in a roughly equal division of community property. Title systems resulted in a very uneven division, because title to property was traditionally held in the husband's name rather than the wife's. In these states, courts might try to balance the property division by awarding spousal support (also known as "alimony") to the wife. Spousal support statutes, however, often required that the wife meet specific other requirements, such as showing special need. The obvious inequities of this system led the legislatures in title states to amend their statutes to require "equitable distribution of marital property" upon divorce. Marital property is roughly the same as community property: property acquired during marriage. "Equitable distribution" is not well defined but seems to presume a fifty-fifty division in most cases.

Community property systems usually do not allow an award of spousal support, but equitable distribution systems do authorize spousal support. The modern trend, however, is to sever all financial ties between the spouses upon divorce (except for child support). Therefore, spousal support statutes require a showing of some necessity for spousal support, and they restrict its availability to a limited period immediately following the divorce. Spousal support might be ordered, for example, for a two-year period to allow a homemaker spouse to obtain training. Extended spousal support might be awarded for lengthy marriages when one spouse could not work because of a disability or another condition.

Many commentators examining no-fault divorce systems have questioned the impact of the division of property and awards of spousal support and have argued that women (and their children) are worse off economically under the no-fault system. Other commentators assert that it is not the change to no-fault divorce that has worsened the plight of women, but other economic factors. This debate is not likely to be conclusively settled, nor is it likely to cause states to jettison their no-fault divorce statutes and return to grounds-based divorce statutes.

Determining who will have custody of the children and what the rights of both parents will be is frequently the most difficult decision for divorcing parents. (James L. Shaffer)

Child Custody and Child Support. No issue in family law raises more debate than child custody and support. Divorcing spouses experience enormous anxiety over child custody issues, and with changing attitudes toward the division of parenting responsibilities in marriage, the determination of which parent should be the custodial parent is not at all clear.

Upon divorce, there must be a determination of which parent (or what combination of both parents) will have custody of minor children. "Custody" is a word for several different things. Of primary importance is the "physical custody" of the child: with which parent the child will be, and when. Also of importance is "legal custody": the right to make legal decisions regarding the child, such as where the child will attend school and what medical care will be given the child. The parent without physical custody is entitled to reasonable "visitation" with the child.

Historically, the mother was awarded custody of minor children upon divorce, in accordance with traditional understandings of the roles of men and women in society. "Custody" in this context meant physical custody. Generally, the father retained the rights to visitation and some legal custody. In response to changing views of the roles of men and women in the 1970's and increased recognition of the need for active fathers in children's lives in the 1980's, legislatures and courts began to eliminate automatic maternal preferences in favor of a "best interests of the child" standard. Under this standard, custody is to be awarded in accordance with the best interests

of the child. While some statutes offer guidance on what this means, most do not, leaving interpretation of this term to the courts.

The best interests standard requires an analysis of which parent is likely to provide the best environment for the child. Courts have focused on the stability of the environment, the emotional state of each parent, the morals of each parent, the willingness of one parent to allow the other access to the children, even the presence of cigarette smoke in the home, and countless other factors. Although the child's preference is rarely invoked by statute, most judges will give children's preferences at least some weight beginning at about age twelve. It is very difficult for courts to determine which parent will be the best parent for the children, and many courts rely heavily on evaluations by psychologists engaged for this purpose.

One trend of special interest is the move toward—and away from—joint custody. Some states have enacted a legislative preference for joint custody, defined as equally shared physical and legal custody of a child. In some cases, when the parents live in the same school district and have a good working relationship, this can ensure maximum contact with both parents. When the parents do not live close to each other or cannot communicate well, joint custody often results in a confusing kind of "shuttle diplomacy" for the child. Some states have changed their statutes to remove the preference for joint custody or have redefined it to mean joint legal custody and shared (not necessarily equal) physical custody.

One issue of special interest in the custody and visitation area is the rights of grandparents and other extended family members to claim custody of, or visitation with, a minor child. Many state statutes specifically recognize the rights of grandparents to visit with children after their parents' divorce. Custody by a nonparent, however, is a more difficult issue. Under all states' laws, the parents of a child are the preferred custodians of that child. Some statutes, however, allow a grandparent or other family member to petition the court for custody of a minor child if it is in the best interests of the child. If, for example, the parents are drug addicted or otherwise incapable of properly caring for the child, it may be necessary to award legal and physical custody to a grandparent or other family member.

The noncustodial parent of a minor child is obligated by statute to make child support payments to the custodial parent. At one time, the amount of child support was determined on a case-by-case basis, based on the needs of the child, the resources of the parents, and other factors. This was a very inefficient system, and awards of child support varied greatly even among children with relatively similar needs and parental incomes. Most if not all states have moved to a system of calculating child support based on tables of parental income. The amount computed under such tables is presumptively correct, but it may be changed when there is a showing of special need or situation of the child.

Collection of child support is a continuing problem in the United States. Although many noncustodial parents do pay support on schedule, too many do not. District attorneys offer child-support enforcement services, and the Internal Revenue Service assists in finding delinquent payers and taking overdue child support out of tax refunds.

Adoption. The natural parents of a child are the child's legal custodians. For any number of reasons, however, they may choose to place the child for adoption. If the parents are

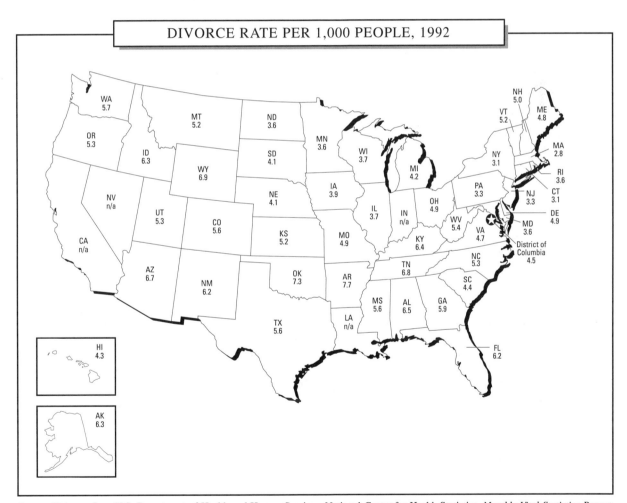

DIVORCE RATE PER 1,000 PEOPLE, 1992

Source: Data are from U.S. Department of Health and Human Services, National Center for Health Statistics, *Monthly Vital Statistics Report.* Washington, D.C.: U.S. Government Printing Office, September, 1993.

Note: The national divorce rate in 1992 was 4.8 divorces per 1,000 people; figures for California, Indiana, Louisiana, and Nevada were not available (N/A).

married, both parents' consent is necessary for a valid adoption. For children born out of wedlock, traditionally only the mother's consent was required. In *Stanley v. Illinois* (1972), however, the Supreme Court recognized the right of an unwed father who had participated in the rearing of a child to object to an adoption. Courts have disagreed on whether this right is extended to fathers who have not participated in their children's lives.

Another issue of particular concern in adoption is the effect of revocation of consent. Most states allow revocation for fraud, duress, or undue influence, and some states allow revocation for any reason. When adoptions may be reversed remains a troublesome question in family law. Other issues include the regulation of private adoptions, the propriety of open adoptions, where the adoptive and natural parents may be known to each other, and the necessity for matching the racial heritage of adopted children and adoptive parents.

—*Gwendolyn Griffith*

See also Adultery; Aid to Families with Dependent Children (AFDC); Battered child and battered wife syndromes; Child abuse; Domestic violence; Family Medical Leave Act; Feminism; Gay rights; *In loco parentis*; Polygamy; Property rights.

BIBLIOGRAPHY

The classic treatise on family law is Homer H. Clark, Jr., *The Law of Domestic Relations in the United States* (2d ed. St. Paul, Minn.: West, 1988). A very readable overview of the issues of family law is Harry D. Krause, *Family Law* (St. Paul, Minn.: West, 1988). Because family law varies from state to state, it is important to focus on the law in a particular jurisdiction, and the state bar associations in most states have compiled "deskbooks" or "manuals" on the family law of the particular state. For a broader perspective on divorce, especially its effects on the participants and children, see Judith S. Wallerstein and Sandra Blakeslee, *Second Chances: Men, Women, and Children a Decade After Divorce* (New York: Ticknor & Fields, 1989); Constance R. Ahrons, *The Good Divorce* (New York: HarperCollins, 1994); and Edward Teyber, *Helping Children Cope with Divorce* (New York: Lexington Books, 1992). Finally, for an in-depth look at the adoption process, see Cynthia D. Martin, *Beating the Adoption Game* (San Diego, Calif.: Harcourt Brace Jovanovich, 1988).

Family Medical Leave Act

DATE: Signed into law February 5, 1993

DEFINITION: Legislation that provided working Americans with guaranteed unpaid time off to take care of a new baby or ill family member

SIGNIFICANCE: This law established federal guidelines for workers' benefits regarding time off for infant care or family medical emergencies

The Family Medical Leave Act (FMLA) grew out of a desire to extend options regarding maternity leave and medically related situations to all workers. First introduced in 1985, the idea of family leave was stalled because of political maneuvering and probusiness lobbying efforts. In 1993, new president

Bill Clinton made family leave a high priority, and the measure passed in early February.

FMLA required businesses with more than fifty employees to provide up to twelve weeks of unpaid leave for workers to take care of a new baby or an ill family member. To be eligible, employees had to have worked at least 1,250 hours in the previous year and must provide advance notice in cases of foreseeable leave. FMLA also provided employees with the protection of secured benefits, including medical coverage.

The Family Medical Leave Act also included provisions for protecting the employers' interests. Specifically, employers can request written verification of the medical condition in question and, if the verification is unclear, can request a second or third opinion. In addition, employers can deny this leave to the highest-paid 10 percent of their employees if such leave would result in "substantial economic injury" to the business.

See also Family law; Labor law; Medical and health law; Sex discrimination.

Federal Bureau of Investigation (FBI)

DATE: Founded in 1908 as the Bureau of Investigation; renamed the Federal Bureau of Investigation in 1935

SIGNIFICANCE: The Federal Bureau of Investigation and its special agents are charged with investigating violations of more than 260 federal laws

The Federal Bureau of Investigation (FBI) as it currently exists is the investigative arm of the United States Department of Justice. Its charge is to investigate violations of federal laws that do not fall within the purview of other government agencies. Such exceptions, for example, are found in the investigation of counterfeiting operations, which are the responsibility of the Department of the Treasury, or offenses involving the U.S. mail, the responsibility of the chief postal inspector.

As it is presently organized, the FBI, under the leadership of a director, maintains fifty-six field offices in the United States and Puerto Rico. It also staffs more than a dozen offices in foreign countries. Of the approximately twenty-five thousand people it employs, about ninety-five hundred are special agents and more than thirteen thousand are non-agent personnel ranging from clerks, custodians, and secretaries to computer programmers, laboratory scientists, and physicians. The special agents constitute the central investigative core of the agency.

Functions. The FBI has two broad functions. First, it is the federal agency designated to conduct general investigations of federal crimes. Its second general function is to investigate breaches in national security.

Of the federal crimes the FBI investigates, the following most frequently come before it: kidnappings; extortion; bank robbery; the interstate transportation of stolen property; interstate traffic for such illegal acts as racketeering or prostitution; violations of election laws; actions that ignore or threaten the civil rights of United States citizens; crimes on Indian reservations, on the high seas, or on aircraft; threats on the life of the president of the United States or other federal officials; and theft of government property.

The FBI has found the distribution of "wanted" posters a useful tool in tracking fugitives. (James L. Shaffer)

The breaches of national security the agency investigates include such areas as espionage, treason, sabotage, and the violation of federal acts designed to protect national security, such as the Atomic Energy Act of 1946. The first group of legal infractions occupies the majority of the agents, although when breaches in national security occur, many agents will sometimes be moved from investigations of infractions in the first group to investigations of the somewhat more sensitive and far-reaching infractions that have to do with national security, which remains a top FBI priority.

Staffing. Although the director of the FBI is currently appointed by the president of the United States with the approval of the Senate, special agents are drawn from a pool of men and women who have taken and passed a detailed and searching written examination. In order to qualify to take the special agents' examination, candidates must be United States citizens between twenty-three and thirty-five years old. They are required to meet at least one of the following criteria: (1) hold a law degree from an accredited institution; (2) hold a degree in accounting, economics, finance, business, electrical engineering, metallurgy, or the physical sciences from an accredited undergraduate institution; (3) be a college graduate fluent in a foreign language appropriate to the needs of the bureau;

(4) have three years of other approved, specialized experience; (5) hold a graduate degree and have two years of full-time work experience; (6) hold a graduate degree in physics, chemistry, geology, biology, pharmacy, pharmacology, toxicology, mathematics, or some branch of engineering; (7) hold a graduate degree in business, public administration, computer science, or the analysis and development of business and financial information systems; (8) have a college degree and three years of experience in biology, engineering, geology, pharmacy, or toxicology; (9) hold a college degree and have three years of experience as a systems or programming analyst who has dealt with business and financial systems.

Essentially, the bureau seeks to hire as special agents people who are capable of logical and analytical thought, who can deal with the scientific aspects of the increasingly sophisticated laboratory work that forensics involves, and who can communicate clearly in English and, when necessary, in specific foreign languages. Not every special agent will possess all of these abilities, but within the organization, large numbers possess some of them.

It is required that candidates be of "good moral character." Because their work is often physically demanding, they must also be in top physical condition. Once selected, potential agents undergo four months of training divided between the FBI Academy, which is located on the U.S. Marine Corps Base at Quantico, Virginia, and FBI Headquarters in Washington, D.C. During this training period, they are schooled particularly in rules of evidence, fingerprinting techniques, investigative procedures, and the kinds of laboratory work upon which the success of their investigations will often depend.

Potential agents are trained in the use of a variety of firearms, including machine guns and other automatic and semiautomatic weapons. They also learn defense techniques to protect themselves in their sometimes dangerous field work.

As their training nears completion, they are assigned to an experienced special agent, working closely with that agent through the remainder of the initial training period. The agents' training continues, however, as long as they are with the FBI through refresher courses, short courses in specialized techniques, and other courses that are readily available for additional training to every agent throughout his or her career.

FBI Directors. The director of the Federal Bureau of Investigation is currently appointed for a term not to exceed ten years. The most renowned director, J. Edgar Hoover, appointed in 1924, served until his death in 1972. His directorship became so autocratic and inimical to the best interests of the country that upon his death, the ten-year limit was established. Hoover was replaced by a Richard Nixon appointee, L. Patrick Gray III, who served from 1972 until his forced resignation in 1973 when he admitted felonious behavior related to the Watergate investigation.

Nixon appointed Clarence Kelley, who served from 1973 until 1978, to replace Gray. William Webster was appointed to the post when Kelley retired and was replaced at the end of his term by William Sessions. Bill Clinton appointed Louis J. Freeh as director upon Sessions' retirement in 1993.

The Beginnings of the FBI. The FBI came into being on July 1, 1908, by questionable means. Charles Joseph Bonaparte, grandnephew of Napoleon I of France, served as the attorney general of the United States from 1906 until 1908. In 1907, he urged Congress to allow a small, permanent detective force to be attached to the Department of Justice.

At that time, the department had no discrete investigative wing and, when it required investigative services, had to borrow agents from the Secret Service, which fell under the jurisdiction of the Treasury Department. This made it difficult for the Justice Department to maintain confidentiality in some highly sensitive investigations. Also, agents on loan were those the Secret Service could spare, seldom their most effective agents. Bonaparte feared that some of these agents, being paid by the job and hoping to stay on at Justice, might go out and create crimes, then solve them for the recognition they would receive, acting as *agents provocateurs* more than as solid investigators.

Bonaparte's request, turned down by Congress in 1907, was resubmitted in 1908. A Congress eager to adjourn and miffed at rumors that Theodore Roosevelt had been using the Secret Service to monitor the lives of some of its more flamboyant

members, again denied the request. Many members of Congress feared the establishment of a secret police in the United States, considering it inimical to the ideals of the founding fathers. Other members, beholden to big business for campaign contributions, were concerned that such an investigative force would accelerate the antitrust activity already being pursued by Roosevelt's administration.

This Congress, completely at loggerheads with Bonaparte, not only denied his request but also added a rider to the Sundry Appropriations Act that prohibited the FBI from continuing its practice of borrowing agents from the Secret Service. Unwilling to accept defeat, Bonaparte, on June 30, 1908, the last day of the fiscal year, used discretionary funds to hire nine men from the Treasury Department as an elite investigative force. They were supplemented by examiners and accountants who brought the full force of investigators to twenty-three.

Bonaparte's elite group, at this point, did not have a name, but when George Wickersham succeeded Bonaparte as attorney general, he dubbed the group the Bureau of Investigation, a name that lasted until 1935, when an expanded bureau was officially named the Federal Bureau of Investigation. The bureau grew during the World War I period, when national security was in the forefront of American minds.

The Ascent of J. Edgar Hoover. The FBI is widely identified with J. Edgar Hoover, its director for forty-seven years. Hoover, a native of Washington, D.C., was provincial, complex, and paranoid. He was a hard worker and a master at handling detail and classifying information, skills he learned during his brief employment in 1913 at the Library of Congress.

Soon after Attorney General Harlan Stone appointed Hoover director of the FBI in 1924, the young lawyer made draconian cuts in personnel, weeding out the weaker agents and muddling through with a reduced investigative force. Hoover also engaged throughout his career in cost-cutting, sometimes requesting a smaller appropriation than he had been granted in the preceding year. This frugality brought attention to him as a competent manager, but harried congressmen often overlooked the fact that the director frequently returned with requests for supplemental funds to deal with crises, many of his own making.

As director of the FBI, Hoover collected voluminous incriminating files on practically every prominent American, including every president under whom he served. He threatened to reveal the contents of these files against those who opposed him, which perhaps accounts for his incredibly long tenure as director. He consistently used his files for his personal advantage and permitted many politicians at the highest levels of government to do so. Upon his death in 1972, the secretary who had served Hoover for his total tenure as director destroyed the most secret of his files. Steps were taken quickly to enact legislation, in effect since his death, to limit the FBI director's term of office.

Under Hoover's leadership, the bureau grew to nearly sixty field offices with an additional 526 resident offices serving the fifty states and Puerto Rico. Hoover's assaults on organized crime were highly effective, although his tactics often were both unethical and illegal. In an average year, the FBI won more than thirteen thousand convictions, an impressive 97 percent of the cases it brought to trial.

The FBI and the Law. As the FBI is constituted, it has no role in making law but is concerned with investigating and prosecuting violations of federal law. Theoretically, the bureau must abide by established laws and must not violate the civil or constitutional rights of any citizen.

Under Hoover's directorship, however, the law was often violated, particularly in such matters as surveillance and wiretapping. While Hoover was director, the bureau admitted no women to training as special agents, nor were blacks, Hispanics, or other ethnic minorities welcome. Although efforts were made to correct these violations of law when the directorship fell into the hands of later directors, documented cases of racial and sexual discrimination against female and/or minority special agents have required official arbitration and legal redress in recent years.

A month after Hoover's death, news of the Watergate break-in became public. Richard Nixon's appointee as director, L. Patrick Gray, who attempted to enact some reforms, including admitting female candidates for the special agents' examination, ultimately admitted that he had destroyed incriminating documents relating to Watergate. He resigned under pressure a year after he was appointed.

Gray's resignation sparked a congressional investigation of the agency that revealed the FBI had conducted unauthorized personal investigations for at least four presidents, two of whom—Franklin Roosevelt and Lyndon Johnson—used the FBI to gather material about the personal lives of some of their critics and political opponents. It was also revealed that J. Edgar Hoover had used FBI employees to do extensive maintenance work on his residence and that he consistently commandeered FBI vehicles for his personal use. The FBI paid for many of Hoover's vacation trips, unconvincingly disguised as professional trips, with his aide and frequent companion Clyde Tolson.

Of all the revelations of Hoover's numerous personal vendettas, the one that is in many ways most shocking resulted in his illegally gathering wire-tap information against Martin Luther King, Jr., and sending King's wife an incriminating tape relating to her husband. He was also behind the sending of a note to King suggesting that the renowned civil rights activist should commit suicide.

The Post-Watergate FBI. Gray's resignation was a blow that the FBI, already suffering from a tarnished image, did not need. Under subsequent directors, however, more meticulous controls and a broader view of FBI functions have helped to restore public confidence in the bureau.

As drug interdiction and the need to control violence have become central public concerns, the FBI has engaged in preventive work with local law enforcement agents and community leaders. Its Safe Streets Program is aimed at fighting violent crime and at directing youth away from crime and gang activity. Among its more successful programs during 1992 were Adopt-A-School, Junior G-Men, a mentor program, and a community outreach afternoon program designed to serve latchkey youngsters.

In conjunction with the Secret Service, the FBI in 1992 conducted its first court-authorized surveillance of data trans-

FBI agents work with other agencies in the field, such as state and municipal police forces; in addition, the FBI forensic laboratory is a valuable resource for those agencies. (AP/Wide World Photos)

missions related to break-ins of computers owned by the Martin Marietta Electronic Information and Missile Group and various telephone companies, violations with substantial implications for national security.

FBI drug investigations during 1992 resulted in 4,361 indictments, 3,419 arrests, and 2,957 convictions, with some cases still pending. In that year, three hundred special agents of the FBI were reassigned from counterintelligence to augment the work of a thousand special agents already assigned to work on violent crime. By the end of the year, seventy-one FBI task forces were at work in forty-five major cities. In California alone, fifty new agents joined antiviolence investigative teams in July, 1992. This infusion of trained personnel resulted in the arrests of 10,777 felons by year's end.

Among the cooperative services in which the modern FBI engages are courses of instruction offered at both the FBI Academy and at other sites throughout the nation and the world for the training of local, state, and international law enforcement personnel. These courses are offered free of charge to qualified law enforcement officers.

Since 1976, the FBI has offered a National Executive Institute, an eighteen-day program at the FBI Academy in Quantico designed specifically for the chief executives of the largest law enforcement agencies in the United States. So successful has this program been that in 1981, the Law Enforcement Executive Development Seminar was established to offer similar opportunities to chief law enforcement executives of middle-sized communities. Faculty at the FBI Academy are also available as consultants to police departments throughout the nation.

The bureau administers the Violent Criminal Apprehension Program (VICAP), a sophisticated, state-of-the-art national data center that collects, collates, and analyzes every element of the investigation of violent crimes. This is in some ways a space-age equivalent of the FBI's "Ten Most Wanted" program, which still exists and which, through the years, has been responsible for the apprehension of thousands of dangerous felons.

The FBI Laboratory. The FBI operates the only full-service national forensic laboratory in the United States. Established in 1932, it has become the best equipped and most sophisticated such facility in the world. It is available to law enforcement agencies nationwide and throughout the world. One of its more recent services is DRUGFIRE, a computerized forensic clearinghouse for drug-related investigations.

The FBI's Impact. In a free society, an agency such as the FBI must be strenuously monitored and controlled. When Bonaparte made his initial request for the establishment of an investigative agency, Congressman J. Swagar Sherley of Kentucky reminded his congressional colleagues that he knew of no government that had perished because it did not have a secret police force but that he could think of many that had been destroyed because they had one. His admonition is one that has been heeded increasingly by both houses of Congress since the leadership of J. Edgar Hoover grew increasingly to have a stranglehold on many Americans.

As violence grows, as the drug culture continues to affect American life adversely, and as international terrorism becomes an increasing threat to a free society, Americans can easily acknowledge the need for a strong FBI. Such an agency, however, must live within the laws it is charged with enforcing and must be subject to the kinds of checks and balances that are the linchpins of any free society. *—R. Baird Shuman*

See also Branch Davidians, federal raid on; Civil liberties; Civil rights; Crime Index; Hoover, J. Edgar; Justice, U.S. Department of; Organized crime; Uniform Crime Reports (UCR).

BIBLIOGRAPHY

One of the most fascinating books relating to the FBI is Curt Gentry's *J. Edgar Hoover: The Man and the Secrets* (New York: W. W. Norton, 1991), a well-documented exposé. Fred L. Israel's *The FBI* (New York: Chelsea House, 1986), part of Chelsea House's Know Your Government series, although directed at a secondary school audience, is concise, accurate, and candid. Among the more interesting studies of the bureau, most of them exposés, are James Bamford's *The Puzzle Palace: A Report on America's Most Secret Agency* (Boston: Houghton Mifflin, 1982), Nelson Blackstock's *Cointelpro: The FBI's Secret War on Political Freedom* (New York: Vintage, 1976), Fred J. Cook's *The FBI Nobody Knows* (New York: Macmillan, 1964), John T. Elliff's *The Reform of FBI Intelligence Operations* (Princeton, N.J.: Princeton University Press, 1979), Harry and Bonaro Overstreet's *The FBI in Our Open Society* (New York: W. W. Norton, 1969), Richard Gid Powers' *G-Men: Hoover's FBI in American Popular Culture* (Carbondale: Southern Illinois University Press, 1983), Andrew Tully's *Inside the FBI* (New York: McGraw-Hill, 1980), and Sanford J. Ungar's *FBI* (Boston: Atlantic Monthly Press, 1976). The *Annual Report of the Attorney General of the United States* provides current information annually about the bureau, which also distributes useful pamphlets about its activities such as *The FBI Mission: To Uphold the Law* (Washington, D.C.: U.S. Government Printing Office, 1989).

Federal Crimes Act

DATE: Became law April 30, 1790
DEFINITION: A law that identified a number of federal crimes and established penalties for their commission
SIGNIFICANCE: This act established the foundation for the U.S. Criminal Code

When the U.S. Constitution was adopted in 1789, it specifically charged the federal government with a narrow criminal jurisdiction, covering only counterfeiting and piracies and other felonies committed on the high seas. Yet the Constitution granted Congress the authority to make laws it deemed "necessary and proper for carrying into execution" the broad powers granted to it. It was by this authority that the first Congress passed the Federal Crimes Act in 1790.

The act specified penalties for a range of federal crimes, including counterfeiting and piracy, as well as treason, murder and manslaughter within a federal jurisdiction, receiving property stolen in a federal crime, bribery and perjury in connection with federal suits, and other crimes. Penalties ranged from three hundred dollars to death by hanging.

Most of the penalties specified by the act have since been altered, and some of the crimes themselves have been redefined. More important, what began as a relatively modest catalog of federal crimes has since expanded to more than one thousand general criminal statutes.

See also Admiralty law; Criminal law; Marshals Service, U.S.; Model Penal Code; United States Code.

Federal Firearms Act. *See* National Firearms Act and Federal Firearms Act

Federal Tort Claims Act

DATE: Enacted August 2, 1946
DEFINITION: Legislation that waives the federal government's immunity regarding negligent acts of its employees
SIGNIFICANCE: This act relieved Congress of the burden of passing thousands of "private bills" to compensate victims of federal negligence; it established procedures that distinguish federal tort claims from other tort cases

The English common-law courts developed the concept of sovereign immunity, whereby the government could not be sued without its consent. Sovereign immunity was incorporated into the laws of the United States.

Yet as government's responsibilities and personnel grew in size, the possibility that a government employee might injure an innocent victim correspondingly increased. The result was that thousands of "private bills" were introduced annually in Congress to compensate these victims. The demands on Congress became excessive. Congress responded on August 2, 1946, by enacting the Federal Tort Claims Act (FTCA), which waives the federal government's immunity for negligent acts committed by its employees acting in the course of their employment. The FTCA did not initially waive sovereign immunity for intentional or strict liability torts, but federal liability now extends to intentional torts committed by federal law enforcement officials.

The statute also includes special procedures that distinguish it from regular tort cases. A claim must be presented to the appropriate federal agency before suit is filed. There is no jury trial in FTCA suits. The applicable substantive law is that of the state where the act occurred. Punitive damages are not available. The federal employee is also not personally liable for the tort.

States have followed the lead of the federal government in limiting sovereign immunity. Many of the statutes are modeled on the Federal Tort Claims Act.

See also Immunity of public officials; Tort; Tort reform.

Federal Trade Commission (FTC)

DATE: Established 1914
SIGNIFICANCE: The Federal Trade Commission enforces antitrust laws and a wide variety of consumer protection laws; it proscribes "unfair methods of competition" and "unfair or deceptive acts or practices"

The Federal Trade Commission (FTC) Act was passed in 1914, the same year the Clayton Antitrust Act was passed. Prior to 1914, enforcement of the Sherman Antitrust Act (1890) was not very vigorous. The only consistently successful application of the Sherman Antitrust Act was to labor unions, an application not even found in the act's legislative history.

Background and Mandate. In the first decade of the twentieth century, there was widespread political agitation against trusts and other business monopolies as well as a general dissatisfaction with the Sherman Antitrust Act and its enforcement. The act was brief, and its language was vague. The courts, moreover, had extremely wide latitude in the interpretation and application of the act. Experience had indicated that a number of predatory competitive practices were, in actuality, anticompetitive. Such acts as stealing trade secrets, misrepresenting the quality of goods, and interfering with competitors' businesses needed to be proscribed. In addition, an independent, aggressive commission was needed to respond to complaints and investigate alleged illegal activities.

The commission was charged with proscribing "unfair methods of competition." The original interpretation of this mandate required that an action needed to injure a competitor, irrespective of any injury to the general public, to be declared an "unfair method of competition." The FTC Act was amended in 1938 to make "unfair and deceptive acts and practices" part of the mandate. Subsequent interpretations of this phrase widened the commission's mandate to include any injury to the general public. It was from this latter concern and the commission's ability to proscribe "deceptive acts and practices" that the commission developed its function of consumer protection. A wide variety of federal antitrust and consumer protection laws are enforced by the FTC. The commission's activities can be divided into the following four categories: maintaining competition, consumer protection, consumer education, and economic analysis.

Maintaining Competition. The Bureau of Competition has primary responsibility, with the support of the Bureau of Economics, for enforcing federal antitrust laws and maintaining competition. The activities of the Bureau of Competition include five separate programs. First is a pre-merger notification program, under which firms of a certain size must notify the commission prior to any significant acquisition. Second is a mergers and joint ventures program, which identifies and investigates those mergers, joint ventures, and acquisitions that are likely to result in a lessening of competition and makes recommendations for possible action. Third, a horizontal restraints program investigates fixing agreements and other types of agreements among direct competitors and makes recommendations for possible action. Fourth is a distributional restraints program that investigates restrictions on the distribution of goods from manufacturers to consumers. Where such restrictions have the effect of limiting supply and thereby increasing prices or reducing quality, a recommendation for action is made. Finally, a single-firm violations program investigates firms for abuse of their market power and makes recommendations for possible action.

Consumer Protection and Education. Maintaining market conditions that allow consumers to make purchases on the basis of informed choice is the goal of the FTC in the area of consumer protection. The activities of the consumer protection mission include five separate programs. First, a service industry practices program brings lawsuits in federal court regarding consumer fraud in a widespread area of service activities, from health care and medical fraud to fraudulent investment schemes. Second, a marketing practices program focuses primarily on fraudulent telemarketing schemes. The FTC has taken administrative actions and filed lawsuits in federal court attempting to stop telemarketing fraud. Third, an advertising practices program takes action against false and misleading advertising as well as unsubstantiated claims in advertising. Fourth, a credit practices program focuses on such issues as equal access to credit, confidentiality of consumer records, and financial histories. Fifth, an enforcement program enforces the FTC's cease and desist orders. The FTC has been given the responsibility, moreover, to enforce a number of special statues, guides, and trade regulation rules, including the labeling of fur, textiles, and wool products as well as the advertising of tobacco and smokeless tobacco products.

The Office of Consumer and Business Education has the functions of consumer advocacy and education. This office develops and implements educational programs aimed at encouraging fully informed consumer choice and business competition as well as educational programs concerning the various activities of the FTC.

Economic Analysis. The primary function of the Bureau of Economics is to provide support for the FTC's enforcement of federal antitrust laws and consumer protection activities. This office studies and analyzes the American economy from the perspective of antitrust enforcement, government regulation, and consumer protection. The office also advises the commission on matters of competition, the impact of government regulation, and the economic merits of various potential antitrust actions. —*Daniel C. Falkowski*

See also Antitrust law; Clayton Antitrust Act; Consumer fraud; Consumer rights movement; Interstate Commerce Commission (ICC); Sherman Antitrust Act; Transportation law.

BIBLIOGRAPHY

For an understanding of the wide scope of the FTC's activities, see the *Annual Report of the Federal Trade Commission* (Washington, D.C.: U.S. Government Printing Office, 1914-). For a good treatment of the historical development of antitrust policy, see Donald Stevenson Watson, *Economic Policy: Business and Government* (Cambridge, Mass.: Riverside Press, 1960). For economic analysis and economic models of antitrust cases, see Eugene M. Singer, *Antitrust Economics: Selected Legal Cases and Economic Models* (Englewood Cliffs, N.J.: Prentice-Hall, 1968), and Eugene M. Singer, *Antitrust Economics and Legal Analysis* (Columbus, Ohio: Grid, 1981).

For cases, see Irwin M. Stelzer and Howard P. Kitt, *Selected Antitrust Cases: Landmark Decisions* (5th ed. Homewood, Ill.: Richard D. Irwin, 1976).

Federalism

DEFINITION: A governmental system in which authority is divided between a central national government, supreme in its sphere, and local or state governments

SIGNIFICANCE: Federal systems allow more local autonomy at the cost of greater complexity and division of authority

When the U.S. Constitution was written in 1787, its framers established a federal system of government. In the political context of 1787 no other choice would have been possible; local autonomy had been part of the North American tradition from the beginnings of English colonization. Consequently, those writing the Constitution had to decide which powers had to be centrally exercised and which powers should be left to the states.

Federal and State Powers. The federal government was granted most of the powers necessary for any sovereign nation. Defense, foreign affairs, the establishment of a national currency, and the regulation of interstate and foreign commerce are familiar examples. The general power to protect the lives, safety, and health of the public, however, was left to state governments. Today the federal government's power under the interstate commerce clause of the Constitution has expanded enormously, and the federal government now has a substantial role in these areas of policy. Even though the balance has shifted over the years, state government still dominates in areas such as education, welfare, child care, and land use. This constitutional allocation of powers also means that the state governments have the primary responsibility for making and enforcing criminal law. Under the original constitution, each state was entitled to establish its own criminal code and to decide what kinds of court system and legal processes were most appropriate. Because the Bill of Rights, which was ratified in 1791, was aimed only at the federal government, none of its limitations applied to the state governments. By contrast, federal law enforcement activities were subject to the procedural requirements of the Bill of Rights. Only with the ratification of the Fourteenth Amendment in 1868 did significant limits on state autonomy in the area of law enforcement come into existence, and these limits were only rarely imposed by federal courts until the late 1950's.

Federal systems are complex. Responsibility and jurisdiction often overlap, and there is often duplication of function and effort. In the United States there are parallel federal and state court systems, prosecutors, and law enforcement agencies. Sometimes even the statutes overlap. For example, bank robbery and kidnapping are crimes under both federal and state law. A person who commits one of these offenses may be tried in either a federal or state court, depending in part at least on whether a federal or state agency made the arrest. At any given moment, a person in the United States is subject to both federal and state criminal laws—and sometimes to municipal ordinances as well.

Fourteenth Amendment and Incorporation. The Fourteenth Amendment limits on state government nearly all result from the command, "nor shall any state deprive any person of life, liberty, or property, without due process of law." The Supreme Court has never significantly altered its initial interpretation of this clause for criminal cases. In 1884, in *Hurtado v. California*, the Court held that only rights "fundamental to a scheme of ordered liberty" were protected. Few such rights were found until Earl Warren became chief justice of the United States in 1953. Rights which the Court does hold to be fundamental are said to be "incorporated" into the Fourteenth Amendment. By the end of Chief Justice Warren's tenure the Court had incorporated all but two of the rights guaranteed in the Bill of Rights as limits on the states. The two exceptions are the right to keep and bear arms of the Second Amendment and the Fifth Amendment's guarantee of indictment by grand jury.

The Court has also incorporated some substantive rights of personal privacy or autonomy. In *Griswold v. Connecticut* (1965) the Court found a fundamental right to receive and use birth control information and devices. In *Roe v. Wade* (1973) the Court established a woman's constitutional right to an abortion in the first trimester of pregnancy.

Federalism and the Appeals Process. The normal jurisdictional pattern for criminal cases which arise in state courts allows a convicted defendant one appeal from his or her conviction. Such appeals go up through the state court hierarchy—normally from the trial court to an intermediate appellate court and then to the state supreme court. The losing party in the highest state court may ask the U.S. Supreme Court to review the case if there is an important issue of federal constitutional or statute law. Federal criminal cases in which there are significant appellate issues can arrive at the Supreme Court by a more direct route through the federal judicial hierarchy.

Several significant changes in American justice have resulted from the expansion of the Fourteenth Amendment's coverage. States have far less autonomy to attempt different or experimental procedural techniques. There are far more appeals than before, and the workload of federal courts has significantly expanded. This is particularly true in death penalty cases, which may go through the appeals process for ten or fifteen years.

—*Robert Jacobs*

See also *Adamson v. California*; American Revolution; Bill of Rights, U.S.; Constitution, U.S.; Constitutional law; *Hurtado v. California*; States' rights; Supremacy clause.

BIBLIOGRAPHY

Any consideration of federalism in the United States should begin with the *Federalist Papers*. These essays, written by Alexander Hamilton, James Madison, and John Jay, were prepared to persuade the public to accept the new federal Constitution. An inexpensive standard edition is edited by Clinton Rossiter (New York: New American Library, 1961). The literature of federalism is voluminous; one particularly good analysis of the historical development and present nature of American federalism is Daniel Elazar's *American Federalism: A View from the States* (2d ed. New York: Crowell, 1972). A profound analysis of what the founders meant by federalism is "The Federalist's View of Federalism," in George C. S. Benson et al., eds., *Essays in Federalism* (Claremont, Calif.: Institute for Studies in Federalism, 1961). A more critical examination of federalism is William Riker's *Federalism: Origin, Operation, Significance* (Boston: Little, Brown, 1964). Finally, Morton Grodzins' *The American System*, edited by Daniel J. Elazar (Chicago: Rand McNally, 1966), argues that American federalism has always involved extensive sharing of functions between national and state governments.

Federalist Party

DATE: Established 1787
SIGNIFICANCE: The fledgling United States prospered during its first twelve years under Federalist administration

Following George Washington's inauguration in 1789, an ideological division arose between the secretary of the treasury, Alexander Hamilton, and the secretary of state, Thomas Jefferson. These two leaders envisioned radically different futures for the new nation. Hamilton, a staunch Federalist, sought to enhance the strength of the federal government by courting the wealthy and by encouraging industry. Jefferson conceived of an agricultural nation whose power derived from and was centered primarily in the individual states.

The economy prospered under Hamilton's plan, and the federal government grew stronger. When Washington retired,

Federalist president John Adams stirred controversy with the Alien and Sedition Acts in 1798. (Library of Congress)

however, the factionalized Federalist party was nearly defeated in 1796 by the increasingly popular Jefferson. The Federalists' image was further tarnished during John Adams' presidency. Struggling to prevent open warfare with France, Adams' administration secured passage of the Alien and Sedition Acts in 1798. Ostensibly designed to prevent treason, the acts were vigorously condemned by Republicans who viewed them as unconstitutional usurpations of individual and states' rights, designed primarily to stifle Republican dissent.

Federalists were defeated in the election of 1880. Before leaving office, however, President Adams made several crucial Federalist appointments to the judiciary branch, including that of Chief Justice John Marshall. By the election of 1824 the Federalist Party was virtually defunct.

See also Alien and Sedition Acts; Chase, Samuel; Jeffersonian Republican Party; Marshall, John; Whig Party.

Felony

DEFINITION: A serious criminal offense, such as murder, rape, kidnapping, arson, embezzlement, or armed robbery, that, according to federal guidelines, is punishable by imprisonment of a year or more or by death

SIGNIFICANCE: Federal and state definitions of felony and misdemeanor vary somewhat, but in all states the distinction is an important one

Criminal offenses are often grouped into two major categories, felonies and misdemeanors, which indicate the seriousness of the crime. Misdemeanors are less serious offenses, such as

FELONY DEFENDANTS IN THE 75 LARGEST U.S. COUNTIES, 1990

Most Serious Arrest Charge	Number	Percent
All offenses	56,618	100
Violent offenses	14,610	25.8
Murder	575	1.0
Rape	798	1.4
Robbery	4,880	8.6
Assault	6,801	12.0
Other violent	1,556	2.7
Property offenses	19,141	33.8
Burglary	5,721	10.1
Theft	8,097	14.3
Other property	5,323	9.4
Drug offenses	18,586	32.8
Sales/trafficking	10,405	18.4
Other drug	8,181	14.4
Public-order offenses	4,281	7.6
Driving-related	1,295	2.3
Other public-order	2,986	5.3

Source: U.S. Department of Justice, Bureau of Justice Statistics, *Sourcebook of Criminal Justice Statistics—1993*. Washington, D.C.: U.S. Government Printing Office, 1994.

Note: Data are from a sample of 39 of the 75 most populous U.S. counties. Percentages may not add to 100 because of rounding.

disorderly conduct; felonies are more serious crimes, such as murder, rape, and armed robbery. Federal guidelines define a felony as any crime "punishable by death or by imprisonment for a term exceeding one year." Most states maintain similar definitions, although some states classify crimes according to the place of incarceration for offenders. If incarceration is to be in a state prison, the offense is a felony; if it is punishable by a term in a local jail, it is considered a misdemeanor. (There are further complications in some areas; in Michigan a few misdemeanors are deemed serious enough to warrant time in a state penitentiary.) In some jurisdictions an offense may be considered either a felony or a misdemeanor depending on a number of factors. Larceny (theft), for example, may be classified as a felony (grand larceny) if the value of the item or items stolen is sufficiently high or a misdemeanor (petty larceny) if their value is relatively small.

Most states maintain separate court systems for felonies and misdemeanors. Felonies are tried in county courts, or courts of general jurisdiction. Misdemeanors are handled by local courts with limited jurisdiction. By far, most criminal cases are handled by local (minor) courts, partly because so many charges are only misdemeanors and partly because felony charges are sometimes reduced to misdemeanor charges before a trial begins. Because the charges and punishments meted out to convicted felony offenders are significantly more serious, the handling of felony cases by the courts is much more complex than the handling of misdemeanors. Felony cases involve pretrial, trial, and post-trial proceedings, and they can take a year or more.

In 1963, in the landmark case *Gideon v. Wainwright*, the U.S. Supreme Court held that defendants charged with serious crimes must be provided with a state-appointed attorney if they cannot afford to hire their own attorney. At first this requirement was applied only to felony cases, but in *Argersinger v. Hamlin* (1973) the Court extended the protection to people accused of misdemeanors if the misdemeanor charge could result in imprisonment.

The exact origin of the term "felony" is unknown, but many scholars trace it to the Latin words *felonia* and *fallere*, meaning "to deceive." In England, a felony originally was a breach of the feudal bond resulting in either the temporary or permanent forfeiture of the guilty party's assets. Gradually the definition expanded. In the twelfth century, Henry II attempted to codify the laws of the realm, and he established forfeiture as one of the penalties for murder, theft, forgery, arson, and other similar criminal acts. Soon all crimes punishable in England by forfeiture of property (eventually abolished in 1870), physical mutilation, burning, or death were considered felonies. In 1967, England replaced the former distinctions with the categories arrestable and nonarrestable offenses, but the felony/misdemeanor distinction remains important in the United States.

See also Common law; Crime; Crime Index; Criminal law; *Gideon v. Wainwright*; Mandatory sentencing laws; Misdemeanor; Punishment.

AMERICAN JUSTICE

LIST OF ENTRIES BY CATEGORY

AREAS OF LAW

Administrative law
Admiralty law
Antitrust law
Banking law
Civil law
Commercial law
Constitutional law
Contract law
Copyrights, patents, and
    trademarks
Criminal law
Environmental law

Family law
Gambling law
Immigration laws
Insurance law
International law
Labor law
Medical and health law
Real estate law
School law
Sports law
Telecommunications law
Transportation law

CIVIL AND CRIMINAL JUSTICE

Adultery
Appellate process
Arraignment
Arrest
Attorney
Bail system
Bailiff
Bankruptcy
Bar examinations and
    licensing of lawyers
Bar, the
Battered child and battered
    wife syndromes
Burden of proof
Capital punishment
Case law
Chief of police
Civil disobedience
Civil procedure
Civilian review boards
Commercialized vice
Common law
Community-oriented policing
Conscientious objection
Coroner
Corporal punishment
Counsel, right to
Crime
Crime Index
Criminal
Criminal intent
Criminal justice system
Criminal procedure
Criminology
Deadly force, police use of
Defamation
Detectives, police

Deterrence
Discretion
District attorney
Domestic violence
Drug legalization debate
Drug use and sale, illegal
Equitable remedies
Equity
Espionage
Evidence, rules of
Felony
Fiduciary trust
Forensic science and medicine
Gangs, youth
Hate crimes
Illegal aliens
Immigration, legal and illegal
Immunity of public officials
Incapacitation
Indictment
Judicial system, U.S.
Jurisprudence
Jury system
Justice
Juvenile delinquency
Juvenile justice system
Labor unions
Law
Law schools
Legal ethics
Legal realism
Lynching
Machine politics
Malfeasance, misfeasance,
    and nonfeasance
Malice
Mandatory sentencing laws

Medical examiner
Medical malpractice
Military justice
Miscarriage of justice
Miscegenation laws
Misdemeanor
Mistrial
Moral relativism
National debt
Negligence
News media
News sources, protection of
Nonviolent resistance
Nuisance
Organized crime
Pardoning power
Pedophilia
Plea bargaining
Police
Police and guards, private
Police brutality
Police corruption and
    misconduct
Political corruption
Positive law
Presumption of innocence
Prison and jail systems
Privileged communications
Products liability
Property rights

Prosecutor, public
Psychopath and sociopath
Public defender
Punishment
Reasonable doubt
Reasonable force
Rehabilitation
Reparations
Restrictive covenant
School prayer
Seditious libel
Self-defense
Sentencing
Sexual harassment
Sheriff
Special weapons and tactics
    (SWAT) teams
Spoils system and patronage
State police
Sterilization and American
    law
Suicide and euthanasia
Ten most wanted criminals
Terrorism
Tort
Tort reform
Vigilantism
Wills, trusts, and estate
    planning
Zoning

CONSTITUTIONAL LAW AND ISSUES

Abortion
Affirmative action
Arms, right to keep and bear
Assembly and association,
    freedom of
Bill of Rights, U.S.
Birth control, right to
Busing
Censorship
Civil liberties
Civil rights
Civil War Amendments
Clear and present danger test
Commerce clause
Constitution, U.S.
Constitutional interpretation
Contract, freedom of
Counsel, right to
Cruel and unusual
    punishment
Double jeopardy

Due process of law
Equal protection of the law
Establishment of religion
Federalism
Incorporation doctrine
Judicial review
Ninth Amendment
Privacy, right of
Religion, free exercise of
Retroactivity of Supreme
    Court decisions
Search and seizure
Self-incrimination, privilege
    against
Speech and press, freedom of
Speedy trial, right to
States' rights
Supremacy clause
Supreme Court of the United
    States
Takings clause

COURT CASES

CRIMES

GOVERNMENT AGENCIES, OFFICERS, AND COMMISSIONS

HISTORICAL EVENTS, MOVEMENTS, AND TRENDS

Rosenberg trial and
   executions
Sacco and Vanzetti trial
   and executions
Saint Valentine's Day
   massacre
Salem witchcraft trials
Scopes "monkey" trial
Scottsboro cases
Selma-to-Montgomery civil
   rights march
Seneca Falls Convention
Simpson, O. J., trial
Slavery
Tax revolt movement
Teapot Dome scandal
Temperance movement
Triangle Shirtwaist Factory
   fire
Vietnam War
Walnut Street Jail
Watergate scandal

LEGAL TERMS AND PROCEDURES

Advisory opinion
Amicus curiae brief
Appellate process
Arbitration and mediation
Arraignment
Arrest
Assigned counsel system
Autopsy
Bench warrant
Bill of attainder
Bill of particulars
Blue laws
Boot camps
Cease and desist order
Certiorari, writ of
Change of venue
Citizen's arrest
Civil remedies
Class action
Color of law
Community service as
   punishment for crime
Compensatory damages
Competency to stand trial
Consent decree
Contempt of court
Declaratory judgment
Deposition
Dictum
Diversion
DNA testing
Electronic surveillance
Eminent domain
Entrapment
Ex post facto law
Expert witness
Extradition
Fingerprint identification
Forfeiture, civil and criminal
Good time
Grand jury
Habeas corpus

Harmless error
Hearsay rule
House arrest
Immunity from prosecution
Impeachment
In forma pauperis petition
In loco parentis
Indictment
Information
Injunction
Insanity defense
Jury nullification
Just deserts
Litigation
Majority, age of
Mala in se and *mala*
   prohibita
Mandamus, writ of
Mandatory sentencing laws
Mens rea
Mitigating circumstances
Parole
Plea bargaining
Polygraph
Posse comitatus
Preventive detention
Probable cause
Probation
Punitive damages
Restitution
Restraining order
Reversible error
Small-claims court
Standards of proof
Standing
Stare decisis
Statute of limitations
Sting operation
Strict liability
Subpoena power
Suit
Voir dire

LEGISLATION AND GOVERNMENT

Age Discrimination in
   Employment Act
Aid to Families with
   Dependent Children
   (AFDC)
Alien and Sedition Acts
Americans with Disabilities
   Act (ADA)
Anti-Racketeering Act
Chinese Exclusion Act
Civil Rights Act of 1957
Civil Rights Act of 1960
Civil Rights Act of 1964
Civil Rights Act of 1968
Civil Rights Act of 1991
Civil Rights Acts of
   1866-1875
Civil service system
Clayton Antitrust Act
Comprehensive Crime
   Control Act of 1984
Comprehensive Drug Abuse
   Prevention and Control
   Act of 1970
Comstock Law
Conscription
Copyrights, patents, and
   trademarks
Employee Retirement
   Income Security Act
   (ERISA)
Employment Act of 1946
Enforcement Acts
Equal Employment
   Opportunity Act
Equal Pay Act
Equal Rights Amendment
   (ERA)
Espionage Act
Ethics in Government Act
Family Medical Leave Act
Federal Crimes Act
Federal Tort Claims Act
Food stamps
Freedom of Information Act
Fugitive Slave Laws
GI Bill of Rights
Great Society
Harrison Narcotic Drug Act
Hatch Act
Hobbs Act
Immigration Reform and
   Control Act
Insanity Defense Reform Act

Judiciary Acts
Juvenile Justice and
   Delinquency Prevention
   Act
Kansas-Nebraska Act
Labor-Management Relations
   Act
Landrum-Griffin Act
Lindbergh law
Louisiana Civil Code
Mann Act
Marijuana Tax Act
Martial law
Missouri Compromise of 1820
Model Penal Code
Motor Vehicle Theft Act
Motor Vehicle Theft Law
   Enforcement Act
National Crime Victimization
   Survey
National Firearms Act and
   Federal Firearms Act
National Labor Relations Act
   (NLRA)
National Narcotics Act
New Deal
Omnibus Crime Control and
   Safe Streets Act of 1968
Opium Exclusion Act
Organized Crime Control Act
Pendleton Act
Political campaign law
Pure Food and Drug Act
Racketeer Influenced and
   Corrupt Organizations Act
   (RICO)
Sentencing guidelines, U.S.
Sherman Antitrust Act
Smith Act
Social Security system
Tariff
Tax Reform Act of 1986
Truth in Lending Act
Uniform Crime Reports
   (UCR)
United States Code
Victim assistance programs
Victims of Crime Act
Violent Crime Control and
   Law Enforcement Act of
   1994
Voting Rights Act of 1965
War on Poverty
Workers' compensation

ORGANIZATIONS

American Bar Association (ABA)
American Civil Liberties Union (ACLU)
American Federation of Labor-Congress of Industrial Organizations (AFL-CIO)
American Indian Movement (AIM)
Anti-Defamation League (ADL)
Black Panther Party
Communist Party, American
Congress of Racial Equality (CORE)
Democratic Party
Federalist Party
Free Soil Party
House Committee on Un-American Activities (HUAC)
International Association of Chiefs of Police
International Brotherhood of Police Officers
Interpol
Jeffersonian Republican Party
John Birch Society
Ku Klux Klan (KKK)
Mexican American Legal Defense and Education Fund (MALDEF)
Mothers Against Drunk Driving (MADD)
Nation of Islam
National Association for the Advancement of Colored People (NAACP)
National Association for the Advancement of Colored People Legal Defense and Educational Fund
National District Attorneys Association
National Organization for Victim Assistance (NOVA)
National Organization for Women (NOW)
National Rifle Association (NRA)
National Urban League
Republican Party
Socialist Party, American
Southern Christian Leadership Conference (SCLC)
States' Rights Party
Student Nonviolent Coordinating Committee (SNCC)
Students for a Democratic Society (SDS)
United Farm Workers (UFW)
Weather Underground
Whig Party
World Court

PERSONS

Addams, Jane
Anthony, Susan B.
Bentham, Jeremy
Black, Hugo L.
Blackstone, William
Brandeis, Louis D.
Brown, John
Bryan, William Jennings
Burger, Warren
Bush, George
Calhoun, John C.
Capone, Alphonse (Al)
Cardozo, Benjamin Nathan
Carter, Jimmy
Chase, Samuel
Chávez, César
Clay, Henry
Cooley, Thomas
Daugherty, Harry M.
Debs, Eugene V.
Dix, Dorothea Lynde
Douglas, Stephen A.
Douglas, William O.
Douglass, Frederick
Du Bois, W. E. B.
Eisenhower, Dwight D.
Ellsworth, Oliver
Field, Stephen J.
Ford, Gerald R.
Frankfurter, Felix
Fuller, Melvin Weston
Gandhi, Mahatma
Garrison, William Lloyd
Garvey, Marcus
Gompers, Samuel
Greeley, Horace
Hand, Learned
Holmes, Oliver Wendell, Jr.
Hoover, J. Edgar
Hughes, Charles Evans
Jackson, Jesse
Jay, John
Johnson, Lyndon B.
Kennedy, John F.
Kennedy, Robert F.
Kent, James
King, Martin Luther, Jr.
Lewis, John L.
Lincoln, Abraham
Livingston, Edward
Long, Huey
Mack, Julian William
Malcolm X
Marshall, John
Marshall, Thurgood
Muhammad, Elijah
Nader, Ralph
Nixon, Richard M.
Pinkerton, Allan
Pound, Roscoe
Randolph, A. Philip
Reagan, Ronald
Rehnquist, William
Roosevelt, Eleanor
Roosevelt, Franklin D.
Rush, Benjamin
Sanger, Margaret
Sinclair, Upton
Stanton, Elizabeth Cady
Steffens, Lincoln
Stone, Harlan Fiske
Story, Joseph
Stowe, Harriet Beecher
Taft, William Howard
Taney, Roger Brooke
Truman, Harry S
Vinson, Fred M.
Waite, Morrison Remick
Warren, Earl
Washington, Booker T.
White, Edward Douglass
Wilson, James
Wilson, Woodrow

SOCIAL JUSTICE AND POLITICAL RIGHTS

Acquired immune deficiency syndrome (AIDS)
Age discrimination
American Indians
Capitalism
Citizenship
Civil rights
Civil Rights movement
Comparable worth
Conservatism, modern American
Declaration of Independence
Democracy
Equality of opportunity
Feminism
Gay rights
Homelessness
Japanese American internment
Liberalism, modern American
McCarthyism
Marxism
Morality and foreign policy
Natural law and natural rights
Nuclear weapons
Poll tax
Racial and ethnic discrimination
Religious sects and cults
Representation: gerrymandering, malapportionment, and reapportionment
Segregation, *de facto* and *de jure*
Sex discrimination
Socialism
Taxation and justice
Veterans' rights
Vietnam War
Vote, right to
War on Poverty
Welfare state
Woman suffrage